Santa
Cruz
CA

WAGONS TO SOQUEL

1732 – 1932

— Photo by the author.

MADONNA OF THE TRAIL
Memorial at Upland CA — California State Society NSDAR.

WAGONS TO SOQUEL

1732 – 1932

by Sidney Glenn Freshour

Glenhaven Press   Modesto — 1995

WAGONS TO SOQUEL
1732 — 1932

Published by:

GLENHAVEN PRESS
2401 E. Orangeburg Ave.
Suite 675 - 109
Modesto, CA 95355

All rights reserved. Printed in the United States of America.
Copyright © 1995 by Sidney G. Freshour.

First Edition — 1995

Publisher's Cataloging in Publication Data
Freshour, Sidney Glenn
Wagons to Soquel — 1732-1932

Bibliography: p.

1. Genealogy—Hans Jerg Froschauer, descendants, 1732-1932.
2. Emigration—Germany to California in five generations. 3. Local History—Penn., Tenn., Missouri, Indiana, Iowa, Calif. 4. Wars—French and Indian, American Revolution, 1812, Civil. 5. Wagon roads—Great Philadelphia Wagon Road, Wilderness Road, National Road, Oregon-California Trail. 6. Wagons—Connestoga, Indiana Farm, Prairie Schooners.

Library of Congress Catalog Card Number: 95-78787
                      Hardcover   ISBN   0-9637265-5-2
                      Paperback   ISBN   0-9637265-6-0

Illustrations by
Lynn Hunt

Typeset with PTI LaTeX

Dedicated to Elizabeth

THE OVERLAND TRAIL

The Plains! The shouting drivers at the wheel;
The crash of leather whips; the crush and roll
Of wheels; the groan of yokes and grinding steel
And iron chain, and lo! at last the whole
Vast line, that reached as if to touch the goal,
Began to stretch and stream away and wind
Toward the west, as if with one control:
Then hope loomed fair, and home lay far behind;
Before, the boundless plain, and fiercest of their kind.

Some hills at last began to lift and break;
Some streams began to fail of wood and tide,
The sombre plain began betime to take
A hue of weary brown, and wild and wide
It streched its naked breast on every side.
A babe was heard at last to cry for bread
Amid the deserts; cattle lowed and died
And dying men went by with broken tread,
And left a long black serpent line of wreck and dead.

They rose by night; they struggled on and on
As thin and still as ghosts; then here and there
Beside the dusty way before the dawn
Men silent laid them down in their dispair,
And died. But woman! Woman, frail as fair!
May man have strength to give you your due;
You faltered not, nor murmured anywhere,
You held your babes, held to your course, and you
Bore on through burning hell your double burthens through.

The dust arose, a long dim line like smoke
From out a riven earth. The wheels went by,
The thousand feet in harness and in yoke,
They tore the ways of ashen alkali,
And desert winds blew sudden, swift and dry.
The dust! It sat upon and filled the train!
It seemed to fret and fill the very sky.
Lo! dust upon the beasts, the tent, the plain,
And dust, alas! on breasts that rose not up again.

THE OVERLAND TRAIL

My brave and unremembered heroes, rest;
You fell in silence, silent lie and sleep.
Sleep on unsung, for this, I say, were best;
The world to-day has hardly time to weep;
The world to-day will hardly care to keep
In heart her plain and unpretending brave;
The desert winds, they whistle by and sweep
About you; browned and russet grasses wave
Along a thousand leagues that lie one common grave.

from *By the Sundown Seas*
by JOAQUIN MILLER

FOREWORD

When I was growing up in my maternal grandparents' home, occasionally I would hear my grandmother refer to "the Freshours." From what she said, I assumed they were related to us in some way, but I never asked. Once she mentioned a "Rutha Freshour." I thought "Rutha" was an odd name — maybe a nickname. Years passed and Grandmother with them. I had all but forgotten the name "Freshour" until one day about two years ago when I had a phone call. It was then that I discovered I had a distant cousin named Sidney G. Freshour. There was that name again, a name I had all but forgotten. Furthermore, this cousin (56th maybe?) is a retired engineer, a history buff, and he has written a book.

Now I have read the book and I am impressed, not only with his painstaking research but also with his ability to make pioneer days live again: from Colonial times right up to Soquel during the 1906 earthquake and Los Gatos in the 1920s. In between, he has delved into the details of pioneer life from the Missouri Trailhead through the Rocky Mountains to the San Joaquin Valley, to Calaveras through the Siskiyous and up to the Rogue River country.

Covered wagons. Conestogas. Did you ever wonder what those pioneer women wore during those jolting trips in those wagons? By the way, that was how she made butter. The 16-mile day-long jolting worked just fine. She didn't have to turn the churn.

For the five-months of hardships on the trail, it was advised that a woman should have "two dresses of English merino and one linsey, two tweed sacks for shawls and two bonnets."

FOREWORD

Rutha Freshour Gann and her husband Nicholas Broyles Gann, crossed the plains with the Hopper Party and arrived in Soquel in 1847. They are buried there in the Pioneer Cemetery. The only roads to Mission Santa Cruz at that time were Indian trails or the one established California Mission trail from San Jose down through the Pajaro Valley. Grizzly bears roamed the Santa Cruz Mountains.

Sid Freshour's book tells it all, including the Civil War politics of the 1860s in Santa Cruz County and the development of the lumber, lime, leather, paper, glue and soap industries.

He even included a story about a Freshour who was accused of stealing cattle in 1877 in Tulare County. Another Freshour who had a wife, five children and the family cow, acquired 160 acres on Laurel Glen road in Santa Cruz County.

And there is the story about a Presbyterian minister who retired to Los Gatos when it was a strictly "dry" town. The minister, who apparently enjoyed a glass of wine with his dinner, labeled his box of wines as "books" and shipped them into Los Gatos that way. It was a fine idea until the "books" began to leak.

WAGONS TO SOQUEL is not only 200 years of family history, it is a kaleidescope of colorful scenes about how America grew, changed and developed, with the opening of the West.

It's a delightful book as well as an informative, well-researched and well-written book.

Cousin Sid, you have done yourself proud as my grandmother would say.

MARGARET R. KOCH
Glenwood
August 10, 1995

ACKNOWLEDGMENTS

The author acknowledges indebtedness to the libraries indicated for permission to use the following documents:

Newton Gleaves Finley, *Memories of travel across the plains in 1852,* Ms., 30 December 1922 (BANC MSS C-D 5182), The Bancroft Library, University of California, Berkeley.

James Findla, *Statement of a few events in early of Cal.,* Ms., 1878 (BANC MSS C-D 79), The Bancroft Library, UC, Berkeley.

Charles Hopper, *Narrative of Charles Hopper, a California Pioneer of 1841,* Ms., 1871 (BANC MSS C-D 105), The Bancroft Library.

Alexander Moore, *A Pioneer of '47, Statement of Alexander Moore of Pescadero,* Ms., 1878 (BANC MSS C-D 127), The Bancroft Library.

Lewis Stout, diary. Oregon Historical Society, Mss 1059. (In the typescript: *The Lewis Stout Family.* Including comments by Ray L. Stout.)

Ira C. Shank, *History of Jenny Lind,* Typescript, Calaveras County Historical Society, San Andreas, CA.

The author expresses appreciation to Connie Foster for permission to use her article *Henry Froshour* in *History of Washington County Arkansas,* 1989, Shiloh Museum, Springdale, Arkansas.

The following libraries provided microfilm of historic newspapers: McHenry Library of UC Santa Cruz, Santa Cruz Co. Library main branch and Watsonville branch, San Joaquin Co. Library at Stockton, San Jose City Library, Palo Alto Library, Yreka Library, Healdsburg Regional Library, Marysville Library, Visalia Library, Southern Oregon Historical Society Library and the Illinois State Historical Library. The newspaper archives of the Gerald D. Kennedy Library of the San Joaquin County Historical Museum at Micke Grove, the Holt-Atherton Special Collections of the UOP Libraries and the Calaveras County Archives also provided historic newspaper items.

Thanks to the Siskiyou County Historical Society for permission to use items from *The Siskiyou Pioneer* and for providing photographs from their collection. The Huntington Library and the Sutro Library receive my thanks for use of rare books. Special Collections of McHenry Library of UCSC receive my thanks for use of the Leon Rowland collection and use of historic photographs. The History Museum of Santa Cruz County provided historic photographs and use of Ernst Otto's newspaper scrapbook. Thanks to the Soquel Pioneer and Historical Association for use of historic photographs and documents.

ACKNOWLEDGMENTS

Thanks to the California State Archives for providing transcripts of State Supreme Court cases, San Quentin prison records and military records of Santa Cruz Co. Militia and to the California State Library, Law Library for providing the State Supreme Court decisions on various cases. The National Archives at San Bruno, CA provided records for the Federal Land Offices at Stockton and San Francisco.

The following genealogical researchers and "wagon train pioneer" descendants have been major contributors to this story:

Theresa Freshour — widow of Terry R. Freshour. Theresa shared information on the Lodi Freshours from the ledger of her father-in-law Henry J. Freshour. Theresa also provided information on five Freshour families living around Jenny Lind in the period 1860 to 1914.

Don and Esther Freshour, who lived for many years on the Klamath River, for their account of the Siskiyou Co. gold rush Freshours. They researched the Evergreen Cemetery of Yreka and shared family records going back to the 1880s.

Norman Dingmore, g.g.grandson of Jacob Freshour of Greene Co., Tennessee. Norman has researched the Solomon Lutheran Church cemetery and the Greeneville Library in Greene Co.

Dorothy Inscho, g.g. grand dau. of William Freshour of Jasper Co., IN. Dorothy has done research on the early Indiana Freshours and Greene Co., Tennessee Freshours.

Patty Neas for information on the Freshours of Cocke Co., TN.

Goldene Burgner for her information on Greene Co. TN Freshours and on the monument placed on John Freshour's grave in the Solomon Lutheran Church cemetery.

Cliff and Nancy Freshour have provided data and photographs on the Henry Freshour line that migrated from Tennessee to Indiana and finally to Iowa. Their research in Jasper Co., IN and Adams Co., IA has been most helpful.

Gail Benson supplied information on the Nicholas B. and Rutha Freshour Gann and family who came to California from Missouri in the wagon train led by Charles Hopper in 1847. Gail shared excerpts from the 1854-1871 journal of Isaiah Horn. This journal is a significant source on the MO Freshours in CA.

The late Leitha Roberts for sharing the Bible of Elias and Lydia Jane Freshour Bradley. Leitha also shared the family photographs dating to the 1860s. Also, for the tape recordings of Leitha's recollections of the Freshour family of Soquel and Capitola.

Lolita Freshour Giddens, who has done quite a search of Missouri and Arkansas for Freshours as well as research on the Pennsylvania Palatine immigrants.

ACKNOWLEDGMENTS

Edward and Bessie Conant for sharing their family history and especially to Ed for sharing his reminiscences of the Gazos Creek Mill and his expertise as a woodsman.

Minnie Freshour, for sharing photos and her recollections of the Freshour family of Santa Cruz and Los Gatos.

Jas.W. Freshour and the late Eddie J. Freshour for details on their grandparents James Wm. and Arabella Atherton Freshour and family.

John W. Freshour of Cox's Mill, WV, Jim Freshour of San Jose, Sue Terrando and Bula Mae Saunders were also helpful.

I wish to express my gratitude to the following people for their generous assistance: Eleanor Brown of the Siskiyou County Historical Society; Carol Champion, Special Collections, McHenry Library, University of California, Santa Cruz. Carol A. Harbison, Library Manager of the Southern Oregon Historical Society; Dr. Bonnie Hardwick, Head, Manuscripts Division, The Bancroft Library, University of California, Berkeley; Alan Jutzi of the Huntington Library Rare Book Department; Archivist Lorrayne Kennedy of the Calaveras County Archives; Rachel McKay, Collections Manager, History Museum of Santa Cruz County; Debbie Mastel, Collections Manager, The Gerald D. Kennedy Library, San Joaquin County Historical Society & Museum, Micke Grove; Richard W. Nutter, President of the Soquel Pioneer and Historical Association; Pamela J. Scott of the Manuscripts department of the Illinois State Historical Library; San Joaquin County historian, Dr. James Shebl; Edith Smith, Curator of the Forbes Mill History Museum of Los Gatos; Archivist Alzora Snyder of the Pajaro Valley Historical Association; Carolyn Swift, Curator, Capitola Museum and Phil Walker, founder of the Capitola Museum, for use of his photo collection.

Thanks to Mary Lou Lyon, History Instructor, San Jose MAEP, for her critique.

I must thank Margaret Koch for sharing her family history which includes Nicholas Broyles Gann and her great grandfather, Charles C. Martin — the founder of Glenwood. Margaret gave me a tour of the vestiges of historic Glenwood. I appreciated this tour and Margaret's Glenwood lore because my great grandparents, the George Conants lived at Glenwood when my great aunt, Alice Conant, died there at age seventeen. Margaret pointed out the cemetery which only she could find — it was reclaimed by the woods. My great uncle, Will Freshour, lived at Glenwood with his family when he was killed in a timber cutting accident nearby. Since Margaret and I both have roots in Santa Cruz County and enjoy its history, we are kindred spirits. Her friendship and encouragement are greatly appreciated.

SGF   8-16-95

WAGONS TO SOQUEL

PREFACE

My father used to tell me that his grandfather and family came to California from Indiana in a wagon train and that his aunt "Jenny" was born at *Devils Gate* on the way out. He told me that his dad had an old chair hewn out pioneer style and held together with pegs and with a woven rawhide seat. This chair came out in the covered wagon and was used by his grandfather. It was almost worn out when my grandfather got it, the legs being worn short, and it finally fell apart and was thrown away. There was some other lore about a log cabin with an earthen floor and a granny who smoked a clay pipe. This oral tradition was about all I had. My dad only knew his grandparents as "grandma" and "grandpa." He could account for his aunts and uncles reasonably well and he also knew his great uncle "Long Joe" Freshour who came out from Indiana with his grandfather. He knew that Long Joe had served in a war but it wasn't clear which one. He also believed his granddad to have served in the Civil War but had no details. My father Everett Edison Freshour and his father Anderson Arthur Freshour were both born at Soquel, Santa Cruz County, California. From this meager start, the extraordinary story of the *Wagons to Soquel* unfolded.

The various geographical movements and land acquisitions of this typical pioneer family were obviously integral to the larger emigrations and settlements of historical record. Much of the material included in this work therefore draws from the ebb and flow of national, state and local history. This was done to explain why they moved from one place to another and what occupied them once they got there. The historical narrative given here may seem overburdened with genealogical data. Or the reader may feel that the genealogical data seems to be buried in historical minutiae. A synergism of the "warp and the wove" to create a congruous and edifying whole fabric is intended. Appendices and notes are used extensively to unburden the narrative.

This account is not intended as another scholarly milestone in Trail or Mountain Men literature. I have not, for the most part, researched primary sources but rather relied on the wonderful body of work already published. My purpose — if any — in this regard is tutorial. This is a literature that I love and in which I would like to interest others.

I have briefly sketched the colonial and early nineteenth century material on the family. This is a subject area worthy of another book. — As is the Renaissance/Reformation and European emigration phase of the family history. This material is included to give the image of our family as perennial movers — pioneers — within the ferment of our national development. Also, scant mention is made of the Ohio branch of the family. — The ones that emigrated directly across the Appalachians from the Middle Colonies. I have entirely neglected those who moved north from the Middle Colonies to New York. My emphasis is on our pioneers who crossed the plains. They were invariably of the Tennessee - Blue Ridge Mountain - North Carolina branch.

I have alluded to the military service of members of the family in the major wars of the country, including the French and Indian War, The American Revolution, the War of 1812 and the Civil War. This also shows the complete involvement of our family in the development of this nation. Our family history is the history of the United States of America in microcosm.

This was an emigrating family that stayed at the edge of America's frontier. When the settlers began building roads and contemplating building a court house of their own, the Freshours would depart. About the only records left by several generations were the census and land records. They kept their own records in family Bibles. Our ancestors' struggle to build a new life in a better place might be mistaken for poverty. It's true, owning a quarter section didn't *ipso facto* make a person immediately affluent by *our* standards. But the privation was incidental to their vision. And they had their own diversions. They enjoyed their square dances and their knee-slappers like the one about "old man Goheen walking the wagon tongue." It's difficult for us to imagine the kind of life these people lived; but, we should make the effort. When we lose our past, we lose our future.

We have an exciting history and a rich cultural heritage. I keenly hope that the reader will catch the spirit and vision of our pioneer ancestors and see resolution of their own struggles in the struggles, defeats and achievements of those splendid men, women and children that preceded us.

The author

San José, California,

August, 1994.

WAGONS TO SOQUEL
TABLE OF CONTENTS

Foreword .... Page i
Acknowledgements .... Page iii
Preface .... Page vii
Contents .... Page ix
Chapter 1 .... COLONIAL PIONEERS .... Page 1
Chapter 2 .... THE TRAIL .... Page 19
Chapter 3 .... MISSOURI TRAILHEAD .... Page 31
Chapter 4 ...... CONESTOGAS TO THE WABASH ...... Page 51
Chapter 5 .... INDIANA PRAIRIE .... Page 75
Chapter 6 .... IOWA TRAILHEAD .... Page 89
Chapter 7 .... OUTFITTING AT OMAHA .... Page 111
Chapter 8 ..... ROCKY MOUNTAIN CORDILLERA ..... Page 127
Chapter 9 .... TRIBULATION IN THE BASIN .... Page 151
Chapter 10 .... WEBER'S TULE MARSH .... Page 167
Chapter 11 .... SAN JOAQUIN TRAIL'S END .... Page 189
Chapter 12 .... UP ON THE CALAVERAS .... Page 211
Chapter 13 .... SISKIYOU GOLD .... Page 227
Chapter 14 .... TO THE ROGUE AND BACK .... Page 253
Chapter 15 .... FROM SONOMA TO SISQUOC .... Page 275
Chapter 16 .... SOQUEL TIMBER .... Page 297
Chapter 17 .... STEAM POWERED SOQUEL .... Page 325
Chapter 18 .... SOQUEL TO HESTER CREEK .... Page 359
Chapter 19 .... OH, THE BEAR WENT OVER .... Page 391
Notes .... Page 423
Bibliography .... Page 477
Appendices .... Page 487

WAGONS TO SOQUEL

TABLE OF ILLUSTRATIONS

Madonna of the Trail .... frontispiece
Map 1 .... The ATLANTIC VOYAGE .... Page 2
Map 2 .... The PENNSYLVANIA FRONTEER .... Page 4
Fig. 1.1 .... A Colonial Map .... Page 9
Fig. 1.2 .... Froschauer Environs .... Page 11
Map 3 ..... GREAT PHILADELPHIA WAGON ROAD ..... Page 12
Map 4 .... The OREGON - CALIFORNIA TRAIL .... Page 21
Map 5 .... OVERLAND TO MISSOURI .... Page 36
Map 6 .... BLEEDING KANSAS .... Page 46
Map 7 .... WILDERNESS ROAD .... Page 55
Fig. 4.1 .... The National Road .... Page 62
Fig. 4.2 .... Wilderness Turnpike .... Page 65
Map 8 .... FREESOIL EMIGRANTS .... Page 96
Fig. 6.1 .... Alfred and Rebecca Ann .... Page 99
Fig. 6.2 .... Charles and Emma .... Page 101
Fig. 6.3 .... Delmar and Mildred .... Page 102
Fig. 6.4 ..... Unidentified Adams Co., Iowa Freshours ..... Page 110
Fig. 10.1 .... Sierra Emigrant Trails .... Page 170
Fig. 10.2 .... The Mines of Forty-nine .... Page 182
Fig. 10.3 .... Panning Gold on the Tuolumne .... Page 188
Map 9 .... ON THE CALAVERAS .... Page 214
Fig. 12.1 .... Returned Ripon Hero .... Page 225
Map 10 .... SISKIYOU GOLD COUNTRY .... Page 230
Fig. 13.1 .... Stage Line Ad. .... Page 246
Fig. 13.2 .... Marion and Mary V. Freshour .... Page 247
Fig. 13.3 .... The Freshour Ferry .... Page 250
Map 11 .... SAMS VALLEY .... Page 268

WAGONS TO SOQUEL

TABLE OF ILLUSTRATIONS

Map 12 .... *SANTA CRUZ MOUNTAINS* .... Page 304

Fig. 16.1 .... *Soquel — late 1890s* .... Page 310

Fig. 16.2 .... Santa Cruz County Sawmill .... Page 312

Fig. 17.1 .... John and Sophronia .... Page 330

Fig. 17.2 .... Frealon Grover with millhands .... Page 332

Fig. 17.3 .... Jerkline Team .... Page 334

Fig. 17.4 .... John Bradley & A.A. Freshour .... Page 334

Fig. 17.5 .... Frealon Grover's record log pull. .... Page 336

Fig. 17.6 .... Loma Prieta bull donkey. .... Page 340

Fig. 17.7 .... Narrow gauge logging locomotive. .... Page 340

Fig. 17.8 .... The Bausch Brewery building. .... Page 348

Fig. 17.9 .... Olive Springs — August 1899. .... Page 352

Fig. 17.10 .... Timber Fallers near La Honda. .... Page 355

Fig. 18.1 ..... Jim Conant driving Grover's bull team. ..... Page 362

Fig. 18.2 .... Grover Mill at Soquel. .... Page 364

Map 13 .... *SOQUEL TOWNSHIP* .... Page 372

Fig. 18.3 .... The Town of Laurel. .... Page 380

Fig. 18.4 ...... Loma Prieta Mill in Hinckley Gulch. ...... Page 384

Fig. 18.5 .... A.A. Freshour Family circa 1906. .... Page 388

Fig. 19.1 .... The Los Gatos Freshours. .... Page 395

Fig. 19.2 .... Place's delivery wagon. .... Page 397

Fig. 19.3 .... Four Soquel generations. .... Page 399

Fig. 19.4 .... Glenn Jones & George Freshour. .... Page 401

Fig. 19.5 .... The Bradleys, Jones & Freshours .... Page 402

Fig. 19.6 .... Mary Ellen Freshour .... Page 421

1

COLONIAL PIONEERS

THE GREAT American migration transformed a fringe of eastern colonies — laboring at the brink of wilderness — into a powerful nation spanning a *continent!* The fledgling congress that forged our government had the audacity to call themselves the *Continental* Congress; although, the frontier at that time was at the Appalachians and no one at that time had any substantive idea of what lay west of the Mississippi.[1] Our Revolution's firebrand propagandist, Thomas Paine, articulated the concept in his drumhead rhetoric against the King.[2] The seminal concept has always been with us. The congress of the new nation created, early on, the methodology for converting raw territory into states.[3] The charters of the earliest British colonies in America granted them the full extent of the land west to the Pacific! Early phantasmic cartography led the grantors to believe that the Balboa experience would be duplicated. The hard reality of French and Spanish occupation of that territory did not dispel the colonial concept of possession from sea to sea. It was implicit in Jefferson's deft Louisiana Purchase and it was explicit in James K. Polk's incisive power politics which secured the far west. Abraham Lincoln spoke of our government as having been "brought fourth on this continent." Lincoln's utmost concern was to preserve the Union that was then in the midst of the very process of occupying this continent.[4]

The story is told here in terms of a German emigrant family who continued to emigrate as the frontier pushed further and further to the west. Hans Jerg Froschauer and his wife Catharina Graff were the progenitors of this family. They with

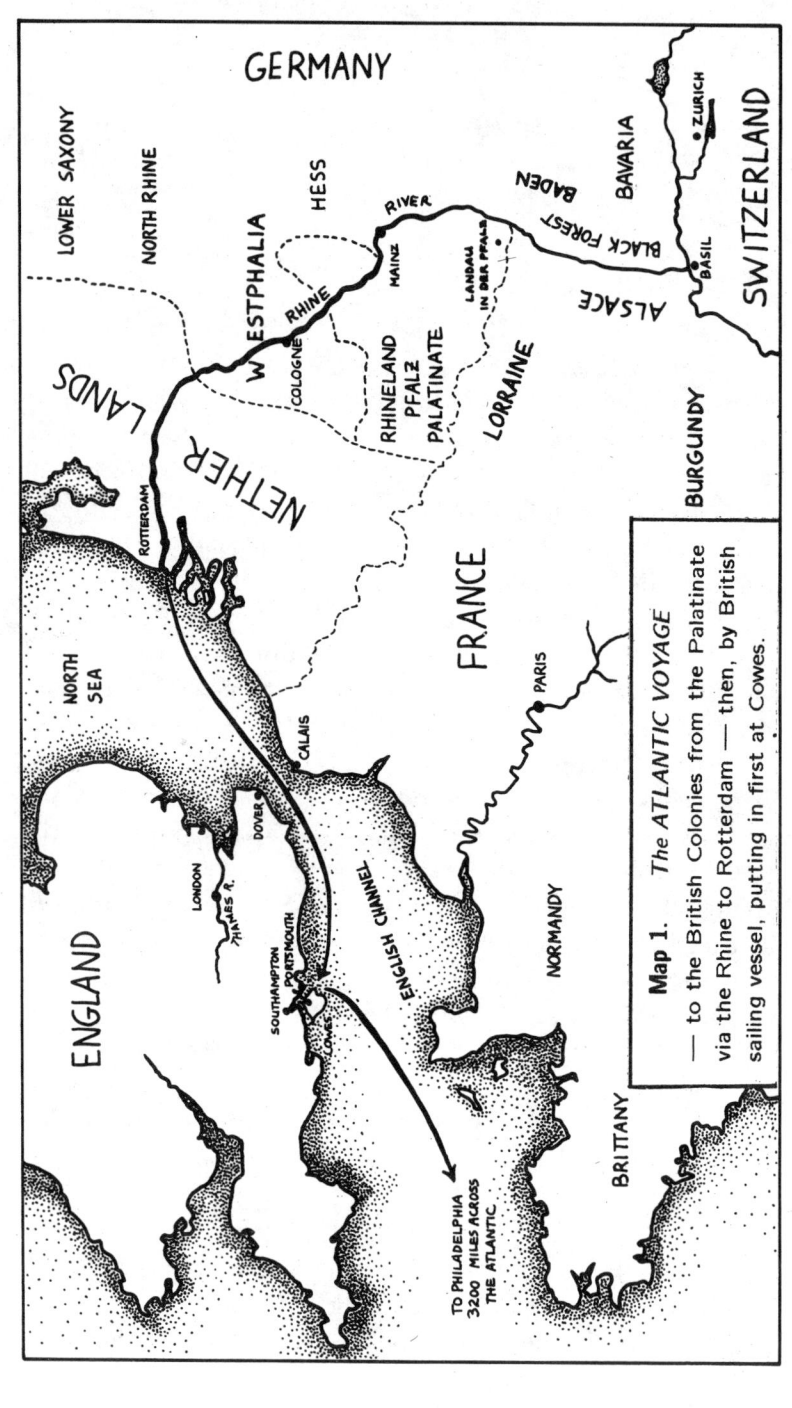

Map 1. The ATLANTIC VOYAGE — to the British Colonies from the Palatinate via the Rhine to Rotterdam — then, by British sailing vessel, putting in first at Cowes.

their children Johan "Vendol" (Wendel) and Anna Maria, disembarked from the ship Mary of London, John Grey, Master, at Philadelphia in the year 1732.[5] They were among the German Reformed Church refugees from the religious oppression in the Palatine (modern Rhineland-Pfalz.) They had accepted the asylum offered by William Penn.[6]

William Penn was soon followed into the Palatine by unscrupulous land promoters who published circulars promising incredible opportunities in Pennsylvania. — A pattern that was to be perpetuated in the American experience. Tolls on the Rhine were opportunistic. Many arrived at Rotterdam in financial straits. Some of the Palatines indentured themselves to pay for the cost of passage to the colonies on British ships. Many died on those horrible ships. These "Redemptioners" were redeemed at Philadelphia. Their obligation was to work for five to ten years.[7] By 1730, half the Germans in Pennsylvania were of the Reformed Church.

When Hans Jerg and Catharina made the voyage across the Atlantic, Catharina was bearing their third child, Johannes, who was born upon their arrival in the Quaker colonies. In that same year, 1732, George Washington was born just to the south in the "Old Dominion" of Virginia. Hans Jerg Froschauer became a loyal subject of the Crown by swearing allegiance upon arrival in Philadelphia.[8] He signed his name. (Many of the Palatines made their mark.) He was 32 years old. Many years later, his son Johannes and Wendel's son John would bear arms in the rebellion against the Crown.

When Hans Jerg and his family arrived in Pennsylvania, the name Froschauer was familiar to the German Anabaptist sects already populating eastern Pennsylvania. (Mennonites, Amish, Schwenkfelders, Moravian Brethren, Dunkards etc.[9]) These had brought the *Froschauerbible* with them to America and published it on the German presses at Germantown and Ephrata. The *Froschauerbible* was a high-German Swiss dialect version published in Zurich by Renaissance printer Chrystoph Froschauer[10] in 1529. The *Froschauerbible* was to the early

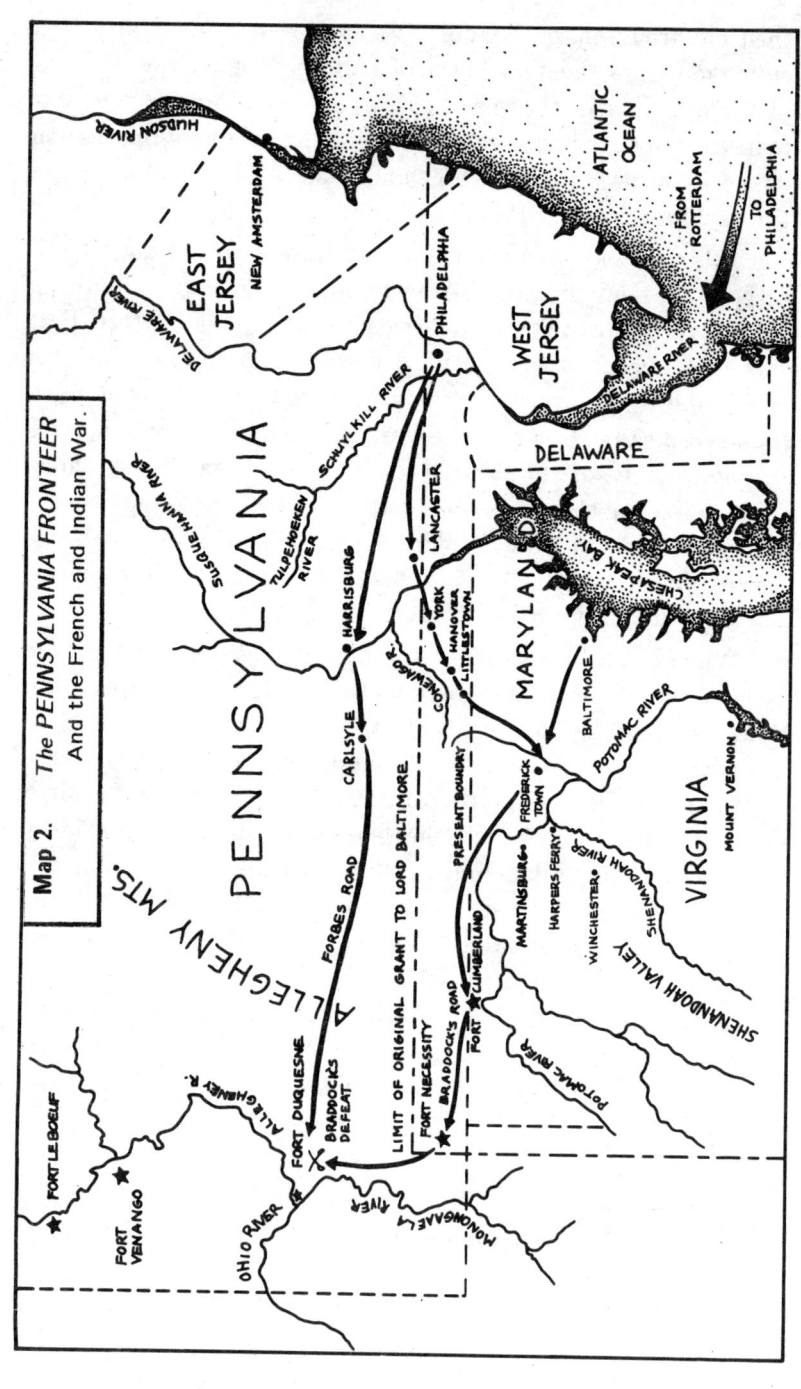

Pennsylvania Dutch what the King James' version with its Elizabethan diction was to the Puritan fathers of New England. It was still in use well into this century by the German speaking Mennonites and Amish.[11] To collectors, the sixteenth century *Froschauerbibles* command very high prices.

The Froschauers settled in the Jerseys but soon left for the frontier. In the 1730s, the Pennsylvania "west" lay just across the Susquehanna — in western Lancaster County which in 1749 would spin-off as York County.[12] The resounding success of Penn's pluralistic settlements of Scots and Rhinelanders had become apparent by 1730 to the proprietor of Maryland. In 1732, Lord Baltimore published a proclamation directed to these newly arriving immigrants in the Quaker colonies "being Desireous to Increase the Number of Honest people" in what he conceived to be Maryland. The enticement was two-hundred acres offered at absolutely no cost to any family locating in the region *between the Susquehanna and the Potomac.* The settlers were exempted from quit rents for the first three years and charged reasonable amounts thereafter. This proposition included assurance that life and property would be as secure as that of "any of his Majesty's Subjects in any part of the British Plantations in America ... " [13] Thus his Lordship exacerbated a longstanding feud with the Penns by generously giving not only Western Maryland land but also Pennsylvania frontier real estate to the arriving Palatines. — Land that the late William Penn had promised to his Indian friends. The Palatinate German dialect *hoch Deutsch* gave the Pennsylvania Germans the name "Pennsylvania Dutch."

A road west to Lancaster was built in 1733 and later extended connecting Lancaster with York. This is where the Hans Jerg Froschauers settled — just beyond Hanover near Littlestown in the Conewago Valley on the Maryland border. At that time it was not certain whether they had settled in Pennsylvania or Maryland. Fifty years prior to the granting of William Penn's charter for his Pennsylvania proprietorship, the first Lord Baltimore was granted the charter for his Maryland proprietorship with the northern boundary set at the 40° N parallel — about nineteen miles north of the present border. It even included Philadelphia![14]

Hanover and the Conewago Valley were well within this disputed region and, for this reason, had a laxity of law enforcement that attracted many lawbreakers. Hanover was known as "Rogue's Rest."[15] Also there were a considerable number of native inhabitants remaining there. The Froschauers had moved from the somewhat civilized Quaker Jerseys to the wild and woolly west of Lancaster County. This was the first emigration west by Freshours. The dispute between the Penns and Lord Baltimore continued for another three decades. It would not be resolved until after the French and Indian War.

Hans Jerg and Catharina Froschauer had eleven children in all. Some of them were christened at the Conewago Christ Reformed Church. As the second generation of Froschauers started their own homes, some of them moved to nearby Frederick County Maryland and on to Frederick County, Virginia which became Berkeley County, Virginia (now Morgan County, West Virginia.)[16] The German names of spouses and sponsors at christenings indicate a close knit German speaking community. Wendel settled at Sleepy Creek in Berkeley County and had property at Bath where Hans Jerg Froschauer is believed to have died. This general area of the colonial Froschauer settlement lies within the disputed area of Lord Baltimore's original charter[17] and was at a longitude central to Pennsylvania. The Pennsylvania frontier moved further west as The Froschauers reared their children in the Conewago Valley.

The Madonna of the Trail standing along the National Road just west of the Monongahela River is a statue of heroic mold. Dedicated to the pioneer mothers of Pennsylvania's covered wagon days, it depicts a bonneted woman with a baby in her arms and a boy clutching her skirt. The colonial western frontier progressed to the western edge of the original colonies. The first glimmerings of "manifest destiny" were evinced as some of the Pennsylvania pioneers pushed even further westward across the Appalachians. This, and the real estate interests of certain gentlemen of Virginia,[18] led to the war of the French against the British colonials. The frontier moved from York County to the western region at the confluence of the Monongahela and the Allegheny Rivers.

While only sixteen years old, George Washington traveled into Ohio lands as a surveyor for Lord Fairfax. The almost impassable trail led to Thomas Cresap's cabin fortress among the Indians on the Monongahela. In 1752, Cresap marked out a 65 mile portage from the Potomac to the Monongahela. Young Washington was convinced that this portage and the Potomac River could be the Virginia commercial route to the Ohio country.[19] He would later have the opportunity to convince General Braddock to build a road there. The French, who were jealous of their Ohio *La Belle Rivière*, instigated Indian atrocities against those settled along its Allegheny and Monongahela tributaries.

Twenty-one-year-old George Washington, a Major in the Virginia Militia, was sent to this area to warn the French that they were erecting fortresses "within his Majestey's dominions." The French were intransigent. Washington won the battle of Great Meadows, but was later forced to capitulate to the French and return to Virginia. Thus, in western Pennsylvania, the terrible French and Indian war erupted.[20] Disaster ensued at the battle of the Wilderness. General Braddock was killed, Colonel George Washington wounded and most of the Virginia troops killed.

There were unspeakable massacres by Indians who were employed as the preponderant French force in this territorial dispute. Thousands of Germans and Scots who had settled in Indian lands were tortured, slaughtered or enslaved.[21] Under William Pitt, the British rescued the colonists from the French and Indians. Wendel Froschauer served with the Maryland troops from Frederick County under Captain John Middaugh.[22]

This war, which escalated into a massive confrontation between global powers vying for control of the North American continent, ended in a humiliating expulsion of the French. This was very expensive for England.[23] The taxation imposed by the British on their colonies to recoup war expense was one factor leading to the Revolution some twenty years later. The Braddock Road and later the Forbes Road were built into the western Pennsylvania region as military roads.[24] The Treaty of Paris in 1763 extended British territory to the Mississippi River.[25]

The French obstacle was removed but not the Indian one.[26] The imposed barrier to western Pennsylvania and Ohio country set up at the Alleghenies left the colonials of York county the handy alternative of Western Maryland with its Potomac and the Shenandoah Valley of Western Virginia. The military roads, particularly Braddock's, fell into disuse.

The border dispute between Maryland and Pennsylvania was finally adjudicated in 1763. Mason and Dixon surveyed, then physically established their line at its present location by placing milestones along the boundry. The coat of arms of the Baltimores and Penns were periodically placed facing their respective Colonies. Completion of this highly visible 233-mile boundry in 1768 resolved the dispute after some eighty-odd years.[27] The settlement of Western Pennsylvania and the neighboring Potomac region of Maryland and Virginia continued. The frontier progressed across the mountains in spite of the 1763 Royal prohibition of settlement beyond the Alleghenies. George Washington and his land speculation partner William Crawford quietly bought up land on the south-east side of the Ohio near the Great Kanawah.

Indians tortured Crawford and burnt him alive near Upper Sandusky. Occurrences such as this dampened Ohio land promotion.[28] The preponderant pioneering thrust was down through the Great Valley of Virginia and into North Carolina and Tennessee. Before, during and after the French and Indian War, emigration was on the path of least resistance southward into North Carolina.

Figure 1.1: North America in a Colonial map of 1778

On the other margin of the continent in 1769, Father Juinpero Serra entered the wilderness to plant the Cross among the Indians of California — and, colonization began. While our colonies struggled to found an independent nation, the Franciscans established missions from San Diego to San Rafael north of San Francisco Bay. The stamp of Spain was upon the land. A vast expanse of *Terra Incognita* separated the two sea coasts.

In 1776 the colonies revolted. The Declaration of Independence was drafted at Philadelphia by Thomas Jefferson standing at his portable writing desk in the second-floor parlor of a young German bricklayer named Graaf.[29]

The Froschauers reared their children in the Conewago Valley of Pennsylvania prior to the French and Indian war of 1755-58 and Froschauers were living in that region through the entire colonial period and after.[30] By the time of the Revolution, much of the family had moved down the Monocacy into nearby Maryland and the adjacent Potomac area in Virginia. In 1770, Wendel moved from Frederick County Maryland to Berkeley

County Virginia. There were two Freshour soldiers serving in the Virginia regiments during the Revolution and one in a Maryland regiment.[31]

Miller gives us some insight into the culture of these colonial frontiersmen in his *Origins of the American Revolution*. The hardened frontiersmen of Virginia were very tough antagonist. Miller quotes *American Archives*: [32] "A formidable company of upwards of one hundred and thirty men, from the mountains and backwoods, painted like *Indians,* armed with tomahawks and rifles, dressed in hunting shirts and moccasins," arrived in Frederick Town, Maryland, during August of 1775. These men were capable of marching and fighting on a simple diet of parched corn over a sustained period of time. American marksmanship could be expected to decimate British troops. Unlike the American colonials, Britons were not acquainted in the normal course of their childhood with firearms. British military training gave them at best mere competence with the smooth bore "Brown Bess" musket. The advanced spiral grooved bore of the rifle was beyond their ken. The British Regulars, according to Charles Lee, were somewhat ignorant of the common musket. One American marksman was generally acknowledged to be equivalent to five British redcoats. An American rifleman, it was believed, could from a distance of over one hundred yards hit a man's nose. The *Virginia Gazette* warned "General Gage, take care of your nose."

Tradition gives Colonial American Johannes Froschauer the anglicized "John Freshour" as his name during his service with Washington's Continental Army. His nephew, Wendel's son John Freshour, who was to settled in Ross County, Ohio, left a remarkable Revolutionary War record. "Vendol" Froschauer, now Wendel Freshour, gave aid to the Revolutionary cause by shipping wheat to the army for which he received over five hundred acres of land.[33] This wheat was grown and harvested by incredibly primitive methods. The metal plowshare was not yet in use. Harvesting was done by sickle and scythe. Threshing by the flail. Production was limited by lack of labor. The

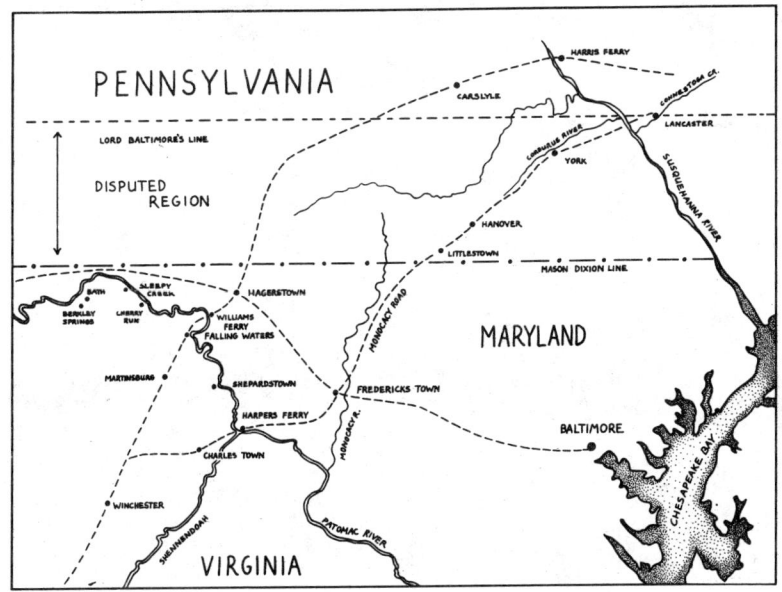

Figure 1.2: Middle Colony Froschauer Environs

notable success of the German farmers was due in part to their womenfolk working in the fields.

Eventually, there was another Treaty of Paris — the one of 1783 — and the Old Northwest Territory and the territory extending to the Mississippi became American.[34] The fringe of colonies confined by the Atlantic and the Appalachians now had a new frontier — and a vast intervening wilderness to conquer.

In 1739, the road from Lancaster to York was eventually extended through the Conewago Valley to follow the Monocacy River south through Frederick Maryland and on south to the Potomac River and the Shenandoah Valley — the Monocacy Road. This road, with its westward extension from Frederick, Maryland to Fort Cumberland, was later used to supply General Braddock.[35] The main road of colonial times was the Great Philadelphia Wagon Road, which continued through the fertile Valley of Virginia and on into the Carolina Piedmont (*i.e.* foot hills.) During the Revolutionary War, when the

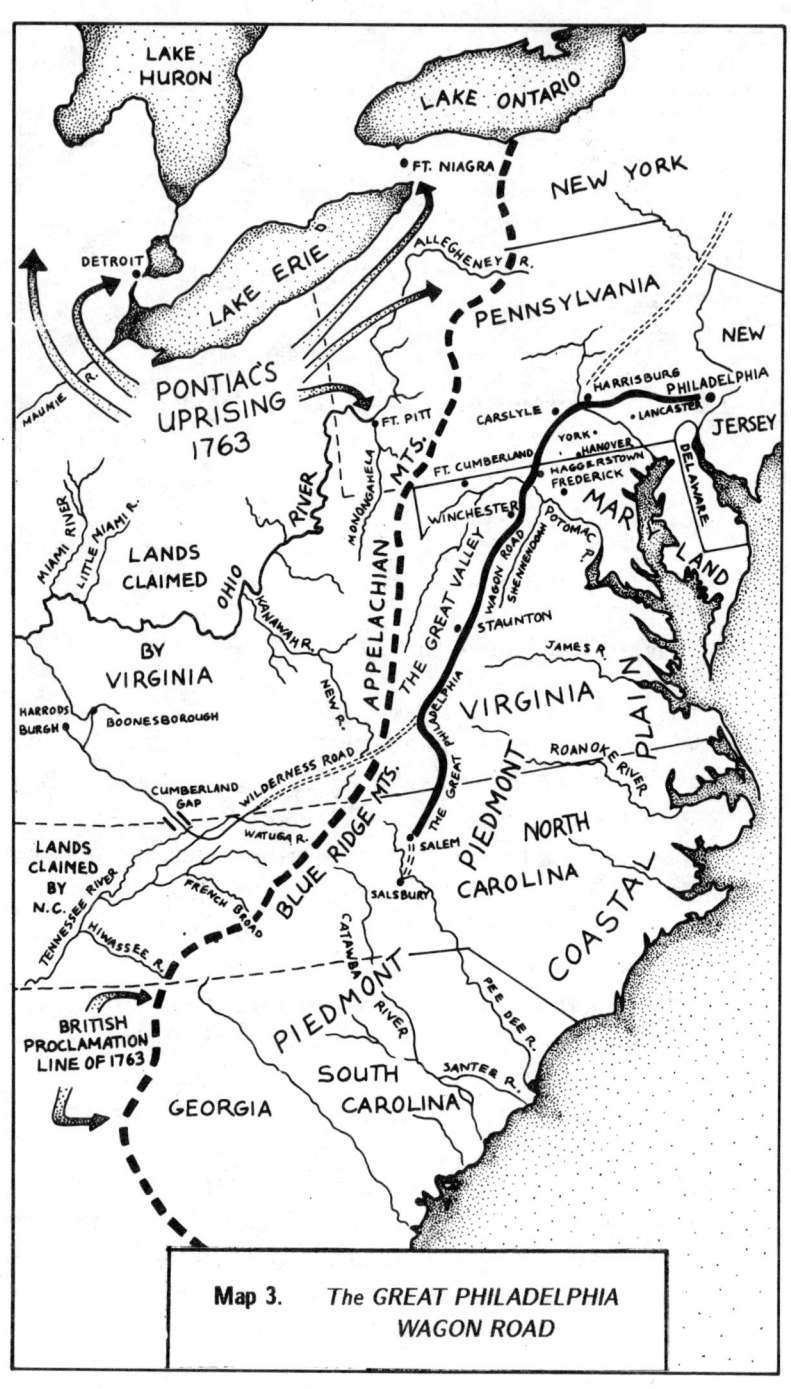

Map 3. The GREAT PHILADELPHIA WAGON ROAD

British occupied Philadelphia, this route was important. The road then ran from the Delaware Valley through Bethlehem and Reading, across the Susquehanna River at Harris Ferry and on through Carlisle and Hagerstown to Williams Ferry on the Potomac. From there, it continued on the southern portion of the Great Philadelphia Wagon Road. The New England Colonies were thus connected by this inland route to the Southern Colonies during the Revolution.[36]

This route was marked by Dutch cities if not "Pennsylvania Dutch" then "Valley Dutch." These extended through Maryland and Virginia to as far south as North Carolina and would include Frederick and Hagerstown in Maryland, Winchester and Staunton in the Virginia Valley and Winston Salem in North Carolina. The two Moravian cities of Bethlehem in Pennsylvania and Salem in North Carolina were connected by the Conestoga wagons traveling regularly on the Great Philadelphia Wagon Road.[37] The route out of the Valley of Virginia to North Carolina went due south from the location of present day Roanoke. Beyond this southward extension of the Pennsylvania Dutch civilization, there was a further thrust down the Great Valley of Virginia southwest into Tennessee. The colonial Froschauer domain participated in this Pennsylvania "Valley Dutch" extension. Place names associated with the Froschauers were Littlestown, Frederick, Hagerstown, Bath (Berkeley Springs), Sleepy Creek, Cherry Run, Shepardstown and Martinsburg. From this general vicinity, the Great Philadelphia Wagon road followed the Shenandoah down the Great Valley of Virginia to either North Carolina or to Tennessee.

As the Pennsylvania back country became well settled, the newcomers who were too poor to buy in Pennsylvania went south into Virginia and the Carolina Piedmont — attracted by land agent advertising. "Pennsylvania Germans" took up land in this region in the 1750s.[38] Two generations of Freshours grew up in the North Carolina back country in the years preceding Tennessee statehood. In 1753, the Boones with son Daniel moved from Pennsylvania to the forks of the Yadkin headwaters of the Pee Dee River. The Freshours seem to have gone to the south fork of the Catawba River. The route into Tennessee was to Asheville and up the French Broad River.

In the decades when Braddock's Road was growing up with brush, when Indians on the western plains of New York barred the way across that state, the road down the Shenandoah was the most practical route to the west.[39] Until after the Revolution, pack trains were the mainstay of this trans-Appalachian emigration and commerce. After the Revolution, the emigrants increasingly used the wagon to transport their family and belongings. The settlers visited Lancaster, York and Carlisle to acquire a Conestoga Wagon, a "Kentucky" rifle and other equipment.[40] Thousands of covered wagons crowded the road to the southwest through Virginia — now called the Wilderness Road after Boone's extension through Cumberland Gap into Kentucky. This road down the Great Valley of Virginia was notable as a good road having crushed limestone roadbed.[41]

After the Revolution, the Ohio country — the Northwest Territory — became the object of territorial development by a government operating under the Articles of Confederation. Washington's dream of turning the Potomac River into a trade route quickened. The "Patowmack Company" canal became the subject of treaties between states. These were illegal under the Articles and the new government had no authority to regulate interstate commerce. This led to the Constitutional Convention.[42] In 1787, fifty-five men endured the appalling rigors of colonial stagecoach travel to assemble in Philadelphia. In less than four months they wrote a constitution that has lasted two hundred years. Briton's Gladstone called it "...the most wonderful work ever struck off at any given time by the brain and purpose of man." The Lancaster Turnpike was built from Philadelphia in the 1790s. — The first actual road, by modern standards, to exist in America.

In 1785 Washington had hired James Rumsey to design the Potomac canal. In 1787 "Crazy" Rumsey demonstrated a steamboat on the Potomac by taking passengers from Shepardstown upriver against the current. It had been the custom to dismantle the river boats at completion of the trip downriver and sell the lumber as well as the cargo. The "Patowmack" canal was completed and a bustling commercial watercourse ran through the prospering Sleepy Creek area where the Wendel Freshour family was established. When Wendel died, there was a mill on his place built by James Rumsey. William's Ferry became Williamsport. Cargoes ran from Cumberland to Georgetown in three to five days. Georgetown remained a busy port until Civil War days. Wendel and the Washingtons bought lots in the fashionable resort of Bath.[43]

Unlike the stopgap Articles of Confederation, the new U.S. Constitution gave our national government an executive branch — The President of the United States of America. George Washington was inaugurated in 1789. His conduct in office defined the American presidency. He won a second term by universal acclaim. During his second term, Mad Anthony Wayne defeated the Indians in the Maumee Valley of Ohio at the battle of Fallen Timbers in 1794. The following year the Grennville Treaty provided for the removal of Indians from Ohio which diminished scalping by the Indians to a level acceptable for the purpose of real estate development in the southern part of the territory.[44] The Middle Colonies' western frontier had moved from the Appalachians to the Maumee Valley. Wendel's son John married Margaret Funkhauser in 1791 in Shenandoah County of Virginia. Wendel's will was probated in 1794.[45] John and Margaret moved up the Braddock road to Ohio settling first in Hocking County and thence to Ross County.[46] By that time — 1795 — Tennessee was admitted to the union and the nation was on the move. Johan and Eave Froschauer and their entire family joined the rush from the Middle Colonies into Tennessee — traveling down Virginia's Great Valley. George Washington's farewell address was published in 1796. John Adams became president in 1797. The century closed with Washington's death in December of 1799. His final utterance: " 'Tis well."

Johan Froschauer became the patriarch John Freshour of Greene County, Tennessee where our narrative starts.[47] "Old John," with his children and grandchildren, emigrated from Pennsylvania, coming on the Wilderness Road through the Great Valley, we can imagine, in Pennsylvania Dutch built Conestoga wagons. We note one family idiosyncrasy. Hans Jerg translates into English as John George. Frequently, the firstborn son of an American Freshour family was named John and the second born son named George. Records in English commonly omit their middle name or initial.

Four generations of Froschauer progeny followed the frontier west. One hundred years had passed since Hans Jerg's pioneering venture into York County. The frontier was now at the banks of the "Wide Missouri." The Indians tribes were now a fractious conglomeration in the "Great American Desert" soon to be known as the Great Plains [48] — later on, Nebraska Territory, Kansas Territory and the ultimate Indian Reservation — Oklahoma. Incremental moves through habitable territory were no longer an option. The move across the wide Missouri was a big one — two thousand miles. The fifth Froschauer generation crossed the plains over the Continental Divide, over the Rocky Mountain Plateau, passed through the Great Basin, climbed over the Sierra Nevada into the San Joaquin Valley and moved on to the Pacific coast. Their descendants are buried in the pioneer cemeteries of Soquel, Santa Cruz and Watsonville and a number of other California pioneer cemeteries. These are wagon train people. They are our ancestors. They moved and lived in community with kinfolks, friends, cousins and neighbors. They were the Himes, the Ganns, the Freshours, the Baucoms, the Masons, the Bradleys, the Macks, the Bausches, the Conants, the Beswicks, the Thompsons and the Goheens. They could have been anyone else who packed up in wagons and headed west.

From the data one can identify at least three wagon trains — i.e. three identifiable years when groups of Freshours, in-laws and neighbors emigrated across the plains.

Four main families originating in Tennessee are identifiable:

Andrew Freshour and Jane Marcum born in Tennessee and Virginia respectively and married in Johnson County Missouri in 1837. Andrew moved to Sonoma County California with his children. They were well known in that county.

Henry Freshour and Elizabeth Hedrick Dunn who married in Greene County Tennessee and reared their family at Fort Wayne and later in Jasper County, Indiana. Their progeny emigrated to Iowa and some moved on to California eventually settling in the Soquel region.

James Rufus Freshour and Francis A. McKelhaney born in Tennessee and Illinois respectively and married in Jackson County Missouri. This couple moved to California with their children and had other children in Calaveras and San Joaquin Counties. They eventually moved to Siskiyou County and were prominent there. They have a number of descendants there.

John Freshour and Elizabeth Smith who married in Greene County Tennessee and reared their seven children in Jackson County Missouri. Most all of their offspring moved as young adults to California to various places in central California including Calaveras and San Joaquin Counties. Many moved on to Santa Cruz County.

We shall give an overview of trail geography and history,[49] establish the emigrant Freshour families at the trail head, describe trail development and the process of traveling the trail, identify the groups that emigrated on certain years and finally trace these families in California up to the early part of this century. Some remarkable individuals and fascinating facts will emerge as the story unfolds.

Each generation moved across country by wagon. The last leg of the odyssey took some north into the Siskiyou to the Klamath or the Rogue. Some stayed on the Calaveras. It took some to Vallejo's Petaluma Rancho. But most of them headed west.

— They took *wagons to Soquel.*

2

THE TRAIL

THE OREGON TRAIL extended from Independence, Missouri to the Willamette Valley and flourished for about five years beginning in 1845. From the 1849 gold rush on, it was in fact the California Trail. There were parties that split up at the Snake River or Soda Springs to go to either destination. Historical perspective gives it both names.[1]

The first leg of the trail is the Great Platte River Road running from the Missouri River across present day Nebraska following the Platte River and extending via Fort Kearny all the way up the north fork of the Platte to Fort Laramie.[2] At it's beginning, the trail is really a system of trails that all finally converge along the Platte. Points of origin along the Missouri were (from south to north) Independence, Missouri (Westport), Fort Leavenworth, St. Joseph, Nebraska City, Plattsmouth, Omaha, Council Bluffs and the Mormon's Winter Quarters. These were the "jumping off" places where civilization was left behind. They were commercial centers that outfitted and provisioned wagon trains. They sold everything imaginable including the hickory bows and the canvas that stretched over them to convert the emigrants farm wagons to "prairie schooners." Some entrepreneurs such as John Studebaker and his brothers built wagons specifically for the trip.[3]

The trains of the mid 40s generally left from Independence. As time progressed, the popular departure point shifted further north. Frequently, the emigrants arrived at St. Louis and came across Missouri with their wagons on the decks of paddle wheelers to debark at their chosen point of departure.[4] Trails were named for their departure points. The Independence Road, the

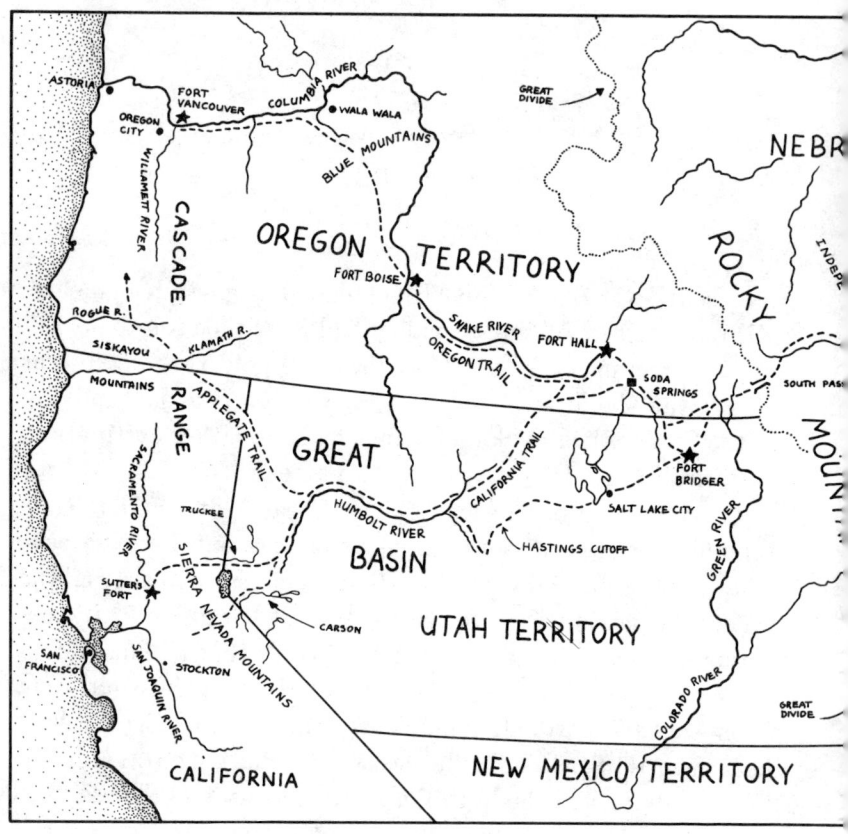

Leavenworth Road, the St. Joe Road, the Nebraska City Road — they all became one road along the Platte by the time they got as far west as Fort Kearny. The road on the north bank of the Platte was known as the Mormon Road since they used it heavily. The Denver Road broke away at the upper corner of present day Colorado following the South Platte. The covered wagons mainly followed the North Platte on up to Scots Bluff and thence across into what is now Wyoming.

The intermediate objective was to get across the great divide via South Pass. Just as the Platte River was a marvelous natural road across middle America, so South Pass was a gentle

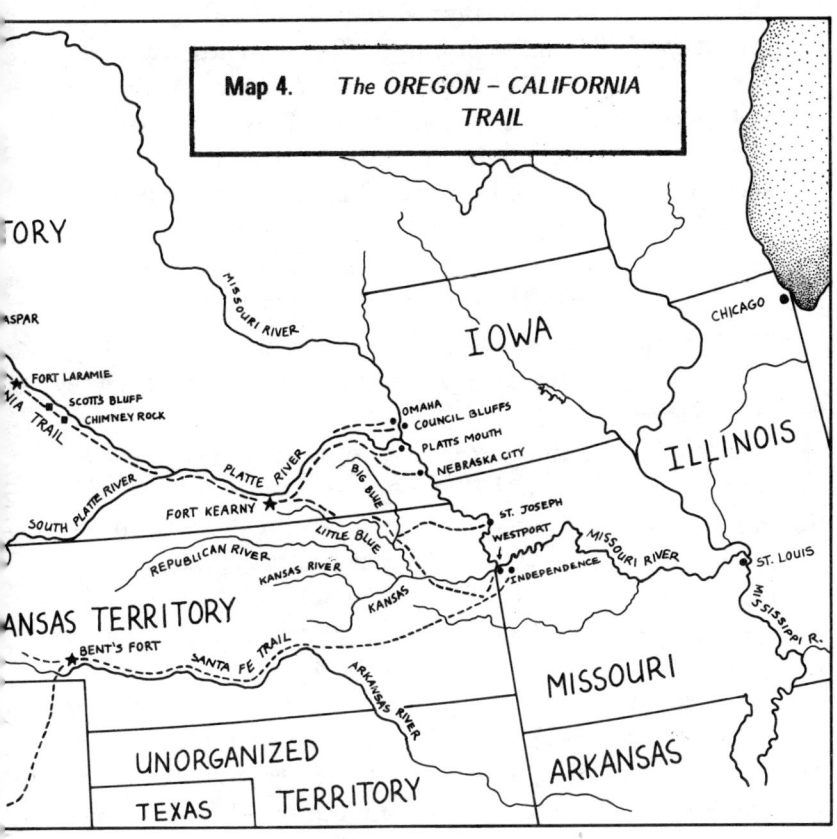

passage through the great mountain range dividing central and western America. The Lewis and Clark route was treacherous and not too helpful in getting to California. A trip through the Colorado Rockies was not likely and the trip via the Santa Fe trail through the arid southwest,[5] although an easy way over the Continental Divide was a very round about trip with a lot of desert and badlands. The favored route to central California and Oregon followed rivers all the way affording water and grazing for the livestock. (They didn't use gas stations much back then.) The trail was opened up by the mountain men doing fur trapping.

The mountain men had trapped and explored as far west as Mexican *Alta California*. Following suit, the French Canadian trappers of the Hudson Bay Company had come south through the Siskiyou to trap in *Alta California*. They rendezvoused at present day French Camp near Stockton. The mountain passages into northern and central California are formidable. Compared to ascending the back slope of the Sierra, the South Pass was a cake walk — toilsome but not harrowing. Captain Bonneville, in 1832 was the first to take wagons over it.

The trip along the Platte had its difficulties. One had to ford the tributaries flowing into it. From Fort Laramie, the trains continued up the North Platte to Mormon Ferry later to become Fort Caspar and now the city of Casper Wyoming. To the southwest of Casper the Sweetwater River flows into the North Platte; its headwaters coming off the great divide to the west. The trail follows the Sweetwater past two famous landmarks — Independence Rock and in plain view further west, Devil's Gate — a four-hundred foot vertical gash in the rock through which the Sweetwater flows. The road climbs the hill at the south edge of Devil's Gate. There are many pioneer graves there. This is where Lydia Jane Freshour was born on July 11, 1857. Fourth of July celebrations were usually held at Independence Rock if your wagon train was on schedule. Thousands of Emigrants carved their autograph into this "Registry of the Plains."

The prairie schooners went on up the Sweetwater, past Split Rock and Ice Slough. One crossing of the Sweetwater remained, a dangerous one, and another ten miles to the summit of South Pass. Although at 7000 feet, one does not realize that they are at a crest. The pass is quite level. The exact summit is hard to locate. Another two miles and the water at Pacific Springs runs west. Narcissa Whitman and Eliza Spalding came through here in 1836, the first women to cross the Pass and continue overland to the Pacific proving that women were equal to the task. The wagon used by the Whitman-Spalding party fell apart and they walked with pack animals over the Blue Mountains into

Oregon. This was the normal method used by the fur trapping mountain men. Years later, the first wagon train conquered the rugged mountain passage into Oregon. Medical doctor Marcus Whitman, his wife Narcissa and twelve associates were massacred in 1847 by the Cayuse Indians at the mission they founded near present day Walla Walla.[6]

To emigrants, South Pass marked the halfway point of the journey. Next came Pacific Creek, the Big Sandy and the Green River. There one could drop down to Fort Bridger on the road to Salt Lake. The trail through this region of the Rockies is in semi-arid terrain devoid of timber or woodland.[7] It consists of hills, buttes, bluffs and river bottoms and long sloping plateaus tufted with small bushes. The trail in places stretched ahead through the knee high shrubbery like a country road disappearing in the distance toward the low slung purple and brown hills.

At Fort Bridger, the west bound traffic heads north west along the Bear river to Soda Springs and then on to Fort Hall in what is now Idaho. The Sublett cutoff headed due west to the Bear River avoiding Fort Bridger. In either case, this put the travelers on the Snake River which could be followed up to Fort Boise and on to Oregon. In the summer of 1845 and again in 1846 John Sutter sent out Caleb Greenwood, an incredibly old mountain man who was "tougher'n ironwood," to travel eastward on this trail to persuade the Oregon bound to come to California.[8] Sutter had a great vision for California.

Soda Springs was at the northernmost part of the Bear River. The Hudspeth cutoff went west from there avoiding Fort Hall and the Snake River. Either from along the Snake or from Hudspeth's cutoff, the California trail followed Goose Creek south crossing into what is now northeastern Nevada. This entire process avoided the Great Salt Lake and what is now Utah skirting north through the bottom of present day Idaho. Years later folks would be confused as to where they had been. They had "crossed the plains" and could give locations by landmarks and rivers. They had traveled through a vast amount of Indian Territory which would become states in years to come. Many places were to be named later.

For the California bound, the plan was to get on the Mary's River, now the Humbolt,[9] and follow it west and south west across the high desert to the Sierra. This is part of the Great Basin which lies between the Rockies and the Sierra. It has a series of valleys and ranges and the soil is thin and alkaline. In the western extent of the Great Basin prehistoric Lake Lahotan once covered the area of the Walker Lake, the Pyramid Lake and the Humbolt sink. The Sierra rivers, the Truckee, the Carson, the Walker and from the north east the Humbolt, run into these lakes.

The emigrants came onto the Humbolt in the vicinity of present day Wells, Nevada and followed it west past Gravelly Ford and the Little Humbolt to Lassen Meadow. The Humbolt offered occasional grassy marshes at present day Winnimucca, Rye Patch and the lush Great Meadow at Lovlock — rendering the route tolerable. The trail went on due west for those going to northern California on the Lassen trail or to the Rogue river via the Applegate Trail.[10] The main trail turned south along the Humbolt toward the Humbolt Sink and the Forty-Mile Desert. The lower Humbolt was calamitous — a virtual *Via Dolorosa*. Broad stretches with no water — hills of crumbly shale — deep trenches of sand and gravel — troughs of alkali or volcanic ash — blistering hot at mid-day — freezing at night. Our travelers finally arrived at the Humbolt Lake where this curious inland river disappeared into the brackish undrinkable water.[11]

From the Humbolt Sink they could continue through this desolate valley of death on one of three routes. Originally the travelers headed west across the Forty-Mile Desert to the Truckee River. The Truckee is named for the Paiute chief who showed the way across the desert to the river to Mountain Man Elisha Stevens[12] who led the Murphy-Townsend party from Council Bluffs, Iowa in 1844.

The Bartelston-Bidwell party leaving the Oregon Trail in 1841 passed just north of Salt Lake. In the Salt Lake desert they abandoned their wagons and as a pack train wandered lost and starving through Nevada and over the Sierra in the vicinity of Sonora Pass and finally with the help of an Indian arrived at the ranch of Dr. John Marsh east of Mt. Diablo. In 1843 the Chiles-Walker party abandoned their wagons in the Owens Valley. Joe Walker organized them into a pack train and led them south skirting the high Sierra entirely and brought them through the Walker Pass on horseback.[13]

The Murphy Townsend party under wagon master Elisha Stevens were the first to bring wagons through the Sierra establishing the Stevens Pass in 1844.[14] The ill fated Donner party followed two years later and the pass was renamed the Donner Pass by popular acclaim. The Murphy party had been stranded at the same place and daughter Elizabeth Yuba Murphy was born nearby. One account says she was named Yuba because she fell in the Yuba River as an infant.[15] A cabin was built at the foot of Truckee Lake and three men left to guard six of the wagons.

The only Sierra trails at this time were Indian foot paths. A few wagons were brought through by making wagon trail where there was none — children rolling rocks aside, the men and women chopping brush, wagons lurching up river bed where possible. The Oxen's feet were bleeding and the men were yelling and whipping them. They manhandled these few wagons through — at one point taking the oxen up a granite precipice and having them pull the wagons up using all the trace chains.[16] Moses Shallenberger ended up staying the winter with the six remaining wagons.

After days and weeks of breaking wagon trail through the Sierra terrain, they arrived at Sutter's Fort only to have the men commandeered for the on going military campaign.[17] They got the remaining wagons down the following year in 1845. They had succeeded in getting the first wagons over the crest of the Sierra. They got to California with no casualties and two babies born on the trip — another Murphy grandchild had been born at Independence Rock.

The Donner party did not fare so well in 1846. They made the mistake of taking a "shortcut" — Hastings cutoff from below Salt Lake to the South Humbolt. They were late and the winter hard — twenty foot deep snow.[18] Before they could be rescued, half of them died near the spot where Shallenberger had survived the winter. They used his cabin.

Nicholas Broyles Gann with his wife Rutha Freshour and their family came through here the following year in 1847 with the Hopper train and saw the Donner party remains.[19] They encountered General Kearny, eastbound from his California conquest.[20] Kearny had his men bury the mutilated remains. The Ganns were part of a group of some four-hundred people, about one half women and children, with one-hundred wagons that left Independence the majority bound for Oregon. The Ganns were among the minority of one-hundred in some twenty wagons that left the trail below Fort Hall and helped pioneer this Humbolt route.[21] This pre gold rush band was led from Fort Hall by Charles Hopper III, "an old mountaineer." Hopper had been to California in 1841 with the Bartelson party and was now returning with his family. The "Donner Pass" route was still being developed, a number variations being tried the first few years until a workable passage was marked out.[22] The Gann's trip was probably not much easier than the Murphy's.

Now, wouldn't you know that Rutha was expecting? In October of 1847 Captain Hopper's company of wagons was reported crossing the San Joaquin Valley on the way to San Jose. While camped at Tuleburg in *El Rancho del Campo de los Franceses* — present day Stockton, William Gann was born — the first American child born in the San Joaquin.[23] After a decade of San Joaquin ranching, the Ganns crossed the coastal range into the Santa Clara Valley and passing through San Jose, they crossed the last range, the Santa Cruz Mountains, to the Pacific Ocean to live near Santa Cruz. Nicholas B. Gann was noted there as an early pioneer. They were close neighbors of the Sophronia Freshour family in Soquel in 1880. The Freshour family had spanned from "sea to shining sea."

In 1848, the Carson Route of the California Trail opened up. The Carson and the Lassen Routes were soon to take most of the traffic away from the difficult Truckee Route. In 1849, James Marshal discovered gold in John Sutter's mill race. John Sutter had his wish. The world rushed in! More than 20,000 men and hardly any women or children. Their destination was the diggings in "Mother Lode" country in the Sierra foothills. The gold rush left "gold rush widows" back east.[24] Their husbands eventually returned. There was always a surprising amount of east bound traffic on the Oregon-California Trail. Pony *express* service wouldn't be established until 1860 but it was possible to send mail home. — the 49ers corresponded with their families back east even though they hardly had express service. The Freshours and Ganns back in Missouri surely received news of California from Nicholas and Rutha. Judging by children's date and place of birth, some came out in 1854. Freshours who arrived in the 50s engaged in mining and some were to participate in the Oregon gold rush. The trail to California was heavily traveled in the early 50s. The traffic thinned down in the late 50s. We know from births of two Freshour families coming out in 1857 and have evidence of several other Freshours or relatives and neighbors coming out at that time. These would have most likely taken a route following the Carson River. Certainly the James R. Freshour family did.

These later groups such as that of John and Sophronia Freshour and their children and brother Joseph Terre Freshour, James R., Martin and Thomas Freshour and their respective wives and children and the parties they were with, headed on south from the Humbolt Sink. They had a more difficult desert to cross to get to the Carson River which went up the Carson Valley to the Carson Pass. Some groups went even farther south through desert to get on the Walker River to go through the Sonora Pass. For those heading toward the Carson River, the hard desert journey continued through chalky formations alternating with stretches of sand. Kegs of water were required.

Overnight travel avoided the intense heat. Eventually, the animals smelled water throwing their noses up and the Carson River would be in reach. There they found large cottonwoods. The first trees big enough to provide shade that they had seen in 1100 miles! A traveler recorded "Men were seen to rush up, half crazed with thirst and hunger and embrace those noble old trees and weep like children, and bless God for their deliverance." They and their livestock drank water from the Carson — "the most delicious water man or beast had ever tasted."[25]

These rivers last mentioned flow off the backside of the Sierra. The Sierra Nevada Mountains ramp up gradually from the floor of the Great Valley that covers the central part of California. It is like a succession of ranges, each successive one getting a little higher. One passes through timber for many miles and finally gets above the timber line. Then there is the almost abrupt drop off the back side into the Owens Valley, the Carson Valley or into Lake Tahoe. This is very rugged terrain. The high desert of Nevada runs about 4500 feet above sea level. The Sierra Passes run 7200 (Donner) to 9600 feet (Sonora). At 8500 feet, the Carson Pass was known as the *Devil's Ladder*. This back slope was a formidable obstacle to the depleted travel worn emigrants that frequently had left half their animals dead and many of their wagons abandoned along the Humbolt. They had a respite at 7000 feet in the lovely alpine Hope Valley before proceeding to the final ascent of the Devil's Ladder.

Once over the crest, they were confronted by granite domes and gorges and bounding rivers and an abundance of tall timber stretching in every direction. The average slope is only about two degrees.[26] Scouting and trail blazing were important. These later parties followed the trail blazed by Kit Carson. Trees he marked were viewable for years after. The wagons had to make it over the Sierra before the first snow flew. It was possible to winter over in the Sierra if provisioned for it. Some of the Murphy party had. James R. Freshour and his wife Francis and their children may have wintered over there.

Their third child Joseph Frank Freshour was born November 4, 1857 in what is now Alpine County.[27] Tradition says near the present town of Markleyville.

Once gold fever had subsided, men started to take note of the fertile great valley — called variously the Sacramento or San Joaquin Valley — and the abundance of water flowing off the Sierra and through it. They understood the potential here that would someday make California the world's sixth largest state in gross national product. The Freshours and their in-laws established ranches in San Joaquin County and were there in the 1860 and 1870 census. They gradually dispersed, some going to the coast to work in the Redwood timber and sawmills and some drifting to Calaveras County and later some going up to the gold of the Oregon-California border region of the Siskiyou.

This in brief is "The Trail" — The 2000 mile route of our pioneers who came to California by wagon train. More about this later. First we will identify and develop the eastern roots of those inveterate movers who followed wagon roads west and ultimately followed the big one — "The Trail."

3

MISSOURI TRAILHEAD

UNLIKE many "greenhorns" who started from further east, they started from the frontier — in Iowa and Missouri where they had settled. From there, various groups of Freshours, friends, neighbors and kinfolk made the great trek across the plains to California in the years 1847 through 1857. The Henry Freshour branch left for California from Jasper Township of Adams County, in southwestern Iowa, sixty miles from the town of Plattsmouth on the Missouri River. They were in the 1856 Iowa state census. Some one-hundred miles south of them, lived the John Freshour family of Van Buren Township in Jackson County, Missouri. They were near to Independence and Westport (present day Kansas City) on the Missouri River — a prime location for departure for California. This family was there for the 1840 and 1850 census.

It was not long after the Freshours settled on the Missouri that the freight wagons were rumbling through on their way southwest to the New Mexico trade at Santa Fé. And there were the rough hewn mountain men fur trapping the wilds beyond Santa Fé. They would come through with their pack animals loaded with pelts on their way to St. Louis. Then these men started trapping the rockies to the northwest. Then "Oregon fever" struck and wagons were being outfitted there for the Oregon Trail. By 1850 the big excitement was the land of the *Calafía* and the *Grizzly*.[1]

There may have been gold seeking excursions to California by some Freshours during the 1849 frenzy but the quest for farm land seems to have been their prime objective. Even when some of them went to the gold country in Calaveras County and later in Siskiyou County and adjacent Jackson County, Oregon, they usually staked out a piece of land to homestead.

The *John Freshour* family of Jackson County, Missouri were pioneers of that area, having arrived in Missouri sometime between 1833 and 1836. John was born in 1790 and his wife *Elizabeth Smith* was born in 1795 — both in Pennsylvania. They were married in Greene County, Tennessee in 1811. Their children were all born in Tennessee except their youngest, Emaline, who was born in Missouri. They had seven children with them in 1840: Nineteen-year-old *Thomas*, sixteen-year-old *Rutha*, thirteen-year-old *Lawson*, eleven-year-old *Malvina*, nine-year-old *Sarah E.*, seven-year-old *Martin* and four-year-old *Emaline*.

John and Elizabeth reared their family at first in Greene County, Tennessee then in Jackson County, Missouri, where they saw most all of them married and grandchildren starting to appear. Rutha married mountain man Nicholas Broyles Gann. "He belonged to the Rocky Mountain Fur Company in 1836 and afterwards joined the forces of John C. Fremont in the conquest of California. He was also a particular friend of 'Kit' Carson the celebrated scout and Indian fighter and was present when Kit Carson fought the dual with the Frenchman, Schuman on Green River."[2] Thomas was married in nearby Lafayette County and there is no such record for Lawson. The entire family including grandma Elizabeth settled in California. Apparently grandpa John either didn't live to make the trip or didn't survive it. The last record of him is a land deed in Jackson County dated in August 1853.[3] There is a deed for his youngest son, Martin Freshour for the same section of land in October 1854 — possibly inherited. The Freshours of Jackson County had several notable neighbors. Charles Hopper (II and III) held several parcels of land in the county. Isaiah Horn is a school teacher living (with his wife Jane Gann and their 7 month old son Marion) in the household of his father, David Horn. There were also Ganns and Baucoms that trace back to Tennessee. Many of these were to take the wagon trail west with the Freshours.

The children of John and Elizabeth, who were with them at trail's head in Jackson County are Tennessee people reared in Missouri. Thomas, Rutha and Lawson had clear memories of Tennessee and the trip to Missouri around 1835. It is quite possible that they traveled most of the way to Jackson County, Missouri on paddle wheeler. By 1819 the first steamboat had puffed up the river to Nashville. The dangerous Muscle Shoals of the Tennessee lay between Knoxville and the Mississippi. A portage railway was used but the channel was cleared and in 1828 the first steamboat reached Knoxville. The steamboat ushered in a new era of transportation. By 1831 there was fairly regular steamboat service on the upper Tennessee and Holston Rivers.[4] Although a meandering course, it was down stream all the way to Cairo. Then up stream to St. Louis and across the breadth of Missouri to Independence. (Mark Twain was born about the time they made the trip so he couldn't have been their pilot.) In 1852, the Isaac Hill family traveled by steamboat from Monroe County Tennessee to St. Louis where they outfitted and proceeded on with a drove of 500 cattle to their Iowa ferry crossing and thence to Oregon.[5]

Prior to the advent of steamboats, flatboats were commonly used. By the Cherokee treaty of 1791 the Indians agreed to allow the whites free and unmolested navigation of the Tennessee River.[6] Flatboats or keelboats were loaded with goods at Knoxville or Nashville and floated to downriver markets along the Tennessee, Cumberland and Mississippi. These boats were often "fitted up comfortably with apartments, and in them ladies, servants, cattle, horses, sheep, dogs, and poultry are floating in the same bottom under the same roof."[7] It is also possible that John and Elizabeth Freshour traveled with their children by flatboat from Greene County, Tennessee at least part way to Jackson County, Missouri just as *Henry* and *Jane Froshour* had traveled by flatboat from East Tennessee to Arkansas in 1832. A flat boat could be arduously poled upriver at about one mile per hour. — A steamboat could do about ten miles per hour going upriver.[8]

In 1832, the Froshours and some of the Finleys migrated to Arkansas. ...For the trip to Arkansas, they built flat-bottomed boats. They left Eastern Tennessee in the spring of the year to take advantage of the high water during that time of the year. They started their journey March 25, 1832 in Calhoun, Tennessee on the Hiwassee River. The original diary of their journey is in the possession of Mrs. Lina Ruth Baker. ...

It took them two months to make the trip. They traveled down the Hiwassee until they reached the Tennessee River. During their time on the Tennessee, the journal records that they 'ran wild' down the river for three days. This surely must have been a terrifying time for them. Upon reaching the junction of the Ohio and Tennessee Rivers, they traveled down the Ohio to the Mississippi, then down the Mississippi to the Arkansas. They traveled up the Arkansas River to where Ft. Smith is now located, then traveled overland to ... Washington Co. [9]

This account depicts a mode of travel from Eastern Tennessee to the frontier. Arkansas Territory, until it became a state in 1836, included Oklahoma. Henry Froshour [10] was granted an eighty acre patent near Evansville and eighty acres just across the border from Evansville in Oklahoma Territory where tradition tells us he raced horses that he brought to Arkansas.

In 1829 Sam Houston resigned as Governor of Tennessee and went to Arkansas to join the Cherokee, with whom he had spent much of his youth in Eastern Tennessee. Prior to 1825, some 6000 Cherokee who were dissatisfied with treaties with the whites went to Arkansas Territory — the Western Band of the Cherokee. Their principal chief, Oolooteki of Hiwassee Island, had adopted the young Sam Houston naming him *Kalanu* — "The Raven." Houston took up the Cherokee cause, going to the nation's capital to plead their case. Houston remained as Indian Agent and full-fledged member of the Cherokee Nation until 1833 when he went to Texas eventually becoming first president of that republic.

The US government had adopted the removal policy in 1825 to create a definite western frontier and by 1835 most Indians were settled in present day Kansas and Oklahoma. The Tennessee River was known as the Cherokee River in colonial times.[11] The lands surrounding the river are the original Cherokee lands. The Cherokee Nation remained established in Georgia and Eastern Tennessee until December, 1835 when some Cherokee signed the treaty of New Echota with the US government. By this treaty of removal, all Cherokee land east of the Mississippi was ceded to the US for $5,000,000 and 15,000,000 acres of land in the Indian territory. The Five Civilized Tribes were forced from their southern plantations by the covetous whites. The US Supreme Court found for the Indians but President Jackson proceeded to hold the Court in contempt — and got away with it. The Cherokee were forced to take their slaves and leave. Another treaty in 1836 paid an additional $1,000,000 and required the Cherokee to clear out of Tennessee in two years. This was enforced by US troops.[12] Among these was Joseph Freshour of Scrugg's Co., 3rd Tennessee Mounted Militia.[13]

In the summer of 1838 many Cherokee were sent by boat. Their route, starting point *and* destination were identical with that of the Henry Froshours and Finleys. But, they didn't use flatboats. Indian agent Nathaniel Smith had large keelboats especially constructed. The Cherokee along with their slaves were conducted to the Indian Territory via the Tennessee, Mississippi and Arkansas Rivers.[14] In the autumn the Cherokee held their last tribal council in Tennessee and the great removal began. The suffering endured by the evicted Cherokee on their twelve-hundred-mile forced march gave to their route the name the *Trail of Tears.* Of the nation of fifteen thousand men, women and children, two thousand died in the detention camp and two thousand more were left in shallow graves along the trail. They were loaded into six hundred and forty-five wagons. The painting of the Cherokee Trail of Tears by Robert Lindneux depicts a covered wagon caravan.[15]

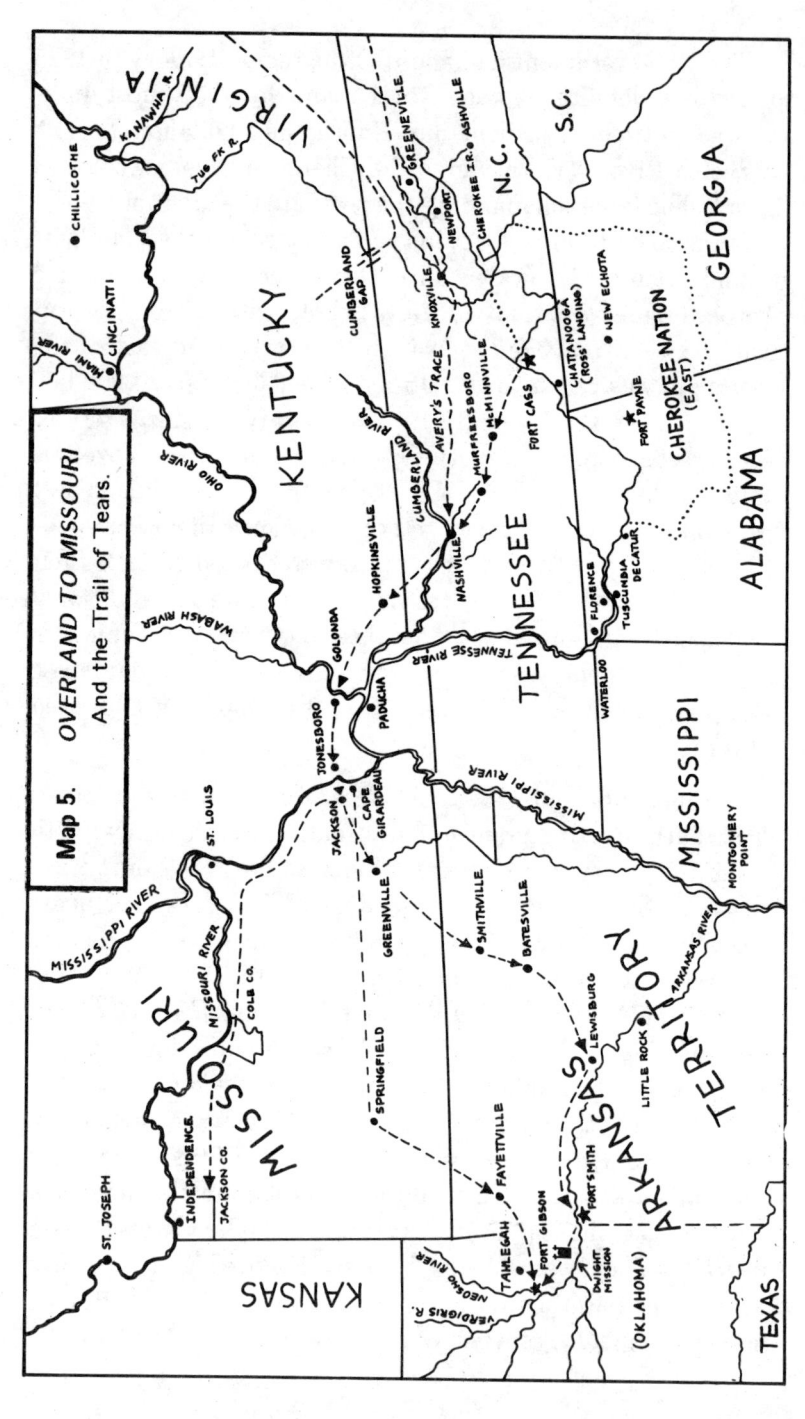

Not all Cherokee submitted. More than a thousand escaped from the forts and fled into the remote mountain regions. Their descendants now occupy the reservation in North Carolina bordering Tennessee. It is interesting that the Greene County Freshours lived in traditional Cherokee lands — the Colonial Cherokee Overhill region — and migrated out of the region in about the same time frame as the Cherokee exodus. They probably traveled by wagon as most of the Cherokee did. Parkman tells of viewing wagon travelers camping along the Missouri as he passed by on a paddle-wheeler.[16]

John and Elizabeth and their family would start their eight-hundred mile wagon journey by traveling the road first from Greeneville to Knoxville and then on to Nashville. The first settlers of Nashville on the Cumberland River arrived during the Revolutionary period via the Cumberland Gap and followed the Cumberland River down from what was to become Kentucky. In 1785, Peter Avery of North Carolina was authorized to blaze a trace to Nashville. The route from Clinch Mountain (near Kingsport) entered the Cumberland Plateau at Emory Gap near Harriman and crossed the plateau to the Cumberland River. In 1791, the Cherokee Nation granted "free and unmolested use of this road from Washington District to Mero District." The Walton Road was completed on this route from Knoxville to Nashville in 1795. Tennessee was admitted to the union in 1796 and in 1804 private companies were chartered to build toll roads. In 1805, the Cherokee granted the Federal Government a mail route through their territory. The Indians owned and operated the inns and ferries along the route charging a nominal fee for their services.[17]

In 1833, the Freshours would pay toll to follow a rough wagon road west to Nashville. From there they would follow the Cherokee route up through Illinois into Missouri. This was a terrible road already strewn with graves even before the ill fated Cherokee trek. In the dry season the travelers choked in dust which in a drizzle became a muddy bog. From the Cape Girardeau region they most likely traveled north to St. Louis and crossed Missouri following the wagon roads along the river. This trip would take six weeks to two months of wagon travel camping in the open. They may have been able to afford the occasional use of an inn.

The verdant woodlands of Missouri are safely inside the newly established frontier and the Freshours travel there with hopes of new opportunity for themselves and their children. The nation was conceived sixty years earlier and Andrew Jackson is now President. The US Constitution is forty-six years old — about the same age as John. Missouri has been in the Union fifteen years now. Samuel Colt introduces a new kind of pistol having a revolving six-shot cylinder. Texas secedes from Mexico. The Alamo will fall the following March. In 1833 Joe Walker had climbed the Sierra from the east and reached the Yosemite Valley in Mexican Upper California. Like the Freshours, Walker was a Tennessean who went to the Missouri frontier. He was one of the founders of Independence and had served as it's sheriff. In 1834 the first missionaries had reached the Willamette Valley. Arkansas will be admitted to the Union next year in 1836. Jackson County, Missouri was pivotal to all this activity — an exciting place to be. The nation is growing and has problems. Martin Van Buren becomes President. By now the beaver market had played out and the mountain men in the west needed a new challenge.

The John Freshour family is counted in the 1840 census in Jackson County, Missouri. Benjamin Harrison is now President and the population of the US is seventeen million — a gain of 17% in a decade. In 1841 the Bidwell-Bartleston party travels overland from Missouri to California and conclude their harrowing journey by being arrested and detained in San Jose for intruding into Mexican Territory without visas.[18] This had been ordered by General Almonte, Mexican Minister of War. News of the expedition had reached Mexico City and incensed at reports of American annexation, he sent orders to Vallejo to forbid immigration without legal passports. A number of the party spent four days in the "calaboose" in San Jose. Although detained they kept their firearms. When Dr. Marsh arrived Charlie Hopper told him "...we are strong, and will fight our way out if necessary."[19] Dr. Marsh interceded with General Vallejo on their behalf procuring the visas and they were finally released to settle in Mexican *Alta California*.

Hopper wintered in the San Joaquin exploring. He visited Yerba Buena (San Francisco) on the way up to Sonoma to visit Yount who provided him and Col. Chiles with dried beef and mules for their journey back to the "States." It was 1842 when Chiles and Hopper conducted a party of nine men back to Jackson County, Missouri. They were caught in a flash flood camping on the San Joaquin River and Hopper caught typhoid and was carried down the valley on a stretcher. He recovered to guide the group on to Missouri via the southern desert and his former hunting and trapping grounds — New Mexico.[20]

Parkman describes a May morning in 1843 on the Missouri frontier.

> Westport was full of Indians, whose little shaggy ponies were tied by the dozens along the houses and fences. Sacs and Foxes, with shaved heads and painted faces, Shawanoes and Delawares, fluttering in calico frocks and turbans, Wyandots dressed like white men, and a few wretched Kansas wrapped in old blankets, were strolling about the streets, or lounging in and out of shops and houses. [21]

By 1843 there was considerable emigration to Oregon outfitted at Independence.

> The emigrants ... were encamped on the prairie about eight or ten miles distant, to the number of a thousand or more, and new parties were constantly passing out from Independence to join them. They were in great confusion, holding meetings, passing resolutions, and drawing up regulations, but unable to unite in the choice of leaders to conduct them across the prairie. [22]

Parkman's account of emigrants of 1843 at Independence is vivid.

> The town was crowded. A multitude of shops had sprung up to furnish emigrants and Santa Fé traders with necessaries for their journey; and there was an incessant hammering and banging from a dozen blacksmiths' sheds, where the heavy wagons were being repaired, and the horses and oxen shod. The streets were thronged with men, horses, and mules. While I was in the town, a train of emigrant wagons from Illinois passed through, to join the camp on the prairie, and stopped in the principal street. A multitude of healthy children's faces were peeping out from under the covers of the wagons. Here and there a buxom damsel was seated on horseback, holding over her sunburned face an old umbrella ... The men, very sober-looking countrymen, stood about their oxen; and as I passed I noticed three old fellows, who, with their long whips in their hands, were zealously discussing the doctrine of regeneration. ...[23]

These were, no doubt, towns quite near to the pioneering John and Elizabeth and their children. They and their relatives and neighbors were undoubtedly keenly aware of all this. It was a constant part of their environment and the local scuttlebutt.

In the summer of 1845 a democratic editor discovered what was to become one of the most dynamic slogans ever coined — *Manifest Destiny.* In this self evident truth the frontiersmen found not only revelation but also recognition. John C. Frémont, along with his wife, Jesse (daughter of Missouri Senator Thomas Hart Benton) was instrumental in forming this policy of the Polk administration. James K. Polk of Tennessee took office in 1845. He hoped to use Texas as a step toward the acquisition of California — if necessary by war. The war with Mexico came and went — opposed by an idealistic young congressman named Lincoln who ruined his political career opposing it.[24] And it did portend acquisition. Dr. John Marsh desired to see California in the Federal Union. He wrote letters to Missouri urging his countrymen to come with all speed to California. California's ownership, he declared, was not to be determined by diplomats, explorers or "manifest destiny," but by settlers in actual possession of the soil. Feverishly, he played the Texas game and dispatched his letters by every caravan going east on the Santa Fé Trail. His letters contained in effect the first overland guide to California. When these letters arrived in Jackson County, Missouri they caused a great commotion.[25] Rubidoux, a returned trapper, painted pictures of California as a perpetual paradise.

Dr. Marsh's strategy worked. The 49er gold rush was *into US territory*. In the celebrated "Bear Flag" revolt of 1846, Frémont and companions announced the establishment of an independent California Republic.[26] Many Missouri frontiersmen fought in California in the war against Mexico. General Kearny assembled his dragoons at Leavenworth for their march down the Santa Fé Trail and conquest of New Mexico. His dragoons continued on along the Gila Trail to San Diego for his campaign which completed the American conquest of Alta California. The old Spanish province came under the American flag in February, 1848 with the signing of the treaty of Guadalupe Hidalgo between the United States and Mexico. The Jackson County, Missouri family of John and Elizabeth Freshour was at a focal point of history.

There is another Freshour enclave located down river to the east in Cole County, Missouri. A very prominent citizen there was Judge *William S. Freshour* born in North Carolina, reared in Tennessee and married in Missouri.[27] The Judge was a merchant and the founder of Centertown. In 1851, William S. borrowed $2500 from his brother *James Freshour* "who had gone to the State of California in 1849 and who returned in 1851 with a fortune that he had made in that State. Afterward he returned to that State, and now [1889] is living there." The Judge operated a store at Centertown until 1860. He owned much of the town. His house became the local hotel when he built his new mansion. He owned vast acreage with a splendid mansion and held slaves until the day he died.[28]

The father of these Cole County Freshours was reported to be *John Freshour*. (Who else?) "*George Freshour* his grandfather was from Germany, but came to America and settled in North Carolina, and later moved to Tennessee and from there to Ohio, where he died." It is not stated exactly where Judge Freshour lived in Tennessee. It is possible that it was Cocke County. The Cocke County courthouse burned, as so many have, making it even more difficult to determine who the early residents were. There seems to be a pattern of the Cocke County Freshours coming from North Carolina and the Greene County Freshours coming from Pennsylvania although they crossed over between Cocke and Greene Counties by osmosis once having arrived. It is interesting that we have here an "Immigrant Freshour" who, it would seem, could have been *Hans Jerg Froschauer*. Or, more likely, Hans Jerg's son George could have gone down to the North Carolina piedmont. It is probable that this is a corruption of the Hans Jerg story.

We do have another *Wagon Train* Freshour found in Jackson County, Missouri — *James R. Freshour* and his wife Frances McKelhany. He presents another enigma. He doesn't fit the John and Elizabeth Freshour family. He is reported to have been born in Hancock County, Tennessee and reared in Missouri. We have his marriage record as evidence that he and Frances were in Jackson County, Missouri in March of 1852. They had two children born some where in Missouri — James Marion Freshour in 1853 and John W. Freshour in 1855. Three other children were born in California — Joseph Frank Freshour on the 4th of November, 1857 in present day Alpine County, Noah (died as an infant in 1861) and Alice Freshour born in 1862 in Calaveras County.

In the eclectic gold rush demographics of 1850, a group of four San Joaquin County households of the Tennessee-Missouri pattern stands out. These families are those of Sampson Hitchcock, Nicholas Gant (sic), Sam'l Campbell and John D. Gann (Nicholas' brother.) Tennessee born, twenty-one year old James "Freasure" is in the Campbell household. The census index gives his name as "Freisare."[29] Hitchcock, Gann, Wm. Fagan, John and son Martin Freshour and Charlie Hopper were neighbors in Missouri.[30] James R. Freshour's obituary states that he came to California in 1847 — returning to Missouri to return again to California in 1857. This data tends to fit the brother, James Freshour, of Judge W. S. Freshour of Cole County, Missouri.

James R. Freshour's son Marion's place of birth is given variously as Centertown in either Jackson County or Johnson County, Missouri.[31] Centertown is in Cole County, Missouri. — Another association of James R. with Judge William S. Freshour. Centertown is just west of Missouri's capital, Jefferson City, in the middle of the state on the Missouri River. One can imagine James R. traveling up river to the west to Jackson County for the purpose of joining a wagon train to California. As a returning argonaut he would pass through there again with romance ensuing.[32]

James R. and his sons had more of a tendency to follow mining in California than any other Freshours that we have tracked at the end of the trail. In his later life, he appears not to have been as gregarious with the other Freshours in California as they were with one another. We may see a dichotomy of [North Carolina - Cocke County, Tennessee - Cole County, Missouri - pro slavery] versus [Pennsylvania - Greene County, Tennessee - Jackson County, Missouri - antislavery] among the wagon emigrants.[33] As we shall see, the Indiana - Iowa branch seemed to be consonant with the Jackson County, Missouri branch — in an extraordinary way.

There is another Missouri wagon train Freshour in Johnson County neighboring Jackson County. *Andrew Freshour* and Jane Marcum were married in Johnson County in March of 1837 both at the age of 27 if one can believe the 1850 census. Andrew and Jane were living in Johnson County in 1850 with their five children. In 1860, Andrew and his children were in California near the town of Sebastapool north of San Francisco Bay in Sonoma County — Wife Jane apparently deceased and eldest daughter Eliza Jane married and gone. This family would have crossed the plains as teenagers. A number of descendants of this family lived in the Geyserville and Healdsburg area in the northern part of Sonoma County. Christopher Columbus "C.C." Freshour, a son of Andrew, was a notable resident. Quite a few Hoppers and a few Horns are notable in this area where Vallejo's Petaluma Rancho once flourished. There is no positive connection of the Andrew Freshour family to other Tennessee-Missouri Freshours either in Missouri or in California.[34]

A California Rancho of the first class was about equal in extent to a small German principality. Although most land was purchased by early settlers, some land had been gallantly given away by the land wealthy Mexicans [35] and in retrospect it appeared to have been simply appropriated (Dr. Marsh's suggestion?) The Federal land offices in California did not sell large tracts of public land as had been done with Indian land in other states. They usually issued patents for land already owned. Land generally was purchased from prior owners just as it had been acquired by Americans under Mexican rule. Land transactions under some of the Alta California regimes were of questionable validity even before American conquest. The Land Act of 1851, pushed through congress by Senator Gwin over the objections of junior senator Frémont, placed *all* Mexican land titles in doubt.[36] Spanish land grants and land title conveyed under Mexican authority required litigation to attain validity under US laws.

Mariano Guadalupe Vallejo, born and educated in California, former military governor of Northern California, delegate to the California constitutional convention, was stripped of much of his land by a US Supreme Court decision.[37] Vallejo went to Washington to plead the Californio cause. Land that he previously had sold and grants he had made as governor now had no clear title. Sutter lost most of his land. Vallejo's son was serving as surgeon with the Union army. Vallejo became good friends with president Lincoln. Even Lincoln couldn't help him. California land buyers were "buying a lawsuit." With this rationale, the ubiquitous squatters were encouraged. Bandit Joaquin Murietta protested, depredating the settlers. He was archetypal. He was killed several times. — Or so it would seem. A medicine show displayed his preserved head.[38]

California was ours — the gold — the land — all of it. The gold was the key. Those finding themselves suddenly rich bought land. The Freshours were not among the suddenly rich. — The name of suddenly rich John C. Frémont [39] appears on page after page of the index of recorded deeds in San Joaquin County. — our manifest destiny.

Brooding in suppression lay an unresolved aspect of that destiny — slavery. Hideous violence would break out between north and south and it would erupt first on the Missouri frontier. California beckoned as a land without slavery and its attendant strife. This gave impetus to the Martin Murphy migration from Missouri to California as early as 1844. Judge W. S. Freshour held slaves. How did the Pennsylvania - Tennessee - Jackson County, Missouri Freshours of German Lutheran heritage feel about that? [40]

The Kansas-Nebraska act introduced in January, 1854 set off a flood of immigration into Kansas. In the spring of 1854, even while the Kansas-Nebraska bill was being debated, the outfitting towns of Westport and Independence were congested with thousands going — not to California, but Kansas.[41] Ohio river steamboats were packed with emigrants from Pennsylvania, Ohio and Kentucky. The entire country had gone mad about Kansas. The bill's passage split the democratic party. — It allowed the new State's populace to choose whether it would be admitted as slave or free. The Republican Party was formed. The race for land was a race between pro-slavery and abolitionist forces. Missourians had not waited for the Nebraska bill to pass. Early in the spring they crossed the "Big Muddy" and staked claim on Indian land. New Englanders settled Lawrence, Manhattan and Topeka, Kansas.

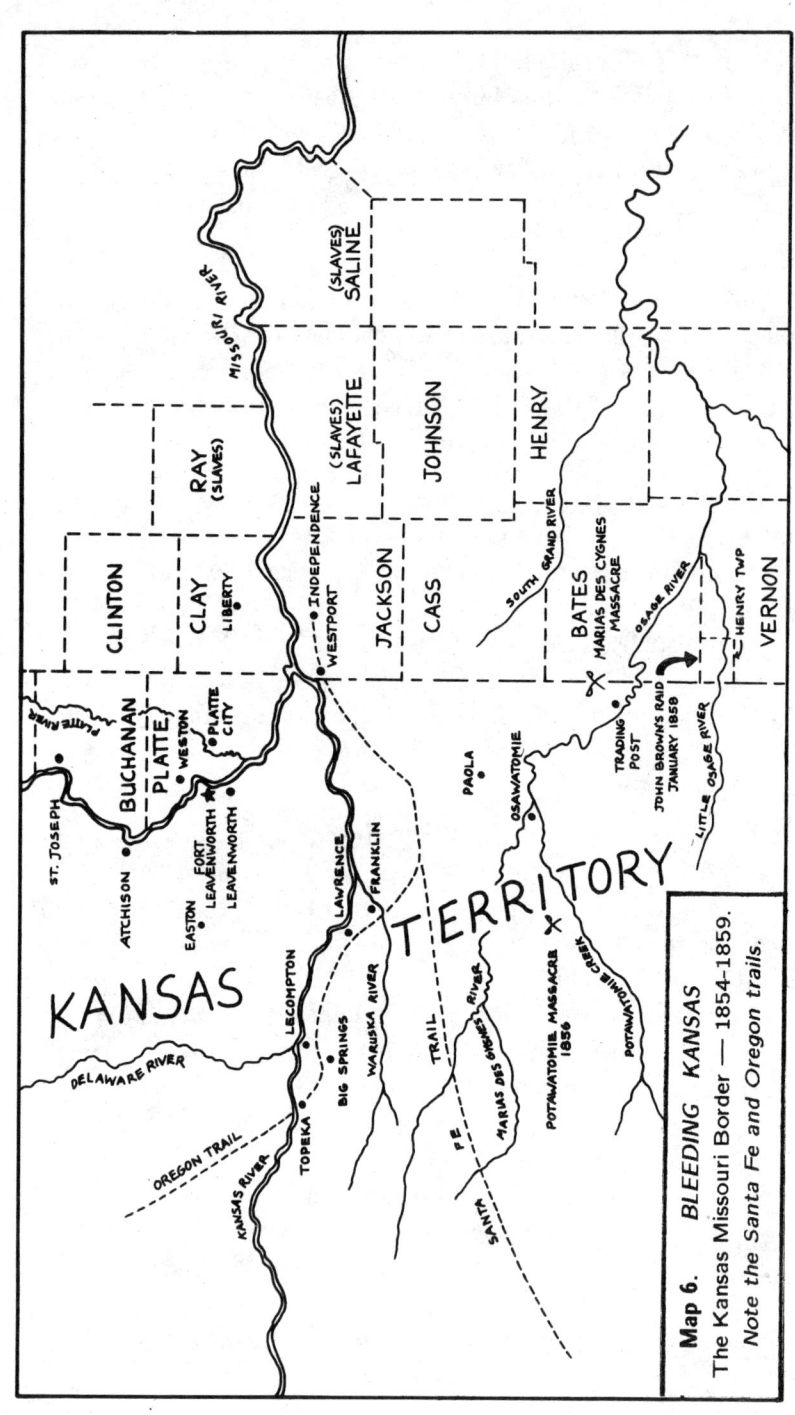

Map 6. BLEEDING KANSAS
The Kansas Missouri Border — 1854-1859.
Note the Santa Fe and Oregon trails.

The Kansas-Missouri border became violent. "Jayhawkers" raided into Missouri murdering, pillaging and looting. The "Border Ruffians" returned in kind. This pent up violence had been building for years. The 1854 rat race between abolitionist and pro slavery forces to take Kansas was the preamble to the War of the Rebellion. An Illinois lawyer named Lincoln decided to re-enter politics.[42]

In February of 1856, on the Missouri and Kansas border, two hundred men, women and children were shot, stabbed or burned to death in the fighting between free- and slave- state settlers and guerrillas. The money loss, in crops burned, cattle and horses stolen or killed, ran about $2,000,000.[43] The sack of Lawrence occurs and in retaliation, Abolitionist John Brown with four sons and others massacre pro-slavery colonists at Pottawatomie Creek.[44] In 1856, President Franklin Pierce issues orders for both Border Ruffians and Free-State men to disperse, but both sides prepare for conflict.[45] President Buchanan has no better luck. In 1857 an effort was made to bring Kansas into the Union as a slave state with fraudulent votes by Missouri residents. It failed. The War of the Rebellion was shaping up. Missouri is half slave and half free. Lincoln gives his "House Divided" speech.[46]

The Freshours of Jackson County, Missouri had a ring side seat to all of this. In the 1850 census John and Elizabeth Freshour had Lawson, Martin and Emaline in their household. Rutha, Thomas, Sarah and Malvina were married. Rutha was in California. Martin and Emaline married in 1853. These young adult Freshours may have understood very well that Missouri and the Nation to the east would be engulfed in a blood bath. They and many of their neighbors appear to have unanimously agreed to go to California.

In a few years, the Missouri governor and Legislature would flee to Arkansas and operate as an exiled government. The state of Missouri never seceded. It was a state of the Union invaded by Federal troops. Local militias had been formed —

many by those pro-union and many by those wanting to maintain a sovereign neutral state of Missouri. To their consternation General Price, commander of the Missouri State Guard, sought Confederate aid and the exiled government joined the Confederacy.[47] The citizens of Missouri had the choice of either a Confederate or Union government both backed by strong military forces warring within the state. The second major battle of the War of the Rebellion and the bloodiest battle in percent of casualties was in September, 1861 at Wilson's Creek outside of Springfield, Missouri.[48] It was followed by the battle of Pea Ridge just to the south in Arkansas. The Union forces of Iowa had moved south and occupied Missouri. The war raged between Union and Confederate forces along the Missouri-Arkansas border until hostilities ceased in 1865.[49]

For years sporadic violence preceded the pitched battles. When the war broke out, the situation worsened. Kansas gangs called "Jayhawkers" ravaged the Missouri border counties between the town Nevada and Kansas City. In response to these attacks, Confederate partisans banded together to fight behind Union lines. The guerrilla fighters were called "Bushwhackers." A few of these were pathological killers who used the occasion to commit savage crimes. Others were more gallant. The Bushwhacker Quantrill and his "raiders" fought on the Kansas-Missouri border. In 1862, the cavalier Quantrill captured Independence, Missouri and was awarded a Captain's commission in the Confederate army.[50] In August, 1863, Quantrill captured Lawrence, Kansas, the abolitionist capital, burned 185 buildings, and killed about 150 inhabitants. In an effort to curb such bushwhacker raids, General Ewing, Commander of the border district, ordered the evacuation of Cass, Jackson, Bates and part of Vernon counties working a great hardship on the Missouri residents and scattering the raiders into central and southern Missouri.[51] Notice that the term "Civil War" is a 20th century euphemism. When this conflict was happening, those loyal to the Union tended to view the Rebels as traitorous criminals to be apprehended and executed. This sometimes occurred.[52] Gen. John C. Frémont was relieved of his command of Missouri Union troops by Commander in Chief Lincoln in November 1861, because of his inflammatory proclamation against Confederates.[53] Prior to this century, Confederate military records were not to be found in the National Archives. They were kept in their respective state Archives for fear of individual reprisal.[54] Captured Confederate soldiers were "paroled" in the sense that convicts are paroled. The Union and Confederate troops in the western regions seldom were in combat against one another. They mostly controlled Indians. A surprising number of California troops were killed by Indians.[55]

When the War of the Rebellion finally broke loose in 1861, the Freshours of Jackson County, Missouri were all settled in California. Most of them appeared there in the census of 1860. That year a political dark horse was chosen as the Republican candidate for the presidency.[56] Abraham Lincoln was elected by a disintegrating country on November 6th, 1860. There were no Freshours and not many Ganns in the 1860 Jackson County, Missouri census.

The Freshour's native lands did not yet exist as the *nation* of Germany. The Prussian Otto von Bismark, a contemporary of Lincoln, would, with a fist of blood and iron, finally forge a loose confederation into a unified German Empire. America was about to see half its Union devolve into a confederation. It would take a man with a different kind of strength to put it back together.[57]

4

CONESTOGAS TO THE WABASH

HOOSIERS from Tennessee? — in Iowa! To the inveterate movers of the three decades spanning the 1830s through the 1850s, that wouldn't seem strange. The other Trail's Head contingent of Freshours — other than the ones in Missouri that is — was actually the Indiana branch. *Henry Freshour* and his wife *Elizabeth Hedrick Freshour* of Greene County Tennessee arrived in Allen County Indiana in 1833 — shortly before John and Elizabeth Freshour left Greene County Tennessee for Missouri. We will leave the relationship of John and Henry as an exercise for the reader. We note that John and Elizabeth Smith Freshour were approximately five years older than Henry and Elizabeth and that John and Elizabeth were born in Pennsylvania and that Henry and Elizabeth were born in Tennessee. If they were from the identical immigration from Pennsylvania to Tennessee, and they probably were, then this brackets that migration between 1795 and 1800. Our concern here is to position California wagon train emigrants at trail's head. In this case Adams County Iowa.

Henry was born in 1799-1800 in Greene County Tennessee and Elizabeth Hedrick was born in 1802 in Greene County Tennessee. *Elizabeth Hedrick* married *James Dunn* and they had one child — J.D. Dunn born in 1820 in Greene County Tennessee. James Dunn died of yellow fever in 1821 and his widow, *Elizabeth Dunn* married *Henry Freshour* in 1823. Twins *John* and *George (Hans unt Jerg!)* were born to Elizabeth and Henry in 1825. *Mary Jane* was born in 1827 and *William* in 1829. When they arrived in Indiana in 1833, they had twelve-year-old J.D., eight-year-old twins George and John, six-year-old

Mary Jane and four-year-old William with them.¹ Henry and Elizabeth reared their family first in Allen County in northeastern Indiana and later in Jasper County in north-western Indiana. They settled near Fort Wayne (Wayne Township) in Allen County Indiana where son *Joseph Terre* was born in 1838. Their first child of record in 9 years! Their children were in two sets. Henry and Elizabeth were in Gilliam Township of Jasper County Indiana for the 1840 and 1850 US census. They moved there in about 1839. Their last two children were born in Jasper County — *Alfred Henry* born in 1841 and *Lydia Ann* born in 1844.

There were other Freshours in Allen and Jasper Counties of Indiana at this time. They mostly emigrated from Virginia and Pennsylvania via Ohio and had no Tennessee connection, but since the Greene County Tennessee Freshours originally came from Pennsylvania they all may have been close cousins. One other Tennessee Freshour was in Jasper County in 1850. *William Freshour* born in 1810 in Tennessee and married in 1830 to *Hannah Robinson* at Allen County Indiana. William was a predecessor of Henry and Elizabeth at Fort Wayne. He may have been a brother. William and Hannah were in Wayne Township of Allen County with four children in the 1840 census. William and Hanna and Hanna's brother Paris and family and a George Freshour family all eventually moved to Jasper County from Fort Wayne and were there in 1850. William and Hanna's son George James Freshour born in 1835 was the father of Paris Freshour.²

Henry and Elizabeth's family grew up in Jasper County and the older children married there. J.D. married about the time they moved there. In July of 1844, Henry and Elizabeth deeded over to their nineteen-year-old son John, in consideration for $100,³ an 80 acre parcel in Jasper County. In 1850, at the age of twenty five, John purchased a small parcel from Paris and Sarah Robinson nearby in Jasper County. Mary Jane was married by the 1850 census and George and John were still in the household of Henry and Elizabeth but would soon be on their own. The entire family then moved to Iowa in 1854. At that time, the three younger children, Joseph Terre, Alfred Henry and Lydia Ann were age sixteen, thirteen and ten respectively. These minor children were shown in the 1856 Iowa census in the households of their older brother and sister. Joseph and Alfred were in the household of John and Sophronia Freshour and Lydia and William were in the household of brother-in-law Perry Mack who was married to Mary Jane. What had happened to Henry and Elizabeth? The Jasper County History of 1883 indicates that "they went to Iowa and died there." [4] In 1854 Elizabeth would have been fifty-two and Henry fifty-four years of age. There are no obituaries or cemetery records for that locale and era. Cemeteries often fall into disuse with no way to identify who is buried in them.[5]

The children of Henry and Elizabeth were reared in Indiana and later positioned at the Iowa trail's head.[6] The movements of the family are interesting. What were the social, economic and political pressures that arose to occasion these geographical displacements? Why would one family leave Tennessee for Missouri while another would leave Tennessee for Indiana? Why did they leave Tennessee at all? Were they just compulsive movers? Did the grass always look greener on the other side of the fence? Why did they pack up and leave Fort Wayne for Jasper County? Where was Henry during the nine year gap?

As we shall see there are some even more bizarre questions that arise in Adams County Iowa. We found strong motives in Bushwhackers, Jayhawkers and bleeding Kansas to repulse all the Freshours out of Jackson County Missouri. How did the Kansas-Nebraska Act and the turmoil preceding the Rebellion effect the folks in Adams County Iowa? And what happened to Elizabeth and Henry? And who was the mystery Henry who married in Jackson County Missouri and bought lots in Brooks Iowa? We expect to shed some light on all this.

The Freshours probably left Tennessee for the same reason that they went there. They emigrated from the vicinity of Franklin County in Pennsylvania to Greene County, Tennessee as pioneers — just as they had pioneered in Pennsylvania. They came to Greene County Tennessee in the flood of populace that

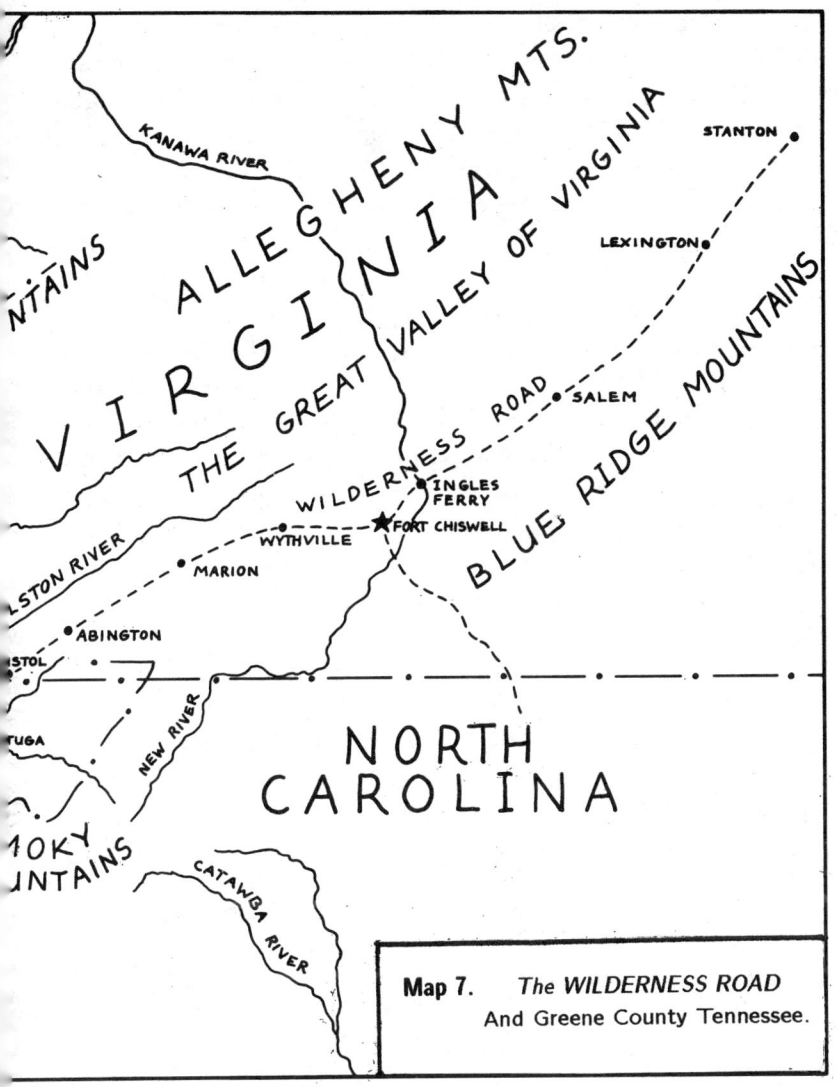

Map 7. The WILDERNESS ROAD And Greene County Tennessee.

surged into the area when it achieved statehood in 1796. It was pioneer territory. It was Cherokee territory. The Indian war path that traverses from Pennsylvania down through the Shenandoah and Great Valleys and the Holston Valley to the Cherokee capital of Chota had become the *Wilderness Road*.

Chota had been located at the present North Carolina border where it is crossed by the Little Tennessee River. (The other war path from Chota up through the Cumberland Gap through Kentucky and Ohio to lake Erie had become Daniel Boone's extension of the Wilderness Road into Kentucky.)[7]

The immediate frontier or "backwoods" for the Freshours of the Conewago Valley was in western Pennsylvania following Forbes's Road up to Fort Pitt and extending across the Ohio. The preferred direction for expansion, however, was down across the Potomac into Virginia and the Shenandoah Valley.

These frontiersmen bit by bit settled along what was to become the Wilderness Road. Their backwoods eventually included lands along the Holston, the Watuga and eventually crossed Cumberland Gap to Boonesborough. The first settlers arrived on foot, then with pack animals. For two essentials, salt and iron, and for whatever "Luxuries" they felt they could afford for their households, the backwoodsmen had to recross the mountains. The pack horses followed the trail in single file with one man on horseback leading and another rider at the rear to look after the packs. Whenever possible, new settlers trailed behind an experienced caravan following pack horses burdened with crooked bars of iron and dangling bags of salt.

> After 1755 Conestoga wagons were following Braddock's road. ...In the valley of the Conestoga River, Lancaster County, a breed of very heavy horses had been developed; perhaps the huge, heavy wagon took its name from its draft horses. No sooner was a road made fit for wagons than a Conestoga appeared on it — one single wagon bearing a family and its household stuff to the West, or a caravan of emigrants. ...these first Conestogas, in western Pennsylvania, were vividly decorated by their proud owners, risen above the status of pack-horse drivers. [8]

The Conestoga horse was believed to be a strain of the magnificent stallion, Tamberlane, and the three brood mares brought over by William Penn. They were 16 to $17\frac{1}{2}$ hands in height and weighed about 1600 pounds. Three span were usually used to pull the Conestoga Wagon with it's eight ton freight capacity. With the passing of the Conestoga wagon, this breed of horse — one of the few breeds to originate in the United States — was permitted to become extinct. These were the commercial freight wagons that traveled the Pennsylvania roads and the Great Philadelphia Wagon Road to the southern states. Sometimes there were trains of fifty to a hundred wagons creeping at twelve to fifteen miles a day, hauling glass, pottery, linen, salt, sugar, grain, flour, charcoal, iron ore and pig iron.[9]

The Conestoga was the grandaddy of all American wagons. These huge freight wagons were covered wagons with eight to twelve hickory bows that formed large arches covered with a hempen homespun canvas that formed an overhang front and rear. The bottom bulged such that no matter how the load shifted, it went to the center. The ponderous rear wheels were five to six feet across. The seasoned oak body was painted brightly with light blue, the wheels, running gear and side boards vermilion, the iron work black and the top white. Bear skins kept the horses warm in the winter. The harness was embellished with Russian style bells mounted in an arch over the horses. These were selected for their tonal quality and served a practical function of signaling the approach of this formidable vehicle. They also indicated the professional ability of the teamster since the price of "road service" was forfeiture of some of the prized bells. This charming bit of *Americana* has given us the enthused *"I'll be there with bells on!"* [10] The left wheel horse — the "nigh-wheeler" — was sans bells because it was saddled to accommodate the wagoner when he wasn't walking by the side of the wagon.

This rig with its team covered a length of sixty feet. A caravan of these wagons was a stupendous sight. The colorfully dressed wagoners were a tough breed who smoked "stogies" and slept in the open air or in rustic establishments devoted to their trade.¹¹ These men had the right-of-way without argument and they established the American habit of driving down the right hand side of the road.¹²

The settlement of Tennessee progressed swiftly. Land-seekers poured in from Pennsylvania, Virginia, the Carolinas, and even from New England. They arrived with Revolutionary War Bounty Land Warrants, from military service or acquired from speculators or veterans. Virginia's Great Valley and Avery's Trace were thronged with "movers" throughout the summer. There were the usual merchants and peddlers with their donkey trains, raw boned sod busters on shaggy plow-nags and fashionable gentlemen astride thoroughbred horses. Household goods were piled high on farm wagons with wide iron tires. Huge topheavy Conestogas pulled by oxen creaked along while others used makeshift sleds with runners of oak or hickory. Immigrants unable to afford ox or horse trudged through the clouds of dust carrying their children and meager belongings on their backs. All were moving west to Tennessee — the promised land. Thousands came by way of the Ohio and poled up the Cumberland or the Tennessee River in keelboats.¹³

Old John Freshour, the patriarch with his children and grand-children came from Pennsylvania. Imagine that entire family with Conestogas coming down the Wilderness Road. Among those coming in from North Carolina were the Freshours of Cocke County. There they found a colony of Pennsylvania Germans settled in 1789 in the "Dutch Bottoms" on the north bank of the French Broad River. The settlers kept coming.

Old John and his party settled in Greene County where he was to build his home and give land to the Solomon Lutheran Church. The Freshours were among its first members. The old log house covered with weathering board is still lived in. A newer church building has replaced the old log church. Old John and Eave and a number of other Freshours are buried in the church cemetery.¹⁴ There were several John Freshours.

John Freshour Jr., apparently Old John's grandson, according to family tradition liked to trade with the Cherokee Indians and was given the Cherokee name "Chucklehead." This is close to the Cherokee word for "Falling Water" which is a common name among the Cherokee. The English spelling that the whites gave the name led to the more recent notion that the Indians called him that because he was always laughing.

The Freshour family prospered in Greene County. They had cattle, geese, hogs, ducks, fruit trees and a big garden. They even had a slave to do the cooking. The farm was in possession by Freshours for several generations but was later involved in extended legal proceedings which kept the church from obtaining clear title until 1940. One of the later owners, Joseph Freshour, had mortgaged everything. The Freshours farmed, were blacksmiths, were proficient in music and interested in schools. There are no longer any Freshours on the church roll. The family spread from there all across the country.[15]

The wilderness had retreated across the Tennessee hills to the Mississippi bottomlands. From the Blue Ridge Mountains of eastern Tennessee to the middle counties of the state, towns burgeoned. Each had its log courthouse and public square. The church served as a schoolhouse on weekdays. Each town had its general store, smithy, gristmill and sometimes a distillery. The roads that webbed the woodlands connected outlying villages and farms with the towns.[16] Soon, the log dwellings were sheathed with clapboards. The churches and courthouses were eventually reconstructed of brick or stone.

In 1800 the Great Revival swept the state. The brawling ferment of frontier days began to pass. The burgeoning US population tripled to 12.8 million in the decades spanning 1790 to 1830. In 1803 Jefferson purchased the Louisiana Territory. Ohio became a state in 1803. In 1804 Old John Freshour died leaving a will mentioning his Greene County children.[17] Several Freshours were among Andrew Jackson's troops when he came into power in Tennessee defeating the Creek Indians, the British at New Orleans in 1814 and the Seminoles in Florida in 1818.[18] He lost the presidential election to Adams in 1824, but became president in 1828 — thirty-two years after Tennessee attained statehood.

In 1825, an illiterate seventeen-year-old tailor moved from North Carolina to Greeneville, the seat of Greene County. His employer had advertised for his recapture. He was a run-away indentured apprentice. Andrew Johnson soon had most of the cloth in town turned into suits. A school teacher named George W. Freshour taught him to read in free night lessons. As a gift, Johnson tailored George Freshour a wedding coat for his marriage to Ailsey Lawson. When Johnson himself later married, his wife taught him to write and cipher. George Freshour never suspected he was tutoring a future US president. The coat became a cherished possession.[19] This George W. Freshour may have been a younger brother of Henry. Henry and Elizabeth may very well have attended Ailsey and George's wedding. The twins would have been three years old then and Mary Jane only one year old. The Lawsons would be there in force to see Aisley married off. John and Elizabeth would not have left for Missouri for several years yet so would have also attended the wedding with their three children, Thomas, Rutha and Lawson. Lawson would have been about a year old. And, of course, the eligible young bachelor, Andy Johnson, would be there — with bells on!

During the decades following Jackson's inauguration, Tennessee became politically and economically the most important state in the Mid South. Manufacturing and commerce flourished as the state became more thickly settled. Henry Freshour who had served Jackson well in the War of 1812-1814 was on his way to Arkansas by flat boat. It was time for Old John's grandkids to move on; John and Elizabeth Smith Freshour to Missouri and Henry and Elizabeth Dunn Freshour to Indiana.

It is not difficult to envision the Tennessee Freshours heading directly west to Missouri. However, Indiana seems more north than west and getting there from Tennessee appears to be an imposing problem. One would not expect a popular movement from Tennessee to the northwest. But, General Anthony Wayne had defeated the Indians at Fallen Timbers. Tyler had won at Tippecanoe. The War of 1812 in America was only a side show to the great events in Europe; but it and the events leading up to it had secured Ohio and Indiana for settlement. The Indians of the Northwest Territory were, as the Indians in the south-east had been, moved out west. *"Ohio Fever"* gripped the New Englander. High land prices and high taxes in New England made the western land look good. By 1817, difficult economics and confining institutionalization impelled the small New England farmer west.

By the time Henry and Elizabeth headed into the Northwest the lower parts of it were well settled. Not only New Englanders and Southerners came into the Northwest Territory. People also poured in from the middle colonies. The Freshour middle colony bailiwick (that includes the Littlestown, Conewago Valley, Pennsylvania area, the Hagerstown, Frederick, Maryland area and the Berkeley Springs, Cherry Run area of present day West Virginia) was located right at the Cumberland Road starting point at Cumberland Maryland. Cumberland was accessed by an established road leading from Frederick.

By an 1806 act of congress the Cumberland Road to the west became the National Road. The first section was the Braddock Road established for French and Indian War logistics. From Wheeling, West Virginia on the Ohio, the National Road followed Zane's Trace to Zanesville being completed in 1826. John Freshour, Revolutionary War veteran son of Wendel, had no doubt followed Zane's Trace on to Chillicothe in Ross County Ohio. The National Road continued to Columbus (1833), Springfield (1838), Indianapolis, Terre Haute and Vandalia in Illinois and finally St. Louis in 1852. The road from Cumberland into Ohio, commenced in 1811, was rebuilt in 1822; the roadbed being a nine inch layer of stone crushed to seven inch pieces for the bottom layer and three inch pieces for the top layer. Trees and stumps were removed to a distance

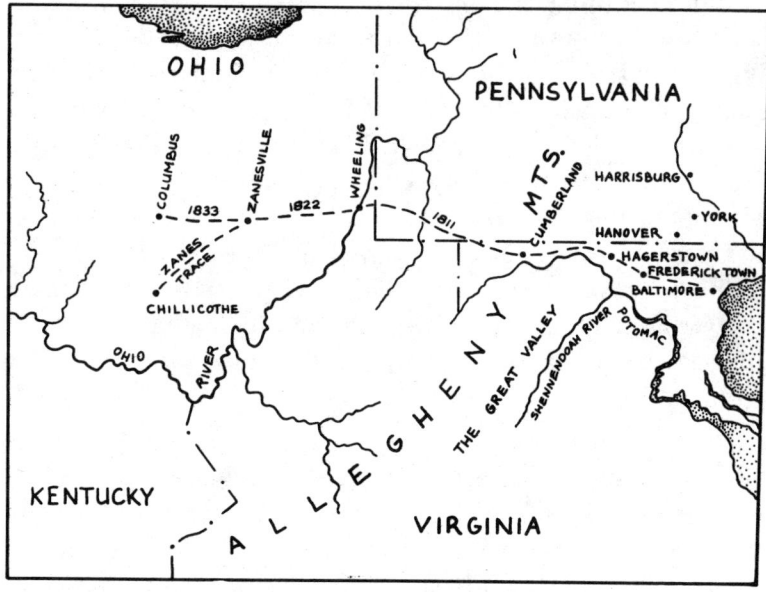

Figure 4.1: The National Road

of twenty feet on either side of the road i.e., forty feet from the center. This was a real road and Conestogas with six or eight horses could haul freight and make good time.[20] Stage coaches could hurtle along at an average speed of twenty-five miles-per-hour with frequent change of foam-flecked horses.[21] It was relatively easy for Freshours to move from their middle colony bailiwick into Ohio and many of them apparently did.

In these years the emigration from the southern states was even greater. The popular idea that the mountainous districts of the South were populated by poor whites pushed from the bottom lands by encroaching plantations fails to recognize that the vernacular, alone, of the mountain folk reveals that they chose their isolated districts before the plantation system began its ruthless expansion in the southern lowlands and in the Kentucky blue-grass country — and fails to take into account the tremendous emigration from the South into the old Northwest. Nor is mention of the dwindling economic opportunity of the small farmer in the slavery district needed to explain much of the emigration from the "southern shore" of the Ohio. The Appalachian backwoods, the Kentucky forest, was the breeding ground of the *insatiable pioneer.* This emigration had by 1820 populated more than half of Ohio, the southern third of Indiana, and the lowlands of southern Illinois. [22]

The old Wilderness Road through Kentucky in the meanwhile had also become a "Turn Pike" which is to say a toll road. Pointed poles (pikes) were used to block the road until toll was paid, then the pikes were turned aside allowing passage. With the cessation of Indian hostilities, the militia stations along the road were abandoned in 1795. Families quickly moved in along the road and eight years later, the wilderness was dotted with homes. Circuit riding Methodist Bishop Asbury was impressed with the need for a Wilderness Circuit. His journal gives his impressions. "What a road we have passed! ... Certainly the worst on the whole continent even in the best weather; yet bad as it was, there were four or five hundred crossing the rude hills ... " Inns began to appear along the road to accommodate the increase of wagoners and drovers. Bishop Asbury found these pestilent.[23]

The Kentucky legislature established the turnpike in 1797 with tollgates at appropriate points. The tolls collected hardly maintained the road. The section out of Tennessee from Cumberland Gap up through Kentucky remained an improved trail. In spite of this, the Cumberland Gap way to the west was more popular than the well developed Ohio River route, the National Road. Moreover, commerce had supplanted exploration and settlement. Eastbound traffic on the Wilderness Turnpike almost equaled that going west. Many Kentucky farmers went to Ohio and Indiana to buy hogs which they raised in Kentucky and fattened in their cornfields for the drive to market in the east. Droves of beef cattle and hogs were driven through the Cumberland Gap to market in Virginia and in North Carolina.

A Virginia visitor to Kentucky in 1825 said of the Road "It was intolerable in most seasons of the year." Although poles had been placed in the worst bogs and sloughs to give it a bed, long stretches were still almost impassable.[24]

Although increased revenue from tolls allowed construction of some ferries and bridges, and the road was widened and straightened in places, the improvements never kept pace with demands. No federal funds were applied. Major R.P. Baker was placed in charge of Kentucky's transportation system in 1835. At Barbourville he observed wagons rumble past in long lines, an occasional big Conestoga drawn by a six-horse team, droves of horses, mules, cattle and hogs on the way to the eastern markets. He saw stage coaches loaded with mail and passengers, creaking and rolling through bogs and chuckholes. He realized the road's inadequacy to carry the traffic of a commonwealth bloated with riches. It had been some sixty years since Boone, Harrod and Logan built their first towns in the wilderness.[25]

Henry and Elizabeth and their youngsters were to leave Tennessee in much the same way that Henry's parents had arrived from Pennsylvania. The most probable way to get to Fort Wayne was by wagon over the Cumberland Gap and up the pike through Kentucky. The commerce of Kentucky extended from the southern parts of Ohio and Indiana, through Kentucky, over the Cumberland Gap into Tennessee, Virginia and North Carolina. The Conestogas on this route found no engineered roadbed. They were the off-road vehicle of its day. The horse drawn freight Conestogas on the National Road were the eighteen-wheelers of their day.

By 1833 when Henry and his family made their trek into Indiana, Cincinnati was a thriving center of steamboat commerce. It had become a boatbuilding city producing the paddle wheelers that plied the Ohio. The Miami and Erie Canal from Dayton to Cincinnati was completed in 1827 and was later extended to Toledo. Henry and Elizabeth with their children would most likely go to the vicinity of Cincinnati and be ferried across the Ohio.

Figure 4.2: The Wildernes Turnpike north into Indiana.

The south-eastern part of Indiana had been sold under the Federal Land Act of 1800 by the Cincinnati Land Office. The northern part was settled by people moving north in the state and emigrants like the Freshours. Fort Wayne was established in 1794 by Mad Anthony Wayne who had defeated the Miami Indians and opened the territory up to settlers. In 1795

General Wayne secured the first land in the Valley of the Upper Maumee. The Indians ceded a piece six square miles at the confluence of the rivers St. Joseph and St. Mary's and a two square mile piece on the portage to the Little River — a tributary giving access to the Wabash. Thus, Fort Wayne was established.[26] The Miami Indians, tract by tract, sold off their land in Northeast Indiana and contiguous Ohio land. There were treaties in 1818, 1826, 1834, 1838 and 1840. The Miamis were finally guaranteed forever a country west of the Missouri river. In 1854 they again ceded their land in Kansas for a cash settlement for which they received 200 acres each and common holdings. Finally in 1868 in spite of all the "forevers" and "pledges," they were required to make a treaty by which they were removed to the Indian Territory (Oklahoma.)[27]

By an act of congress in 1822, a land office was established at Fort Wayne. The land ceded by the Miamis was surveyed, a receiver appointed (under president Monroe) and in 1823 the Fort Wayne land office opened at the fort for sale of lands to the highest bidder. A section of land was purchased and laid out as the original town of Fort Wayne, embracing 118 lots. Additions were subsequently laid out.[28] This land sold for $1.25 per acre. The old fort grounds — forty acres — were reserved for use of the Indian Agency. The Indian Agency was moved from Fort Wayne to Logansport in 1828. The land office at Fort Wayne continued sales until 1844. In the first few years there were only two-hundred odd entries on the land books and the country around for a great distance was an almost unbroken wilderness. Allen County was organized in 1823 and the county seat set up by commissioners in 1824.[29]

In 1827, congress granted to the state of Indiana, "for the purpose of constructing a canal from the head of navigation on the Wabash to the foot of the Maumee rapids," every alternate section of land equal to five miles in width on both sides of the line to be fixed for the canal. It was not until 1830 (under president Jackson) that an office for the sale of lands was opened at Logansport, and not until October 1832, that the Fort Wayne office did business. The minimum price of these lands was $2.50 per acre. The proceeds were used for canal construction.[30] Thus there were two land sale activities going on in Fort Wayne. When Henry and Elizabeth and their children arrived in 1833, there was enterprise that might offer not only employment but a commercial basis for a thriving community. The ceremony attending the commencement of work building the Wabash-Erie canal was on Washington's birthday in 1832. The first contracts were let in June 1832. Laborers were employed in great numbers. In 1835, the section uniting the sources of the Wabash with the Erie was completed. The canal promised to open up distant markets for farm production. Henry, William, John and George Freshour held Wabash-Erie land.

William Freshour was in the vicinity of Fort Wayne for some time prior to his marriage to Hannah Robinson there in 1830. It is not hard to imagine correspondence back to Greene County Tennessee telling Henry and Elizabeth of these developments. It is interesting that the canal was the first civilized means of transport into the area. Overland travel still occurred on Indian "traces;" the St. Joseph trace that passed by Wolf Lake and went through Elkhart prairie and followed along the St. Joseph river towards Lake Michigan, the Robinson trace which went due north from Richmond to Fort Wayne, and the Wayne Trace that followed the Mary's river passing near Wilshire. The harrowing experience of O.H. Smith campaigning for congress in 1826 and following the Robinson trace, reveals a trail through wilderness virtually impassible by wagon. The Hon.O.H. Smith might not have survived had not his horse been a good swimmer. He never would have arrived in Fort Wayne had not an Indian constructed for him on the spot, at the Wabash crossing, a canoe from the bark adroitly peeled from a very large hickory tree.[31]

The year 1827 was memorable as the date of the survey of the first road from Fort Wayne, "the river road" that extended to just east of New Haven and was later extended to Defiance, Ohio as a stage road. The mail service during the 1830s was by horseback on this route. Later the state of Indiana was to construct a highway from Vernon in Jennings County by way of Greensburg, Rushville and New Castle to Fort Wayne.[32] The most direct route for Henry and family would have been on the Robinson trace. A more likely route would have been north from Cincinnati along the Miami river or possibly the Miami-Erie canal to St. Mary's and from thence on the Wayne trace.

For the Freshour children this trip north into North-eastern Indiana was a wagon trail experience that was a precursor to a trek across Indiana and later a much longer trail they would follow as adults with their own children. It is not unlikely that they used a Conestoga or similar large wagon. They arrived at the canal construction boom town — a rustic settlement located in the midst of a sparsely inhabited countryside.

The first task would be to secure land and the next to build the traditional log cabin. Even though employment may have been available, subsistence farming would be a necessity. The surrounding woodlands were home to all manner of wild life affording game for the table. The principal predator was the wolf, of which there were still vast numbers in the northwest. Their barking and howling could be heard during the night in the settlement around the fort.

> The forests of northern Indiana have long been celebrated. Nowhere was walnut found of a finer grade or in more plentiful quantity. Great oak trees of the white and red variety had lifted their strong arms in the gales of a century and nodded to the straight hickory, the graceful popular and the stalwart ash. The early settlers who set about hewing farms out of the wilderness gave to the business of saw-milling its early prominence, and at many points where a water power could be had by damming the streams, the sawing of logs into lumber was extensively carried on, the farmer being glad enough to rid his land of an encumbrance so great as a grove of walnut trees. Where the distance to the saw-mills was too great these trees were cut up into rails, or oftener still, were burned. [33]

In 1835 the first steam saw-mill in northern Indiana was built by Benjamin Archer and his sons on the St. Joseph river, two and a half miles north of Fort Wayne. A water powered saw-mill was built the same year. Clearing of the land was progressive. It started with ...

> ...cutting away the undergrowth of briers, grapes, haws, spice, gooseberries, pawpaws and the like. The bushes were cut down or grubbed out; the smaller trees were chopped down, and their bodies cut into lengths of twelve to fifteen feet, and the brush piled in heaps. The large trees were left standing, but "deadened" by girdling. In a dry time the brush heaps were burned over; a large area was scorched by the burning of the leaves, and the soil underneath would then be especially fertile. Sometimes the brush would be piled about the larger trees, which were easily killed in the same operation that removed the undergrowth. To get the logs out of the way, there would be a "log-rolling," to which the neighbors were invited, who came with wooden hand-spikes, and put all the logs in heaps to be burned. The trees that did not fall were gradually cut down, and so the clearing proceeded hand in hand with tillage of the fields. [34]

Plowing was done with a bar-share — a bar of iron about two feet long with a broad share of iron welded to it. The moldboard was of wood split out of winding timber or hewed into a winding shape. Sown seed was brushed in with a sapling with a bushy top, dragged butt forward. The harrow or drag was of primitive construction, and was sometimes made of a crotched tree. The grain was harvested with a sickle until the land was entirely cleared and the threshing was done with a flail, two sticks of unequal length fastened together with a thong, with which the inexperienced were in more danger than the wheat piled on the threshing floor.[35]

In the six years that Henry and Elizabeth Freshour lived at Fort Wayne, the young settlement burgeoned and matured into a town. Their children also grew. Their eldest J.D. Dunn at eighteen years of age was in the teaming business making long hauls on the road that followed the Wabash-Erie canal from Toledo on the Erie to Logansport in north central Indiana. The old fort was situated in the middle of a rich farm area which would in the years to come become the city of Fort Wayne. This would include Wayne Township where the Freshours lived. Fort Wayne was not incorporated as a city until 1840, shortly after Henry and Elizabeth had packed up with their young ones and headed west.

The canal, it was expected, would one day provide access to markets for cash crops. But, an immediate concern of the Indiana pioneer was the presence of Indians and the lack of transportation. In addition to the individual efforts of the farmers to make hauls with their wagons, there were opportunities for entrepreneurs such as J.D. Dunn to get hauling jobs that led him to range over northwestern Indiana. He may have hauled provisions into sparsely settled territory recently purchased from the Indians and sold by government land office. As his biography indicates, J.D. found ample opportunity to land speculate while plying his teaming trade.[36] Being young and single, he at first returned home to Fort Wayne from his excursions bringing the story of the newly opened Indian land to Henry and Elizabeth. The Delaware, Potawatomie and the Miami had been progressively moved further west opening up more land for sale.

Work on the Wabash-Erie Canal was delayed by financial difficulties, but managed to proceed at a slow pace. Funding became an embarrassment. The engineer for the project took it upon himself to have notes printed, bearing interest and receivable for canal lands. These were given the picturesque name "White Dog" and became part of the currency of that era. The excitement of the Wabash-Erie canal enterprise had lapsed into the doldrums and the entire nation was heading into the economic recession of 1837-43. Completion of the canal was finally celebrated at Fort Wayne on the fourth of July, 1843. Packet boats traveled between Fort Wayne and Dayton until 1854. The canal enterprise eventually went bankrupt. The canal was then filled to form the roadbed for the Wabash Railroad. The Henry Freshours never witnessed this train of events. They left in 1839. Although industrial and agricultural growth was not as spectacular as the Wabash-Erie promoters had envisioned, the struggling village that gathered about the historic fort would one day emerge as the prosperous and wealthy city of Fort Wayne.[37]

"Old Hickory" Andrew Jackson had been president for eight years. The inflation which occurred during his administration was driven by the sale of public lands. In his farewell address, Jackson condemns paper currency and speculation. He hands over a monumental economic disaster to his surrogate, Martin Van Buren. In the spring of 1837, stock and commodity prices crash bringing on the general economic collapse known as the Panic of 1837. Failure of wheat crops, ravaged by the Hessian fly, sent grain prices soaring. Gamblers in western lands had borrowed the shaky currency of "wildcat banks." [38]

> The land speculator goes forth with a guide and a pack horse; and for weeks perambulates the uninhabited forest ... When he has selected some tracts of virgin soil, ... he returns to the land office and pours his *all* into the coffers of the government. ... He meets the tide of emigration and endeavors to direct it toward the spot of his predilection. If he succeeds, he realizes in a short time a ten-fold profit, and begins again with enlarged capital.
>
> Interlocking with speculation in lands was the mania for canal-building in the western states after the completion of the Erie Canal (in New York.) Canals were authorized to be built through unsettled regions, on the ground that population would immediately increase, creating taxable values that would soon warrant the outlay. Here again the West was borrowing overconfidently against the wealth of the future. "By the winter of 1836-1837, every Western state, like every western citizen,

...had pledged its future upon the success of speculative ventures, whose mere continuance was contingent upon free access to capital and the perpetuation of good times." ... The war between President Jackson and the second Bank of the United States ... again brought a period of deflated capital and capsized schemes. The westward movement suffered a momentary lull — then rushed ahead without waiting for prosperity to catch up. [39]

Van Buren only lasts one term. He was our first president to be born under the American flag. His predecessors had all at one time been subjects of the Crown.[40] This national scenario explains the difficulties that befell the Wabash-Erie canal project at Fort Wayne. The Ohio section of the canal had similar problems. It is a credit to the Indiana pioneers that they pushed the project through to completion. Although short-lived, the Wabash-Erie canal was a vital force in the development of northern Indiana. Financial doldrums were not the only discouragement encountered by the Fort Wayne pioneers. Their plight was exacerbated by mother nature.

The summer and autumn of 1838 were signalized by a drought of longer duration and greater geographical extent than had been experienced since the first settlement of the country. On the estuary of the Maumee no rain fell from the 3rd of July to the 15th of October, and at Fort Wayne there was no rain-fall of any consequence from July to Christmas. The St. Mary's was so low that no provisions could be brought down from Ohio, and the supply of provisions in town was finally reduced to two barrels of flour. It was not until the next March that three flat-boats came down, laden with flour and bacon and whisky, and the arrival of these necessities was duly celebrated.

During this drought all the smaller streams throughout the region were exhausted and their beds became dusty. The wild animals of every kind found in the forests collected on the banks of the rivers, and even approached the town. The wet prairies became dry, the wells failed and even the bogs of the Black Swamp below, dried and showed great cracks in the muck. The excavation of the canal was then going on in the lower valley and the mortality among the laborers was frightful. [41]

Our inveterate pioneers pulled up stakes again. Now the family had a new infant — Joseph Terre — born in 1838 at Fort Wayne. Joseph was a frequently used Freshour name but Terre was innovative. It is reminiscent of Terre Haute — *high land* in French. Perhaps J.D. had hauled along the Wabash to Terre Haute. The children that came with them from Tennessee were now the teen-age twin boys, fourteen-year-old John and George, twelve-year-old Mary Jane and ten-year-old William. This trip across Indiana would be a memorable one for these youngsters. It was wagons again. Henry and Elizabeth probably found the trip easier than the pike going north from Cumberland Gap through Kentucky. J.D. had been hauling on this road and it was no doubt a definite road that assumed the Indian trace attributes as it reached north-west beyond Logansport into the pioneer territory of Jasper County.

They were headed into ......

5

INDIANA PRAIRIE

SCORES of people have perished on the prairie — simply from being lost. They traveled for many hours, ending up right where they started — having made a huge circle in the vast sea of grass. It was best to follow the Indian trails. An Indian, by definition, was never lost.

Jasper County is just north of the Wabash river basin — on the Illinois border. The southwestern part is gently rolling prairie. The northern and northeastern part has oak openings and prairies interspersed with knolls and ridges. Until 1832, this country was not open to white settlers.[1] At that time, it was in a wild state, scarcely disturbed by the hand of man. The Pottawatomie Indians gathered here every spring and fall to hunt and fish. The Iroquois river swarmed with the largest fish and the prairie supplied innumerable deer and grouse. The Pottawatomie nation occupied the northern part of Indiana. They were a bold war-like people, and were generally found allied against the whites. They were allied with the French against the Iroquois and English, with the English against the Americans, and took a prominent part in Pontiac's conspiracy, yielding to the general pacification which closed the war of 1812. They finally became fast friends to the whites and sided with them in the Winnebago outbreak of 1827 and the hostilities of Black Hawk in 1832. The French priests were remarkably successful in their missionary labors among this nation. In 1834 Vincennes was made the See of a bishop, who provided the Indian mission with a priest who labored among the Indians with wonderful results. Several tribes of the Pottawatomie nation made their home in Jasper County. The whites found their way here on hunting and fishing expeditions. The larger part of the Pottawatomie nation was removed in 1838 by the Logansport treaty to a reservation in Kansas.

The first settler came to what now is Gilliam Township with the treaty of 1832. The next settlement was made at the Falls of the Iroquois in 1834. These settlers from Illinois used the front wheels of a wagon and a yoke of oxen and exploring the river, reached the rapids. They prepared a cabin and returning with the oxen, brought the family in 1835. In 1834, Thomas Randal and George Culp of Virginia arrived at the "new purchase" which had just been surveyed and selected land at the forks of the Pinkamick and Iroquois. In May following of 1835 they returned with their families and made the settlement at the Forks. In the following year several other families followed.

In 1834-35, the Indiana Legislature dealt with the disposition of the unorganized area of the Northwest Territory. An act was passed forming fourteen counties extending from the Ohio border to the Illinois border. This included the counties of Jasper and Newton both touching the Illinois border. The original county of Jasper (named for a hero of the Revolution) included all of the present Benton County and most of present Newton County. The county lines later shifted as new counties were formed. In 1838, Jasper which had been an administrative part of White County was formed as an independent County, Newton County being administrated at this time by Jasper and White. In 1839 the Legislature passed an act establishing a town named Newton located at the Iroquois Falls as the county seat of Jasper County and combined the two counties abolishing Newton County which was reestablished in 1859.

There were no newspapers and no railroads and very poor roads here until about 1854. Due to its remoteness, the growth of this part of Indiana was greatly retarded until after 1850.

Henry and Elizabeth Freshour arrived here in 1839 with their family. J.D. Dunn was to settle here as well as William Freshour and his wife Hannah Robinson.[2] Other Robinson family members settled here. The Mason family, descendants of Lewis Mason of Ohio, moved here.[3] Isaac and Cathrine Mack

of Pennsylvania settled in Iroquois Township. Some of these settlers became prominent Jasper County residents. Most of them finally moved west. Some of the Masons, Macks and Freshours ultimately settled in California.
The History of Jasper County states:

> The blacksmith shop opened by Henry Freshaur, in 1839, was patronized from far and near, until that of Rial Benjamin and others south of the Iroquois and Pinkamink, divided his trade. [4]

The 1850 census gives his occupation as blacksmith. This was real pioneering. The local store was in a log cabin located on Casad's farm. In this settlement also was the first brick building in the area erected by Thomas Randall. It especially attracted the Indians who came on begging errands much to the discomfiture of Mrs. Randall. Her corn cakes were their especial admiration. They would take them warm from the griddle, lay down a quarter and leave in silence. The squaws were frequent visitors. It was not an infrequent sight to see two or three papooses stood up against the outside while their mothers were inside.

The early lines of travel were along the Indian trails. These were clearly defined paths, about eighteen inches wide, and worn into the sod of the prairie, sometimes to the depth of eight or ten inches. One of these led down from Lake Michigan across the Kankakee river to the Indian village in Newton Township. Another connected this village with one to the east, crossing the Iroquois and recrossing it to the east. From there the trail extended east crossing the Monon river and on to the Wabash river. These and similar trails served as the principal guides to travelers until regular roads were established. Blazed and staked roads pioneered the way for roads that were regularly laid out. Congress had passed a "three percent fund" for building roads and bridges. In 1835, Thomas Randall was appointed agent for Jasper County and regular road building commenced. It was many years before the county had decent bridges. These primitive roads were impassable through much of the year to heavily loaded teams attempting to reach the closest railroad. The first legally established road was the State road leading from Williamsport, the head of early navigation on the Wabash River, through Jasper County and on to Winamac in Pulaski County, important in the early days as the location of the land office.

The breadth of northern Indiana is about one-hundred and forty-five miles. The Freshour's trek across Indiana from Fort Wayne to Jasper County spanned most of this distance. The seventy mile trip from Fort Wayne to Logansport would be on a well established road. — The one used by J.D. Dunn as a teamster. They may have gone the twenty-five miles north from there to Winamac to do business at the land office there. In 1839 the road from Winamac to Jasper County would have been fairly primitive. This last thirty mile leg of the trip would be across open country. — They were in Indiana Prairie.

Henry and Elizabeth were in their late thirties — almost forty years old. The 1840 census would be next year. The year that "Tippicanoe" Harrison was washed into office on a wave of hard cider and the log cabin came into vogue as a political motif. Steam boats were here to stay and the Iron horse was becoming established in our more civilized parts. By now Henry had developed into a capable blacksmith perhaps having apprenticed at the trade in Tennessee and working at blacksmithing at Fort Wayne providing the worked iron used by the canal building community. A blacksmith was necessary to other craftsmen in a critical supporting role. A wheelwright needed iron tires and the iron bands that bound together the shaped pieces of oak that formed the wheel hubs. The wagon undercarriage and the pivot mechanism were from the iron worker as were the iron parts of the single trees and double trees. Perhaps he even forged the trace chains. A smithy was very important to any small pioneer community. A smith could shoe their horses or oxen, repair their wagons, hammer out plowshares and even square nails on his anvil.

The Freshours were from a pioneer tradition and had been trained to meet and conquer the difficulties of a new country. They were to find unfamiliar problems here. The timber that skirted the margins of the rivers and sent out spurs here and there along the banks of the creeks and marshes, divided the vast open plain of grass and flowers in two great divisions. North of the Iroquois, beguiling meadows were circumscribed by timber, while on the south the broad expanse of the grand prairie, marked here and there by a stray clump of undersized trees, stretched away toward the south, unbounded except by the horizon, and the pioneer with his little retinue of wagons was lost in this luxuriant wilderness like a covey of sloops in midocean.

The nature of these conveyances varied according to the tradition and origin of the pioneer.

> The pioneer from Pennsylvania, Ohio, or the Southern States, betrayed his nativity and prejudice in the schooner-shape wagon box, the stiff tongue, the hinder wheels double the size of the forward ones, and closely coupled together, the whole drawn by a team of four or six horses, which were guided by a single line in the hands of a teamster riding the "nigh wheeler." His harness was of gigantic proportions. What between the massive leather breaching, the heavy hames and collar, the immense housing of bear skin upon the hames, the heavy iron trace chains, and the ponderous double-tree and wiffle-trees, the poor beasts seemed like ... some terrible monsters that human ingenuity could scarcely fetter securely.
>
> The Eastern immigrant, from New York or further east, was marked as far as his caravan could be seen by a long-coupled, low-boxed, two horse wagon, provided with a seat, from which, with double lines, the driver guided his lightly harnessed pair of horses. there was about each part of the outfit evidence of the close calculation of means to an end, and an air of utility which left no room for doubt as to the purpose of the maker in every part of it. [5]

These vehicles were the progenitors of the Indiana farm wagon.[6] The small farm wagon was developed to permit every farmer to get his product to the nearest mill or shipping point. Also, the use of oxen as draft animals came into prominence on the prairie. J.D. Dunn commenced hauling with a "breaking team" of five oxen in Jasper County.[7] The primitive roads of these early Indiana farm communities were atrocious for hauls with large heavy wagons and teams. The answer was farm wagons which were the pick-up truck or 2 ton flat-bed of the day. For the pioneering farmers of northern Indiana, these sturdy agile vehicles were the means to haul their corn to the distant flouring mill or their surplus crop to the canal for transport to markets in the more developed areas to the south and east. For the next generation of pioneers these smaller wagons were to replace the Conestoga as the choice of vehicle to traverse the plains, ford streams, struggle over loose sliding shale and immense rugged granite slopes. The occupation "wagonmaker" occasionally appeared in the 1850 Indiana census. Originally, these wagons were built by country blacksmiths or by the pioneer himself.

> The pioneer ... arrived with all his worldly possessions on wagons, and making selection of a farm, chose a site for a cabin, and set at once to build it. Trees were felled, logs of proper length chopped off and drawn to the chosen site, and willing neighbors for miles about invited to the raising. Rude as these structures were, it needed no little handicraft to rear them. ... The logs, trimmed, "saddled" and properly sorted, were placed in the pen-shape of the cabin; the gable ends were run up with regularity, shortening logs, shaped at the ends to allow for the shape of the roof; ... the roof which was made of clapboards, riven by a froe from bolts of oak, laid in place ... Then followed the sawing-out of the door-way and windows, the chinking of the cracks with pieces of riven timber; the caulking with a mixture of mud and chopped hay; the construction of floors and a door from puncheons, and the building of a chimneys of "cat and clay."

Hinges were supplied from raw hide, and the wooden latch, reached from the outside by means of an attached leather latch-string passing through a hole in the door, was often the only protection against forcible entrance. Later experiences introduced the use of heavy wooden bars; but the proverbial expression of early hospitality was the hanging out of the latch-string. [8]

The pioneer after constructing a shelter usually found it necessary to manufacture tables and chairs. Hand tools were frequently part of the load, but in their absence the ax sufficed. A section of a good sized log smoothed with an ax and fitted with legs served as a chair. A rude bedstead was often constructed in the corner strung with deer hide thongs. Upon this the tick was filled with leaves until the first crop supplied corn husks.

In the wide fire-place the "crane" hung with iron pots and kettles, and the Dutch oven, half submerged in coals furnished the meal at the end of the day. The frontier home, as a rule, contained but one room, which served all the domestic and social purposes of the family. Curtains arranged about the beds formed sleeping apartments, while the cheerful blaze of the fireplace afforded an unstinted glow to the whole establishment. The single window was closed with greased paper to let in the daylight. At first there was often no floor but the ground, but generally slabs split out from unseasoned timber were smoothed with the ax and made to do service as a floor. This was probably the phase of our Freshour family history that tradition has with a granny smoking a clay pipe and living in a cabin with a clay floor which she swept with a broom every day as if it were a real wood floor.

The surplus product of the frontier farm supplied a slender stock of tea, coffee, sugar and spices, black powder and lead, with an occasional hat for the man and a calico dress for the woman — all else must be derived from the soil. This was accomplished by the flax-wheel, brake, spinning-wheel or loom. To card and spin, to dye and weave were skills that all women possessed. Diversion was provided by camp-meetings, large weddings, and spinning and husking bees.

Farming was done with rude agricultural instruments. Corn was the only crop planted at first and this furnished food for both man and beast. This was crudely processed with mortar and pestle until "crackers" were put up in some communities where people would bring their corn and patiently wait for their "grist." But for flour, the only resort was to La Fayette, an older settlement that had a "flouring mill." The bee was easily domesticated the settlers capturing swarms and placing them in hollow logs to secure a constant source of sweetener for the culinary work of the cabin. The early settlers found a good substitute for fruit in the pumpkin. The long flintlock rifles furnished game for the table. Most of the settlers brought horses and cows. The horse generally gave way to oxen for working purposes.

Life in this new country was everywhere subject "to the misery of malarious disease." The location of cabins along the lowlands that formed the margin of the streams exposed the settlers to the miasmatic poison fog that hung over the stagnant water of the sluggish streams. The lack of good water exposed the settlers to the bane of "fever and ague." To have a severe case of malarial fever or several seasons' run of the ague, was expected by each new-comer. But the greatest disappointment was the utter lack of markets. There was a market at Chicago at this time, where fair prices could be had for the surplus crop. There were also markets to the east and south in Indiana but the lack of roads hindered their accessibility.

Neighbors were spread out. A Journey of fifteen miles was not considered a great undertaking for an afternoon's visit. In a country without continuous fences and few landmarks, it requires some skill to cross even a small prairie in daylight. Crossing the uncultivated prairie at night was a very uncertain venture even to the most expert. The tendency is to move in a circle, and when this is once begun and observed by the traveler, the only recourse is to camp and wait for morning. Each family had its signal light, which served to mark the place of the cabin. It was a frequent practice to erect a pole by the chimney, upon which a lighted lantern was placed. Others had a light in the window, which often saved a dreary night's experience on the open prairie. Such experiences, unpleasant in mild weather, were too often fatal in the winter season.

Within fifty years of the arrival of the first settlers this land was to be transformed to a pleasant rolling area of thrifty farms. The open land was originally covered with a rank growth of prairie grass; on the high lands the grass was short, while on the lower lands it frequently reached a height that would conceal a horse and rider. The occasional clumps of trees were devoid of undergrowth due to the annual fires that swept the prairies. These fires which kept the beautiful panorama of prairie unobstructed, were to the settlers the most dreaded of scourges.

> Those only who have been awakened at the dead hour of the night by the lurid light of the approaching flames can appreciate the horror connected with such an event. The feeling of utter helplessness, in the face of the unequal combat; the wall of fire, from ten to fifty feet in height, advancing with the speed of a race-horse; the winged denizens of the prairie flying affrighted and screaming before its approach; the maddening rush of the deer, wolves and other animals, forgetting all other fear in the presence of this overshadowing calamity; the terrible grandeur of its irresistible advance; the suffocation and heat of its presence; the charred and blackened waste which marked its fateful course; the bewilderment of the isolated family grouped on the only bare spot that offered safety; all this cannot be imagined, it must be felt to be appreciated. The excitement of its approach, passage and retreat, followed by the contemplation of the smoking ruins of a house and improvements which cost months of toil, or of a crop that was the only hope of sustenance during the approaching winter, burns upon the brain of an interested spectator, a sight never to be forgotten, and one the farmer took pains never to see repeated. [9]

The modicum of government enjoyed by these pioneering communities had no responsibility to record vital statistics. This was the responsibility of the head of every household. The common means for keeping family records was the family Bible, frequently given as a wedding gift for such purpose. This would have a set of record pages to be filled out. Several generations of Freshours stayed at the leading edge of frontier life, moving along with it and thus staying beyond the regions where civil institutions perpetuated historical data. The sparseness of early settlement and pioneering rigors precluded general literacy. Information is very sparse for these pioneering Freshours. The only records left by them in Jasper County and at Fort Wayne, Indiana are land records and census data. We can only speculate on things like child mortality and familial relationships. The loss of a family record in a prairie fire would be an incalculable loss to succeeding generations.

> From the time the grass would burn, which was soon after the first frost, usually about the first of October, till the surrounding prairie was all burnt over, or, if not all burnt, till the green grass in the spring had grown sufficient to prevent the rapid progress of the fire, the early settlers were continually on the watch, and as they usually expressed the idea, "slept with one eye open." When the ground was covered with snow, or during rainy weather, the apprehension was quieted, and both eyes could be safely closed....[10]

A common precaution was to plow several furrows around a strip, several rods wide, outside the improvements, and then burn out the inside of this strip in July. The grass would start afresh immediately, and the cattle would feed it close preferring it to the older grass. In a few years, this process repeated would run out the prairie grass which was replaced with blue grass, which would not burn to any serious extent. A prairie fire driven by a high wind would often leap such a barrier. We can visualize Henry Freshour with sons John, George and William plowing firebreak and fighting fire.

> The usual way of meeting advancing fires was to begin the defense where the head of the fire would strike, which was calculated by the smoke and ashes brought by the wind along in advance of fire. A road, cattle-path, or a furrow is of great value at such a place; ... On the side, nearest the coming fire, of such a road or path, the grass is set on fire, which burns slowly against the wind until it meets the coming conflagration, ... This is called "back-firing" ... The head of the fire successfully checked, the force of fire-fighters divide, part going on the right and part to the left, and the back firing continues to meet the side fires as they come up. ...
> Various implements were used to put out a side or back fire or even the head of a fire in a moderate wind. ... A bundle of hazel brush, a spade or shovel were often used with effect. The women frequently lent their aid, and dexterously wielded the mop, ... The physical efforts made ... protecting one's home from this devouring element, were of the most trying nature, not unfrequently resulting fatally. [11]

Not only would the debilitating effects of ague and the peril of prairie fires be a constant cause for concern, but also routine life would not be easy for the Freshours in Jasper County. Schools would be few and far between. Every child was a farm hand. There would be corn to be planted, cultivated, suckered, picked, cribbed, shucked, shelled, cracked and perhaps milled, cows to milk, wood to be cut for the winter and all the inevitable activities required to carve out a home and livelihood in the prairie. J.D. was married and on his own. John and George lived with their parents from the 1840 to the 1850 census when they were twenty-five years old – two farm hands who had helped Henry Freshour farm the prairie. William was twenty-one in the 1850 census and was also living with his parents — a third farm hand. As grain production shifted from corn, on which the Indians before them had subsisted, to wheat, there would be fields to plow, harrow, sow, reap and thresh. As wonderous as corn is, it does not have the gluten of wheat that makes the dough so important to the European cultures. There was a big market for wheat.

The Indiana prairie became highly productive with new American technology. In 1837, blacksmith John Deer invented a plow with a steel moldboard which he formed from a circular saw blade. This replaced the wooden moldboards with cast iron share. The new plow could turn the heavy stickey prairie soil and was self polishing. This revolutionized prairie farming. Cyrus McCormick in Virginia in 1834 patented a mower-reaper that was superior to others. After much competition and mechanical refinement (and a lawsuit won with the help of illinois lawer Abe Lincoln) the McCormick mower-reaper emerged by 1847 as a very effective machine available to the prairie farmers who by 1850 needed it to keep up with the price of wheat.[12]

Mary Jane was married to Perry Mack by this time. Perry and Mary Jane had four children, six-year-old Mary, five-year-old John, four-year-old George and one-year-old Alice.[13]

Sophronia South was eighteen years old and living with her parents William and Prada South in Aubbnaubber Township in Fulton County some forty miles east of Jasper County. She was the fourth of nine children reared in Hocking County Ohio. John was to marry Catherine Golesberry in Jasper County — a tragically brief marriage. Catherine died in July of 1852. Within a year John was remarried — this time to Sophronia. William Henry was born to them at the end of January 1854. Twin George had married Elizabeth Ann Davis and their first child Henrietta was two years old in 1854.[14]

Thus Henry and Elizabeth had six grandchildren at this time. They had been in Jasper County fifteen years. They had in their household in 1854: sixteen-year-old Joseph T., thirteen-year-old Alfred Henry and ten-year-old Lydia Ann. These last three were Hoosiers with no memory of Tennessee or Fort Wayne. Their entire world was Jasper County. William was probably still living with his parents. John, George and Mary Jane and Perry Mack were established with their own households and property. These young adult Freshours had vivid memories of the trip from Fort Wayne as teenagers.

The *insatiable pioneer* was to come forth again. The entire family of Henry and Elizabeth was to take to their wagons again! They were to head across Illinois and Iowa to just short of the Missouri river. Curiously, many people started from Indiana and made the trek all the way to California. John Mohler Studebaker joined a wagon train organized at South Bend.[15] There are accounts by wagon train emigrants who traveled overland from Indiana to Council Bluffs, outfitted there and continued on west. It was also possible to proceed by riverboat down the Wabash to the Ohio and on to St. Louis and via the Missouri to the outfitting towns. Then there was the National Road which in its furthermost western extent went through Terre Haute and on to St. Louis.[16]

In 1852, the Studebaker family, forth-generation Pennsylvania German wagon makers, arrived in South Bend to the north east of Jasper County and opened their blacksmith shop. Financed in 1858 by J.M.'s earnings in the "diggings," they started wagon production. These were smaller than the Conestogas their great-grandfather had built in Pennsylvania.[17]

The Freshours were of the Indiana farm wagon culture and they no doubt headed across the Illinois prairie country in wagons. With the Freshours alone there would have been four families with at least four wagons and there is reason to believe there was a sizable caravan. One would infer that the Freshour move was part of a more general exodus from Jasper County, Indiana to Adams County, Iowa, since the Township in Adams County in which the Freshours settled was named Jasper Township. The majority of original settlers went west at this time being replaced by Hollanders and Norwegians.[18]

Signs of civilization were appearing in Jasper County. The first jail was built in 1847. In 1853 the county Commissioners were planning a court house. An architect was secured from La Fayette and the contract let in 1854. The record vault requirements were modified in the contract to save money. The structure was accepted in 1856. The Henry Freshour family left for Iowa in 1854.

In 1864, the court house caught fire and was partially destroyed. The fire was first discovered about 11 o'clock at night, and at that time the flames had got beyond the control of the facilities which the town afforded for checking it. It was generally supposed that the fire was the work of an incendiary, who was interested in the destruction of the records, and suspicion pointed generally to one man who left the county about that time, though no evidence was obtained to fasten the guilt upon anyone. The whole interior and roof of the structure was burned and all the papers and records of the county were destroyed save such as were rescued and thrown out of the burning building. The cheap vaults proved no protection, ... [19]

The walls survived undamaged and the court house was rebuilt, this time with proper vaults.

The Henry Freshour family's Indiana sojourn of twenty-one years saw the development of northern Indiana from Indian Territory to the productive rural Americana of *frost on the pumpkin and corn in the shock* tradition. Iowa, Indian Territory until 1821, was admitted to the Union in December 1846. The Mexican War had come and gone and California was now American Territory. The gold rush had come and gone and the number of wagons going to California had dwindled. Heading west our travelers found Illinois every bit as civilized as Indiana. Abe Lincoln was riding around in his one horse buggy practicing law and politicking as was his wont. He ran for congress and lost again in 1854. He usually lost. In May 1854, the Kansas-Nebraska Act is passed. Lincoln speaks in Peoria Illinois condemning slavery and favoring gradual emancipation of slaves. He denies that the Kansas-Nebraska Act is a slaveholders conspiracy, [20] Over the Great Plains moved the wagon trains, a traveler counting 459 wagons in ten miles along the Platte River. A Peoria newspaper in 1854 counted 1,473 wagons in one month, movers going to Iowa.[21] The wagon train Freshours were on their way to settle at trails head in Iowa.

6

IOWA TRAILHEAD

HENRY AND Elizabeth Freshour were living, in 1850, in Jasper County Indiana with John, George, William, Joseph Terre, Alfred Henry and Lydia Ann living in their household. Only their eldest daughter Mary Jane had married. By 1854, in just four short years, the entire family was in Adams County Iowa. The twins, John and George, and their sister Mary Jane are married with their own households. Their brother, William, and their minor brothers and sister are listed in 1856 in the households of John and Sophronia and Mary Jane and Perry Mack. Their parents, Henry and Elizabeth, are not listed in this census or any subsequent one. The exodus in which these Freshour families had been caught up is described by Branch.

> Access into the rich lands of Iowa had been made easy by the railroads, land companies were making alluring inducements, emigrant guides were being published by the score. The summer of 1854 brought severe drouth to the Ohio Valley and the states eastward, and another epidemic of cholera. And farmers harkened to the literature about healthful, fertile Iowa, sold their old holdings, packed their goods. "The immigration into Iowa the present season is astonishing and unprecedented," reported an Eastern journal in June, 1854; "For miles and miles, day after day, the prairies of Illinois are lined with cattle and wagons, pushing towards this prosperous state." The ferries at the principal points of the Iowa-Illinois border did business limited only by their maximum capacity; emigrants and their wagonloads of household stuffs and their droves of live stock sometimes waited two or three days for their turn at the ferry. At

Burlington "20,000 emigrants have passed through the city within the last thirty days, and they are still crossing at the rate of 600 and 700 a day"; Dubuque, MacGregor, and Keokuk as points of entry recited similar accounts. Over the Chicago & Galena Railroad, it was estimated, more than three thousand emigrants came into Iowa each month...."[1]

The Freshours, kinfolks and neighbors arrived, in 1854, on the East Nodaway River in Adams County. When the trail weary immigrants moving west found the beautiful little valley so peaceful and well supplied by a clear meandering stream and with plenty of wood and rich soil, it must have seemed like paradise. Some of them decided to settle and built log houses in a group for protection and named it Canaan City. The US Government conveyed title to the land the colony was occupying to William Shield in 1854. The village was renamed Brookville, perhaps because of the stream of good water. In 1855, Shields conveyed the land title to Silas Riggs. The following year the town was platted as Brookville. The Methodist Church built a seminary at Brookville in 1857 naming it Simpson Seminary in honor of Bishop Simpson of Council Bluffs. When a US post office was established in 1860, it was named Simpson because the name Brookville could not be used as it was already in use in Jefferson County. The seminary moved to Indianola and the post office assumed the name of Brooks in 1871.[2]

We have no record of Henry or Elizabeth's death. The Jasper County Indiana history of 1883 says that they moved to Iowa and died there. This is probably the understanding received from J.D. Dunn at that time.[3] Joseph Terre Freshour stated in a Civil War pension affidavit "That my parents had a family record in which were recorded the dates of births, marriages and deaths of the family, that said record was burned in a fire which burned our home in Iowa; ..."[4] "Long Joe" gave this loss as the reason for his uncertainty about his age. Who knows what record would be in the Henry Freshour family Bible. It would likely be a source of information about Henry's parents identity. Something on which we presently can only speculate.

George Freshour and his wife Elizabeth were to live out their lives in Adams County Iowa as were Perry and Mary Jane Mack and Alfred Henry and Rebecca Ann Freshour. Lydia Ann married twice in Adams County Iowa.[5] Both men were Iowa Union soldiers in the Civil War. Her first husband was killed in the war in 1864 and she married another Union soldier, Samuel Young, in 1866. The Youngs moved to Beloit Kansas in 1873 and in 1883 they moved to Fort Collins, Colorado where they lived out their years.

We have no further data on William after the 1854 Iowa census.[6] John and Sophronia and Joseph Terre Freshour were to travel to California in 1857. Unlike the Jackson County Missouri Freshours who unanimously hit the trail to California, the Adams County Freshours for the most part seemed to have settled down there in Iowa. This is understandable in view of the fact that they arrived only three years previously and had just gotten established on their property. John and Sophronia owned a lot in newly platted Brookville and acreage nearby. In the case of Joseph Terre, a venturesome single nineteen-year-old, the trip across the plains would be a natural inclination. But John had always been together with his twin brother up until now — they had hit the trail together in wagons three times — from Green County, Tennessee to Fort Wayne, Indiana in 1833, from Fort Wayne to Jasper County in 1839 and finally from Jasper County, Indiana to Adams County, Iowa in 1854. What prompted John and Sophronia to sell their recently acquired property[7] in Iowa and take out for California with two toddlers and Sophronia expecting? And, the twin brothers would be two-thousand miles apart!

Another aspect of this question is why they stopped in Iowa at all? The main thrust of the emigration through Illinois and Iowa was primarily into Kansas or, for the truly venturesome, onward to California. An 1870's editor said of Brooks:

> There are few, if any, towns ... of equal size to Brooks, that can rival her in general prosperity and thrift. It is what is termed a solid town, not built on imaginary resources, but founded on that safest of all cornerstones — agricultural prosperity. Hardly a score of years has passed since all this country was a vast prairie and was supposed by many to be of no value. Thousands of emigrants passed over these prairies with hardly a glance at them on their way to what they thought was the finest farming land in the world — Kansas and Nebraska. To-day some of the finest farms in existence are made on this same "worthless prairie," ...[8]

Not everyone who passed by Brooks was headed for Kansas and Nebraska. Many folks who pulled up stakes in Indiana outfitted at the Missouri river and kept going. Council Bluffs was a primary "jumping off place." The *Kanesville Frontier Guardian* listed 1400 names and twenty-one different wagon trains in 1850. Folks would register and send back home copies of the paper to show that they had reached Kanesville safely.[9]

The Medely family left Clark County, Missouri (on the Iowa border and the Mississippi River near Keokuk) in 1852 after several years of planning their trip to California. They visited family in Scotland County then followed the Chariton River up into Southern Iowa and "We traveled along until we arrived at Council Bluffs." Southern Iowa was so sparsely settled that there was little there to impress the memory of ten-year-old Mary Medely. She vividly remembered the crowded wait for the ferry crossing at Kanesville.[10]

Lewis Stout and his sister Rebecca kept diaries of their 1852 trip to Oregon from Van Buren County, Iowa (contiguous to Clark and Scotland Counties, Missouri.) Their day by day accounts of the westward trek across Southern Iowa describes camping, fording streams and geographical landmarks. There were few towns to speak of. They left Birmingham, crossed the Des Moines River and arrived at Chariton. They mention the Grand River, Nodaway "Creek," Nishnabotna River (and ferry,) Silver Creek and Kanesville.[11]

The following year in 1853, William R. Brown traveled from Madison, Brown County, Indiana to Sacramento California. His company went first to Indianapolis, joined others and traveled overland through Terre Haute, Paris Illinois, Springfield, crossed the Illinois River at Meredosia and went through Clayton to Quincy. They were ferried across the Mississippi and went overland through Monticello, Memphis, Lancaster and on to Chariton in Iowa. The route of this Indiana company crossing Iowa was like that of the Medleys and the Stouts. Brown's company camped at farms across Indiana, Illinois and Missouri but in Iowa they mostly camped in open country. They met many other emigrants on their way across Iowa but encountered few towns or settlers.[12]

The trail through Iowa fanned in from points up and down the Mississippi with trains crossing Illinois from points ranging from Chicago to Terre Haute. This was the alternative to river travel through Saint Louis and across Missouri by steam boat.

In 1853, John Mohler Studebaker traveled from South Bend Indiana to Hangtown, California (Placerville) with the wagon built by him and his brothers at their shop in South Bend. He left South Bend in March and would have crossed the Missouri at Council Bluffs in May making the entire trip in the same year.[13] Of course, the timing had to be right. The Mormons had their *Winter Quarters* just north of Council Bluffs.[14] The trail across the prairie immediately to the west would be soggy in early spring with Platte river tributaries swollen and even more difficult than usual to cross. The calendar of the trail had an optimum departure time which minimized the opportunities to get stuck in the springtime mud and yet allowed arrival at the Sierra before danger of the first snowstorms in the fall. They could not leave until there was sufficient grass on the prairie for the oxen.[15] It would make sense to travel across Illinois and Iowa in one season and lay over the winter and get outfitted in the spring. But their objective may have been new land and the newly plated towns of southwestern Iowa. The trip to California in some cases was an after thought.

What was the impact of the Kansas-Nebraska Act on this part of Iowa? It had the immediate impact of people moving into the newly opened territory of Nebraska.

> As the word went out in 1854 that Nebraska would soon be organized as a territorial government and its lands thrown open to settlement, speculators and restive Westerners gathered in Council Bluffs and the other Iowa towns on the Missouri. In March, 1854, Indian commissioners persuaded the Omahas and Otoes to withdraw from the greater part of their hunting grounds; and squatters ventured across the river to blaze the boundaries of some choice field. On the twenty-fourth of June President Franklin Pierce formally let down the barriers, and the land-hungry mob rushed into the Territory. ...
>
> Until land offices were opened, the proof of ownership of a claim was a cabin and a shotgun....[16]

There was a secondary impact of the Kansas-Nebraska Act on this part of Iowa. That was the Lane trail through Iowa to Kansas. The entire Kansas Territory lay west of Missouri and for the most part this slave State was separated from it by an imaginary line. To the south no natural frontier existed. The northern part of the boundary was formed by the Missouri river flowing sinuously southeast to Independence and Westport. At this point the six contiguous counties of Platte, Clay, Ray, Jackson, Lafayette and Saline embraced the major slave population of the state. It was popularly believed in this region that Kansas was to be made slave and Nebraska kept free. (See the "Bleeding Kansas" map in chapter three.)

This region of Missouri also held a monopoly on the services required by emigrants into Kansas.[17] There were problems in moving slavery into Kansas. If moved from Missouri, slavery was further weakened in Missouri. Slaves were being moved into places such as Texas where there was no contention on the matter. It was pointed out by a Missouri citizen that it cost $1200 for a slave in Missouri and the cost of capital on that amount would be $120 per annum plus the slaves keep. But a freesoil settler could hire an intelligent, efficient, industrious German for $100 a year, and get twice as much out of him.[18] It appeared that slavery in Missouri was having a hard time holding its own. The New England Emigrant Aid Company was equipping and sending in hundreds of freesoil emigrants into Kansas. News of the "five-million-dollar" Emigrant Aid Company reached western Missouri. The Missouri slaveholders, becoming alarmed, organized in opposition.[19]

The pro-slavery forces on the Missouri (including those in Cole County) had the advantage of being able to obstruct free-soil emigrant passage westward either on the river or on overland routes through Missouri. Even before the sack of Lawrence or the Pottawatome massacre, travelers on the Missouri river boats had been threatened or turned back and shipments of weapons seized.[20] As this situation worsened, a flanking route through Iowa and Nebraska was developed.

> To Missourians the emigrants who swarmed into the Territory across the Missouri were an army of dangerous abolitionists, smuggling guns into Kansas, intent on driving out every squatter who dared bring in a slave. The "border ruffians" laid a strict embargo on the Missouri River, boarding and searching steamboats, breaking into baggage, insulting and maltreating passengers; but the emigration simply changed its course a bit, coming into Kansas by way of Iowa and Nebraska.[21]

The westward route passed through Iowa City, Oskaloosa, Osceola, Quincy in Adams County, Nebraska City and thence south into Kansas. The "Grim Warrior," James Henry Lane, one time lieutenant governor of Indiana, now a resident of Kansas, toured the north as a "fugitive" from the boarder ruffians. As a speaker he was a spell binder. In speech after speech he raised funds and volunteers to go to Kansas.[22] Chicago became the outfitting town for parties from the east. They left by train, their covered wagons on flatcars to be unloaded at Iowa rail-heads for the final leg of their journey to Kansas. [23]

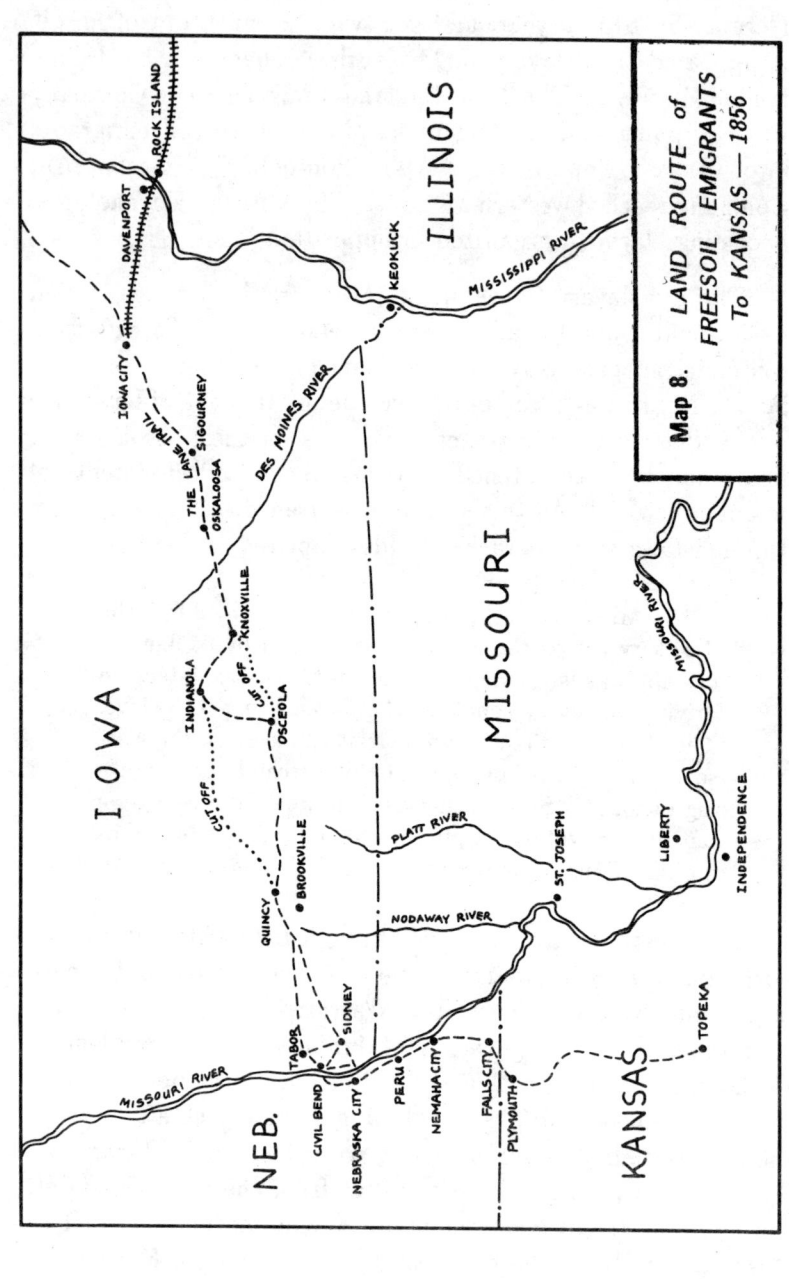

In July of 1856, an army of four-hundred passed through on the "Lane Trail." This "army" passed peacefully into Kansas and established the towns of Plymouth and Holton.[24] Several other "armies" passed through that summer. One was armed with cannon and small arms supplied by the Iowa State Arsenal. Most of this armament was seized by federal troops, but the emigrants were permitted to swell the ranks of Kansas free-soilers.[25] In the meanwhile, since the Indiana Freshours had arrived in Iowa in 1854, the mayhem and massacres continued in the Kansas-Missouri border region with "Old Brown" attacking and being attacked.

John Brown was born in Connecticut in 1800, reared in Ohio and spent years conducting abolitionist projects in Pennsylvania. He traveled the Lane Trail through Iowa in 1855 following his five sons into Kansas territory — the center of the antislavery - proslavery maelstrom. Old Brown conceived the idea of raiding into Missouri, freeing slaves and transporting them through Iowa.[26] He had the help of Iowa Quakers who founded Salem, Iowa in 1835 and by 1850 had thirteen other settlements in Iowa. John Brown set up headquarters at both ends of the Lane Trail — at the Quaker settlements of Tabor and Springdale — making Iowa the center of his activities for three years. John Brown's house is an historical site in the town of Tabor along with a nearby underground railway house used to hide slaves on their way north to freedom. Old Brown spent the fourth of July 1857 in Davenport while bringing in supplies for his last foray into Kansas before the Harpers Ferry incident. His men spent the winter of 1857-58 in Springdale.[27] John Brown then went east to organize the raid and capture of the US Arsenal at Harpers Ferry, Virginia. He was captured there, given a fair trial and hung in November of 1859 giving the abolitionists a martyr.[28]

The eyes of the entire nation were on "Bleeding Kansas" and the Iowa Freshours were precariously close even though safely in a free-soil state. They were located right on the Lane Trail. There was already a de facto civil war in the region to the immediate south. The nation was polarized. Iowa would fight for the Union. The Iowa troops would march into Missouri singing *"John Brown's body lies a-mould'ring in the grave."*

But, for all anyone knew at this time in 1856, the War of the Rebellion in that region could have been fought on the Iowa-Missouri border. The Mason-Dixon line parallel, when it is projected westward from the Pennsylvania-Maryland border, runs between Iowa and Missouri.[29] The Kansas-Nebraska boundry falls slightly to the south of the Mason-Dixon projection. Moreover, there is a natural economic division between these western regions relating to markets and transportation. The Central Missouri region was associated by steam powered riverboat with St. Louis, the Mississippi, and New Orleans. They had the slavery based agriculture geared to this southern commerce. Iowa, on the other hand, was linked by northern railheads at its border to the Chicago market place and eastern industry. Their large families were farm hands and they were quick to adopt technical innovation. The southern motor was slavery and the northern motor was McCormack and John Deer.[30] Steam power appeared on the plains to pull gang plows and combines. These transport and market delineated regions were radically different in ethos. The ideological line was near the Iowa-Missouri border.

Missouri was potentially a Confederacy stronghold. The bold incisive action of General Lyon, when he rushed from Fort Leavenworth at the outset in 1861 capturing Jefferson City, secured the Missouri Arsenal and Missouri for the Union.[31] He allowed the Governor and Legislature safe passage through his lines to travel into Arkansas to operate in exile there. General Lyon was killed shortly after in the hideous carnage at the battle of Wilson's Creek.[32] Four years of strife and pillage ensued. The Union troops of Iowa were to occupy Missouri and wage war along the Missouri-Arkansas border.

Alfred Henry Freshour was in combat and wounded at the battle of Pea Ridge, Arkansas. He and Andrew Dow, his sister Lydia Ann's beau, enlisted at Quincy on October 28, 1861.[33]

— Courtesy of Cliff Freshour, Prescott, IA

Figure 6.1: Alfred and Rebecca Ann Freshour.

They served in Company H of the Fourth Iowa Regiment of Infantry under Colonel Grenville Dodge at the Battle of Pea Ridge on the Missouri-Arkansas border. Colonel Dodge had three horses shot from under him and was severely wounded. The Iowa Fourth and Ninth lost almost a hundred men each the first day of battle. The loss of officers was heavy on both sides. The men slept on their arms and the battle continued at daybreak.[34] Alfred received a slight wound in the hip. The Confederate forces withdrew at mid-day leaving the field to the Union troops on March 8, 1862. In the ensuing campaign, Batesville, Arkansas was taken May 3, 1862.[35] Alfred was hospitalized there and found to have an enlarged heart which the army surgeon judged to be a longstanding problem. He was given a disability discharge in July of 1862 at St. Louis. At the age of twenty he returned to Iowa farm life as a veteran of some of the fiercest combat the Iowa troops ever saw. Alfred later married Rebecca Ann Evans in February of 1865.

Major General William Tecumseh Sherman commanded the newly organized Department and Army of the Tennessee which included the Fifteenth Army Corps commanded by Major General Frank Blair. Iowan, Brigadier General Peter Osterhaus, commanded Blair's First Division which included the second Brigade, entirely Iowans, under Colonel James A. Williamson. Alfred's buddy, Andrew Dow, continued to serve in Company H of the Fourth Iowa Regiment now commanded by Lieutenant Colonel George Burton.[36] Andrew Dow was wounded in the hand at Chickasaw Bayou in September of 1862. He mustered at Rolla, Missouri in November of 1862. He was on leave in Iowa to marry Lydia Ann Freshour in April of 1863. We can imagine all the Freshours attending the wedding at Brookville. Perhaps Alfred was best man and Rebecca Ann a bridesmaid.

The next big event for the Iowa Fourth was Vicksburg which fell in July of 1863. Andrew mustered out on December 31, 1863 and reenlisted on January 1, 1864 at Woodville Alabama. Then the Fourth went sixty miles northeast to Chattanooga and the Ringgold campaign. The Iowa Fourth was again in fierce combat. Andrew was severely wounded by gunshot in the line of duty on August 31, 1864. He was in the hospital at Rome, Georgia in September. Andrew Dow died on September 20, 1864 in the hospital at Marietta, Georgia. He was buried in the National Cemetery at Marietta. Lydia Ann Freshour Dow was a widow at age twenty.[37]

In 1856 however, the war probably wasn't fully expected in Iowa even though it existed as civil warfare in the contested Kansas border region — "Bleeding Kansas."[38] Folks hoped that things would settle down. Perhaps Kansas would be admitted slave and Nebraska free and the status quo maintained. Surely this war would never come to Free-soil Iowa! They did their best to go about their task of building their frontier homes and farms.

— Courtesy of Cliff Freshour, Prescott, IA

Figure 6.2: Charles E. Freshour, son of Alfred and Rebecca Evans Freshour, married Emma Hays. They appear here with their children. From left to right are: (front row) Ada, Emma, Charlie and Rewa Freshour. (back row) Boyd, Delmar, Ivan, Warren, and Nate.

The Freshours of Southwestern Iowa are generally the descendants of George Freshour or Alfred Freshour, two sons of Henry Freshour. After the Civil War, much of the general populace left the Old Northwest Territory and settled in Iowa, Kansas and Nebraska and eventually drifted further west. A Freshour family came from Ohio after 1868, the year their daughter Orpha May was born. Their son, Albert Vincent Freshour, was born in 1872 at Winterset. He is the ancestor of the Bloomfield and Ottumwa Freshours in Southeastern Iowa.

— Courtesy of Cliff Freshour, Prescott, IA

Figure 6.3: Delmar and Mildred Freshour of Adams Co. IA

Delmar Olin Freshour, grandson of Alfred and Rebecca Freshour, married Mildred C. Farris. Their children, appearing in from top to bottom are: Cliff, Jerry and Joan.

In 1856, another emigrant Freshour from Tennessee makes a Melchizedekian appearance at the trail head frontier — turning up out of nowhere — not having parents, kith nor kin. This is the peripatetic Henry Freshour who freely ranged back and forth between Jackson County, Missouri and Adams County, Iowa and finally settling down in Adams County. Henry Freshour married Amanda Henning in March of 1856 in Jackson County, Missouri. Their eldest child, Lucinda, was born in 1857 in Missouri, Emiline in 1858 in Iowa and Thomas in 1861 in Missouri.[39] In 1866, Henry bought three lots in Brookville, Iowa (now Brooks) that were on sale at the court house in Quincy for back taxes. Henry paid 79 cents apiece for these and waited three years and, since they weren't redeemed, the county deeded them over to him in 1869. In 1870 Henry and Amanda and their three children were in the Iowa census in Jasper Township of Adams County. Since Henry's age was given as 60 at that time, it was thought that he was another Henry Freshour.

It is curious that this Henry turned up in Jackson County in 1856 right after we lost track of the documented Henry at Adams County, Iowa. It is also curious that he seemed to commute back and forth between the only two localities on the frontier that had Green County Tennessee Freshours in residence at that time. Our Henry would have been about 56 years of age in 1856. Age discrepancies from census to census are not uncommon. Ten years is stretching it a bit. Is it *possible?* Do you suppose that Henry has *recycled* himself here? Amanda is checked off on the census form under [deaf, dumb, blind, idiot.] It is difficult to relate this Henry to the Henry of Indiana. But his daughter's relationship with Joseph Terry Freshour in California indicates that they were very likely family.

Henry and Amanda's daughter Emiline married Lewis T. Mason in Santa Cruz, California in July 1886 at the age of twenty. They were neighbors of Joseph Terre Freshour in Soquel at the time they were married and were executors of his estate in 1915.[40] It was thought that she was J.T.'s niece but she possibly could have been his half sister! Henry apparently lived out his years in Brooks. Emma and her brother, Tom, brought Amanda out to California after Henry passed away. Tom died in 1909, Emma in 1922 and L.T. died in 1923, all at Los Banos in Merced County. Amanda (Henney) Freshour died in 1913 at Palo Alto, California and was interred at Los Banos, Merced County, California.

The 1870 census shows Henry's occupation as "peddler." This may very well explain his movement up and down the frontier. He may have been in Jackson County as early as 1854 and he may have made reunion with the Green County, Tennessee Freshours there — particularly John before he passed away. It seems likely that the Jackson County, Missouri and Adams County, Iowa Freshours were second or possibly first cousins. The older ones of both families had remembrance of Green County, Tennessee and surely knew one another as children there. It appears that Henry may have become a widower in 1854-5 and taken up a different lifestyle and trade. Since he spanned both localities it is likely that the two Freshour groups were aware of one another and in communication. Surely the Iowa Freshours knew in advance that their Missouri kin were pulling out and heading for California. They could easily have visited back and forth. Young Joseph Terry was to later live on the Martin Freshour ranch during the 1860 census in San Joaquin County, California. They could have been acquainted in Missouri. J.T. could easily have made an excursion down there between 1854 and 1857. The two branches of the family were to intermingle later in California.

Of the Green County Tennessee Freshours that had migrated to the frontier and were located at trail's head, we can identify definitely three different years during which a group of them made the trek across the plains. We know that Nicholas B. Gann and his wife Rutha went to California in 1847 preceding the gold rush of 1849. Jas. R. Freshour also came out that year for the first time. This wagon train has been identified by family tradition as the Charles Hopper wagon train described in the journal of William Alexander Truebody. He recounts the trip from Lafayette County Missouri to Sutter's Fort, California.⁴¹ Hopper had traveled the Southwest as a trapper living the perilous life of a "mountain man." This was Hopper's second trip with an emigrant party; the first being that of the Bartleston-Bidwell party in 1841. Hopper returned to Jackson County Missouri to bring his family to California.⁴² Nicholas was uncle to Jane Gann who married Isaiah Horn. Isaiah fondly referred to him as "Uncle Nick." The Horns went to California in 1854. Uncle Nick and Rutha visited Isaiah Horn and his father-in-law John Gann near San Jose in 1854. In September, 1856 Isaiah Horn took his family to visit Nick Gann's on the Calaveras River. On a visit to Russian River to visit his mother in 1856, Isaiah had gone by way of his Uncle Nick's on the Calaveras River and then on up through Sacramento and on to Napa where he stayed with "Old Man Hopper."⁴³

Noted historian Bancroft mentions the Hopper train passing through the present location of Stockton in 1847 and the birth there of William Gann (a Freshour grandchild.) This probably came from the 1878 statement of Alexander Moore of Pescadero — a member of the Hopper train.⁴⁴ Some of the train apparently went to San Jose where Isaiah Horn settled. The Ganns settled at Stockton where we found them in the company of James "Freasure" who was no doubt James R. Freshour, a brother to Judge Freshour of Cole County Missouri.⁴⁵

The trail conditions were terribly crowded in 1850 (50,000 emigrants) and 1852 (60,000 emigrants). In 1854 the traffic had subsided to 18,000 and the camping conditions and forage for the livestock were not as stressed. The cholera scare was over.⁴⁶ The Humbolt trail and the Mormon-Carson route over the Sierra were established. Word from California would tempt other family members to come on out. The Thomas Baucoms definitely came out in 1854 which is the second most likely time for a group of Freshours with kinfolk and neighbors to have been on the trail. Isaiah Horn and his family and parents of Jackson County also were in the 1854 group.[47] Lawson Freshour, William Fagan and wife Malvina Freshour most likely came at that time. They are all mentioned in Horn's diary.

The third group of Freshours identifiable as wagon train pioneers who made their trek across the plains were the ones of 1857. We can identify this group by family tradition and the established fact of two babies born on the trail that year. John and Sophronia had Lydia Jane Freshour, born July the 11th, 1857 on the Sweetwater near Devils Gate. This is recorded in Lydia Jane's family Bible and mentioned in her obituary.[48] James R. and Francis A. had a son, Joseph Frank Freshour, born in Alpine County, California on November 4, 1857.[49] A strong family tradition says that he was born at Markleeville, although Markleeville did not yet exist in 1857. Neither, for that matter, did Alpine County. But Marklee may have been running his toll bridge on the "middle fork" of the Carson river at that time. There was no government entity in the region then to which one could apply for land ownership — except possibly the Indians. Marklee filed his land claim in Douglas County, Nevada in September 1861 — the same year the US Territory of Nevada was created. Marklee was shot dead in 1863. His killer had to be taken across the Sierra to the nearest court which was in Amador County for trial. Alpine County, California was formed in 1864. In 1857, when the Freshours came through this region on the back side of the Sierra, it was not readily apparent where the California border was. Silver was found there the next year in 1858 and in a few years Silver Mountain City boomed — only to peter out as boom towns do. Eventually, Markleeville emerged as the principal town.[50] The James R. Freshour family, having spent some time there when Joseph Frank was born, probably took notice of and identified with any newsworthy development of that area. They may have known Marklee. The tendency of James R. and his sons to follow mining in later years, leads to speculation that he might have been prospecting there. As is the case with so much pioneer history, retrospection tended to convey certain facts to the succeeding generation as anachronisms. At any rate, this establishes reasonably well that James R. Freshour and family had arrived (barely) in California in 1857.

Joseph Baucom and his wife Emiline Freshour had a child in Missouri in 1857 and one in California in 1859. The Martin Freshours had a child in Missouri in 1856 and one in California in 1859. George W. Himes and his wife Sarah Freshour had a child in 1857 in Missouri and the next one was born in California in 1859.[51] These young families would have been traveling with infants and toddlers. The Himes would be traveling with one-year-old James Rufus Himes. James Rufus Freshour must have been a great hero to these folks. Perhaps he was their captain for the 1857 trek. Many of the pioneer women set out on the trail expecting. Some of the Freshours may have come out to California in 1858. We can only bracket the date. Some such as Thomas and Harriet Freshour had large gaps between children so could have come out anytime between 1854 and 1860. Andrew Freshour and family came out from Missouri when Christopher Columbus Freshour was fifteen years old according to C.C.'s obituary.[52] This would place them on the trail in 1857. Their youngest child Nancy was two years old in the 1850 census but listed as fifteen in 1860.[53] It is probable that Jane Marcum Freshour died shortly after 1850.

There are numerous journals and memoirs of wagon train travelers. These people had a keen sense of destiny and historical importance about this migration of the 1840s through 1850s. Some actually took the trip for the purpose of writing about it. Historian Francis Parkman did just that in 1846.[54] The famed artist Albert Bierstadt traveled making oil sketches while accompanying surveyor Lander in Wyoming.[55] Also, this was an era when journal keeping was in vogue. Any number of trail journals have appeared in print. A multitude of such journals remain unpublished. Some of these journals are written in amusing pioneer colloquialisms. Much of this raw Americana is reposited in university or museum libraries.[56] Some remain the cherished possessions of the descendants. Alas, no such Freshour journal or memoir has been passed down to us so we can only extrapolate from the writings of those who did leave a record.

One such diary was that of William H. Frush. In 1850, Frush traveled from Knox County, Missouri to St. Joseph and found his train had left him behind. He pushed on to Fort Laramie, a 600 mile ride on horseback, in eighteen days. He laid over there for eleven days cataloging all manner of data about the fort's operations and data gathered from other travelers on trail conditions, death and notable incidents. Frush identified trains and people. He met Kit Carson while there and was advised that the best way to California was to first go to Oregon. Thus he and his brother, John, made the trip to Portland, Oregon. He made friends easily, so traveled on horseback past most of the trains on the road, mooching a nights lodging with a different train each night. Thus he met and made record of an extraordinary number of people. His voluminous account is written in tiny script in a small notebook. Magnification is required to read it. The original is at the Beinecke Library of Yale University.[57]

The various Missouri and Iowa Freshours who traveled to California could well have traveled in different years and even in the same year in different trains. From the documented trains we know that it was common for relatives and neighbors to move in community. The Hopper train of '47 exemplified this. The Hopper train had, besides "Old Uncle Charlie Hopper — the Captain, cousin Thom Hopper, cousin Will Hopper, brother Dave Hopper, son Thomas Hopper and his son-in-law, his wife and his daughter." There are numerous Hopper descendants in Sonoma County. All of the Hopper family (except one that returned to North Carolina) eventually left Missouri for California.[58] Not only did the Freshours clear out of Jackson County, Missouri, but most of the Gann family apparently did so. Many Ganns ended up in Calaveras County, California where they took out numerous homesteads.[59] There was a

Ganns Station located there on the old turnpike coming down from Ebbits Pass. The site, now known as Ganns Meadow, is located between the Bear Valley ski slopes and Dorrington.

These are Freshour kinfolk and fellow travelers of North Carolina, Tennessee, Missouri and California. The same can be said to some degree of Baucoms, Himes, Horns and Fagans. Thus we take the years 1854 and 1857 on the basis of what evidence we do have, as years that are prototypical of Freshour treks across the plains, over South Pass, through the Great Basin and over the Sierra. From diaries and reminiscences of kindred spirits, we have vivid pictures of their journeys.

Figure 6.4 Unidentified Adams County, Iowa Freshours.

— Courtesy of Cliff Freshour, Prescott, IA.

7

OUTFITTING AT OMAHA

MOST LIKELY the Iowa and Missouri Freshours joined forces and traveled together. There are two probable plans they could have followed. The Missouri Freshours could have taken the Independence road across Kansas to Fort Kearney on the Platte and joined the Iowa Freshours there. The Iowa Freshours would have followed the Old Fort Kearney road from Plattsmouth or possibly left from Kanesville (Council Bluffs) and followed the Council Bluffs road along the Platte to the rendezvous at Fort Kearney.[1]

Another scenario would be for the Freshours to rendezvous at Omaha. In 1857, Omaha was an exciting boom town. The Omaha *Times* gleefully announced that they had surpassed Council Bluffs. In the decade since Nicholas and Rutha had departed from Jackson County, Missouri, the favored jumping off place had shifted progressively northward with the development of paddlewheeler commerce on the upper Missouri. The summer of 1857 saw 174 steamboats deposit 13,000 tons of freight at the wharves of Omaha. The town was ringed at night with the campfires of travelers temporarily camped with their tents and wagons. What the steamboats did not bring, the ferry boats did, transporting thousands of wagons across the Missouri.[2] In February 1855, Congress appropriated $50,000 for the improvement of the "Old Mormon Trail" between Omaha and Fort Kearny. The work began that summer and continued until the end of 1858. A major feature of this improvement was the construction of wooden bridges at the fords. Commercial ferry service at the tributaries had been established early on. In 1857, road construction had begun from Fort Leavenworth to Fort Kearny through the bog-lollies experienced in 1846 by Parkman when he traveled through the Kansas grasslands. The prospects of an improved road from Omaha would be a strong incentive for the Jackson County Freshours to go north for their rendezvous and departure westward. As early as 1844, the Martin Murphy party of St. Joseph, Missouri had gone north to rendezvous at Council Bluffs with an Oregon bound party which they would accompany as far as Fort Hall on the Snake River. From there, captain Elisha Stevens would lead them on to California.

There were a number of north-south roads in this area. The Nebraska-Kansas end of the Lane Trail went from Nebraska City to Nehama City along the western bank of the Missouri and thence south to Topeka. A road went from Nebraska City to St. Joe on the east bank of the Missouri. Not all the people trekking across Iowa in 1854-6 were going to Kansas nor were the rest going up the Platte. Notably the Freshours and associates were going to south-western Iowa. The Platte Purchase region just south of there in north-western Missouri had opened up to settlement. The Iowa, Fox, Sac and Potawattomie Indians had been moved across the Missouri River and St. Joseph became the trading center for the developing farm region. Families were dropping down off the Lane Trail from Osceola or Quincy into Gentry County, Missouri and environs on the Iowa border. There were wagon roads developed through this region and on down to St. Joe. Certainly the mobile Henry Freshour had been traveling these routes, probably overland, through the years.[3]

All manner of advice would be available to the prospective emigrant Freshours. James R. Freshour had been to California and back as an Argonaut and thus could relate first hand the nature of the journey and the preparation and provisions required. Of course, the outfitters had plenty of advice and recommendations. Generally they highly recommended what they were selling. Regular mail service had over the past decade been established by contract with stagecoach companies with

Salt Lake being a focal point and the "Mormon Corridor" being a reliable route.[4] By now, many California newspapers had been established and exchanged articles with papers to the east. Newspaper articles and letters to the editor dealt with trail vicissitudes and dangers. The outfitting towns were vigorously competitive and printed scurrilous things about one another.

Washington Irving's *the Adventures of Captain Bonneville* had been in print since 1837. Francis Parkman's notable work *The Oregon Trail* had been avidly read for a decade. Edwin Bryant's *What I saw in California* had been in print since 1849 and Alonzo Delano's *Across the Plains and Among the Diggings* had been in print since 1853.[5] There were the official reports of John C. Frémont's exploring expedition to California and Oregon which had been used by Ware to produce his 1849 guide book used by the gold seekers. This successful guidebook was followed in 1852 by those of Child and Horn and that of Steel in 1854.[6] The Freshours may have read some of the extended works or at least come under the influence of the related lore. They or someone in their party may have had guide books with them and consulted them for pointers on preparation. They probably were almost as comfortable about the journey as we would be with our trusty Rand McNally Road Atlas and our AAA Tour Guides. This was not the same daring venture that the Ganns faced a decade earlier. A mountain man guide was redundant now except for the leadership and discipline a "captain" could provide.[7] Perhaps the reason that no Freshour journals or memoirs were produced was that this trip was no "big deal." John and Sophronia had hit the trail in wagons three times before. The journey had become standard drill in the decade since Nicholas Broyles and Rutha Freshour Gann had made the trek across the plains with Kit Carson cohort Nicholas as "Wagon Master."

A primary item of utmost concern would be the vehicle used. By 1856 it was well established that many inferior wagons were strewn along the trail. In 1846, J.M. Shively had advised emigrants to buy a light strong wagon made of the best seasoned materials. The guide book of Ware also recommended, "Let your wagons be strong, but light, with good lock chains and the tire well riveted through the fellowes — if not thus fastened, you will have to wet your wheels every day to prevent them from coming off" ; as did that of Child.[8] They were also told to check the wheels for sturdiness, ensure that the key points were reinforced with iron and that the bed be straight sided with a strong canvas cover. The running gear was the heart of the wagon. The "falling tongue" was important as its articulation allowed traversing irregular terrain. The wheel, axle and running gear designs were amazingly "high tech"[9] for their day. The wagon box was nine to ten feet long, about four feet wide and about two feet high. The five or six bows supporting the top were generally of bent hickory and were hooped to a height of about five feet from the wagon bed. There were a variety of coverings but the best were made by sail makers. Most were white giving the "Schooner" appearance but others were of diverse colors. Some were emblazoned with mottoes.[10]

In St Louis, Joseph Murphy, famed as the Santa Fe Trail "monster wagon" builder, also built emigrant wagons. In 1830, Samuel Weston opened a blacksmith shop and wagon factory in Jackson County, Missouri. Independence and Saint Joseph had wagon builders as well. The South Bend wagons would be in short supply until the young Studebaker Argonaut returned from the mines to finance the operation. For the most part, the wagon was a farm rig built by a country blacksmith or by the emigrant himself. A "tar" bucket would be hung from the rear axle with a mixture of tar and tallow to grease the wheels. A tool box and water barrel would be mounted on the sides. The emigrants would be prepared to repair their wagons en route. The choice of stock was controversial. Mules were best for a fast trip but cost more. The oxen were slower and more durable on necessarily slow trips.[11] Besides they were more edible.

Mary Medley was ten years old when she traveled from Clark County, Missouri with her parents and family in a party of ninety — a train of twenty wagons. She recalled:

> The first thing father did was to go to Keokuk and ordered two strong wagons which were made with long wagon beds and then corded with ropes the length of a mattress ... Tall bows were placed over the wagon bed with two covers of heavy canvas made to fasten tight in front and back to keep out the rain. A large tight box was made behind the wagon bed with a lid on hinges to let down, which could be used as a table. ...
>
> The front of the wagon was tall enough to allow one to stand up straight in it. This was the family wagon. In the other wagon our provisions were stored to last through the journey. [12]

Some advised a very tight wagon bed to "ferry in."[13] From their Iowa border origin the Medley train traveled to Council Bluffs passing through the southern counties of Iowa.

Dr. Anson Henry, who successfully traveled from Springfield, Illinois to Oregon, wrote back home to a friend at Springfield:

> Now, if I were in your place, with my present knowledge and experience, I would have made to order in Springfield, two light two-horse wagons, (wide track) close coupled, with short beds, and I would have them covered with *"cotton top sail duck,"* with aprons front and rear, that you could open or close tight, at your pleasure ... I would have side boards, and my bows and covers so arranged that they could be shipped and unshipped at pleasure; and I would have the beds constructed in the same way. I would have patent locks, with two light lock chains to each wagon, for the patent locks ... are not as safe in bad rocky places as chains. Have a box one foot wide in the front of each bed with a strong cover, that will answer for seats: you will find these very convenient for stowing furniture. [14]

The going price for a light wagon was about $90. Oxen ran about $50 per yoke, large mules (15 hands) at about $70 *apiece*, horses ran about $50 each and cows $10 to $15 a head. One experienced traveler in Oregon noted that he hardly saw any dead horses or mules in route but had seen thousands of dead oxen.[15] But oxen prevailed as the most popular choice of wagonmotive power due to economics.

Note that John and Sophronia had sold their forty-six acres for $150 (a $45 profit) and their lot in Brookville for $10.[16] They had come overland from Indiana two years previously and may have been able to use the same wagons and stock. Nevertheless, $160 was not a lot of capital to outfit with. One emigrant who took his family from Indiana to Oregon in 1853 spent $846 on the trail. There were ferry and bridge tolls and the cost to replace stock and other items at trading posts. This was excluding the cost of wagons, stock and most of the provisions. His total expenses ran about $1500. Hopefully he would arrive with the value of some of this retained for use or sale on the other end.[17]

So much for the rollingstock. Provisions would be required. The frontier Freshours had an advantage being residents in the area. They could decide well in advance to make the trip and deliberately prepare over a period of time and out of the immediate vicinity of the sharp dealings of the outfitters. They could follow the accounts over the years such as the article in the Saint Louis *Daily Missouri Republican* by Edwin Bryant (author of *What I Saw in California*) who had gone to California with the Donner-Reed party in 1846. A letter in the Independence *expositor* written by Colonel Wm. Gilpin in 1849 again gave outfitting advice to 49ers and included his "List of Necessities." [18] These articles described outfitting typical of a military expedition with men sleeping in bedrolls and riding saddlehorse with the necessary logistic support for the sustained march carried in a few light wagons. After all, they were going for the gold. An individual rider could join the group with a horse and two pack mules. A man traveling with his sometimes pregnant wife and his children, including toddlers, would outfit differently.

The question of provisions occupied the emigrants through the spring. Five women, twenty seven children and twelve men of Saline County, Missouri were led by Newton Finley. Their transport included eight wagons drawn by oxen, two carriages propelled by mule teams and several saddle horses. They were drovers with stock amounting to three-hundred head of cows, extra oxen and twenty mules. Each family formed a mess, cooking for themselves and taking care of their own food. Each family had tents of a standard design having a ridge pole supported by two upright poles. Ropes and stakes secured the canvas. Tents were necessary for sleeping quarters, particularly for the women and children. Finley wrote:

> ...Our supply of food was bountiful and of the best grade ...consisting in part of: Cornmeal, Flour, Buckwheat flour, Ham, Bacon, Sausages, Dried Beef, Beans, Peas, Potatoes, Rice, Coffee, Tea, Sugar, Honey, Syrup, Milk, Butter, Dried Fruits, Apples (Green), Walnuts, Hickory Nuts, Hazel Nuts, etc. ...We had fresh milk daily, butter fresh daily; procured simply by placing milk at morning in the churn, put it aboard the wagon, at night we had the genuine article. [19]

Dr. Anson Henry wrote his friend back home at Springfield that a family numbering seven with three drivers would require:

> ...You will need for mule or horse teams the following quantities, with one-third added, if you come with cattle: — 700 lbs of flour, and 200 lbs of good butter crackers, in tin boxes, sealed up; 400 lbs bacon, *hog round;* 50 lbs of lard, in tin can; 50 lbs salt with mustard and pepper in proportion, with as many pickles, sweetmeats, &c., as you can afford to buy and haul; 100 lbs white crushed sugar, and 5 gallons of syrup; if you omit the syrup, 150 lbs sugar, 60 lbs coffee, 6 lbs tea, 40 lbs soap; 10 lbs sperm candles; 40 lbs of butter, put up in 8 or 10 lbs cans, sealed up. [20]

Remember that at sixteen miles a day for six days a week (a grueling pace for families with ox teams and driving livestock,) they would be on the road about five months and the prices at trading posts were exorbitant.

Dr. Henry continued:

> I would bring nothing in the shape of clothing that will not be needed on the trip. Each girl should have two good linsey dresses and three good calicos, with plenty of underclothes, (especially socks, which, bring by the dozen,) and one pair of light boy's boots, with three pairs of shoes. Do not omit the boots for the females, for they will frequently have to wade half way up to the tops through mud and water. Let them lay in plenty of coarse needles, thread, yarn and combs, and all the little fixings women are always wanting....
>
> Each boy should have one pair of coarse kip boots, made large, for when they are wet they always shrink one or two sizes, (if made wrong,) and at least two pair of shoes made to order, if store shoes three pair, and at least a dozen pair of good woolen socks — two good stout suits of clothes, with an extra pair of pants, and four or five hickory shirts. Good stout box coats are very comfortable after leaving the Platte ...
>
> Do not load yourself down with sheets, table cloths, bed quilts, &c., but bring plenty of blankets and coarse towels. Each man should have an india rubber coat ...and two blankets, and an india rubber carpet for the floor of your tent. — Get your tent made in St. Louis, ...have it made of the best top sail duck, with very strong cords and stakes, and when well "pitched," it will stand any of the storms on the Platte. ...Get Armstrong to make you a camp table ...and get half a dozen camp stools and have them covered with duck. ...Have plenty of buckets and tin cans. [21]

The distaff side recommended:

> ...that a lady should have two good strong English merino or linsey dresses, with three or four dark calico wrappers; two tweed sacks in place of shawls; one good silk hood, and two bonnets, with three pair of good buckskin gloves — you should have three pair for yourself for the akali dust is hard on the skin. Each man and boy should have a good hat and cap ...[22]

Another traveler suggested having the family physician put up your medicine chest, but better yet, if the son in law is a doctor, bring him along. Also lay in a good stock of patience and perseverance.

Such advice would be avidly read by the Freshours and a topic of comparisons pursued with friends, family and storekeepers. The outfitters, stock dealers and large wholesale grocery stores at trail's head were very competitive.[23] The dried fruit was very important for the purpose of disease immunity. They faced many months without fresh fruit or garden produce. Trail cuisine would tend to get very monotonous.

One very important aspect of equipping a wagon train relates to the fact that it was — particularly in the 1840s — a semi-military organization. The *Iowa Capital Reporter* advised in 1843 that a train should have not less than 100 men armed and equipped each with

> ...a good rifle gun of large bore carrying not less than 60 bullets to the pound — 4 pounds of powder, 12 of lead — (flint locks to be preferred,) caps and flints in proportion — and a good knife and a small tomahawk ....[24]

It is surprising how anachronistic one's thinking in this matter can be. Surely they used "old timey" rifles and pistols such as those used by movie heroes portraying the "old west" — lever action breech loading carbines carried in scabbards on the saddle and the low slung six guns using smokeless powder cartridges. Although these old weapons originated in the 19th century, they are of post Civil War gun technology and the wagon train era was predominantly ante bellum.

John Bidwell in 1841 carried a flintlock on the advice of old hunters that the new percussionlocks were unreliable. Most emigrants carried percussion firearms which, contrary to Bidwell's informants, were more trustworthy than the temperamental flintlocks.[25]

Many outfitters made or sold guns. In 1850, there were twelve firms making and selling firearms in Saint Louis including the Hawken shop. Eastern firms such as J.J. Henry had been selling guns to trappers and Indians. In 1849, Congress authorized sales to emigrants at cost directly from the US arsenals. These were commonly the Model 1841 US Rifle in .54 caliber, also known as a "Mississippi Rifle." Also available in 1849 were .52 caliber Hall breechloading carbines, the first breechloader adopted by the Army. By 1850, the Sharps and other breechloaders were becoming available. Eliphalet Remington developed a great combined manufactory of arms and farm implements, turning out rifles, carbines and pistols. But, the most famous of rifles was the Sharps. One model which he manufactured in quantity in the middle fifties was widely regarded as the most effective small arm in existence, for it was simple, easily cleaned, capable of ten shots a minute and of deadly precision at a quarter mile. Many of these Sharps rifles traveled the Lane Trail through Iowa. In Kansas they were known as "Beecher's Bibles."[26] but it was not until the mid 1860s that breechloaders, including various repeating types, started rapidly replacing muzzleloaders. Shotguns were also popular and could be used with a single large ball or with shot. They had the advantage of providing two shots before reloading.[27]

Emigrant sidearms included single shot holster pistols or colt revolvers which started replacing the "pepperbox" in 1850. The pepperbox was a cluster of gunbarrels that rotated — the Allen revolver. A Colt revolver cost $50 or more.[28] It is hard for us to appreciate the importance of the revolver to these men. We tend to associate six-guns with western outlaws and lawmen and the "oat-eater" motion picture industry. The accurate large bore rifles are of obvious importance it would seem to us for both hunting and firing at circling whooping "Injuns" from the circled wagons. Actually, the rifles were of limited usefulness against the Indians. The Indian tactic was to draw fire and then swoop in while the hapless plainsman was reloading. The Indian could let fly with several arrows in the time it took to reload a muzzleloader. — or close in for hand to hand combat. This is why a small hatchet was advised.

Martha Hill described her girlhood recollections of Indian fighter weaponry of 1853.

> Every fighter carried, hung from his shoulder, a powder horn, which was made from a cow's horn, the big end being made air-tight by a piece of wood fitting into it, and the little end stopped with a cork. First the powder was put in the barrel of the gun and packed down tight with a ram rod; then the bullet, wrapped in a strong piece of cloth, was pushed down to meet the powder. When the trigger was snapped on a small piece of flint, it set sparks a-flying, caught the cloth around the bullet, ignited the powder and sent the bullet on its way. This process had to be gone through every time the gun was fired. Another inconvenience was that no two guns were alike and bullets had to be moulded to fit each gun. The lead came in bars about one foot long; this was put into a ladle over a fire, and when it came to a white heat, was run into bullet moulds.[29]

The Texas Rangers were losing almost every skirmish with the Comanches. Many units were entirely wiped out until they obtained Sam Colt's "six-shooters" as they named them. The long rifle was an excellent weapon in the eastern woodlands where it earned its reputation. It also served well in the mountainous Northwest. It was a good weapon to have when on foot. Combat on the plains usually took place on horseback. The plains Indians were consummate horsemen riding very fast horses that they would ride into combat with one leg slung over the horse, the horse's body shielding them. They could swing up at the critical moment and hurl their lance with devastating force and accuracy. The plainsman would have to dismount to effectively use his long rifle. The Indian could release arrows in rapid succession while on horseback riding at full gallop. The revolver answered the requirement for a rapid fire repeating weapon suitable for horseback.[30]

Ranger Samuel Walker worked with Colt in redesigning the revolver into the gun that was not only to turn the tide against the Comanches, but also to win the Rangers widespread fame in the Mexican war. After the war, the story spread about the phenomenal fighting Texas Rangers and the marvelous side arms they carried.[31] This was the obvious weapon for the plainsman on horseback. As late as 1865 bull train drivers were molding bullets for their muzzeloader Colt Arms revolvers. By then metallic cartridges could be purchased for the breechloading guns designed for them.

Ware's guide suggested five pounds of powder, ten pounds of lead and a few pounds of shot per man. Lead was purchased in "pigs" or bars and the emigrants molded bullets over the campfire. The emigrants took the armament requirement all too seriously and each man became a "walking ordinance department." This presented a safety problem. There was a tendency to stick the huge revolvers into the belt and handle the rifle by the muzzle end. The problem was to get these men to California before they killed themselves. The guide books were uniformly careful in advising gun safety in explicit detail. Some emigrant companies adopted rules against carrying guns primed or capped. This advice was widely ignored.[32] The aboriginal threat prevailed.

The leading cause of trail death in the years 1840-1860 was cholera. The second most common cause was Indian clashes, although the emigrants gave slightly better than they received in that regard; wagon train massacres notwithstanding.[33] Death by freezing and starvation was frequent and drowning occurred regularly. Seven percent of the deaths were due to other accidents with firearm mishaps most common. There were approximately 20,000 deaths during the migration of 250,000 persons to the west coast.[34] They would be spending some five months traveling two-thousand miles through country where the only law was the guns they carried and their mutual commitment to collectively provide for one another's welfare. This journey would be entirely through Indian territory and, although most of the Indians were only a nuisance, some would be hostile.[35] The innate nobility of the red man was not a favorite topic among the emigrants. That has been reserved for the present generation. Some emigrants were destined to die at the hands of Indians in 1857 as they had in previous years.

The other consideration taken for granted was the necessity of guns for the hunting of game to relieve the monotonous diet of the trail.

The Freshours would no doubt arm each man with a rifle most likely of the muzzle loading percussion cap type and many would carry a Colt muzzle loading six shooter. They would no doubt lay in a stock of lead and black powder and bring along bullet molds to use at their camp fires. John and Joseph Terre Freshour would later in the 1860s proudly wear the Colt revolvers issued to them as California Militiamen serving in the Santa Cruz Cavalry. Bullet molds were part of the arms issue to the unit.[36]

The most dreaded peril of the trail, cholera, apparently began in India in 1816 where it burned slowly, reaching the Ganges delta in 1826. It was carried to the Caspian Sea and became pandemic passing on in 1830 to the Black Sea and up the Danube. Throughout Europe in the years 1831 and 1832, the pestilence was terrible. In 1831 it was all over the British Isles. Irish emigrants brought it to Canada in 1832 and it made its way up the Saint Lawrence and spread along the canals and waterways with commerce. The entire interior valley down to New Orleans suffered terrible outbreaks in 1832 and again in 1833. The disease would die out, mutate and recur. In 1833 the recurring epidemic at Saint Louis went by steam boat up the Missouri River to Independence. Doctor Marcus Whitman fought it among Fontenell's men at nearby Bellview in 1835.[37]

In June of 1835, Fontenelle's party experienced the first signs of cholera. These familiar symptoms were to become the dread of wagon trains on the plains where it was easily transmitted by lack of sanitation. The first signs are diarrhea, restlessness, nausea and chills. In a few hours the victim develops violent diarrhea, painful vomiting and muscular cramps, thirst and circulatory failure resulting in collapse. Severe fluid and blood loss shrinks and wrinkles the patient's skin. His face grows hollow and his nose seems to sharpen. He turns blue. In a few hours of extreme agony he dies — or turns the corner to convalesce for several days. Relapse back into the disease may happen if the patient is not allowed to fully recuperate. Without modern medicine, the mortality rate is 50 percent. The disease is transmitted by bacteria from the stools of the afflicted. A gift to all the wagons that follow. Epidemics still occur in primitive environments.

Cholera continued to smolder on the frontier with an occasional local outbreak. It was epidemic again during the emigration of 1850 — even worse than it had been in 1849. Some died on the paddlewheel steamboats on the Missouri River before they even got to the frontier. The pioneers on the frontier in Iowa and Missouri were to be devastated by it and it may have caused some of them to postpone plans to strike out across the plains for Oregon or California. Those who were stricken on the trail suffered greatly because they lacked both comfort and medical help. The emigrants were not far from the frontier when the cholera epidemic overtook them, completely debilitating entire camps of covered wagons. A correspondent wrote to a Missouri newspaper in 1850 from the Platte River, reporting that they had counted forty graves in a span of sixty miles. West of Plum Creek they had seen three wagons in a company from Saint Joe, with only one man able to sit up. The company of twelve had suffered six deaths with four others in the throes of death, one had measles and one was suffering from exhaustion. The week following, he encountered a train in which sixteen out of seventeen were sick. In two other trains, all but one had died. Within fifteen days, approximately two hundred and fifty people had died in the distance he had traversed along the Platte.[38]

No one could mistake what was wrong with the first victim. The group of prairie travelers must have felt the awful dread that made the well as wretched as the sick. Some would turn back rather than face the mountains and the desert with only a few survivors of their party. Others would consolidate forces and move on. It should be remembered that some 44,000 people traveled to California in 1850.[39] Percentage wise, the number of cholera deaths was not that great.[40] The ones still on the frontier, having survived, could start west when the scourge subsided. This would be the case in 1854. By 1857, cholera in epidemic form was history.

John and Sophronia Freshour sold their property in Iowa in the late summer of 1856. This left them about eight months to prepare for the trip. Their preparation must have been careful and deliberate and included all of the factors cited. Apparently Joseph Terre Freshour was included in the plan. To the south, in Jackson County, Missouri, similar activities were taking place. The main part of the company was being put together there. They needed about 100 wagons. Perhaps they planned to go to Omaha and seek an alliance with other groups that had consonant purpose in order to get the critical mass required to move out. One could expect advertisements in papers soliciting small groups of emigrants to join forces with well organized emigrant companies.

Thus we see a company grouping at trails head in the spring of 1857, including Freshours, Ganns, Himes and Baucoms. There were no doubt many other family names involved. They were anxious to join the relatives and friends who had preceded them to California in the trains of 1847 and 1854. They would perhaps join groups from Ohio, Indiana and Illinois. This could have included the Bernard Thompson family from near Quincy, Brown County Illinois. The Thompsons ended up in San Joaquin County near French Camp in California. These families would spend day after day living as a community on wheels. They would forge fast friendships that would persist for many decades in California as they built new lives there. They would populate the land and make it strong and productive. They would meet with old friends and laugh about the things good and bad that happened on the trail. They would tell grandchildren "I came across the plains in '57."

8

ROCKY MOUNTAIN CORDILLERA

JEDEDIAH STRONG SMITH, foremost among "mountain men," and Thomas Fitzpatrick led a group of trappers across the Rockies discovering South Pass in 1824. Jedediah Smith explored the far west as a fur trade entrepreneur — mapping previously unknown areas as he went. He drafted a letter to the US Secretary of War telling of the potential for settlement of the Willamette and Columbia river Valleys of Oregon. This letter, also signed by his partners David Jackson and William Sublette, was published by Congress. He sold out and returned through South Pass in 1830 to pursue the Santa Fe trade. He was killed by Comanche Indians in May of 1831. Today, his explorations and cartography are ranked with those of Lewis and Clark. They show the Green River as a Colorado River tributary.[1] Actually, Jedediah Smith *rediscovered* South Pass and was the first white man to travel *westward* through it. Robert Stewart, one of John Jacob Astor's *Astorians*, traveled east from the Pacific via South Pass to Saint Louis in 1812-13 traversing what was to become the Oregon trail.[2] Stewart was the first European to use the route that was first trekked, in aeons past, by migratory stone age foragers of the plains, themselves burdened and aided by packed and travois-trailing dogs. At the dawn of historic time, with the acquisition of the horse, these tribes flourished — developing into the culture we know as the Plains Indians.

The first wagon train to follow the Platte across the plains of Nebraska and travel over South Pass was that of West Point trained Frenchman, Captain Benjamin L.E. de Bonneville, a soldier turned mountain man — later to become a distinguished

veteran of the Mexican war.³ William Sublette had taken a few
wagons to Popo Agie at the foot of the Wind River mountains,
but lost all enthusiasm for the method. The fur traders were
devoted to the use of pack animals which had to be unloaded
and loaded at each camp. Bonneville saw wheeled vehicles as
a natural for traversing the plains which were relatively unimpeded. He set out with one hundred and ten men and twenty
ox and mule wagons — leaving Fort Osage near Independence,
Missouri in May 1832. He ran the wagons in two columns
— one under the command of Joseph Redford Walker. They
used wagons smaller than the later prairie schooners and much
smaller than the standard freight wagon. The goods thus carried over South Pass by the Bonneville expedition provided for
two years trade at Fort Bonneville established on the Green
River.⁴

Not all the terrain was easy. By the time Bonneville's expedition reached the vicinity of Laramie Fork, the arid climate
was playing havoc with his wagons. — An experience that was
to plague hordes of wagons through the succeeding years. The
wood shrank and warped and the wagons commenced falling
apart requiring constant repair. The worst effect was on the
wheels. As the spokes shrank, the iron tires came loose and
initially had to be secured with wooden wedges. The entire
wheel would eventually disintegrate if something wasn't done.
A blacksmith could shorten the tire, but the most expeditious
remedy was to remove the wheels and soak them overnight
in a stream where possible. As they progressed they encountered gullies, hillsides, canyons, bluffs and tributaries that were
impossible to ford. For these they again removed the wheels
to make bull-boats of the wagon boxes by sheathing them in
hides. They did not have the mobility of a pack train but the
experiment was nevertheless quite successful.⁵

This was the 1830s — the era of fur trapping, mountain
men and their famous annual rendezvous. The mountain men
were trapping the *Tierra Incognita*. Jim Bridger discovered the
Great Salt Lake on a bet. By riding a "bull boat" — a wooden

frame covered with hides — down the Bear River. His report of the Great Lake's salty water on his return to winter camp at Green River led the trappers to believe that he had been to a Pacific bay. The locale was the Wyoming Basin. Bonneville, there ostensibly as a fur trader, pursued his military specialty from this strategic location. Cline maintains that he had a delusion of riches to be made in furs.[6] He made a survey of the territory which included sending Walker with a brigade to explore the Mary river. (So named by Hudson Bay Company's Peter Ogden, later renamed the Humbolt by Frémont.) They discovered the Humbolt Sink and crossed the Sierra Nevada to California. Bonneville produced the maps published by Irving. At that time, Bonneville was credited with the discovery that the Great Basin had no outlet to the Pacific — contrary to the Spanish legend of *Rio Buenaventura*.[7] As late as 1841, Bidwell had brought along boatbuilding tools because it was common knowledge that one could take a boat down river from Salt Lake to San Francisco.[8]

The Bonneville-Walker expedition did make a major contribution. — they demonstrated the trail along the Humbolt River as a direct route into California. A decade after the Walker Brigade tour, the more overt explorations of the *Pathfinder*, Captain John C. Frémont, would commence. His meticulously recorded volumes brought immediate fame to himself and his main mountain man Christopher "Kit" Carson.[9] The mountain men were living among the Indians — trading with them, employing them and adopting much of their culture and mores. Bonneville and Joe Walker became squaw men as was frequently the case among the mountain men. Regular caravans brought the furs to market at St. Louis and returned supplies to the rendezvous of the trapping and trading mountain men living in Indian territory.[10] The Bonneville venture of 1832-5 introduced wagons into this milieu.

The Delaware were vanquished by the Iroquois warriors and denied the privilege of calling themselves a tribe. They were, however, superb soldiers and found significant service as mercenaries on the plains both by the mountain men and the horse soldiers. Among the elite body guard for General Frémont, when he commanded the Union army in Missouri, were a contingent of Delaware.[11] They loved soldering and combat. Bonneville hired Delaware and had them pirated away by Fontenelle who coveted their services.[12] Parkman describes the Delaware transplanted in Kansas as living in squalor but traveling clear across Kansas to the Rockies to battle indigenous tribes.[13]

Bonneville encountered a war party of Crow Indians who were out to avenge some of their kin killed by the Cheyenne. Bonneville's group found them very friendly. In fact, the Crows repeatedly embraced them and pilfered all their loose personal belongings. The Blackfoot were by far the meanest of all the Indians the mountain men dealt with. Armed by McKenzie of the American Fur Company, they vowed to surge south to take territory and exterminate the Flathead Indians. This lead to the shootout at Pierre's Hole.[14] William Sublette, who had taken command, was severely wounded. A number of mountain men were killed and scalped in the initial onslaught and "horribly mutilated." This discrete Victorian phrase so often found in frontier reports meant that when the Indians took scalps from dead men they usually took the male genitals also to use with their ritual incantations when they danced around the scalps in victory celebration.[15] Often they took scalps from the wounded preferring to leave them to agonize in a lingering death. Frontier medical practice included treatment to encourage the skin to grow back over bare skull bone.[16]

The Blackfoot set out to hunt down and kill any white man trapping in their territory. They nearly did so to Fitzpatrick in a now legendary episode. They later killed Vanderburgh of the AFC, stripped his bones of flesh and threw them into the stream he and his men had been trapping.[17] Washington Irving, traveling in 1832 with a government commission to inspect lands designated for dispossessed tribes,[18] met William Sublette and his mountain men on the upper Missouri, traveling back to Saint Louis with their pelts. They had carefully chosen their route out of the mountains to avoid the Blackfoot and had made the frontier in safety.

> ... Their long cavalcade stretched in single file for nearly half a mile. Sublette still wore his arm in a sling. The mountaineers in their rude hunting dresses, armed with rifles and roughly mounted, and leading their pack-horses down a hill of the forest, looked like banditti returning with plunder. On the top of some of the packs were perched several half-breed children, perfect little imps, with black eyes glaring from among elf locks. These, I was told, were children of the trappers; pledges of love from their squaw spouses in the wilderness. [19]

The mountain men had learned the requirement of traveling in a large armed force. Indian marriages also gave safety, at least from one particular tribe, but subjected one to an inordinate in-law problem — the entire tribe it would seem.[20]

The Flatheads killed many Blackfoot at the Pierre's Hole fracas and subsequent encounters, frustrating Blackfoot ambition. But the Blackfoot met their ultimate match in the Crow who established a southern containment for the Blackfoot "Lebensraum." The mountain men considered the Crow to be superior to all other plains and mountain tribes — the Sioux being superior in numbers only. [21] Mountain man Jim Beckwourth became a Crow war chief. He led the Crow in the annihilation of a band of thirty to forty raiding Blackfoot that they had tracked down. He threw his rifle to the ground, stripped himself naked and like the Indians themselves, took up a hatchet and ran across the prairie with forty or fifty young warriors close behind, to storm the Blackfoot breastwork and slaughter the Blackfoot in hand to hand combat. The Indians exultation in the glory of war is set forth in Parkman's description of this incident.[22]

This scene was to attract missionaries. The supply caravans of the flourishing fur trade of the 1830s routinely followed the Platte River road. Packing along with the fur traders in

1834 came a party of five Methodists headed by Jason Lee. The Reverend Samuel Parker, a Congregationalist pastor from Massachusetts, and Doctor Marcus Whitman, a Presbyterian medical missionary, arrived in 1835. Doctor Whitman battled a cholera epidemic that broke out among Fontenelle's men and removed an arrowhead that had been lodged in Jim Bridger's back since 1832. The greenhorn doctor thus gained acceptance of the profane and raucous mountain men. Reverend Parker and Doctor Whitman had been commissioned to investigate the receptiveness of the Nez Perce and Flathead Indians to the Christian gospel. The Indians were eager and wanted the missionaries to continue with them. They decided that Parker would stay on and Whitman would return to the States and mount an expedition equipped to establish a mission. The greenhorn Reverend Parker mounted his horse and with his Greek Testament and unfamiliar sidearm traveled out among the Indians. He progressed up the Snake river enduring illness and hardship and teaching among the Indians as he went — arriving at Walla Walla in October.[23] He went by dugout with three Walla Wallas down the Columbia to Fort Vancouver to stay the winter with the "Father of Oregon" — the Hudson Bay Company's director Doctor John McLaughlin.[24]

In 1835 Whitman and Parker had traveled from Liberty (across the river from Independence) crossing the plains to the Green river area of the Wyoming Basin with the American Fur Company's Lucien Fontenelle. The missionaries using pack mules had joined Fontenelle's pack train of about sixty men with about two hundred animals and six wagons — after Bonneville's precedent. The wagons strongly interested Whitman for he foresaw the possibility of ridding himself of pack mule responsibility and possibly transporting mission supplies all the way to Oregon. Marcus Whitman returned the following year in 1836 with his new bride Narcissa in company with the Reverend Henry Spalding and Mrs. Eliza Spalding.

The annual pack train of the American Fur Trading Company, under the command of Thomas Fitzpatrick, arrived at

South Pass on July the fourth, 1836. The train of over seventy men and some four hundred horses and mules came through the Pass this year with the Company cart and a light four wheeled wagon without springs. This now famous wagon was with the adjoined missionary group, which included fourteen horses, six mules, fifteen head of beef and milk cows. They camped that evening at Pacific Springs.[25]

A monument in the pass commemorates the religious service held there by Dr. Whitman. He knelt to pray with an American flag in one hand and a Bible in the other. One hundred years later, people would be touring through in their model A Fords. The monument is pointed out in *The Oregon Trail* road guide of the *American Guide Series* written by history professors put to work during the great depression by president Roosvelt's Works Progress Administration.[26]

Narcissa and Eliza were the first white women to cross the great divide at South Pass. — Riding side saddle. In heavy boots and swathed with yards of skirt. At times one or the other of them would ride perched on the baggage in the wagon. These two women were the first of many thousand. Two days later they reached the rendezvous at Horse creek (a tributary of the Green river near Fort Bonneville) and the annual jubilation. The mountain men put on quite a show. The Nez Perce, the Flatheads, the Bannocks and a whole village of Snakes were there. This was their first encounter with white women. Their squaws greeted Eliza and Narcissa profusely.[27]

The Whitmans and Spaldings joined a Hudson Bay Company train to continue their journey to Oregon. Just past Fort Hall, an axle breaks. Baggage and supplies are discarded and Marcus converts the wagon into a two wheeled cart. At Fort Boise, the cart has to be abandoned and they continue with precious possessions on pack animals and driving their cattle. They continued the trip Indian style without midday rests — living on jerky. Narcissa and Eliza stoically trudging mile after mile over the rough mountainous trail — at times nearly fainting from the heat and exertion — the stony path at times swimming before their gaze. Again, the first of many women to follow.[28] They walked through the Blue mountains to Fort Walla Walla. A perilous journey down the Columbia brought them to Fort Vancouver and the hospitality of Dr. McLaughlin. Marcus and Narcissa established their mission at Waiilatpu where Marcus was the resident physician to twenty thousand square miles.

In the following ten years, the commercial impulse of the fur trade and the altruistic impulse of the missionaries would be replaced by the land cravings of the inveterate pioneer.[29] This would be lubricated with the trendy manifest destiny doctrine. In 1840, Joel Walker took his family to Oregon as an avowed emigrant as distinguished from the missionary families he accompanied. They traveled under the protection of a fur trade caravan. This signaled the beginning of emigration as such. It would be seven years after the Whitman wagon was abandoned before wagons were successfully brought across the Blue Mountains into Oregon. Up till 1843, the wagons were left at Fort Hall and pack trains went on in from there. The hospitable Hudson Bay men at Fort Hall truly believed passage by wagon was impossible.[30]

Thomas Fitzpatrick piloted the first two emigrant trains into Oregon. In 1841, one of these trains was joined by a party of three Jesuit missionaries led by Father de Smet. This party had included with it a party of young folks — most were under thirty, the oldest being forty-one year old Charlie Hopper — who were resolute in their determination to go to California. "Broken Hand" Fitzpatrick, the fur traders and the Jesuits continued on to Oregon, parting ways with this Bartleson - Bidwell party. Five men returned to the States.[31]

"Oregon fever" strikes in 1842-3 and many wagons with women and children regularly travel to Oregon as graphically described by Jessie Applegate's *A Day with the Cow Column*.[32] An American government is formed in Oregon in July 1843 provoking a dispute with Britain. President Polk's inaugural address in 1845 asserts US title to Oregon. In May of 1846

President Polk exacts a treaty from Britain establishing the present Oregon boundary.[33] His war with Mexico is brewing. The "Bear Flag Republic" is promoted by the exploring Captain John C. Fremont and his party of mountain men.[34]

When Nicholas and Rutha crossed the plains in 1847 with the Hopper wagon train, the Oregon trail was well established — The California trail was nascent. They were pioneers in the sense that they were very dependent on their mountain man turned captain to guide them through desolate territory — particularly once they left the Snake river to follow the Humbolt river. Hopper guided them across the Great Basin and over the Sierra. They were dependent on their careful provisioning, their armed strength and their dogged persistence. They traveled as a disciplined quasi-military caravan with outriders and sentries. They also relied on Captain Hopper's experience in dealing with the Indians en route. It had been only three years since the first wagons had struggled over the Sierra and the routes were still in early development. The experimental route of the Donner party across the great basin the previous year had culminated in a notorious disaster. Under Captain Hopper's capable guidance they would take a sure route and arrive without any major calamity. They certainly wouldn't wander lost and starving across the Great Basin and over the Sierra as the Bartelston-Bidwell party had done six years previously. Hopper had learned that lesson well as a participant.[35]

The wagon trail to Oregon was not without friction with the various Indian tribes. The fur trapping mountain men had many narrow escapes and were frequently killed by Indians. Etenne Provot had seven of his men killed at the present site of Ogden just prior to Walker's trip up the Mary. — Something Walker had in mind at the time. Jedediah Smith lost most of his men in an Indian attack — the Umpqua massacre — on a trek up the Oregon coast in 1828.[36] The mountain men had an occasional pitched battle with the Indians, such as the battle at Pierre's Hole in 1832. Irving concludes *The Adventures of Captain Bonneville* with the observation that the work clearly manifests the requirement for military posts and a mounted force "to protect our traders in their journeys across the great western wilds ..." [37]

This was implemented in May of 1846 by an act of congress authorizing the establishment of military posts along the road to Oregon. Three thousand dollars each was appropriated to purchase from the Indians rights to the necessary land for posts and seventy-six thousand five hundred dollars for mounting and equipping a regiment of Mounted Riflemen to consist of ten companies of sixty-four privates each. These troops were diverted to the Mexican war where, in eighteen engagements, they lost four officers and forty-five men in action and had thirteen officers and one hundred eighty men wounded. Aside from combat, one officer and two hundred eighty men died. Fourteen officers won brevets and eleven men were advanced in rank.

They mustered out in 1848 and commenced reorganization for the original mission. At the beginning of 1849 preparations for the departure of the Mounted Riflemen from Camp Sumner near Fort Leavenworth began. The Mounted Riflemen would be the first military unit to travel the entire length of the Oregon Trail. The assembled train, when ready to march, consisted of seven hundred horses, twelve hundred mules, a number of oxen and one hundred seventy-one wagons loaded with provisions to establish posts. Major Osborne Cross was to command the supply train and establish quarters for the regiment in Oregon. This he did — returning to the United States[38] in February of 1850. His official journal and the diary of George Gibbs who accompanied the Mounted Riflemen are published in a fascinating account of the 1849 gold rush throng on the trail.[39]

The Trail was becoming a Road. The stretch following the Platte river across Nebraska accommodated travelers to Oregon, to California, the Mormons to Salt Lake and those taking the South Platte, branching south-west to Denver. The hard packed prairie clay made natural roadbeds up either side of the Platte to form what is known as *The Great Platte River Road*.[40] Up until 1855, the government contribution to trail improvement was channeled through the Army Corps of Topographical Engineers — John C. Frèmont being their most illustrious explorer.[41] During the early 1850s, there was much reconnaissance relating to the Pacific Railroad Surveys; an attempt to locate the optimum route for the transcontinental railroad. — The construction of which was delayed by the Civil War. Sections of the road west were constructed as military roads. Bridges were constructed and commercial enterprises including trading posts and ferries across streams were established for the emigrant trade. Fort Bridger and Fort Laramie offered goods and services including a forge.[42]

For the Freshours traveling on the road through the newly formed Nebraska Territory in 1854, there would be difficulties even that early in the trip such as: lost or stolen livestock, broken down wagons and possibly dissension in the group involving the pace traveled and leadership of the group. Major Cross reported broken down wagons and discouraged parties turning around to return to the States. As early as 1846, Parkman had seen abandoned along this road "shattered wrecks of ancient clawfooted tables well waxed and rubbed, or massive bureaus of carved oak." [43] Wrecks of disabled wagons and abandoned furniture and belongings were to be found along the entire 2,000 mile length of the trail.[44] Many of the diaries give a running account of dead animals and those left to die, wagon iron and general wagon train debris; including discarded clothing and worn out shoes. One woman wore out ten pairs of shoes on her trip to Oregon. Many were comfortable walking barefoot and saved their shoes. Many of the wagons were outfitted with a stove, and the use of dutch ovens for cooking was common. The stoves were frequently left on the trail when the going got tough after leaving the Platte River.[45]

The loss of livestock could be disastrous. Seldom less than ten oxen were used to pull a wagon at the start of the journey in 1849 according to Major Cross. Lavender indicates three yoke as normal for a family wagon. A family usually had two wagons plus other livestock driven along and perhaps a saddle horse or two. Each evening, if possible, they would have to camp where they could let these animals graze. Each days travel usually had an objective — taken from a guidebook or the captains experience — that hopefully would satisfy this requirement.[46] Lost, stolen or dead animals would eventually force them to abandon a wagon and some precious possessions. Broken wagons could be repaired with parts scavenged from abandoned wagons. When a wagon was stopped for repairs or if a member of the party was too ill to move or in the last stages of dying, all the wagons stopped. A wagon left straggling was an obvious target for the Indians.[47] The emigrant's safety was in numbers. But the worst vicissitude would be the tedium of the daily routine of a 2,000 mile journey traveled at twelve to twenty miles in a day. The oxen were driven by bull whackers who walked alongside them. Walking twenty miles a day over prairie in the hot sun is a hard days work. Women and children walked to relieve the burden to the animals in rough terrain or to relieve the boredom of an endlessly slow ride. "Are we there yet, mamma?" — "No, dear, we have a few miles to go." The travelers were to universally benefit from the salubrious effect of a perpetual outdoor existence. Many literally walked to California. More than one elderly lady attributed restored health to the walk to California.[48]

They were awakened at daylight by a bugle or a gunshot by one of the sentries standing the last watch of the night. They dressed, built fires with buffalo chips and cooked breakfast, took down and packed tents and stowed everything in the wagons, rounded up and yoked the oxen and broke camp. Everyone had their assigned task. Two hours after daybreak they would be rolling. They would stop at a likely place for a noon time rest and cook lunch. Generally the only shade was from the wagons. They would press on until late afternoon allowing enough daylight to make camp. They would again tend to the livestock and cook their evening meal with buffalo chips, mend things, socialize around campfires comparing observations about the days journey and speculate on the morrow. The distasteful *bois de vache* was necessary because the plains are not wooded and what little fire wood there was got used up by the multitude of travelers.[49] The livestock would be cared for and sentries set for the night. Each new landmark on the horizon marked their progress. Many of these already famous landmarks were described in guide books and other written accounts. Life would be very "daily." Inevitable hours of boredom fell between the moments of excitement. Parents brought along small libraries and created lessons to fill these hours.[50] Indians were rare. They were in a corridor — Pawnees to the north — Cheyenne to the south.

George Gibbs aptly describes the Platte river two days march beyond Fort Kearny. This typifies how it was experienced by the emigrants.

> ... The Platte is, I imagine, alone among rivers. Straight and swift, shallow and muddy, it is unfit for navigation, bad to ford, destitute of fish, too dirty to bathe in, and too thick to drink, at least until custom habituates one to it. Rivaling in length and breadth what are called great rivers even in our own land, running with a current equal to the East river at Hell Gate, draining a country in extent one fourth the continent, an Indian canoe cannot even float upon its broad waters. Excepting for quicksands and occasional holes a horse may wade it without wetting his saddle girths, even where, as here, it is a mile in width. Where cut up with islands, as is often the case, it extends double or treble ... It is easily swollen by rains, running almost level with its banks, ... Timber is rarely found upon its banks, although the islands are covered with willows and cottonwood. Ash trees are found only upon the ravines which come down from the bluffs. The islands are ... low and narrow, they are often of great length....[51]

They forded the south fork of the Platte. It was fearsome looking because of its breadth. It was like going out to sea. It was usually only two feet deep, but if it was high the travelers would wait for it to fall.[52]

Parkman graphically described the climate and blustery weather of late spring on the Platte. In the years to come, women travelers reported having their tents literally blown away — getting soaked to the skin and spending the remainder of the night trying to sleep in the shelter of the wagons.[53] Six-year-old Jesse Applegate experienced one of the famous Plains thunderstorms which he described in his later years.

> Some-time during the night, I suddenly awoke. The rain was pouring down my face, my eyes were blinded with the glare of lightning, the wind was roaring like a furnace, and the crash of thunder was terrible and almost continuous. I could see nothing but what looked like sheets of fire, and hear nothing but the wind, the pouring rain and the bellowing thunder. [54]

This was the land of the warrior horsemen – the Sioux. The wagons were carefully circled at night and the guards set with stricter instructions. The Sioux came into camp to trade or beg. A conspicuous show of arms kept this from turning into bullying.[55] This was their territory. The children were aghast at the scalps on the Indian belts. They were in great herds of buffalo now and could enjoy buffalo steak. It was possible to pass through without encountering Sioux since they lived in symbiosis with the migratory herds of buffalo. Parkman came here to live among the Oglala Sioux.[56]

The boy Jesse Applegate saw a great war party mustering at Fort Laramie to fight the Blackfeet.

> As I remember this army of Sioux warriors, they were all mounted on nice horses, bucks and squaws all painted about the face, and armed with bows and arrows encased in quivers slung at the back. Some had spears, some war clubs, but no guns, or if any, very few. This war party, as I see the picture now, looking back sixty years, marching or halting in close array, covered several acres of prairie. It was a gay and savage looking host, and sometimes when a squadron of those warriors would break away from the main body and come toward us shouting the

war whoop, urging their ponies at full speed, I thought
it a grand display indeed, although I fancied I could feel
the hair rise on my head. Several of the Amazons of this
war party visited our encampment. They were dressed
and painted and armed like the men. Some of them
were very fine of figure, had pretty faces, and eyes soft
and bright as the antelopes on those wild plains. They
were all young women, and, as I thought, made love to
our young men with their eyes like city damsels, but
in the excitement of battle I suppose they became very
furies and those lovely eyes flashed fire. Their small,
shapely hands and small feet clad in beaded moccasins
were admired even by our women ...[57]

Trubody describes a band of eight hundred Sioux encountered in 1847 by the Hopper train near Fort Laramie. The Sioux were heading south to combat their traditional enemies, the Pawnees. He notes that the Sioux were numerically superior and eventually just about annihilated the Pawnee. On this occasion, as usual, the Sioux smoked the peace pipe with the white men.[58]

Parkman describes his mistrust of a young Sioux when he was living with the Oglala. The lad, Hale-Storm had yet to take his first scalp. His status was no better than that of a squaw and his prospects for marrying an Indian maiden were slim, until he had used his scalping knife. Parkman, wanting to keep his own scalp, kept a close eye on this young man. The Indians would take a scalp any way they could. They dug up the dead, buried by wagon trains traveling through, to take their scalps and their clothing and any valuables left on the body.[59] Undoubtedly, far more Indians were killed by contact with the bodies of cholera victims than ever were killed by the white man's guns. The early trains buried in the trail so the graves would be obliterated by wagon tracks, thus preventing this desecration.[60] The mountain men in trading with the Indians had wiped out vast numbers with the small pox. They diligently tried to explain the danger to the Indians and enforce quarantine. But, the concept of communicable disease was as abstruse to the Indian as the concept of an unarmed society. They thought they were being cheated out of the opportunity to trade. They considered the pestilent deaths the result of white man's magic. This was why the Cayuse killed the Whitmans. (As DeVoto points out, neither the Europeans nor the Native Americans knew about "*no-see-ums*" at this time since Louis Pasteur hadn't invented them yet.)[61] The wagon train emigrants seldom killed Indians but had an impressive ability to do so — and would if necessary. This the Indians could understand. They very seldom killed the emigrants — only on opportunistic impulse.[62]

It is possible to drive most of this trip on modern highways. Driving west along the Platte on Interstate 80 and breaking away onto US 26 at Ogallala, the author stopped to pay his respects at the Ash Hollow cemetery then drove west through some horribly parched desolate country on a July afternoon. Finally, way in the distance, he could distinctly see the famous landmark, Chimney Rock. He drove for more than an hour with it in view. When he got near he stopped every few miles and took a picture. The sky blackened with clouds. Finally, as he got to where he had a full view of the entire natural structure, the random flickering of a lightning bolt dazzled the darkened sky — seeking out the tip of the chimney — followed by a thunder clap and downpour. One wonders how many wagon travelers had witnessed this. Certainly these sudden Platte River storms were common. It was clear that the wagon travelers spent perhaps days with this curious monument in view. Many described it, investigated its geology and sketched it.[63] Major Cross speculated that it appeared to be formed by erosion of a bluff similar to those nearby.[64] Trubody claimed that thirty feet had been struck off the top of the chimney sometime during the 1850s reducing it to less of a land mark than it was when he came through with the Hoppers in 1847. Jim Bridger claimed it was lightning that blasted it off.[65]

Later, the author came over a rise and viewed the orange glow of the bluffs in the afternoon sunlight as an immense stage back-drop to the town of Scott's Bluff. Another famous landmark. What a picture. The road way overlooked and descended into the town at this point. When he finally found a spot to pull over, the composition was spoiled; he turned around to re-acquire the vantage point. But to his chagrin, the moment of charm was a fleeting one. The entire vista was enveloped in a large cloud — a dust cloud. Such are the vicissitudes of the fickle Platte River Road.

During September of 1851, more than 10,000 Plains Indians gathered at Horse Creek in council with Indian agent Thomas Fitzpatrick to sign the Fort Laramie Treaty of 1851. Fort Laramie was thirty-four miles to the west. Horse Creek provided the necessary grass for the thousands of horses. The treaty outlined each tribe's territory and they agreed to no longer fight each other. They recognized the right of the government to build roads and forts on Indian lands. In return, the Army was to protect the Indians from white depredations. With exception of hostilities following the Grattan massacre late in 1854, tribes along the trail remained peaceful until the Indian Wars of 1864.[66]

At Laramie fork, the crossing of the swift Laramie river is difficult. It is named after Jacques La Ramie, the Canadian fur trapper who's body was thrown into the river when he was killed by Indians near here in 1821.[67] Fort Laramie, the fur-trading post, had Sioux camped about looking for a chance to trade. Wagons that had been abandoned or sold could be purchased here. In August of 1854, Lieutenant Grattan, rashly attempting to discipline the Sioux for the theft of a stray cow, rode out with twenty-eight men. The young Lieutenant foolishly ordered his men to fire on the peaceful Indians.[68] He and his men were wiped out by the Sioux precipitating warfare with the Indians that brought trail traffic to low ebb in 1855. Everyone knew there was war on the plains so waited at Council Bluffs to build strong well armed parties before starting out.[69]

In spite of all the hard toil and dangers of the trail, amenities accompanied the tribulations as the emigrants adapted to a way of life that was a variation of the American cultural theme. They had always provided their own entertainment, and the fiddle, banjo and the jews harp came with them.[70] After the Mexican war, the guitar was heard on the trail. There was music, singing and story telling around the camp fires. Lasting friendships were formed. As the days passed, the geography and the character of the river gradually changed. The landscape started to pitch and roll and the trail looped away from the river constantly returning to it. At Fort Casper they found Mormon Ferry with hundreds of wagons lined up to cross the Platte. Brigham Young established this ferry in 1847 and Major Cross recorded in 1849 that $4 per wagon assured that the wagon and its contents would arrive safe on the north side.[71] Delano describes the ferry as a single flimsy raft. It had lost its rope which was replaced across the swift stream by persistent attempts. If the emigrant failed to remove the canvas top, it acted as a sail to tilt the raft dumping the wagon into the swift current. The draft animals and droves swam across. The emigrants pitched in to help one another across.[72]

Various traders came here to do business while the travelers awaited their turns. Kit Carson was here in June of 1850 with a herd of horses and mules to sell. By 1854 this north Platte ferry had been replaced by a bridge of hewn timbers.[73] Lewis Stout recorded on June 30 of 1842 "Left the Platte river for good, none of us shedding any tears, for we were all tired of it. We have traveled up it for 750 miles and longed for change." [74] A woman can place the Platte River in perspective by imagining waking up in a tent in the morning with morning sickness and opening the flap to look out on the Platte. Many set out on the trail pregnant.[75]

The trail took them through a forced march of 30 miles without water to a camp at Willow Springs. The wagons, cattle, horsemen and droves formed a continuous procession through blinding suffocating dust with no way to get around them in this desolate stretch over Rattlesnake Hill. Many struggling oxen dropped in their yokes. Here travelers commenced to lighten their loads to spare the dehydrating animals. They passed Poison Springs where the black water killed the animals allowed to drink it. They finally arrived at Willow Springs and good water. Some celebrated the fact that they were no longer on the Platte with its rain squalls and ailments. One group fiddled and danced all night long.[76] A few more miles and they would find grass. The next camp would be on the Sweetwater River.

They came to the famous land mark, Independence Rock, where the emigrants continued the custom established by the mountain men by adding their autograph to the behemoth rock. They laid over here several days and prepared a celebration feast for Independence day. The men went out for a day's hunting to put fresh game on the table. In one party the ladies even sewed a flag so the speechifying ceremony could be done in the presence of *Old Glory* rippling in the breeze.[77] The pie from the dutch ovens on this festive occasion was superb — even if the pie dough had been rolled out on the wagon seat. On occasion, weddings were held here.

Here the children could spend a day playing together instead of walking the trail. Whenever they had the chance they would play button-button, London Bridge, leap-frog and run-sheep-run. Girls and younger boys chanted handed-down rounds and rhymes and made necklaces and wreaths from wild flowers — a favorite pastime until the present century. The older ones would run up to the top of the rock as they still do today. It was a relief to get away from foul water and camp rations, but they longed for fresh fruit and vegetables. They brought along dried fruit to ward off scurvy. A boy of eleven recommended dried apples for economy. "You need but one meal a day. You can eat dried apples for breakfast, drink water for dinner and swell for supper."

Widower Andrew Freshour from Johnson County Missouri would be traveling through here in 1857 with his five children. The eldest, Eliza Jane, would be going on twenty years of age — marriageable, but as it turned out, she waited until they were settled in Sonoma County. This marriage could well have been the result of a trail romance. William F. would be eighteen years old — a good age to drive the oxen of the second wagon or to mount up and do outriding while his fifteen year old brother Christopher Columbus "C.C." drove the oxen. Thirteen year old Mary M. was probably a tomboy and may have run up "the rock" with her ten year old sister Nancy C. — Andrew's youngest. They may have had sad moments when they missed their mom. Eliza Jane probably had the distaff responsibilities thrust upon her.[78] Over all, it was probably the adventure of their lives. They probably had many wonderful tales to tell their own children in later years. The men inventoried, assessed, repaired, anointed sore hooves and padded yokes that were making ugly sores on the necks of the oxen. They knew the roughest part of the journey lay ahead and critically estimated their animals ability to bring them through. Previously they had abandoned niceties such as furniture and trail comforts such as stoves. Here they discarded things important to a new start in California. The area around Independence Rock was strewn with anvils, bellows, plows, bar iron, kegs, axes, and even extra wheels and axle trees.[79]

A man with a pick-up truck loaded with posts and fence building material stopped to let his boy run around for a bit. He was headed for Montana to work on a ranch property he had acquired. He made the mistake of asking the author what the "rock" was. Eventually, as he edged away to round up his kid, he commented that he wanted to teach his boy some of this western history.

Looking up the meandering Sweetwater across the grassy flat to the west, one can clearly see the massive granite cleft of Devil's Gate with the Sweetwater emanating from it.[80] A fine memorial site allows modern travelers on Wyoming SR-220 to also view Devil's Gate from a western vantage point overlooking a prosperous bottom land ranch — posted naturally. While reading the various historical plaques there, the author was joined by a tour bus full of retired folk. They were

Mormon he discovered. They shared ancestral nostalgia. This was their trail too, the author was reminded. He recited the fact that his great aunt was born here. This was not uncommon. The typical pioneer woman got married in her late teens and had babies continuously until in her forties. No sooner was one weaned than another was on the way. One can trace the westering of the family in their family record by noting where the children were born. Ten children was par for the emigrant wife who was often to become mother and grandmother in the same year — as the eldest children started their families. Sophronia was on the trail with two-and-one-half year old Will and eighteen month old Joseph Alfred and gave birth to Lydia Jane at Devil's Gate on July 11, 1857. The odds were that several women of each wagon train would deliver a baby along the trail. At Coy's writing circa 1930 he reported an active *Covered Wagon Babies' Club* with a large membership. The women tended to one another on these occasions. The older more experienced ones performing as midwives — a task they all sooner or later were called upon to perform. Babies were generally delivered under a wagon with the women of the party surrounding and attending.[81] Birthing, dying and marrying were all part of the earthy trail life just as they had always been part of the pioneer experience.

The mountain plateaus of Wyoming exposed the travelers to relentlessly piercing solar rays. One can stop off at Lander to replenish their ice chest and buy medication for their hands which scorch from gripping the steering-wheel in the July afternoon sun penetrating the windshield. The trail along the Sweetwater was relatively easy with good pasture and water. Sometimes the animals would stampede along this stretch.[82] It has a number of landmarks such as Split Rock and Ice Slough. We can envision thirty-two-year-old John Freshour walking alongside the oxen "bull whacking" with Sophronia and little Will occasionally walking while newborn Lydia Jane and toddler Joseph Alfred rode in the wagon. Nineteen year old Joseph Terre Freshour would drive the second bull team.

Martin Freshour and his wife Mary Ann and their first little girl Sarah were no doubt along on this 1857 trip.[83]

The winding Sweetwater had to be crossed seven times; the final crossing being rather difficult. The Sweetwater was a Rocky Mountain stream of icy water. In spite of the intensity of the hot sun, one could get pneumonia from washing clothes or bathing. Even in July, the weather can be very chilly. The men would be in the water up to their waist and even armpits — positioned on either side of the wagons guiding them. Sometimes some of the oxen would be brought across first in order to pull with ropes from the far bank. Many of the travelers had the foresight to equip with block and tackle. Wagons were sometimes upset here.[84] The Sweetwater, according to tradition, got its name from a wagon load of sugar being dumped accidentally into the stream from an upset wagon. This could have been a trader commodity since the Indians were very fond of this wonderful substance from the white man. At Strawberry Creek there is a monument to the Mormon handcart party marooned here in 1856. This party of 576 European converts and other saints in wagons totaling about 1,200 in all, started late in the year and they met a blizzard. One by one they gave up and were strung along the route here for miles. This was the Mormon equivalent to the Donner disaster. Their animals died and their carcasses were eaten by ravenous wolves. The storm lasted for a week. Brigham Young sent out a relief party, but it was inadequate. Over a hundred died near here in nine days. Their huddled bodies were left under great protecting blankets of snow. They were buried in a trench two miles above Devil's Gate.[85]

Our pioneers traversed the expansive slope extending out of the shallow valley that was the imperceptible crest of South Pass.[86] The young lad Jesse Applegate, gazing far off across a dreary sage plain "got to wondering where we were trying to get to." "To Oregon" he was told.[87] The trip through South Pass wasn't necessarily anticlimactic. They were at that point at an altitude of seventy-five hundred feet in the midst of the Rocky

Mountains of Wyoming. If these wayfaring pioneers happened to get caught in one of the horrendous thunder storms common to the Rockies, the whole flat mountain top would be incandescent with electricity and instant thunderous explosions.[88] It was clear to the terrified lowlanders that they had climbed the last rise and adventured onto earth's zenith to stand in the very presence of Almighty God. This was, in fact, North America's continental backbone — the Rocky Mountain Cordillera.

> ...When you cross the Dry, or Little Sandy, instead of turning to the left and following the river, strike out across to the Big Sandy, twelve miles. If you get to the river along through the day, camp til near night. From the Big Sandy to Green river, a distance of thirty-five miles, there is not a drop of water. By starting from the Sandy at the cool of the day, you can get across easily by morning. Cattle can travel as far again by night as they can during the day, from the fact that the air is cool, and consequently they do not need water. ... By referring to the large map, you can see that you save nearly five days travel by following what I have taken the liberty to call *Sublette's Cut Off.* [89]

On they toiled. They went over Sublette's cutoff, crossing Green River and Fontenelle Creek, then they followed the Bear River to Soda Springs. Pushing on, they crossed Hudspeth's cutoff to the "City of Rocks." They had crossed the Rockies — the land of the Mountain Men — another 355 miles of difficult trail since leaving South Pass. They were in Oregon Territory.[90] This was constant outdoor living, with tents, bed-rolls, latrines, doctoring trail-worn oxen and cooking over open fires — oh, how they longed for hearth and home. The diaries express such yearnings. The twin spires of the City of Rocks eventually earned the name "Cathedral Rocks." [91] From thence they rolled down Goose Creek into Utah Territory and the Great Basin.

9

TRIBULATION IN THE BASIN

THE WORST was ahead for the emigrants and they were trail weary. They would spend August following the Humbolt to a forty mile desert crossing and then assault the towering eastern approach to the Sierra. The first week from Cathedral Rocks and nearly a hundred miles brought them to the head of the Humbolt. From here we can drive high speed Interstate 80 west along the wagon trail through present day Nevada.[1] If one thoughtfully appraises the terrain they are whizzing through, they are appalled. Tempers would be shorter and there would be more cursing. There would be weeks between baths but no one would complain of the feculence since the odor of rotting mules and oxen was even worse. The pioneers would travel one-hundred-seventy-five miles through this terrain to Lassen Meadows at present day Rye Patch. At this point they had covered the area of the Great Basin that, apparently not taken into account by Bonneville, had already been thoroughly trapped prior to his notion to send Joe Walker on his 1833 expedition through here.[2] But from this point at Lassen meadows, Walker's brigade would experience several *Firsts*. They would be the first group to follow the Humbolt to its sink and beyond crossing the Sierra to California. They would be the first to fight off the depredations of the "Digger" Indians. They would be the first to travel in the Yosemite high country and see the *Sequoia gigantea* Big Trees below on the Tuolumne.[3]

Jedediah Smith had explored the Great Basin from 1824 to 1830 and accurately mapped the hydrographic details of the western regions of the Rockies; particularly as they relate to the Great Basin. He identified the Green River as a tributary of the Colorado.⁴ The Mojave Indians directed him across the desert to California.⁵ He gave up his original belief in the Rio Buenaventura myth as a result of his California explorations. He showed the Sierra to be a barrier between California and the Great Basin. Smith had crossed the Great Basin west to east, but, in 1833, the Walker brigade was first to travel the route that in a few years many wagons would follow. And they experienced the same hardships. They recuperated on the California coast. They explored, then returned over Walker Pass and back up the Humbolt the next year.⁶ This was a horse and saddle venture. Walker was to repeat this journey ten years later with the Chiles-Walker train which burnt its wagons near Owens Lake and packed on over the southern margin of the Sierra.⁷

Joe Walker's first encounter with the Diggers along the Humbolt was to tarnish his reputation as was his later endeavor in this locale in the "previously owned horse" commerce. DeVoto flat out calls him a horse thief — albeit with tongue in cheek.⁸ Walker was actually moderate in his dealings with these Indians on the lower Humbolt, but had been given the reputation of shooting up Diggers for sport. The trappers traveling with Walker killed Indians vengefully without his knowledge because the Indians were stealing their traps to obtain the metal. The trappers contrived to do this without Captain Walkers knowledge because they knew the "Cap'n" would not permit it. This devastating first assault did not deter the metal craving Indians for long and the incident was repeated and Walker discovered it. The small brigade was tracked by a growing number of Diggers who had been nonplussed by the severe retribution for practicing their principal virtue — thievery. The presence of these fabulous white men and their extraordinary riches was to soon attract a vast hoard of Indians.⁹

The term Diggers is an epithet rather than a tribal designation. Several tribes had remnants that fell into this category of Great Basin destitution. Cline eschews the vulgarism, designating the Indians that Walker encountered as Paiutes. These pint sized Indians were quite unlike the tribes from which they had degenerated. They lived without shelter or in small huts woven of sage brush. They had few clothes and those were made of woven grass. They fed on what was at hand — carp and suckers from alkali streams, seeds, bulbs, roots, grasshoppers, black beetles and grubs of flies that bred in alkali pools. Many of them had no way of making fire. They had only rudimentary artifacts. They were the most primitive of the American stone age aborigines. They skulked along the route taking the traps that the trappers bought at Saint Louis for $20 apiece. Individually, with your eyes upon them, these Indians were harmless. They were dangerous in numbers or at night. Mark Twain described them as "treacherous, filthy and repulsive."[10]

By the time the Walker brigade reached the Humbolt Sink, a dreadful number of Indians were gathered. Walker had his men demonstrate their fire-power by shooting birds, game and targets. The Indians persisted and wanted to smoke. Walker judged this to be a delaying tactic. The number of Indians continued to grow. The situation was dangerous and out of control. Walker decided that he must act decisively while he still was able. He unleashed his trappers and they opened fire killing about fourteen Indians. The Indians dispersed and no longer troubled them. This situation was to repeat itself on the brigades return via the Humbolt route the following year. Thus a precedent was established. Normal practice was to take pot shots at any group of Indians congregating in the vicinity of the trail.

Hopper sent out outriders when his party came through here in 1847. They were sent ahead by Hopper every day to choose camping places. In the morning he would go around to see if everyone was ready, and when the teams were yoked would sing out, "Roll out." The team ahead one day would be put in the rear the next. An equitable practice because of the dust the train stirred up. "Oregon rules" were put into effect — corraling, men mounting guard, double guard when Indians were ugly. Men on guard had to walk around through the camp from evening 'till daylight, then slept in a wagon the next day. The outriders discovered an Indian roadblock set up as an ambuscade and took punitive action. [11]

The question arises as to why the "Diggers" would live in such horrible circumstances. The answer lies in the Indian culture in general which has as its principal component latent tribal warfare. This was a very low technology culture. They were stone age tool makers. They had not discovered the wheel, preferring the travois as so carefully illustrated in the oil sketches of Bierstadt. Bierstadt accompanied the surveyor Lander among the Sioux. He illustrated their adaptation of tepee poles to this usage. This was their only utilitarian use of the horse, so recently introduced among them by the Spaniards. Its main use by them being for their normal pursuit of warfare and hunting. They followed animal trails making no improvements on them. Roads and wheels were of no interest to them. These were a higher technology beyond their mastery, since they were based on metal smithing. The impoverished Indians along the Humbolt had not even acquired the horse.[12] This is why they would consider the Truckee river a route over the Sierra.[13] It was a difficult footpath — it was a poor horse trail and the worst possible route for a wagon. Viewing it when driving off the top of the Sierra towards Reno on Highway 80 and visualizing a wagon train in that terrain makes your hair stand on end. The only technology of Indians was stone age tool making, principally for hunting and warfare. They dressed in animal skins and animal skins stretched on the poles were their housing. They made dwelings such as their stone axes permitted. They had no written language. Their principal industry, beyond physical subsistence, was warfare. This was the job title of every adult male — *brave* or warrior. The Indians that managed bare survival in the Great Basin were the vanquished — the losers. The victors secured a better habitation for themselves with a superior standard of living and banished the Diggers to a dried up primordial lake bed. — an Indian "third world."

Guerrilla warfare on the wagons following the Humbolt was a wonderful welfare program for the Indians up and down the entire length of that curious landlocked river. It gave them summer employment. This was just compensation for the fact that their ecology and the choicest part of their habitat had been disrupted by these strange houses on wheels. Violence on the part of the Indians wasn't always the case. The Utes on the upper part of the Humbolt were fairly well behaved. Instead of killing the emigrants, they would more likely rob them of everything they had, particularly the livestock, and leave them half naked and on foot.[14] The Shoshones would sometimes come into camp calling "Gee!" "Haw" and "Whoa!" which they understood to be a form of emigrant communication. Communicating with draft animals would not occur to them since they immediately ate any animals within their grasp. The wary emigrants kept an eye on them. Friendliness was a preliminary to thievery.[15] Parkman's Oglala used their dogs on occasion for culinary purposes. Parkman once eradicated an obnoxious cur by giving a feast of dog stew for his Indian friends.[16] The Diggers weren't that sophisticated. The breeding stock would be eaten. The key to Digger behavior besides their lack of ethics, was the fact that they were in a perpetual state of quasi starvation. Even if the emigrants were fortunate enough to avoid Digger hostility, they were sure to lose livestock. The Diggers were particularly partial to mule. Ownership was not an issue. They would take one off the trail and settle down around the carcass, gormandizing until they had slicked up every morsel or the animal started to stink.[17] They would then procure another.

The wagons following the Humbolt on occasion took a short cut, but always returned to the river following its big bend without any major cutoffs. The Humbolt flowed forty feet wide and eighteen inches deep typically and was frequently forded to a better camp or trail on the other side. The first wagon to cross would be vulnerable when it was isolated from the remainder of the train just as it came up on the far bank. Eight men were killed at Gravelly Ford. Five were put in a common grave there.

Donner party dissension occurred at Gravelly Ford. John Snyder was killed there by Jim Reed in an altercation that ensued when Reed interfered with Snyder's beating his oxen up the hill. Reed was expelled from the party and went on ahead making it over the Sierra. With his leadership, the Donner Party might have survived the Sierra.[18]

The Piutes on the lower Humbolt were the nastiest. An emigrant party got into a fracas with them and one of their members named Sallee sustained wounds so severe that he soon died. He was properly buried but the Diggers dug him up. The next party coming through reburied Sallee and he was again dug up by the Diggers. This went on for the rest of the season. No matter how often the Diggers dug him up, they never disturbed the note left on a stick by his party because it was white man's medicine. "Sallee's grave" became a principal landmark and the knowledge of it became the certain mark of a veteran who had run the Digger gauntlet that year.[19]

The Mormon Battalion, recruited to serve with General Kearny when he marched his dragoons via Santa Fe to California, was deployed from Santa Fe down the Rio Grande and across New Mexico to Tucson. From there they proceeded along the Gila River cutting a road through the mesquite, cottonwood and palo verdes of the river bottom.[20] These road building skills would soon be put to use in the Sierra. General Kearny left a major contingent of the Mormons Battalion in California when he marched back east.[21] Their normal connection to Salt Lake City was along the "Mormon Channel" into southern California.[22] Some of the Mormons who were employed by John Sutter established a shorter route to Salt Lake. The geological feature of the Sierra that makes a large ramp running from the vicinity of Placerville up to Carson Pass was used in 1848 by the members of the Mormon Battalion returning to Salt Lake by the Humbolt route and thus the name Carson-Mormon immigrant trail. Three of these Mormons were killed by Indians on this trail at Tragedy Springs. Kit Carson had blazed the trail but the Mormons Battalion turned it into a wagon road.²³

Some of the Mormons were still in Sutter's employ when Marshall discovered gold and the Mormon Corridor mail route was undoubtedly the path of the leaked out information that set off the gold rush of '49. Soon the gold itself was to travel up that corridor as gold mining became a Mormon activity. Eagle Station was established in 1851. It was later named Carson City after the river named by Frémont. Mormon Station was established near the present site of Genoa. Except for wagons taking the Lassen route into northern California or those branching north into the Rogue River country of Oregon on the Applegate trail, most of the emigrants after 1848 would take the lower Humbolt to the Carson river and continue on the Carson-Mormon route or its more southerly variants.

In 1850 there were more women on the trail than in 1849 and people traveled lighter; having heard about overloading. Unfortunately, many did not bring enough provisions to last out the trip. On the lower Humbolt, people were destitute and starving. Again there was harassment from the Paiutes. There were a number of suicides. — Three men and two women drowned themselves in the Humbolt. — Driven past the point of endurance by the suffering of their children. Then they came to the desert crossing to the Carson. An 1850 account recorded 9,771 dead animals and approximately three-thousand abandoned wagons. Traders were selling water. A relief party was sent out from California. The majority of emigrants walked on in across the Sierra.²⁴ There was Cholera on the trail again in 1850. Many had lost loved ones along the way — 936 graves along the length of the trail by one count. The stories of hardship were so terrible that hardly anyone emigrated in 1851. But, 1852 was a boomer. The peak years for numbers on the trail to California were 1849 through 1853. By 1854 the traffic had dwindled to twelve thousand.²⁵ The Grattan massacre was related to late season Mormon travel; so, the California travelers were in the Great Basin by the time the Sioux were riled back on the plains.²⁶ Good travel practice was established and conditions were not exacerbated by overcrowding. The Ganns, Horns, Fagans and Freshours on the trail in 1854 had picked a good year to travel.

They would camp at the Lassen Meadow (at present day Rye Patch) where the road to Peter Lassen's ranch, in the Sacramento Valley, headed off to the west. Actually, Lindsay Applegate, older brother of Jessie Applegate of Oregon Trail fame, opened up this trail into Rogue River Oregon country just north of California. Lassen's trail branches south at Goose Lake. Nobles' Road also branched south off the Applegate Road to give a shorter route than Lassen's which was very circuitous.[27] The choice here was between the lower Humbolt and the Forty-mile Desert to the south or the Indian infested northern California mountains. They headed south on a well established trail that had proven to be the quickest. There was never a chance of losing this trail as there had been for the early California bound emigrants of the 1840s. By 1854, the emigrants had only to follow the wreckage and debris. Another forty-five miles of terrible Humbolt travel brought them to the Great Meadow — a lush alkaline swamp where they could rest and gather feed to get their cattle past the Humbolt Sink and over the Forty-mile Desert to the Carson River — another forty miles across blistering desert sand.[28] They could make coffee or tea at Boiling Springs without a fire.

By 1854 it was well known that this desert must be crossed in the cool of night. The wagons left the last slough crossing in late afternoon. By the time they were well into the dunes they were enveloped in dark starry night — each company straining in isolation in the eerie darkness. The desert was drained of its latent heat by the bitter cold sucked down from the snowy Sierra peaks. As the stock failed, the abandoned wagons were burned and the weary travelers rested from their slogging through the sand in the warmth of the fire. They would heat up coffee to warm them and stimulate them through the long exhausting night. They would consolidate their load on remaining wagons and proceed. The flames of a preceding wagon would at times act as a guiding flare. They were burning "purdy good" wagons. The junkier ones were left further back on the trail as they had switched to choicer abandoned wagons. The route is strewn with dead animals. Wagon after wagon stops, the failing ox or mule being unyoked or taken out of harness and fewer wagons reteamed with the strongest animals. Loads are redistributed; the lighter loads going to the animals that might barely make it to resuscitation at the river. The weakest are left to die in agony as they broil in the desert sun. The desert becomes a junk yard interspersed with animal carcasses.[29]

In the forenoon they would finally come in view of "Ragtown." The name came from the ragged wet clothing put out to dry on the bushes along the Carson River. They knew it was just ahead because the scent of water had quickened their animals. At last, wonderful water — melted Sierra Nevada.[30] They had itched continuously from exposure to alkaline dust. Even at the lush Great Meadow the water had been alkaline. Salt crystals had sparkled on the lower stalks of the marsh grass. Now they washed the alkaline dust out of their clothing and bathed. They were emaciated and haggard and their lips split and the membrane in their nostrils fried to paper by the weeks in the hot desert air. They had labored around the clock and suffered loss of stuff carried almost all the way to California. They were all bunged up from their dogged toil on the Humbolt and unloading and loading wagons in the desert. Now they rested. Good water with which to cook and water the stock seemed miraculous.[31]

They followed the Carson River up the Carson Valley. — They were nearing California. The Mexican governors presided over an Alta California that encompassed virtually the entire Mexican territory acquired in the Treaty of Guadalupe Hidalgo. However, they barely managed to administer that which was west of the Sierra. The California constitutional convention of 1848 set the present eastern border to exclude the Great Basin and its Mormons.[32] The Mormons formed the state of *Deseret* from the residue but it was never admitted to the Union. It became Utah Territory in 1850. The Mormons would later content themselves with Utah proper, the Great Basin being divided into Utah Territory and Nevada Territory.[33] For the emigrants California meant the other side of the Sierra — the "Diggins," the burgeoning valley towns and the ranch lands. Nevada was *also* to the west — on the *other* side of the Sierra in the Northern Diggings. In the 1850s, Nevada, the seat of Nevada county, was the largest city in California. It had several large hard rock mines riddling the granite, on which it was built, with miles of shafts and tunnels. It had an opera house, sumptuous hotel and the impressive home of a US Senator. With the discovery of the Comstock Load, many of its important citizens were to cross back over the Sierra to participate, in 1861, in creating the US Territory that was to become the 36th state to enter the Union — Nevada.[34] So called after its namesake, Nevada California, which was renamed Nevada City to obviate the inevitable confusion. What our emigrants were leaving behind was the Great Basin, then Utah Territory. If you were to ask them where they had been, they would tell you that they had been on the Humbolt in Indian territory. It had been pure hell. They had just been luxuriating on the grassy meadows along the pure melted snow of the Carson River and were now in the upper Carson Valley. They had another job of work just up ahead. They were almost in California.

The upper Carson Valley narrows into a small winding canyon with rocky jutting walls — no place for wagons. They struggle in the river bed in a steep climb that in places allows for switchbacking among the boulders and timber at the margin of the river. Injured stock and smashed wagons commonly occurred here. As many men as could get ahold of a wagon would get in the stream and literally carry the wagon over the bolders, the poor oxen falling down again and again. This was repeated for each wagon in turn.[35] It took an entire day to go four miles. — A difficult days walk for the women and children. The men collapse from the strenuous days work. Another hour of travel and they emerge into groves of aspen at the lower end of Hope Valley. A respite in the successively tiered meadows flanking the gliding river and another days journey brings them to the upper end of Hope Valley at the foot of Devil's Ladder. This is the drive on US-88 from Minden, Nevada to the Carson Pass. You can stay at an Alpine lodge in Hope Valley and take a guided hiking tour of the wagon trail. You may noticed that the door jamb at the entrance to your cabin is entirely decorated across the top and down both sides with funny looking horse shoes. These turn out to be oxen shoes. Earlier in the century, they could be picked up by the bucket full. There are block and tackle marks on the trunks of trees. One can discover the trail by rusting iron wheel tire marks and grooves in the granite. The switchback grade of Devil's Ladder is perceived by the boulders and rocks pushed and thrown to the down hill side by the women and children going ahead of the men laboring with the wagons. They used twelve yoke of oxen to haul one wagon up at a time. A single yoke took a wagon down the other side to camp. The men held back from the rear with chains. Another days work. [36]

In 1854, William Finley made his ninth plains crossing. His first was in 1847. Apparently he made two trips in one year. This was possible by pack train or in light wagons using mules and without droves. Huge herds of cattle were driven to California since the Mexican longhorn cattle weren't sufficient for the demand. The hide and tallow trade had depleted them. The Mexican Ranchos raised beef for tallow and hides to be shipped to foreign markets. Soon they were doing a brisk business with the square rigged sailing vessels coming around "the horn" from New England.[37] The slaughtered longhorns were skinned and the tallow rendered in huge iron pots just as was done with whale blubber. The tallow was poured into sewn up hides called botas to be shipped with the bales of hides. The carcasses were mostly allowed to rot. There was only a small market for edible beef in Alta California and salted beef was not profitable as a shippable commodity.[38] This all changed with the burgeoning Anglo population. The emigrant droves provided stock for beef ranches as well as meat for California tables. Herds of sheep and even turkeys were also on the trail. Finley reported that 1854 was his worst trip of all. His party of one hundred included women and children and a large herd of cattle. They were caught in a two-day storm on Carson Pass. Five hundred of the cattle died. Traders saved the rest with very costly hay.[39]

A days journey past the crest of the Carson Pass in the timber overlooking a vast granite gorge, lies

> Rachel Melton,
>
> died October 4, 1850,
>
> native of Iowa.

A State Historic Landmark sign says *MAIDENS GRAVE*. The grave is cobbled with granite stones and a carved granite headstone was placed in 1908 by friends of Kirkwood. There are most always flowers on the grave. It is customary to stop to pay one's respect and invariably catch cold — the kind that makes one's eyes water — the cold mountain air perhaps. This young lady endured the trip along the Platte and through the Wyoming mountains and the severity of the Humbolt — the agony of the desert and the struggle to the crest of the Sierra. She had arrived in California.

> *Do not weep for me; I am not dead;*
> *I've only gone — just up ahead.*
> *You've arrived in the land of gold;*
> *I've arrived where I'll never grow old.*
> *Do not weep for me; I am not dead.*

In another week to ten days Rachel's bereft family would arrive in Placerville or Sacramento having come off the high Sierra slopes without her. Our pioneers coming through here in 1854 may very well have stopped to pay their respects.

The year 1857 only had about four thousand emigrants. The trail along the Humbolt had become dangerous. The Paiutes had grown bolder. — By now, they were equipped with horses and firearms. The early parties coming through in 1857 had shot up the Diggers pretty bad so they were in a nasty mood. A party of seven men, two women and a baby camped by themselves — something they should never have done. When they started to move about in the morning, gun shots and arrows felled several men and one woman. One man fired back and fled wounded. The Indians killed a man who lay sick. The remaining woman, still in her night gown, was hiding in a tent with her baby. She started to run with her baby but fell wounded. The Indians took the baby girl and dashed her brains out on a wagon wheel. They pulled the arrows out of the woman and thrust them into her again. She feigned death. They stripped her naked and scalped her. They looted the wagons and were rounding up the stock when another emigrant train approached routing them.

The wounded man recovered as did the scalped woman who's husband and baby were dead. The Indians in their flight had dropped her scalp. She had a wig made of her own hair. She never fully recovered — eventually losing her mind. She was the subject of newspaper interviews in later life in California. There is a photograph of her wearing the wig.[40]

Indian lawlessness was probably equaled by crimes of emigrants among themselves. The criminal activities of Indians and emigrants alike reflects that this was lawless territory. Something, that in years to come, the legendary western lawmen would deal with. The troops along the main trail to Oregon afforded a degree of safety, but they were spread too thinly to assume responsibility for the majority of emigrants. Occasionally, a US Cavalry escort was provided for a careless, poorly led group in an effort to instill in them the proper discipline required to continue through Indian territory.[41] Once the emigrants had left the Oregon Trail to descend into the Great Basin, they would be on their own. As far as crime among themselves was concerned, there was no court that had jurisdiction once they left the frontier and entered Nebraska Territory; nor, for the entire trip until they reached the state of California. It would not do to arrest a murderer and conduct him to California. No court there would have jurisdiction. He would be set free unprosecuted. They were only subject to the Indian version of *Lex Talonis*. The answer was a form of ad hoc law later to manifest itself in California as vigilante law.[42]

Nor was all the jeopardy found on the trail. Trail's head larceny tended toward swindling, cheating and hornswoggling in general. Crime could take the ugly form of murder for profit. J.M. Studebaker was to see a gambler, who had cheated him out of his savings playing three-card monte, tried and hung for murder by the emigrants gathered at Council Bluff. Studebaker remained in an impecunious state until he found employment at Hangtown in the northern mines. Apparently there was lawlessness at trail's end to boot.[43]

When things got tough after several grueling months on the trail, men would get testy and tempers would flare over trivia. The pioneers were surprised by violence and murder occurring spontaneously among themselves. There were several ad hoc trials sometimes from several wagon groups assembled together to insure impartiality. Sheriff and judge would be elected, a jury carefully empaneled and the murderer dealt with. In the infamous case of A.E. Brown, the trial coincided with a 4th of July celebration and the defendant was acquitted by the celebrants. They didn't even bother to adjourn the court.[44] In some cases, the emigrants were cowed by the murderer and there was no confrontation. The murderer simply went free. The Donner party expulsed Jim Reed for what could have been manslaughter or second degree murder. Murder in the process of armed robbery became common — the renegade whites sometimes masquerading as Indians or leading Indians in the attack. The brigands were usually apprehended and dealt swift justice.[45] Many of the emigrants had liquidated their assets and intended to invest when they got to California

— another reason to conduct the enterprise as a heavily armed expedition. Bringing cash also saved hauling the burden of equivalent goods.

The *San Joaquin Republican* reported the arrival of Thomas Cook and son, five drovers and 285 head of loose cattle. This was Cook's fourth cattle drive across the plains.

> Mr. Cook's party, being very strong, have come through unmolested, and report and confirm previous advices in reference to robberies of stock &c., and think that a regular organized system has been adopted under the leadership of white men to harass the emigrants. ...
> ... Reports have been continually brought in of the suffering on the Truckee route by emigrants who had been influenced to take that route by a trader named Blackford, who has a post on the Desert. Nearly every party which has taken that route, and not been strong enough for self protection, has been robbed of all or a portion of its property. [46]

By 1857, a number of traders were established along the Humbolt and it was common knowledge at Carson Valley that men named Haws and Tooley had supplied the Indians with a wagon load of rifles, powder and lead. The wagon train of Holloway & Rector of Napa Valley lost 45 head of cattle at Goose Creek on the upper Humbolt to a band of Indians carrying new rifles.

> They (H. and R.) are confidant that these Indians were led on by white men, for they distinctly heard voices of the three men who spoke the English language freely. They swore in English ... are at the head of these Indian cattle thieves. ...
> Holloway and Rector say that if any more attacks are made by the Indians on the emigrants, the latter will hang every trader in that neighborhood. They believe that if these traders can live with impunity among these savages, while the emigrants cannot even pass through the country without being attacked, that these traders must be friends of the Indians and are prompting their attack upon the emigrants. They fear ... [47]

Two months later, most of the incoming emigrants had received benefit of indigenous Great Basin welcoming committees — orchestrated by jailbirds fled east from California.

> The emigrants, it is said, from the depredations which have been committed on them, are perfectly exasperated. They have shot and hung several men who were detected and caught stealing their stock, and some of these, it is said, have been recognized by the traders as abandoned characters from California; no doubt some of them are the escaped convicts from the State Prison, seventy of whom are now running at large, who have escaped within the last eighteen months. They go with the Indians, dress in their costume, head their companies and direct their movements in attacking immigrant trains; and some of these have actually been caught and proved to be white men.[48]

This lawless state of affairs led to the inevitable vigilante activity and a flurry of excitement in Carson Valley to bring in law and justice by way of petitioning the Fedral Government to create a US Territory extending westward through the Great Basin to the California border.

The emigrants also had to deal with those turned criminal in their midst. In several cases the murderer was tried, convicted and executed — usually the next morning. Since there were no trees in the terrain along most of the trail, Wagon tongues of two wagons were put together to form a gallows.[49] Sometimes a firing squad was put together in the normal military fashion. Nowadays, we are disconcerted with this lack of an appeal process. European travelers expressed surprise at this grass roots due-process-of-law exercised in the absence of any governmental authority. The trail was another experiment in American democracy in microcosm — like its archetype, imperfect but somewhat functional.

10

WEBER'S TULE MARSH

JOE WALKER wasn't at his best trying to run *wagons* over the Sierra. He was famous as the first man to run a *pack train* down the Humbolt and over the Sierra. This fame resulted from Washington Irving's account of Walker's exploration published in 1837 in Irving's *Captain Bonneville*. Walker is credited with discovering Yosemite on that trip with Bonneville's trappers, but he didn't then get a chance to actually explore Yosemite Valley. He viewed it from Tuolumne high country. His group was reduced to eating their mules and struggling to get down out of that primeval glacial grandeur and into the civilization of Alta California.[1] His mission was not to explore the Sierra generally, but to find a direct route into California. The emigrants usually called this ultimate mountain barrier the "Sierra." To be precise, the mountains of Lassen Volcanic National Park and those extending on northward are part of the Cascade Range. This range consists of high plateaus capped by lava ridges and volcanic cones with rivers like the Pit and its tributaries cutting deep twisting paths. Mt. Shasta and Mt. Lassen are two immense volcanic cones serving as timeless guides to travelers.

In contrast, the Sierra Nevada, imposed squarely across the direct routes from the east, is a tilted megalith on the earth's surface overlaid with remnants of an ancient mountain range. The upraised eastern edge forms steep escarpments rising to a serrated glistening crest that lends the range its name. The mountainous surface of this megalith, sloping toward the central valley, has been carved by glacial and hydraulic forces into an irregular topography of ridges and canyons. Yosemite, — with its Lyle Glacier, the expansive glacially polished granite pavements, the vast high country meadowlands with timber groves, its concatenation of valleys, lakes and canyons with the thundering Merced and Toulumne Rivers, its granite domes and sculpted granite walls, its punctuation with spectacular water falls, — is the consummate example of the primordial Sierra process.

When he piloted the Chiles-Walker train, Cap'n Walker again ended up presiding over a pack train struggle over the Sierra. Trail veteran Chiles brought his contingent and their wagons in by the volcanic Cascade route via Ft. Boise and down through south-eastern Oregon.[2] As a matter of fact, the first emigrant trains coming directly into California from the east were pack trains. The feat of Elisha Stevens in bringing a wagon train through on the Truckee in 1844 was extraordinary. They had to build road as they went — as did many emigrant trains in the years to follow. The Mormon Battalion returnees, following Carson's blazed trail, worked at making a road just to get their wagons through. The westbound emigrants lost no time in putting this new road to use and were soon adding improvements and variations. Over the next decade, many wagon trains exploring various routes out of the Great Basin into California would be building road as they went.

The California terminus fanned out into a system of trails just as a system of trails fanned out to the outfitting towns at trail's head. As new routes came into use and older routes were given up, what might be considered real wagon roads started to develop out of the cumulative efforts of successive emigrant trains. Several factors led to the choice of route. Its directness was important. Natural approaches such as the principal rivers on the eastern slope of the Sierra Nevada, either the Truckee, Carson or Walker was another factor. They followed the course of the river to the final escarpment and scrambled up it as best they could. The choice of low gap or pass at the summit became another factor. The emigrants found this word curious because the "Pass" was frequently hardly "passable."

Those taking more northerly routes through the Cascades would avoid the steep escarpment, but would have to travel much farther through dry and generally inhospitable terrain.

And, most important, the choice of destination dictated the route. There were folks who wanted to go to southern California. They would come in by the Mormon Corridor from Salt Lake or via Santa Fe and the Gila or Old Spanish Trail. That Southern California has its own strong pioneering traditions[3] is attested to by the ubiquitous Madonna of the Trail statue erected in San Bernardino County.[4] For those coming into Central California, the specific route over the Sierra would be influenced by the choice of mining town or a principal city such as Sacramento or Stockton.

Frémont's Mariposa mine marks the lower boundary of what is regarded as the southern mines region. A line extending from the confluence of the Sacramento and San Joaquin Rivers and up into the Sierra along the Consumnes River divides the northern mines region from the southern mines. The northern mines region extends up to the mines along the Feather River at the southernmost edge of the volcanic Cascade region. The mines further north on the Klamath River in the Siskiyou were actually part of the Oregon gold rush which soon followed the rush of '49. The southernmost pass used by the emigrants into "the diggins" or Central California in general was the Sonora Pass. The horrendous Tioga Pass in Yosemite high country was part of a later silver mining enterprise as was the Tioga toll road — now SR-120.

The tilting megalith forming the Sierra also tilts north to south with passes such as Mono and Kersarge being well south of the central mining regions and at altitudes progressively higher than the Sonora Pass. The highest jutting corner of the slab is the pinnacle of Mt. Whitney — the highest peak in the Sierra and in California.[5] Walker's Pass at the attenuated southern end of the Sierra Nevada can be considered to be in Southern California; affording a shortcut into the Mormon Corridor — another means of avoiding the High Sierra. Hopper and Chiles with seven companions left Sutter's Fort in 1842, traveling south through the San Joaquin Valley, and traveled through Walker's Pass on their return trip to Missouri via Santa Fe.

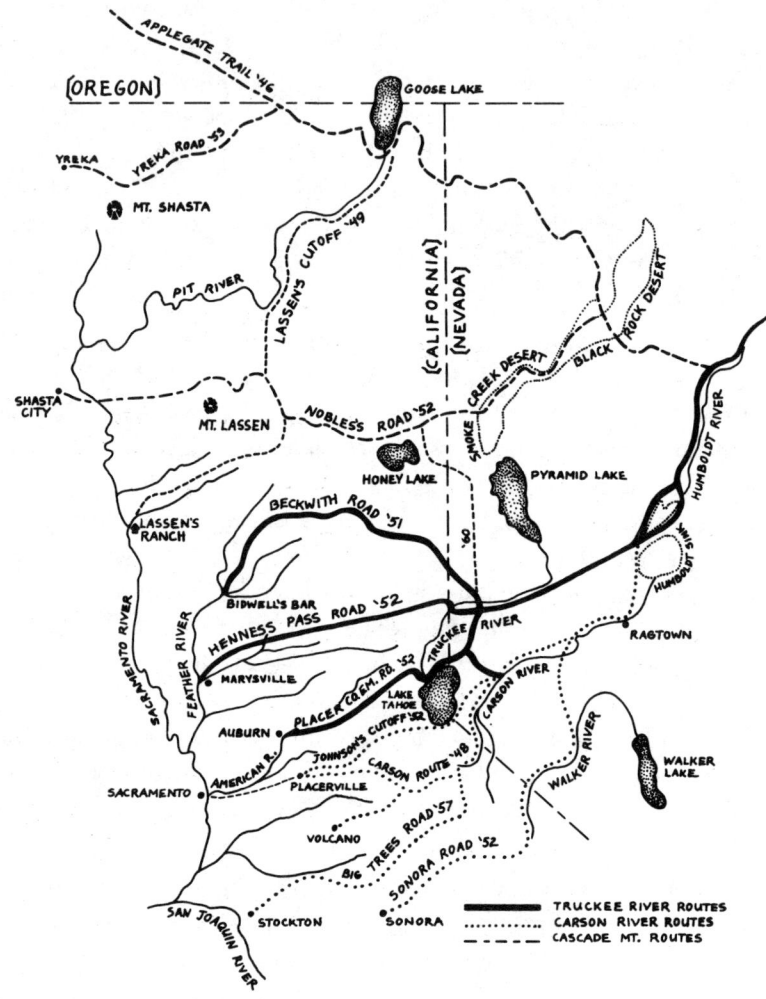

Figure 10.1: Sierra Emigrant Trails

The Walker River route led into the Sonora Pass and had as its terminus the town named Sonora by its founding Mexican forty-niners. The Carson River led into the Carson Pass and the Carson-Mormon trail that had Placerville as its main terminus in the mines. The Pennsylvania cutoff led to Volcano and other towns in the southern mines. Later the Johnson cutoff from the Carson Valley followed a more northerly route over Echo Summit to Placerville, avoiding Carson Pass. This was to become the main road to Sacramento. Another Carson River route cut south just below Carson Pass to cross over "Border Ruffian" Pass and proceed through Bear Valley, down the north fork of the Stanislaus and past the Calaveras Big Trees to Murphy's. This was to become the main road to Stockton.[6]

The Truckee River route led to Truckee Meadows (Reno) and branched to the south on the Placer County Emigrant Road which skirted the north end of Lake Bigler (Tahoe) and terminated in Auburn in the foothills above Sacramento. The main Truckee route was the Henness Pass road to Downieville, Nevada City or Marysville. The northern branch of the Truckee route, Beckwith's[7] road lead to Bidwell's Bar on the Feather River. Beckwith's route was the northernmost of roads in the Sierra Nevada proper.

Northern California was reached by entirely avoiding the trying lower Humbolt and the Sierra and following the original Applegate trail that lead through the California Cascades to Applegate Oregon. This was later designated by its California destinations as the Lassen Trail or the Yreka Road. Nobles' Road left the Lassen Trail at the Black Rock Desert in Nevada and proceeded via Honey Lake, skirting north of Mt. Lassen, to Shasta City. Nobles' Road provided an optimal northern route into the Sacramento Valley.

Commercial communities developed in the Great Valley to support the mining industry of the Sierra. The southern mines and the northern mines were distinct districts each with its major supporting commercial city. Sacramento, with its paddlewheel riverboats plying the Sacramento River to San Francisco and back, linked the northern mines to the larger world.[8] Then there was Tuleburg blossomed into Stockton located in *El Rancho del Campo de los Franceses.* This modern inland sea port that loads Russian grain ships with wheat has long had a dredged channel through the San Joaquin delta islands.

Known as "Muddville" (where the mighty Casey struck out) before a diverting canal stopped the perennial flooding, the city featured old victorians stilted to put them above high waters. The channel through the middle of the city was filled. A spacious boulevard — Weber Avenue — was in sharp contrast to the funky old horse-and-buggy Main Street paralleling it a block over. Captain Weber's enterprise had blossomed out into the commercial center that supported the southern mines with river access to San Francisco. The magnificence of the construction of the Sacramento riverboats and the opulence of their accommodations rivaled that of the Mississippi riverboats[9] — complete with riverboat gamblers and ladies with derringers in their garters. — An inevitable result of the wealth flowing down out of the Sierra.

When Nicholas Broyles Gann and his wife Rutha Freshour Gann traveled into Alta California in 1847, Their wagon train captain had his extended family along on the trip. Besides Hopper brothers, sons, cousins and in-laws, Charlie married a Hopper cousin so he had a cousin cum brother-in-law. Charles Hopper III our venerable captain was "big" Charlie to his family to distinguish him from cousin "little" Charlie. This was the Hopper train. A sizeable portion of it was Hoppers. The captain not only knew the trail, he knew many of the people they would meet when they got there. Even though Nicholas and Rutha and the other friends and neighbors who had come along were arriving as foreigners in a foreign land — Americanos in Mexican territory — they would find many friends who were well acquainted with their captain. Charlie Hopper was returning after a five year absence. His companions of his previous trip to California had accomplished many extraordinary things in the interim. We can gain an appreciation of the arrival of Nicholas and Rutha into Alta California in 1847, and the prospects they found there, if we view the settlement of their Missouri forerunners of 1841.

When the Bartleson-Bidwell party came into Alta California in 1841, they were a group of young American adventurers — most of them were in their twenties. The oldest among them was Charlie Hopper at the age of forty-one. He and Joseph Chiles would return in 1842 to Jackson County, Missouri and, later, they would both lead wagon trains to California. Schoolteacher John Bidwell remained in California to work for Sutter and was to become a leading citizen of the state. He owned properties including *Arroyo Chico* Rancho where the town of Chico now stands. Nancy Kelsey married Benjamin Kelsey at the age of fifteen and accompanied her husband as an eighteen year old mother. She rode into the Sierra on horseback with babe in arms, walking barefoot in the high country where it was too rough and precipitous for horseback. The Kelseys went on to Oregon and also tried Texas but returned to California. The nefarious Talbot Green stayed to work for Larkin becoming the model of entrepreneurial propriety and a leading citizen. He stayed because he dared not go back. He finally had to because he was recognized and denounced by a late arrival in the midst of his bid to become Mayor of San Francisco.

Witty and generous philanderer Grove Cook, also a member of the 1841 party of "foreigners," worked for Sutter, then wandered about California becoming a Mexican citizen in 1844. His first wife, Sophronia Sublett of the fur trapping Subletts, divorced him when he left for California. He made several fortunes, none of them permanent. His affluence was generally of the fluent variety. His first wealth stemmed from his assistance to Talbot Green who was struggling in 1841 to bring his booty through the Sierra.[10] Cook built a whiskey still at Sutter's fort in 1845. He was married by John Sutter to Rebecca Kelsey "who presently had some reason to regret it." He settled at Pueblo de San José in 1846 where he served on the alcalde's committee. He bought the *Rancho de los Capitancillos* becoming the first American owner of the property that was to become the fabulous New Almaden quicksilver mine.[11] There was an urgent demand for mercury up in the hardrock mines where the gold, embedded in the crushed rock coming off the stamping mills, was extracted by being dissolved in mercury. The gold laden metallic fluid was then distilled, the golden residue cast into ingots and the recovered mercury reused.

Charles Weber, a young German from the Bavarian Rhineland had arrived in New Orleans in 1836, served under the Lone Star flag against Mexico, then travelled to the Missouri frontier to join the 1841 adventurers. Weber also remained in California to attain prominence as an important pioneer.[12] Charlie Hopper would again meet Weber when Hopper conducted the family wagon train into California. Charles Weber worked through the winter for John Sutter who had signed his bond on his arrival in California in 1841. He settled in San José in 1842 as miller, baker, trader and later on became a salt producer and cobbler. Weber conducted most of these enterprises in partnership with blacksmith William Gulnac. They also owned cattle and land. Charles Weber married Ellen Murphy a daughter of Martin Murphy Jr., owner of the 4000 acre *Pastoria de los Borregas* rancho north of San José and just north of Santa Clara.

William Gulnac and Maria Ysabel Cesena de Gulnac had been married for eighteen years and had seven children. This made Gulnac a Mexican citizen in good standing and allowed him to acquire California land under the Mexican law. Young Weber, not inclined to jeopardize his naturalized US citizenship, urged Gulnac to obtain, in Gulnac's name, a grant for the partnership. The land chosen was at a strategic location in the Great Central Valley, midway between Sutter's New Helvetia and the major pueblo of San José and the northern capital, Monterey. The flag over Alta California changed from Spanish to Mexican in 1822. Spain's final effort to secure California for itself was to advance the settlement of it and to them this meant establishment of more missions. In the decades prior to 1822, the interior river system of the great valley was explored for this purpose.

The heroic explorer of this era was Gabriel Moraga who explored and gave names to the Sacramento and San Joaquin Rivers and most of their tributaries. The exploring padres and soldiers concluded that the interior was worthless for civilized purposes. Their explorations became increasingly punitive in nature, dealing with runaway mission Indians who were stealing horses and cattle from the missions and ranchos. The padres concluded that any mission built in the central valley would need with it a strong *presidio*. The indefatigable Moraga had explored the Calaveras from its headwaters to its San Joaquin confluence — the location chosen by Gulnac and Weber for their Mexican land grant. Moraga found no location there amenable to settlement.[13]

Because this spot was central to the Sierra river system, the French fur trappers of the Hudson Bay Company had chosen it as their rendezvous. This was the first Anglo settlement in Alta California since Ewing Young and his trappers came in from Santa Fe to trap on the San Joaquin and its tributaries and camped there. But it was the French for whom the camp was named in Spanish. This was the site that Weber urged Gulnac to claim. In 1833 Young and his trappers went up the Sacramento Valley trapping and exploring into the Siskiyou and back. One of California's short violent winters with its torrential rains had swollen the Sierra rivers and by the end of winter in 1833, the Central Valley was a great inland sea. When Young's party returned in the fall they were shocked. The Sacramento and San Joaquin flowed through a valley of death. Clouds of mosquitoes, including the Anopheles, were everywhere. Many of the Indian villages were abandoned. The Indians fell dead in their sweat huts — the only medicine they knew. The stench of death was everywhere. The malaria stricken Indians finally decided to burn the bodies in heaps by the hundreds. This was another episode of the white man's inadvertent germ warfare against the Indians. Smallpox would soon follow. Malaria was a common experience of the beaver trappers. The Hudson Bay man La Framboise traveling the Siskiyou trail into the San Joaquin carried quinine.[14]

Governor Micheltorena signed, in January of 1844 at Monterey, the grant to Don Guillermo Gulnac and his family for the eleven square league *El Rancho del Campo de los Franceses*.[15] The Mexican Government required all grantees to settle at least twelve families on the land within one year after granting the land. Weber immediately planned a settlement. Weber made arrangements for Gulnac and his son and Peter Lassen to drive livestock and horses from his *Rancho Cañada de San Felipe* near Madrone, south of San José, to the new rancho in the San Joaquin. The Hudson Bay trappers at French Camp were expected to afford protection, but they had dispersed for the season. Gulnac sought help at New Helvetia and Sutter armed them with a swivel gun to frighten off the Indians. Weber thought it prudent to do as Sutter had done at New Helvetia and make a treaty with the local Indians. The treaty was signed with the captain of the local tribes, José Jesús, who would later lead his braves under Captain Weber against the Mexicans in the war that followed. These Indians remained friendly and never caused the white settlers any problem.[16] Earlier in 1832 and 1833 when the American trappers followed the San Joaquin River trapping beaver, the huts of these Indians glowed red with the salmon drying in the sun.

After the treaty, James Lindsay was left in charge of the settlement with some Indian and Mexican vaqueros. David Kelsey with his wife and two small children and his son-in-law William Buzzel also settled. In 1845 the dreaded small-pox struck the Indians in Northern California. Vallejo's friends, the Suisuns, were wiped out except for a few individuals including Vallejo's loyal companion Chief Solano.[17] The pox raged among the Indians on the San Joaquin. Lindsay's vaqueros fled to the coastal hills. Kelsey tried to help a sick Indian friend and contracted the small-pox himself, transmitting it to his family. Kelsey died and his wife and son lay too sick to bury him. Everyone had fled. The friendly Indians fled into the Sierra foothills. Kelsey's little daughter, America, sought help of passing travelers. They buried Kelsey and found Lindsay floating full of arrows, the stock gone and all the tule huts burned. The Polo Indians from up on the Toulumne, discovering the stock unprotected, had swooped down in a raid killing Lindsay and driving off the stock.[18]

The partnership with Gulnac was dissolved. Gulnac was alleged a drunken sot. He sold his share of the Rancho to Weber in 1845 to retire a $60 grocery debt.[19] Gulnac and Ysabel and five of his children signed the conveyance of Grant to Don Carlos Maria Weber. The story of Lindsay's murder was known throughout the pueblos. Weber managed to convince seven families to settle under the leadership of Napoleon Schmidt, but Frémont who had taken upon himself the conquest of Alta California, had the settlers come to Santa Clara for military protection. They settled there and lost interest in Schmidt's settlement at "Weberville." [20]

Weber participated in the turmoil leading to the conquest of California apparently making enemies of both sides. He was imprisoned by Sutter in 1844 during the Micheltorena War. He became Captain of militia in 1845 and was later taken south as a prisoner of Castro. Micheltorena capitulated and left California with his *cholos*. After Weber's release by Castro he eventually returned north to supply horses[21] for the California Battalion in which he declined to serve because of his antipathy towards Frémont. He served as Captain of volunteers in 1846 in the final campaign. He discharged his troops in February of 1847 and returned to settle on his French Camp Rancho. He needed to colonize. Later that year Weber rode into the Sierra to persuade travelers to settle on his property.

Hopper's wagon train was coming out of the Sierra on the Stevens-Donner Trail in early October of 1847. They met an acquaintance of Charlie Hopper from his 1841 trip — Captain Weber. Weber invited them down to his French Camp settlement telling them of the land opportunity there. He offered 80 acres and a town lot.[22] On their way down to Sutter's Fort they arrived first at Johnson's Ranch[23] and were visited there by John Bidwell who also knew Hopper from their 1841 trip. Bidwell apparently also rode out to meet the incoming crop of fall emigrants for recruitment purposes. Bidwell remained a loyal employee of Sutter at Sutter's Fort even though by then he was a naturalized Mexican citizen and had two grants of his own — *Ulpiños* and *Colusa* ranchos. The Hopper party split up at Sutter's New Helvitia with Hopper taking the main contingent southward into the San Joaquin Valley with the intention of going on to San José by way of Weber's settlement. The

San Francisco California Star reported on October sixteenth that Captain Hopper's company of sixty emigrant wagons had crossed the San Joaquin River on the way to San Jose. [24] The Trubodys sold their oxen and stayed on with Sutter to help him build his flour mill.

Weber was determined to get eleven more settlers on his French Camp Rancho and here came the covered wagons of all the Hoppers along with the Moores, the Findlas, the Fines, the Eastins, the Angels, Gerke and the Ganns. They halted there and made camp and were entertained hospitably by Captain Weber. Weber had built a house, partly of adobe, and a warehouse and dock were constructed of materials delivered by boat. It was possible to come upstream on the San Joaquin River by sailing vessel from San Francisco. More frequently small craft such as wailing boats were used. The local Indians made tule rafts. Weber had to take strict measures to keep Indians from stealing his horses. Tuleburg was a small cluster of tule huts. The only semblance of a house prior to Weber's place was Buzzel's Tavern — a log cabin with a tule roof. No bridge or ferry then existed to cross the San Joaquin River. Travelers more often arrived by boat. When Lindsay was killed, the tule huts were burned leaving Buzzel's Tavern as the only building standing in Tuleberg.[25] But, Weber had land to offer — much land. He could make an offer hard to turn down.

Alexander Moore, Captain Hopper and five or six others decided to take the deal. Moore helped his father, and the others who were going on, to get across the San Joaquin River. They made a large raft of willow pole framing stuffed with tules and a willow pole deck. One of the party swam the river with a rope and they pulled the raft back and forth across the river as a ferry with a wagon or a pile of their goods perched on the willow deck. It took all day to get the wagons and loads across. Moore's father wasn't satisfied with the notion of settling there and went back over with a span of mules and got Alexander's wife and belongings. Others changed their mind also. "Wm. Gulnac had undertaken it [settlement] but was cleaned out by Indians and small pox in 1846." Weber's deal fell apart.[26]

Moore reports that, before they left, "a Mrs. Gann was delivered of a little boy on the 11 of October ..."[27] The Ganns camped at Tuleberg until Rutha and baby William were ready to travel. Captain Weber convinced them to stay the winter.[28] They then followed the other families of the Hopper train to San José and on to Santa Cruz.

Most of the Hopper train settled in the vicinity of San José initially. The Findlas and Gerke went on to Yerba Buena (San Francisco.) The Angels went to Gilroy. The Eastins settled out toward Los Gatos Creek. Some of the party including Alexander Moore contracted with "Ike Brennan" to build a sawmill on Los Gatos Creek at the foot of the Santa Cruz Mountains just above the present town of Los Gatos.[29] This developed into the town of Lexington. Alexander Moore took the Indian-Mexican trail through the Santa Cruz mountains to look over Santa Cruz. On his way over the hill he encountered "Capt. Graham" and "Joe Majors" coming over from Santa Cruz recruiting settlers. Isaac Graham and Joseph Ladd Majors were mountain men who followed the Santa Fe trail trapping and hunting in 1833-4 to settle at Natividad near present day Watsonville. Joe Majors became a naturalized Mexican citizen in 1839 and married Maria de Los Angeles Castro soon after. Maria inherited part of *Rancho Refugio* and Joe Majors was granted *Zayante Rancho* in 1841. Majors, Graham and Peter Lassen operated a sawmill at Zayante. Lassen went north and Graham acquired this property. Joe Majors became the first Santa Cruz alcalde under the new American government.[30]

Alexander was impressed with Santa Cruz. The recruitment of the Moores and Hoppers was successful. Alexander's father, Eli Moore, bought the Santa Cruz property on which he lived out his years. The Moores, Ganns[31] and Hoppers moved over by way of San José, Gilroy and Pajaro — the only route open to Wagons. They were driving sheep they had brought all the way from Jackson County Missouri. They camped one night where Watsonville now stands. The Ganns settled along the San Lorenzo River on the *Rancho Carbonero* granted to Guillermo Bocle (William Buckle) in 1837. The Moores lived in an adobe on Jose Bolcoff's part of *Rancho Refugio* until they got their own house built. The Russian Bolcoff married Candida Castro in 1822 and served as Alcalde three terms and was later *juez de paz*. Moore went into the milling business with "Mr. Balcoff" in May 1848. Charlie and Thomas Hopper started in the lumber business, but didn't get far. Everyone went to the mines in '48-'49 and got more or less rich. Thomas Hopper built a boat to take with him to get across streams. He found the mines too rough for his family; so brought them to stay with George Yont while he mined. The Hoppers went from the mines to Sonoma and Mendocino Counties.[32] Alexander Moore returned from the mines to profitably finish Bolcoff's mill then went up the coast to settle at Pescadero.[33] Nicholas and Rutha left Santa Cruz in 1849 to join the gold rush and stayed to settle on the Calaveras River.

All of the Hoppers and most of their entourage had passed by Weber's tule bog for the really nice settlements of California. Weber also failed to recruit the John Doak party. They were crossing the country in the fall of 1847, five months and seventeen days out of Illinois. Weber met the party of 100 persons and thirty-seven wagons in the Sierra and tried to induce them to locate on his land. He agreed to give them 160 acre parcels, but said Doake, "I would not give ten dollars for all the land between Stockton and Sacramento." [34]

It is not difficult to see why a man, who had been talked into diverting his energies from a thriving enterprise in the Pueblo de San José to a God forsaken uninhabitable swamp that was infested with treacherous thieving Indians, would turn to drink. But young German knuckleheads are made of sterner stuff. Undaunted, Weber settled on the land himself with his family — something Gulnac had never done. The more mature Gulnac mellowed out in the comforts of Pueblo de San José absolutely convinced that young Don Carlos Maria Weber was beating a dead horse. Weber platted a town and named it Stockton — An American name for an American town. The treaty of Guadelupe Hidalgo had been signed on the 2nd of February, 1848.

The visionary German's fiasco assumed sudden plausibility when the mania for California's gold galvanized the entire state and drew miners from all over the world. The madness was contagious. Weber led his motley crew of settlers and friendly Indians off towards Sutter's Mill. They started prospecting at the Mokolumne finding some "color" and finally established diggings at Weber's Creek.

At the close of 1848, some nine thousand people had taken up the search for gold. Their success was greater than that of any subsequent year. The only methods they knew were primitive and inefficient. They "creviced" with knives prying the gold out of surface rock. They "panned" with large sheet iron pans filled with dirt and sluiced in circular motion at stream's edge — the classic stereotype of the '49er. Usually the miners of shallow diggings along ravines on tributaries — "placer diggings" — used a cradle. The dirt was dumped into the "riddle" at the top and water sloshed on the dirt which washed down the length of the long sloping box over "riffle bars." The fine gold was caught in a canvas apron at the bottom of the riddle or in the riffles as the box was rocked and water sluiced through it. The nuggets could be picked out of the gravel left in the riddle — a kind of sieve device.[35] If flowing water was abundant it was channeled through a fixed sluice box.

The miners of '48 swarmed over the land skimming the cream off the diggings. They took out gold to the tune of ten million dollars. Nuggets weighing several *pounds* were found! A hundred dollars a day was a pretty good days work. Days when they made five to seven hundred happened fairly often. Then there was the "Dry Diggings." The earth was taken out of ravines in the hills and packed to the nearest stream for sluicing. Pack animals or wagons were used but some men simply carried the dirt on their backs from one to three miles. (Studebaker wheelbarrows later proved helpful.) An average cart load brought $400. Some would dig and haul dirt and sell it to sluice operators. A five-cart load was once sold for 47 oz. ($752) and was sluiced out for a yield of $16,000. Men were known to carry earth on their backs and make $1500 a day.

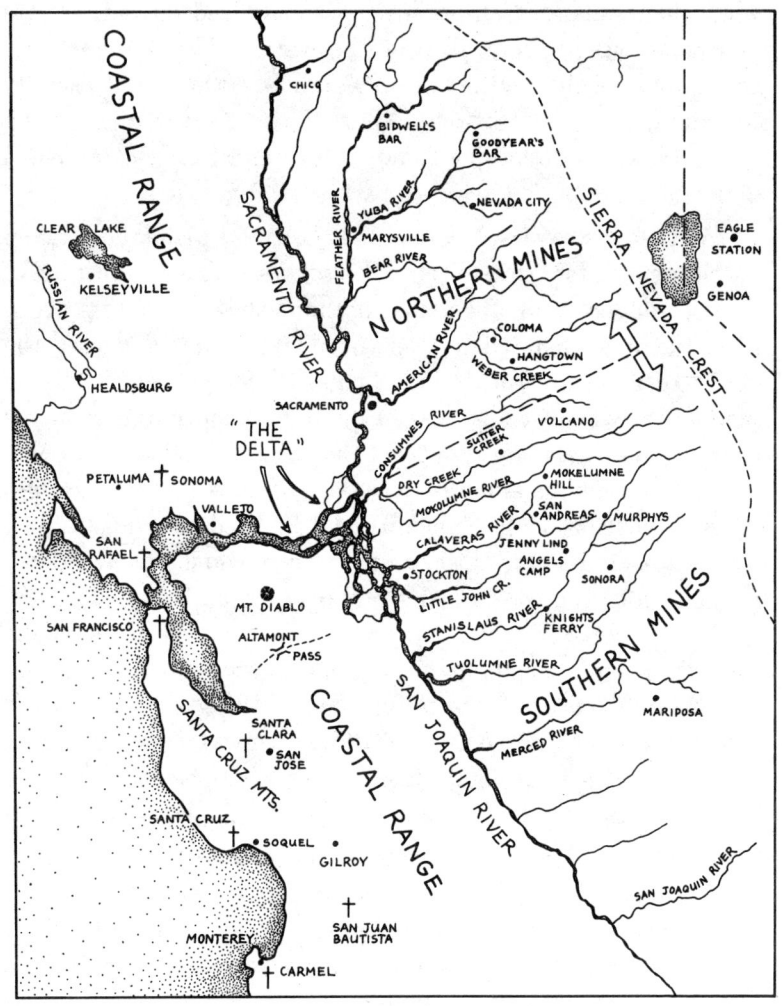

Figure 10.2: The Mines of Forty-nine.

Weber now found it easy to find new recruits. Even José Jesús and twenty-five of his braves learned gold prospecting under the enterprising Weber. He sent his Indians back to the Stanislaus River to start prospecting around their rancheria.

The results were spectacular. Weber formed the Stockton Mining Company.[36] Word reached the Dry Diggings about the new placers discovered on the Stanislaus River and some two hundred miners prepared to leave earth worth four hundred dollars a load for the promise of even better "pay dirt." Newspaper accounts started appearing on the east coast in the fall of 1848. By the close of that year, the furthest reaches of the civilized world had received the news. Every scrap of information on California was sought after. Special editions of guidebooks went to press.

A traveler in California's Central Valley passed through Stockton early in 1849 and returned through there in May of that year. He noted that it was not then possible to see the snowy outlines of the Sierra Nevada because of the hazy air made more dim by the burning of the tule marshes. He observed:

> A view of Stockton was something to be remembered. There in the heart of California, where the last winter stood a solitary ranch, I found a canvas town of one thousand inhabitants, and a port with twenty-five vessels at anchor. The mingled voices of labor around, the click of hammers, the shouts of mule-drivers, the jingling of spurs, the jar and the jostle of wares in the tents, almost cheated me into the belief that it was some old commercial market familiar with such sounds for years past. Four months only had suffered to make the place what it was, and in that time a wholesale firm (amount of a dozen) had done business to the amount of $100,000. It cost this firm to erect a common one story clapboard house $15,000. ... Launches were arriving and departing daily for and from San Francisco, and the number of mule trains, wagons, etc., on the way to various mines with freight and supplies, kept up a life of activity truly amazing.[37]

Rutha and Nicholas Gann were undoubtedly in the vicinity of Stockton[38] during this dramatic growth and Nicholas couldn't have been immune to "gold fever." Nicholas and Rutha settled on the Calaveras River, a tributary coming out of the Sierra and flowing through San Joaquin County to the San Joaquin River; the confluence being just northwest of burgeoning Stockton. James R. Freshour had arrived in either 1847 or 1849 or conceivably could have gone back in 1848 and returned in 1849. In October of 1850 the Nicholas Gann family, the John D. Gann family, the Hitchcocks and the Campbell family with James "Freasure" in their household, are all living in four adjacent households in the Stockton District — the only district listed in the county in 1850.[39]

The John D. Gann family came to California in 1847. These are Jackson County Missouri families originating in Tennessee. An interesting thing about this group is that, except for the Gann families, no wives are listed and the families are all boys. One could surmise that Campbell and Hitchcock brought their boys out on a lark to dig for gold — with every intention of returning home to mama. They may have driven sheep or cattle from Missouri. Gann and Campbell are listed as drovers, John Gann as blacksmith and Hitchcock as Farmer. Good money was to be made in the commerce supporting the mines.

Some of Weber's men established diggings bearing their own names. John Murphy of Murphy's Camp, Angel of Angel's Camp, Woods of Wood's Creek and Sullivan of Sullivan's Creek left their mark on Calaveras County — the Sierra county above San Joaquin County and its seat, Stockton.[40] The locale received widespread publicity with the publication of Mark Twain's first book *the Celebrated Jumping Frog of Calaveras County* in 1867. Bret Harte's *The Outcasts of Poker Flat* published in 1870 portrayed life in the Calaveras mines. In the years following the gold rush, this became Freshour-Gann country. As gold fever lapsed into "the mining industry,"[41] agriculture emerged. The marshy delta land west of Stockton would be engineered into "the islands" using thousands of Chinese coolies to build levees. The islands quickly became of great agricultural importance. The expanse of ranchland to the east of Stockton extending to Calaveras County gave Stockton as much or even more immediate credibility than the gold higher up. California wheat was shipped around the horn by square rigger to England.

Mining towns such as Sonora in the southern mines and Placerville in the northern mines had sponsored trail development activities for commercial reasons. The incoming emigrants meant growth and expanded trade. The Sonora trail was built by a wagon train that was seduced by Sonora merchants into a near disaster. The stranded emigrants requested trail building tools to be sent with the relief supplies sent out from Sonora. (Relief Valley and Reservoir thus derived their names.) Merchant hornswoggling of emigrants has its precedent in the "forts" such as Jim Bridger's with associate "Old Vaskiss" diverting the commercial trade to the route past Ft. Bridger. The most flagrant example is that of Hasting's fraudulent representation to the Donners in an effort to establish traffic past his proposed trading establishment. Joe Walker went out of his way to warn the Donner party and was assailed by them as a meddling "puke." — The Mormon epithet for their Missouri tormentors.[42]

It was natural for American enterprise to put its stamp on the California trails over the Sierra. Indeed, some of the trails themselves were an overt exercise in capitalism. The Beckwourth and Lassen trails were each developed by individual entrepreneurs. The Sonora trail was promoted vigorously by the towns of Columbia and Sonora in the southern mines. Nobles' Road was constructed under the auspices of Ft. Reading and Old Shasta City. As is wont to happen in a selection of enterprises, two of these were fiascoes. Most just petered out. One was a flash in the pan. One showed repeated promise but never really sparkled. One became a "cash cow."

The most promising trails were those relating to the Truckee and Carson Rivers. The negative publicity of the Donner Party and the lack of commercial development at Truckee Meadow in contrast to the successful winter crossing of the Sierra by Frémont and Carson plus the commercial development of Carson Valley led to the dominance of the Carson River route. The Mormons created Mormon Station, soon to be the town of Genoa, at the base of the Sierra in the Carson Valley as their western establishment in Utah Territory. Eagle Station and Ranch, prominently located for the convenience of incoming emigrant trains, was established in 1851. In 1858 it was purchased and platted as Carson City — named for the nearby river.

The earliest of the entrepreneur trails was Peter Lassen's "Horn route" over which he diverted many emigrants to his trading post at the mouth of Deer Creek in Tehema County. The trail he blazed went as far northward as Goose Lake in Modoc County, crossing the Warner Range by Fandango Pass — where the Wolverine Rangers danced the fandango late into the night with Mr. Smith's three attractive daughters — then via Big Meadow (Lake Almanor) to the destination Lassen had chosen for them.[43] The wily Dane had phony endorsements published in eastern papers for the benefit of the gold crazed forty-niners. He put up a billboard at Lassen Meadows and dispatched agents on the trail to divert the forty-niners onto his "cutoff." Nearly 10,000 forty-niners followed this trail and so many sent letters home warning about "Greenhorn Cutoff," "Lassen's Horn Route" or the "Death Route" that in 1850 — the peak year for trail traffic — only about 500 took Lassen's Cutoff. A glance at the map (Fig. 10.1) will show the humor, or tragedy, related to the name "Lassen's Cutoff." This and Hastings Cutoff led to the dictum "Don't take no cutoffs."[44]

Jim Beckwourth, mountain man of Crow Indian fame,[45] tried his hand at prospecting in the Sierra and rather than striking it rich he discovered Beckwourth's Pass. In 1851 he was guiding emigrants over the trail he had improved bringing them into Marysville. He built a trading post and hotel on his route in 1852 and the following year he was set up at Humbolt Sink attempting to redirect the wary emigrants past his enterprise.[46]

That same year, 1853, G.W. Patrick, Mayor of Sonora, "a man of considerable persuasive power and not too much regard for the truth,"[47] stationed himself at the sink of the Carson River warning anyone that would listen against any route but the "Sonora Immigrant Road." The road had been opened the previous year by the calamitous Clark-Skidmore party led by charismatic rapscallion, General Joseph C. Morehead who represented the mining town of Columbia.[48] The hardship suffered by the Clark-Skidmore party is memorialized in the names Emigrant Basin, Emigrant Lakes, Relief Valley and Relief Reservoir. It was soon apparent that this is not a very direct route. The Sonora Wagon Road is now in Wilderness Area and only passable on foot or horseback. Both Beckwourth's Route and the Sonora Road faded into oblivion.

In 1851, William H. Nobles scouted a route that left the Humbolt at Lassen's Meadow and followed the Applegate Trail to Black Rock Desert. From there he turned west along Smoke Creek Desert and crossed over Honey Lake basin. Then he proceeded west to cross the plateau at the head of the Susan River and passed through what is now Lassen Volcanic National Park and on past Manzanita Lake and into the Great Valley to Shasta City. Shasta City donated $2,000 for improvements made in the spring of '52 and the usual representatives were sent out on the main trail to entice the incoming emigrants.[49]

Now the commercialism had culminated at trail's end. The rivalry between Sacramento and Stockton, each seeking to become the principal terminus for the wagon road traffic coming from the east, developed to the point where they each sponsored road construction. Ultimately, the transcontinental railroad would upstage the wagon roads reducing Stockton and Sacramento to whistle stops. But in the 1850s, surveyor expeditions were still searching out the optimal transcontinental rail route. And the Civil War and antebellum politics would force more than a decade of delay in western railroad construction. This was pie in the sky to the folks doggedly following the Humbolt through the Great Basin. What they needed now was a decent road over the Sierra.

— Courtesy of Julia Engles, Fresno, CA

Figure 10.3: Panning Gold on the Tuolumne.

11

SAN JOAQUIN TRAIL'S END

JAMES RUFUS Freshour had returned from the mines of California and married Frances McKelhany in Jackson County Missouri in 1852. Upon his arrival in Missouri, J.R. no doubt visited Nicholas' and Rutha's families to convey regards and give a thorough account of his California sojourn with Rutha and Nicholas. There would be a multitude of questions asked about California, about the trail, about the Indians, about the terrain, about what equipment would be important, about the crossings, about the forts, about the time it would take, about the cutoffs, about the Sierra, which Sierra road to take and where they would find a good place to settle — at least until they could reconnoiter the best opportunities of the day.

Of course, J.R. was on his way down river to Centertown in Cole County to join his two elder brothers settled there. J.R. returned from the mines with significant financial resources and no doubt was nicely established in Centertown when his two sons James Marion and John William were born there in 1853 and 1855. J.R.'s brother, William S. Freshour, borrowed $2500 from the prosperous argonaut and commenced flourishing himself — later becoming Judge of the county court in 1879. At this time, in 1854, the nearby Missouri River was blocked to free-soilers by the "border ruffians" and the wagon trains were coming through Iowa. A few were attracted by Iowa publicity and some were determined to outfit and continue across the plains; but most were Kansas bound free-soilers. The Judge was a slaveholder giving rise to speculation about the Cole County Freshour's attitude and possible support of the border ruffian activity on the river. Judge Freshour was a benevolent master, giving freedom to his slaves in his will — long before Lincoln's emancipation proclamation. J.R. probably had a *laissez-faire* attitude towards slavery. His Illinois born wife, Frances, perhaps influenced him against it.

While James R. was settled in Cole County in 1854, the Henry Freshour wagon train crept it's way across Illinois and Iowa, taking the Lane trail to Adams county to settle on the Nodaway River. The Freshours were on the move. A train left out of Jackson County Missouri that same year bound for California. Lawson Freshour and William Fagan and his wife Malvina Freshour went west in 1854 with the Horns and Ganns. Daniel and Catherine Horn with twenty-year-old Greenberry and fifteen-year-old Elizabeth, their school-teacher son Isaiah and his wife Jane Gann with their four-year-old son Marion, accounted for two or three wagons in the train. Jane's parents John and Juda Gann were along with a number of their children — all of them adults born in Tennessee except the two youngest born in Missouri. This Gann family emigrated from Tennessee in about 1833, perhaps with John and Elizabeth Freshour. They were close neighbors of the Horns, the John Freshours and the Fagans in Missouri in 1850. Now, in 1854, they would account for several wagons. Thomas Baucom with his family may have been in the same wagon train. Baucoms were numerous in Jackson County and Emaline Freshour married Joshua Baucom in 1853. Joshua Baucom would follow his brother Thomas to California in 1857. We know about this 1854 emigration from Isaiah Horn's journal which was written after he and his parents and the senior John Ganns and son William Gann settled in San José.

The wagon trains coming off the Sierra in 1854 had passed through a 2000 mile civil void into a bustling civilization equivalent to that of the midwestern states. It was a maritime ordered economy with newspaper coverage predominantly devoted to ship arrivals with details about equipment, commodities, passengers and most important, the news gleaned from the eastern newspapers and mail sent by ship. Except for an occasional item on wagon train activity during the late summer and early fall, the tenor of the press was that of an island community awaiting the next ship from the mainland. The Spaniard's designation of this land as the Calafía's Island had it's rational. The newspapers carried an extraordinary amount of commercial advertising indicating many city blocks of stores selling hardware, groceries, dry goods, farm and mining machinery, equipment and supplies, furniture, pianos, musical instruments, jewelry, books and anything else that might have newly arrived by ship. The ships also brought immigrants who came from the eastern states the easy way. Others came from the far east. The *San Joaquin Republican* exclaimed "STILL THEY COME" giving details of large groups of Chinese arriving.[1]

The major mining towns had their own newspapers which were a source of news items for the metropolitan papers. The papers of Sacramento, Stockton, San Jose and San Francisco carefully read one another, repeating or rebutting stories and haggling over California political issues. The eastern papers provided national and international news. A telegraph line between Stockton and Sacramento clacked with hot news items. The Stockton to Sonora Telegraph Company was organized in 1854. The bucolic mining communities provided continual news. The Stockton to Knights ferry stage line was extended by a new company to Columbia and Sonora. A weekly "passenger train" service by horseback was offered from Placerville to Carson Valley for $12 per person. And of course there were a few items on the shady lady of the mine town theaters — Lola Montez. A road was built from Murphys to California's premier tourist attraction, The Mammoth Tree Grove. There was violence in the mines — accidents, robberies and murders.

Tempers frequently ran hot and were satisfied by gun fights. The metropolitan newspapers tended to be politically polarized. Stockton had, besides the *Republican,* the *Stockton Journal* (a whig paper) and the recently established democrat paper, the *Stockton Daily Argus,* giving them briefly three newspapers. Joseph Mansfield, an owner of the *Republican,* was shot dead on the street outside his office in a confrontation with John Tabor, editor of the *Journal.* Tabor was arrested leaving the scene. The *Journal* was reported in the *Republican* as defunct, its materials acquired by the *Argus.*[2]

There were only seven items in the *Republican* on wagon train arrivals in 1854.[3] Those running late in 1853 who laid over at Salt Lake were reported on June 28th as arriving at Carson Valley where they found a good wheat crop and a flour mill to provide 500 barrels of flour to 1854 emigrants. The potato crop was likewise good there. Another item lists "Beckwith's party." Two men arrived at Ragtown around the first of July to report "a large immigration on the way." Sixteen trains of the Salt Lake layover arrived in Sacramento in mid July with 1000 sheep and 80 cattle. They reported grass along the Humbolt scarce because the river was high but the Indians were friendly. On the 21st of July, the Montgomery and Lowery train came in on the Truckee route through Auburn with 70 horses, five wagons and fifteen men bound for Sutter County. This was obviously a fast moving group without droves, women or children traveling military style with spare horses. Arrivals via the Sonora route were listed on 16 October. And a Nobles' Pass train was announced on 20 October. This last group used the Cherokee rout, coming via Ft. Gibson, up the Arkansas river and via old Ft. Atkinson up the foot of the Front Range and into Ft. Bridger to join the main California trail.

The Horn-Gann party probably followed the Carson route which was still very much in use in 1854.[4] They could have taken the Pennsylvania cutoff (opened in 1852) to Volcano and on through Jackson down into Stockton. Or they could have paid the toll and taken the Johnson cutoff through Placerville and gone down the valley to Stockton. Isaiah, his parents and his father in law ended up in San José. They visited uncle "Nick" on the Calaveras River on arrival — Nicholas Broyles Gann being the younger brother of the patriarchal John Gann. The "Broyles" distinguished uncle Nick from fourteen-year-old nephew Nicholas just arrived with his parents. The family of Nicholas and Rutha now included thirteen-year-old Mahala Jane, seven-year-old William H., three-year-old Mary Elizabeth and newborn Martha.

After the death of his father, Daniel Horn, at San Jose, Greenberry Horn and his mother went to the vicinity of Santa

Rosa in Sonoma County. They may have been influenced by their former Missouri neighbor "Old man Hopper." The senior Horns and the Hoppers were from North Carolina originally. Charlie Hopper could very well have directed them on into Sonoma County which was Hopper country. Thomas Baucom settled in San Joaquin County as apparently did the Fagans and most of the Ganns — Frazier (Adam) Gann, Tom Gann, John Gann Jr., and a brother-in-law Elkins.

Lawson Freshour was in San Jose in 1854-5. Isaiah Horn and William Gann went into farming in the vicinity of San Jose. Isaiah frequently worked at harvesting wheat and barley crops. The Isaiah Horns traveled about a bit visiting all the Ganns in San Joaquin County and going up on the Calaveras River to visit Nicholas and Rutha. Isaiah also traveled up to Sonoma County to visit his mother and Greenberry, staying over with Charlie Hopper on the way. He paid a lot of ferriage — there were very few bridges.

The state was growing and changing in 1854. Legal notices ran continuously in the *Republican* concerning the formation of Stanislaus County. The state capital was moved from Sonoma to San Jose in October. The California Land Commission was busy sorting out land claims. If a Mexican land grant was disallowed, the land became public land which the "freeholders" (*i.e.* squatters) could then legitimately claim. On June 12 the following item appeared:

> C.M. WEBER'S CLAIM – Several persons have enquired of us why the claim of Mr. C.M. Weber to eleven square leagues in San Joaquin County, was placed by the Board of California Land Commissioners at the foot of the calendar. We have ascertained that Mr. Weber was most anxious to bring the claim to trial, but the US Attorney said he was not ready. [5]

The US Attorney was busy taking depositions from anyone who had ever lived on the *Rancho del Campo de los Frances*, or camped there, prior to 1849 or conversed with Gulnac or Weber prior to 1849 regarding its status.[6] Depositions were obtained from anyone who had ever surveyed the property.

All the original spanish documents and related correspondence were included in the US Attorney's evidence.

The published abstract of Nicholas B. Gann's deposition says:

EVIDENCE
IN THE WEBER LAND CLAIM

Nicholas B. Gann has lived in the vicinity of Stockton since 1849, and knew it as early as 1847. (Witness describes the settlement in 1847.) "I understood there were Indians scattered about there, but saw only two vaqueros." [7]

The freeholders were an organized and vociferous lobby. They considered US Law Agent McKuen their champion. McKuen had meticulously built his case against Weber's claim for *El Rancho Del Campo de Los Frances*. In a long carefully crafted argument incorporating the data he had solicited in depositions, McKuen made the case that Weber's claim was invalid because the land was not settled within one year as required and the Indians were friendly and did not constitute a reason for extension of time. He used surveyors depositions to make the case that Weber was claiming fifteen leagues when granted eleven. He alleged that the wording in the conveyance had been altered from "Un Rancho" to "La (sic) Rancho." McKuen's entire document was published in the fall of 1854.

The Board of US Land Commissioners were very busy in the spring of 1855 handing down decisions on Land Claims. The *San Joaquin Republican* regularly announced the results. In April of 1855, the *Republican* printed the full text of commissioner Seth B. Farwell's decision.[8] Farwell gives the salient points of Weber's petition and opposing arguments and cites the duties of the Commission as defined by the 1854 act of Congress, then concludes:

It is evident that Congress never designed these cases to be decided upon strict technical rules of common law, but that a wider scope should be given, so as to enable all claimants to have their rights adjusted according to the laws and usages of Mexico, and the principles of equity.

I have no doubt that under the liberal policy of the Mexican government, this claim would be recognized as good, as laid down by our rules of practice, the results would be the same, and that a decree of confirmation should be entered, which will accordingly be done.

Confirmed.

On May 11, the list of other confirmations and denials included:

BOARD OF US LAND COMMISSIONERS

CONFIRMED

No.333 Charles M. Weber, for *Cañada de San Felepe y Las Animas,* two square leagues in Santa Clara Co. ...Confirmed by commissioner Farwell.

On May 17, the confirmations included Sutter's claim. On May 24, the confirmations included two for Mariano G. Vallejo. The settlers met, decrying commissioner Farwell's decisions and lauding Agent McKuen's defense of the "freeholders" rights.[9]

San Joaquin and Calaveras Counties are original counties that participated in California's constitutional convention in 1849 and could have recorded deeds at their county recorder's office upon California's entry into the Union in 1850; however, deeds were of dubious validity, because of Senator Gwinn's act, until the US Land commission declared yea or nay on the validity of the Mexican land grants. Now that the conundrum was solved, an entire daisy chain of land transactions were legitimized and could become public record. The County recorder had a flurry of business. Among the transactions to become public record at this time was the original Mexican government grant by Governor Micheltorena to William Gulnac dated

July 14th, 1843. Also a deed granted by Guillermo Gulnac to Charles M. Weber on April 3rd, 1845. J.H. Tamm and Wife in May of 1853 granted N.B. Gann part of sections 64 and 65 of the oversized boundary skewed township surveyed as C.M. Weber's ranch. This was a large piece of land that the Ganns sold off piecemeal through the years.[10] "Nicholas B. Gann and Ruth Malinda his wife" sold and quit claim to part of this parcel to C.M. Weber in August of 1855. Nicholas and Rutha were at Stockton in 1850 and lived "on the Calaveras" until their return to Santa Cruz in 1858. They may have occupied land as "Freeholders" — a common practice prior to the decisions of the Land commission.[11] More Freshours and Ganns would appear in San Joaquin County in 1857. First, some Sierra wagon road would be built. It would take a typical rambunctious California brouhaha to get it done.

Poor Marlette was left holding the bag in the California Wagon Road game. Marlette held the critical post of state Surveyor-General in California in 1855-7. At that time the issue of wagon roads over the Sierra was a hot one. Back in 1850 a network of railroads in the eastern states extended as far west as Chicago. It was apparent that financing was the only obstacle to extending rails to the Pacific. In California, the topic of transportation was a celebrated public cause. The only practical commercial link to the "states" was by square-rigger. Federal assistance was needed but withheld because of regional rivalry and political interests. The suitability of the various routes being touted was then actually unknown. An act of Congress in 1853 provided for "A careful reconnaissance of the proposed routes for a railroad from the Mississippi Valley to the Pacific Ocean."

Five routes were surveyed, only one of which crossed the mountains in Northern California. This one reached the eastern border in the vicinity of Honey Lake. It was thought that the railroad could be built to reach the Sacramento Valley either along Nobles' Road or through Madeline Plains and along the Pit River. This was not really a Sierra route but rather a California Cascade range route. No consideration whatever was given to Donner Summit, which ultimately became the route of the first transcontinental railroad, or to the Beckwourth Pass through which the Western Pacific was later built.

The report of the explorations signed by Secretary of War, Jefferson Davis, stated that any route across the Sierra was impractical because of the deep snows. The recommended route swept in a great arc down to the Mexican border and back up to San Francisco — a route hundreds of miles longer. The folks in California soon realized the nature of the pre Civil War political climate they were confronting. They knew that an immediate agreement on the route for a transcontinental railway was very unlikely.[12]

They turned their energies toward the building of a transcontinental wagon road. Public agitation for a road from the Sacramento Valley to the Missouri River via Salt Lake resulted in mass meetings in San Francisco, Sacramento, Marysville, Placerville and other towns in 1854 and '55. The California Legislature passed the Wagon Road Act which was signed by Governor Bigler in April of 1855. The act authorized construction of a road from Sacramento to Carson Valley at a cost not to exceed $105,000. It stated: "the Surveyor-General of the State shall cause to be surveyed a good wagon road over the Sierra Nevada Mountains at an expense not to exceed $5,000 ..." There was just one hitch! The legislature failed to appropriate the $5,000. Surveyor-General S.H. Marlette was left "holding the bag."

In desperation Marlette called upon public spirited citizens for help.[13] The following advertisement appeared in Sacramento papers:

> Wanted immediately, on the credit of the state, $500 to enable the undersigned to complete the explorations for the Emigrant Wagon Road. Any gentleman who is willing to advance the above-named sum and will signify the same, will be called upon immediately by the undersigned.
>
> S.H. Marlette
> Surveyor General

Marlette's fund raising had produced sufficient funds by the summer of 1855 to launch Sherman Day, civil and mining engineer and State Senator, on a survey of the Carson Pass and Johnson cut-off routes. Considering the snow clearance problems on the Carson route, a problem that persists to this day, Day recommended the Johnson route. Marlette also had George H. Goddard make a survey of the area at the behest of the Mormon Territory of Utah which wanted to establish a local government in Carson Valley and wanted information including the location of the border. The Goddard and Day reports give accurate accounts of these two emigrant routes. Colonel J.B. Johnson opened the route from Carson Valley to Placerville in 1852. Due to its lower elevation and relative freedom from snow, the Johnson cutoff became very popular, but by 1854 the main Carson route was carrying more traffic in protest to the tolls charged at the Echo Pass.[14] There was little doubt among the northern mines interests that the Johnson route was the most practical route over the Sierra. But opposition from other interests prevented the legislature from appropriating the funds. The constitutionality of the State Wagon Road Act was challenged and the US Supreme Court declared it unconstitutional in December of 1856.

The year 1856 passed without any substantive work done on the route surveyed by Day. Petitions went to the congress. In February, 1857, President Pierce signed a wagon road act. It was a political football. The southern or border route (the Gila Trail) received $200,000 and the Salt Lake route received $300,000. There was just one glitch in the appropriation. The terminus of the Intercontinental Wagon Road was to be Honey Lake and not Carson Valley which was favored by Sacramento and Stockton alike. The California Stage Company moved to Marysville. In spite of this act of the Federal Government, most Californians persisted in fighting for a more direct route to Carson Valley.

All of California's interior towns wanted to be the ultimate terminus of the first transcontinental road. A reconnaissance of the Henness Pass route was submitted to Marlette. A similar survey was submitted for the Beckwourth Pass route. O.B. Powers of Calaveras County submitted to Marlette a surveyed route from the Carson road in Hope Valley to the Calaveras Big Trees. Proposals continued to be thrust forward. Placer county touted the Placer County Emigrant Road. Marysville wanted a road that went through Humbug Valley to join Nobles' Road to Honey Lake. Routes other than this Marysville one would connect to Honey Lake via a north-south link through Truckee Meadow to Carson Valley.

Several San Joaquin Valley counties joined in a meeting at which newly-elected Surveyor-General John A. Brewster and "Snowshoe" Thompson spoke of the superior advantages of the Big Trees Route. Construction work started on this route with funds raised locally and the *Calaveras Chronicle* of August 23, 1856 stated that this road, "the first over the Sierra," was ready for travel. This emigrant road ran from Murphy's in Calaveras County up through Bear Valley to Hermit Valley where it angled north over the divide — later named Border Ruffian Pass — to pass through Faith and Charity Valleys to join the road through Carson Canyon. The grade over the pass was reasonably moderate and it was relatively free from snow the year round. The Big Trees road was used extensively following its completion in 1856 and again during the summer of 1857.[15] It completely replaced the incredible Sonora route as the way into the southern mine environs of Sonora, Columbia and Murphys. After the discovery of silver on the *Comstock*, the Big Trees Road provided Nevada the most direct access to Stockton's wharves on the San Joaquin River.

The Stockton-Southern-Mines faction managed to create the first actual wagon road over the Sierra in 1856 while the State Legislature was deadlocked. However, a considerable amount of work was done on the Johnson route in the summer of 1857 by private subscription. By legislation passed in May, 1858, a Wagon Road Commission was appointed with power to award a contract for the construction of a road following Day's survey of the Johnson route. The contractor was unable to complete his contract. It was alleged that the contractor, one L.B. Leach, who just happened to be from Stockton, was a fictitious person who could not be held accountable. Leach had won the contract with a very attractive low bid. The remaining work had to be relet. Meanwhile, the Calaveras Big Trees route was booming. The Northern-Mines folks cried *"FOUL!"* claiming that enemies of their route had connived to submit the exceptionally low bid in order to delay construction. The work on the Johnson Road was completed in November of 1858.[16]

Stockton and Sacramento newspapers kept up a running account in 1857 of activities in the mines and road conditions and travel in the Sierra.

A Trip over the Big Tree Road

Mr. Travers, Agent of Wells, Fargo & Co. at Murphy's, a few days since made a trip of observation to Carson Valley and back, over the Big Tree road. ...
... we extract the following memoranda of Mr. Travers trip: "Whole time from Murphy's to Carson Valley, 47 hours; driving time, $21\frac{1}{4}$ hours; returning, whole time, 36 hours; driving time, 18 hours. ..."

"... I drove a two horse Concord wagon. The weather on the return trip was most unfavorable; raining, snowing, and blowing nearly all the way. The snow was two or three inches deep, for several miles. I think that, in dry weather, the trip can be made easily in fifteen hours." [17]

This trip was during the last week of June — the earliest one would attempt traveling through a Sierra pass. A month previous, the snow would have been many feet deep. The crest of the Sierra is stormy all summer long — mostly rain storms. The following report appeared July 4th in the *Republican*.

From Carson Valley

Messrs. Peters and Bowen, of this city, returned yesterday from Carson Valley, for which place they left last week on a tour of business and observation. They went over in a single buggy, and drove the same horse the entire distance there and back, and had no difficulty in making the trip. They fully confirm the uniform reports of the excellence of the road, and represent the entire practicability of making it a thoroughfare for all kinds of vehicles, from a light buggy to a heavy merchant wagon.

... on the return trip the party suffered some inconvenience from rain and snow, which fell in considerable quantities ... [18]

Carson Valley Expressman, John A. "Snowshoe" Thompson, at this time made regular mail runs to Mokelumne Hill and back.[19] He was a constant source of reports on the traffic and conditions of the Big Trees route — particularly its branch that departed at the head of the North Fork of the Stanislaus and passed through the small mining community of West Point and on to Mokelumne Hill. The main Big Trees route followed the Stanislaus down to Murphy's. Thompson's reports appeared in the Calaveras *Chronicle* and were picked up and rerun by the *Republican* in its *From Carson Valley* column. Usually this newsy column contained reports on the progress of Shearer's road crew that was working it's way over the summit. There were also reports of Kirk's crew out of Placerville that was working on the section of road common to both the Big Trees route and the Carson Pass route — the rugged Carson Canyon interposed between Hope Valley and the Carson Valley.[20]

There was considerable freight on the Big Trees road in 1857.

Rich Copper Mines in Carson Valley

"Uncle Billy" Rogers arrived in Sacramento the other day, says the *Bee* of that city, from his extensive copper vein in Hope Valley, east of the Sierra summit. He brought in a wagon, by the Big Tree route, 1,300 pounds of the ore, which, he says, will yield seventy per cent. of pure copper. ... [21]

By September of that year, the prosperity of Uncle Billy was such that he had opened a hotel and his newspaper notices spoke of "Col. Rogers."

By mid July both the *San Andreas Independent* and the *Calaveras Chronicle* had reported that Mr. Sherer's Big Trees road crew was out of cash. Another $3,000 was needed from subscribers in order to complete improvements on the road from the summit to Hope valley before the incoming emigrants arrived. Snowshoe Thompson reported some unusual freight on his arrival at Mokelumne Hill on the evening of Thursday, July 23rd.

Latest from Carson Valley

Mr J.A. Thompson ...
...On his way eastward, on Saturday last, at the head of the Stanislaus, met two brothers named Hatch, from Eagle Valley, with two four-horse teams loaded with wagon tires, which they picked up on the Humbolt desert, where they have been accumulating since the memorable exodus of '49 and '50.

The labor which Mr. Kirk and his company expended in the cañon, Mr. T. says has placed that part of the road in very good condition for loaded wagons. He is convinced that $1,000 more would make it good as desirable.

Mr. Kirk left Carson Valley on Saturday 18th inst., with nine heavy teams and seventy laboring hands, for Honey Lake, where he will commence to mark out and locate the overland wagon road. He will work eastward from that point. ...[22]

The last item of the July 26th column states: "Mr. Thompson will not return to the Valley until the arrival of the Atlantic mail, at which time he will take over a threshing machine to thresh out the grain now growing in Carson and Wassau [Washoe] Valleys."

The articles in the southern mines press continued week by week to compare performance of buggies, coaches and freight wagons on the northern mines routes to the superior performance of the Big Trees Road and to boast of progress in road improvements. Then, the emigrants started arriving and news from the plains became the principal topic.

By the end of 1856, James R. Freshour and his wife Annette had made up their minds to leave Centertown, Missouri and repeat the trip J.R. had made to California ten years previously. The same decision was made up river in Jackson County by the Freshour families headed by Martin and Thomas Freshour and their brothers-in-law Joshua Baucom and George Washington Himes. Andrew Freshour and his teenagers in nearby Johnson County were of the same mind. North of there, at Brooks, Iowa, John and Sophronia and Joseph Terre Freshour made the same decision. We can only speculate on the coordination of their plans. We do know that they were associated in California and arrived in 1857. On J.R.'s first trip to California, the eastern approaches to the Sierra were devoid of civilization. Now J.R. and company arrived at the Carson River and headed into Carson Valley.

There they found a settlement on the order of the one J.R. had left behind in the San Joaquin Valley less than a decade previous. Eagle Station was a busy enterprise supplied by freight wagon connections to the wharves and warehouses of Stockton and Sacramento.[23] An agricultural community spread across the Carson Valley. Sierra ramparts towered over the Mormon town of Genoa centered among splendid farms. The Mormons were selling out at panic prices to return to Salt Lake. The Francher party taking the Mormon Channel south to California from Salt Lake were massacred by Mormons at Mountain Meadows near Cedar City.[24] The entire nation was outraged. Brigham Young, fearing a Military reprisal, called all Mormons back to Salt Lake from the outlying settlements in far western Utah Territory and Southern California. The hastily departing Saints liquidated some very fine ranches which were snapped up at bargain prices by the gentiles.[25] Brigham Young was arrested by US troops and the "war" was peacefully ended.

The incoming emigrants had a choice between the Carson Valley or the wagon road over the Sierra. Kirk's road crew had commandeered Carson Valley men to finish the Carson Canyon section and information on the state of the roads to Sacramento and Stockton was stock in trade at Eagle Station and Genoa.

The other inducement to stay on the eastern side of the Sierra was the mining activity going on there. The electrifying silver discovery that was to create Nevada Territory had not yet occurred; but, minor strikes such as Uncle Billy's copper mine were going on. Hall, the discoverer of gold on the Walker River was leaving from Genoa with fifteen men and enough provisions to last the winter. A group in Placerville was also outfitting to prospect the Walker River. Hall's strike was 80 miles south of Billy Roger's mine and both mines were at the edge of the Sierra escarpment and Hall's discovery also had large deposits of copper as well as gold. This led to speculation that the veins were linked and this in turn sparked prospecting along a line between the two mines.[26] Probably one of the prospectors was Jacob J. Marklee who eventually set up a toll bridge on the Middle Fork of the Carson River — now Markleeville Creek. The only means to make a claim there at that time was to settle on it with a shotgun. When Nevada Territory was established, some four years later, Marklee recorded at Douglas County, Nevada his 160 acre land claim — a tract that was to later embody the Townsite of Markleeville.[27] It is easy to imagine J.R. deciding to stay over and do some prospecting in the area. Apparently the prospecting didn't "pan out" as a reason to stay there. The Walker River strike turned out to be only "a flash in the pan." One positive result of their sojourn was the birth of Joseph Frank Freshour on November 4th, 1857. The family was settled in Douglas Township of San Joaquin County in 1860.

In late September the *Sacramento Union* published a letter from Genoa in the Carson Valley estimating the overland emigration for 1857 at 25,000 to 30,000 strong, of which two-thirds were women and children. Most of the trains brought with them loose stock. From 5,000 to 6,000 head of emigrant and California cattle were expected to winter that season on the east side of the Sierra Nevadas.

> The emigration this year is by far the most valuable that has ever crossed the Plains in any one season.
> The emigration really exceeds in number any previous calculation. It is truly immense. Carson Valley is all alive with men, women and children. Wagons, horses, mules and cattle are everywhere to be seen. From this fact Genoa is full of trade and activity.[28]

John and Sophronia proceeded over Sierra wagon road to San Joaquin County with little William Henry, Joseph Alfred and baby, Lydia Jane, who had just spent the first two months of her life rocking over mountains and desert in a wagon. They apparently passed up the Calaveras mines and foothill ranching and went on to the agriculture of the flat lands. They settled in O'Neal Township with Stockton as their Post Office. Rhoda Ann was born at Stockton in February of 1859 and George Wesley was born in O'Neal Township in November of 1860. Martin and Mary Ann and one-year-old Sarah Ann also had come over the Sierra wagon road through Calaveras County and settled near John and Sophronia in O'Neal Township. They were living there in 1860 with four-year-old Sarah Ann and two-year-old Martha Jane. John's brother, Joseph Terre, was in their household working as a ranch hand. Rutha and Nicholas lived, until 1858, in O'Neal Township just east of Stockton near the Linden road leading to Jenny Lind and the Sierra wagon road. Their daughter, Mahala Jane, married Kelsey Hobbs there in September of 1857. It is likely that John and Martin looked them up and that the families all lived in close proximity during the following year.

Thomas and Harriet Freshour settled with their children, thirteen-year-old Sarah E., seven-year-old James W. and baby Thomas I., in Elkhorn Township of San Joaquin county north of the Mokelumne River and northeast of Lodi. Harriet's brother, James Offitt, was in their household. Thomas' sister Emaline and her husband Joseph Baucom with three children settled nearby with grandma Elizabeth Freshour in their household.

They had been preceded by Joseph's brother Thomas Baucom who was now a neighbor. Thomas and Harriet purchased 160 acres in 1866 and another 80 acres in 1868. This Elkhorn Township group of Freshours were some forty miles north of Rutha and Nicholas' location in O'Neal Township.[29] The objective of the Freshours and kin arriving in the San Joaquin Valley was the firtile farm land. They would have to buy at this late date. There were no deeds recorded for John and Sophronia or for Martin and Mary Ann in O'Neal Township.

The James R. Freshour family came down the Big Trees Road and through Calaveras County and settled just over the San Joaquin county line on the Calaveras River on the road running past Jenny Lind and Bellota on the way from Mokelumne Hill to Stockton. The terrain is rolling hills studded with a few scrub oak. The winter rains turn these hills emerald green. Although in the early days of settlement, wheat was grown here, it is typical California cattle country. The Calaveras flows out of the Sierra through Calaveras County and crosses the very tip of the triangular northern boundary of Stanislaus County and flows immediately on through San Joaquin County on its inevitable course to join the San Joaquin River at Stockton. The northern boundary of Douglas Township intersects the Calaveras boundary at a point just above the apex of Stanislaus County. J.R. Freshour's property was located at this peculiar junction of several boundaries. He held a 160 acre parcel pieced together from two 80 acre parcels in different sections such that his land was a quarter mile wide and one mile in length north to south. The county line cut diagonally through this property such that the upper 80 acre parcel was mostly in Calaveras County. The two sections straddled the Douglas Township boundary to the extent that they were in San Joaquin County. Thus part of the lower 80 acres was in Douglas Township.

In 1860, James and Frances were living with their children, seven-year-old James Marion, five-year-old John William, and two-year-old Joseph Frank, in Douglas Township of San Joaquin County — apparently on the lower end of their property. Deeds were recorded in both counties for these straddled properties and the census takers took pot luck. J.R. had settled where he could both ranch and work in the "Lower Diggins" which were a short distance away in the vicinity of Jenny Lind. He was also on the busy wagon road running from Mokolumne Hill and other southern mines towns to Stockton. He was up on the Calaveras — a locale that would attract other Freshours in the years to follow. It appears that the emigrant Freshours who were channeled into San Joaquin County by the Big Trees wagon road eventually left for the coastal redwoods or doubled back to the mining and ranching of the Calaveras foothills.

In spite of the entrepreneurial machinations and vigorous industry on the part of Stockton and associated southern mines communities on behalf of their fine wagon road, the Johnson route ultimately became the premier Emigrant Road. A lack of legislative support, however, resulted in its being taken over by private capital following the discovery of the great silver deposits in Nevada. Excessive traffic from Sacramento over the Sierra to the Comstock and other mines resulted in one way traffic with return via the lesser routes including the Calaveras route.[30] The Johnson Route became the Sierra Wagon Road and its tolls paid huge dividends to its operators. The other contenders eventually became secondary roads or grew over with grass. The Calaveras Big Trees Road became the route to Silver Mountain City[31] via the Ebbits Pass and soon became the Big Trees Turnpike. The section from Hermit Valley over Border Ruffian Pass did go to grass. When the trans-Sierra railroads appeared with all their associated lesser railroads, the teamster wagons crossing the Sierra all but disappeared and the wagon roads more or less went to grass — until the advent of the automobile. Silver Mountain City faded into a ghost and Markleeville took its place.[32]

The year 1857 marks the last year that the trail to California existed as such. Early in the 1850s, road was built from Fort Leavenworth to the St. Joe trace and in 1856-8, road was built from Ft. Leavenworth via Ft. Riley to Ft. Kearny. The road extending west from Ft. Kearny was targeted with $300,000 by the US Congress for road construction beginning in 1857.

Three sections of the road were designated: Fort Kearny to Independence Rock, from thence to the City of Rocks and the last leg through Nevada to Honey Lake. Honey Lake is inside the California border some seventy-five miles north of Lake Bigler (now known as Lake Tahoe) as show on Britton & Reys map of California published in 1857.[33]

President Buchanan's friend Magraw proved incompetent to run a road building operation in 1857 and Frederick Lander got the project properly underway in 1858. Lander built a fine road from South Pass to City of Rocks. This road reduced the travel time over that distance by five days. He hired a mountaineer to direct traffic over the road and went east to Washington. When he returned his employee had been killed in a gun fight and traffic was being directed to the old trail. He stationed a soldier there with printed guide books. Lander claimed 13,000 emigrants used the road in 1859. In 1860 Lander worked on the last link to Honey Lake.

President Buchanan finally sent dragoons west to deal with the Mormon problem. Col. Albert Sidney Johnston arrived in Utah Territory in June of 1858 with an expedition to establish Camp Floyd forty miles south of Salt Lake. For the next two years the largest single concentration of US military power was at Camp Floyd. Col. Johnston sent 100 dragoons and 50 infantrymen to patrol the length of the Humbolt. Military aid and escort for emigrants became common. Indian and Mormon problems abated. Johnston led an escort for a military supply train sent from St. Joseph, Missouri to the barracks at Benicia, California. A battalion of engineers under Johnston's command made improvements on the Johnson Cutoff en route. In 1860, the forces supporting secession in California led by senator Gwin arranged for Johnston to take command of the California State Militia. He was replaced by Unionist General E.A. Sumner who brought troops down from Oregon and squelched the armed secessionists of California. Gwin was arrested and exiled during the war and Albert Sidney Johnston became a Confederate General. He died in combat at Shiloh. The Mormon conflict died down to smolder for years to come.[34]

In 1858 and 1859, Captain James Hervey Simpson of the Topographical Corps of Engineers surveyed a route through Nevada from Salt Lake to Carson Valley that entirely avoided the course along the Humbolt. Simpson then supervised the work of grading, timber cutting for materials and construction of the new road that cut 288 miles off the old California Trail. On the traditional route, Lander was constructing his road to the north of Sublett's cutoff through to the City of Rocks.

Although these construction projects loomed imminently, the 1857 California Trail — well defined with wagon ruts, forts, trading posts, ferries, familiar landmarks, wagon iron, Indians, river fords, discards, and fresh graves — was none-the-less the *Trail*. Travelers were "crossing the plains by covered wagon." — A romantic sentimentality that they relished even then and one that has become one of the legends of western American culture. The emigrant wagons would continue to come even after transcontinental railway service was established; but, from now on, they would travel among the commerce of large freight wagons and stage coaches and even buggy traffic.

Orion Clemens and his brother arrived at Carson City in 1861 by stagecoach from St. Joseph Missouri. It took twenty days to journey west, and they had paid one hundred and fifty dollars apiece for tickets for the 1900 mile passage. Orion had been appointed to the post of Secretary to the new Territory of Nevada, and brought his brother along to be nepotisticly employed as his scrivener. His brother, Samuel, later wrote the book *Roughing It* describing the coach ride west. He used the nom de plume, Mark Twain.

The *Trail*?
    — Well, it became a yarn
                      — spun by elderly folk.

12

UP ON THE CALAVERAS

CALAVERAS County got its macabre name from its river so named *en español* by Moraga, who found its banks lined with skulls, ghastly reminders of the bloody conflicts that took place among the Indians for possession of the "salmon water." It may just as well have been named for the super macho madness of the Mexican *calaverónes* who would frequently squander their mining proceeds on celebrations including bull and bear fights, cock fights and vaquero contests such as riding at full speed and reaching down from the saddle to snatch the head off a live chicken buried with only its head sticking up. Their wild drinking, gambling and knife fights were appalling even to the boisterous gringo forty-niners. There was no love lost between the two groups. Much of the early crime in the county consisted of reciprocated malevolence.[1]

Calaveras County lies on the Sierra slope between the North fork of the Stanislaus at its southern boundary and the Mokelumne River on the north. It narrows to a blunt apex that borders Alpine County at the crest of the Sierra and spreads on its lower western boundary along the Sierra foothills at the Stanislaus and San Joaquin boundaries. The Mother Lode runs through the lower parts of the county at elevations of one-thousand to twenty-five-hundred feet. The Yaqui miners from Mexico first mined a gulch there in 1848 and put up a little church which they named San Andreas. In a few years there were about a thousand Mexicans there. They were soon outnumbered by the American forty-niners.[2] Other diggings such as Mokelumne Hill and Angels Camp developed in this region where Charles Weber and associates made their fortunes.

The county seat was briefly at Double Springs [3] but "Moke Hill" was the first county seat of note and it lost out in 1863 to

San Andreas. The lowest altitude at which gold was mined, in those days before dredging, was at the county line in the region of Milton and Jenny Lind. Jenny Lind was first known as "Dry Diggins" or, more specifically, "Lower Diggins." [4]

The first settlement in the Dry Diggins was at Pleasant Valley in 1850. A road house and later a post office was established there on the mail route from Stockton to Murphys. After 1856, the road house was moved down to Stone Corral near the county line and the Pleasant Valley settlement vanished; all its inhabitants having moved to Lower Diggins. The Swedish Nightingale toured Eastern America in the years 1850-52 and was well known by many who had come west. The legend of her having sung to the Dry Diggins miners is charming but untrue.[5] Perhaps the renaming of Lower Diggins as Jenny Lind was the whimsical touch of homesick miners. The placer miners with their sluice boxes were limited by the seasonal availability of water until 1857 when the famous engineering feat of the Jenny Lind suspension aqueduct by the Jenny Lind Ditch Company brought water to the Lower Diggins. The towers supporting the high flume were blown down by gale force winds several times in the winter of 1858-9. Reconstruction was almost a continuous project that winter.[6]

Freighting into and out of the mining camps came to be a leading occupation in the years following the gold rush. It was no easy task to handle the great teams of horses or mules hitched to large, heavily-loaded wagons over the rough roads and up the steep grades of the Sierra Nevada. It should not be surprising that the freight rates were very high. The road house at Stone Corral was a stopover for teamsters hauling freight from Stockton to the towns of the southern mines. About 1860, a black teamster by the name of Boss, a popular citizen of Jenny Lind, was hauling freight from Stockton and stopped over at Stone Corral. He and six other teamsters were killed by a band of Mexicans who robbed and burned down the road house. One man escaped and hid in a ditch until the robbers left. None of the gang was ever caught.[7] Repetition of such robbery and mayhem and the resultant abuse of the Mexican population by the intolerant mining communities led the Cherokee writer, John Rollin Ridge, to set the beginnings of his fanciful yarn about Joaquin Murietta in San Andreas.[8]

Several "Joaquins" were ensconced among the Mexicans of Calaveras County as they were throughout not only the Mother Lode but most of California. The state legislature responded by creating Captain Harry Love's California Rangers for the purpose of hunting down the rascal. Love's Rangers killed a Mexican in the hills west of Fresno in 1853 and collected the reward. The Joaquins of Calaveras County were some years later driven out by organized citizens. A posse shot it out with the *bandidos* at Yaqui Camp two miles south of San Andreas. The camp was totally destroyed but the wily Joaquin escaped. In his haste he left his red sash which by legendary process is now "Joaquin Murietta's sash." [9]

During the dark days of civil strife between the North and South, California supplied troops, mostly to control Western Indian uprisings; but, California itself was spared the scenes of bloody combat. The loyalty of its troops, the leadership of governors Leland Stanford and Frederick Low and the adroitness of its people in saving the state from internal warfare, enabled California to further the development of its resources while pouring treasures into the Union. By the close of the Civil war, ships were entering the Golden Gate in ballast to load grain, flour, lumber, wool, hides, mineral ores, quicksilver and other products. But it was California's gold that supplied an indispensable element of strength and steadiness to national finance. General Grant stated "I do not know what we could do in this great national emergency were it not for the gold sent from California."[10] A French writer asserted "It is the gold of California that has dealt the fatal blow to the institution of slavery in the United States." Every demand made by the federal government was met without delay or question.[11] These war times were no doubt prosperous for the San Joaquin Valley farmers.

Sacramento and Stockton during the 1850s and '60s reigned over the state's dominant population centers. Nevada City in

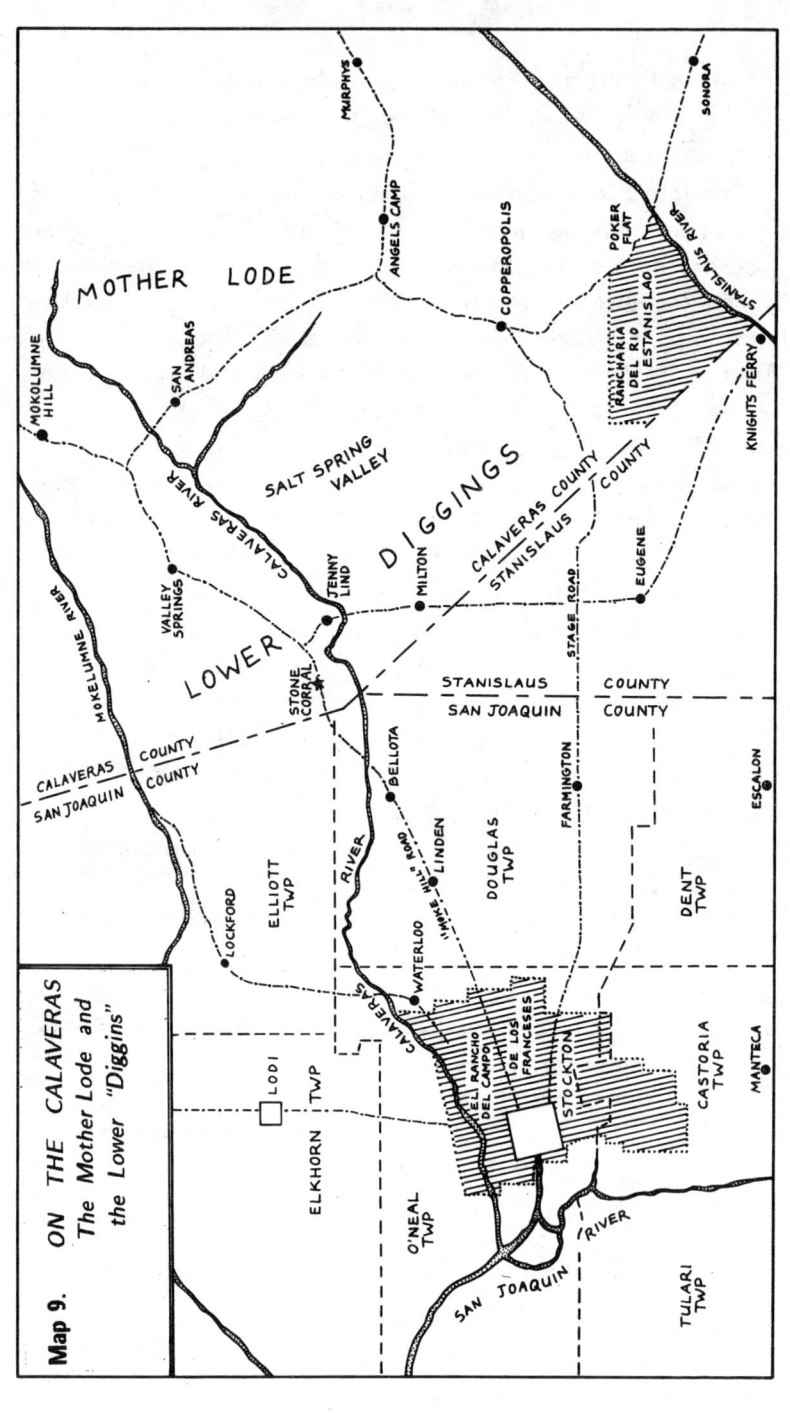

the Northern Mines had a population of over one-hundred-thousand people and Mokelumne Hill in the Southern Mines was almost as large. Many of the Mother Lode towns that are now quaint tourist attractions or, in recent times, quiet retirement communities, were in the last century the most populous towns in California. These large mining communities clamored to become the state capital but the traditional coastal cities had prior claim.[12] Sacramento won as the central location with the large mining population on the Oregon border balancing southern California. The sought after farming flatland of the San Joaquin was generally located between the San Joaquin and Sacramento river delta and the populous Mother Lode. Many of the emigrants who were channeled into San Joaquin County by the Big Trees wagon road remained there through the Rebellion years — 1860-65 — then some of them doubled back to the mining and ranching of the Calaveras foothills. Homestead land had become available there and there was work in the mines.

While the apocalyptic "War of the Rebellion" devastated the eastern states, the Great Valley of California underwent an equivalent cataclysm as the usually beneficent Pacific-Sierra hydrological cycle ran amuck. This phenomenon periodically turned the entire valley into a vast lake. The most destructive flood of record in the Great Valley was the flood of 1861-2. Captain W.H. Brewer, employed as a surveyor, made this journal entry in January of 1862.

> The great central valley of the state is under water — the Sacramento and San Joaquin Valleys — a region 250 to 300 miles long and an average of at least twenty miles wide, a district of five thousand or six thousand square miles, or probably three to three and a half million acres [is inundated]! [13]

Captain Brewer estimated one-fourth of the taxable property of the state to have been destroyed. The State Capitol at Sacramento was once more afloat — raising the question of moving the capitol to a location less disposed to flooding.

The Chinese shanty towns were washed away. The loss of life included some fourteen hundred Chinese reported drowned in various parts of California. The destruction of property and life was accompanied by a terrible loss of livestock. — some drowned but most starved from loss of feed. Loss of 100,000 sheep and 500,000 lambs was reported. Cattle, horses, hogs, gophers and ground squirrels were all alike drowned.[14]

The winter storms of California can at times be bitterly cold or tropically pleasant depending on origin either in the Aleutian region to the northwest or from the sub-tropics to the southwest. The winter weather turned warm, melting the Sierra snows deposited earlier. The normally swift Sierra rivers turned into raging torrents that flushed away bridges and ferries and swept entire mining operations down river. The rich valley soil was an accrued benefit of alluvial deposition, but this was of small comfort to the valley farmers who had to clean up and rebuild.

Following the sun spot cycles, the climatic pendulum swung to the dry years that inevitably follow to produce a meager and incidentally very fine vintage. Drought had a different significance to cattle ranchers. The great flood of 1861-2 was immediately followed by dry years that destroyed the Mexican cattle industry. The Mexicans tended half wild long-horn cattle running on equally wild open range. They were absolutely subject to the vicissitudes of climate. They never provided for the dry years by developing dams for water storage or raising hay crops for storage in barns. The Spanish cattle barons, who had never heard of irrigation, began to fade with the drought of 1855-6. Over a million cattle were lost in the state. Thousands of wild horses were run off cliffs and killed to save the pasture for the cattle. The introduction of superior American stock and ranching practice assisted in wiping out the Mexican ranchero. The drought of 1862-5 was the coup-de-grâce.[15]

The flood of 1861-2 was an incentive to move to the coast and the subsequent drought of 1862-5 was no doubt a factor causing valley ranchers to move into the Sierra foothills. John and Sophronia left the vicinity of Stockton right after the War started. By 1862 John and Sophronia, their five children and Joseph Terre had moved over to the coast to live among the redwoods in Santa Cruz County. Shortly after, the Joshua Baucoms left the San Joaquin for coastal Santa Cruz County. James and Frances Annette Freshour had not gone to the Valley but had settled on their border-straddling quarter section on the Calaveras River. The Stone Corral was just up the road from their ranch. It is likely that they lived there when the *bandidos* raided the road house in 1860. They spent the war years rearing their children there along the Calaveras in the rolling grassland punctuated with chaparral. The election of 1864 was of special interest to the California Freshours since their roots were in Greene County Tennessee — the political origin of the war governor of Tennessee who was now Lincoln's running mate.

The care worn Abraham Lincoln, weary and facing a task even more burdensome than the painful catharsis of war, the onerous burden of reconstruction — had at last found peace. He lay at rest in his burial vault in the Oak Ridge Cemetery at Springfield Illinois. An old proverb of the woodsmen was fitting: "A tree is best measured when it's down." [16] To the Greene County diamond in the rough, Andrew Johnson, lay the task of applying Lincoln's "Rosewater" reconstruction policy. Many eastern cities were devastated and needed to be rebuilt. The entire nation needed to be restructured politically and economically. The North was vindictive. A southern democrat, Johnson served in a republican administration. He had not been elected. Johnson's long suit was not tact and diplomacy. He served one rocky term during which the reconstruction was transmuted into a military occupation. The South was overrun with scalawags and carpetbaggers. The national debt engendered by the war and the adjustment to a peace time economy meant austerity everywhere including California.[17]

Martin and Mary Ann Freshour moved from the Stockton area to the Douglas Township region near Bellota on the road to Mokelumne Hill and just north of the Calaveras River. Martin traded properties from time to time tending in an easterly direction. In the early 1870s, he had acquired four quarter sections — close together but not a contiguous square mile. Martin and Mary Ann were the nearest neighbors to Annette Freshour with seven-year old Alice and her three teen-age boys in 1870. James R. was absent — no doubt in the mines. Soon James and Frances Annette left for the Siskiyou and Martin homesteaded their borderline property. Martin also held two 160 acre parcels east of Jenny Lind in Salt Spring Valley of Calaveras County.

In 1860, there were a number of Ganns in Castoria Township south of Stockton.[18] They too developed an interest in the Calaveras area east of Jenny Lind. There were twelve 160 or 80 acre parcels homesteaded by various Ganns in Salt Spring Valley which is above the present day Hogan Reservoir. A Ganns Road is located there.

The road house at Stone Corral was never rebuilt but the old corral was in continuous use for many years. The land at Stone Corral was purchased by Jacob Shank and Victor Gilliam in 1870 and a school was built on their property about a half mile to the south-west of the corral. Originally, the school was called the Douglas School. It was later called the Chaparral School and was moved across the Calaveras River to the Kirk property just over the hill from the Kirk Family Cemetery. From there it was moved to Stone Corral. The historic site served as the community center for gatherings, such as weddings. Martin and Mary Ann Freshour's children and grandchildren attended the Stone Corral School.[19] The children of James and Annette Freshour no doubt also attended the school in the war years when it was on the Kirk property. In those days they opened with prayer and Bible reading and saluted the flag. The older children would know the names of all sixteen presidents starting with George Washington. Imagine the shock they felt when the telegraph brought word to California that president Lincoln had been killed.

General Ulysses S. Grant was elected president in 1868. Reconstruction cruelty ground forward under his direction. The burgeoning industrial age brought with it prospering corporations and millionaire opulence. Corruption was commonplace. Grant's administration was rife with corruption and scandal. He was reelected in 1872 and the panic of 1873 brought the American economic establishment down like a house of cards. California felt the full force of this fiscal calamity.[20]

Thomas and Harriet sold out in 1873 and moved with their family and her brother, James Offitt, from Elkhorn Township of San Joaquin County to the Calaveras border near Jenny Lind.[21] James Offitt homesteaded 160 acres straddling the San Joaquin-Calaveras boundary and located to the north of Stone Corral — a parcel which he purchased from Martin Freshour. Thomas' sister Emaline and her husband Joseph Baucom and family along with grandma Elizabeth Freshour had moved to Santa Cruz county by 1863. The panic of 1873 was followed by long years of depression and deflation. In spite of Grant's ineptitudes, and the economic woes that befell the nation, the robust young Republic surged forward with expansion in the west and industrial growth.

Quartz mining at first was questionable as a profitable industry. Eventually, the technology was perfected for taking ore from deep within an immense megalith and crushing it to a state that permitted extraction of the gold. California manufacturing firms, some located in the mother lode, produced this machinery which was used by large mining corporations whose stock was sold by eastern investment brokers. Laborers sweated at the stamping mills and the work of hauling the ore. Deep under the surface, mule skinners wearing carbide lamps urged their animals pulling the ore carts along tracks laid in the cold stony corridors, bringing the quartz out from where it had been blasted loose and heaved chunk by chunk into the carts deep in the interior of the stone mountains. Once a blithe spirit alongside a stream with his gold pan, the California miner was now an industrial employee.

Placer mining expanded with the civil engineering projects that dammed streams, built canals and tunnels and hillside trestles supporting the flumes delivering the continuous flow through summer and fall for sluicing operations. The lower diggins were supplied water from a dam at Salt Spring Valley and a tunnel and aqueduct – one of several such projects centered around Jenny Lind.[22] The wooden flumes had to be replaced after a few years service. This and the large timbers used in mine tunnels gave additional business to the Sierra lumber industry. Such corporate projects later created the devastating water cannon of hydraulic operations and at the turn of the century the ultimate ecological catastrophe, the dredgers. These gold ingot producing activities provided a mother lode industrial base that had some immunity to the vicissitudes of the agriculture industry. There were some quartz mines in the Jenny Lind area, but the big corporation mines were higher up.

In the 1860s and 1870s there were five Freshour voters registered in the 1866-87 "Great Register" of Calaveras County.

> *James Rufus Freshour*, 39, Tenn., miner, Jenny Lind, removed 1867.
>
> *Marion Freshour*, 22, Missouri, farmer, Jenny Lind, registered 1875, removed 1875.
>
> *Martin Freshour*, 38, Tenn., farmer, transferred from San Joaquin Co., 1872.
>
> *Thomas Freshour*, 46, Tenn., farmer, Milton, transferred from San Joaquin Co., 1875.
>
> *James William Freshaur*, 23, Missouri, farmer, Jenny Lind, registered 1875.

Marion was the eldest son of J.R. Freshour. Annette and J.R. sold most of their land in 1868 moving to a small plot just across the line to Douglas Township of San Joaquin County, where they were neighbors to Martin and Mary Ann while J.R. worked in the mines. They moved up north to Yreka in 1872. Marion was in Calaveras County in 1875 and was in Siskiyou County by 1877. Martin acquired J.R.'s former ranch and moved across the County line in 1872 — possibly by building a house at the other end of the property. James William Freshour was Thomas Freshour's eldest son. He homesteaded and built a cabin on 160 acres just east of Stone Corral School.

James W. married Arabella Atherton, daughter of Englishman William Atherton, a neighboring farmer of Jenny Lind.

Following the anti-dictator tradition of the two term limit, the Republicans cast about for a successor to Grant and finally settled on Ohio governor Rutherford B. Hayes, a combat veteran who rose through the ranks to become a major general, having been wounded several times in the process. The fetid, cigar-reeking atmosphere of the white house was aired out in 1877. The Hayes had daily family prayers. "Lemonade Lucy" Hayes served no alcohol. Hayes courageously ordered the last federal troops out of the South. An idealistic purist, characterized as a "Queen Victoria in breeches," Hayes threw out the spoilsmongers and restored integrity to government. The cyclic depression and recession following the 1873 panic culminated in the turbulence of 1877. Hayes had to call out federal troops to deal with labor violence. The farmer continued to experience depression. Hayes was unable to read the deeper economic currents of the new industrial age that were bringing monopoly to business and injustice to labor.[23]

The labor unrest swept to the Pacific Coast where the dry winter of 1876-77 resulted in general failure of the grain crop, and thousands of cattle perished. Idleness abounded. Tramps seemed to be everywhere. Seven thousand people in San Francisco needed public relief. By 1877, fifteen thousand men were idle in the metropolis. Hot headed labor leader Denis Kearney harangued the workingmen to arm themselves and suggested that "a little judicious hanging" would be the best course of action against the robber capitalists. The "Celestials" became the butt of the unemployed laborer's wrath. Many Chinese, who at that time comprised about ten percent of California's population, had their precious pigtails cut off and some were murdered outright. The excess of cheap Chinese labor became the principal issue in California politics culminating in the Treaty of 1880 regulating, but not prohibiting, admission of Chinese laborers. The Exclusion Bill of 1882 finally suspended emigration of the Chinese.[24] The gravel of the lower diggings had been worked and reworked from the first scrambling opportunists

of 1848, and the various stages of placer operations until the
Chinese, left without work by the completion of the railroads,
took to patiently sifting the diggings one last time. Typical of
the census in all the California mining communities, the 1870
Calaveras County census shows page after page of male Chinese.
They were listed as laborers in what appeared to be very
large bunkhouses with an occasional cook and less frequently
a female among them was frankly listed as prostitute. Among
the white mine laborers there was an occasional household of
several white females discreetly listed as "fancy ladies."

The unemployment problem of 1877 led some to seek more
profitable lines of work. At that time a sequence of mother lode
stage coach robberies began and continued until November of
1883. The *modus operandi* was established in 1877. At a spot
carefully chosen such that the horses would be slowed to a walk
by the grade, a hooded figure would leap out in front the lead
horse halting the team. Shielded by the horse from gunfire from
the coach, he leveled a double barreled shotgun at the driver
and rasped "throw down the box." Once the box was thrown
down he waived the coach on its way then forced open the box
then disappeared with the loot. On his first robbery in 1877
the lone bandit left a note in the box.

> I've labored long and hard for bread,
> For honor and for riches,
> But on my toes too long you've tread
> You fine-haired sons of bitches.
> . . .
>
> Black Bart, the PO8.

Twenty-eight robberies followed this pattern — except for
the poetry — over the next six years. The robberies were frequently
reported with a reprint of the original doggerel lending
legendary literary status to Black Bart the "Po-ate." His last
robbery, on Funk Hill on the Sonora-Milton road went awry.
A lad out hunting with his rifle encountered the robbed driver.
The driver had been sent on his way with just the team. Black
Bart was working on the safe bolted into the coach. He was

driven off by whistling rifle bullets. He left a handkerchief with a laundry mark and was soon tracked down.

Black Bart was none other than Mr. Charles E. Bolton of San Francisco — a quiet and perfectly proper gentleman who was known to make business trips to his mining properties in the gold country. He was brought back to San Andreas for trial. He was actually a Civil War veteran named Boles with a wife and child at Hannibal, Missouri. He was a fine citizen who never drank, swore nor smoked and he dressed nattily. He had never fired a shot in twenty-eight robberies. He was sentenced to six years in San Quentin, got time off for good behavior, made some remarks to reporters as he left prison then completely vanished. True to his word, he never troubled Wells-Fargo again.[25]

Black Bart's "mining" career brings into focus the fact that the Mother Lode was a strong industrial center through the last half of the 1800s and continued as such into this century to finally peter out in the 1940s. Wells, Fargo & Company rapidly emerged as the main freight company to service the industry. Its unassuming service oriented drivers were usually hard working family men lacking in flamboyance. But they put their lives on the line with each bullion run. Unlike Black Bart, many stage robbers shot up the coach, driver and passengers as a matter of course. A number of drivers were killed or maimed. An even worse injury, some suffered a loss of dignity.

The San Andreas-Milton stage was robbed by two masked men in May of 1880. they were unable to blow the safe on the stage so took money and watches and stole the driver's boots.[26] At the end of the run the driver would have to respond to droll queries as to why he was driving in his socks. To add injury, as the stage rolled into town a young lady sang out "Yoo hoo — I see somebody's big feet." Never mind the robbers were foiled. Such was the *Calaveras Chronicle* newspaper fare of Martin Freshour and family of Jenny Lind.

Neither James W. Freshour nor his father Thomas were any longer in Calaveras County in 1880. The Great Register for Calaveras County in 1888 had only Martin Freshour registered.

The grain growing farmers of the Jenny Lind region and lower Calaveras County generally did not survive the 1870s economics. The cattlemen became dominant by buying up the land of the failing grain farmers. They had the ideal arrangement of owning acreage scattered from the San Joaquin line to the Sierra meadow lands higher up in the county. They could graze their herds into the higher altitudes as summer arrived in the Sierra and the foothills turned hot and dry. The Ganns of Salt Spring Valley grazed their herds above Dorrington on the Big Trees Turnpike. Charlie Gann staked out land there and built the place known as Gann's Station now called Ganns.[27] There is a Gann's trail from there to the river where Charlie traded with the Indians.

Martin Freshour was a close neighbor to pioneer John W. Kirk who came to California in 1847. The Kirk family established a family cemetery which was used by their neighbors. Annette and J.R. lost an infant son Noah — buried in Kirk's Cemetery in February of 1861. The farmers up on the Calaveras petitioned the San Joaquin Board of Supervisors for a local county road. Written in December of 1861, by July of 1862 it was recorded with some one-hundred and twelve signatures, including those of John W. Kirk and Martin Freshour.[28]

Martin and Mary Ann tragically lost two of their children. Their stones in the Kirk Cemetery tell us that seven-year-old Sarah Ann died in August of 1863 and ten-year-old Martha Jane died in November of 1868.[29] Their son William A. Freshour married Julia E. Wright, both from Stone Corral, in 1885 at Stone Corral. Their daughter Clara E. Freshour married A.A. Neal in 1888 at Stone Corral. Stone Corral School is now a State Historical Location. Daughter Emma R. married William H. Wolfe in 1886 in Jenny Lind.

Pioneer wife Mary Ann Gentry Freshour, born in North Carolina, married as a very young girl in Missouri, traveled the plains as a young mother, died in August of 1896 at Stockton.[30] Martin Freshour died in September of 1914 in San Andreas, a resident of Jenny Lind, born July 14, 1831 in Tennessee. He was in California for 47 years. He was buried in Kirk Cemetery.

Daughters Mrs. Minnie Ellen Christy and Mrs. Clara Eviline Neal were living at Jenny Lind and daughter Mrs. Emma Rey Wolf was living at French Camp near Stockton. Martin's son William Andrew Freshour was living with his family at Ripon south of Stockton on the Stanislaus County line.[31]

America was losing its pioneers and it was about to lose its innocence. In another two years America would be plunged into "World War One." Martin's grandson Rollin G. Freshour would survive combat on a June day of 1918 by being buried under his comrades bodies. The Germans unpiled the bodies and the wounded soldier spent six months in prison camp until the armistice was signed and he was liberated skin and bones and not entirely recovered from his shrapnel wounds. He returned to duty and when he finally returned to Ripon in August of 1919 he collapsed with pneumonia and died a week later.[32]

— Courtesy of University Of Pacific Library

Figure 12.1: From the *Stockton Daily Evening Record.*

America had emerged as a nation of international importance — and had fields of crosses row on row to secure the claim. Rollin is buried in the Liberty Plot of the Park View Cemetery on French Camp Road. His parents and other Ripon Freshours are buried in the family plot there.

The *Calaveras Prospector* copied Rollin's obituary from the *Stockton Record*. Since Rollin was reared at Jenny Lind and had attended Stone Corral School, he had many friends there in Calaveras County. His father, William A. Freshour, and his grandfather, Martin Freshour, were very well remembered around Jenny Lind.

Rollin's brother, Arthur D. Freshour Sr., carried on the family name at Ripon. Arthur's sons, Martin Freshour's great grandsons, David R. and Arthur D. Freshour, grew up at Ripon. Twenty-two-year-old Corporal Arthur Freshour was killed in action on November 7, 1951 in the Korean War. He had attended Ripon Union High School, worked at the Nestle's Milk Plant and married Joan Black of Salida. His brother David, had been discharged from a five year hitch in the US Navy the previous summer. Arthur's body was repatriated from Korea and interred in the Freshour plot in Park View Cemetery.[33] Dave R. Freshour died in 1989 and was survived by his son Russel A. Freshour.[34] The name "Freshour" disappeared from Jenny Lind when Martin died in 1914. All that remains of the gold rush town are a few ruins. The Stone Corral School is still in use — as a Church.

13

SISKIYOU GOLD

GOLD NUGGETS GLEAMED in the mud dribbling off the rain soaked clumps of uprooted grass clamped in the teeth of Abraham Thompson's mules as the spitting critters attempted to feed on the rain soaked herbage. Thus began the gold rush into the Siskiyous — following hard on the heels of the rush into the Sierra Nevada in '49.

Siskiyou country stands surrounding the Oregon-California border separating the Rogue River from the Klamath River. The Rogue runs westward through Southwestern Oregon to the Pacific. The Klamath, which has its head waters in the interior of Southern Oregon, curves southwest into California and meanders through Siskiyou County in a westerly course that takes it to the Pacific. The Siskiyou[1] is a mountainous land mass formed as sea bottom and folded and raised into what geologists know as "Siskiyou Island." The island extends from Red Bluff in California to Roseburg, Oregon in the north and the east-to-west expanse extends from inland Yreka to Eureka on the Pacific. The sea left strata of fossil-bearing sediments. Gold bearing strata were exposed by river erosion and glacial action. The freed gold became concentrated in the river beds and bars of the Siskiyou. The deposition of these riches in the chaos of rugged Siskiyou canyons was accompanied with the growth of lush conifer forest.

The eastern "shore" of Siskiyou Island is an ancient seacoast that forms the boundary between the young formation of the Siskiyou and the old formation of the volcanic Cascades. Sea creature fossils are found along this ancient shore that runs along the Shasta River Valley. Fossilized Mastodon bones were

227

unearthed near Hilt and elephant fossils found just west of Gazelle both in this sandy formation. Little gold was to be found in the old volcanic formations.² The entire Siskiyou was rich in gold. The Oregon gold rush of 1852 was into present day Jackson and Josephine Counties in Oregon and adjacent Siskiyou County of California.

The Siskiyou Trail, as established by the French-Canadian trappers of the Hudson Bay Company, extended from Doctor McLoughlin's headquarters, located at Fort Vancouver where the Willamette joins the Columbia River, to the rendezvous of his *bourgeois,* Michael La Framboise, with his *engagés* in their camp at the river delta of California's great central valley.³ In the years 1826-7, the Hudson Bay's Peter Skene Ogden hunted beaver in the Rogue River Valley and crossed the mountains to the Klamath "Buenaventura" which he explored for beaver. In 1827, using an Indian guide to find the best path over the mountains, Ogden returned to the Klamath and made his way along its Shasta River tributary down past Mount Shasta to the Pit River which he explored and trapped. He named the Indians and their river for the deadly "pitfalls" which they dug to trap large game. Ogden's men, mounted on their horses, fell into these artfully concealed traps more than once.

Had Ogden opted to follow this "Buenaventura" south, he would have been on the Sacramento River, since the Pit River is actually the main fork of the upper Sacramento. Ogden returned to Ft. Vancouver in August of 1827 with some two thousand beaver pelts. He had traveled from the Willamette into Northern California — past Mt. Shasta to the upper reaches of the Sacramento River.

While Ogden was trapping and exploring the Rogue, the Klamath and the Pit, Jedediah Smith had traversed the Great Basin into Southern California and was trapping beaver in the "tulares" or bull rush swamps of the central valley and exploring the river system of the Sierra seeking the "Buenaventura" — the name he finally applied to the Sacramento. Smith shipped his furs by Yankee trader square rigger and purchased a *remuda* then headed up the Sacramento Valley. His view of the snowy Shasta range led him to take what appeared to be an easier course to Oregon — a disastrous decision. He missed Ogden's newly blazed trail.[4]

Jedediah followed the Trinity River to the Pacific hoping to follow the surf into Oregon. This not being feasible, he led his band of trappers overland to the Pistol river and continued to the Rogue where they built rafts to cross. They camped at Coos Bay and then proceeded north to Winchester Bay at the mouth of the Umpqua River. Smith left his party camped there while he and two of his men went on reconnaissance. When they returned, they found the main party massacred by the Kelawaset Indians who also attacked them. They escaped and made their way to the Willamette and thence to Ft. Vancouver. The White-headed Eagle, Doctor John McLoughlin, already knew of their plight for one survivor of the massacre, Arthur Black, had preceded them in wounded and desperate condition.

The ever hospitable and compassionate Doctor McLoughlin had an opportunity to feather his own nest. He agreed to purchase the pelts Jedediah's men had gained as they trapped their way from California and to deal with the Indians for the purpose of recovering the pelts, equipment and stock that were lost in the Umpqua massacre. The dividend received was Smith's reconnaissance and maps of the California beaver country. Through no small effort, over several months, the furs, horses and equipment were recovered even down to paper and pencils and the precious journals, notebooks and maps. By the time Jedediah was on his way back to Green River, McLoughlin had launched a California beaver trapping expedition greater than his Snake River Operation. Thus, the Siskiyou pack train trail was established. Jedediah Smith's South West Expedition had been wiped out. The Mojaves had killed ten of his men, fifteen more had been murdered on the Umpqua and two had deserted in California. Jedediah's incidental reconnaissance of the Willamette Valley received the attention of the US Congress.

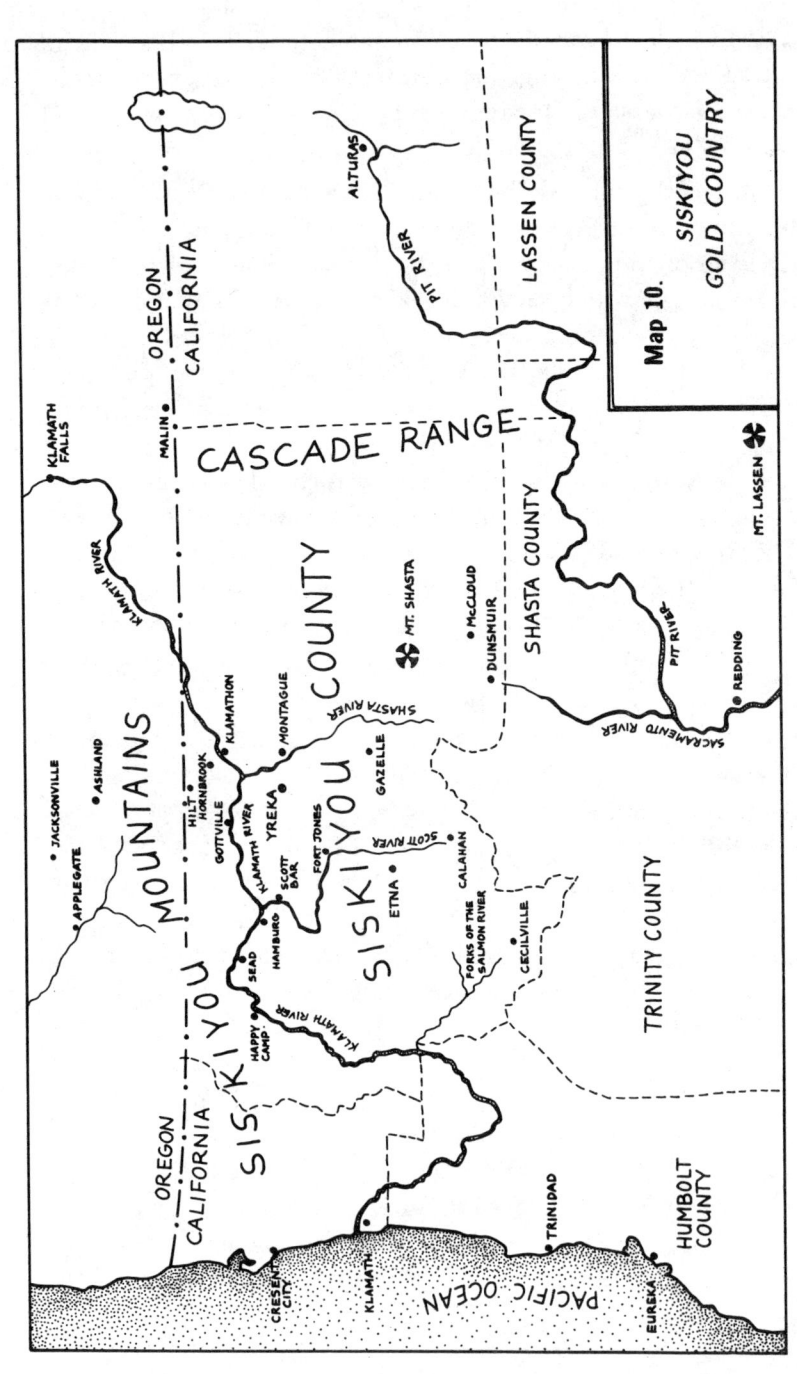

The French-Canadian trappers found Ewing Young and his company, including George Yount, and a number of other American trappers busy in the San Joaquin Valley.[5] Ewing Young went up the Siskiyou trail to settle in the Willamette Valley. He had an altercation with McLoughlin when the Mexican governor complained to McLoughlin that he was a horse thief. McLoughlin had a breeder herd of cattle brought in by ship. He was parsimonious with his breeding stock and there was hardly any beef to be slaughtered, so the meat available in Oregon was mostly game. This led to the practice of the emigrants driving loose cattle in their trains from Missouri and a cattle drive up the trail from California. By the time the 1830s drew to a close, Michael La Framboise was recognized as "Captain of the California Trail."

In 1841, the US Exploring Expedition mapped the trail from Oregon to California. In September of 1841, the Emmons pack train traveled the trail to Sutter's Fort. In the train was the Joel Walker family. Walker had with him his wife, his sister and his three boys and two girls. They were the first family to come across the plains to California — albeit via Oregon.

The Hudson Bay operations petered out around 1845 and grass started to grow on the moccasin pounded trail over the "Siskiyou" — the name given it by the *engagés* packing over it. In 1845, James Marshall followed the trail from Oregon to Sutter's "New Helvetia." Marshall discovered gold in Sutter's mill race. It was not until 1848 that the traffic on the trail picked up again.[6] Foremost among California's Argonauts were men from Oregon's Willamette Valley.

The prospectors of the forty-nine gold rush fanned out over California looking for pristine deposits of the maddening gold metal. The first strike in the Siskiyou was at Scott Bar on the Scott River tributary of the Klamath in November of 1850. Miners came from everywhere. They came in from Nevada on the Applegate trail.[7] They came down from Oregon and up from the Sacramento Valley. They disembarked at Trinidad beach and packed in from the coast. A group coming down into the Siskiyou from the Willamette Valley was caught in a three day rain storm which they weathered at a campground at Ieka Creek. Abraham Thompson was on watch that day with the stock set to graze on the flat above the camp. The serpentine formation there was thinly covered with the soggy soil which the critters pulled up in clumps, spitting dirt and grass. Thompson noticed glimmering pieces of yellow in the mud dribbling off the bottom of the rain soaked clumps as the animals fed. Thompson got his gold pan and started panning the soil. The men all staked out Ieka Creek claims. A town of tents and brush shanties soon sprang up.

Ieka, the center of the Klamath River strike of March 1851, was soon the base of supplies for the prospectors digging for gold all over Northern California. It wasn't long until the Ieka strike settled down to a dull roar and the adventurous started prospecting over the mountains in Rogue River country. Gold was found along the Applegate River tributary to the Rogue and soon the town of Jacksonville was booming. Confusion arose as to the exact location of the Oregon-California border. It was even rumored that Ieka was in Oregon. The miners conveniently neglected to pay taxes in either state and, being zealous as citizens, voted in both states. After several contested California elections, T.P. Robinson was commissioned, in 1854, to settle the issue with a survey of the boundary.[8]

Martha Hill and her sister Mary, living with their parents Elizabeth and Isaac Hill at Ashland in the Rogue River Valley, traveled to Yreka in 1854. Martha recalled:

> Our Aunt Kelly wrote inviting us to Yreka to spend the Fourth of July, so three of our friends came for us and we started for Yreka early on the morning of the third. It took some time to travel the distance, a good sixty miles. Part of the way was over the Siskiyou mountains, but when the road was level we ran our horses, for all were good riders and enjoyed the sport. About two miles from Yreka, my friend said he thought we had better stop by a little stream and refresh ourselves. So we

girls took off our little bonnets, washed our faces, then
started on, and in a short time I saw a man coming
toward us on horseback. When he saw us, he turned
his horse around and went dashing back. I asked my
friend if he thought the man took us for Indians, but he
only grinned in a rather a sheepish manner, and we soon
found the cause. Coming toward us was a hayrack filled
with men who, when they joined us, headed their horses
back for Yreka. To our utter amazement, the men on the
hayrack formed a brass band from town, which escorted
us through Miner Street and up to our aunt's home. As
we passed along, the way was lined with red and blue
shirted miners, and thus we began the celebration.

We danced until four o'clock in the morning and even
then did not feel like stopping. ... They had two fiddlers
and a drummer ... Sometimes they played in tune and
sometimes not, but we did not seem to mind and went
laughing through the quadrille. [9]

The prevailing style of dress for the miners was red flannel
shirts, trousers stuffed in the top of heavy boots, wide brimmed
slouch felt hats, and everyone wore long whiskers as it was too
much trouble to bother with shaving.

Martha's father, Isaac, had made his fortune digging out
gold at Humbug Creek on the Klamath and left the Kellys
there when he returned east with a pack mule laden with gold.
He had the gold made into coin at the mint at St. Louis and
used the money to finance moving his family from Tennessee
to the Rogue River Valley.

In 1857, six years after Abraham Thompson's mules discovered gold there, Ieka's 5000 citizens incorporated as the town
of Yreka.[10] They soon had the streets of Yreka illuminated by
gas lights and received electric power from the nearby Shasta
River, also a tributary of the Klamath. By now the wagon road
following the Sacramento River extended from Redding in the
timbered foothills, up a rugged two-thousand foot mountain
climb past Mount Shasta and into the Shasta Valley, ending at
Yreka. This wagon road was soon traveled by stage coaches.

Commerce at Yreka would one day yield to the lumber industry and farming, but in its early days, mining was so dominant that the purchasing exchange was gold dust. Alex Rosborough recalled:

> Buying of things from the stores was paid for with mined gold, and a little set of gold scales at the end of the counter was a necessity, even in the days when I was a boy in Yreka. The use of silver, which was gradually increasing with time was mostly confined to "four" or "two bits" ...
>
> Labor of all kinds found its remuneration in gold dust. Tom Orr owned a placer claim just west of the Gold Discovery Monument now near the west boundary of Yreka City on the sloping flats, and every day, at closing time, he paid each man working for him in his mine one ounce of gold. When the trappers and Indians came to bargain with a storekeeper for sale of bear, beaver, otter, mink or other fur skins, a price was agreed on and then payment for them was made in mined gold. Years afterwards, in 1898, when I went to Alaska as a "sourdough," the same use for gold as money was in vogue.[11]

James and Annette Freshour with their children, seventeen-year-old John, fifteen-year-old Joe and ten-year-old Alice traveled down into the central valley from Jenny Lind and made their way north past Sacramento and continued up the Sacramento Valley past Mount Lassen and its towering alter ego, Mount Shasta, and climbed into the lovely sylvan heights of the Siskiyou. It was wagons again. — A three-hundred mile journey following the Oregon-California stage road. They arrived in the mining metropolis of Yreka in 1872. James [12] was forty-six and Frances Annette [13] was thirty-six years of age. Apparently their eldest son, Marion, had some involvement at Jenny Lind that kept him there when his parents went north.

The first claims filed were in 1852, the year following the big strike at Ieka. A rip roaring gold rush in the Siskiyou region surrounding the Klamath River engendered small mining settlements given whimsical names or named for the miner that got there first. The boom days soon passed when many of the miners rushed to the Frasier River strike in British Columbia in 1858. The Freshours moved in 1875 from Yreka to Honolulu, on the Klamath downriver from Humbug, a few miles northwest of Yreka. Honolulu was in the midst of the Klamath River Placer and granite mines. The big mine at Honolulu and principal employer was the Centennial Placer Mine operated by William Gott. There is a Kanaka Bar a ways upstream and the nearby schoolhouse is identified as Honolulu School, so there must have been quite a Kanaka settlement there.[14] The first miners at Honolulu may have been Hawaiian Portuguese. That there was a large Portuguese settlement in Siskiyou County is shown by the list of uncollected Portuguese letters regularly published in the *Siskiyou News*. Barton lists the "Kanaka P.M. [Placer Mine] — Freshour's ranch, Virginia Bar," among the Klamath River Mines.[15]

Marion was registered as a voter in Jenny Lind in 1875 at age twenty-two. He joined his parents at Honolulu in 1877, worked there in the Centennial Placer Mine for two years, then started working as "the Honolulu express man."[16] In March of 1881, Marion and his brother Joe (Joseph Frank Freshour) started operating the stage line between Yreka and Gottville, Virginia Bar mining district and Lower Humbug. They also ran pack trains to the mines.[17] In November of 1882, Joe married Sarah O. Waggoner and the couple settled at Honolulu.

There was a marriage of a John Freshour to a Mary J. Wright by a JP in Jackson County, Oregon, just to the north, in 1878. Nineteen-year-old Mary Freshour with one-year-old baby William lived at Jacksonville in 1880. Alice Freshour married Jesse W. Hubbard of Oak Bar.

The year 1886 was an eventful one for the Freshours of Honolulu on the Klamath. In January of that year, the bond of James R. Freshour was accepted by the Siskiyou Board of Supervisors and license granted to "keep a ferry across the Klamath River."[18] Joe Freshour appeared in the list of Trial Jurors. The hard winters of the Siskiyou made mining difficult.

> Mr. Marion Freshour, the Honolulu expressman, is now using his stage teams in hauling lumber to the Klamath, as the express business and passenger travel will be very light until work is resumed at river mining in the spring.[19]

There was a regular *Quartz and Placer Mining* column in the *Siskiyou News* during the 1880s. the mining operations at "Freshour's bar" were frequently mentioned.

> ...At Freshour's bar, just below Humbug Creek, on the Klamath, the Chinese are busy putting in new wheels to replace those washed away last winter. ...[20]

Joe felt the pangs of grief in August of that year. Joe's wife, Sarah, not yet twenty, succumbed to typhoid fever in 1886 leaving Joe a single parent to three little children, Walter, Robert D. and one year old Mae. On Sunday, August the 8th, Mr. and Mrs. William Gott and the other residents of Honolulu were in Yreka for the funeral. Sarah's sister, seventeen-year-old Margaret Waggoner, was engaged to marry Marion but this was not meant to be. — She followed Sarah in death within three weeks — also stricken with typhoid fever. She is buried in the Freshour family plot in the Evergreen Cemetery at Yreka. Marion did not soon marry. He remained single for the next fourteen years. The shared grief of the loss of the two young Waggoner sisters formed a bond between Joe and Marion. Three years later, in 1889, Joe married Bessie Finley. Joseph Freshour Jr. was born to them in 1891.[21]

The name "Honolulu" faded into history when the new post office, established there sometime after 1886, was named Gottville after the area's most illustrious citizen, William Gott.

James R. Freshour and his three sons filed some 34 mining claims in the years 1881 through 1906.[22] Only one of these was filed for J.R. and it was in 1887. There was a robust mining industry going on in the area when the Freshours arrived. By the time they arrived, the "easy pickins" on the surface were depleted and the claims filed were classified as either Placer or Quartz. The claims were developed to a point where their potential was demonstrable and then sold to a corporation having the capital required to bring them into production. The Freshours kept a hand in the gold prospecting game even though gainfully employed in other endeavors. The locations of their claims were predominantly at Virginia Bar with three at "Klamath River" and occasional mention of Humbug, Deadwood, Beaver Creek, Oak Bar and Gottville. The *Siskiyou County Mines* column in the *Siskiyou News* reported in 1898 on Marion's development of his porphyry and quartz vein on Empire creek.[23] Joe had a quartz ledge named the New Era mine at Virginia Bar. Joe and Marion frequently filed joint claims, the most notable one being their quartz prospect near Virginia Bar.[24] There were four claims for John W. Freshour from 1887 to 1898.

The *Siskiyou News* reported in 1906 that more than three million dollars had been taken from the river mines at "Honolulu diggins."[25] Between 1905 and 1909, James R.'s grandsons Walter and Robert "Bob" and Joseph Jr. filed claims. In 1911, Joe Freshour [Jr.] filed a claim in Jackson County Oregon near the border in the Elliott's Creek Mining District.

Joe and Marion were close and shared in mining claims, a fifty acre farm at Empire Bar and the operation of their stage line in which business they were partners for twenty-five years. In all this time there was never a harsh word between the brothers and "never the scratch of a pen, as they kept no books." [26] Marion had no family of his own but was a father to his nieces and nephews. He was well known throughout the county for his generosity to the poor and his financial help to miners down on their luck. Marion's biography appeared in the *Siskiyou News* in May of 1898 in a section titled *Some Prominent Residents*.

The Siskiyou county line extends for one-hundred-fifteen miles along the Oregon border. The county has an area of six thousand square miles — the combined areas of the states of Connecticut and Rhode Island. There are a few productive farm valleys, but five-thousand square miles are mountainous timber region. The Sheriff of Siskiyou County was responsible to maintain law and order in this large sprawling terrain and all the mining communities within it. This formidable task made the Sheriff the most important official in Siskiyou County in 1898. Marion Freshour, proprietor of the Honolulu stage line, threw his hat in the ring in June of 1898 as Democratic candidate for Sheriff.[27]

In September of that year, the slate of candidates selected by the Democratic convention was printed on the front page of the pro Democrat *Siskiyou News*. Heading the slate was: For Sheriff — MARION FRESHOUR — of Klamath River. The *News* printed several articles boosting his campaign. Marion was elected sheriff of Siskiyou County in November of 1898.[28] He had many friends, Republicans as well as Democrats, so he won handily. In a year when Republicans swept the California and national election, Siskiyou with its strong Democratic slate went solidly Democratic chortled the *News*. Marion made an excellent officer and spared no pains or expense in capturing criminals. He pursued one man all the way to Austin, Texas and brought him back for trial.[29]

The great Siskiyou jail break of November, 1899 provided a front page feature story for *The Siskiyou News*. The droll episode involved all three Freshour brothers. It happened on this wise. Sheriff Freshour's two boarders were a man named Brown who was a halfbreed Indian and was probably jailed for that offense and a slippery character named Rivera who had escaped from the Klamath County jail where he had been incarcerated for burglary. He had been recaptured in Siskiyou County. The two were let out of their iron cages at mealtime and Friday evening at suppertime they dug a hole in the wall above the cages and were gone when Sheriff Freshour came to lock them in at six p.m. The Sheriff dispatched deputies to places to which the fugitives were likely to go while he himself went to Hornbrook.

John McCarton was sent down to Honolulu where he arrived at 1.30 a.m. Saturday morning. In company with Joe Freshour of Honolulu, McCarton went up the Klamath to watch the footbridge at the mouth of Dutch Creek. Here they found fresh tracks leading across the bridge, surmising that they were the tracks of the fugitives they followed a short way from the mouth of Dutch Creek where they suddenly came upon the men wanted but before the officers could get near enough to get the drop on them the fugitives made their escape into the brush, Freshour taking a shot at one of them but doing no damage. As it was not yet daylight and the brush being so thick the officers were unable to follow.

They spent the rest of the day tracking the fugitives who split up. By the end of the day they had the Indian holed up in John Ladd's cabin. He was told to "elevate" and was tied up and taken to Honolulu by McCarton who took him to Yreka Sunday.

In the meantime Al Lash, the Honolulu stage driver, [who] had been making inquiries along the road learned from a Portuguese that Rivera had taken dinner with him Saturday. Lash lost no time disposing of the mail, and his team started back up the river in company with John Freshour. They had proceeded but a short distance when they spied the Mexican across the river, who was all but played out from his long tramp and exposure, consequently no difficulty was experienced in taking him.

The officers took their man to Henley and returned him to Yreka Sunday. They ended up with three prisoners. The young men deputized by Marion at Hornbrook had caught a burglar robbing a store there Saturday night. The man was arrested and brought to Yreka and jailed. He was also wanted in Oregon for robbing a railroad office. It was a busy weekend for the Sheriff and all his deputies. The *News* indignantly pointed out the dire need for a new jail of the caliber capable of holding the type of desperados with which Sheriff Freshour had to deal.

A Year later, the *News* reported the completion of "one of the best jails in the State." [30]

The twentieth century was ushered into the Siskiyou by an epic snowstorm. On Wednesday the 2nd of January, the *Siskiyou News* reported 40 inches of snow. The following days, Yreka and surrounding countryside had five to seven feet of snow and in the mountains as much as twelve feet was reported. The telephone, telegraph and electric power went out. Eight engines were required to get a train from Ashland to Hornbrook. By Saturday, delayed passenger trains were fully able to get through from Dunsmuir to Ashland. Newspapers were brought in from Montague on snowshoes and sold in Yreka for the outrageous price of ten cents. All wagon travel was stopped. Meat was brought in on horseback for the butcher shop. Every able bodied man was put to work shoveling snow off of walks and overloaded roofs. Gold rush relics such as the Last Chance Saloon on the Humbug Trail collapsed under the snow.

On Wednesday the 3rd of January, John Freshour, Edward Eastlick and Harry Hart Smith started out at 11 a.m. for Yreka from Humbug. When they started, they were in only three to four feet of snow and expected to make it to Yreka by 6 p.m. It kept on snowing and they got into snow six to ten feet deep. They struggled on all night finally getting in sight of Lemos ranch about 9 a.m. During the twenty-three hour ordeal, young Smith had given out and they couldn't get him to keep on and decided to send help back. Marion led a rescue party but they had to give up and got back to Yreka at 10 p.m. The next morning they started out again and lost one horse to the elements but kept going and got to Smith by noon. They had to carry the body a half mile to the horses and got back to Yreka at 3 p.m. Smith had been sent by his father from their mine to help his mother staying at Yreka, not wanting her to endure the storm alone. It had snowed continuously the entire time. The rescuing party had placed their lives at risk. The losses of the great storm included Mrs. Smith's son.[31]

On more than one occasion, labor conflicts at the larger mines led to riots. An article headed RIOT AND BLOOD SHED describes how Sheriff Freshour and his deputy broke up a riot by taking the leader at gunpoint. The man who was brought to Yreka broke free and "attacked Chas. Chochran in the blacksmith shop and sustained severe injuries on his head having come in contact with a bar of iron." [32]

The sheriff was mentioned in connection with the murder of Wesley Dollarhide at Klamathon. In April, Marion "advised" two confidence men posing as detectives to return to Oregon. They went. In June, the sheriff picked up a prisoner in Alturas. Marion's name was frequently mentioned respecting real estate records involving his own mining properties and in his official capacity. Another item headlined A MURDEROUS ATTACK, reads "...Sheriff Freshour brought the prisoner to town today."

Smallpox broke out with a vengeance at Callahan fifty miles south of Yreka on the Scott River. The State Board of Health threatened to quarantine the entire county if it did not stop the outbreak. At a special session of the board of supervisors, "Sheriff Freshour swore in the following deputies who were sent to Callahan Saturday night and will remain there until the quarantine is raised ... [ten names.]" The town was restrained from transmitting the disease to the outside world.

Sheriffs from other counties would pursue fugitives into Siskiyou County since the remote mountainous regions were sparsely populated and seemed to be a likely place to evade the law. Marion spent several days in the Salmon River region helping the sheriff from Marin County track down a murderer. The headline read HUNTING FOR MURDERER KING. King was soon apprehended.

The century had ended. It was September of Anno Domini 1900. Marion was, at 46 years of age, popular, successful, of sound reputation, a loyal family man and as Sheriff was a very prominent citizen. Most of all, he was *eligible*. The inevitable happened.

The Siskiyou News chronicled:

PRISONER FOR LIFE

Sheriff Marion Freshour Makes an Important Capture

When Sheriff Freshour departed from Yreka Monday he said he had important business down the railroad. He had an air of mystery about him and from the happy look of expectancy he wore it was thought he had got track of some noted criminal and could see visions of a $1000 reward floating in the air.

Our Sheriff is a methodical sort of a fellow and never makes any fuss about what he intends doing; so his friends anxiously awaited developments.

It came Tuesday night. The message said: "Marion Freshour and Mrs. Mary Monroe of San Francisco were married Tuesday in this city." Mrs. Monroe is a former resident of Yreka and a sister of P.O. LeMay.

We extend congratulations to Sheriff Freshour and his estimable wife and hope their pathway in life may be strewn with roses and sunshine.[33]

In 1901 the sheriff conducted business as usual:
"...Sigmund Wetzel ...was arrested early Tuesday morning by Sheriff Freshour. When the Sheriff appeared Wetzel came to the door of his cabin with a Winchester rifle, but the officer took the weapon away from him and brought the man to jail." Wetzel was taken before a "commission of lunacy" and committed to the Napa asylum.

The Chinese population had crime problems. Sheriff Freshour sent out notices when a Chinese killed "an aged Chinaman" with a cleaver at Happy Camp. The sheriff went up to Grants Pass and secured the prisoner apprehended there.[34]

In an article titled CHINESE HIGHBINDERS we are given the following story:

> For the past week Sheriff Freshour has had, in the female quarters at the jail, a Chinese woman. ...she was very much frightened and her appeals for protection were earnest and pitiful. ...Chinatown has been in a fermented condition for some time, and the law abiding, well meaning inhabitants of that portion of our town have been terrorized by the presence of four or five genuine highbinders, who's business it is to levy tribute from the industrious and well disposed Chinamen. They think nothing of taking life and will kill anyone without compunction, for gain or revenge. There are two or three loyal and faithful Chinamen, who keep Sheriff Freshour informed, of the presence of suspicious characters here. A known convict was recognized by the sheriff the other day in Chinatown ... War may break out there any time, and there may be work for the Coroner ...[35]

May Freshour was graduated from the 8th grade at Honolulu in June of 1901 and in August the Joe Freshour family vacationed at Sisson where they took in the Log Rolling.[36] Joe had a problem in November. His ferry was swamped.

> The sinking of the ferry boat on the Klamath River last week did not prevent Joe Freshour from making his trip, he swam across and arrived here all right. The boat was raised and is serviceable again.[37]

In January of 1902 there was an article headed "Bloody Affair at Henly." There was a barroom fight between gamblers over a woman. "Sheriff Freshour departed at once and visited the scene and Rhodes was brought to Yreka ... " In July, two men who were drinking and fooling around made off with a horse and buggy in jest. The owner didn't think it was funny and shot them. Sheriff Freshour made the arrest.[38]

A.D. 1902 was an election year and L.F. Miles of Montegue was announced in March as Democratic candidate for sheriff in the primaries. Marion's ad announcing his candidacy for sheriff appeared on July 31st with those of the other Democratic candidates. The August 28th *Siskiyou News* had a front page spread on the Democratic County Convention.

> In a rousing speech which reviewed the efficient services, the well deserved popularity and the numerous good qualities of the present incumbent, E.H. Autenrieth, of Sisson, placed the name of Marion Freshour before the convention. It was greeted with prolonged applause, and, on motion, the secretary was instructed to cast the ballot for Marion Freshour as the nominee for the convention.

The second page listed the DEMOCRATIC TICKET with Marion Freshour heading it. Under "A STRONG TICKET" an extensive editorial gave the endorsement of the Democratic *News* to all the candidates. Their enthusiastic endorsement concluded "All who have had dealings with Marion Freshour, either in his official or individual capacity, have always found him honest, obliging and just and his popularity throughout the county is due largely to his pleasant and affable manner."

The campaigning was heavy in September and October. A September advertisement proclaimed "For Sheriff, Marion Freshour of Klamath, Regular Democratic Nominee." Euphoric endorsements appeared regularly in the *News*. An example:

> The brave man is always generous. The generosity of Marion Freshour is proverbial. There are many who can testify to his deeds of kindness. No worthy man ever called upon him for aid in vain, but he is a terror to the evil doer or law breaker. Quiet, unassuming and ever courteous, yet prompt, fearless and determined in the execution of his duties, Marion Freshour has made a model officer and the people will show their approval by re-electing him to the office of Sheriff.[39]

A front page item stated that the Hon. Thos. S. Ford had addressed a Democratic rally at Fort Jones. In the course of a rousing speech, Ford invoked applause by citing the performance of various incumbents. The mention of Marion Freshour produced a large ovation. The *News* commented "Coming as it did from the neighborhood of the enemy's country, it was particularly gratifying ..." On October 23rd it was reported that Marion's supporters were "indignant at the questionable methods being employed to injure him ..."

Republican candidate Charles B. Howard of Quartz Valley, just east of Fort Jones, ran a tough, no-holds-barred campaign. The contestants for sheriff were in a dead heat on election day. The November 6th issue of the *News* had the headline:

Sweeping Democratic Victory
ENTIRE COUNTY TICKET ELECTED EXCEPT SHERIFF.

The initial tabulation given showed Howard winning by about 100 votes out of some 3700 votes. The final tabulation was published on November the 13th. Howard won by only 62 votes. Less than one percent of the voters had decided the election. Controversy ensued about the integrity of the election. A recall was demanded by Marion's supporters. The lawsuit went to the California Supreme Court — all to no avail.[40] Meanwhile, Marion had quietly returned to his Gottville-to-Yreka stage line business and his mining prospects.

Prominent among the advertisements appearing in a column on the front page of the *The Siskiyou News* was that of the Yreka & Gottville Stage Line — Marion Freshour, Proprietor. Near it ran the notice for the YREKA BAKERY of pastry and palindrome fame. Marion was elected marshal of Yreka in the spring of 1906 but lapsed into "quick consumption" (pulmonary tuberculosis) and passed away shortly after taking office. People came from all over the county to pay tribute to this tough peace officer who had been their kind and generous friend.

Most of a century has passed and people in the Siskiyou are still talking about Siskiyou Sheriff Marion Freshour and his fabulous memory. This item appeared in the *Pioneer Press*.

MARION FRESHOUR

Memory sheriff

Marion Freshour of Gottville parlayed a photographic memory into a term as Siskiyou County Sheriff in the late 1890s.

Freshour drove a "mud wagon" or a small stage driven by two horses. Freshour's trip went from Yreka to Frogtown (Hawkinsville) over the pass to Humbug Creek, hitting the towns of Gottville, Beaver Creek, Oak Bar and Horse Creek.

Much of the road was so narrow along the Klamath River "that the waters of the river lapped at the wheels on the one side, while the cliff scraped the other side."

The popular Freshour often would take "pokes" from miners to the bank in Yreka, and without notation could tell who the gold was from, how much it weighed and where the diggin's are located.

In addition, miners would often give orders for merchandise, which he was able to rattle off from memory.

In 1898, incensed by an incident in which his brother was robbed, Freshour ran for county sheriff and was easily elected.[41]

Chester Barton admired this piece and commented that his dad had told him about this wonderful memory that Marion had. Chester, a mud wagon mail carrier himself, with passenger and freight service early in this century, recalled that they had to do the shopping for men, women and children. When they got to Yreka their work just started, putting in all the orders, then getting them loaded the next morning for delivery. Chester said that the difference between Marion and the rest of the carriers was that they had to use notebooks and even then usually forgot something.

Yreka & Gottville Stage Line

First-class Accommodations for Passengers.

Stages Leave Yreka at 7 a. m. on Mondays, Wednesdays and Fridays returning Tuesdays, Thursdays and Saturdays.

Particular attention paid to parcels or packages left in our care.

Marion Freshour, Propr.

Figure 13.1   Stage line Ad.

— Courtesy of Siskiyou County Museum

Figure 13.2: Marion and Mary V. Freshour.

He recalled this in 1981 with the usual clarity of hindsight, saying he forgot most everything except happenings of fifty years past. Using his power of recall, Chester corrected some anachronisms in the piece. His friend Jesse DeAvila started school as a six-year-old in 1906 — crossing the Klamath in a cage on a cable and walking up a trail to school. His father Antonio DeAvila started building the road down by Vesa Creek in 1906 with a contract at $1000 a mile. He built the road on the south side of the river through to Little Humbug Creek where it tied into the road from Yreka to Oak Bar. So, Marion couldn't have driven below Gottville.[42]

The small concord coach making the run along the river from Gottville to Humbug on its way to Yreka had a difficult course. Sometimes the exuberant miners would bury the roadway with mine tailings or, worse yet, dig an excavation through it. The driver would simply detour off road over rocks and through muddy holes giving the stage the name "mud wagon." In winter the roadway would ice over and a horse could slip and snap a leg in a frozen hole in the road. The driver would shoot the suffering animal and make his way as best he could to the next stop where he could secure another horse.

Chester drove his mud wagon run from Hamburg to Yreka on this road following the Klamath. He crossed the Klamath on DeAvila's cable bridge and changed horses at Joe Freshours. There he had dinner with Joe and his wife Bessie before rolling out to finish his run to Yreka. (This was before we succumbed to fancy eastern jargon. "Dinner" was at noontime and "supper" was at day's end.) Walter Freshour had the ferry there on the Klamath at that time. The stages traveled from Yreka three times a week — Monday, Wednesday and Friday — and returned on Tuesday, Thursday and Saturday.

In June of 1907, the year following Marion's death, his brother John was accidentally killed at fifty-one years of age by a railroad train at Stockton.[43] The body was removed to Yreka. John seems to have been, if not the black sheep, a loner. Of the four claims registered to him, the first was filed the same day, October the first, 1887, as his father's only registered claim — both Placers at Virginia Bar near Gottville. He filed two claims at Humbug, one Placer in 1894, one Quartz in 1897. His last claim was Quartz at Virginia Bar in December of 1898. He is not noticed in Marion's rather effusive obituary. He may have left the area by 1902. His brother Joe acted as head of family and made funeral arrangements. — A Methodist funeral and interment at Evergreen Cemetery at Yreka. His father, James R. Freshour was eighty-one years old at this time.

> John William Freshour ...
> ... was a resident of Siskiyou County for many years. He was born in Jackson County, Missouri and came to Oregon with his parents when a child and in 1857 went with the family to Calaveras County, this state. The

greater part of his life however was spent in this county.

He was the brother of the late Marion Freshour and Joseph Freshour who survives him.[44]

As usual with death certificates and obituaries, there is a strong component of dysinformation. His surviving father is not mentioned nor is there any mention of spouse or children. He appears to have been for the most part unmarried.

Gottville — now extinct — was located about 18 miles from Yreka, "Down River" on the Klamath. Ferry boats were a common sight on the Klamath in the Siskiyou region prior to 1914 when the first bridge was constructed. Pearl Freshour of Yreka had nostalgic memories of those ferry boat days.

> ... "Down River" was her home for many years, from 1907 on, to be exact, when she hired out to help at the ranch of her future father in law, Joe Freshour, one of the pioneers of the Klamath River ranching country. She was 15 years old at the time, Pearl Wallace, from Etna. She helped with the many chores that were required of the pioneer women, and girls learned young to do all that was required. She went to school there for a time and in July 1908 she married to [sic] Walter Freshour.
>
> As a wedding gift his father gave them the "Ferry Place" near Gottville. This was the location of one of several ferries that crossed the river ... Other ferries crossed the river at the Lucas place (near the present Hornbrook), Quigleys and Hamburg. Others were used further down.
>
> The main road from Yreka, the county seat, crossed over Humbug Mountain, down to the river and followed the stream on its south side. Since most of the ranching country was on the north side of the river, ferries were required to get to them. The young Freshour couple lived about 1½ miles from the post office of Gottville ... The fare on the ferry at Gottville was 25 cents per single person or a man on horseback, 50 cents for a two horse buggy and $1.00 for the stage or a four horse wagon.[45]

— Courtesy of the Siskiyou County Museum

Figure 13.3: The Freshour Ferry taken from the north bank of the Klamath River; Marion Freshour driving. (ca. 1896-7)

The ferries were constructed by the people living near the river and governed by them. The one near Gottville was considered the property of Joe Freshour. The person employed as ferry tender kept the fares collected as his wages.

> A bar had to be put across the ends of the ferry to guard the occupants of the ferry from slipping off when it lunged across the river, which was often rough. Once this was neglected and the two horse buggy, and the two young people occupying it slipped off into the river and the horses and people all drowned before they could be rescued. This happened before 1894. ... The bodies were not found until 3 weeks afterward.[46]

Walter's grandfather, James R. Freshour pursued farming

as well as mining at Gottville. He is listed in Oak Bar Township in 1900. His daughter, Alice Fogassi,[47] and grandchildren, John and Bertha, are in his household. Annette apparently deceased sometime after 1880. J.R. lived at Gottville for most of the thirty-three years before his death there in December of 1908. He was preceded in death by his wife, Annette, and two of their four children, Marion and John. He can be truly considered a California pioneer since he had arrived before the treaty of Guadelupe Hidalgo. He was living near Stockton with the Ganns in 1850. This is born out by his obituary.

> At his home in Gottville on December 15, James R. Freshour, a pioneer of Siskiyou county, died at the advanced age of 82 years, 8 months and 11 days. The funeral was held at the M.E. church in Yreka Wednesday afternoon and the interment made in Evergreen cemetery. ...
> ...In 1847 he crossed the plains by ox team to California, settling in the central part of the state. He was the friend of Marshal, Sutter and other historical characters of that early day. ...
> He was a miner and farmer all of his life, and lived as he died with the respect of all who knew him.[48]

Joseph Frank Freshour, the youngest son of Annette and James R., "born in a wagon just after they crossed the line into California" on November 4, 1857, passed away at Yreka in July of 1931. He was in his seventies and was considered "a Siskiyou pioneer, having made his home at Gottville for many years. He was well known as a rancher and cattleman and was interested in mining." [49] The Freshour name was well established in Siskiyou County by his three sons, Robert of Yreka and Joseph Jr. [50] and Walter of Gottville. Alice Hubbard, daughter of James R. and Annette, died in Oakland, Alameda County, in 1935. She is interred in Evergreen Cemetery at Yreka. The Freshour genes in many localities have been dominantly female and the name has died out. James R. Freshour of the Siskiyou produced robust male progeny. The name is still prominent in Siskiyou County and carries with it proud traditions.

14

TO THE ROGUE AND BACK

OREGON'S ROGUE is a river. The infamous whitewater Rogue is protected by the Wild and Scenic Rivers Act. The thirty-two miles, cutting through the coastal Siskiyous is one of the most remote river courses in the nation. Zane Grey, who had a cabin in this area, reflected "The happiest lot of any angler would be to live somewhere along the banks of the Rogue River ... " The river teems with chinook salmon and steelhead trout.[1] The Applegate River, a major tributary, flows northwest from the California border into the Rogue Valley.

Years ago, the Rogue River Valley belonged to the Rogue Indians. Gold was discovered in 1852 and miners thronged to the Valley of the Rogue in search of nuggets and were followed by farmers attracted by favorable climate and fertile soil. Small towns sprang up overnight with their ubiquitous grist mills and the forests of Douglas-fir and ponderosa pine inspired saw mills. Isaac Hill had been so impressed with the Rogue River Valley in 1850, when passing through on his way to prospect the Klamath River in California's Siskiyous, that he determined to head back to Tennessee to bring his family to settle in the Rogue. He did return to Tennessee in 1851, gold laden pack mule in tow, after successfully mining Humbug Creek. The Hill family traveled the Oregon Trail from Tennessee in 1852. Hill's daughter, Martha, then 19 years of age, later wrote an account of the journey and early settlement in the Rogue River Valley.[2]

The 1849 rush into California had depleted the original Oregon populace. Many of the 49ers were from Oregon. Congress fixed this problem by passing the Donation Land Act in 1850.[3]

The large tracts of Oregon land given to settlers at no cost caused a resurgence of Oregon Trail traffic. The immense immigration which crossed the plains in 1852 experienced great suffering and hundreds slept the sleep of death in that vast solitude. Doctor Anson Henry doctored people through the whole route to Oregon for Cholera Morbus, Bloody Flux and Mountain Fever — all very serious diseases which kept many convalescing through a crisis as they traveled. Many of the dead could have been saved with proper diet and care and the use of Dr. Henry's Cholera Pills.[4] After alkali dust, hardship, diseases and much toil, the Oregon bound survivors arrived at the Dalles of the Columbia in time for six weeks of incessant rain; Then, it commenced to snow through the entire winter. The settlers, waiting out the winter so they could find and settle a claim, wrote letters back east discouraging friends from coming. The grass was iced over with frozen snow and since winters were normally milder, no provision had been made to feed the stock through the winter. The only forage was the tips of hazel bushes. Hundreds of cattle and horses perished. Many late arriving emigrants were destitute. Snow was ten feet deep in the Calapooya Mountains, standing between the Willamette Valley and the Siskiyou Island, cutting off communication with the Rogue River mining districts.[5]

The following spring, one emigrant, in a letter from Oregon Territory, described his findings beyond the Calapooya Range.

> I have at last seen the Umpqua, and will attempt to describe it. The largest valley I saw in the Umpqua was four miles wide and six long. William Churchill lives in this valley. He has a good claim. The main Umpqua runs through this valley. There are many smaller valleys. It is a good grazing country and plenty of water in winter and dry in summer; timber very scarce, and poor — black oaks generally. The country does not suit me. I have also visited the Rogue river valley. It is the best country I have seen in Oregon. It is some 30 or 40 miles wide and 35 or 40 miles long, with many strips of timber

running through it; and the mountains are covered with fine timber, and generally are of easy access. The valley is only tolerably well watered. Though several fine streams run through it, springs are scarce. It produces splendid grass. The snow which commenced falling on the 12th of December, was generally in all the valleys. It lay on the ground until the 4th of January, during which time the weather was very cold. Many streams in the Willamette valley were frozen over, much stock was lost, and many persons frost bitten.

Since the snow has gone the nights are very cold. The mice have destroyed nearly all the wheat, and little seed is left in the country. The emigrants cannot get work. How they are to keep body and soul together, I know not. I pay ten dollars a week for my board. I am now down upon the country. It will never have as good society as there is in the States.

I was at Isaac Constant's, in the Rogue river valley, during the snow storm. He lost one cow. He has 18 cows and heifers, 15 yoke of cattle, 3 mules and one horse. The last emigration are generally dissatisfied with the country; and I would frankly advise my friends in Sangamon County to stay where they are. My advice is stay away! [6]

Dr. Henry patiently pointed out that one idyllic Oregon summer would dispel this gloom.

The sawmill town of Merlin had been left with a few scattered inhabitants and a large mountain of sawdust as its central feature when the Everett Freshour family moved there in 1938. The Freshours moved into the old remodeled church which they rented from the venerable Mr. Dukes. Pioneer octogenarian Dukes lived in the back apartment and presided over the back porch and its integral well with rope and bucket. This rustic Rogue River community is located on Jumpoff Joe Creek a few miles from where it flows into the Rogue. Old man Dukes was not only landlord but a living history book and avid story teller.

In the open field across the road stood a greenapple tree oddly surrounded by a whitewashed fence. The fence stood as a mute invitation to children to climb over and bring on themselves the dreaded green apple malady. A consultation with Mr. Dukes brought fourth the conclusion that the owner of the apple tree had jeopardized the general populace and that it was therefore proper that the Freshour denizens should strip the tree in order that Mrs. Minnie Freshour might make apple sauce and pie. "Ole' Duter" came from next door to help. (His folks wanted their boy to have a biblical name so they called him *Deuteronomy.*) This left the more ponderous question of why the owner was never apparent and why such a pedestrian tree was ornamented with its very own fence.

Old man Dukes waxed eloquent. "Pioneers was *massacreed* under that tree by *Injuns!*" The tree has since gone through several more cycles of self propagation and the white fence has likewise been perpetuated. In fact, this is virtually the only feature of the bucolic little berg that has survived the passage of half a century. Since the venerable Dukes can no longer proclaim the tree's purpose he has been replaced by a large sign with the narrative:

> Homestead where the Haines family were Massacred. Mr. Haines was found murdered and scalped. His young sons were killed with tomahawks. Mrs. Haines and a daughter were taken captive, later killed and their bodies thrown into the Rogue River near Hellsgate. Volunteer militia found this horrible scene duplicated many times in the Rogue River Valley on that tragic day October 9 1855.[7]

There had been skirmishes with the Rogues as early as 1851. A full scale Rogue Indian War occurred in 1853 as vividly chronicled by Martha Hill Gillette who experienced it as a young woman living with her parents on their donation claim in upper Bear Creek Valley — present day Ashland.[8] The Rogue Indians made their last stand near there on Table Rocks. The Rogue winds its way past the plateau formations of Upper and Lower Table Rocks serenely standing like islands overlooking the surrounding valley. Just beyond lies Sams Valley. Chief Sam of the Rogues signed a treaty with Governor Joe Lane here in 1853 temporarily ending hostilities in the Rogue River Valley. The gold seekers continued to come and find gold. Jacksonville boomed through 1854.

Minor skirmishes with the Rogues resumed culminating in the massacres memorialized by the apple tree. This final Rogue Indian War involved the Applegate Creek and Illinois River branches of the Rogue River nation inhabiting the lower Rogue River. The settlers fought against overwhelming odds suffering many atrocities and impoverishment from the continued strife but the Indians failed in their attempt to drive them out. Sufficient military force was brought to bear and the Indians that did not elect to die were sent to reservations. The last battle was fought at Oak Flat on the Illinois River just above its entry to the Rogue. The Rogue Indian Wars lasted over a five year period.[9]

In the early days of the Oregon gold rush, the rustic mining settlements had little supporting agriculture and depended on supplies shipped into the coast and carried inland by pack mule. Odd as it may seem to us, in the days of sailing vessels it was easier to get to the coast of the northwest via Hawaii. The ocean currents and prevailing winds along the Pacific coast are established by earth's rotation to be contrary to sailing northward up the coast. The Manila Galleons of New Spain had used this principle, usually traveling west on a tropical course and returning by a more northerly route to follow the Pacific coast southward. Thus, in the 1850s, many of the Oregon miner's supplies arrived from Hawaii. Coastal shipping was changed years later by the brute force of steam power.

It was inevitable that local wheat fields would remove the need to use flour shipped thousands of miles. Sams Valley became the bread basket of the Rogue Valley. Sams Valley supplied not only grains and produce for the miners but also provided dairy products and livestock. Early Sams Valley farmers were men who came on the Oregon Trail in 1853 to take up donation land claims. The town of Moonville was established by Alexander Moon, who arrived in Sams Valley in 1859, and Dr. Arad Stanley who arrived in 1875. A lithograph shows Sams Valley Hall occupied in 1884 by the A.C. Stanley Drug Store and A.S. Moon — General Merchandise. Moon's store also served as the post office. The establishment of the post office occasioned renaming Moonville "Sams Valley." Perry's blacksmith shop and W.H. Runnells' tin shop rounded out the thriving little village of the 1880s.[10]

Of the three Calaveras Freshour families, two appeared in the vicinity of Sams Valley in its boom years. The first record of California Freshours appearing in Rogue River country was the organization of the Chimney Rock precinct in April of 1878 with the voting place at M. Freshour's house.[11] Seventeen-year-old Mary J. Wright married John Freshour in Jackson County in June of 1878.[12] He was twenty three. She was Oregon born and from a pioneer family well represented in the Rogue Valley. Her father, Francis Wright, had traveled the Oregon Trail from Missouri as a young man. In August of 1878, just two months after John and Mary were married, the *Democrat Times* of Jacksonville reported that John Freshour, of the Chimney Rock precinct, was arrested at Butte Creek on a charge of stealing cattle in California. He was taken to the California border and turned over to the sheriff of Siskiyou County.[13] The *Yreka Union* also gave an account :

> ARRESTED FOR CATTLE STEALING. — A Deputy Sheriff of Tulare county, arrested near Jacksonville last week a young man named John Freshour on the charge of stealing cattle in that county about two years ago. While in Oregon the Deputy Sheriff also discovered that Freshour's brother Joseph, whom he also wanted on the same charge was living at Virginia Bar in this county, and he engaged the services of Deputy Sheriff John Hendricks and went over and arrested him last Sunday. The

arrests astonished our citizens considerably as both the Freshour boys are well known here and have always bore a good character. The eldest, John, is married and his wife lives in Oregon where he was arrested. It is reported they in company with another man stole cattle, and shipped them to Oakland and sold them. The other party being arrested turned state's evidence.[14]

When James and Annette Freshour left Calaveras County to travel to the Siskiyous, their teenage sons along with their eldest son, Marion, apparently decided to strike out on their own. Marion was in Calaveras County in 1875 and John and Joseph were far to the south in Tulare County in November of 1876. When the inveterate gold miner, James R. Freshour, decided to move to the Klamath River, where working small claims was still a regular activity, his sons may have stayed on in Calaveras County. They may have drifted down to Tulare County from there or they could have looked over the Siskiyous and decided to return to their old stomping grounds. In 1875, Marion was twenty two, John twenty and Joseph eighteen years of age. They were from the Calaveras cattle raising region and no doubt had skill as horsemen. Single young men on horseback could venture over a tremendous amount of territory simply because it was there. There was no war to fight and they were of the age to assert their independence. In any case, they found work chopping wood south of Visalia.

The Visalia newspaper frequently ran an advertisement for wood choppers. Railroads, including the *Atchison Topeka & Santa Fe* and the *Southern Pacific*, operated in Tulare County. The railroads had not yet switched to western bituminous coal. The fire boxes of the insatiable locomotives were fed with fire wood piled in the tender. Hundreds of men were employed cutting firewood. While so employed, the Freshours struck up an association with W.L. Randall — a native of Arkansas who had been reared at Visalia. He was about John's age. This casual acquaintance was one the Freshour brothers would regret for the rest of their lives.

On a January winter's day in 1877, John and Joe helped Randall drive a herd of cattle up to the railroad at Kingsburg — a days work. The freight agent there later reported dealing with a man named Hogan (an assumed name) regarding the sale of these cattle. He recommended a buyer in Oakland and telegraphed Tulare to the south to see if an empty cattle car was available for the next northbound train. None was. Hogan made arrangements for the agent to care for the cattle and ship them as soon as possible. When the cattle were received by the Oakland firm, they were evaluated and payment by the agent at Kingsburg duly authorized. Hogan returned to collect the check which was subsequently endorsed and presented at the Bank of Visalia. R.E. Hyde, the president of the bank, refused to cash the check unless it was cosigned by someone he personally knew whereupon Hogan fetched Randall and the transaction was completed. Hyde had known Randall since he was a boy.

Randall was arrested a short while later for stealing horses and a buggy at Visalia. He was promptly indicted, tried and sentenced to prison. While this was going on, an investigation of cattle thefts from two ranches in Tulare County had connected the cattle stolen to the cattle sold by Hogan. The firm in Oakland had recorded a description of each animal including brands and ear notches. Randall was incriminated by his cosignature on the check and was soon being interrogated at the county jail where he was being held during his trial for the theft of the buggy and horses. This led to indictments for theft from A.T. McGee of four steers and five young cows and for theft from J.T. Willis of fifteen steers. Indicted were W.L. Randall, John Doe and Joe Doe. Randall's memory improved with the suggestion of possible leniency in the impending prosecution. The indictments were hastily copied with the names John and Joe Doe changed to John Freshour and Joseph Freshour.[15] The indictments were recorded on March 9, 1877. W.L. Randall entered San Quentin Prison on March 26, 1877.[16] The ledger gives his occupation as *vaquero* — a flamboyant touch. He was sentenced to six years for stealing the horses and buggy. He was also under indictment for cattle theft which could add an additional sentence — possibly an additional ten years. That trial would have to await the capture of the Freshour brothers. They had disappeared.

Randall was destined to spend a year and a half in the daily San Quentin grind before he heard more about his ill fated cattle rustling enterprise. The sheriff of Tulare had no doubt put out a circular stating that John and Joseph Freshour were wanted in Tulare County. Sooner or later it came to light that a number of Freshours had been located in Calaveras County in the vicinity of Jenny Lind. The only Freshours at Jenny Lind by then were Martin Freshour and progeny. It was probably known there that the families of Thomas Freshour and James R. Freshour had headed north to the Klamath and the Rogue in the Siskiyou region. The Freshour boys were ultimately tracked down giving the *Tulare Weekly Times* cause to chortle:

> J.W. Freshour and J.F. Freshour were landed in jail this week under the charge of cattle stealing. Our efficient Sheriff J.H. Campbell "got wind" of the whereabouts of the supposed thieves some time ago, and sent deputy Sheriff Ellis after them, J.W.F. was captured in Jackson county Oregon, by the Sheriff of that county and turned over to Ellis. J.F.F was captured in Siskiyou county.[17]

Witnesses were subpoenaed. District Attorney Edwards took the train to Richmond and crossed the bay by ferry to San Quentin over in Marin County. His case against Randall and the Freshours would be difficult to prosecute without Randall's cooperation. It had been the better part of two years since the Freshours had spent their brief stay in Tulare County. Hardly anyone there knew them. The freight agent, the banker and others subpoenaed to witness at the trial had only seen John Freshour on the occasion of the cattle sale and check cashing if indeed they had ever seen him at all. The only positive connection of the Freshours with the cattle rustling was Randall's candor. Randall and the DA conferred under the watchful eye of the prison guard. Although the three men were named together on the indictments, it would be normal procedure to try them separately and since there were two indictments — one for theft for each of the two ranches — there were potentially six prosecutions. Randall's trials could be deferred according to the priorities of the DA. If the people of California were given a conviction for the crime, the deterrence that the harsh penalty afforded would suffice. The DA would go for a conviction of John Freshour with Randall as the key witness.

A jury was summoned. W.L. Randall was brought from San Quentin to Tulare County on September 30, 1878. A jury was selected from a venire of twenty citizens. The trials of John Freshour on the two cattle theft indictments were conducted by Judge John Clark through the month of October. J.E. Marshal, the freight agent, positively identified John Freshour as having been present during his dealings with Hogan but was uncertain whether or not John had used the name "Hogan" or had signed that name. The agent who issued the check could not definitely identify any of the parties involved. (It had been almost two years since this single brief episode had happened.) The banker, Hyde, couldn't swear that John Freshour had signed the name "Hogan" or that John Freshour was the man who had cashed the check. "Levi" Randall was called to the stand. Apparently Randall was known by many in the courtroom by his nickname which ended up in the trial transcript.

Randall denied paying the Freshours $10 to drive the cattle. He claimed that he had received only a one-third share of the proceeds. He "disremembered" whether it was he or John that negotiated the sale of the cattle. He claimed the cattle were taken from open range also "disremembering" taking down any fence and driving the cattle through. He refused to answer questions, no matter how couched, about exactly who planned and directed the cattle rustling — on the grounds that a response would "criminate" him. Judge Clark sustained this over the persistent objections of the defense. On cross-examination by the defense, Randall denied that he had bargained with the prosecution for any special treatment in exchange for his cooperation. The jury knew better. They knew that there would never be a prosecution of Randall under this indictment — and there never was. If there was ever to be a conviction for this crime it would have to be their finding in the case at hand. They solemnly returned to the courtroom and the foreman handed a slip of paper to the clerk. John Freshour was found guilty as charged. The trial on the second cattle theft indictment quickly ensued with Randall again refusing to "criminate" himself over the insistent objections of the defense. The verdict was:

"We the jury find the Defendant Guilty and recommend him to the extreme mercy of the Court.
H.C. Stanley, foreman."

Judge Clark sentenced John to eight years on the first charge and three years on the second — eleven years in all. The case of the People vs. Joseph Freshour was continued for the term. The venire was discharged and the trial of criminal cases adjourned for the term. Atwell and Bradley, the defense attorneys, drew up a thirty-two page bill of exceptions which was sent with their appeal to the Supreme Court of the State of California. They pointed out that Judge Clark's allowance of Randall's testimony only to facts that would not incriminate himself was "against law." The fees for the defense of the Freshour brothers were well beyond their means. The fifty-three dollars garnered from the illicit cattle sale was paltry compared to the expense of the resultant legal process. A gold miner from the Siskiyous might be able meet the expense. James Rufus Freshour rode up the Shasta Valley and out of the mountains into California's Great Valley. He traveled hundreds of miles down its length into the ranch land that was known for its tule marsh or Tulare. He saw to it that his boys were properly represented. He had hired the best law firm in Visalia.

Having obtained a conviction, the District Attorney was not inclined towards further prosecution on the indictments — at least not until the Supreme Court decision was known. Randall was sent on his way back to San Quentin in the custody of a deputy. He gave the deputy the slip. He was captured a few days later by the sheriff down in Kern County and "sent to San Quentin where he belongs." [18]

J.R. Freshour returned to the Klamath River with his son Joe. John was left in the Tulare County jail awaiting the appeal results. The news of his sentence appeared in the Yreka and Jacksonville papers.[19] Mary Wright Freshour remained near the Wrights at Jacksonville. She must have corresponded with John. Surely he knew the details of the birth of his son. The wheels of justice ground slowly at Sacramento. John was kept in the Tulare County jail until July of 1880 when he was taken to San Quentin.[20] But the wheels had ground exceedingly fine. A few days later John's case was reversed and remanded back to the Tulare County Court for retrial. Supreme Court Justice McKinstry, citing several precedents, declared the rulings of Judge John Clark to be a travesty. Justices Ross and McKee concurred.[21] The *Tulare Times* gave this cogent summary:

> John Freshour, who was sentenced by Economy Judge John Clark, now defunct, has been given a new trial, after two years in the county jail. It will be remembered that through the prejudice, stupidity or ignorance of Economy Judge John Clark he was kept at the expense of the county in jail. Atwell & Bradley, so confident of injustice on the part of that prejudicial Judge carried the case to the Supreme court, and will doubtless on the second trial clear the prisoner. It is a mighty good thing for the tax payers that John Clark is defunct. ... [22]

John was never booked at San Quentin. John's case came up in the Superior Court of Tulare County. Star witness, Levi Randall, would have to answer questions in compliance with the Supreme Court's opinion. Randall wasn't about to lengthen his prison term by another eleven years. He remained safely in San Quentin.²³ The District Attorney was left without a prosecutable case. He dropped all charges against the alleged cattle thieves. John Freshour was left sitting in the county jail in legal limbo. A petition for a Writ of Habeas Corpus was signed by John Freshour on August 30th of 1880. It was submitted to Judge C.H. Marks who wrote:

> ... said John Freshour is illegally imprisoned and restrained of his liberty ... It is ordered that said John Freshour be restored to his liberty and said Sheriff M.J. Wells is hereby directed to release said Freshour from his custody.²⁴

John was free. His reputation had been ruined and his life left a shambles. He had been taken from his bride to spend two years in jail. She had born his first child and lived alone — awaiting his return. The 1880 census showed J.R. Freshour with his son Joe living on the Klamath while Annette with son Marion was at Yreka. Mary J. Freshour and one-year-old William were living at Jacksonville Oregon. She was sick with chills and fever. John was in jail in Tulare County. In a matter of weeks — on the first of September, 1880 — John was free to return again to the Rogue River Valley. Free to return to his wife and to the child that he had never seen.

The next record of John is his October, 1887 mining claim at Virginia Bar on the Klamath where the Siskiyou County Freshours were settled. Acquaintances there knew him as an unmarried man. He remained there working claims until his brother, Sheriff Marion Freshour, was voted out of office in 1902. A nasty rumor was spread that the Freshour brothers had been cattle rustlers. This slur caused Marion to be edged out in a bitterly fought campaign. John seems to have left the Siskiyous then — perhaps feeling that he had once again cast a pall over the family name. He appeared at Stockton in early 1906 and found employment there until his untimely death in June of 1907. The *Stockton Record* tells us the story: ²⁵

JOHN FRESHOUR KILLED BY TRAIN THIS MORNING

Rancher's Team Became Unmanageable While on the West Lane Crossing of the S. P. and Swiftly Approaching Train Completed the Awful Tragedy

A team of horses balked on the Southern Pacific railroad grade at El Pinal, near West's winery, this morning and a bloody tragedy resulted. John Freshour, the driver, was killed and both horses were horribly mangled. The wagon was reduced to kindling wood.

Freshour was driving north on West's lane en route to the Calaveras river after a load of wood. His outfit consisted of a team of large beautiful bay horses and a heavy wagon with a hay rack on it. the railroad crossing is about four feet above the grade of the road and just as the horses reached the middle of the track, they balked.

All unmindfull of the early Lodi train which was approaching, Freshour remained in his seat and urged the horses on. It was then 7:12 o'clock and the train, being a few minutes late, the engineer was running more rapidly than usual.

Mr. Looper, who drives the sprinkling cart, was approaching on the north side of the and seeing the unfortunate man's peril, he cried loudly for him to jump. But Freshour did not heed the warning.

An instant later, the engine crashed into the team with terrific force. The two horses were hurled in opposite directions on the one side of the track, while the driver and the wagon were knocked different directions on the other side.

Freshour's body was not mangled, but he was hurled nearly fifty feet. He struck on his head and died three minutes later without regaining consciousness. The near horse was ground almost to a pulp and blood, flesh and bones were strewn along the track for over 100 feet. The off horse was also badly mangled.

The wagon was completely wrecked.

When the engineer saw that there was no hope of averting the accident he did not attempt to slow down, knowing that the train would be more apt to keep the track running at a high speed. The cow catcher of the engine was demolished but all wheels remained on the track. The train was quickly stopped. Deputy Coroner Oscar Pope was on the train, returning from a visit to Lodi, and he immediately took charge of the remains. The train was in charge of Conductor Whitney.

John Freshour came here over a year ago from Yreka, Siskiyou county, where his brother, Marian Freshour, was formerly a Sheriff. He was about 50 years of age. For nearly a year he was employed by Supervisor George French. Recently he was in the employ of G. M. Pock. The deceased formerly held an associate membership in the Woodsmen of the World, but his card ran out last December.

The horses which the dead man was driving were valued at $500.

Although firmly established in Siskiyou County, progeny of the J.R. Freshour family made one other sojourn into Jackson County, Oregon. On the 13th of October, 1911, Joe Freshower (Joseph Freshour Jr.,) a resident of Jackson County, Oregon, discovered in that county a Quartz Claim in the Elliotts Creek Mining District. It was the second Northerly Extension to the "Silver Night Queane." [26] In 1918, when his son, Don Freshour, was born, Joseph Freshour Jr. was living in Applegate Oregon. Joe's wife, Betty Head, was a native of Applegate. Joe later moved back to the Klamath River with his family.

In the 1880s, another Freshour family settled in Sams Valley. Thomas and Harriet Freshour and son James W. Freshour with his family left Calaveras County about the same time that the Siskiyou County Freshour brothers did in the late 1870s. The families had no doubt known one another while they were in Calaveras County. James W. Freshour and his wife Sarah Arabella left Calaveras County sometime after 1875. Eddie, Minnie and Lillie were born to them at Jenny Lind and two-year-old Minnie died there in December of 1876. Charlie,[27] Henry James, Willi and Addie were born to them somewhere in California — most likely in Sutter County or perhaps in Butte County.[28] Eddie died in April of 1883 at eleven years of age. They and their five surviving children, ages one through nine, arrived in the Rogue River Valley around 1885. Hattie was born in June of 1886 at Sams Valley and died four months later.[29]

The Oregon & California railroad construction started in the 1870s and progressed as far south as Roseburg where it halted for a ten year hiatus before surging south again in 1883. Construction extended south through Grants Pass and reached a point on the Rogue River near Sams Valley where the bridge crossing the Rogue was constructed. The construction of a station on the north end of the bridge led to the platting of the brand new town of Gold Hill there in January of 1884. This rail shipping point near Sams Valley was a stimulus to that farm community through the 1880s, but eventually the

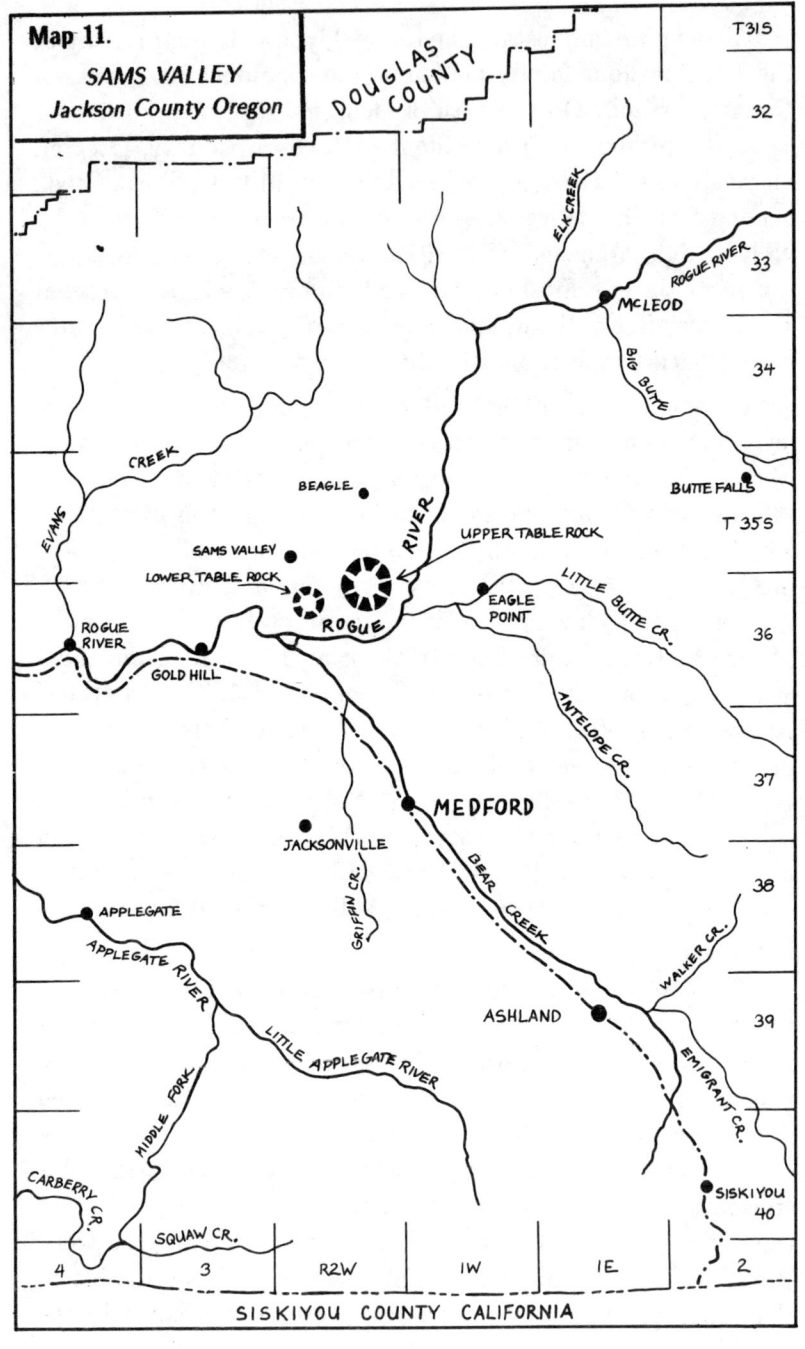

success of the town of Gold Hill led to the demise of Sams Valley as a town. In 1892, Arad Stanley finally moved his enterprise from Sams Valley to Gold Hill where he had taken up residence. Jacksonville suffered a similar fate losing its bid to become the route of the railroad. Instead, the O.& C.R.R. ran through "Middle Ford" which burgeoned as the new town of "Medford." Medford was so successful that the county seat was moved there from Jacksonville. Railroad construction through the Rogue River Valley triggered a new wave of prosperity that attracted newcomers to the area.

The Freshours lived at Sams Valley a number of years before securing land titles for themselves. In September of 1889 James W. Freshour deeded eighty acres, located two miles northeast of the Sams Valley store, to his wife Sarah A. Freshour. This created a deed for the property so that, in September of 1893, President Benjamin Harrison was able to grant a homestead patent on the same parcel to James W. Freshour.[30] Grandpa Thomas Freshour homesteaded nearby — further over towards Beagle. He was granted the land patent by President Benjamin Harrison in May of 1890.[31]

Frank Walter Freshour was born to James and "Bell" in November of 1887 at Sams Valley and Myrtle arrived in June of 1890. In November of 1890, eight-year-old Willi died leaving James and Bell with six surviving children of the ten Bell had born. Willi and Hattie probably occupy two of the unidentified graves in the nearby Pankey Cemetery. There are three family cemeteries in Sams Valley that eventually became public cemeteries. The only records were the gravestone catalogs made in this, the twentieth century. Many of the simple wooden markers had long since disappeared.[32] Dollie was born in June of 1893 probably at Sams Valley. Fred Leon was born in January of 1896 in California.

Grandpa and grandma Thomas and Harriet were living in Butte County, California in March of 1896 when Thomas died. James W. Freshour arranged for his father's burial in the cemetery at Chico. There is not a family plot. Only a single grave for the only Freshour buried in Butte County. There are a number of Athertons in a family plot. They may have been relatives of Arabella. Harriet Alice Freshour, widow of Thomas Freshour, sold the 120 acres in Sams Valley to Helen A. Walker of Butte County. The deed was executed in Butte County and recorded at Medford in Jackson County, Oregon. The Freshours were never well established in Butte County. Their presence there seems to have been a stopover as they traveled through.

Fur trapper, Nicolaus Allgeier, traversed this Sacramento Valley region in 1839 when Alta California was still Mexican territory. Allgeier was born in Frieburg, Baden in 1807. He came to America in 1830 and "was employed by the Hudson Bay Company in the wilds of British America." While in their service he trapped in California in 1839-40. Allgeier was soon employed by John A. Sutter to establish and operate a ferry on the Yuba River just south of the confluence with its Rio Oso tributary. The ferry was necessitated by the cattle drives of the huge herds of Sutter's New Helvetia. When not moving cattle across the river, Allgeier trapped animals along the streams. This incurred the wrath of local Indians and nearly cost him his life. He escaped to Sutter's Fort and John Sutter placated the Indians. Sutter also established his Hock Farm nearby. For his service, Sutter gave Nicolaus Allgeier a large piece of land on the river below the ferry.[33]

When the wagon trains started arriving in Sutter County, Allgeier parceled out his land and did some profit taking. The town of Nicolaus was soon plated. The surrounding judicial township of 130 square miles took its name from the town. In the mid 1890s, after their Rogue Valley sojourn, the Thomas Freshour progeny settled at Nicolaus. Many of the local citizens were immigrants from Germany. Nicolaus is now a quiet little village on a back road. The flood of 1955 took out its bridge, further contributing to its diminution. It still retains the post office that serves the outlying area. The Nicolaus Cemetery is a nicely maintained county cemetery rich in local history.

W.M. Parker started across the plains in April of 1853. He settled on 160 acres[34] in Sutter County with his Post Office at Nicolaus. Born in 1824 in Montgomery County, Indiana, he grew up near Rock Island in Mercer County, Illinois. He married Miss Keziah Rogers in November of 1864. She came to California from Illinois in 1858. They had three daughters and two sons. George William Parker was born in 1872. He married Miss Lillie A. Freshour in September of 1894. Both were residents of Nicolaus. She was seventeen and married with her father's consent on record. Phil Drescher, J.P. of Nicolaus Township officiated.[35]

James W. Freshour was in California in the year 1900 and living in the household of his son-in-law, George Parker, near Nicolaus. Addie Freshour, age seventeen, and Henry Freshour, age twenty, were also in the Parker household. "Ma Bell" and Cecil, Fred, Dollie, Myrtle and Frank W., ages one through thirteen, were again mysteriously missing.[36] In 1900, Harriet Freshour was living at Scottsburg on the Umpqua River in Douglas County, Oregon. Her grandson, twenty-one-year-old Charles Freshour was in her household. The Charles Johnsons with their seven children lived next door. They were Indians — true natives of the Umpqua. The next neighbor was the Clark McAfee family. Mrs. McAfee was her mother's namesake, Harriet Alice Freshour, who had married Clark McAfee in 1880. She now went by the name of Alice and was thirty-eight years old. Alice had born two children — both of them living. The youngest, Maria, was thirteen years old and had been born in Oregon. Their eldest had left home. The McAfees owned their farm free and clear. Grandma Harriet had come up from Butte County, California, to live near them. Charles acted as man of the house enabling Harriet to maintain a separate household, thus avoiding mother-in-law problems for the McAfees. Among the other neighbors were three families with parents that had emigrated from Germany. Eventually, Charles moved down to Nicolaus in Sutter County, California. His grandmother, Harriet, probably came with him to be near her granddaughters

Lillie and Addie. George and Lillie Parker bought 80 acres near Nicolaus in October of 1900.[37]

In March of 1901, the following caption headed an item in the *Marysville Daily Appeal*.

May and September Mate

County Clerk Gordon Bowman issued a marriage license last evening to David Hilko Cramer, aged 68, of Nicolaus, and Addie Freshour, aged 18, of Nicolaus. The ink was not dry on the license before Justice of the Peace I.N. Aldrich pronounced them man and wife in the County Clerk's office.

The bridegroom is a rancher.[38]

David H. Cramer was listed in 1900 as the rancher next door to George and Lillie Parker. The sixty-seven-year old widower was a native of Germany. It is interesting that they crossed the river from Yuba City to Marysville to be married in Yuba rather than Sutter County. This elopement must have astounded the Freshours. The bridegroom didn't last long. He died in August of 1906 and is buried next to his Brother, George Cramer in the Nicolaus Cemetery. He left a twenty-three-year-old widow — hopefully a rich one.

In October of 1906, George and Lillie sold their ranch to his brother Frank C. Parker and moved to Placer County near Lincoln which is on the road running due east from Nicolaus. In July of 1907, Charles Freshour purchased a place on First Street of Nicolaus.[39] In March of 1908, Charles purchased a plot in Nicolaus Cemetery. The occasion was the death of his grandmother, Harriet Offit Freshour. Her husband, Thomas, had been laid to rest at Chico. Harriet was buried at Nicolaus. They had traveled to California by wagon with two of their children in 1857. As a small boy their son, James W. Freshour, had traveled with them from Missouri. Now, their grandson, Charlie, was the man assuming family responsibility.

There is scant evidence of this Sams Valley Freshour family in California in 1910.[40] Lillie and George Parker were living at Lincoln. He was absent, working at Nicolaus as a farm hand. Henry James Freshour was at Lodi with his wife Elizabeth and their infant son Terry. In 1920, other progeny of Thomas Freshour had settled in the San Joaquin County town of Lodi. Henry James, Elizabeth and ten-year-old Terry were living on East Elm. Charles T. Freshour, his wife, Bessie Connoly, and their five children lived in Lodi on Stockton Avenue. Grandpa, James W. Freshour, at age 68, was in the household of his son Frank W. Freshour who was living on Eaton Avenue with his wife, Annie C. Bianchinni, and son, James W. Freshour. Grandma, Belle S. Freshour, age 64, was head of the household which included her sons Fred L. and Cecil C. Freshour.

James W. Freshour died on December 6th, 1922. He was buried in the Freshour plot in Nicolaus Cemetery. A proper gravestone was then erected for him and his mother, Harriet.[41]

Engraved on the stone:
HARRIET FRESHOUR 1824 - 1908
J.W. FRESHOUR 1852 - 1922

Mr. Leo Michel, seventy years old in 1994, native of Nicolaus, was a trustee of the cemetery. He stated that people around Nicolaus remembered the Freshour name. There are none of these Freshours remaining in Sutter County.

Sarah Arabella Atherton Freshour and her sons, Charles, Frank and Fred, lived out their years at Lodi. Henry and Cecil lived nearby at Stockton. Charles Thomas "Charlie" Freshour worked for the City of Lodi for 25 years and was a park foreman in their city parks. Electrician, Fred Leon Freshour, was an electrical contractor in Lodi. Frank Walter Freshour worked for the City of Lodi in the Water Department. Henry James Freshour ran a fruit and produce business in Stockton. They were a close knit family. "Ma Bell" Freshour died in Lodi on December 30th, 1937. These Lodi Freshours are buried in the Cherokee Memorial Park or in the Lodi Memorial Cemetery with the exception of Cecil Chester "Dock" Freshour. He is buried in the Golden Gate Memorial Cemetery at San Bruno.[42] Dock served with a Medical Detachment in WWII. He never married. A number of Freshours continue to live at Lodi. They are mostly descendants of Charles Thomas "Charlie" Freshour. Charlie's brother and sister-in-law, Frank W. and Annie C. Freshour, were highly successful in real estate around Lodi. For the years 1936-41, their names appear in the grantee index at the county recorders for more than forty properties.

James W. Freshour of Modesto recalled his grandfather, James William Freshour, telling that he arrived in the Lodi area of the San Joaquin in a covered wagon. He would have been five years old in 1857 when Thomas and Harriet Freshour traveled the California Trail from Jackson County, Missouri to California's San Joaquin Valley.

15

SONOMA TO SISQUOC

RUSSIA HAD ITS imperialistic eye on the cornucopia that was *Spanish Arcadia*, as Nellie Sanchez so romantically described it. Originally their purpose was fur trapping just as was the purpose of Britain and the United States. Just as John Marsh coveted this land for his countrymen, so too must the British and Russians have coveted it. This Arcadian gem was *muy lejos* — far beyond *La Fronteria* — to the inept bureaucracy in Mexico. Father Kino's frustrated attempts to establish a road from Sonora to Alta California was a conscious effort to bring this vast wealth into close economic unity with mainland Mexico. — something that could not occur as long as California remained the *island* of the Calafía.[1] Father Kino's dream died with him and, as surely, California was slipping through the loose grasp of an ineffectual administration. This Vallejo knew very well and he was not inclined to let the British and especially not the Russians seize upon this windfall. The same observation was being made by Doctor Marsh.[2]

But, Vallejo had the Russians right at the back stoop of his *Petaluma Rancho*. That is to say at the Russian River which was immediately to the north of his Rancho. The Russians built Fort Ross there on the coast around 1812. The introduction of silk hats, of the variety that Lincoln made famous, wiped out the beaver pelt market — just in the nick of time for the hapless beaver which were being relentlessly trapped in California by Mountain Men and the Frenchmen and Britons of the Hudson Bay Company. Americans found reasons, other than fur trapping, to be in California. *Los Rusos Indios* as the

Mexicans called the Russian's Aleut fur hunters, ranged down the California coast far south of Fort Ross.[3] The Russians also found more important things to do in California. Fort Ross was established by the Russian-American Company as their otter hunting base but it soon became a provisioning base for their frigid North American territory. The Russians emulated the Mexican ranchos in order to supply hides, tallow, meat and grain to Alaska. Fort Ross was a model of organization and productivity. This was much more than a trappers camp. Vallejo was sent into the region north of the bay to checkmate the Russians.[4] The Russians, frustrated in their attempts to expand their holdings, decided that their enterprise was not viable. They sold out to John A. Sutter who overextended himself to snap it up right under Vallejo's nose. The Russians got even with their Californio antagonist who had coveted their Rancho. Vallejo had offered them payment for their livestock but not for Fort Ross because Governor Alvarado insisted that the Russians had been occupying Mexican territory.[5]

Exeunt *Los Rusos*. — Their logistics were unfavorable for empire building. And, they feared running afoul of the actively enforced Monroe Doctrine. Without its California base, Alaska was not as useful to the Russians; so, they sold it to the new owners of California in a transaction[6] dubbed "Seward's Folly."

Early in 1833, Governor Figueroa dispatched the twenty-four-year-old commandante of the Presidio of San Francisco, *Alférez* Mariano Vallejo,[7] to pay an official visit to the Russians at Fort Ross and to reconnoiter the territory north of the bay with a view to establishing a presidio there. At the same time, Figueroa sent additional troops to defend the missions at San Rafael and San Francisco Solano. Vallejo's report to Figueroa described a "promised land" and excoriated the friars for their management of the missions there. The following year, Vallejo was granted ten leagues in the "Oh Fair Vale" — *Petaluma* in the Suisun tongue. While at Petaluma, Vallejo made a treaty with the Cainamoro tribe that was maintained for many years.

A turf battle between Figueroa and the friars ensued. Initial colonizing efforts including those at Petaluma and Santa Rosa failed. Governor Figueroa was determined to carry out the instructions from the government in Mexico to colonize this *fronteria del norte* and arrest the progress of the Russians. He entrusted this enterprise to the young lieutenant not yet turned twenty-eight, Don Mariano G. Vallejo. In a letter, Figueroa conferred on his protegé the title *Military Commander and Director of Colonization of the Northern Frontier*. Instructions to establish a pueblo in the valley of Sonoma were included. This document, of June, 1835, was the instrument under which Vallejo granted land.

Vallejo had made a number of excursions north of the bay to explore the Sonoma and Napa valleys. When Vallejo and his soldados first faced the Carquinez Strait it gave them pause. If they traveled upstream they were met with the Suisun Bay which expanded inland for many miles to blend into the delta marshes. The entire Sierra watershed flowed into the half-mile wide strait where the current surged deeply and swiftly. The Mexicans of Alta California habitually swam their horses across streams but this was the granddaddy of all California streams. Vallejo and his men debated whether their horses could swim across this torrent while mounted. The courageous lieutenant rode into the water with his men plunging their mounts in after him. They had their remuda in tow. They were fortunate to struggle out on the opposite downstream shore with only one mishap. The lieutenant lost a mare — swept down stream in the swift current and no doubt drowned. They camped nearby on the bank of the Napa River that flows into the San Pablo Bay at the western end of the Carquinez Straits — the site of the present day city of Vallejo. The opposite bank of the Napa was a small peninsula cut off from the mainland by sloughs to form an island. One of Vallejo's men spied a large animal on the island. Further investigation proved this to be the lieutenant's missing mare. The island was thus named *Isla Yegua* — Mare Island.

They followed the Napa River north to Suscol Creek where they forded the river and proceeded east to the Mission San Francisco Solano on Sonoma Creek. Here Vallejo established a military barracks and soon the pueblo flourished there under his protection. The peaceful charm of the Mexican colonial town, blended with the nostalgia of American pioneering, delight the wine tasting tourists of today. Vallejo built a fine but modest home in Sonoma where he and Benicia reared their children. To the east Vallejo established his Petaluma Rancho. This was not a modest ranch house — it was a fortified outpost. Cattle ranching of the hide and tallow trade variety was pursued there with great enterprise; but, the Russians were to the north and the Petaluma plain was inhabited by large numbers of Indians. Ranching was done from within a large fortress complete with outlying breastworks. It survives today as a state historical park.

Vallejo fostered development in the Napa Valley through his amicable association with one of Ashley's beaver trappers who neglected to return to his family in Missouri. In addition to his education in Spanish, Vallejo had become proficient in French and English under his mentor Richardson while a cadet at Monterey. He had surreptitiously availed himself of foreign books proscribed by the Spanish authorities.[8] He was reasonably well read in English and fascinated by the American culture and its attendant achievements. Now the trapper, George Yount, arrived at Sonoma in 1835 and asked Vallejo for work. Vallejo asked him what he could do. The Mexicans were roofing their buildings with massive terra-cotta tiles suitable for the timberless regions of Mexico. Vast stands of timber were at hand in Alta California. Yount was soon busy making shakes to roof Vallejo's new adobe. Yount requested a half league of land and the use of a few heifers to start cattle ranching. Vallejo generously granted Yount two leagues — 11,814 acres — of prime Napa Valley land in March of 1836. This was the Caymus Rancho named for the Indians that lived in their wiki-ups across the Napa River from Yount's Rancho.

Vallejo had a major task in Indian management. He handled this well to the mutual benefit of the Indians and the settlers but not without difficulty. In a pitched battle with the Suisuns, he defeated them and met with their chief to talk terms. Chief Sem Yeto was a six foot seven giant determined to keep the white men out of his territory. The chief was impressed with the young lieutenant's confidence and the decency of the terms offered. The two leader's respect for one another developed into lasting friendship and loyalty. Chief Sem Yeto converted to christianity and was christened "Solano."[9]

When Joseph Chiles and Charlie Hopper arrived in the Bartleson party of 1841, they looked up their old Missouri neighbor George Yount. Yount was overjoyed to receive news from his family in Missouri and provisioned Chiles and Hopper for their return to Missouri the following year sending mules with them for his family. They were to receive land in return for bringing his family to California. Colonel Chiles made good his word in 1843 bringing Yount's two daughters in the Chiles-Walker expedition. Chiles was ceded the Catacula grant in 1844. The Chiles Valley is located between Napa and Berryessa Valleys. Hopper arrived with his own family in 1847 to settle with his cousin Thomas Hopper in Santa Cruz.[10] After a fling at the gold mining of 1848, Charlie returned to Yount's domain. Although he hadn't brought any of Yount's family from Missouri, Yount was nonetheless grateful and offered Hopper free land. Hopper was cagey enough to pay for the land in order to establish the validity of his claim. He purchased 560 acres at $1.50 per acre from Yount in 1849.[11] Thomas Hopper took his family to the mines in 1848 but the mining towns were too rough so he left his family with George Yount while he mined in the dry diggings in 1849. He settled with his family in the fall of 1849 in Sonoma County and farmed there. By 1879, he owned fifteen thousand odd acres in California, most of it in Sonoma County. "Little Charlie," another cousin also held land in Sonoma County. David Hopper who apparently came from Missouri with the Horn-Gann Party, acquired some seven to eight thousand acres near Healdsburg and eventually moved to Mendocino County. Such were the opportunities in Sonoma County in the 1850s.

Despite his favoritism towards Americans, Vallejo did not always receive proper respect from them. The swashbuckling Fremont had Vallejo arrested during the bear flag revolt and placed in Sutter's custody — much to Sutter's dismay. Sutter knew that Vallejo was favorably disposed towards American occupation of California. Both Vallejo and Sutter served as delegates to the California Constitutional Convention for which they were rewarded by having vast amounts of their property taken over by squatters. Apparently Freshours, Hoppers and Horns were among those "freeholders" that settled on Vallejo's land. Of course, he had an inordinate amount of land. The Mexican government paid him in land since they had no ready cash.

The lands of Mariano Vallejo had become Napa and Sonoma Counties. Greenberry Horn moved up to Santa Rosa in Sonoma County in 1856. The Horns had settled at San Jose when they first arrived in the fall of 1854. Isaiah Horn was farming there with his family and his brother, Greenberry, was living with his parents nearby. Isaiah's wife was Jane Gann. Her parents lived nearby and her brother, William Gann, was farming there. Lawson Freshour was also part of this San Jose community transplanted from Jackson County, Missouri. Upon settling, Isaiah dug a well striking water at forty-five feet. Isaiah's diary gives 1855 accounts of cutting, binding and threshing wheat and barley and hauling and selling the sacked grain or having it milled. The neighboring farmers worked together as threshing crews.[12] Isaiah mentions "Ringstaff" [Rengstorff?] in regards to threshing. They seem to have immediately prospered in the Santa Clara Valley growing grain. The apricot and prune orchards had not yet become dominant in this area. Daniel Horn died in August of 1855 leaving Greenberry to care for his widowed mother. A year later, Greenberry and his mother were living in a rented house at Santa Rosa.

At the end of July of 1856, Isaiah Horn with his family and the elder John Ganns traveled by horse and wagon from San Jose to Stockton. They reached the San Joaquin River and camped overnight. The mosquitoes bit the children awfully. The ferriage was $1.50. They stayed at brother-in-law Elkins and John Gann's parents stayed with him. Having deposited his family at Stockton, Isaiah started out for the Russian River accompanied by "Frazier" Gann[13] They stopped off at uncle Nicholas Gann's and stayed two days while Frazier hunted for a horse to ride. Both properly mounted, they traveled on north to Elk Grove House where they stayed the night. They traveled through Sacramento and crossed over the toll bridge. They were tired by the difficult travel so put up before dark at the Half Way House at the cost of $2.25 each. They went on to stay the next night at "Old Man Hopper's" near Yontville. Three drinks and gambling losses cost Isaiah $0.50. The next day they left Hopper's and crossed the mountains to Santa Rosa. "Late at night, we arrived at Jack Esbey's after a hard days ride over the roughest road I have ever seen." (And he had crossed the plains from Missouri.) Notice the circuitous route from Stockton avoiding the delta marshes. It would be years before the dikes would be built to form the delta islands and California's rivers would be tamed by hydroelectric and flood control dams. The next day they arrived at "Mother's." It was Sunday. They had been on the road for one week.

Saturday they went for a ride to check out "Poor Man's Flat." They spent the next four days helping Greenberry build a house. The weekend was spent enjoying a camp meeting then they departed for Stockton. At Carneros Creek Isaiah and Frazier part. Frazier went to William Fagans and Isaiah took the Suscol Ferry and put up for the night at Suscol House. The next day he went to Benecia and took the ferry across the strait. He went through the "Ramona Valley" and stayed the night at a private house. His horse was worn out so he swapped horses with the man where he stayed. He got a horse that had been worked or rode but little. He mounted without difficulty and reached French Camp about sundown on a tired horse.[14] He found his family well. The new horse worked well when harnessed to the wagon. After staying variously at Elkin's, Tom Gann's, John Gann's and uncle Nick Gann's,[15] he made preparations to leave with his family for the Russian River.

On the 9th of September they departed passing through Stockton where they "got some grub etc." The "grub" included eleven pounds of bacon for $2.75 and the "etc." included a fry pan at $0.50 and a hat for Billy at $1.50. They traveled until dark then camped "on the plains." The wind blew too hard for a fire so they went to bed without supper. They traveled in a high wind for the next three days. Each night notation was made "Wind blew too hard to have a fire." The Sacramento River was crossed by ferry boat. They "Came to a sheep ranch on the plains and stay all night with the shepherd." They bought crackers at a store at Suisun Valley. The Napa River was crossed by taking the Suscol Ferry. The next morning, they finally got out of the wind and were able to stop and cook breakfast. At Sonoma, they bought more crackers then continued on to "Mother's" at Santa Rosa arriving at ten o'clock Saturday night. There they "contented ourselves" for the next three days. The five days travel on wagon road included four nights camping with little opportunity to fry the bacon. They had munched crackers along the way.

After three days of contentment, Isaiah started for San Jose with Greenberry and they got as far as Suscol House. The next day they stayed at a man's house letting their horses stand at his hay stack. Friday they crossed the strait and they arrived at William Gann's at San Jose around 3 o'clock on Saturday. Isaiah went to San Jose Monday and "Bargained some wheat to Dutch Mike for a horse, valued at $77.50." The next three days were spent weighing out and selling Isaiah's wheat and barley and hauling wheat to Hank's Mill for some of the buyers. After settling accounts Isaiah netted $117 in cash. Thursday, he stayed about William Gann's "fixin to start." On Friday, September 26, 1856, Isaiah started for the Russian River with the "plunder" and accompanied by Greenberry, William Gann and Lawson Freshour. They traveled without difficulty but slowly because of their livestock. They encamped along the way. Sunday they crossed the Carquinez strait by ferry paying $8.50 ferriage for one wagon, two horses, three cows, a mare and a horse. Monday they paid $2.24 to cross the Suscol ferry. One of the cows calved on the way. They got to Santa Rosa on Wednesday and found everyone doing well.

After a few days rest, the men traveled north to hunt land staying at G.B. Byrd's on the way. They crossed Soda Springs ridge heading towards Russian River which they crossed near Heald's. They picked out land and "concluded to settle on it." They went back across the Russian River and followed it south to return to Santa Rosa. "About dark Mother's cow fell in the well — about twelve feet deep — and we worked nearly all night to get her out but I think she will die." Isaiah worked about his mother's place for a few days while "Green, Wm. Gann and Freshour went up on Dry Creek to work on claims." Isaiah became uneasy when Greenberry was late in returning. "Green came home with rather unfavorable news. The Spaniard would not sell or asked too much for their land. We intend to settle anyhow. The old cow got up and walked." The next day, Isaiah went up to Dry Creek with a "load of plunder." He moved his family to Mark West. He bought of Heald one pound of nails — $1.50 and one ball of twine — $0.20. By now it was mid October and they started to get some rain. Isaiah built a corral for his stock and started building a house and in about ten days had a roof on it and started laying the floor. He went down to Mark West with his wagon to move his family up with part of the plunder. He went to Heald's and stocked up on groceries. By the end of October he was putting a chimney on the house.

Isaiah's diary entries for the summer of 1858 reveal a transplanted midwestern farm economy. Mutually assisted wheat farming activities thrived as they had at San Jose — Greenberry and William Gann being frequently mentioned. He noted threshing out two sacks of wheat to take to the mill and later going to get his "grindings." His wife, Jane, baked with flour from wheat grown by her husband. Isaiah also grew a large crop of corn. Some was hauled in for fodder and the rest was "cut and set up." He made himself a corn sheller. A craftsman, Isaiah was always making something. He "Got out some timber to make some cradle fingers." — A device for gathering wheat into shocks as cut. He "ironed a bucket" for a neighbor and he noted the details as he built a wagon for Green. Butchering hogs was a regular activity. "Helped Green kill a shoat." He was also in the chicken and egg business. Shopping was now done at Geyserville. In July, 1858, Isaiah noted "The assessor came and assessed my stuff. Paid poll tax — $3.00."

By this time, the 1857 wagon train Freshours were settled around Stockton. In August of 1858, Isaiah notes "Nicholas Gann and Martin Freshour came here today." Uncle Nick had come to visit his nephew, William Gann, and his niece Jane Horn. Martin, a Missouri neighbor, had come to visit his old friends and his brother, Lawson, who was presumably still in the vicinity. Its likely that Martin hadn't seen Lawson since Lawson had left Missouri in 1854.

In the autumn of 1859, Isaiah's diary shows the same farm life with cooperation with William Gann and other neighbors. The chicken and egg business had become more pronounced with William Gann hauling their chickens to Petaluma where there was apparently a market for poultry. His brother and mother were off to a camp meeting. He went to Healdsburg to get leather, found none, so, got it in Geyserville. He made shoes for his children. Frazier Gann and two Frazier brothers came to visit from Stockton. Isaiah recorded a Certificate of Purchase for his "Unsurveyed Land Grant" in March of 1862. He paid Forty dollars of the two-hundred owed for the quarter section and sixteen dollars interest on the amount owed. The following year, he recorded an identical certificate but only paid the interest.[16] The squatters were thus eventually legitimized by the Federal Land Office in San Francisco. In a deed filed in 1863, Isaac M. Lewis granted to Greenberry M. Horn a quarter

section of land for fifty dollars gold coin. This was a mile
and a half east of Isaiah's land.[17] These were the only land
records for the Horn brothers. There were none for William
Gann or Lawson Freshour. Lawson was at Corralitos in Santa
Cruz County in 1867, registered to vote as a thirty-eight-year-
old farmer. Nick Gann and his wife, Rutha Gann — Lawson's
sister, had moved to Santa Cruz around 1858. Lawson's mother
and two of his other married sisters had moved over there from
the San Joaquin Valley in 1862. Lawson may have moved there
around that time.

Andrew Freshour, and his family arrived in Sonoma County
in 1857. They had arrived from Johnson County Missouri.
His daughter, Elizabeth, was nineteen and the following year
in November she married Benjamin W. Scott at Santa Rosa.
William F. was eighteen and Christopher Columbus was fifteen
when they arrived. Daughters Mary M. and Nancy E. were
twelve and nine years old. They settled in Armalloy township
with Sevastapool as their Post Office. David Hopper and his
wife Nancy both of Missouri lived near by and were probably
the influence that led Andrew into Sonoma County. There
is no land record for Andrew in Sonoma County but this is
no surprise since the County seems to have been populated
to a great extent by "freeholders." Andrew's daughter, Mary,
married Daniel G. Wright shortly after 1860.

The census of 1860 was followed right away by the War of
the Rebellion and in California the Great Valley was inundated
by the flood of 1861. These events were declared by clergymen
to be the scourge of God to reward California for its wickedness.
Although there was an exodus from the region devastated by
flood, dry years immediately followed and California thrived in
the years that its gold fueled the Union war machine. People
commenced drifting into the San Joaquin Valley to join those
who had stayed on after the flood to farm the rich soil. Andrew
Freshour of Petaluma and his sons moved to the interior during
this time. Andrew's son, William, may have been the soldier
serving at Camp Bidwell at Chico from November of 1864 to

June of 1866. Sixty-year-old Andrew is registered to vote as a farmer in Liberty Township of San Joaquin County in October of 1868. In April of 1869, "C.C." married seventeen-year-old Eunice Lavina Rice, with her mother's consent, at Woodland in Yolo County just east of Sacramento.

In 1870 Andrew is in Salinas township of San Luis Obispo County with the D.G. Wright family next door with their sons Andrew, David and George. Newly married Christopher and his wife, Eunice, and their month old son, are in Andrew's household.[18] Eunice's Mother, Sarah Rice, with her ten-year-old son, Andrew Rice, are next door. The David Hopper family are neighbors. These folks got their mail at the Hot Springs Post Office — present day Paso Robles. In 1874, Andrew was assessed for taxes on land located near the Estrella School.[19] The same year, Lawson Freshour was also assessed for land near Paso Robles.[20] Lawson had left Sonoma County earlier to spend a few years farming at Corralitos before moving on south. In the 1870s there seems to have been a general movement from the bay area to San Luis Obispo County. Albert Jones, former Sheriff of Santa Cruz County moved from Santa Cruz to the Cholame Valley to the east of Paso Robles. Federal homestead land attracted people of Santa Cruz County to this region of San Luis Obispo County.[21] They simply went to Watsonville in the Pajaro Valley and then followed the Salinas River south through the Salinas Valley to its headwaters. "Hot Springs," now Paso Robles, is located on the upper Salinas River.

The trip to San Luis Obispo County made by the Andrew Freshour family and neighbors would be of the same nature as the travels of Isaiah Horn and his family earlier on. They would camp along the way. This would be a small train of wagons — and another wagon road trek. They would pass through San Jose and travel south through the Santa Clara Valley to follow the Pajaro River to the coast. It would take them at least a week to get from the San Joaquin Valley to Watsonville. Longer if they were bringing milk cows. This first leg of their journey followed the primordial route of the Sierra watershed to the

Pacific. From the Carquinez Strait, these waters flow south through San Pablo Bay into the main bay of San Francisco and continue out through the Golden Gate into the Pacific. But, in prehistoric times, the ridge forming the Santa Cruz Mountains and San Francisco Peninsula was continuous, entirely enclosing the San Francisco Bay. The Bay was above sea level. The San Joaquin was a marshy lake and the Bay engulfed the present day Santa Clara Valley to flow out through the Pajaro delta lands to the Monterey Bay. Great fanned out alluvial deposits extend out into Monterey Bay giving evidence of the former geology. The mountain ridge was rent in a colossal cataclysm worthy of Indian legend. An earthquake sheared a schism through which poured the pent up bay. Earth and boulders were sluiced, opening the Golden Gate and lowering the bay to form a tidal extension of the Pacific. Often shrouded in ocean fog, this slight gap in the coastal ridge is hardly discernible to ships threading their way between the Farallon Islands and the tricky shoreline. The Santa Clara Valley thus emerged with its Guadelupe River to form the southern margin of the Bay. The massive river flowing into the Monterey Bay dwindled to a local stream — the Pajaro River and its creeks — draining the southern end of the Santa Clara Valley.

The foregoing enthralling story is just that — a story. It is folk geology that unfortunately still persists in some quarters of the local history curriculum. Modern geology tells us that the undersea canyon formed by the stream flowing out of the Golden Gate is among the most ancient features in this region. The alluvial fans are also a fiction not to be found on modern maps of these coastal waters. Actually, the San Francisco Bay has always been part of the Pacific with ocean tides flowing through the Golden Gate. The Santa Clara Valley streams feeding the salty bay drain the northern end of the valley as they ever have.

Continuing south from San Jose to Morgan Hill, our travelers reach a point in the Santa Clara Valley below Mount Loma Prieta where there is a subtle divide beyond which the streams draining the southern end of the valley flow into the Pajaro River. The main tributary of the Pajaro River is the San Benito River. The San Benito drains a sizable area and is a major contributor to the Monterey Bay, the Salinas River being the main contributor. The furthest reaches of the Salinas River flow from the Carrizo Plain in the interior of San Luis Obispo County. The river flows north through the rich plain of the Salinas Valley. These streams marked out near-sea-level routes for trails and wagon roads used by California's early pioneers and eventually by the railroads.

This route follows the coastal valleys where the Franciscan padrés established their missions. Our Sonoma travelers passed down the east shore of the Bay to pass by Mission *San José*. Another ten miles brought them to the pueblo, by then the town, of San Jose with the Mission *Santa Clara de Asís* close by. Traveling on south through Gilroy they would skirt Mission *San Juan Bautista* and follow the Pajaro River to Watsonville. Following the coast of the Monterey Bay south they would head inland above the Salinas River to follow the general course of the river through the Salinas Valley. They would spend several days following this large coastal valley south from the town of Salinas. The uninterrupted flat plain provided the solitude enjoyed by the Mission *Nuestra Señora de la Soledad*. Passing on, another day's travel took them past Mission *San Antonio de Padua* to the west. The large valley narrows down to follow the river through hills where they encountered Mission *San Miguel Arcángel*. A few more miles brings them to Hot Springs. The missions of California were spaced a day's travel by the padrés on mule. This was the *El Camino Real*. — The Royal Road.

This route following the Salinas River has a gradual grade bringing the traveler into a system of minor valleys and hills on the upper reaches of the river. The Santa Lucia Range separates this region from the small valley on the ocean where the Mission *San Luis Obispo de Tolosa* is nestled. The padrés traveling from Mission San Miguel to Mission San Luis Obispo would pass over the Santa Lucias at the 1522 foot summit which they called *La Cuesta*. The altitude at Hot Springs is 730 feet and, upstream through rolling hills some fifteen miles, Santa Margarita at the base of the mountain is at a thousand feet. This altitude would not be noticed since it was attained gradually over a one hundred and twenty mile trip from Watsonville. The five hundred foot climb from there to the summit is not much of a challenge — obviously a small hill. The descending 1500 foot Cuesta Grade when thus encountered is breathtaking. *La Cuesta* towered over the sleepy Mexican sea-level village and could be seen from the front steps of the mission.

The Sonoma Freshours traveling this route in the late 1860s would notice that the missions had gone to rack and ruin. This decline was well underway in 1848 when the Americanos took over. The Mexican Secularization Act of 1833 had produced an immediate ruinous effect. This act took the missions away from the church. Abraham Lincoln restored the missions to the churches in California in 1862 with a grant to the Bishop of Monterey in letters of patent signed by President Lincoln and issued by the General Land Office.[22] The Soledad Mission was reduced to eroding adobe walls by the 1900s. By the mid 1900s, a mound of earth was all that remained. Archaeological digging was required to commence restoration. A new carefully researched replica now stands on the site. The caved in and abandoned Soledad Mission would have been viewed by the Sonoma Freshours trekking through here in the Late 1860s. Mission San Miguel was then fully functional but dilapidated. The wagon train from Sonoma no doubt enjoyed a stopover there just as modern travelers do. It is a trip into California's charming past.

San Luis Obispo is located in one of a series of fertile valleys running inland from the coast in the region between the Salinas Valley and Santa Barbara. The southern end of this region is marked by the *Santa Ynés* mission, two days journey on the El Camino Real traveling south from San Luis Obispo. The Santa Ynez Mountains block the path between *Santa Ynés* mission and the *Santa Barbara* mission. The region between San Luis

Obispo and Santa Ynez is bisected by the Santa Maria River which marks the boundary between San Luis Obispo County and Santa Barbara County. Just north of the river lies the Nipomo Valley and across the river in Santa Barbara County lies Santa Maria in its bountiful valley. The mission *Purísima Concepción* lies south of Santa Maria at present day Lompoc. Mission *Santa Ynés* is to the east at present day Solvang.

Sea captain, William G. Dana, cousin of Richard Henry Dana of *Two Years Before the Mast* fame, took command of the brig *Waverly* in 1826, to engage in the "Sandwich Island" trade. He arrived in California eight years before his famous cousin and became a Mexican citizen in 1835. Captain Dana was granted the 37,887 acre Rancho Nipomo on which he built an adobe house where he and his wife reared their twenty-one children. The area of Lompoc [23] in Santa Barbara County was to be settled as a temperance colony by people from Santa Cruz County. The important means of transportation into this area was by ship. In the 1860s and 1870s, the wagon travel through the Salinas Valley was limited to those going to settle in the upper plateau of the Salinas River. Once settled at Hot Springs, they could visit the county seat, San Luis Obispo, by taking the mule trail of the padrés over Cuesta. Transportation to San Luis Obispo or the Santa Maria Valley was usually by ships plying the coastal waters.

The first wharf was built at San Luis Obispo Bay in 1855. Before that, small boats were used to carry goods from the ships anchored safely offshore. Cooperage was very important then since barrels were the packing crates of that era. Not having fork lifts, they used man power and the round barrels could be rolled easily. Since the barrels were water tight, it was common practice to roll them over the side and let the waves drift them onto the beach. In 1869, Peoples Wharf on San Luis Obispo Bay opened for business and, in 1873, it had a competitor in Harford's Wharf, located in the lee of San Luis Point with a horse railroad and tunnel connecting it to the road from Peoples Wharf to San Luis Obispo. The Avila brothers platted a town on San Luis Obispo Bay in 1874 giving the port a town. Steam powered rail travel arrived when the San Luis Obispo & Santa Maria Valley R.R. was completed in 1876. Eventually "Port Harford" had rails running from out on its pier to San Luis Obispo thus connecting with the Santa Maria Valley. The Pacific Coast Company was then organized as a steamship company which included other narrow gauge rail extensions in the Puget Sound area and at San Diego.[24] The Pacific Coast Company's S.L.O. & S.M.V. R.R. reached its furthest extent at Los Olivos in 1887. A stage line ran from Los Olivos to Santa Barbara.

Lawson Freshour and the Andrew Freshour family settled in the vicinity of Hot Springs and were living there in a horse and wagon pioneer farm community in 1874. The padres traveling through there on the El Camino Real called the region *El Paseo del Robles* — "The Pass of the Oaks." Rancho *Paseo del Robles* was granted to Pedro Naverez in 1844. It was purchased by D.D. Blackburn and associates for the purpose of developing it into the Paso Robles Hot Springs resort. The Post Office was named "Hot Springs." The modern town was incorporated as "Paso Robles." Stanford's Southern Pacific was gradually making its way south from San Jose with the plan of eventually completing a coastal railroad route to Los Angles. In 1871, the S.P. reached Pajaro near Watsonville; and, in 1873 the S.P. had reached Salinas. It would be another eighteen years before the S.P. reached Templeton, just beyond Hot Springs. In 1874 the Hot Springs community was somewhat isolated from the steam powered industrial revolution going on over in the sea level part of the county.

With the arrival of S.P. at Templeton in 1888, a wild and woolly stage coach line took passengers the last twenty-four miles to San Luis Obispo. The Concord coach drawn by six horses galloped through Santa Margarita and over La Cuesta summit. The road down Cuesta Grade wound its way down the side of the large gulch extending down the mountain.[25] On one occasion, a top heavy coach rolled over on a curve plunging the driver and three topside passengers over a precipice to their doom. The passengers in the coach were badly shaken. On another occasion, the stage was held up on the Cuesta Grade by a lone bandit who got away with the Wells Fargo box in true Black Bart style. The stage line was short lived — 1888 to 1894.[26] The S.P. reached Santa Margarita in 1891 and began the horrendous task of constructing the system of tunnels and tracks that ran in a giant switchback path on the mountainside in order to maintain the gradual grade required by railroads. The tracks reached San Luis Obispo in 1894.

Andrew Freshour and his daughter and son-in-law, D.G. Wright, and family were in Arroyo Grande in 1880. Grandpa Andrew was seventy-one years old. *Arroyo Grande* or "Big Gulch" is located south of San Luis Obispo and at that time was on the narrow gauge rail line going south to Santa Maria. They hadn't waited for the rail and stage coach development at Hot Springs. They left sometime after 1874. Perhaps the development of the S.L.O. & S.M.V. R.R. offered them economic opportunities. Daniel G. Wright was a county supervisor in 1880. Andrew Parker Wright and his brother Daniel William Wright, grandsons of Andrew Freshour are registered to vote in Santa Barbara County in 1890. They resided at Sisquoc. Also registered was Lawson Henderson Freshour of Sisquoc who had left Hot Springs seemingly after 1874. *Sisquoc* means "Quail" in the native Chumash language according to Robert Bickett's *Chumash Place Names.* — Onomatopoeia to those who have heard the California quail wail — or the sisquoc squawk if you will. The eleven league Sisquoc Rancho was originally granted to Maria Dominques Cabrillo. The town of Sisquoc was located on a branch of the Santa Maria Valley Railroad. The gravel quarries of Sisquoc provided gravel for roadbeds.

The S.P. continued to creep south reaching Casmalia in 1896. The construction crew was then sent south to work on the section extending north from Santa Barbara. The "Gap" in coastal rail service from San Francisco to Los Angeles was the stage service from Santa Barbara to Los Olivos. The S.P.

next extended their line from Casmalia to Surf at the mouth of the Santa Ynez River and built a branch east from there to the village of Lompoc. Lompoc became the terminus for the Santa Barbara stage cutting Los Olivos and the narrow gauge line out of that business. Finally, in 1901, the last spike was driven near Gaviota and the "Gap" was closed. S.P. tracks ran along the coast from San Francisco to Los Angeles. San Luis Obispo's narrow gauge line running through the Santa Maria Valley went into decline. S.P.'s freight and passenger service drove the coastal steamship lines out of business. The small narrow gauge lines, even though they upgraded to standard gauge, eventually faded into history. An era had passed.

Evidently the bloom faded from the promise of Hot Springs in the mid 1870s and people drifted over the Cuesta Grade for the opportunities offered there or they took the wagon road back up north through the Salinas Valley. "C.C." Christopher Columbus Freshour and his wife Eunice returned to Sonoma County. A similar trend was occurring at Sonoma County as people were drifting north into Mendocino County. David and Nancy Hopper and their family, who had been neighbors to Andrew Freshour at Armalloy Township in Sonoma County in 1860 and were neighbors to Andrew at Hot Springs in 1870, were in Arma Township of Mendocino County in 1880. David Hopper was working there on a railroad and his eldest son was making ties.

Christopher Columbus Freshour and his family settled at Alexander Valley and later at Geyserville. C.C. and Eunice reared eight children and lived out their years at Geyserville. The family was well known thereabouts. Daughter, Fannie, died in January of 1894 at age twenty one. Eunice died in 1915 and C.C. spent his last year at Healdsburg with his daughter, Mrs. Grace Corria. He died in 1917 and is buried in Oak Mound Cemetery. Other surviving children were Mrs. Sarah Fitch of Healdsburg, Mrs. May Brooks of Windsor, Charles E. Freshour of Yountville, and three brothers at Healdsburg, Harvey C., Willard C. and John L. Freshour.[27]

Charles E. Freshour married Minnie Rose in 1898. She died in 1910 at Geyserville leaving five children. Their children were Irene M., born in March 1899, Elton, born in 1902, Gertrude, born in 1904, Leland Franklin Freshour, born in November of 1906 at Geyserville and Allen, born in 1908. In 1910, Charles E. Freshour is living at Napa with his four younger children and his new wife Mabel (1885-1925) and mother-in-law, Catherine Hill. Elton died at age seventeen.

In May of 1905, John L. Freshour (1879-1935) of Windsor married Frances P. Cobb (1885-1908.) Frances died at twenty three years of age after three and a half years of marriage apparently, without issue. John L. lived in Sonoma County and remained single until his death at age fifty six.

The name "Freshour" seems to have died out in Sonoma County, but there are many descendants of wagon train Tennessean, Andrew Freshour, and his wife Jane Markam, living in Sonoma County. The same may very well be true of Arroyo Grande and San Luis Obispo County as well as towns in the Santa Maria Valley of Santa Barbara County. Andrew spent his last years down there with his daughter, Mary M. Wright. His genes have been propagated by his Wright grandchildren living there at the turn of the century.

Andrew's eldest daughter, Eliza Jane Scott, with her husband, Benjamin William Scott, lived nearby at Santa Maria. They were there in 1880 with seven children ages eleven months through sixteen years. Ben and Eliza lived out their years there, both of them dying in 1909 — Eliza in January and Ben three months later. They are buried in in the Santa Maria IOOF cemetery. The family plot was purchased in August of 1884 and one grave is occupied by an infant. Another is occupied by their son Frank A. Scott who died during Christmas of 1897. Their daughter, Ada May Scott, had her shingle hung out as a stenographer and bookkeeper in Santa Maria in 1900. She died in 1910 and is buried in the family plot. Her brother, Will, was a teamster living in Santa Maria in 1900. The Scotts also produced Andrew Freshour descendants in the Santa Maria Valley.

Mahala Jane and Sam Hobbs left San Joaquin County sometime around 1870 and traveled with their six children to present day Orcutt in the Santa Maria Valley. Mahala Jane's parents, Rutha and Nicholas Gann, were living at Santa Cruz at that time. Considering the difficulties of the overland route from Stockton to Orcutt in 1870, one might expect them to resort to the waterways. They may have been part of the general exodus from Santa Cruz County to Lompoc. The Lompoc settlers traveled by ship from a landing at Watsonville. In any case, the Hobbs settled at Orcutt where Mahala bore seven more children. She frequently reminisced about the wagon train trip to California in the Hopper wagon train of 1847. There are numerous Hobbs descendants in the Santa Maria Valley, among them Gail Benson of Lompoc. The Hobbs family remembered "Uncle Loss" who lived a few miles away at Sisquoc. He was a younger brother of Rutha Gann. The extended Hobbs family appears to be the only family that Lawson had during his last days in the Santa Maria Valley.

Lawson Henderson Freshour seems to have had a strange aversion to the census takers. We have traced him from 1854 to 1890 by means of Isaiah Horn's diary, tax and land records, and voter registration. The census data is sought after because it would list wife and children. It appears from what little information that can be found on Lawson, that he was unmarried and had no offspring. Lawson failed to pay the taxes on his 160 acres near Paso Robles for the year ending June, 1876 and the land was deeded over to the state in March of 1877. When he paid his taxes in 1874, he gave no residential address. He also let 80 acres located ten miles east of Sisquoc[28] go to the state for $6.75 owed in taxes for the year ending 1878. He wasn't alone. There were many such deeds recorded in Santa Barbara County in 1879. They must have been going through hard times. Lawson seems to have owned both of these properties in the same time frame. He was probably land speculating. His death record indicates that he arrived at Sisquoc in 1871 and resided there until his death in 1897.

Lawson also owned 160 acres located on the north fork of La Brea Creek east of Sisquoc[29] and just north of his other Sisquoc property. In 1885 he sold this property to John Thomas Goodchild and James Wilson Goodchild for $500. Lawson registered to vote in Sisquoc precinct in 1890. It is amusing that the folks at Sisquoc spelled Lawson as "Losson" or "Loson." Generally he went by L.H. Freshour. He apparently outlived everyone who knew how to spell his name. Loson H. Freshone, age 72, died of apoplexy in the County Hospital at Santa Barbara in September of 1897. He was single. The index gives his name as Losen H. Frishour. He was buried in the small cemetery on the hospital grounds at Cacinque and Salinas Streets. The hospital along with its cemetery was moved in 1917 when the property was sold. A list of the bodies moved was compiled by the county in 1964. It gives "Lasen Freshone" and indicates a headstone so marked.[30] Most public records and obituaries in the late 1800s and early 1900s gave incomplete and misspelled names and frequently gave nicknames. However, the registrars of voters in the late 1800s were sticklers for exact and complete names in order to qualify the voter. (Men only — woman's suffrage was not yet accomplished.) The Great Registers of Santa Cruz and Santa Barbara County give Lawson's name precisely and in agreement.

Lawson Henderson Freshour was born in Tennessee and reached manhood in Missouri. He had taken the California Trail across the plains from Missouri in 1854. The end of his wagon road was at Sisquoc. One of the remarkable things about these wagon people was their mobility in moving about the state when transportation was primitive. Where they spent weeks camping along trails, we now traverse the same terrain in a few hours in the comfort of our sleek automobiles. From Sonoma to Sisquoc would for us be a long day's drive — or better yet, three leisurely days along *El Camino Real* doing a mission tour.

16

SOQUEL TIMBER

THE SECRET BAY was hidden to experienced sea dogs and galleon captains who for centuries had sailed this shore. And it was virtually right under their noses. The epic discovery was made by Catalan soldiers traveling overland on the coast. Drake had marked his bay. Sebastían Vizcaíno had urged that the "fine port"— which he named Monterey in 1602 — be used as a base for the protection of Spain's Philippine trade. Neither Vizcaíno nor any of the other seafaring Spaniards plying the California coastline had found the obscure outlet emanating from the huge hidden bay and the river that fed it.[1]

Captain Gaspar de Portolá was appointed governor of Baja California in 1767 and tasked with establishing a military presence in Alta California to head off the Russians. Junípero Serra was sent with him to establish missions. Their main task was to locate Monterey using Viscaíno's information and to establish a fort and mission there. At this time the entire California coastline had only been explored by ship and was occupied only by Indians. Portolá mounted a three-hundred man expedition in Mexico at San Blas including three ships to carry them across open sea to the Gulf of California. Portolá and his soldiers and missionaries landed at La Paz then traveled overland the length of Baja to arrive at San Diego while others went by ship.

They arrived after many harrowing months which included scurvy, desertions, the loss of one ship at sea and death in the inhospitable Baja terrain. About one-hundred and fifty debilitated survivors established *Misión San Diego de Acala*. They depended on supplies shipped from San Blas through the turbulence and head winds at Cabo San Lucas.

Portolá then mounted an overland expedition northward to Monterey. Arriving at the Salinas River on Monterey Bay, in September of 1769, the scurvy ridden and exhausted group failed to recognize the bay described by Vizcaíno. Onward they trekked. They crested a ridge and were startled to see a huge bay hidden from ocean's view by intervening peninsular mountain ridges. Portolá's soldiers were excited. They explored its perimeter and determined that they had found the long sought Strait of Anián.[2] An exploratory coup! As a disciplined military man Portolá was dejected because he had failed his mission — to find the Bay of Monterey and build a mission and fort. The starving group returned to San Diego eating their mules as they went.[3] Their supply ship returned that winter giving their San Diego base a new lease on life. The following year, 1770, Portolá returned to rendezvous with Serra's ship, at last, at Vizcaíno's port. The presidio and mission were inaugurated. Portolá's task was done. Serra's was only beginning.[4]

Don Gaspar de Portolá's foot-soldiers with their pack mules scouted their way through the terrain now known as Soquel during his famous 1769 expedition marked by his discovery of the large estuary later to be known as San Francisco Bay. They encountered very primitive Indians living in small groups or "rancharias" — a term coined by Portolá. Each squalid little group had a unique rudimentary language, thus there was no general Costanoan tribal tongue to perpetuate. Soquel is one of the few local Indian names to survive. Its meaning has not been preserved. Soquel Rancho took its name from the Indians once living on the *rio de Bravo o Shoquel* later known as Soquel Creek. Portolá and his soldiers moved on to camp at a river they named San Lorenzo.[5]

Conquistador Portolá was accompanied into the Spanish Alta California frontier by Franciscan college professor Serra, a veteran of twenty years service in the missions of New Spain, who poured out the last fifteen years of his life in austere mission service dying in 1784 at Carmel at the age of seventy-one.[6] Serra presided over priests and soldiers in a system dependent on tenuous logistics. Conversions were few. At times they were near starvation and survived on bear meat. The precious livestock were saved for breeding stock and they survived using the milk. There was only one blacksmith in all of Alta California and he had little or no iron since it had to be sent from Spain. Many decades would pass before the missions would approach the agricultural productivity for which they were later known. It was thought in Mexico that this ill advised experiment in territorial expansion would soon fail due to its isolation and need to be provisioned. Under the perceptive aegis of Spanish Viceroy Bucarelli, Serra's plight was ameliorated.

The incredible Juan de Anza expedition brought overland from Sonora two-hundred and forty men, women and children, soldiers and their families with over a thousand animals, to settle in Alta California. They saved the San Diego mission from certain annihilation by an Indian uprising and arrived at Monterey in 1776. Anza ordered the founding of San Francisco mission and presidio by José Joaquín Moraga who had brought his wife and young son Gabriel with him in the Anza expedition. The superb leadership of Juan Bautista de Anza opened the overland route from Mexico and infused viability into the faltering Alta California establishment[7]

Serra's successors, Father Palou followed by Father Lasuén, nurtured the missions into self sustaining establishments. Father Lasuén, crossing the Monterey peninsula from the mission at Carmel, had traveled up the coast of Monterey Bay, in 1791, to inaugurate *Misión La Exaltación de la Santa Cruz*, at the place where the San Lorenzo flows into the Pacific.[8] The pueblo Villa de Branciforte was established across the San Lorenzo River from the Santa Cruz Mission in 1796. The establishment of three pueblos in California that were non-religious and non-military was ordered by the Spanish government of Madrid in reaction to fear of Russian expansion from Alaska or military aggression by the French or English. These were *el Pueblo de Nuestra Señora de los Angeles, el Pueblo de San José de Guadelupe* and the third was *el Pueblo de Villa de Branciforte.*

The site for *Branciforte* was selected by Lieutenant Alberto de Cordova of the Spanish Army Corps of Engineers as an ideal location for a large population center. It was named for the Spanish Viceroy in Mexico. Corporal Gabriel Moraga was appointed to build and administer the pueblo. The 1834 Mexican land grant of Soquel and its 1844 *Aumentación* are a few miles south of Villa de Branciforte.[9]

Eight persons convicted under Spanish law were given, as an alternative to imprisonment at Guadlajara, the opportunity to colonize in Alta California. In 1797 they were sent with wives and children such as they had to be *los pobladores* of Villa de Branciforte.[10] To these were added, as further defense against hostile intrusion, *los Inválidos*. — The young soldiers who were pensioned upon completion of their ten-year enlistment at the presidios. The Indians were led into a system of peonage by the mission.

The pobladores, rather than taking up residence on the lots platted by Lieutenant de Cordova, established estates along the coast to the south. Their baronial Pacific vista was the great sweeping beach line forming the Monterey Bay. Seen dimly on a clear day, far across the bay, was the northern capital of Alta California — Monterey. Sargento retirado, Marcelino Bravo, arrived around 1800 to become the first caucasian resident of Soquel. The profane community of Villa de Branciforte, including its countryside villas, accommodated the sacred community of Santa Cruz (Holy Cross) by providing padrinos for Indian baptisms. Ultimately, Branciforte, as platted by Lieutenant de Cordova, was subsumed into the City of Santa Cruz.

Spanish Arcadia flourished in the coastal hills and valleys of Alta California and reached perhaps its finest flower on the shore line of Monterey Bay — just over the Santa Cruz Range from the idyllic Santa Clara Valley with its pueblo de San José on the Guadalupe River. The competing Santa Cruz coastal region became extraordinarily wealthy in a remarkably short time in the Mexican measure of wealth — cattle. The livestock brought by Portolá and the stock surviving Anza's trek became so numerous that they could no longer be contained in corrals. California's verdant valleys and rolling hills were open unfenced rangeland. The horses originally lost by Portolá and Anza filled the San Joaquin Valley with great herds of wild horses. The semi-wild cattle belonging to neighboring ranchos intermingled on the range. They were branded using *el fierro para herrar los ganados* to identify their owners. The large numbers of the christian Indians used to tend the half-wild stock were skilled *vaqueros* — the antecedents of the American cowboy. This was by far the most important industry in Mexican California bringing great wealth from the British and the "Bostons" in the 1828 to 1846 era of hide and tallow trade.[11]

Leon Rowland depicts the forty-four cattle brands registered by the *juez de campo* of Branciforte in the 1820s.[12] Among the prominent second generation pobladores registering cattle brands were the Rodrequez, the Robles and the Castros. As a portent of things to come, several rather strange spanish names also appeared — among them the Russian Jose Antonio Bolcoff, Samuel and Guillermo Bocle (William Buckle,) Jose Mechacas (Joseph L. Majors) and Isaac Graham. Four Branciforte residents had deserted from British privateer, Lord Chocrane, who had been participating in South American revolutions against Spanish rule. Others were Tennessee-Missouri types who came trapping along the old Spanish trail and the Gila.

It was this coastal region that welcomed Cap'n Joe Walker and his mountain man brigade, sent out by Bonneville in 1833, and entertained them with bull and bear fights. It appears that two of Walkers men may have stayed here. Charles Hopper knowing San José from his Bartleston-Bidwell adventure of 1841, was determined to settle there when he brought his extended family out from Missouri in 1847. The P.R. work of Cap'n Majors and Isaac Graham induced the Hoppers, the Moores and the Ganns to immediately move on to Santa Cruz. At that time countless thousands of half-wild cattle and horses fed along the coast and in the draws of the wooded foothills from Pescadero to the Pajaro river. Until the discovery of gold, the rangy long-horned Mexican cow was worth little. Suddenly, the beeves had a ready market. Hides and tallow became incidental but not unimportant. The hides formed the basis of a major Santa Cruz County industry — its tanneries.

The Spanish cattle baron began to fade from the picture when the winter of 1855-6 passed with little rain. The streams, wells and watering holes dried up and the trampled rangeland blew with dust storms. Thousands of horses were run off cliffs and killed to save the range for the cattle. Incredibly, the drought was preceded by a flood year but the rancheros never stored water or provisions — having never known the necessity. Over 100,000 head of cattle were lost in the county. Introduction of superior stock by American cattlemen furthered the demise of the Mexican rancho. The recurrence of drought in 1863-4 thoroughly completed the job. One million cattle perished in California. Hay sold for $150 a ton. Bleached cow bones covered the terrain. "Every ciénega became a Golgotha." Germanic animal husbandry thrived.[13] Miller & Lux emerged as cattle barons in the San Joaquin rangeland encompassing Los Banos in western Merced County. The american cowboy had arrived — followed several decades later by the film crew of Thomas Edison who made silent "oat-eaters" at Los Banos.

In Santa Cruz County the disappearing rancho and vaquero were replaced by hacienda endeavors such as vineyards, potato farms, apple orchards and finally sugar beets. The local germanic baron was the sugar baron, Claus Spreckels. The thick walled adobe ranch house crowned with an expanse of red terra cotta became the eloquent artifact of California's Spanish origins. The american proclivity to build structures crafted of wood was satisfied by the huge *palos colorados* encountered by Portolá when he traveled north from the *Rio del Pajaro*. The Santa Cruz Mountains and the Pacific Ocean form the local hydrological system producing streams and the rain loving redwoods on the slopes facing the ocean. Redwood sawmills have been a continuous part of Santa Cruz history from the Mexican days to well into this century. By the 1860s when the

Freshours, Baucoms and Himes left the San Joaquin for Santa Cruz County, the lumber industry was booming.

At the arrival of the Hopper-Gann party in 1847, with the exception of Sutter's New Helvetia at the confluence of the American and Sacramento Rivers, the settlements in California were in a small fringe along the coast. The fringe can be defined by mapping the missions strung like beads along *El Camino Real* — The Royal Road.[14] Portolá, with his troops, muleteers, padres and engineer, traveled the length of this fringe and back in 1769 — without benefit of a road or lime juice. These would come later.[15] The only road to Santa Cruz, until American enterprise created others, was the El Camino from the Pajaro River to Corralitos to Soquel to Santa Cruz Mission. This differed little from Portolá's route.

The San Andreas fault is a giant seam between continental plates. The fault line forms the Santa Cruz Mountain ridge that defines the boundary between Santa Clara and Santa Cruz Counties. The fault runs through the Carrizo Plain along the Temblor Range to the east of San Luis Obispo, north through the Salinas Valley, along the length of the Santa Cruz Range and up the San Francisco Peninsula to form the cleft filled with Crystal Springs Reservoir and passes out into the Pacific Ocean just to the east of San Francisco. The crest, viewed from the Santa Clara Valley as a blue green skyline, can be driven on roads giving access to mountain parks such as Portola State Park. Saratoga gap is at an altitude of 2634 feet and the summit of the modern as-the-crow-flies highway from San Jose to Santa Cruz is at 1800 feet. The dark eminence of *Loma Prieta* looms at 3900 feet over a panorama including the Santa Clara Valley and the Monterey Bay. Hecker Pass on the road from Watsonville to Gilroy is at 1300 feet. From there southward, the range tapers into small hills that occupy the region between the Santa Clara Valley and the Salinas Valley and spread across the fault to Watsonville and the ocean. The Pajaro River extends through these hills to bisect the great arc of the Monterey Bay shoreline making a natural route from the southern end of

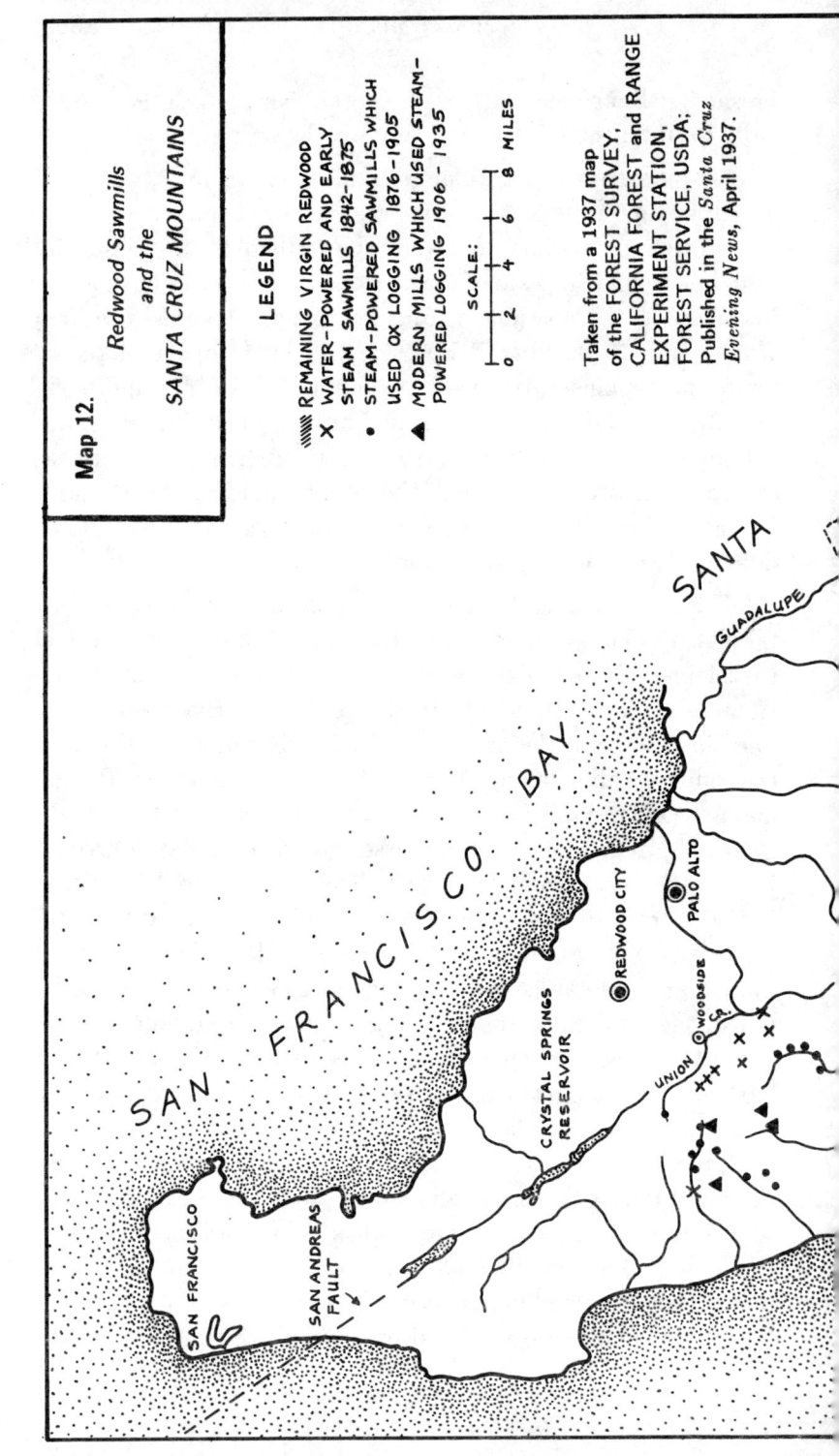

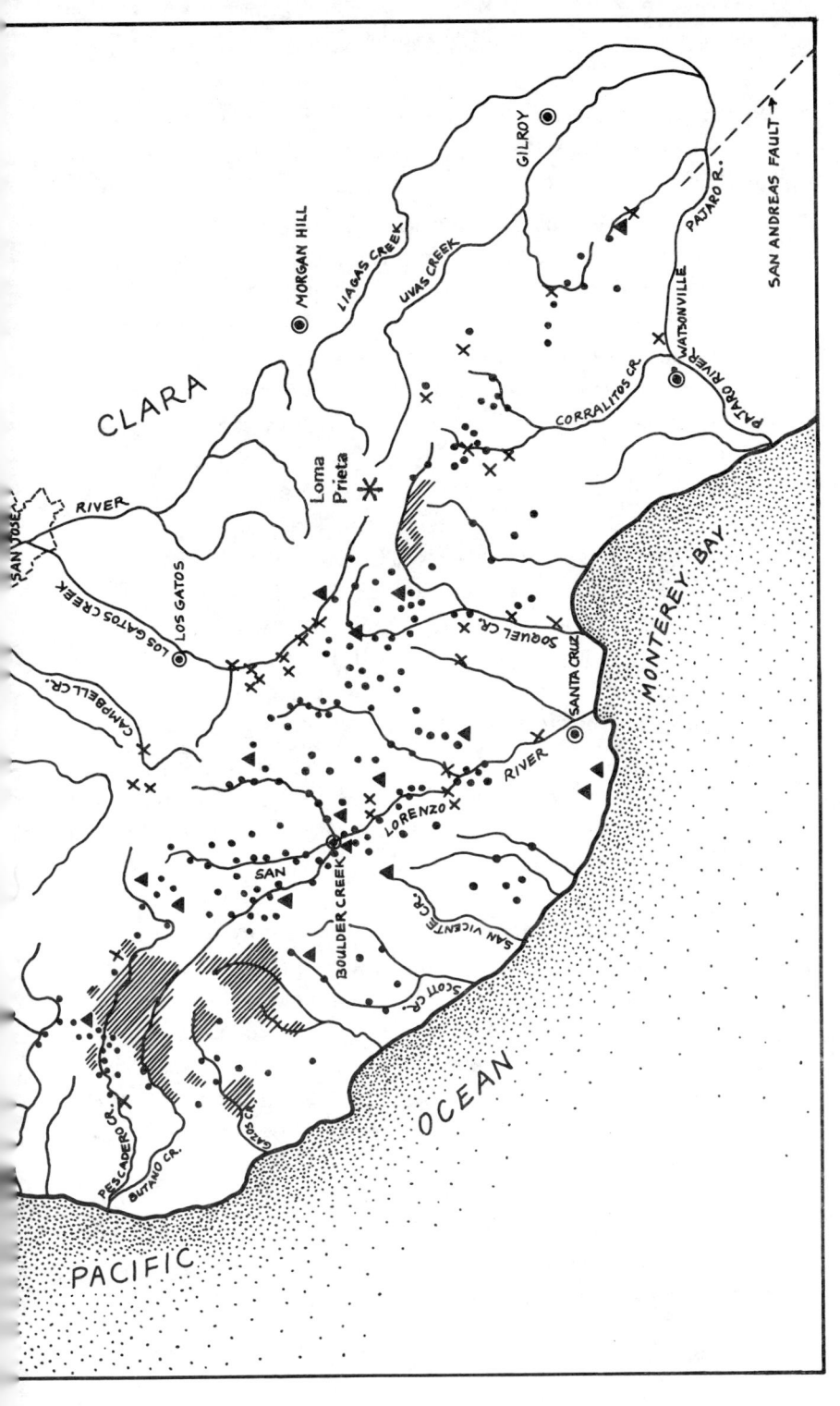

Santa Clara Valley to the ocean. This forms the end-around route from San Jose to Santa Cruz taken by the Hopper party in 1847 as described by Alexander Moore.

The gold rush shifted development into the Sierra and its supporting Great Valley communities. Nicholas Broyles Gann and his wife Rutha Freshour Gann who, with the John D. Gann family, were in the Hopper party apparently were at Santa Cruz briefly but returned with many of the Santa Cruz settlers to the interior for the gold rush. They were at Stockton with the John D. Ganns and Jas. R. Freshour in the 1850 census. Nicholas Gann and several other men who were also involved in Captain Weber's San Joaquin Valley enterprise and the southern mines had maintained their Santa Cruz interests. This is known from their 1850 Santa Cruz County testimony in the case of Willard Buzzell vs. Jackson Bennett.[16] The gold engendered boom burst in 1854 with a panic and subsequent economic doldrums. The economic development in the coastal communities that had been eclipsed in 1848 now assumed new importance. California had natural resources other than gold.

The Indian trails across the Santa Cruz Mountains became the horse trails of the Spaniards and Mexicans. They remained thus for the first decade under the American flag as Cornelius Cole and his new bride discovered in the summer of 1853. The young couple departed from Sacramento to visit some friends in Santa Cruz. They arrived at San Francisco by boat and continued to San Jose by stage coach, arriving in mid-afternoon. Not appreciating the distance nor the difficulties, they resolved to proceed at once, hoping to reach their destination that night. The trip could only be made on horseback. But horseback riding was not new to either of them. Procuring the best mounts available, and a guide to bring back the horses the next day, they skimmed over the eight or ten miles of intervening valley and were in the late afternoon shadow of the mountain before arriving at its base. As there was no sign of a settlement anywhere near, the only alternative was, either to plunge into the mountain forest at dusk or return to San Jose.

"...From now on the way was a single tortuous bridle path up the gradual mountain slope, through a dense growth of large overhanging trees. The moon was shining, but its light was almost entirely cut off by the foliage, so that we were compelled to ...trust to the instinct of our horses for the right road.

"After groping our way up the trail for an hour or more, our progress was suddenly interrupted. The horses stubbornly refused to proceed any further ...We soon learned that a large grizzly bear had camped directly on our line of march. There was no possibility of circumventing him by a flank movement, nor in any other way. ...the guide and myself, with lighted torches hastily prepared, advanced with due caution ...The only thing in all the world that will intimidate a full grown grizzly is a blazing fire. Our good generalship prevailed. The enemy in a hesitating mood slowly retreated before us, going further up the trail, but finally moved off to one side, so that Mrs. Cole, in the light of our torches, was able to bring up the horses, which we mounted and without further delay proceeded up the grade, but not without some apprehension ....

"The remainder of our jaunt that night, seemed almost interminable. It may have been near midnight when finally we arrived at the cabin-home of Mountain Charley at the summit. To go further then was out of the question and we remained there till morning. Charley had been living at this highest point on the Santa Cruz trail for years, leading almost a hermit's life. ...His domestic animals, for he tried to keep a few, had repeatedly been attacked and destroyed by the grizzly bears, which in early times infested this range of mountains to a frightful extent. Owing to their depredations Charley determined to make war upon the monsters ...to hunt and destroy them." [17]

The Coles descended into "the cozy valley of Santa Cruz," and passed through a "grove of mammoth trees." They had in fact traced the route taken by Frémont in his campaign a few years earlier. They found Santa Cruz in 1853, to be more of a scattered settlement than a concentrated village. Except on the ocean side it was hemmed in by mountains and quite isolated from the rest of the world. The only outlet for it, except by the mountain path leading over to the Santa Clara Valley, by which they had come, lay, skirting the ocean, — the route of Gaspar de Portolá.

Charles McKiernan finally tangled with the wrong bear. The Irish born McKiernan served in Australia with the British Army, rushed to California in 1850 and made his stake in the mines, ran a supply train from Trinidad to the Siskiyou mines and was nearly killed when this enterprise was wiped out by Indians. He found the best land around San Jose taken; so he settled on the Santa Cruz Mountain summit above Los Gatos and, being unable to raise stock due to the depredations of grizzlies, made a living as a professional hunter for the San Francisco market. He and a friend came suddenly upon a grizzly and her cubs while hunting on a May day of 1854. Charlie fired, wounding the rapidly closing bear, then beat her over the head with his gun until it broke and continued the battle with his hunting knife. He suffered the loss of his left eye and a crushed skull. His dog attacked the cubs, thus saving his life. After rescuing her cubs, the bear covered him with leaves and left him for dead. His friend had run for help and encountered Joseph L. Majors who helped secure a doctor and hammered out the silver Spanish coin which was placed to cover the hole in Charlie's skull. One can imagine the disappointment of the bear when she returned to eat Charlie and found him gone. Charlie married the lady that nursed him back to health and they reared seven children up on the mountain. Famed as one of the rare men to survive hand to hand combat with a grizzly, "Mountain Charlie" owned 3000 acres of timber and put in a toll road and later an inn for the stage coach trade.[18]

It was not until 1858 that the first stage coach road over the mountains was built by the Santa Clara Turnpike Company of Soquel. The competing Santa Cruz Turnpike used the Graham Road and the Mountain Charlie Road. The Soquel company won the competition. They finished their road first and it became the main route to San Jose.[19] It was upgraded into a wagon road that is now the "Old San Jose Road."

The railroad would later use the Pajaro River route for the same reasons that it had been the preferred freight wagon route from San Jose — because it was a well traveled near-sea-level grade. The stage coach road through the mountains initially was a pair of wheel tracks precariously following the ridges through brush and timber. The Santa Clara Turnpike, built in 1858, remained a stage road also used by buggy traffic, lumber wagons and logging operations. The steep winding grade had narrow cuts in the hillsides with turn outs to allow wagons to pass. It forded Hester and Soquel Creeks at twenty-five places between the summit and Soquel. Tolls were charged.

When Nicholas and Rutha moved from the San Joaquin to Santa Cruz in 1858, they probably took the El Camino down the Santa Clara Valley from San Jose to Gilroy and along the Pajaro River to Watsonville and thence north to Santa Cruz. This was yet another wagon trip heading west. When John and Sophronia and Joseph Terry Freshour moved from the San Joaquin in 1862 they could have used the Watsonville route or the more adventurous route over the summit. The Baucoms with grandma Elizabeth Freshour and the George Washington Himes had the same options.

After New Spain became Mexico, Irishman Michael Lodge settled with his wife, Martina Castro on the *Rio Shoquel* and built a three-room adobe overlooking Soquel Valley. Martina Castro Lodge was granted the half square league Rancho Soquel in 1834 by Governor Figueroa and *Shoquel Aumentación* was granted to her in 1844 to increase her holdings to about eight square leagues — the largest rancho in the region. Rancho Soquel produced long-horns for the hide and tallow trade and the Augmentation encompassed the *Rio Soquel* watershed with its vast stands of *Palos Colorados.* Martina's father, *inválido* Joaquin Castro, was granted San Andres Rancho and Raphael, her brother, was granted the Aptos Rancho.[20] Michael Lodge was murdered for his gold on his way back from the mines in

Figure 16.1 View of Soquel looking west towards Santa Cruz. (Late 1890s.)

— The History Museum of Santa Cruz County.

1849. Martina divided her land into nine equal sections; one for herself and eight for her children. Debts, litigation and lawyer's fees engendered by the US Land commission's hearing, caused most of this land to slip from their grasp. Much of this land was acquired, in the 1863 partitioning of the Augmentation, by Frederick Augustus Hihn who thus became the German lumber baron of Santa Cruz County. He improved Soquel Landing and developed it into the town of Capitola.[21]

The ford at *Rio Soquel* used by travelers between Corralitos and Villa Branciforte became a village when the first American settlers started using the water power of the stream for sawing lumber which they moved down river to Soquel Landing for shipment. In those early days much wheat was grown along the Santa Cruz coast. Although hardly a river, the stream, now called Soquel Creek, was adequate to power several grist mills and a flouring mill. In the early 1850s the population in the vicinity warranted the formation of Soquel Judicial Township. Edward and Ben Porter and a number of their cousins arrived in 1853. Edward and Ben established a tannery in Porter's Gulch, just east of Hihn's Capitola property. They shipped leather from Capitola Landing to San Quinten where the inmates manufactured boots and shoes. By 1865, the Porter tannery was producing enough leather per month to make 3000 boots. Later, in 1872, Claus Spreckels purchased land in Aptos Rancho just east of Porter's Gulch.[22]

In the 1860s, the Grover brothers, Frealon, Lyman and Whitney, natives of Maine timber lands, came to Soquel. The Grover Company acquired the nearby property along Bates Creek for the purpose of harvesting its large stands of *Sequoia Sempervirens*. In the 1860s and 70s Grover's Gulch, just outside of Soquel Village was the scene of a booming redwood sawmill business.[23] In 1868, the audacious little berg made a serious effort to get the State Capitol moved to Soquel. They were turned down. In the 1870s, Soquel boasted 11 saloons balanced by one Congregational Church, one flour mill, four sawmills, two tanneries, one sugar factory and a chair factory.[24]

Figure 16.2 Santa Cruz County Sawmill.

— Special Collections, McHenry Library, UCSC.

Soquel was a thriving community by the time the floods devastated California's Great Valley in 1861-2. Rutha and Nicholas had no doubt related to Rutha's sisters the virtues of Santa Cruz when they left the San Joaquin in 1858 and they had no doubt corresponded with their kin folk in the San Joaquin after settling at Santa Cruz. The flood gave impetus for the move to Soquel and those who did so arrived just as the community was beginning its boom. The men may have ridden over and staked out a place to settle before starting out from the San Joaquin with wagons loaded with household goods, women and children and all their earthly belongings.

John and Sophronia pulled into Soquel with their loaded wagons carrying five children; eight-year-old Will, almost-seven-year-old Joe, five-year-old Lydia Jane, three-year-old Annie and year-and-a-half GW. They would have the family milk cow along and probably some other stock including saddle horses. John's twenty-four-year-old Brother Joseph Terry would be driving the second wagon. Sophronia was thirty and John was thirty-seven. Some of the furniture and household goods and perhaps the wagons had come across the plains with them five years before. They acquired 160 acres above Soquel on the Laurel Glen Road. They soon had little Emily born to them in November of 1862. The George Washington Himes family arrived in the same style and settled nearby. The Joseph Baucom wagons pulled in with grandma Elizabeth and all their children. They acquired property in Soquel Township near Corralitos.[25]

Sacramento lay half submerged and at the edge of a vast lake as the Sacramento River swelled over its banks in the winter of 1861-2. Cornelius Cole and his wife had fond memories of their 1853 visit to Santa Cruz and had kept in contact with friends and relatives on the coast. The flood had risen to three feet above the floor of their house located well above expected high water level. This was reason enough to pack up three small children and all their household belongings and make the move to the security of coastal Santa Cruz. There was another reason of more lasting importance on Cornelius Cole's agenda.

When the young lawyer came west in 1849, he practiced law briefly in San Francisco then moved to Sacramento to become partner with McClatchey in the ownership of the Sacramento Times. In 1858 Cole became District Attorney of Sacramento County. He had joined with California's "big five," Leland Stanford, Charles and Edwin Crocker, Mark Hopkins and C.P. Huntington, in forming the California Republican Party and was well connected in Washington. Lincoln's secretary of state William H. Seward had been his law professor and mentor.[26] Cole's brother-in-law, Colonel Whiting — the port authority of Monterey, urged him to come to Santa Cruz as there was little "congressional material" in this district that reached as far south as Los Angeles.[27]

As a young congressman, Lincoln had blistered James K. Polk on the floor of congress for his aggression against Mexico. A later mellower Lincoln realized the necessity of political concessions as a choice of lesser evil. Polk was confronted with a powerful southern block determined to take Mexico and carve it into a number of slave states. Their appetite was wetted by the admission of Texas to the Union in December of 1845. Rather than all of Mexico they were tacitly allowed a large piece of it as potential slave-state admissions to the Union — all of New Mexico and Utah Territory and California — while Mexico proper was generously allowed to retain its national sovereignty. The Compromise of 1850 made Texas a slave state with slavery as an option for the remainder of the acquired Mexican territory except California which was admitted to the Union as a free state.[28] California was demographically a "border state" — half slave and half free. The California legislature, after heated debate in 1852, gave everyone who had brought slaves into the state prior to acceptance of its constitution, a year to emancipate them. The law was extended in 1853 and extended again in 1854. California's "free state" status became a cynical joke. Greeley's *New York Tribune* growled at the indulgence.[29] California was important to Lincoln's political schemes. Keeping California in the Union was of crucial importance to him.

Senator Gwin had represented California since 1849. Tall, courtly and southern by origin, Senator Gwin spoke before the US Senate in December of 1859:

> "I say that a dissolution of the Union is not impossible, that it is not impractical, and that the northern states are laboring under a delusion if they think that the southern states cannot separate from them either violently or peaceably; violently if necessary." [30]

California's anti-slavery senator Broderick was gunned down in a rigged duel by California's secessionist Chief Justice David S. Terry giving California two senators who favored secession.[31] The clandestine *Knights of the Golden Circle* was organized in California — some 24,000 of them, each required to equip himself with a rifle, revolver, bowie knife and ammunition.[32] The Knights defiantly responded to Lincoln's election by flying their palmetto flags in Southern California. After the Union defeat at Bull Run, the California secessionists fully expected to elect their own governor.

Under Gwin's influence, Albert Sidney Johnston was placed in command of the Western Military District. It was reported to McClatchey that Johnston was plotting to turn over the state's ordnance to the Knights, given the opportunity. Hooves pounded across Nevada high desert. The Pony Express rider, buckskin fringes fluttering in the breeze, strained forward in the saddle urging his horse on, carrying the urgent dispatch for President Lincoln. Lincoln quickly replaced Johnston with E.A. Sumner. General Sumner rushed loyal troops down from Fort Vancouver and the Oregon District of Washington Territory to suppress the armed secessionists. Sumner had Senator Gwin arrested for recruiting US Army officers for Confederate service. Confederate troops from Texas invaded and occupied New Mexico Territory. They were defeated at Glorieta Pass by US troops from Colorado and New Mexico and the California Column drove the remnants well into Texas.[33]

Although southern forces failed to take over the former Mexican territories, they remained as a guerrilla threat and

California was isolated from the Union which was not winning the war at this time. The grisly specter of the guerrilla warfare going on in Missouri frightened Californians. The California legislature voted in 1862 to form the California Militia, under Governor Stanford as their commander-in-chief, in order to deal with this threat of internal insurrection. The militia was funded for two companies of infantry and one company of cavalry for *each* county. This addressed the lack of adequate rail transportation to move troops around the state to deal with guerrilla outbreaks. The citizen soldiers of each county using arms supplied by US Arsenals would be prepared to handle any local insurrection. The very presence of these troops would obviate the threat.

As an avid horseman, Cornelius Cole would be sure to encourage organization of a cavalry unit in Santa Cruz County. He would also promote the organization of Union Clubs within the county to militate against any laissez faire attitude towards the seceded states. The "Peace Democrats," who wanted to stop the killing and permit the Confederacy to coexist with the Union with the vague hope of future reconciliation, were more of a political threat to the Union than outright secessionists, in the view of Republicans. Cole would have as a paramount objective to become the Republican Congressman from Santa Cruz to prevent this prize from falling into the hands of the strong Peace Democrat following in the county. Quite an agenda — and Cornelius Cole, the new lawyer in Santa Cruz, was just the man to handle it.

Before jumping into the fray of Civil War politics in Santa Cruz County, Cole decided to visit his family in New York and secure his political ties in Washington. He had been in California for fourteen years. He embarked at San Francisco in February of 1863 for the trip via Panama. From there the voyage, designed to avoid Confederate interception, took them to Jamaica and via the Atlantic into safe Union territory. He visited troops in the field and briefed Seward on the state of affairs in California. His return overland journey in April was relatively civilized until he reached Denver. For eighteen days and nights he was confined to the stagecoach that traveled from Denver to Carson, with only brief stops at the outposts where the horses were changed. The driver on the preceding stage had been killed in an Indian attack and a passenger drove the stage on in to the next station.[34]

A baby daughter was born to the Coles at Santa Cruz on the first of June. The venerable Santa Cruz County Judge, R.F. Peckham, certified Cornelius Cole to superintend the organization of a cavalry company on the 12th of June 1863.[35] Cole had a legal notice of the organizational meeting published ten days prior in the *Santa Cruz Sentinel* and posted in three public places. The State Republican Convention commenced at San Francisco on June 17th. Cole sent a legal document, dated June 22nd at San Francisco, appointing Lucian Curtis Esquire to organize the cavalry. The Republican candidates, including C. Cole for Congress, were listed under the masthead of the *Sentinel*. The organization petition of the Santa Cruz Cavalry Company and the proceedings for election of officers are dated June 23rd. The sixty-one petitioners included John W. Morgan, J. T. Freshour, Jacob Parsons and William Reed of Soquel. The first name on the petition was Albert Jones who operated stables on Mission Street in Santa Cruz. He was elected first Lieutenant. Cornelius Cole was elected Captain. Cole signed the sworn and certified oath required for his commission as a Captain in the California Militia. Since Cole was nominated as a candidate for Congress, it was not likely that he would be available for Militia service after the November elections.

Santa Cruz County burgeoned during the war years with most of the 4600 residents working at manufacturing lumber, leather, lime, paper, glue and soap. Shipping was from the landings at Santa Cruz, Capitola and Watsonville. Santa Cruz County commanded the leather and lime markets of the State but its largest business was lumber. Dairy farming and wheat production were important and John Hames was running his flour mill at Soquel. The bustling populace followed the war news and newspaper notices of Santa Cruz troops in service with the US Army. These included the exploits of "Albert Brown's" cavalry company serving with the California Column and news of Captain Tidball's infantry company serving in the Southwest. These units provided security for the stage coaches carrying US Mail and for the travelers on wagon roads. The Pony Express had been replaced by the telegraph which also needed to be secured against the Indians who needed the wire for handicrafts.

Terse telegraphed eastern reports of the War were printed in the weekly papers at Watsonville and Santa Cruz. Detailed accounts were cribbed from the eastern papers which arrived by ship weeks later. The Freshours of Soquel had more than a passing interest in the war. From correspondence with their brothers and sisters in Iowa they knew that their brother, Alfred, had been wounded at the battle of Pea Ridge and their brother-in-law, Andrew Dow, was wounded at Chickasaw Bayou.

Independence Day was celebrated by Santa Cruz in 1863 with a rural barbecue that included reading of the Declaration of Independence and an oration. After dinner there were toasts responded to by Cornelius Cole, William Anthony and John Nutter. The Santa Cruz Volunteers with their Ladies where honored. Actually, organization of the California Militia was just getting started when the July 8th telegraphed dispatch from Lincoln's Secretary of War was published in the *Sentinel*.

> Hon. F.F. Low — In three days battle at Gettysburg, Lee's army was beaten, and retreated through mountain passes to the Potomac. Lee is today in Williamsport trying to cross the river ...
>
> Vicksburg surrendered to Grant on the fourth of July.
>
> EDWIN M. STANTON

A UNION CELEBRATION on the Santa Cruz Plaza included speeches and a torchlight parade which ended with patriotic songs by a group of ladies. Banners, it was reported, included "The Union Forever" and a bespectacled ass labeled "Neutral." This was the turning point of the war. The North had been without a notable Victory. — Now they had two. The *Sentinel* of August the 8th Carried a full page account of the Gettysburg Battle taken from the New York Tribune. European powers took note. England withdrew its support of the Confederacy. Lincoln now had a chance of winning a second term running against the intensely eloquent Vallandingham who had branded Lincoln as a despot who rejected reasonable offers of peace in his determination to liberate blacks and enslave their masters. Lincoln's unpopular policy now assumed credibility. Cornelius Cole noticed a like change in the political climate in California. The latent Confederate threat in California diminished. The Union Clubs and the California Militia had made their mark on public attitudes. Preservation of the Union was becoming popular. *One* Nation, *indivisible,* ...

The cavalry company got off to a slow start because Cole was busy campaigning. The members of the company supplied their own horses and saddles and the California Militia was to supply the uniforms and the Colt pistols, sabers and accoutrements. The company had not faced the fact that their officers had to post a sizeable bond before the State Arsenal would ship the arms. While in this organizational muddle, the company supplied its own fatigue uniforms and commenced weekly squad drills and met once a month for company drill. On November 28th of 1863 under the headline SANTA CRUZ CAVALRY the *Sentinel* reported: " — this Company of young men paraded through our streets on Thursday. They are fine riders and even without uniforms made a fine display."

It was finally apparent that Cole's politicking had left them in limbo. They had not even filled in a Muster Roll nor sent it in to Brigade Headquarters as required. An election of new officers was held on October the 5th according to the *Sentinel* but was not reported to Brigade — it was no doubt contested. The men were upset because nothing had been done to obtain arms and uniforms and the future availability of Cornelius Cole was problematical. Ranks were reduced to forty-three members. The November congressional election determined that Cornelius Cole would be in Washington. The company finally got off to a belated start as a proper military organization with the November 13th election of Deputy Sheriff Orville Root as Captain. George Anthony of Santa Cruz was First Lieutenant. Blacksmith, Jacob Parsons of Soquel was Second Lieutenant. Soquel's young lawyer, Henry P. Stone was First Sergeant. John W. Morgan, a Soquel farmer was Second Sergeant and Joseph Freshour, mill hand from Soquel was Third Sergeant. A vigorous round of correspondence between Captain Root and the Adjutant General of California determined the bond requirement to be $5,000 and details about obtaining arms and uniforms were clarified. By March of 1864, evidence of the bond was supplied to the Adjutant General in Sacramento and arms were requisitioned. The company rented Farnham Hall in Santa Cruz as their Armory.

The Santa Cruz Cavalry mustered March 8th in 1864 and sent the Muster Roll to 2nd Brigade HQ in San Francisco — a list of fifty-six men and four officers. There were, besides the Lieutenant and the three Sergeants, a number of privates from Soquel. — Among them Joe and Reese Baucom, Lewis P. Bates, John Freshour, Ephriam Hattery, Calvin Johnson and Edward Smith. The number of men had been reduced by some resignations and "pulsions" and they had been furnished no uniforms nor arms. They mustered a month later with an issue of fifty sabers with saber belts, fifty pistols with holsters, twenty-five bullet moulds and spare parts and tools. The weekly squad drill was held at the armory and, once a month, Saturday afternoon was given to parade drill. Most of the time these men were employed at their regular work in mills or farming. The Soquel boom continued. Titus Hale and Ed Briody put in a new tannery on Holcomb Creek located three miles from the wharf. There was an abundance of tanbark in the immediate vicinity. Tradition has it that John Freshour worked for the Porter Tannery.

In June, Captain Root requisitioned uniforms and the company was able to parade on the fourth of July in full regalia — uniformed and mounted and proudly wearing their sabers and Colt revolvers. Many from Soquel and Corralitos would go to Santa Cruz for the Parade since their "boys" were riding with the Cavalry Company. The Freshours and Baucoms would be there for sure.

The Citizen Soldiers of the California Militia operated under democratic principles. They annually elected their officers, commissioned and non-commissioned. In February of 1865, 2nd Lieutenant Jacob Parsons became 1st Lieutenant and Sergeants Stone and Morgan became 2nd Lieutenants giving the Santa Cruz Cavalry all Soquel men as commissioned officers except for Captain Root who was invariably re-elected. The Muster Roll of March, 1865 was reduced from sixty-one to forty-seven men. Captain Claremont Smith was recruiting at Watsonville for Company A, Eighth California Infantry of the US Army. This was a chance for full time soldiering beyond county or state boundaries. Among those young men who jumped at the chance was Joseph Terre Freshour. His older brother John remained in the Santa Cruz Cavalry along with the other older men who had families to look after.

Joseph Terry Freshour enlisted for a term of three years of service in the Eighth California Infantry on the 12th of November, 1864 at Watsonville and mustered in on November 17th at Fort Point, San Francisco as a Private. He was appointed Sergeant on November 25th. His height was given as six foot two inches; his eyes, hair and complexion were given as dark; his occupation as farmer. The Eighth California Infantry was sent to Fort Vancouver, Department of Columbia, District of Oregon, Washington Territory. Brigadier General Ben Alford commanded the District.

General Alford was charged with establishing fortifications, including eight inch and ten inch guns, at the mouth of the Columbia River to prevent enemy incursions. A wharf was to be built there to facilitate the task. General Alford sent a detachment in March of 1864 to Cape Disappointment to commence the work which continued through 1865. Most of the troops provided security for the populace. Joe spent July and August of 1865 on Detached Service at Cape Disappointment. Company A of the Eighth California Infantry was back at Fort Point and mustered out of US service on October 24th, 1865. J.T. Freshour mustered out with his company.[36]

The War of the Rebellion had passed through its final phase in 1865 with Lee surrendering the Army of Northern Virginia to U.S. Grant on April the 9th and Joe Johnston surrendering to Sherman on April 26th. The large Union Army was no longer needed and general demobilization followed. California reorganized its Militia. The new National Guard of California took its place. All CM companies were mustered out of service in October of 1866.

The Santa Cruz Cavalry reorganized as a California Guard company on October 11th. Joe Freshour rejoined and served with his brother John as a Private. Their Soquel neighbor, Joseph Frey, joined them. The officers remained the same — Orville Root as Captain with his three Soquel Lieutenants. Santa Cruz founding father, Elihu Anthony, a charter member of the company was still with them as treasurer. The Santa Cruz infantry company — the Butler Guard — disbanded at this time. Some of its members, such as Duncan McPherson of the *Sentinel*, joined the cavalry company. Horse soldiering was becoming popular. George Otto joined. When the Santa Cruz Cavalry mustered, in January of 1867, its ranks included some prominent Soquel citizens: miller, George Washington Giles, blacksmith, William H. Harrison Green and the lumberman, Frealon Grover. Soquel's hotel owner, Thomas W. Mann was now Fourth Sergeant. This was the last time John and Joe Freshour rode together with the cavalry company.[37]

The primitive roads of Santa Cruz County were made impassable by the winter storms of 1866-7. Captain Root reported that men from outlying regions couldn't get into Santa Cruz for weekly drill because of swollen streams. John rode into town, the 31st of January, after a physician to see Sophronia. Returning that evening, near Porter's tanyard, a bridge broke through with him. "He got his horse out – and felt uninjured himself; proceeded home, sat down for a while, and then went to the stable to see if his horse was hurt. While examining the horse he fell dead." [38] John died at age fourty-one of a heart attack. Tradition has him dying while mounting his horse at Porter's tannery. He left Sophronia with seven children ages two to thirteen and twins on the way. Anderson Arthur and Rutha Malinda were born two months later. John also left Sophronia a quarter of a section of land. John's brother, Joe, bought the Freshour plot at the IOOF Cemetery in Soquel and John was the first of the family to be buried there. John had left Tennessee as a child, just as had Sarah Freshour Himes and Rutha Freshour Gann. Emaline Freshour was married to Joseph Baucom from Tennessee and Elizabeth Freshour, who lived with them, had born most of her children in Tennessee. Rutha, Sarah and Emaline were her daughters and her son, Lawson Henderson Freshour was then farming at Corralitos. John's funeral was an occasion to reminisce together on their Greene County Tennessee origins and their pioneering across the country. One of the strong ties they had with John and Sophronia was the overland trek they had all made in covered wagons. Ten-year-old Lydia Jane, born on the Sweetwater, was there as a reminder of the joys and hardships they had shared on the trail. John's family in Iowa would have to know. Joseph Terry would write to his brothers and sisters. The terrible news went east in the overland mail.

The Santa Cruz Cavalry mustered in September of 1867 at full strength, complete with its Soquel officers and enlisted men, but they were troubled by delinquent reimbursement from the California Guard. The officers of the company were footing the bills. The financially troubled State had to down-size the Guard. Governor Low decided that Santa Cruz County Guard companies were dispensable. Joe Freshour had signed their organization petition in 1863 and now, he rode for the last time with his Soquel friends as the Santa Cruz Cavalry mustered out of service in January of 1868. The muzzle loading Colt six-shooters, sabers and uniforms were returned to the State Armory but the camaraderie was theirs to keep forever. The cavalrymen of Soquel had paid their respects at the funeral of their comrade, John Freshour a year earlier.

As her portrait attests, Sophronia at thirty-six years of age was a very handsome widow. Sophronia Freshour married Alfred Musgrave at Soquel in July of 1868.[39] Martha Ellen Musgrave was born in May of 1869. In 1870, Sophronia Musgrave headed the Freshour household. Her eldest son, sixteen-year-old Will, was listed as a wood chopper and shingle maker, Joseph T. Freshour, lived nearby. Alfred Musgrave was working elsewhere as a hired hand.[40] George Washington Himes, his wife Sarah and their children were Sophronia's neighbors. Nicholas Gann and his wife Rutha lived in Santa Cruz. Sophronia's three-year-old Rutha was no doubt named after Rutha Gann. Thirteen-year-old Lydia Jane was working as a domestic that summer for Baden farmer, Adam Martin, and his family in Pajaro Township. Sophronia had five children in school and a five-year-old and the three-year-old twins at home. It's hard for us to see how she got by. She was surrounded by caring friends, neighbors and kinfolk. Joseph T. probably helped considerably.

In 1872, Will and Sophronia sold her one-hundred and sixty acres to Jose Maria Carravajal and Mariano Soto. Justice of the Peace, Lambert Clements, wrote up the deed.[41] Over the remainder of the century, Sophronia would see her children grow up and marry — most of them in Soquel. "Ruby," as Rutha was called, remained single. Sophronia lived to enjoy her children and grandchildren well into the 20th century. She outlived John by almost half a century. She rests beside him in the Soquel Pioneer Cemetery.

17

STEAM POWERED SOQUEL

SANTA CRUZ WAS, in 1857, as remote as Shangri-La. It was at the end of a circuitous two-day stagecoach ride from San Francisco. The round-about route from San Jose went through San Juan Bautista and followed the Pajaro River to Watsonville and then went up the coast through Corralitos and Soquel to Santa Cruz. The shorter stage routes through the mountains were developed in 1858 when the first stage over the "Soquel Turnpike" rattled into Soquel.[1] These coaches plunged through groves of timber with tree branches slapping the sides of the coach and careened down mountain ridges. Where they had slow uphill climbing, they were prey for armed stage robbers.[2] The San Jose Stage screeched to a stop in front of Tom Mann's hotel and, the stopover completed, lurched out with the driver's whistle, pop of the whip and guttural "gee-dap" — headed west for the last few miles to Santa Cruz. The stage route through Corralitos to Watsonville continued to provide connections to Monterey, Salinas, Gilroy and, for those wishing to go end around, San Jose.

The stagecoach routes continued to be the overland method for getting into the isolated communities of Santa Cruz County through the Civil War years and through the remainder of the 1860s. The dominant method of freight transport was by coastal ship. Among the first rail systems on the west coast were those extending from the wharves of the shipping companies to the towns in the small coastal valleys. It was common for the rails to run out on a pier where the vessels docked.[3] The great river system of California's central valley afforded natural freight channels for the many valley farm towns located on river banks where barges and boats could carry their commodities to market. This dominance of freighting on the waterways was to be superseded in California, as it had been earlier in the east, by the "iron horse."

It was in Omaha in 1859 that Lincoln had picked the brains of Grenville Dodge, the engineer who had surveyed west from Omaha for the Pacific railroad. Colonel Dodge was wounded leading his Iowa Infantry at Pea Ridge and rapidly rose in rank. While serving under Sherman at Atlanta, Brigadier General Dodge was severely wounded. While recuperating, he was called to the White House by Lincoln to discuss their ambition to build the transcontinental railroad. With southerners no longer in congress to deadlock legislation over the choice of route, Lincoln had easily gotten his railroad to California enacted into law. He signed the Pacific Railroad Act in July of 1862. Dodge was placed in command of the Western Department at the edge of the plains. His ability to organize and lead men was later put to use in driving the Union Pacific up the Platte Valley, across Wyoming and down the Wasatch into Utah — a route he designed.[4]

Meanwhile, in California, Leland Stanford and his cronies threw their resources into an achievement that was equal, in its day, to putting a man on the moon in the twentieth century. Stanford drove the golden spike connecting his *Central Pacific* with the *Union Pacific,* near Ogden, Utah, in 1869.[5] This brilliant feat of civil engineering did the unthinkable. It crossed the Sierra crest in the locale where the Donner Party had perished — the most direct route through the most hostile terrain. This achievement was made possible when the new explosive, dynamite, was applied where blasting powder had been ineffectual. Nor would it have been possible without the Chinese.[6] California was now tethered to the Eastern States by a pair of steel ribbons — demonstrating the solution to the geographic isolation problem but hardly solving it.

It was finally in the 1880s that the U.S. was bound coast to coast by an adequate rail system. The *Northern Pacific,* connecting Seattle to Duluth on Lake Superior, was finished in 1883. The *Atchison, Topeka & Santa Fe* spanned from the Missouri River to Southern California in 1884 — the same year that the *Southern Pacific* finally connected Los Angeles to New Orleans. The five transcontinental railroads were completed when the *Great Northern,* running north of the Northern Pacific, had its final spike hammered home in 1893.[7] The railroads were for the most part privately owned. They created a new moneyed aristocracy — also known as "robber barons."

The great iron horse, and steam power in general, began taking over in California during the 1870s. Stanford's Southern Pacific coastal route, going south from San Jose to Los Angeles via Santa Barbara, made its way gradually during the 60s from San Jose down through the Santa Clara Valley to Gilroy and, in the 70s, followed the Pajaro River west from the Santa Clara Valley to reach the town of Pajaro near Watsonville. From there it followed the Salinas River inland to Salinas in 1873. This brought the iron rails into Santa Cruz County. The stage coach line running from Soquel to Watsonville provided railroad connections to San Jose — and, to San Francisco.

To Frederick Hihn and Claus Spreckels, the two wealthiest men in Santa Cruz County, this was an opportunity to get into the railroad business themselves. Hihn had tried for years to interest Santa Cruz in a railroad to San Jose and now managed to get a public subsidy on the ballot for a simpler project connecting Pajaro to Santa Cruz. The *Pajaronian* was scathing in its criticism. Since the citizens of Watsonville were a short wagon haul to the S.P. depot at Pajaro, they voted the subsidy down. Hihn stubbornly persisted with the construction of "Hihn's railroad." He spitefully laid out a route through his own properties and bypassed not only Watsonville but Soquel and Corralitos as well. A court injunction forced him to change the route to go through Watsonville. Work on the roadbed started in 1874 and rails were laid in 1876.[8] The tedious two-day stagecoach ride of 1857 from Santa Cruz to San Francisco could now be traveled in a few hours by rail.

Sophronia and the Himes and the Baucoms reared their children in Soquel and Corralitos through the Civil War years and the 1870s. As they grew up, they witnessed the development of roads and stagecoach lines. The wagons hauling lumber from Grover's Gulch to Soquel Landing were a common sight for them. The cutting of tanbark and hauling it to the curing sheds at the tannery was to them a familiar industry. Sophronia had spent her formative years on the frontier and signed her name with an "x." Soquel had a school where her children and the Himes' children learned the "three R's." Even though John was gone and she had to go it alone, they had come to a better life in a better place. The industry of the community provided work for loggers, bull whackers and mill hands and there was plenty of work for teamsters and farm hands. The boys grew up learning how to wield an ax to chop wood and how to grease skids so the logs pulled down to the mills by bull teams would slide over the skid roads but not slide out of control endangering the oxen. When they came of age they would work as bull whackers and mill hands or at felling trees. As teenagers they were familiar with steam powered mills and as young adults they saw the railroads come into use in the timber. They also saw the stationary steam engine with winch and cables — the "donkey engine" — replace the skid road oxen. They would all go down to Aptos in May of 1875 for "The Event of the Season" as the *Sentinel* billed it. A premature grand opening was staged for the partially completed Santa Cruz Railroad to allay the apprehension of the stockholders. Among the dignitaries of the day were Claus Spreckels and Frederick Hihn who were heavily invested in this narrow gauge short line. Hihn was its president. Governor Pacheco rode the construction train pulled by the diminutive narrow gauge locomotive "Betsy Jane." At the Aptos ceremony, Spreckels invited the crowd to a celebration and ball at his Aptos Hotel. Governor Pacheco and Spreckels exchanged toasts and the communities of Watsonville and Santa Cruz were reconciled by the gala event.[9]

In the spring of 1876 the Soquel citizenry would go down to Capitola to see the wondrous sight of the wood-burning Baldwin eight-wheel locomotive belching smoke as it rumbled over the 670 foot span of the bridge towering over Soquel Creek. In tow were two passenger cars with waving passengers celebrating the completion of the railroad connecting Santa Cruz with Watsonville. As the train puffed into view, it rolled past Spreckels sugar mill and then, at the approach to the bridge, it passed the tents of Hihn's Camp Capitola.[10]

Rail transportation had come to Soquel — well, almost. Another stagecoach enterprise bit the dust. Among the festive crowd enjoying the excitement that day would be Sophronia, her sons, Will, age twenty-two, Joe, age twenty and his uncle, "Long Joe" and the rest of the Freshour bunch including Elias and "Liddie" Bradley with one-year-old John Wesley.

Thirty-nine-year-old Elias Bradley was farming in Soquel in 1867. Elias was from Geauga County, Ohio. He had come to California driving an eight-mule team.[11] Bradley was an unmarried farmer without land in 1870 at Soquel — probably farming rented land. To make ends meet Sophronia took in boarders. This may have been how she encountered Musgrave. Elias and Sophronia would have made a good match were it not for her unresolved Musgrave entanglement. Sophronia's eldest daughter, seventeen-year-old Lydia Jane, was marriageable. Elias Bradley and Lydia Jane Freshour were married in April of 1874 at the residence of the bride's mother. Soquel Justice of the Peace, Lambert R. Clements, officiated.[12] He would serve the Freshour family in this capacity on a number of future occasions. J.T. Freshour was the witness. The bride and groom were presented with a splendid new family bible elegantly inscribed in its record pages with a record of Elias and Lydia Jane's wedding and records of John and Sophronia's family. This timely gift restored, as much as possible, the records lost when the family bible was burned in the fire that destroyed their home in Iowa.

Photos this page — Leitha Roberts Collection.

Rhoda Ann & Lydia Jane

Elias Bradley

John Freshour

Sophronia

Figure 17.1: Soquel Freshours & Bradleys.

The Bradleys settled in Grover's Gulch.[13] That year, Hihn graded the roadbed for his railroad from Watsonville. Grover's steam powered mill was busy and running wagons loaded with lumber to the Soquel Landing. *La Playa de Soquel* landing was three miles from the town of Soquel. Soquel's Main Street runs parallel along the east side of Soquel creek and continues up into Grover's Gulch — the small canyon now identified by Glen Haven Road. The hilly little canyon, nine miles in length, is drained by Bates Creek, a branch running from north east into Soquel Creek. It is bounded on the east by the ridge of Aptos Creek and on the west by the ridge separating it from Soquel Creek. The northern dead end of Grover's Gulch is at Hinckley ridge. The Grover brothers acquired the huge stand of redwood timber along Bates Creek and commenced logging it in 1860. The Grovers at one time were operating four sawmills in the county as well as a large commercial establishment in Santa Cruz and they even owned an ocean going vessel to transport their sawmill products. Frealon "Godfrey" Grover managed and lived at their operation at Soquel. A God fearing family man, the nearest he ever came to cursing was the euphemism, "Godfrey," hence, the nickname.

The Grover sawmill on Bates Creek was relocated twice to keep the skid roads to reasonable length. The third and last mill in Grover's Gulch was at the head of Bates Creek near the base of Hinckley ridge. The first mill was at the end of present day Prescott Road, originally a Grover Company wagon road. The huge felled redwoods were trimmed of limbs and cut to length and the logs thus formed were drug down the slopes over narrow skid roads that had been laboriously pick-axed by hand. Peeled limbs of madrone or oak hardwood were embedded across the trail at four to ten foot intervals to act as skids. Tallow was smeared on the crosspieces so the trains of giant redwood logs chained end to end and pulled by yokes of oxen would more easily skid down the road to the mill pond. The logs floated in the pond waiting their turn on the carriage that ran the log back and forth over the whirling circular blade

Figure 17.2 Frealon Grover with Millhands.

— Courtesy of Special Collections, McHenry Library, UCSC.

under the sawyers expert control. The make-shift building next to the pond housed the boiler and steam driven pistons that revolved a system of shafts, belts and pulleys that enlivened the workings of the mill.

The mill had a payroll of some fifty to sixty men including a few teenagers. They lived in rustic cabins built of rough lumber and slept on straw filled burlap mattresses. They worked twelve hour days for $1.50 per day, fifty cents of which went for room and board. They ate in a mess hall presided over by a Chinese cook. As the days grew short they worked by lantern light and when the rainy season set in the mill closed for about two months. A company store was close at hand to provide sacks of flour and other staples, single and double bit axes, ax handles, kerosene and wicks for lanterns, sacks of grain to feed the draft animals, plug tobacco, Bull Durham, red flannels, overalls and other needs peculiar to woodsmen to busy to go to town.

A small settlement was nestled around the mill. Besides the general store, there was a blacksmith shop, barns with corrals for oxen, mules and horses and wagon sheds. Homes with newly planted orchards sprang up on the hills at the west side of the road. All the buildings were of vertical rough sawn board walls, battened to seal out the weather. The buildings were roofed with redwood shakes. They could be given more class by tacking cheese cloth to the inside walls and wallpapering them. Locally produced lime could be used as whitewash on the exteriors to give the homes greater refinement. Stud walls and linseed oil paint were for the more permanent dwellings of the affluent.

A youngish Frealon Grover rode with the Santa Cruz Cavalry in the days when the first mill centered this village in Grover's Gulch. In 1869, Frealon Grover brought his new bride from Maine to live in a seven room house in his Gulch. Their first three children were born there. At about the time the Santa Cruz Railroad started running through Capitola, Frealon built an earthquake-proof two-story house in Soquel. Two more children were born to the Grovers there.

— Soquel Pioneer and Historical Association.

Figure 17.3: Jerkline Team of D.W. Grover hauling from the Grover Eldorado Sawmill on Bean Creek. Note mounted driver.

— Leitha Robert's Collection.

Figure 17.4: A.A. Freshour and John Bradley.

John Wesley Bradley was born to Elias and "Liddie" in Grover's Gulch in February of 1875. He would grow up in Glen Haven, as Grover's Gulch was later named, and he would, as a teenager, work as a "swamper" on an eight-horse team lumber wagon for Frealon Grover. John and his sister, Lydia Ann (named for her great aunt,) walked to the school in Soquel until the Glen Haven School was built in 1888.[14] A Dr. Taylor had built a sanatorium which he romantically named Glen Haven to evoke the Elysian beauty of its environs. "Grover's Gulch Sanatorium" wouldn't have been very attractive to ailing folk. Dr. Taylor's venture fizzled out but it gave its euphonious name to the new school and hence to the community.

By 1887, the Grover Company had prospered so much that Frealon and Sarah Grover and their children moved to a superb Victorian mansion on Walnut Street in Santa Cruz where his brother Lyman Grover had his mansion. Frealon continued to direct the operations in Grover's Gulch. The mill had moved up Bates Creek and the jerkline teams were hauling lumber down Slab Alley. The dusty wagon ruts began to turn muddy from watering trough overflow that decided to follow the ruts; so, slabs from the first cut on logs were placed in corduroy pattern along the narrow roadway making for a very bumpy ride. This was typical of logging roads in Santa Cruz County at that time.

Oxen managed by a bullwhacker were used to haul logs down skid roads but lumber was hauled by wagons pulled by five to eight span of horses or mules. The team pulled on a chain attached to the wagon tongue and was guided by a single rein handled by a teamster riding the saddled nigh wheeler. The jerkline team is reminiscent of the connestoga wagon teams even down to the melodious chiming of the hame bells mounted on iron bows. But the jerkline teams were trained with "pointers" and "leaders" to negotiate steep winding logging roads up hill and down hill. The superb skill of the animals and their driver commanded great respect.[15] Loads of lumber were hauled through Glen Haven for thirty-six years. Grover's third mill in

— Special Collections, McHenry Library, UCSC.

Figure 17.5: Frealon Grover's record 600 ton log pull at his "Minni-Ha-Ha" property. Chris Ifert is the bull driver. Judge Logan later purchased the property and built Brookdale Lodge.

the gulch was closed down in 1896. The Grover Company had other operation such as their Bean Creek mill. The lumberjacks and mill hands followed the mills leaving Glen Haven as a quiet little farm community with a lot of stumps and redwoods too small to cut. John Bradley found work on the Cowell ranch over in Santa Cruz.

The year 1876 was a notable year for the Soquel Freshours and their kin folk. It had been one-hundred years since the English speaking people of North America had decided to independently develop the Continent. Now, several generations later, the children that had traveled with their parents across the plains, the ones born on the trip and the Native Sons and Native Daughters born after they arrived, had come to their majority years and were getting married. Rhoda Ann "Annie" Freshour, age sixteen, and Charles Morrison, both of Soquel, were married in March of 1875 in Soquel. Judge L.B. Clements married Joseph Alfred Freshour and Agnes C. Mack at the residence of the brides parents near Soquel in March of 1876. Irena Beswick married William Freshour at the residence of the brides parents at Soquel in April of 1876, Justice Clements again officiating. Nineteen-year-old Annie Morrison, née Freshour, of Soquel and Irena's brother, Richard Beswick, of Gilroy were married at Soquel in September of 1878. Joe and Agnes were the witnesses.

Agnes Mack was the adopted daughter and only child of the William L. Macks, who had made the 1854 wagon trek with the Freshours from Jasper County, Indiana to Adams County, Iowa.[16] William Mack's brother, Perry Mack, of Brooks, Iowa, was married to Mary Jane Freshour. The W.L. Macks made the trek to California in 1866. They returned to Iowa and were with the Perry Macks in 1870. In 1875, William and Sarah Mack again traveled with Agnes to California to join the Freshours at Soquel. Younger brother, Indiana born John A. Mack, also arrived from Iowa with his wife and children including eight-year-old W.P. Mack. Joe and Agnes were living in Aptos in May of 1877 when their first child Caliste was born. In 1880, the William Macks and the Joe Freshours were neighbors to Sophronia and her household. The John A. Macks were living nearby. W.P. Mack became a Capitola photographer in the 1890s. Sophronia's four eldest children were married by May of 1876 when the first train from Watsonville was able to cross the bridge at Capitola and roll into Santa Cruz.

The year 1876 was not only a year marked by beginnings but it also marked the end of an era. Elizabeth Smith Freshour passed away in 1876 at the age of eighty-one. Her death went unnoticed and she lies in an unmarked grave. The important people receiving notice represented America's industrialization. Her life epitomized the westering of America. She was born in Pennsylvania in 1795. The United States Constitution was then only six years old and George Washington was president. Her parents brought her down Virginia's Great Valley to Tennessee. She grew up in Greene County and married John Freshour there in 1811. John's family fought in Andrew Jackson's Indian Wars. Elizabeth and John reared six children in Greene County. They knew Andrew Johnson when he was a tailor. They traveled overland with their children in 1833 to Jackson County Missouri where their youngest child Emeline was born. Elizabeth's children were married there. She saw Santa Fe traders, Mexican War troops and the fur trappers come and go. Her eldest daughter, Rutha, married fur trapper Nicholas Gann. She witnessed the conflict over slavery in Bleeding Kansas. John passed away and she travelled by wagon train across the plains in 1857 with her youngest daughter and grandchildren. She travelled down the Humbolt and over the Calaveras Big Tree route into the San Joaquin. She saw more grandchildren born on a San Joaquin ranch and saw the devastation of the great flood. She packed up with her family, the Baucoms, and traveled the wagon road to their new home in Corralitos. Her son-in-law, Joe Baucom, rode with the Santa Cruz Cavalry. More grandchildren arrived at Corralitos. Her lifetime spanned from coast to coast. She saw the development of a few eastern states into a continental whole piece — one nation, indivisible. But, as a pioneer woman, her focus was always on the needs of those about her. She had touched many lives along the way.

Joseph Baucom bought a family plot in the Watsonville IOOF Cemetery. Grandma Elizabeth was the first of his family to be buried there. Sophronia, Long Joe, all the Freshours, the George Washington Himes and all their family, the Ganns and all the Baucoms would be there to comfort Emeline on the loss of her mother. Emeline's sisters, Rutha Gann and Sarah Himes, were there but her brother Lawson had moved down the Salinas Valley to Hot Springs (present day Paso Robles) in San Luis Obispo County. Word of his mother's death would have to be sent to Lawson and to his brothers Martin and Thomas at their Jenny Lind Post Office.

Sophronia deeded her home in Hihn's Soquel Addition back to F.A. Hihn in 1879. She was then living with her daughter, Mrs. Anne Beswick, at Gilroy. The following year she was again at Soquel. George Wesley "G.W." Freshour, at age nineteen, was the man of the house in Sophronia's household in 1880. Curiously, John Freshour was listed as the head of the household — even though he had been dead for over thirteen years! Sophronia, although listed with John as his wife, was also listed in the Charles H. Ryder household as a boarder and housekeeper. No doubt Sophronia had left her teenagers, Emeline and Mary Francis at ages seventeen and fifteen, to keep house while she was employed at the Ryders. The census taker apparently never asked if their father was living. The twins and Martha at ages thirteen and eleven were in school. The Himes had been neighbors until 1872, when Sophronia sold her 160 acres on the Laurel Glen Road and moved down to Soquel. Mahala Jane Himes had married William Ryder at the house of the bride's father at Soquel in 1864. Now, in 1880, William Ryder and his brother Charles prospered on Soquel ranches near Porter's tannery.

At her own household, Sophronia's immediate neighbors were Joe and Agnes, the Macks and Nicholas and Rutha Gann who had moved from Santa Cruz. The Gann's granddaughter, Malinda Richey, was in their household. The Richey's children attended Glen Haven School with the Bradley children. Joe was also listed in the crew of Jared Comstock's sawmill as a teamster. His uncle, Long Joe, was listed as a mill hand at the W.A. Young sawmill. In 1882, G.W. voted as a Soquel woodsman.

— Courtesy of Phil Walker.

Figure 17.6: Loma Prieta bull donkey.

— The History Museum of Santa Cruz County.

Figure 17.7: A narrow gauge logging locomotive.

The first sawmills in Santa Cruz County were the sawpits that produced the timbers and planks used by the Spaniards in the terra cotta roofed adobe buildings of *Misión La Exaltación de la Santa Cruz* and those of *el Pueblo de Villa de Branciforte*. A pit was dug under a felled tree and planks were "whipsawed" by a two-man saw worked by a man below in the pit and his companion above. Square beams were, in those days, made from a round timber, of approximate required size, by a man "walking the beam" with an adz. The surface was thus hewn roughly flat and the log rotated and the process repeated until the timber was hewn square. The first water powered sawmill was the "muley" mill built by Peter Lassen for Joe Majors and Isaac Graham on their *Zayante* Mexican land grant located about seven miles up the San Lorenzo canyon from Santa Cruz. A muley mill was a wooden frame with a vertical blade driven by water power — a mechanization of the earlier whipsaw. Such were the improvisations of the Californios.[17]

After California passed into the hands of the Americans, all manner of machinery and equipment started making its appearance. This was accelerated by the gold mining industry which was in itself an industrial revolution. Steam power arrived on the waterways and in the mines. The circular saw blade driven by steam arrived to meet the prodigious demand for lumber. It took half a century to completely harvest the redwood — first in the gulches and then up the canyons and finally up the farthest slopes of the Santa Cruz Range. At first the mills were close to the landings and water transport. Steel cables and steam powered winches replaced the oxen and skid roads. Then the mills put in their own railroads. The circular saw was upstaged by the band saw. Ultimately the log carriage was replaced by a steam propelled "shotgun" carriage. Mills contested who could produce how many thousand board feet per day. A few small mills worked minor stands of timber or did second cutting. Industry giants such as Frederick Hihn and corporations like the Santa Cruz Lumber Company at Felton cut huge amounts of timber well into this 20th century.[18]

Several thousand redwood ties, imbedded in gravel ballast, supported each mile of California's railroads. Massive timbers supported the puffing engines and cars hurtling over trestles and bridges. The railroads in turn hauled redwood timber to such important industries as the New Almaden Quicksilver Mine where the mine shafts and tunnels were timbered with redwood. Indeed, as the redwood logging industry matured, railroads were incorporated into operations where skid roads and oxen and flumes had sufficed in their early days. As the railroads extended into the less developed areas of the state, they carried redwood to build the two-story Victorian ranch houses and redwood barns. The synergism between redwood timber and railroads was soon apparent in Santa Cruz County. Sawmill operations in the Bolder Creek-Lorenzo region used the San Lorenzo Flume & Transportation Company to move their lumber fourteen miles from their sawmills to Felton. The last eight miles of hauling to the wharf at Santa Cruz was done by the Santa Cruz & Felton Railroad built in 1875.[19] At first flimsy and poorly designed, and forced by city ordinance to pull its cars through town by horse, the SC&F was rebuilt and rerouted in 1876.

This dowdy little railroad was destined to blossom into a great boon to Santa Cruz when, in 1877, two Comstock Lode millionaires, James Fair and Alfred Davis, decided to forge the South Pacific Coast Railway from Alameda to Santa Cruz. They fulfilled Hihn's dream of a railroad over the mountain to San Jose. The two millionaires used their monetary might and mine tunneling expertise to put two tunnels through the mountains. The first one tunneled under Mountain Charlie's to come out in upper Soquel Canyon where Frederick Hihn was starting to cut timber. From there the second tunnel punched through to Glenwood and the tracks were then laid to Felton via Zayante. With the purchase of the Santa Cruz & Felton line, the South Pacific Coast Railroad was complete. In March of 1880, three years and eight million dollars after Jim Fair and Alfred Davis struck their bargain, SPC trains were running the narrow gauge tracks from Alameda to Santa Cruz. A ferry trip across the bay completed the route to San Francisco.[20]

In 1881, Stanford's Southern Pacific Railroad purchased Hihn's narrow gauge line, running from Pajaro via Watsonville and Capitola to Santa Cruz, and beefed it up to the standard gauge of Southern Pacific.[21] Southern Pacific had become very interested in tourism and had purchased Hihn's line for that purpose. The South Pacific Coast line had been conceived by Fair and Davis as lumber transportation and its flat cars were indeed loaded with lumber destined for Bay Area markets.[22] Soon the South Pacific Coast line was giving Stanford a run for his money in the tourism market, dropping fares and reducing transit times, for the trip from the "City" to the "Switzerland of America." The remote community, once ensconced behind the Santa Cruz Mountains, was now a short train ride from Los Gatos, Santa Clara and San Jose. One-day excursions to the beaches and redwood forests of Santa Cruz County were now possible. The county was transformed from a community peopled with wagon train folk to that of the young steam engine generation of America's industrial expansion.

The synergism between steam, redwood and rail had never been more dynamic than it was at nearby Aptos Creek. The rivalry between the Loma Prieta Lumber Company and Hihn's Valencia Mill stimulated logging that made the Grover's Gulch operations look tame. The two Aptos Creek mills made claim and counter claim of astronomical amounts of board feet per day of redwood lumber they had sawn. Hihn had used narrow gauge and the little pufferbelly Betsy Jane to log his Aptos Creek holdings in the Augmentation. The logs were hauled to his sawmill and finishing mill at Aptos which became a booming mill town. Once the area immediately above Aptos was logged off, sawmill operations on Aptos Creek were moved to the higher slopes. Southern Pacific rebuilt the Santa Cruz Railroad in standard gauge by 1883 making it an extension of their rails running through Pajaro. No sooner had the Southern Pacific taken over the Santa Cruz Railroad from Watsonville than a railroad was built from Aptos station up Aptos Creek to the mills cutting logs coming from as far as the base of Loma Prieta. The five mile Aptos-Loma Prieta Line was built by Southern Pacific not only to transport lumber to market but also to feed its insatiable craving for redwood ties being used in its drive to place rails down the Salinas Valley towards its ultimate goal — the coastal route to Los Angeles.[23]

Once the large trees of the Aptos Creek and Loma Prieta slopes had been logged off, Hihn still had timber remaining in the Soquel Augmentation including the stands of redwoods on the slope of Hinckley Ridge on the east branch of Soquel Creek. Hihn proceeded with a plan to put Betsy Jane and his narrow gauge rails to work again. Soquel would have a railroad! It would run from the S.P. station in Capitola, through Soquel, through the western edge of the Grover's Glen Haven tract and on up Soquel Creek to Olive Springs. Right of way was secured and the forty foot wide grade was completed to within seven miles of Olive Springs. The grade with its abutments was still viewable in the early decades of the 1900s. It is marked on surveyor's maps as "Hihn's Railroad Grade." [24] This was Soquel's "Almost Railroad." It was never built.

Hihn's grading crew had removed Frederick Wilding's fence along the right of way. In fact, they ran the grade on Wilding's property since an error in surveying the neighboring property, which had been sold by Hihn, neglected to leave nearly enough right of way. Hihn's crew compensated for the error by appropriating a strip of Wilding's land. They cast Wilding's fence aside allowing the neighbor's cattle to trample his vines and newly planted orchard. This was the last straw for Wilding. He had been in contention with Hihn over a right of way across Hihn's property that Hihn had agreed to sell Wilding. Hihn had reneged. There had been a sharp exchange over the matter. Wilding filed a suit against Hihn in September of 1891.[25] The jury found for Hihn and Wilding's appeal was denied in May of 1892. He appealed to the State Supreme Court. The court negotiated a settlement between the two Fredericks. An order stipulated that the suits be dismissed. It also ordered that Hihn be allowed use of the Grade for his railroad without any fee and Wilding be given free use of "Hihn's Railroad Grade" as a right of way. Frederick Wilding and F.A. Hihn signed the agreement in July of 1892 and the Supreme Court Judges signed the order that August.[26] By then, Hihn was concentrating on his summit timber lands at the head of Soquel Canyon where the town of Laurel shipped lumber on the South Pacific Coast Railroad. The Loma Prieta Lumber Company moved over to Hinckley Gulch a few miles above Olive Springs. The Glen Haven folks could tread the wooded path over Hinckley Ridge at the end of Grover's Gulch to work for the Loma Prieta Mill. The Loma Prieta relied on teamsters to haul their lumber to Opal for rail shipment. No pufferbelly ever puffed along the grade bisecting Glen Haven and Soquel.

With two railroad terminals and several millionaires in residence, Santa Cruz was no longer a modest pioneer settlement. Some of John and Sophronia's offspring gravitated into Santa Cruz. In April of 1883, nineteen-year-old Emeline Freshour of the Town of Branciforte and twenty-two-year-old George H. Bausch of Santa Cruz were married at Soquel by the Reverend L.N. Barber. George Bausch was employed in his father's brewery located on Bridge Street at Ocean Street. Bridge Street got its name from the covered bridge placed over the San Lorenzo River. A steam powered pile driver drove pilings for the bridge. From Ocean Street, the Soquel Road ran over the hill through open countryside on its way to the village of Soquel. When the covered bridge was replaced by a modern concrete structure, Bridge Street was renamed Soquel Avenue.

George Henry Bausch, of Hesse Darmstadt, was known as "Henry." He arrived in Pennsylvania in 1849. Henry walked from San Francisco and over the Mountain trail into Santa Cruz in 1853 and started brewing beer. He was naturalized in 1859 and married Hannah, a native of Cork, Ireland. The Henry Bausches had six children; George Henry Bausch (Jr.,) Mary (died as an infant,) Sophia, Alice "Allie," Mary and John.

Hannah died in 1878. Henry then married thirty-one-year-old Annie McDonald. He was fifty-two.[27]

Henry Bausch's properties included two in East Santa Cruz. In 1866, he owned what is now county property along Ocean Avenue at Water Street. Bausch Street divided this lot on which the court house now stands.[28] The modern Ocean Street did not then exist. The Branciforte "River" ran through open farm land and into the San Lorenzo River. Cooper Street crossed the San Lorenzo at this confluence and continued towards Soquel. This route ultimately became Soquel Road. It ran along the southern edge of Henry Bausch's other East Santa Cruz property — his farm.[29] The Branciforte River formed the northern boundary of this triangular parcel which extended from its apex at the San Lorenzo to its broadest extent at the top of the hill. Henry worked mostly on his brewery. His fields about the brewery were at times planted in barley to be used for brewing. These fields eventually became part of Branciforte — now east Santa Cruz. Much of the surrounding acreage was planted in barley for the Santa Cruz breweries in the late 1800s. Hops came from the Pajaro Valley.[30]

T.W. Wright surveyed and mapped Henry's farm in 1867, laying out Ocean and May Streets and the "Bausch Tract." By 1873, the new covered bridge was in use. Ocean Street was established from Water Street to Soquel Road and Henry's farm was thereby divided. The Bausch Tract contained the Bausch home above the proposed May Street.[31] Henry Bausch built his ultimate brewery in 1873. The *Sentinel* announced:

> "Mr. Edward Hubert, the carpenter, has just completed the fine, large, new brewery for Henry Bausch. This is one of the largest and best buildings yet erected in Santa Cruz, for manufacturing purposes. The cupola is completed, surmounted by a tall flagstaff, with a golden beer keg for a ball, ... The building is painted white and the entire outside work is completed. Active brewing will not commence until about April, when all the departments will be plastered, painted and bricked, ready for use.[32]

The brewery included a bar and a room with tables for family gatherings. The covered bridge on Bridge Street was nearby. Most of the folks of Santa Cruz patronized the brewery, if not for delivery of beer, then to get yeast for bread. Dried yeast was unknown then. On Saturday mornings, lines of children could be seen crossing the bridge on their way to Bausch's Brewery with pails to get yeast which they delivered earning a nickel per pail. One of those youngsters was Ernst Otto who was known later as the beloved newsman and historian of Santa Cruz. Beer was delivered about town by horse drawn wagon. A large service yard behind the Bausch Brewery was stacked with cords of firewood used in the brewery.[33]

Brewmaster Henry Bausch died in 1884 leaving his house on Soquel Road to his wife, Annie, and his remaining estate to be kept intact by an executor until his son John, then age twelve, attained age twenty-one. The executor, John Werner, let the brewery to Theodore Beck and Louis Koehn during the nine years he administered the estate.[34] The grounds west of the brewery, along the banks of Branciforte Creek, were developed by George Bausch. Bausch's Garden was a grove of trees, gardens, many walks, summer houses with tables and climbing roses on their latticework, a dance hall and above Branciforte Creek was a long bowling alley. During this time, George's sister, Sophia, married Louis L. Rogge. George and Sophia received half ownership in the brewery real estate between them when the estate was finally settled in 1893. Allie died in 1890 unmarried and childless, so the estate was distributed as four equal shares. Louis and George formed the Bausch Company which then took over the brewery operation. At that time, the Bausch Gardens became the Vienna Gardens and the brewery became the Vienna Brewery.

The Soquel Freshour clan would gather at the brewery to enjoy the hospitality of George and Emma. These good times were fondly remembered many years later by the family.[35] The George Bausches had three daughters and a son Eddie. Louis Rogge died in August and George Bausch in December of 1904

— Special Collections, McHenry Library, UCSC.

Figure 17.8: The Bausch Brewery building circa 1886.

leaving sisters-in-law, Emma and Sophia in ownership of the Bausch Company. Emma was appointed executor and finally had George's estate settled in 1907. The Bausch Company, the brewery real estate and the brewery equipment were sold to a group that operated as the Santa Cruz Brewery with Carl Beck as brew master.[36]

The Santa Cruz Brewery was in business until 1919 when an amendment to the US Constitution established prohibition. Breweries and bars were closed. The old Bausch Brewery became a feed and grain store.[37] The roaring 20s with fast cars, speakeasies and bootleg booze ended in the stock market crash of twenty-nine. Prohibition was repealed in 1934.

In 1884, Irena and Will Freshour were in Soquel Township and Will was working as a teamster. Woodsman, G.W., was still single and with Sophronia and her teenagers in Glen Haven. Mary Francis was at Branciforte working as a domestic. By 1884 rail travel had become common place and although there were still many people touring over the landscape by wagon, a person traveling light could relocate by railway.

Elmer Ellsworth Mack, the schoolteacher son of Perry and Mary Jane Mack of Brooks, Iowa, decided to visit his relatives way out in California. He had been born in 1861, after the wagon train Freshours were in California but, his parents and aunts and uncles in Iowa had been in correspondence with their family in California so Elmer had the assurance that he had kin in California. Elmer's mother, Mary Jane Freshour Mack, had passed away in 1869 when he was eight and his father remarried in 1875 when he was fourteen. In those days, it was possible to become a schoolteacher by virtue of having completed grammer school with excellent grades. Elmer taught school for a few years then decided to venture west to California.

Instead of months on a wagon trail or weeks in a stagecoach, Elmer could get to Soquel in California in a couple of days. He would visit his Uncle, William Mack, and family and make the acquaintance of Aggie and Joe. He would visit his mother's brother Joseph Terre Freshour and his aunt Sophronia and meet all his Freshour cousins in and about Soquel. Elmer was about twenty-one or two years old when he arrived and his cousin, Anderson Arthur "Blond" Freshour was fifteen or sixteen years old. They became fast friends and tradition has it that Elmer taught A.A. "booklearning" in the evenings. A.A. was reported to have claimed three years of schooling — the same year on three different occasions. This is a sample of the Freshour Tennessee German humor which seems to have been derived from excessive association with mules. The school system at Soquel was as good as any in its day and the 1880 census shows the twins, A.A. and Ruby, in attendance.

After 1888, the Glen Haven residents had their own school. In 1890, the Santa Cruz *Surf* reported the monthly honor roll of Glen Haven School. In March, Lydia Ann Bradley was at the head of the class, in April she tied for first, in May she was third in the class and in June she tied for second. Her scores ran 94 to 97 — a very bright girl. Her brother J.W. Bradley contributed to the success of a Glen Haven School "Fishing and Dancing Party." In another entertainment, Perry Mack and Ed Hartley were in a concert where they played a Banjo and Mouth Organ duet. Could this have been Elmer's father out from Iowa for a visit? Elmer Mack retained the formal bearing of a school master. He invariably called A.A. Freshour "Anderson." Elmer found some pretty good reasons to stay in the Golden State, one of them being George and Sarah Himes' daughter, Clarissa Francis. Elmer Mack and Clara Himes were married in 1884.

Henry Freshour of Adams County, Iowa probably died prior to 1880. In 1882, His widow, Amanda Freshour, traveled from Brooks, Iowa to Soquel with her son, Thomas A. Freshour, and daughter, Emiline Freshour.[38] It is quite probable that they traveled with Elmer Mack. Other Adams County, Iowa people may have come out to California at that time to visit their Soquel relatives and, after a wonderful vacation on the Pacific Ocean, returned to their midwestern flatland. Henry's family stayed. In 1900, Thomas A. Freshour was at Soquel working in the timber. He had no family but his mother, Amanda, was in his household. They were living among the Bradleys, the Masons and the Soquel Freshours.

Emma Freshour, age 28, and Lewis Tracy Mason, age 29, were married in July of 1886. Both were residents of Soquel. This Emma — not to be confused with Emma Bausch — was the daughter of Henry and Amanda Freshour and was reared by them at Brooks, Iowa. Lewis and Emma lived at Soquel where his father, Sylvester, and older brother Charles were prominent ranchers, together owning 270 acres known as "Mason's grove" located north of town on Soquel Creek. The Masons were from Ohio via Jasper County Indiana. L.T. was named for his grandfather Lewis T. Mason of Ohio. The family came across the plains in 1857 or earlier and were living at Gilroy in 1860. L.T.'s brothers Charles and Frank were wheelwrights in Sylvester's household at Soquel in 1870. Their neighbors were G.W. Himes and J.T. Freshour who each owned a quarter section just up the road. Emma Mason was somehow related to J.T. Freshour through her father, Henry Freshour. In 1890, Charles and L.T.

Mason sold 120 acres of the Soquel land formerly owned by their father, each retaining a small ranch. C.S. Mason, J.T. Freshour and William Oliver were appointed by the County Superior Court to appraise the estate of George W. Himes, deceased in August of 1903.

Sophronia's children were all on their own by 1890, her youngest, Martha Ellen Musgrave, being twenty years old. "Ella Mosgrove" married Charles B. Barden in July of 1890. Both were residents of Santa Cruz. Barden worked for the Bausch Brewery and the couple lived across the street from the brewery on Ocean Street. The Barden's had a son Earl and, a number of years later, daughters Zay and Thelma.[39]

Mary Francis "Mae" Freshour lived nearby on Branciforte Avenue. Mae was a member of the Salvation Army. She and a fellow soldier, Charles Carrington, were married in January of 1895 in a quiet wedding at the Advent parsonage in Santa Cruz. They were attired in their uniforms. By this time Sophronia was living in a cabin built for her on John Bradley's property in Glen Haven. Mae Carrington was born there and was cared for by Sophronia for several years until the Bardens became her foster parents.[40] Mary Francis died shortly after her daughter Mae was born. Services were held at her home on Branciforte Avenue. She is buried in the Soquel IOOF Cemetery.

G.W. married Martha Jane "Mattie" Speaker in San Joaquin County in December of 1890. He was twenty-three and she was thirty-five. Martha Jane Buchannan had married Melville A. Speaker in 1875. "Widow Speaker" had six sons. The couple moved to Santa Cruz where they resided at 18 Trescony Street. They had three children; Clyde, Birdie and Gladys. Birdie was born in September of 1891 and Clyde in June of 1893, both at Santa Cruz. They were living in Santa Cruz in 1897. They were at Santa Rosa in Sonoma County in 1900 with teenage Melvin Speaker in the household. Gladys Marie Freshour was born in February of 1901 at Santa Rosa. G.W. and Mattie lived in Santa Rosa until 1910 — the year Mattie died there on Easter Sunday. The *Santa Cruz Surf* ran her obituary.[41]

— The Soquel Pioneer and Historical Association

Figure 17.9 Olive Springs — August 1899. Men (L to R) are: Frank Reanier, Clarence Angel, Lewis T. Mason, Joseph A. Freshour, Clarence Schelling, George Hart and Bill Hart.

Joseph Alfred Freshour took up driving team during the 1880s, hauling for the sawmills of the Santa Cruz Mountains. He had occasion to haul over the Soquel-San Jose road over to the Santa Clara Valley towns. By 1890, Joe had moved with Agnes and the children over the summit to the hamlet of Los Gatos — now thriving as an important station for Stanford's South Pacific Coast R.R. The road running from Soquel up Hester Creek to the summit and down Los Gatos Canyon to Los Gatos was a popular buggy drive with hotels along the route for tourists and vacationers. Camping and hunting in the Santa Cruz Mountains was becoming popular. Joe would occasionally return to Soquel to visit his relatives and to go hunting with his Soquel cronies. Aggie's parents, the William L. Macks also moved to Los Gatos as did the Elmer Macks. Joe worked for the San Jose Water Company which used water taken from Los Gatos Creek above Lexington in the canyon above Los Gatos.

Ruby, single and living in Santa Cruz in 1897, appears to have been in the Salvation Army. Her twin, Anderson, was married and living at Soquel. Will and Irena and their son Harvey were living in Santa Cruz in March of 1897 when Will got a job working as a woodsman with Bowen's Mill located near Glenwood on Stanfield's claim. Will moved his family to Glenwood and was working at falling timber with Nick Gann Jr. and John Keough. The men were working together in the timber on April the eighth at four-thirty when a sudden gust of wind brought the redwood tree Will was about to fall crashing down unexpectedly.

The redwood trees that are logged nowadays are seldom very large. They are lopped off with chain saws by woodsmen standing on the ground without the bother of springboards. The trees being cut in Santa Cruz County in the 1800s were virgin timber and were anywhere from four to seven feet in diameter or greater. Many tons of green wood towered into the sky above the woodsmen who worked with two man cross-cut saws. The sawing was not possible without wedges because the weight of the tree would settle and bind the saw fast. Very thin wedges with a long taper were driven in behind the saw using metal shims to make a bearing surface. When the cut was raised a fraction of an inch behind the saw to relieve the binding, the movement of the top of the tree would be many inches. As the sawing progressed, the wedges were driven in further and further until the center of gravity of the huge tree would cross over the line of the under cut and the tree would start "talking." As the men worked at this they moved around on planks supported by "springboards" mounted on the tree.[42] There is much skill involved in this process. It is *very* dangerous work. The Santa Cruz newspapers of the 1800s often reported death in the woods.

The base of a redwood tree for the first few feet above the ground is of a wavy burl like formation. The cut is made above this to get a log with normal grain to the wood. The trees were invariably on a mountain slope so the springboards, pounded into axe cuts, were anywhere from one or two feet to four or five feet above the terrain as one moved around the tree. Planks were placed on the springboards to form a continuous platform. A determination was made as to where the tree was to fall and a bed for the tree planned so that the tree would not be broken with sheared grain breaks that would bind the saws cutting it into logs. A tree could be reduced to scrap if improperly felled. The under cut was first put in with thin, razor sharp felling axes with long handles to reach well into the deep under cut. The line formed through the center of the tree, at the innermost part of the big wedge shaped cut, is what establishes the direction of the tree's fall — usually on an uphill slope.

An axe handle placed with the axe head in the center of the under cut, will point in the direction of the fall. The saw cut approached the under cut above the line of the under cut and parallel to it. The trunk would break off making a stepped edge that the tree would be stopped against as it swung towards the earth. The impact of tons of tree reverberated along the length of its trunk. The men stood on the springboard planks as they

— San Mateo County Historical Museum

Figure 17.10: Timber fallers near La Honda. The undercut is finished and they are ready to start sawing on the backcut.

chopped the under cut and later as they alternately sawed and drove the wedges. Once the undercut was made and the saw cut started, the massive redwood was balanced overhead under the control of the woodsmen. The woodsmen usually had in back of their mind which way they would jump to in case they had to get out of the way.

Working in the timber was risky. The "widow makers" caused many a woodsman's death. When felled, a large tree would sometimes have branches broken off from falling through the limbs of an adjacent tree. A branch would sometimes get caught in the branches of the still standing adjacent tree and remain dangling precariously. These "widow maker" branches were sometimes quite large and heavy. They would gradually pull loose from their own weight or with the help of a wind gust and come plunging down on a hapless woodsman. Of course, the remaining tree with the widow maker in it would soon be a prospect for the woodsmen's springboards.

The handles on the two-man cross cut saw were detachable allowing the removal of the saw from the cut by detaching one or the other handle and pulling the saw out from the opposite side. If the sawing got tough, they would interrupt their work to file and "set" the teeth of their saws using a "spider" to check the set and a gauge to get the "rakers" to the proper height to clear the sawdust out of the cut. Once the tree was down it had to be pealed and trimmed of limbs and cut into logs and the logs drug to the skid road. Falling the tree was the first step of a laborious process.[43] Incredibly, the census takers usually listed these men as common laborers. They were laborers to be sure; but, they were most uncommon.

On that fateful afternoon in April of 1897, William Henry "Will" Freshour had his tree to the point where he could drive the wedges in a bit further to bring the tree down. Nick Gann was ten feet farther down the hill falling a pine tree. The tremendous gust of wind caused the large redwood to break away and Will knew from the sound that there was trouble and he had better get out of the way fast. He jumped to the ground to scramble behind the pine tree below. "His foot caught in the brush causing him to fall. The falling tree struck him across the breast and he was killed instantaneously."[44] The following day the coroner went to Glenwood and returned to Santa Cruz with the body. A coroners inquest was held and the jury returned the verdict "that Freshour's death was caused by accident."[45]

Will died at forty-three years of age leaving Irena widowed at the age of thirty-six. The funeral was held at the residence of his brother George (G.W.) Freshour in Santa Cruz and he was interred according to the wishes of George and Emma Bausch, in the Bausch family plot in the Santa Cruz IOOF Cemetery. He was also survived by his sisters, Miss Ruby Freshour of Santa Cruz, Mrs. Bradley of Soquel, and Mrs. Beswick of Gilroy. His mother, Sophronia, was residing at Los Gatos. She had born Will in Indiana and brought him to Iowa as an infant then across the plains as a toddler. It had been thirty years since Will's father John Freshour had died in Soquel. Will had been the role model for his younger brothers. His death was a sudden shock and great loss to the family. The following year, Irena's son, twenty-year-old Harvey Freshour, visited her and his friends in Santa Cruz, then returned to San Jose.[46] Harvey L. Freshour with wife, Birdie is in San Francisco in 1910. In 1920, he is in San Jose on Delmas Avenue with wife, Birdenal, and daughter, Lelabell. His mother, Irene, was then living on Autumn Street.

In November of 1902, Rutha Malinda "Ruby" Freshour underwent surgery. At that time, blood transfusions were not practical. The discovery of blood types in 1901 led eventually to modern hematology and routine blood transfusions. Ruby never recovered from the surgery. She gradually weakened and died. A few years later, with the use of donated blood, she might have recovered. It had only been a hundred years since doctors routinely sent patients to the barber shop to be bled. A vestige of the practice is the striped red and white barber pole. Ruby died at thirty-five years of age. She never married. She was buried near the Bausch plot in Santa Cruz and some years later, Ruby's remains were exhumed and reburied in the Bausch plot. George Bausch died in 1904 at Santa Cruz and Emma died in 1936 at Soquel. They are buried in the Bausch family plot. Thus, three of John and Sophronia's offspring — Will, Emma and Ruby — were buried together in the Santa Cruz IOOF Cemetery.

By 1907 there were no Freshours left in Santa Cruz. May, Will and Ruby tragically had died; G.W. and Mattie had moved to Santa Rosa. Emma Bausch was a widow and had moved to San Jose then San Francisco where she lived during the 1920s. Eddie Bausch ran a bar in San Jose prior to prohibition. The three Bausch daughters died at an early age; Mamie in 1901, Eva in 1903 at age seventeen and Ruby (named for her aunt) in 1908 also at age seventeen. The brewery eventually became a feed and grain store and the covered bridge was torn down. The Freshours and kin continued to thrive around Soquel or Los Gatos — habitats apparently better suited to them than the cosmopolitan Santa Cruz.

By the turn of the century, the timber had played out at Glen Haven. The last jerkline team plodded down Slab Alley in 1896. Frealon Grover dismantled his mill and quietly moved off to Bean Creek.[47] The forest was left to recover, the great redwood stumps sprouting encircling rings of suckers that, over the past century, have become large redwoods. Some of the stumps were removed and the remaining rich forrest humus planted in orchards and vineyards. Soquel became a farm town with a fruit packing and shipping industry. The roaring 20s were spent. Emeline Josephine Freshour — Emma Bausch — finally returned to Soquel — her native Soquel of fond girlhood memories. The Bradleys and the Joneses were close by. Emma lived out her years there among family.[48]

18

SOQUEL TO HESTER CREEK

ANDERSON ARTHUR MET MINERVA JANE when the Conant family moved over to Soquel from Glenwood. Minerva Jane was the daughter of George Horace Conant and Elizabeth Ellen Thompson Conant. George H. Conant was from an old New England family dating back to when Roger and Christopher Conant of the Devonshire Conants emigrated to Plymouth, Massachusetts in 1623 on the ship *Anne*. It is presumed that Christopher returned to England after 1630. Roger Conant eventually moved with his family to Salem.[1] There were many descendants in Massachusetts and some in Maine, Vermont and Connecticut.[2] George H. was the youngest of nine children born to Noah and Mary Conant of Townsend Harbor, Middlesex County, Massachusetts.[3] The family owned the water powered mill on the Squannacock River at Harbor Pond near Townsend — about twenty miles further inland from Lowell and near the New Hampshire border.

The New England Conants were quite adventurous. Some of them went to Mexico to live. The first Conant to appear in California was Vermont born Charles Conant who was at Stockton in 1850 with a Mexican wife and five children — ages one through nine — all born in Mexico. In 1860, two of George H. Conant's older brothers, Benjamin H. Conant and Josiah Conant both married, were living at Stockton. Subsequently, George H. arrived with his furniture on board having sailed "around the Horn by sailing vessel" as he liked to reminisce. He married Elizabeth Thompson at Stockton in May of 1871.

Elizabeth Ellen Thompson came to California by wagon train as a little child. She was born in 1852 as the youngest of the six children of Bernard and Clary Thompson of Brown County, Illinois. Their nearest town was Quincy. Widower Bernard Thompson, with his two youngest children, Elizabeth and James W., were living at French Camp, near Stockton in 1860. Bernard was living there in 1857, so, a likely time frame for their trek across the plains would be 1854-56. They would have taken the ferry across the Mississippi at Quincy and traveled northwest to follow the Chariton River into Iowa. From Chariton they would have traveled west across Iowa to Council Bluffs where they would cross the Missouri River by ferry. From there they started up the Platte River Road for the two-thousand mile trek across the plains. Elizabeth Ellen spent her childhood and grew into womanhood in the environs of Stockton. She married George H. Conant in May of 1871 when she was eighteen and he was close to thirty-eight.

Minerva Jane was the third of the four children born to George and Elizabeth Conant. Alice Elizabeth was born in April of 1872 and James Crozier was born in July of 1874 both at French Camp.[4] Minerva Jane was born in October of 1878 and Mabel Agnes in January of 1881 both at the City of Merced in Merced County. The Conant family was living at Glenwood in February of 1887 when daughter Alice died at the age of fourteen years and ten months. A photograph of Alice was taken at a studio in Los Gatos shortly before she died. Her obituary in the Santa Cruz *Daily Surf* added the notice "Jacksonville, Oregon and Lowell, Mass. papers please copy." — and the final lines:

Asleep in Jesus' blessed sleep.
From which none ever wake to weep.

George Conant was employed by the South Pacific Coast Railroad at Glenwood. His job was to take a hand car between Glenwood and Wrights, going through the two long tunnels, fixing things such as loose spikes and inspecting generally. His trip through the mile long tunnel from Glenwood would bring him out at the railroad and logging town of Laurel at the head of Soquel Canyon. After a respite at the Laurel depot and store, he would continue his inspection through the tunnel under the summit to come out at the town of Wrights. He probably used a carbide lamp to inspect the tunnels.

George Conant was working for a very successful railroad. By 1887, Albert "Hog" Davis, the tough Nevada Comstock Lode millionaire who had hammered the South Pacific Coast Railroad into existence, had the road running to perfection. His success was in part due to his hiring experienced railroad men away from Southern Pacific. George Conant may have had some railroad experience prior to moving to Glenwood. Both the Southern Pacific and the Atchison, Topeka and Santa Fe ran through Merced. The S.P.C.R. was so successful that Davis' silent partner, Senator James Fair, took control and leased the operation to Stanford. A year later Stanford's Southern Pacific took over the S.P.C.R. to continue it as a narrow gauge until the quake of 1906.[5]

Sometime around 1890, give or take some, the Conants moved from Glenwood to Soquel. George H. continued at his track walking job with the S.P. which by then owned all the railroads in the county. Elizabeth may have had some contacts with Soquel wagon people with whom her parents had traveled, or, she may have been acquainted with some of the folks from around Stockton who had moved to Soquel in 1863. She may have been related to either of the Thompson families living around Soquel. In 1890, Jim Conant would have been about sixteen years of age, Minerva Jane would have been twelve going-on thirteen and Mabel would have been nine years of age. Jim Conant started work greasing skids for Godfrey Grover's bull teams and made the acquaintance of twenty-three-year-old A.A. Freshour, who by then was a woodsman. The two became life-long friends. Jim Conant became "Conant" and A.A. became "Frenchower." Jim Conant had the humorous habit of giving his own nicknames to all his friends. Conant soon moved up to the position of bull whacker working for Grover at first and later hauling lumber with his own team.

Figure 18.1 Jim Conant driving Grover's bull team.

— Soquel Pioneer and Historical Association. (Donated by Jim Conant)

A.A. and his brothers were no doubt among the role models in woodsmanship that influenced Jim Conant's development in the craft. A.A. himself had grown up without a father, but his brother Will was thirteen years old when A.A. was born so he served as role model for his kid brother. Then there was A.A.'s uncle, Long Joe and brothers Joe and G.W. who all at various phases of A.A.'s development served as manly examples. A.A. had learned the skills of a logger and of a mill hand and perhaps some about farming; but, he developed an abiding fondness for draft horses — perhaps from his uncle, Long Joe Freshour. Joseph Terre "Long Joe" Freshour had become a prominent citizen of the community of Soquel and was a fine example to his nephews. J.T. Freshour appears in an 1892 photograph of the Soquel Odd Fellows Lodge with Anderson Freshour standing near him.[6]

Long Joe had more land dealings than any other Freshour in Santa Cruz County. There are eleven surviving records of his land dealings. Five of these survived the fire that swept the town of Santa Cruz, in 1894, destroying the courthouse. There are no records of how he acquired some of the land that he sold or deeded over after 1894. This is generally true of much of the land in Santa Cruz County. This is true of the land John Freshour left to his wife, Sophronia. The 160 acres sold by Sophronia and Will in November of 1872 to Carravajal and Soto was apparently sold in turn by them to Francisco McColl who some fifteen months later, in March of 1874, sold the very same 160 acres to Joseph T. Freshour. It seems that Joseph T. was finally able to acquire the land that formerly belonged to his brother. The price had gone up from $100 to $175 in the intervening fifteen months. He applied to the US Land Office in San Francisco for his land patent on this quarter section. It was granted to him in April of 1880 by President Rutherford B. Hayes.[7] Across the road, his neighbor, George Washington Himes also owned a quarter section which he likewise patented. These properties were located on the Laurel Glen Road off the San Jose Road to the north of Soquel.

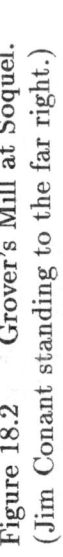

Figure 18.2 Grover's Mill at Soquel. (Jim Conant standing to the far right.)

— Soquel Pioneer and Historical Association. (Donated by Jim Conant)

The biggest dread of all for those living in timber country is a forest fire. In September of 1886, those living on the Laurel Glen Road had reason to dread. From the *Soquel Journal:* [8]

> For some days past a heavy fire has raged in the forest hills over the country owned by Messrs. Lynam, Freshour, Dakin, Hall, Calhoun [Cahoon?], and Walker and at this writing Friday morning Sept 10 the end is not yet. Teams and wagons from all directions have been busily engaged in hauling out timber, grain, hay, etc. from the endangered district ...

The Soquel Road running westward to Santa Cruz crossed "Doyle's Gulch." John Doyle, in the 1860-70s, owned 160 acres on Rodeo Creek about two miles north of the Soquel Road. In August of 1887 a new bridge was being built on Soquel Road in Doyle's Gulch — later to be known as Rodeo Gulch. Roadmaster, J.T. Freshour, had a crew of men grading and filling the approaches to the bridge. In those days, Santa Cruz County property owners commonly paid their road tax by working on the road crews. They were paid with a receipt. Long Joe had a narrow escape, while working about the bridge. A falling timber just missed him. A large spike in the timber ripped his boot open its entire length as the timber rolled over his foot. He escaped with a slight bruise.[9]

Long Joe, as roadmaster of Soquel Township, sometimes filed lawsuits because the county roads that he improved were often viewed as private property by land owners since the roads had been created originally as logging or wagon roads across their land. The early mountain roads such as the Santa Clara Turnpike and "Mountain Charlie's Road" had been privately built and operated as toll roads. In the 1880-90s, the courts were enforcing public right-of-way law. Claus Spreckels put up a gate and fence, in 1886, blocking the "Wharf Road" running along Aptos Creek. Roadmaster J.T. Freshour's complaint, filed in October of 1890, averred that the road had been a public thoroughfare for twenty years prior to being blocked and asked that the obstruction be removed by court order.[10]

A month later, Long Joe was in Superior Court again with a complaint against his neighbor, A.F. Himmelmann who had barricaded "Samuel's Road" claiming it to be private property. A venire of twenty jurors was impaneled. In December of 1890, *The Weekly Surf* reported "In the matter of J.T. Freshour, roadmaster, and A.F. Himmelmann, the jury found a verdict for the plaintiff." [11]

These were among a spate of such cases engendered by an ordinance enacted in May of 1889 by the Santa Cruz County Board of Supervisors directing the Clerk of the Board to record the particular roads in question into the Road Records of the county as public highways. This ordinance was in accordance with the Act of 1876, titled: *An act to establish and maintain public and private roads in the County of Santa Cruz.* As the foremost landholder in the county, Frederick Hihn was a natural target of the ordinance. A battle of the wills was thus precipitated between F.A. Hihn and County Board of Supervisors. Enforcement of this ordinance was the task of newly appointed roadmaster, Joe Freshour. The altercation came into court as *J.T. FRESHOUR, Road Overseer of Soquel Road District, Plaintiff vs. F.A. HIHN, Defendant.* The case ended up in the Supreme Court of the State of California.[12]

Under instruction from W.T. Cope, the manager of Hihn's Soquel Wharf property, a fence and gate were constructed barring the road customarily used by the local teamsters to access the beach by crossing over F.A. Hihn's property. Leon E. Jones had charge of the gate. The fence and gate were constructed on or before the first of May, 1889, and the Board of Supervisors responded with their ordinance three weeks later. On the 8th of June, J.T. Freshour acting in his official capacity as Road Overseer[13] served a document to Jones and left a copy at Hihn's residence in Santa Cruz "with the defendant's servant girl ... she saying to me that she would give it to the defendant; ..." (F.A. Hihn was in Yosemite at the time.) The legal notice informed Hihn that the fence and gate were an encroachment on a public highway and must be removed.

Push came to shove. As one of the witnesses, J.T. Freshour further testified:

> I opened the gate on the 8th day of June, 1889; the next day I found it closed again, and locked as before. Mr. Jones, who represented to me at that time that he was the agent for the defendant, and in the charge, possession and occupancy of the premises traversed by the road, as such agent told me that he closed the gate, and that he was authorized by the defendant to keep it closed. It so remained until the 19th day of June, 1889, when I again opened it and removed the fence the width of the road. It was replaced again by Mr. Jones, who said to me that he would continue to replace it as often as I removed it. I told Mr. Jones that I had opened the gate, and in what capacity I was acting; Jones knew that I was there in the capacity of Road Overseer. ....[14]

Among the witness, besides J.T. Freshour and F.A. Hihn, were quite a number of Soquel old-timers. C.H. Ryder, resident since 1850, Road Overseer for the eight years preceding J.T. Freshour's election to that post, was an expert witness for the plaintiff. T.W. Wright, County Surveyor since 1850, gave a history of road development on the Soquel Wharf property. Charles L. Pioda, surveyor, testified that he had helped Wright survey the Soquel Wharf property in 1888. W.R. Ryder came to Soquel in 1853 and had hauled freight from the Soquel Wharf property since 1860. He had been given permission "last spring" by Irvin Grey to use the road to go down and get a load of sand. Wharfinger, N.A. Bixby, lived at Soquel Landing from 1869 to 1874 and had always known the road to be open, used and traveled. Barber Darling had lived at Soquel twenty years. He testified "The road has been used and traveled by people generally during the past 14 years. I have teamed over it during that time, and have seen others using it for the same purpose." He had worked on the road in 1880-81 under Road Overseer Ryder. D.C. Feeley knew the road since 1863 to have been used for hauling sand or wood or to go bathing and it was not obstructed until May of 1889. It was Feeley who had petitioned the Supervisors to open the road. S.A. Hall, the ships carpenter who had built for Hihn and managed Capitola for him for a few years, testified that the road was freely used from 1866 to 1879. Henry Daubenbis testified on behalf of the plaintiff. A resident for 35 years, he had been Supervisor of the Soquel Supervisor District for the past 6 years. He knew the road to be located in the same place for the past twenty years and had gone over it several times a week during that time. S.F. Grover had been in the county since 1866 and had used the road "from 1876 to about three years ago."

The case was tried without a jury. Hihn protested the charge for jury fees. He had waived jury trial after a jury had been called. The trial commenced in December of 1889 and lasted through 1890. The decision was against Hihn. The court ordered removal of the encroachment and fined him $10 per each day that use of the road was denied — a total of $870. Notice of appeal was filed in the Santa Cruz Superior Court in April of 1891 and the case was submitted to the Supreme Court of California in January of 1892 and briefs were submitted to that court through 1892. Hihn's case was soon followed in Santa Cruz by those of Spreckels and Himmelmann in the autumn of 1890.

The California Supreme Court handed down its decision at the end of August in 1893. The upper court reversed the order and judgment.[15] The Board of Supervisors had erred in causing the road to be recorded as a highway since it had not been "duly laid out or erected" and no breadth had been specified in the plaintiff's evidence. The lower court erred in admitting this record as evidence. The $10 per day penalty for encroachment pertained only to a highway "duly laid out or erected." The road was not a "highway" but a public road by reason of usage and the court should have ordered the gate removed as a public nuisance. Hihn had won a Pyrrhic victory. He was acustomed to winning his numerous legal battles. His attorney, Charles B. Younger, was outstanding.

Frederick Hihn was often in court not only as defendant but also as plaintiff. Eleven times his name appeared as plaintiff and appellant at The State Supreme Court.[16] Among others, he sued Claus Spreckels and the City of Santa Cruz (twice.) Long Joe Freshour was not as comfortable in the court room. He spoke in a combination of colloquialisms and legal jargon that no doubt came from the prompting of legal counsel. He was more at home out grading roads and repairing bridges.

In the 1890s, the ranches of J.T. Freshour and G.W. Himes typified the transformation of the foothills into orchards and viticulture. This process was progressive, complimenting the movement of timber harvesting which was in its final phase in nearby gulches. Joseph T. deeded the remaining stumpage on his property to Frank R. Dana in 1893.

The *Santa Cruz Weekly Surf* in those days had a special feature:

RURAL LIFE
Quiet Country Homes Among the Foothills where — Peace and Prosperity Reigns.
— From Laurel Glen to Vine Hill —
"Crescent" and "Union Vineyards."

Leaving the Laurel Glen Fruit Farm early in the morning and riding up the road on the west side of More's [sic] creek in a few minutes the visitor reaches a "fork" in the road. On the right side is the 160 acre ranch owned by Mr. Geo. W. Himes, the oldest surviving settler in this valley. Mr. Himes took up this claim twenty-five years ago and now enjoys the leisure of his old age with his wife, their children being scattered through the country. The soil on this ranch is good, the hay crop being large, the fruits and grapes doing well, and the vegetables — especially the potatoes — "beating anything outside of Watsonville."

Close to the entrance to the Himes' place is the Palo Alto Rancho, owned by J.T. Freshour, who is roadmaster in this district. Mr. Freshour is a N.S.G.W.[17] and owns a ranch of 80 acres set in fruit and vines. The dwelling house is a neat, plain building. The stables and barn are large and well kept. At the entrance to the barnyard is a large gate, over which are displayed the antlers of a dozen deer, all killed in this vicinity.

...On the road leading up to the creek, and about one-eighth of a mile beyond the Palo Alto is "Spring Vale" ranch, owned by Mr. J.O.W. Rielly and leased by Mr. A. Whitman. This property has changed hands several times, each occupant improving it somewhat, until now it is in good paying condition, being planted, for the most part with fruit trees and vines.

Mr. Whitman's residence is located a little above the road on a spacious terrace, with a pretty flower garden in front and a clump of fine redwoods, affording a grateful shade. There is an abundant supply of water on the place as, indeed, there should be, More's [sic] creek flowing a steady stream through the place from its sources, not far above this ranch.

The Laurel Glen Road forked off from the San Jose Road at old sea captain Benjamin Cahoon's place.[18] The road ran from there to the Himes and the Palo Alto ranches. At that point, a road ran up Moore's Gulch but the Laurel Glen Road continued as the Mountain View Road, crossing Rodeo Gulch past Fitch's property and extending to the Junction of Vine Hill Drive and Branciforte Drive. Jarvis Road branches off from Vine Hill Drive to run up Blackburn Gulch. The travelogue continued.

Returning to the Palo Alto ranch, your correspondent took a left hand road leading up over the range of hills that enclose this valley on the south and west. A short ride brought him to the "Fitch" vineyard, leased by the Rostrom brothers. there are sixty five acres in this estate, thirty of which are in vines, ten being young and not yet in bearing. Passing through the main portion of the vineyard one cannot but notice the great size and length of the vine trunks and branches. These are some twenty-five years old and are in vigorous bearing. As the cultivated land covers a succession of curved slopes the vineyard has been called the "Crescent." It is very favorably located, being but seven miles from Santa Cruz by the "Blackburn Gulch" road. Besides grapes a fair crop of prunes has been gathered this year. Anderson, the famous fruit packer, has his men gathering the table grapes for shipment East, and very busy they were at the time of our visit.

A description of the Blackburn Gulch property of County Supervisor J.W. Jarvis with its fruit trees, "Union" vineyard and winery is given. Jarvis was a pioneer in this "Vine Hill" region and has left a road with his name. Erdman's place was on Jarvis Road.

> There is a road through the Union vineyard that leads up to the summit of the ridge where Mr. William Erdman has his ranch of eighty-seven acres overlooking the Union vineyard on the south ... Thirty acres of this place are in vines and fruits — of the latter the peaches and apples being exceptionally good. The Tokay grapes netted $45 per ton this season, and the Verdels — which are just being gathered — command good prices. There is a well arranged wine house built on the hillside ... [19]

The modern reader who has driven these roads some one-hundred years later will find the enthusiastic report of lush productive ranches given above to be utterly fantastic. Today the landscape consists of the thick vegetation of woodlands that would appear to have lain unchanged since they were the habitat of Costanoan Indians and grizzlies. The land has been repossessed by the woods. The hills and gulches have been thickly overgrown with oak, laurel, toyon, poison oak, pines and manzanita. (The redwoods of course, will require an additional 2000 years to achieve their former glory.) The few inhabitants have little or nothing to do with agriculture. At the turn of the century, however, Soquel had a fruit packing industry. There was a footpath leading from Glen Haven to the packing sheds of Soquel. The Bradley, Jones and Freshour womenfolk were among those seasonally employed. Phylloxera wiped out the grape vines in 1906-7. The market for fruit became so glutted

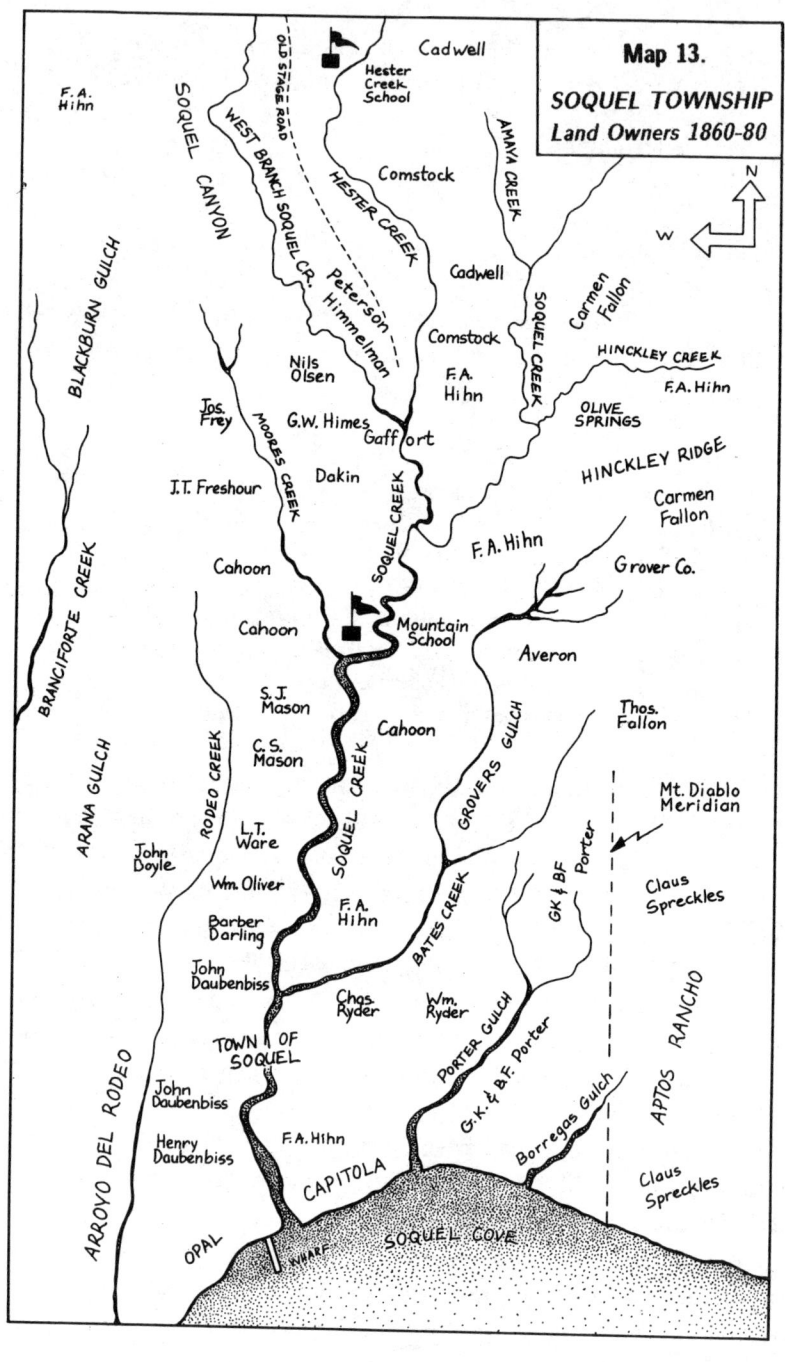

that the price would hardly pay the freight costs. The packers closed down and these orchards and vineyards fell into disuse.

Because of his years of experience as shingle maker, mill hand and woodsman and because he had made a significant number of land transactions in the vicinity of Soquel, fifty-year-old Long Joe Freshour was considered to have expert opinions on those topics. The Santa Cruz *Daily Surf* told of Frederick Hihn's fight with the tax assessors in July of 1891 over his timber holdings.

TIMBER LANDS
THE MAGNIFICENT TRACTS OF THE F. A. HIHN COMPANY

Information Concerning Their Extent and Value Brought Before the Board of Equalization

---

As patiently and attentively as jurors, the members of the Board of Equalization sat all day Saturday and listened to testimony concerning the value of the timberlands of the F.A. Hihn company, ... the Assessor introduced J.T. Freshour, L.T. Mason and Nathan Hart Sr., of Soquel and Wm.E. Emory, and E.B. Morrill of Highland.

Evidence was taken upon the character and amount of the timber and the general value in the immense tract known as the Soquel Augmentation Rancho, and every witness was called upon for his estimate of what the land should bring if offered for sale at auction. Nearly all the witnesses agreed that good redwood timber land would sell for $50 per acre at auction. Mr. Morrill valued a considerable part of the timber in Hihn's Highland tract at $100 per acre, ... Mr. Emory estimated good fruit land in Highland at from $50 to $75 per acre ... [20]

There were about 1,400 acres of redwood timber in Soquel Canyon in 1891. Hihn's main contention concerning the upper

Soquel tract was its inaccessibility. Because it would require the construction of seven miles of railroad to reach it, Hihn claimed it should be assessed at a lower value.

J.T. Freshour appeared before Charles Craighill, J.P., to file a *Declaration for Invalid Pension* in October of 1891. He was partially unable to work because of a lame side caused by pleurisy. He had served in the War of the Rebellion as Sergeant in Company A of the 8th California Volunteer Infantry.[21] An affidavit followed giving his disability as muscular rheumatism contracted near Soquel during August of 1882 while logging in the redwoods. In neighbors' affidavits of December, 1891, Nathan Hart and Henry Daubenbiss of Soquel stated that they had known J.T. Freshour for twenty-five years. The three men appear in the 1892 photograph of the Soquel IOOF Lodge. Emma and L.T. Mason appear as prominent members.

Periodically new applications were filed with affidavits by other neighbors. In 1896, Long Joe put in another pension claim giving an additional disability stemming from an accident that occurred on Memorial Day in 1893. An early riser, he had gotten up especially early that morning — two a.m. in fact — to feed his horses and to make preparations to participate in the Memorial Day celebration. We must remember that farm folk in those days before electricity "went to bed with the chickens" and got up before daybreak to make maximum use of daylight. Joe was a member of the Wallace Reynolds Post of the GAR and participated in their patriotic activities.[22]

In Joe's affidavit written in his own hand in November of 1896, he stated that he was a farmer, aged 56, and he dealt in wood some. He described the accident of three years previous. In passing behind one of his horses in the barn he received a kick that jammed his left hand against the barn breaking two fingers and generally lacerating the hand. He returned to the house ten minutes later after feeding the horses and called out to his hired hand, William Strickland, who got up and looked at the hand, wrapped it and took Joe to the doctor who dressed his hand. It did not heal very well and developed into a crippled condition. Storekeeper, Theodore Wiest, of Soquel described Joe in a July, 1897 affidavit as having a halting walk and a fractured crippled left hand. In March of 1907, Joe again made Declaration for Pension. He was living at Soquel and gave his age as sixty-four.

By 1896, Long Joe had moved closer to Soquel to a small piece of property between the San Jose Road and Soquel Creek. By 1897, Joe had parceled and sold his Palo Alto Rancho and most of his other property.[23] Maytie Woods recalled that "He had a little home a mile or so above the Soquel Cemetery. ... He had a team and done light hauling — mostly wood." [24]

Long Joe had moved closer to The Freshours and Bradleys living in Glen Haven — just across Soquel Creek. At this time, the L.T. Masons lived in Soquel on First Street.[25] By 1893, Long Joe's nephew, Anderson Arthur Freshour had taken notice of Minerva Jane Conant who was rapidly growing into a young woman. With her mother's signed consent, they were married in March of 1893. She was fifteen-and-a-half and he was twenty-five. C.H. Darling, pastor of the Methodist Church, performed the ceremony. The witnesses were Nelson Jones and Miss Lydia Bradley. Two years later Nelson and Lydia were married at Soquel. Nelson Jones was from Carlton County, New Brunswick, Canada, just fifty miles north of the Grover's home town of Wesley, Maine. Nelson's attraction to Soquel may have been the timber since, like the Grovers, he came from north-eastern timber country. He may have known the Grovers there. Nelson Jones built a house on Porter Avenue — the San Jose road – and he and Lydia reared their family there. The next generation was getting married. It had been over twenty years since Long Joe had witnessed the marriage of his niece Lydia Jane and now her daughter, Lydia Ann was married. Years later, Minerva's sister Mabel "Maime" Conant married George French. He and A.A. would also be lifelong friends. In a short time, George French was to have quite an influence on the lives of Jim Conant and A.A. Freshour.

George French was the son of Massachusetts born forty-niner, Jaret N. French, and Julia S. French. George French studied at Healds Business School of Santa Cruz. He picked up the trades of sawyer and millwright in local sawmills. C.B. "Curt" Miracle had left Grover's Soquel Mill in January of 1890 and was sawing laths with his brother at their Bean Creek mill. The Soquel Odd Fellows Lodge of 1892 included C.B. Miracle, Conductor and George French, Financial Secretary.[26] The French and Miracle mill was started in 1893 at the old Jerd Comstock mill site.[27] It was up on Hester Creek on the San Jose Road. When the Soquel Augmentation was divided by the US Land Commission, one of the recipients was Craven P. Hester. The creek running through his land was named for him. C.P. Hester succeeded John H. Watson, of Watsonville fame, as district judge. Judge Hester removed to San Jose where he made his mark as District Attorney and Judge. A street and neighborhood are named for him in San Jose. The only impression left by Judge Hester in Santa Cruz County seems to be his creek.[28]

Hester Creek is the central branch of Soquel Creek. The larger western branch of Soquel Creek flows through Soquel Canyon from its headwaters near Laurel. The eastern branch of Soquel Creek forks to form Hinkley Creek as its easternmost branch. The ridge running down from the summit and separating Hester Creek from Soquel Canyon is the ridge followed by the old stage coach road running down to Soquel. The newer San Jose Road runs along Hester Creek on the eastern slope of the ridge. This was the location of the French-Miracle Mill. The mill was first located about two miles above the road into Hinkley Gulch. It was moved in 1897 about a mile up the road near the present day Stetson Road. The Conants, Frenches and Freshours lived up and down the San Jose Road in the vicinity of the mill. About a mile below the junction with Stetson Road was the small ranch of James and Mary Simpson. Jimmy Simpson, with the help of his son Boyed, pulled stumps and planted a prune orchard plus a variety of other trees for family use.

Simpson worked for a while for the French mill. Across a gulch just below the Simpsons was the ranch of Nils Peterson. Below Petersons was the George H. Conant place, later occupied by Lee Isaac. Below the Conants was the Reed place occupied by the Freshour family. Alice Edith[29] and Everett Edison were born to "Blond and Min" on the Reed place. They continued to get their mail down at Soquel; so, E.E. claimed Soquel as his birthplace. The Simpsons shipped their fruit from Wrights up over the summit so they used Wrights as their Post Office.

The Simpsons and Petersons sent their children up to the Skyland School some two-and-a-half miles above. A former school teacher from Riley County, Kansas, Mary Simpson home schooled her young ones until they could make the mountainous up-hill hike to the school. Mrs. Simpson circulated a petition and presented it to the County Supervisors in January of 1907. The Hester Creek School District was created and the school built about a mile above the Simpsons — a much easier walk. The Freshours sent their children down the road to Mountain School located near Cahoons just above where Laurel Glen Road [30] branches off the San Jose Road.

Jim Conant and A.A. Freshour were working for George French at his mill putting in ten hour days six days a week for thirty dollars a month. They lived in rustic mountain houses. But no log cabins, these. They were built with lumber. They had glass windows and even wallpaper. Some of the houses in the mountains were truly fine; But, the people working at farming or in the small mills along Hester Creek were the hillbillies of the Santa Cruz Mountains. When they hitched up the wagon and went to town, they bought supplies such as flour, potatoes, pinto beans and coffee by the fifty or hundred pound sack. Lard was bought by the bucket. The empty bucket served as a lunch pail. Bacon was bought by the slab and pieces sliced off for frying. Folks roasted their own coffee beans. Coffee was made in a great enamel pot on the wood stove. More water and coffee, freshly ground in a hand mill, were added each morning. Sunday was special. They rinsed the pot and made new coffee.

Another Sunday activity was to give one another haircuts. On one occasion Jim Conant was trimming A.A.'s hair. A.A. had developed a fine handlebar moustache which he waxed to points. Conant was standing behind the chair snipping away when he excitedly exclaimed "whup! whup! — look out, Frenchower! look out!" and when A.A. turned his head to see what was happening Conant lopped off one end of his handlebar. Conant delighted in harassing "Frenchower" just to hear him cuss.

The Soquel people living up on Hester Creek called Nils Peterson "Nils Pete." This probably distinguished him in their minds from Nils Olsen who lived below off the Laurel Glen Road. Nils Peterson's wife was a Goheen. Banner and Adelaide Goheen lived across from Hotel De Redwood. When Nils' wife died, the Goheens took in their granddaughter, Dolly, and reared her as Dolly Goheen. Nils married a Mexican lady. She would drive their wagon down the winding mountain road into Soquel at full gallop. Min would warn her children as she sent them off to school; "If you see that Indian a coming you get off in the brush. She ain't got no sense. She'll run over you." To the Simpson children, the "Indian" was Mrs. Peterson. She and Mary Simpson shared the large oval shaped copper tub on the fire place built down alongside the creek where they washed their clothes. Folks then thought it necessary to boil clothes which was the purpose of the copper tub. Great wooden tongs were used to handle the hot clothes. They had a clothes line rigged up there alongside the creek.

Runaway horses were a common cause of death and injury. Lydia Emeline Mason, wife of C.S. Mason of Soquel was thrown from a buggy and killed near the Dakin place when her frightened horse ran.[31] Jim Conant was hauling a load of lumber down to Soquel with a four horse team when a limb got caught in a front wheel and kept slapping the ground. — right behind one of the wheel horses. The wagon was lightly loaded. Conant let 'em run. He pulled them in down in Soquel to deliver the load after a wild ride.

Banner Goheen, sixty-three years of age at the turn of the century,[32] was recalled by A.A. and Jim Conant as "old man Goheen." The hard working crew at the Miracle-French Mill had their times of fun and comic relief. E.E. Freshour recalled a story he had heard many times in his youth. He was laughing so much while telling the story that some details were hard to make out.

> He [Conant] never had any fear. ... Him and my dad [A.A.] and Old Goheen — they were down on the beach getting mussels; and they had a jug of wine and Goheen was — was a dipping these mussels in this bucket of wine and they — they were eating them off those — they got those whiskers — they hook onto the rock with — they pulled that off and throw it away — and they claim Goheen was eating them. 'By hedges' he says 'I thought something was a scratchin my throat.'
>
> They started home and Conant and Goheen was in the front seat — Conant was driving — my dad was in the back of the spring board wagon. And Conant just threw the lines over the side and he come with — over that — that buggy whip over these horses — Old Goheen 'By hedges! you'll kill us all!' — he got out there and he got his hand on the rump of them horses and he walked up that little bit of pole up — then — then he stopped 'em. — My dad'ed tell that and old Conant — tears would run down his cheek — [33]

Minnie Simpson Freshour recalled the detail that Goheen severely remonstrated the young bucks for their treatment of the horses. He didn't think it was funny to run them till they were exhausted. Years later Banner Goheen suffered paralysis and arthritis and couldn't walk. He would crawl to the well to get a drink of water. He wouldn't bother people unnecessarily. Goheen spent his final years up on Hester Creek. He died in March of 1915 and is buried next to Adelaide in the Peterson plot in the Soquel Cemetery. A.A. was still telling the knee slapper about how Old Goheen walked the wagon pole years after Goheen was laid to rest.

Figure 18.3 The Town of Laurel.

— Special Collections, McHenry Library, UCSC.

In January of 1901, twin girls were born to the Simpsons. One lived only a few days. They had a private funeral and buried the little one on their ranch. The surviving girl was named Minnie. The neighbor women performed as midwives for one another and helped out with the newborn and mother. Maime French helped out and the Freshours visited to see the new little girl.

Min and Maime's parents, George H. and Elizabeth Conant lived nearby. He was still working inspecting the tunnels for the S.P.C.R. which required him to go over the ridge to Laurel. All the people living on the San Jose Road along Hester Creek went to Laurel to catch the train. There was a footpath going over there for those using "Shank's mare." The Terrace Grove Hotel would send a buggy over. Elizabeth worked as cook at the Miltonmont Hotel at Miller Road where the San Jose Road crosses Skyland Ridge. The Thompsons were big sturdy people. Tradition has it that she would take a sack of flour off the springboard wagon, flip it over her shoulder, and march into the kitchen with it. Not that she was inelegant. Photographs show her to be a very handsome woman. She had a long walk down from the hotel to where they lived. On one such occasion in October of 1901, she was caught in a rainstorm and arrived home soaking wet. She took sick and died at age forty-nine. Her gravestone at Soquel Cemetery reads:

> *Asleep in Jesus*
> *blessed sleep*
> *From which none*
> *ever wake to weep*

She had lived to see her son Jim marry Ida Gibson in Hollister that summer. George Conant retired from the railroad at age seventy in 1903 — the year E.E. Freshour started school.

George French married Maime Conant in 1905. Neighbors celebrated by giving them a "shivaree." French built a house at the mill that was one great long room with a back bedroom. Family and neighbors would come over for an evening and this usually meant fiddling, singing and dancing way into the night.

The house had a hardwood floor. They would push all the furniture to one side, shave some soap flakes onto the floor and dance. Jimmy and Mary Simpson and their children would come and Jimmy would bring his fiddle. A.A. played what they called an accordion. We would call it a concertina. It was great fun for the kids but they would soon tire and be bedded down on the floor in the back bedroom. One of the children's favorites was when A.A. played his accordion with his foot flapping to keep time and he would rare back and sing:

> *Oh, the bear went over the mountain.*
> *The bear went over the mountain.*
> *The bear went over the mountain.*
> *To see what he could see.*
>
> *Oh, the other side of the mountain.*
> *The other side of the mountain.*
> *The other side of the mountain.*
> *Was all that he could see.*

That was the whole tune as E.E. recalled. A.A. sang it over and over until he wore the bear out. Simpson was great at singing ballads but the kids really loved when he fiddled and A.A. called the dances. They thought it was a wonderful game. Their parents had a lot of fun too. The calls went something like:

> *Sides and in*
>   *Forward and back*
> *Alaman left*
>   *Right hand to your partner*
> *Grand right and left*
>   *Swing em on the corner.*

They would end up with coffee and cake, collect their children off the floor, and make their way home.

George French's love for music blossomed with the arrival of the Edison Gramophone. He was among the first to have one. This was the type with a small oak rectangular case with the record cylinder drive at the top and a beak like stylus that drove the great tin horn that looked like a giant morning glory.

So impressed was he with this technological achievement that he named his first son Thomas Edison Alva French.[34] Min and Blond were likewise impressed by folk hero Thomas Edison. They named their son Everett Edison Freshour. George had to have the latest recordings and eventually he collected several boxes full of the cylinders. They were packaged in a paper tube with an identifying label. The machine could also serve as a record cutting lathe. All one had to do was to perform facing into the horn. George soon had A.A. with his accordion set up before the contraption lustily singing you know what. The bear committed some sort of indiscretion midway through and A.A. was flustered by the flub. He suddenly realized he was being recorded and he blurted out, "Stop the damn thing! Stop it, I say! Turn it off!" This resulted in the most famous gramophone out-take in the history of Hester Creek. People came from miles around to hear A.A. cussin on the Edison.

The Miracle-French Mill ran from 1893 to 1905. The A.A. Freshour family moved down to the Donovan place and Blond started working down at the Loma Prieta Mill which had moved to Hinkley's Gulch in 1905. The Donovan brothers of Santa Cruz built their place up on Hester Creek originally as a retreat where they could get rip snortin drunk without upsetting their city neighbors.[35] The extended Conant family continued to live up on Hester Creek until the earthquake of 1906. Mabel had started attending Mountain School with E.E. and Alice. They had been warned about mountain lions. These big cats were very common in the Santa Cruz Mountains.[36] They have a call that sounds like a baby crying. People have been known to rush into the timber on impulse to investigate — only to be confronted by a big cat. E.E. hid in the brush along the road and let out a yowl like a mountain lion. The two girls ran all the way home. E.E. made quite a story out of that — they got so excited they kept knocking one another down as they scrambled up the road. E.E. arrived to hear them excitedly tell their mother, Min, about the lion. He had great fun teasing them about the timber cat that almost got them.

Figure 18.4 The Loma Prieta Mill in Hinckley Gulch. Mill hands posing the day before the 1906 earthquake.

— Soquel Pioneer and Historical Association.

"Old Dolly" suddenly balked and braced her feet out as if to keep from falling. A.A. was startled by the mares behavior. *Earthquake !* The two wheeled cart was pitching and shaking. The frightened mare wouldn't budge so A.A. jumped out of the cart and ran up the road to get out from under the bank where the new road had been cut through. He heard a strange swishing sound. He looked up and saw the redwood tree tops whipping in the air. — It was five in the morning, April the 16th, 1906. A.A. was on his way to work. The San Andreas Fault running along the summit had slipped. Boulders bounded downhill. Landslides cut loose. Great clumps of redwoods slid downhill the trees upright and a quiver. Earth, trees, rocks and boulders rumbled off the slope and into Hester Creek with a roar and cloud of dust. A.A. coaxed the frightened horse around and whipped her back up the hill. Cracks were opened up everywhere in the earth. He made his way through rubble and cracks in the road and wheeled into the yard to see the chimney bricks spilled across the yard and a gaping hole in the side of the house where the chimney had stood. Min and the kids were all right. She had been in the kitchen at one end of the house. There was a long room with a fireplace and a bedroom at the opposite end. The chimney was banging against the house and every thing was flying off the shelves. Furniture skidded across the floor. The fireplace flew into the yard kicking bricks back into the room. At first she stood rooted in terror then remembered "Oh my God, the kids!" She made her way through the bricks to the children and gathered them all on the big bed. She told the kids "maybe the Lord's coming." The shaking finally stopped and she surveyed the mess. Min looked up the hill towards the Frenches and saw dust swirling upward from a slide. Her sister and father were up there. Then Blond wheeled into the yard.

She told him, "We're all right here. Get up there and see if Maime and dad are all right." The Frenches house was built on a slide. An intervening slide made it appear that they had gone down with it. A.A. mounted the mare and rode up since the terrain was too torn up to take the cart. A.A. found George and Maime French and George H. Conant had survived without any serious injuries; so, he returned down to Min and the children to help clean up and straighten things out there. After awhile a man in a buggy came rattling in — his horses whipped into a lather. "The mill's buried in a slide. Get on down there. We're diggin 'em out." The steep slopes of the narrow Hinkley Gulch came thundering down to bury the lumber mill under an estimated sixty feet of earth. Thirteen men lost their lives in the gulch. In the cabins nine men including Charlie Joon, the cook, were buried under ten to fifteen feet of earth, rocks and timber that slid down from above. They used the water from Hinkley Creek to sluice out most of the dirt. Laborious digging for several days yielded all the bodies except one. One body was found draped over a pipe above the mill under a foot of dirt. He almost got out. All they found of Charlie Joon was a hand and wrist and his queue.[37] Uncovering the mill's installations was more difficult.

Up the road the Simpsons were awakened by the quake and tried to get out of bed but were thrown to the floor every time they tried to get up. They could hear the four girls screaming. Minnie and Bertha in one room had their beds bang together then slam to the walls then bang together. The same thing was happening to Elvira and Beatrice in the next room. The cistern behind the house was sloshing water all over the house and getting them wet. The cistern ruptured and flooded the yard. The big iron kitchen stove was skittering from wall to wall and stopped against the door barricading the parents in their room. When the shaking stopped Jimmy went out a window and went around to move the stove to let Mary out. They found everything in their house thrown to the floor and the cellar an indescribable mess. Jimmy was also called down to help dig out at the Loma Prieta Mill. They moved into Peterson's barn with the Petersons until they got a tent for camping. They built a shed to cook in. Everyone was camping out for fear of having their houses collapse.

They had been a few miles from the epicenter of a Richter Scale 8.3 shock. — A cataclysmic event. Refugees started arriving to report the major cities destroyed and burning. After shocks occurred daily — sometimes several in a day. These were quakes themselves by normal standards. The children delighted in running and jumping across the great cracks opened up in the ground. Then an after shock would close those cracks and open others. On May 27th, Mary reported that it had rained for four days. June the 4th they had just had another big rain. "I never saw so much rain this time of the year." Camping out was miserable. On June 5th she reported "The heavy rains we have had has settled the ground that was broken up so badly by the quake. We have decided to fix up the house and move back into it. We have not had any shakes for over a week."[38] They had camped out for two months!

Nelson and Lydia Ann Jones and their children, Leitha, Wilbur and Glen, were awakened by the clatter of the brick chimney rolling brick by brick down the roof of their house on the main street of Soquel. The first shock apparently took down every brick chimney in Santa Cruz County with the exception of Frealon Grover's. He had been through the terrific earthquake of 1857 so built his house in Soquel to be earthquake proof.[39] Eighty-five years later Leitha Jones Roberts recalled:

> Papa grabbed a little brother and mamma grabbed the baby and they started downstairs yelling "Come on Leitha — come on — get up and get out." ... We all made it to the street and papa was laughing at one of our dignified neighbor ladies in her kind of short nightie when he happened to look down, and he saw he was in only his red flannel nightshirt. We did not dare laugh at papa, but it was sure funny. He did go back upstairs (even if the house could have fallen down) and he got some pants on. Boy, that was the day! We kids stayed out all day under the cherry tree — We were afraid to go in as the place was still "ashake." We had no brick chimney after that — Papa had a terra cotta one instead.

— E.E. Freshour Collection.

Figure 18.5:   A.A. Freshour Family — circa 1906.

A.A. covered up the hole left by the fallen chimney using boards and battens. An old photographer, who had his home and shop built on a horse drawn wagon, eked out a living taking pictures of the mountain families. The Freshours posed for their photograph using kitchen chairs placed across the road in front of a redwood tree. Their quake battered mountain home wasn't very photogenic. The hardships in the Hester Creek District following the quake caused the Conant-French-Freshour group to look down hill to the Mountain District just north of Soquel. A.A. moved his family down to the old Himes' ranch[40] putting them closer to A.A.'s job in Hinkley's Gulch. George French likewise moved his family down to be near the finishing mill he was running with Herman Peterson.⁴¹ Twin girls, Ione and Irene, were born to George and Maime in July of 1906 at French's Mill near Soquel. Mary Simpson attended and sent her daughter, Elvira, over to help in the following days. Irene died a month later and is buried in the French plot at Soquel Cemetery. Inez was born in June of 1907 at Soquel. E.E. as a young lad milked a cow at Lou Gafforts every evening to get milk for the French twins. Mrs. Gaffort, a short, stout lady who spoke a mixture of Swedish and English, never failed to have E.E. in for a big piece of plain cake and a glass of rich milk ladled from a pan. She seemed to have a boundless supply of cake — and kindness for a young country boy.

Once the Loma Prieta Mill was unearthed it was dismantled and moved up the coast to Mill Creek above Swanton. A.A. helped take down and move the mill and set it up at Swanton. A.A. worked filing saws at the mill at Swanton until 1909 or 1910. He moved his family to the Munceford house over in Capitola. By that time the Bradleys and Sophronia had moved to Capitola Heights. The Ocean Shore Railroad was built through from Santa Cruz to Davenport, four miles south of Swanton, in 1905. A.A. must have commuted between the mill and Capitola. E.E. recalled attending the school across from the Park House in Soquel in those years. The school district must have included Capitola Heights. Close family ties were formed between the Bradleys, Jonses and the Hester Creek Freshours. The Soquel Cove of the Monterey Bay was close by with its beaches affording family outings. E.E. recalled rolling up his pants legs and wading out with an abalone iron to take abalone from the shallow rocks. He also learned to fish up along Soquel Creek for the small black trout that were then common there.

For big city excitement, there was the beach at Santa Cruz. Fred Swanton's Neptune Casino burnt down in June of 1906 but he had a new one built within a year. Swanton's flamboyant promotion of the Santa Cruz beachfront as a vacation spot won it the title "The Atlantic City of the Pacific." Just as pleasurable but lower key was Hihn's Capitola development with its hotel, boardwalk and esplanade with its dance pavilion, skating rink, shooting gallery, billiards room and bowling alley. Hihn's hotel beach was open to local residents in the off season.[42] New Brighton Beach was nearby. Soquel was an exciting place for youngsters. It had mountains, beach and the fun of family gatherings all close at hand.

19

OH, THE BEAR WENT OVER

THE MOUNTAIN, to see what he could see. The pickings got pretty slim around Soquel as the logging went into second cutting by smaller mills then went into a continuing decline. The orchards, fruit packing sheds and vineyards took up the slack for a while until wiped out by market glut and vine killing disease. There was an exodus from the area first by lumbermen and then by the fruit growers. The Santa Clara Valley beckoned just over the summit. The Soquel Road to San Jose led over the summit and down through the Los Gatos Canyon through Alma and Lexington and into Los Gatos at the foot of the grade. Across a short stretch of flatland lay Campbell. Or, one could take the train up the San Lorenzo Canyon through Felton and on through the tunnels between Glenwood, Laurel and Wrights to again follow the Los Gatos Creek Canyon into the hamlet of Los Gatos.

Curt and Lottie Miracle had settled in Campbell by 1900. The Miracle-French mill was run at Hester Creek by French while C.B. ran the Campbell lumber yard. Jim Conant hauled lumber from Hester Creek to Campbell and met his wife, Ide, at a dance at Lexington while so employed. In April of 1907, C.B. bought a cannery in Los Gatos on Lyndon Avenue for use as a lumber yard. George French, again set up the mill works for Miracle. In those days, sawmills mostly rough cut lumber and "finishing mills" did the necessary planing, routing and cutting to length and even made such things as doors and windows. Modern sawmills tend to be wood products manufacturers and the lumber yards retail outlets. Lumber yards were once a natural employment alternative for millhands. That's enough right there to cause the bear to go over the mountain.

A.A.'s brother, Joseph Alfred took a job with the San Jose Water Company in 1890 and moved over to Los Gatos with Agnes and their children. Joe and Aggie were the first Soquel Freshours to migrate over the summit to Los Gatos. They were joined by the rest of the Freshour-Mack clan. Aggie's parents, the W.L. Macks, also left Soquel to join Joe and Aggie. Cousin, Elmer Mack, and his wife Clara Himes Mack and their children, soon followed his uncle. Aggie died in February of 1892 at age twenty-nine and was laid to rest in the Los Gatos Cemetery. The family had a nostalgic memory[1] of kidding Aggie about wanting more gravy for her "taters." With both Aggie and her father deceased by 1900,[2] J.A. Freshour and his two young adult children, Effie and Edwin, were in the household of grandma Sarah Mack. Calista Freshour had married Fred Barryman and the young couple had an infant son. Charles and Martha "Myrts" Barden also moved over from Santa Cruz with their children including teenager, Earl. Myrts' mother Sophronia and four-year-old Mae Carrington also came with the Bardens when they moved to Los Gatos. In 1902, Deputy Marshal, Joseph A. Freshour, became Fire Chief of Los Gatos.[3]

A.A. was still filing saws at the mill above Swanton on Mill Creek in 1909, when his brothers-in-law got him to come over to Campbell. A.A. would hitch up the team to the wagon and haul his family along the San Jose Road over the summit. "Oh, the bear went over the mountain, to see what he could see." Although living over the hill in Santa Clara County, the A.A. Freshour family would maintain strong ties with Sophronia, the Joneses, the Bradleys and Long Joe. They were only a short ways apart by the train. Min would be close to her sister and dad. Her children attended the school located at Winchester and Campbell Avenues. They lived in Campbell about a year.

Miracle moved A.A. and George French over to his mill at Los Gatos. Jim Conant went to Colorado to homestead. Blond and Min moved their family into the Carr house on University Avenue then to the Lauser House up on Taite Ave. The going rent then was $6.00 to $8.00 a month. Then they moved to a house across from the lumber yard. E.E. and his brother George slept in a screened tent house in the back. They were living there in March of 1912, when Charmion was born. Blond had an Ingersol railroad watch which he would ceremoniously pull out of his watch pocket and flip open to pronounce the time. Sometimes this impressive process went awry and the back of the watch would flip open leaving him looking at the works. This was handy for adjusting the lever to correct the speed of the movement, but one had to take care to have the watch "right-side-to" when checking the time. A.A. would fume and fuss while making a second try. Min would laugh and say "Having trouble with your Ingersol, Blond?" This was part of a regular repartee that went on between them.

With Sophronia there as the maternal bond, the Los Gatos Freshours, Bardens and Macks were close. By 1910, Sophronia was getting along in years and had moved back over to Capitola Heights to live with the Bradleys. Martha Musgrave Barden died at Los Gatos in November of 1911.[4] She was buried in the Barden plot in the Santa Cruz IOOF Cemetery. G.W. and family had moved down from Santa Rosa after Mattie died in 1910; so, all of the Freshour brothers were in Los Gatos at this time. Elmer Mack exercised his political convictions as a noted soap box orator in the park across from the bank in Los Gatos. He continued to live on Pennsylvania Avenue in Los Gatos until his death in 1938.

Anderson Arthur Freshour had a premonition one morning that something dreadful was going to happen so he told Min that he wasn't going over to the mill. It didn't make any sense to her to have him staying home for no good reason, so she sent him off to work with the assurance that nothing was going to happen. He was working on a shingle mill in those days, that had a circular sawblade rotating in the horizontal plane and a carriage that was pushed back and fourth over it with the shingle bolt gravity fed down to the blade. The operator, A.A. in this case, would shove the carriage back and fourth slicing off a shingle on each pass. The carriage was rocked to one side then the other between passes to tilt the bolt to give the taper to the sawed shingles. There were stops set to give the proper taper each time. Although the operator was to keep both hands on the carriage handles, he usually pushed down on the bolt with one hand to get positive downward feed of the shingle bolt. This practice got chancy on the last few passes. A.A. trimmed the fingers on his left hand off even loosing the index finger at the first knuckle. That was the end of his accordion playing.

Min developed a goiter that, in 1912, was becoming life threatening. Surgery was scheduled in October when Charmion was only six months old. Min had a premonition that she would "go to the hospital in a buggy and come home in a wagon." She died on the operating table. Minerva Jane was taken over the hill and buried in Soquel Cemetery in the plot with her first-born, Jimmy, and Mary Francis Freshour Carrington. The family was comforted by their Soquel relatives including the Bradleys and Sophronia. Reverend Robert Whitaker of the Los Gatos Baptist Church officiated.[5] Elias Bradley died the same year and was buried in the John Freshour plot.

Blond had promised Min that he would never make her children live under a step mother. The family photographs taken over the next few years always show him holding Charmion. Seventeen-year-old Alice was left with the task of rearing her baby sister. Alice would take baby Charmion down to Doctor Anthony for electric treatments for neuritis. Alice would carry her on a pillow because of her painful condition. A.A. lived as a widower until about 1929 when Charmion was seventeen. The house was filled with memories that made Min's absence even more painful for Blond. He moved the family over to the Wright house on Taite Avenue. This was a good sized house with modern plumbing. "Uncle George" (G.W.) with his youngest child, Gladys, moved in and helped with the $8 a month rent. They moved across the street to the Patterson house; then, A.A. built a big house on Ashler Ave. This was a fine house with cement foundation and all hard wall plaster.[6]

Figure 19.1: Los Gatos Freshours: (Front) Mabel, Gladys, Hazel, George, Alice, (back) E.E., A.A., Charmion, and G.W.

The Freshour children went to the school on University Ave next to the library — in recent times commercially developed as "Old Town." E.E. received his diploma in 1913. The chorus performed selections from Donizetti's Lucia de Lammermoore. E.E sang tenor. He was encouraged by his teacher to go on to high school but A.A. would not permit it. A.A. and Elvert Place of the Place Furniture Store and Funeral Parlor, were Odd Fellows. A.A. was in debt to Place for Min's funeral. E.E. was on his way to the Post Office to pick up the mail and old man Place stopped him and asked "Are you looking for a job?" E.E. allowed that he was — sort of. Place: "How'd you like to work for me?" "I don't know who you are." "Place, the undertaker." "How much does it pay?" "Nine dollars a week. You be there and help us open at seven in the morning and you close up at six every evening." At the end of the first week, E.E.

went in to turn in the keys. Place shoved four big silver dollars across the desk. "Here Ev." "No, me and my dad — we talked it over and I'm going to put it all on my mom's bill." Place: "I wouldn't do that to you. If you want, I will keep five one week and four the next until the bill's paid. Or, if you want, you can have it all." The bill was around $150.00. That was for a highly varnished redwood box with a lid that was closed with screws — no hinges — and plain crinoline lining with a taffeta ruffle around the top. That was standard in that day. Place had a fine silver-trimmed horse-drawn hearse handcrafted in San Francisco around 1900. It was replaced with motorized equipment around 1915.

E.E. drove the delivery wagon for Place delivering furniture all around those parts — even to Senator James Phelan's great mansion on the road to Saratoga.[7] The head gardner there was the brother of Place's furniture finisher and mattress maker, Louie Fetch. E.E. picked up the fine art of finishing furniture from Fetch. He also helped Happy O'Neal lay carpet. One evening, after a day of laying cork cloth with Happy at the Novitiate, he was closing up Place's place. He made his way through dim light to the back door and stumbled over a body on the cooling slab. He rushed out the back door with his heart pounding and then stopped. He decided that the dead ones can't hurt you so he bravely went back in and closed up.[8]

E.E. never lost his yen to fish in Soquel Creek. He and Charlie Gibson would take the train from Los Gatos over to Santa Cruz and then take the electric car to Opal Station just short of Capitola. From there they walked up to the old Mason place and slept overnight in Mason's barn. They would get up early and go down to Soquel Creek and fish upstream all the way up to the falls above Nils Olson's place. Then they would fish back down to Hester Creek and fished it some. On one occasion, they fished up most of Hester Creek and came out on the road above and walked over to Laurel to catch the train to Los Gatos. They met Jimmy Simpson cleaning out gutters along the road with a shovel and wheelbarrow. The slides along

Figure 19.2: E.E. Freshour driving Place's delivery wagon

the mountain roads were cleaned up by hand in those days. Simpson's family was running the Terrace Grove Hotel on the San Jose Road on Hester Creek and Jimmy picked up odd jobs. He spoke of his daughter Beatrice, "his fiddler," and invited the boys over to visit his family. Simpson later left the slim pickings of Hester Creek to follow the bear over the mountain. He went by train to the mines of Amador County and returned to winter with his family in the Santa Cruz Mountains. E.E. and Charlie went into Napier's store at Laurel and for a dime bought a box of soda crackers and a big chunk of cheese which they ate while awaiting the train to Los Gatos.

On another trip, old Lou Gaffort stopped his wagon and offered them a ride as they were walking the road past the Soquel Cemetery. He knew Charlie but E.E. had grown up and Lou, not recognizing him, named off all of A.A.'s family and asked what ever happened to them. E.E. enjoyed fishing so much that he acquired a fine split bamboo rod, a good reel, a wicker creel and rubber hip boots. He became expert at fly tying. The hip boots were last seen hanging on Lou Gaffort's gate. He expected to come back by and get them, but never did. The trips sometimes ended with a visit to the Joneses or Bradleys and grandma Sophronia. The electric car took him to Santa Cruz where he boarded the train for Los Gatos. The conductor would call out "Felton! Change cars for Mount Hermon, Ben Lomond and Boulder Creek." He called in turn: Glenwood, Laurel, Wrights, Alma, Los Gatos, Campbell and San Jose, as E.E. mimicked years later. After the earthquake, Southern Pacific had rebuilt the railroad as a broadgauge. E.E. recalled when it had three rails to accommodate both gauges.

The year 1915 marked the end of the trail for three Soquel wagon train Freshours. Sophronia was 83 years old. Lydia Jane, her daughter, had been born on the trail 57 years past. Long Joe, who was bull whacking in that wagon train and was present when his niece, Lydia Jane, was born, was now 77 years old. They had started this newfangled Rural Free Delivery.[9] Long Joe was living at a Santa Cruz Rural Route address in October of 1912 when he made his last Declaration for Pension. Long Joe was compelled in an affidavit of April, 1913, to explain his conflicting birth dates given in previous affidavits and records.[10] His affidavit explains "That my parents had a family record in which were recorded the dates of births, marriages and deaths of the family, that said record was burned in a fire which burned our home in Iowa." In May of 1915, he slipped on the steps at his home and fractured a thigh and went into Seabright Sanitarium. He died on June 16, 1915. His affairs were attended to by Emma and Lewis T. Mason of Los Banos. Long Joe had deeded his remaining property on Soquel Creek to his niece, "Jane Bradley ... for and in consideration of the love and affection the party of the first part has and bears unto the party of the second part."[11] He left the deed to be recorded, upon his death. Sergeant Joseph Terre Freshour, Co. A, Eighth California Infantry, was buried in the family plot in the Soquel IOOF Cemetery. A Union Army headstone marks his grave.

— The Leitha Roberts Collection.

Figure 19.3: Four Soquel generations: Sophronia Freshour and (L to R) Lydia Jane Bradley, Leitha and Lydia Ann Jones.

Ironically, niece Lydia Jane could not attend her uncle Joe at the Seabright Sanitarium because she herself was dying. Her family doctor had prescribed medicine for a stomach ailment but her condition steadily worsened. Surgery revealed carcinoma of the stomach. She was sewn up and sent home to die — standard treatment in those days. Her daughter, Maytie, tended her in their Capitola Heights home. Maytie did double duty because her grandmother, Sophronia, was also dying from a broken hip and the general rigors of old age. June and July was a harrowing time for twenty-four-year-old Maytie Bradley. Gangrene set in on Sophronia's leg and the smell was oppressive. E.E. took the train over from Los Gatos to pay his last respects to his grandmother. Leitha Roberts recalled visiting her grandmother, Lydia Jane, and her great grandmother Sophronia. In 1914, Leitha with her mother, Lydia Ann Jones, had posed for a four-generation picture with Lydia Jane Bradley and Sophronia.

During her last days at Capitola Heights, Lydia Jane looked across the road into a field of strawberries and spied a large ripe strawberry and sent Leitha over to get it for her. When Leitha got over there, sure enough, there was the large ripe berry just as Lydia Jane had said — a remarkable feat of visual acuity. She had those Cherokee eyes right up to the end. Leitha also remembered the awful gangrene odor. Sophronia responded to questions about the tradition of Cherokee blood in the family with "You ain't got any Injun in yuh. I'm not a Cherokee — I'm a Yankee!" This was true of course. Her father was a South and her mother, Prada, was of some sort of Slav origin by way of New Jersey. This showed in Sophronia's features in her last days. The Indian blood would be on the Freshour side.

"Liddie," as Elias called her died June 21, 1915 — just five days following the death of her uncle Joe. She was laid to rest next to Elias. Sophronia died a month later and was laid to rest beside her husband John who had preceded her by 48 years. There were three fresh graves in the plot that Joseph Terry had bought when his brother and comrade in the Santa Cruz Cavalry had died nearly half a century before. A.A. came over the mountain three times that 1915 summer to grieve with his family at the gravesides of his uncle, sister and mother. His brother G.W. would be there with the family. The only surviving Freshour of that 1857 trek across the plains was Joseph Alfred Freshour of Los Gatos. He, no doubt, attended with the Macs. In 1916, Jerrit French was buried next to his wife and daughter in Soquel Cemetery. George French was sole survivor.

A graveled road, canopied over with large oaks, ran through the Soquel Cemetery as it does today. When John was buried, in 1867, the road was lined with the buggies and horses. In 1915, steam power was still in its heyday. The road over the summit by then was in such an improved state that Santa Cruz was a couple of hours by buggy from Los Gatos. E.E.'s younger brother, George, would trot a one-horse buggy over the hill to spend the day fishing with Glen Jones. The more precocious

— The Leitha Roberts Collection.

Figure 19.4: Glenn Jones with his catch and George Freshour driving his buggy.

youngsters were becoming enamored with the horseless buggy. In 1903, these obnoxious contraptions were outlawed on mountain roads; but, by 1905, the Supervisors had repented and, in deference to realtors, legalized motor traffic in the mountains.[12] By 1915, an automobile trip from Los Gatos to Soquel was almost as likely as a buggy ride. The gravel road in Soquel Cemetery would be, during the 1915 funerals of the wagon train Freshours, lined with a mixture of conveyances including the self propelled type. This bewildering new technology had been witnessed by Long Joe and Sophronia who could clearly recall walking the two-thousand miles across the plains, desert and mountains using vehicles propelled by very slow oxen. Now they had seen everything — and been appropriately laid to rest along with "trail baby," Lydia Jane.

Long Joe's property was thus left to all of Lydia Jane's heirs. Tradition tells us that it was sold to a party that dug up most of Long Joe's orchard looking for buried treasure. They never found any that anybody heard of. A rumor of unknown

— The E.E. Freshour Collection.

Figure 19.5: Los Gatos Freshours visit Capitola. L. to R. (standing) Lydia Jones, Charmion held by A.A., Leitha Jones, E.E., George, Maytie Bradley, and Alice. (kneeling in the sand) Irma Jones, Hazel, Mabel? and Glenn Jones.

origin told of this cache and greased the skids for the liquidation of the property. The story was considered hilarious by the Freshour descendants of Soquel — namely the Bradleys and the Joneses. If a gold mine can be salted, so can an orchard.

When the Freshours and kin visited back and forth across the hill they would entertain one another with knee slappers from their communities. A.A. was credited with saying "If you're goin' to tell a story, you might as well make it worth tellin'." A favorite tale from Los Gatos, possibly apocryphal, was the story of the leaky books. It was often narrated by E.E. who retained the story teller's art of the days before we all became the passive receptors of media sleaze. His stories were a dramatization — He laughed his way through all the roles with old timer's rusticity, mimicked mannerisms and implied quote marks.

> He was a retired Presbyterian minister — Sproul was his name. You see, Los Gatos was dry. Nobody in Los Gatos could sell any liquor. — They couldn't have it in a hotel. You could buy it in San Jose and ship it in on the interurban car that stopped right there in town. And this preacher, he had it shipped in on the train — Wells Fargo Express — and no label on it, just his name. And, them fellows got kind of reckless with that case of whiskey and they threw it around; and, pretty soon, one of them books start to leakin' — and the express man called him up and told him "Reverend, you better come down here and get your books! One of 'em' a leaking." It wasn't two days till that story was all over town.
> He was a big man — taller than I was a whole lot. — And a real kind old fellow. ...I took furniture up there and took stuff out of there to refinish. — I knew him for years. — I never saw 'em that I could detect that he was under the influence of it. ....[13]

The train ran literally right through the middle of Los Gatos which is located on Los Gatos Creek right at the entrance of Los Gatos Canyon. The principal street of Los Gatos is Santa Cruz Avenue which runs out to Campbell and the main cross street is Main Street which leads to San Jose. University Avenue runs parallel to Santa Cruz Avenue and between it and the Creek. The railroad came down out of the canyon and ran parallel between University and Santa Cruz Avenues. The business men on the east side of Santa Cruz Avenue could go out of the back doors of their businesses and be on the tracks. The railroad ran smack between the bank and the Ford Opera House. The bank was on the corner of Santa Cruz Avenue and Main Street and the opera house was the next establishment down towards the creek on Main Street. Photographers could get dandy pictures of the train highballing into Los Gatos by getting on the roof of the opera house.[14] The lower floor of the opera house building became a department store and the Opera House was upstairs. E.E. could recite an account of every business along the three block business district of Santa Cruz Avenue during 1913 to 1916 when he was delivering there. He did the same for Main Street. The undertaker parlor and furniture store were on the west side of Santa Cruz Avenue in the middle of the block going towards Campbell from Main Street. Two blocks down from Main on the east side of Santa Cruz Avenue was the plumbing shop that belonged to Fred Barryman who was married to Caliste Freshour, Joe and Aggie's daughter. From there on down to the intersection with the Saratoga Road there was open countryside — just a barn and some horses. At the Saratoga Road, there was a very large cannery on one corner and the cemetery on the opposite corner. E.E. helped move the cemetery. Notice was given and a few bodies were moved at the request of next of kin. Most were left there. Generally, there wasn't much left of the remains. Bodies decompose after a few years and all that is left is some hair and objects buried on the body according to E.E.

In the genetic roulette game some interesting surprises are produced in siblings. Caliste Freshour had a fair complexion but her sister, Effie, and brother, Eddie, were dark-complected with straight dark hair and dark eyes. The children of Fred and Caliste were distinctly Indian in appearance. E.E. claimed that Joe Freshour's Indian blood had come out in them.[15] G.W. was dark-complexioned but his brother, A.A., was known as "Blond." G.W., claimed Cherokee blood. E.E., described his father as a "blockheaded Dutchman." A genetic side effect seems to be that the blond characteristic was accompanied by extreme myopia. A.A.'s pride kept him from wearing glasses when he was a youth, so, he was unable to recognize friends waving to him from across the street. This led people to think of him as a mite peculiar. The dark-complexioned members of the family tended to have phenomenal eyesight. They would naturally conclude that the fair members of the family were not too bright. Those with keen eyesight tended to have cataracts with advancing age. This genetic prank persists to this day with its deleterious effects and associated misunderstandings.

The tradition that the family had Cherokee blood in them led A.A. and Elmer Mack to seek Oklahoma land offered at that time to the Cherokee. Anderson and his Iowa cousin were found to be without identifiable Cherokee ancestry.[16] They wouldn't have qualified in any case. At least one-quarter Cherokee blood was required to qualify. Their grandmother, Elizabeth Hedrick Freshour, was possibly half Cherokee. One can always skirt this issue by claiming "Black German." The issue gets a little sticky when one discovers that the Cherokee from Tennessee, and especially Georgia, owned negro slaves. The Cherokee fought as Confederate troops in the War of the Rebellion.[17] When forced by the Emancipation Proclamation to free their negroes, they made them members of the tribe. The Cherokee records list many *Cherokee Freedmen*. Neither "Black German" nor "Black Cherokee" rings true for the Tennessee Froschauers. Eastern Indians and fair skinned Europeans have intermarried since the earliest colonial days. Wendel Freshour's descendants living around Martinsburg, West Virginia showed evidence of Indian blood.[18] Intermarriage particularly occurred with regard to the "Civilized Tribes." More Americans are probably of Cherokee blood than is generally known.

Seeking out farm land became a trend. The flood control and water management of the San Joaquin Valley had made it attractive to farmers. Annie and Richard Beswick had followed the bear over the mountain to take up farming near Lathrop. The L.T. Masons were living on First Street in Soquel when the 1906 earthquake hit. That did it! They bought ranchland at Los Banos in Merced County. They were followed by Tom Freshour, with mother, Amanda Freshour, in June of 1908. L.T. bought the Mason plot in the Los Banos Cemetery when Tom died in April of 1909. The Masons and grandma Amanda lived in Palo Alto from 1911 to 1914 while Lewis Jr. attended Stanford. Amanda died at Palo Alto in March of 1913 and was interred in the Mason plot in Los Banos Cemetery. The Masons returned to Los Banos where they sold their ranch and purchased another from Miller & Lux.

George and Maime French moved to Turlock to take up farming. French filled a rainy day giving vent to his literary bent by filling an entire onionskin tablet with prose, political analysis, weather reports, doggerel, eulogies, the state of Turlock agriculture, limericks and family affairs. He removed the cardboard back and stuffed the entire tablet into an envelop addressed to A.A. Freshour of Los Gatos. A.A. would read a page or two, rip off a few oaths and slam the thing down and storm outside. He couldn't leave it alone and would return to repeat the cycle. Aunt Maime was taking care of her nieces, Hazel, Mabel and Charmion. A.A. wanted to see his kids and E.E. thought it would also be nice to see his aunt Maime again.

The first Excelsior owned by E.E. was a one-lunged belt driven model without a clutch. He had taken his dad to San Jose on it a couple of times but it was pretty gutless — wouldn't pull a hill with two people. He then bought a new two-speed 1914 Excelsior twin (two-cylinder.) It had a lot of power. He set out for Turlock with A.A. perched on the back. On the road going up through Mission San Jose E.E. slowed down to a walk to shift gears on a hill. Just as A.A. started to climb off E.E. gunned out leaving him on his hands and knees in the road. A.A. expostulated "We're going to put this damned thing on the train at Niles and ride the train." They needed a bolt to fasten the tandem up stronger. Not finding one at Mission San Jose, they avoided the old Mission San Jose grade and headed for Niles. E.E. got a bolt at Niles and installed it and coaxed his dad back on for the trip up through Niles Canyon. The hilly Vallicitos route from Sunol to Livermore was under construction so they went by way of the flat land route through Pleasanton. They got behind a water wagon. The adobe road was slick and the cycle was slipping and sliding so they were going along slow and E.E. had both feet down. Then, *"Hoo-whee!"* They were both left sprawled in the 'dobe. A.A. got up and ran over and asked "You hurt?" "No. I ain't hurt!" He started to pick up the cycle. E.E. yelled "Leave it alone!" The Excelsior was on its side and in gear with its rear wheel whirring. It was laying on the clutch so they couldn't get it out of gear. E.E. pulled the plug wires and they got it upright. A.A. wasn't going to ride anymore. "You're a long ways from nowhere out here." He finally got on.

The Excelsior buzzed up the road following the rails through the Altamont Pass. They sailed into Turlock in a grand finale. The main stem was covered with straw and sand had drifted forming small sand dunes. They discovered this when they both went over the handlebars. E.E. thought it was just a hump in the road. They cautiously proceeded in on West Main and there was aunt Maime in the street waving.

> "She had a Buck-board with two horses on it — one they called Tar — had two horses on it and she had Eddie there. Eddie had a hernia and she bought a truss there in the drug store and laid 'em right down there on the sidewalk and fit the truss on 'em and pulled his pants up and turned 'em loose again. My dad got in the spring wagon with her and I'd ride down the road a piece and I'd let them catch up with this old Tar — and wait there — and pretty soon why they'd come — I would sit there and wait some more and they'd get down and I'd take off and pass 'em again — and finally got home."

French had a big field of watermelons. They would scoop the hearts out and eat their fill and throw the rest to the hogs. French would take the wagon out and load it up with watermelons and bring them in and heave them over the fence to burst open among the guzzling hogs. They had been there about a week and had pretty much healed up from the trip over; so, they were ready to return to Los Gatos. A.A. said "I'll ride with you, but by ♮⋆♭, you promise you'll go slow." They went out of their way to get to the Crows Landing Road. It was black top. — a pretty good road. They followed that up to Tracy. They did pretty good all the way back to Los Gatos. A.A. said "By ♮⋆♭, you could drive it that way all the time if you wanted." He thought the rough trip over was done by E.E. for meanness.

San Jose had its own version of the Eiffel Tower at this time. Not to be climbed, it was a local triumph of Edison's incandescent bulb. So successful was the illumination that it caused roosters at the edge of town to crow at the wrong time of day. More notable for youngsters, Alice and Everett Freshour of Los Gatos, was the establishment at its base that served a hamburger for a nickel and, for the second nickel, a draft to wash it down. "That one was so good we had to have us a other one." Then they got back on the Excelsior and tooled their way back to Los Gatos.

E.E. quit the job with Place in 1916 and went to work for the Curtis Brothers driving one of their two Studebaker busses on the run from San Jose to Los Gatos. He drove on their San Jose - Santa Cruz stage run during the brief time that Santa Cruz permitted it. They used a Hudson "Super-Six Phaeton." on that run. A custom built pleasure car, it was an immense machine. The huge engine had a cast iron pan that "must have weighed 500 pounds." It had to be going fifty miles an hour in order to shift into fourth gear. In those days engines weren't balanced so there was a lot of vibration, rattling and banging from under the hood. This stage run was up over summit and down the old San Jose Road into

Soquel — an experience not unlike the stage coach trips of the previous century. (High gear was never used.) He also drove their Palo Alto run which had a stop in the town of Mayfield. The Railroad Commission governed their schedules and regulations. The Studebaker busses had governors to keep them from going too fast. The Curtis Brothers went big time and bought a third Studebaker but had problems keeping them running because there weren't many experienced drivers and the Studebakers were frequently "fritzed up" by new drivers. E.E. would sometimes have to use the Hudson since the other drivers couldn't drive it. Anderson Arthur Freshour continued to make a living with the horses he loved so much but his son was of the emerging automotive age. The world was plunged into a war that would use trucks. — An era quasi automotive, quasi equine. The days of the Cavalry were drawing to an end. Trucks then used hard rubber tires.

In September of 1916, Curt Miracle and three Campbell associates formed the Campbell Redwood Lumber Company and bought the defunct Bloom Mill and its stumpage on the Gazos Creek on the coast near Pigeon Point. Pescadero is just to the north. This locale was originally the northernmost part of Santa Cruz County but, in 1868, San Mateo County took some thirty square miles including Pescadero and Half Moon Bay from Santa Cruz County.[19] George French moved his family over to Mountain View and served as mill wright and head sawyer once again for Miracle. The Simpsons had moved from Hester Creek to Locust Street in San Jose. Mary Simpson maintained her friendships with former Hester Creek neighbor Maime French. Ione French egged her cousin E.E. into visiting the four Simpson girls, ages twelve through eighteen, with a box of chocolates. He gave all four in turn a ride on the Excelsior. Ione's matchmaking came to naught.

E.E. recalled taking French over through La Honda to Gazos Creek on his Excelsior. The road up the Gazos to the Mill had bark filled ruts so trucks wouldn't get stuck. The ride was treacherous. "Yipp!" French would put his long legs down as the cycle slithered. He finally said "Moze, I'm walking half the time anyhow, so you go on ahead." French saw that E.E. was fed at the mill mess hall before going back. The squirrels running across the road going through La Honda would run through the Excelsior's wheels and get wove into the spokes. Jim and Ide Conant had returned from their Colorado venture and Conant was recruited by Miracle to work at the Gazos mill. A.A. came over from Los Gatos to cut timber. By the spring of 1917 they had the mill running. The Campbell Redwood Lumber Company went broke in 1918 and closed permanently. Jim Conant and his family moved out to Pigeon Point.[20]

In July of 1918, E.E. turned twenty-one and could do as he pleased. He joined the Marine Corps. Boot camp was at Mare Island on San Pablo Bay up near Vallejo. He qualified as sharpshooter on the Springfield rifle. He went across country in a troop train to take further training at Quantico, Virginia. For military secrecy reasons, they were confined to the train and had to keep the blinds drawn when passing through towns. A number of nice men wanted to teach the young and innocent looking E.E. how to play poker. He had a nice roll when he got to Quantico. The favorite sport of the Los Gatos Freshours was poker. The war ended before he could be sent overseas. He was discharged on February 28th, 1919.

A.A. found an opportunity to lease land at Bean Hollow between Gazos Creek and Pescadero. This land along the coast with its summer morning fog and sea mist was ideal for growing peas and beans. E.E. had bought a house in Los Gatos and arranged for the rent to be applied on the mortgage by the bank. He sent his power of attorney from Quantico to A.A. to sell his equity in this and use the money to lease the Bean Hollow ranch. His discharge papers were sent to the Post Office at Pescadero. He came home to his folks at Bean Hollow where he helped his dad farm.[21] He spent his service bonus check on a cow to provide the family with milk. The ridge next to Bean Hollow was known to the local folk as Freshour Ridge. Hazel and Charmion Freshour attended Gazos School.

In 1918, pandemic influenza struck the US. People living out in the mills and farms were by nature of that circumstance fairly well quarantined. People in the cities were dying at a terrible rate. Coffins could not be made fast enough. Railroad platforms had large numbers of stacked shipping crates awaiting shipment. They contained bodies being shipped by rail to be buried in their native soil. Half a million people died in the US. People wore gauze masks when they had to leave their dwellings. George French commuted between his home on "Sawdust Alley" in Mountain View and the Gazos, dividing his time between the mill and his family. The flu epidemic hospitalized Aunt Maime, and her daughters, Inez and Ione. While Maime lay in a coma, Inez and Ione, died. George French, distraught and not knowing where to turn, went to see Maime's dear friend, Mary Simpson, then living in her apartment house at 76 Julian Street in San Jose. Minnie looked after Eddie while George unburdened himself in Mary's kitchen. Mary Simpson tried to comfort him and encourage him to go on. Maime had pulled through and come home. She was asking for her girls. He had to break the news to her. She was devastated with grief. She was consoled by her Adventist neighbors and took refuge in that faith. George and Maime were left with Eddie and later were blessed with George Junior. Grandpa Conant lived out his years with them at Villa Street in Mountain View.

The Freshours farmed for a few years on the coast. They lived briefly at White House down the coast then moved on down into Santa Cruz County to Scott's Creek above Swanton. Here fifty-three-year-old A.A. had the opportunity to teach his sons some woodsmanship. E.E. was twenty-three and George was eighteen. A.A. would size up a redwood, deciding by the pattern of the bark if it would split well. They would plan exactly where they wanted the tree to fall and chop in the undercut accordingly. Standing on the springboards they would start making the cut with the two man saw. Nowadays, this is done by gasoline powered saws. Then, the saw was powered by grub such as steak and beans.

A.A. roasted and ground his own coffee then. Every morning a few beans were ground in a small coffee mill, the freshly ground coffee falling into a little wooden drawer at the bottom. A small brush was used to get every bit of the fresh coffee into a great enameled pot. Each morning more coffee and more water was added. On Sunday he emptied and rinsed the pot and started a fresh one. A.A. woke up his boys and his "kids" in the morning with the rattle of stove lids and banging of pots and pans. Wood was stuffed in the firebox of the old wood stove and a couple of glugs of "coal oil" from a jug wet the wood for a quick start. Steak in those days was a large round steak that filled the big black iron frying pan. The steak was thoroughly "tanned." They didn't believe in rare meat. The other pan was filled with boiled pinto beans spooned from the souring pot and fried in bacon grease. E.E., found it difficult to get himself around a huge plate of roundsteak and refried beans before daylight. A.A. would grumble "By ♮♭, you got to eat, boy, if you're goin' to work."

They would occasionally visit the Conants up the coast. One time George told Jim Conant that he had to get home and boil some beans. Conant asked him how he knew when the beans were done, George responded "Oh, I just pinch em." After that, Conant would razz him by saying "You goin home to pinch the pink ones?" He gave George the nickname "Pinchem." When E.E. was small, Conant named him "Moze."

Once the tree was felled, they had to lop off the limbs and then use the two man saw to cut the tree into logs of the proper length to split into grape stakes. A.A. couldn't wield an ax without grunting on each swing. *"Haugh," "Haugh," "Haugh."* He was standing with one foot braced on a bent over redwood sucker as he was limb lopping. A ring of small redwood trees sprout up around the stump of a redwood after the tree has been cut down. They were working among these "suckers." The particular sucker he was braced on chanced to have a hornets nest fastened to it. With each stroke of the ax he went *"Haugh,"* and the sucker flapped, banging the hornet's paper nest on the ground. Hornets came swirling up A.A.'s pant leg and he chucked his ax and went hopping and cussing down the slope swatting hornets and peeling off his clothes as he went. He ended up standing down in the road below in his shirt tail. E.E. and George whooped in hilarious enjoyment as the old man yelled at them from the road below. They got his trousers and swatted the hornets and picked the dead ones out and brought the trousers down to him. "By ♮✳♭, you wouldn't think it was so damned funny if you had hornets in *your* pants." E.E. laughed "You looked like September Morn." (Coca Cola tray art of the day.) They laughed some and sweat much. Once the tree was trimmed and cut into logs, the bark was peeled off and wedges and malls used to split each log into grape stakes. They toiled at this brute labor from sunup till sundown. Their pay was for the large load of grapestakes they had split. By day's end they were "purdy gaunt." Steak and beans sounded "purdy fair."

Scots Creek and Mill Creek, both above Swanton, branch off the same stream. It's as if A.A. had returned to the site of the mill he had left eleven years earlier. Perhaps he wanted to show his boys something about the woodsman's trade. After a brief stint at making grape stakes, they moved on further south to Laguna Creek to do some more farming. Bonny Doon was the nearest town. E.E. had sold his Excelsior when he quit working for Place. They had been farming using a six-horse plough and used the same team to pull the "wood wagon" full of grape stakes. During this time it seems that E.E. acquired his father's passion for draft horses.

> That was a team of colts — Percheron — part Percheron — crossed, they weren't pure. That one blue roan — he had a white blaze down his face — and his nose was pink — and he had four white socks to his knees. Called 'em Dewey — The other one Bessie was a strawberry roan. I used to drive them down Pacific Avenue in Santa Cruz and — they'd stop and look at 'em — and, boy, they're right up and a comin'.

He had trained them to "high step." They would raise each hoof up hesitating in mid step to show the bottom as they pranced up the street.

They hadn't had a rope on 'em when I got 'em. Three hundred and fifty bucks. "aye ♮⋆♭, I knew you were crazy, but I didn't think you were that bad." "awah, you ain't seen nuthin' yet." No harness. I'v't take my own rope and halter. I lead 'em. I put a war bridle on 'em. Take a whip and get 'em out to the end and sit down on 'em and turn 'em wrong end too a few times — and, purdy soon they come right up to me — and I led 'em home.

We had six other horses and I took one uh the — I took a set of harness belonged tuh the big ones (th're big.) — I had a big set of — Well the — I guess they were part Clydesdale — they weigh two-thousand pounds, big suckers. [What kind of work did you do with them?] Plough, harrow, disc, haul lumber, haul wood. I put them two colts in that six horse plough. I put one in the wheel and tied 'em down to the doubletrees; and I put the other one i'the swing — tied him down to the doubletree — and they shakin' and jump. — I first put the harness on 'em and turned 'em loose in the corral, they'd buck! and kick! and jump! and whinner — *eh - eh - eh* — and kick and run. They're out there 'bout half-a-day and — they got used to that harness – 'nd it wasn't so bad. Then I put 'em in the plough. — Then I put em in the wagon — one at a time. Oh I – I played with them two or three weeks. [You mixed them in with the horses you already had.] Yeah. I – I played with them two or three weeks 'n I put 'em together — on the wagon and drove 'em – 'n' I work 'em together — right out in the lead – all the time.

Yea-up a *nice* team.

I had a wood wagon. It's got the seat comes up over there and kinda – goes ahead – out way over the tail of the horses. Got a long bed back there about twelve fourteen feet — haul four foot a wood on it. [What, firewood?] Yeah. Bolts 'n firewood , ties, grapestakes. Yeah, they were sure purdy. I kept 'em good.

While A.A. and his boys were farming on the coast, eighty-nine-year-old George Horace Conant died in Mountain View. One of his last wishes was to see his grandson in his Marine Corps uniform. E.E. visited his aunt Maime and uncle George French in Mountain View where they were caring for the old Massachusetts gentleman who years ago had come to seek his fortune in California. E.E. had just arrived from Quantico and was in his Marine uniform. His grandfather again recounted how he had come around the "Horn" in a "sailing vessel." George Conant was interred in the Soquel Cemetery next to his wife, Elizabeth, in March of 1920.

In the summer of 1920, the last of the Soquel wagon train Freshours died at Los Gatos. Joseph Alfred Freshour, A.A.'s older brother, was going on two years old when his parents brought him into California in a covered wagon. He arrived in Soquel when seven years old and spent his youth there working in the timber and sawmills. He lived his last thirty years around Los Gatos. Joe was employed by the San Jose Water Company which got its water from Los Gatos Creek up in Los Gatos Canyon. They had a lower reservoir at Lexington and a redwood flume ran from there down the side of the canyon to Los Gatos. The reservoir has been replaced in modern times by a much larger earthen dam which has created a lake which covers the old towns of Alma and Lexington. Up until the early 1960s one could still view from the modern highway the old flume supported by trestle work running along the opposite side of the creek. Joe would walk the flume checking and maintaining it. Joe remained single for many years after Aggie died but eventually remarried. He and his wife, Scotswoman Belle Cassels, lived at Alma in 1920.

The main San-Jose-to-Santa-Cruz road then was the wagon road going through Alma and Lexington and through Wrights and up over the summit and down Hester Creek into Soquel.[22] Being sixty-three years old at the time of his death, Joseph Alfred was of the horse and buggy generation. Joe drove this road in his buggy as part of his water company duties for many years. His luck finally ran out. On July the 11th of 1920, two autos suddenly met on the narrow winding road and both swerved to avoid a head on collision. One of them slammed into the rear of Joe's buggy throwing him up against the dash. The driver, Louis H. Gibbs, stopped to assist. Joe was badly shaken but apparently not seriously injured. Over the following weeks he complained of stomach pain then took a turn for the worse in August. He died on August 4th, 1920. An autopsy revealed cause of death to be a torn liver. A coroner's jury found his death to be accidental. He was buried in the Freshour-Mack plot of the Los Gatos Cemetery.[23]

Joe was survived by his widow, Mrs. Belle Freshour, and daughters, Mrs. "Clista" Berryman and Mrs. Effie Mason, of San Mateo. He was also mourned by his sisters, Annie Beswick and Emma Bausch, and his brothers, A.A. and G.W. Freshour. They were "sons and daughters of the Golden West" — all born to John and Sophronia in California. The last Soquel wagon train Freshour was gone. "The Trail" was now being driven by automobiles.

Joseph A. Freshour's son Eddie continued to work for the San Jose Water Company. He later moved to the Sacramento Valley to take up farming. His Soquel roots are born out by his obituary in the *Santa Cruz Evening News* of February, 1941.

> Edward J. Freshour a member of a pioneer Santa Cruz family with its home up the Cahoon Gulch on the way to Mountain View Ranch, died on Sunday at Colusa and was buried yesterday at the Los Gatos Cemetery.
>
> Freshour was born at Soquel, son of Mr. and Mrs. Joseph Freshour. His father drove team for the timber companies when the Santa Cruz mountains were humming with mill activity.
>
> Freshour had been a dairyman and alfalfa grower at Williams.
>
> He is survived by a widow, Mrs. Maria Freshour and two step sons and two sisters, Mrs. Fred Berryman of Los Gatos and Mrs. George Mason of Burlingame.[24]

A.A. and his boys farmed at Bonny Doon through 1921. Once again opportunities beckoned over the hill at Los Gatos. A.A. had come full circle. The bear decided to go over the mountain again. About this time E.E.'s mechanical proclivities resurfaced. He sold his team of colts for three-hundred and fifty dollars — not the greatest return on his investment, but, he saw a motorcycle in Santa Cruz that he had to have. A big Chief Indian that had been completely rebuilt. It had a reground camshaft and was really fast. They only wanted two-hundred and fifty. "You could put it in second gear and give it the gun and it'd pull you right off the seat." It could "freeze" the speedometer at its maximum of one-hundred miles an hour. Typical of engines with racing cams, it was very rough idling. "You had to break the throttle on it and get it up there running purdy good before it would even out. It was fighting against itself until you got it up to speed." The shift to high gear was made at thirty MPH and it would cruise very smoothly.

When he arrived at Los Gatos, A.A. moved his family into the place across from Casaletto and made an arrangement to keep his horses in Casaletto's barn. He later moved to a place on Chester Street where he had a house and barn and some land from which to operate his teamster business. He was joined by G.W. and Barden who drove team for him. A.A. took teaming jobs well into the 1920's. At one time he even hauled grain for Miller-Lux from Firebaugh to Stockton pulling two wagons with sixteen horses on a single line. He also went by saddle horse into the Trinity mountains to hunt deer. The people of the horse and wagon era were remarkably mobile. Trains and automobiles only added the dimension of speed.

E.E. eventually sold the souped up Indian to an ex speed cop, Carl Balch. Carl had graduated a few years after E.E. from the Los Gatos Grade School. His father and Case owned the bank in Los Gatos. Carl became the local California Highway Patrolman. The state provided him with a badge and a big Harley-Davidson. He kept bragging to E.E. about how hot the Harley was. He didn't know much about E.E.'s Indian.

The Indian had a "barn door" muffler — an opening ahead of the muffler with a cover that, when slid aside would vent the exhaust straight past the muffler. E.E. was heading out through town on Santa Cruz Avenue. He shifted into second gear, flipped the barn door and cracked the throttle, rattling everything in downtown Los Gatos. He glanced behind and here came the speed cop. He cracked it wide open in high gear and kept right on a going. This became a recurring event. He and Carl had a lot of fun — much to the consternation of the Los Gatos business men. Balch never did catch the Indian. He quit the CHP and opened the auto supply store on Santa Cruz Avenue.[25] He wanted that Indian real bad. E.E. kept the Indian until after he got married and a new baby necessitated a family style vehicle — a model T. He worked for a while for the Gurnsey & Doyle mill and cabinet shop in Mayfield and cruised down El Camino on the Indian. He took the Indian on hill climbs at Meteor Rock near Alum Rock Park. He gave his aunt Maime a ride up Castro Street, Mountain View's main stem, much to her embarrassment, after swearing he wouldn't. He also gave "aunt Lottie" Mericle a ride past the preachers house in Campbell after promising to take her straight home. It so happened the preacher and his wife were porch sitting. The word got around not to get on "Ev's 'cycle" — especially in a skirt. Aunt Maime called him a "dirty bugger" — the worst her religion would allow.

A.A. took his two sons into his teaming business which was billed as *A.A. Freshour & Sons*. E.E. acquired another team for that purpose.

> That team I bought in Los Gatos. I go by that roller down there when they were rollin' Santa Cruz Avenue — well I was going down there with the gravel wagon — I had these two big horses on there — these two big [clumps?] — weighed about eighteen hundred apiece. And we got down to this roller and — that one horse turned around and wanted t' climb on the seat with me. 'nd I had that shot whip under my jumper — I took that

out and laid it on his ribs pretty good – 'nd *swishtt* —
he took off. He — he went by that roller all right — in
a dead run. And I had a — spring seat on this gravel
wagon with — a tail gate up in front — a little higher
than the side boards. See 'nd I just slid back over that
thing — and got a good hook on that with my butt —
I let em go! When they got all done runnin', I give em
some more. And he won't run no more — so, I got down
— got down in the gravel pit 'n I was half loaded – 'aye
th' time my dad 'nd George got down there.

"By ♮×♭, unhook 'em and I'll lead 'em back!"
"No — no — no — that's *my* team."
"You ain't a goin' to work 'em!"
"Yeah, I'm gonna work 'em. I'm goin'a fill that thing up
with gravel and I'm goin' right back by that steam roller!"
"By ♮×♭, You ain't!"
"Yes I am."

Well, we got done. I took the — I had some chains
on the inside the checks — and I put them through the
bridle – the bit. And, hooked them over on the other
side. And the stay chains back on the double trees — I
tightened 'em up tight so they didn't have any give in
'em. And, — we got up by the roller — and, George,
he wouldn't have it no other way; he was going to ride
there. So, I said: "O K, you ride. You take the break
rope. Don't put that break on unless they go to get away
with me. If they gittin away from me, why, why put the
break on. But if they – they just gonna run, — let 'em
go."
So we got up by that — roller again — and the guy
stopped the roller — and, and — got up by it; and, old
Prinz, he looked over at it and he's a crowdin' the pole
and I come down with that — shot whip on 'em again;
and, he began t' tighten up and dance up and down —
and he went by it — but, he went by it pretty smooth.
And it wasn't, oh, I guess, — a week — he trotten by
there 'nd he wouldn't look at it. *Somebody let 'em get
away.* The man that owned 'em.

The previous owner had cautioned E.E. "He'll kill you!" "No he won't. — No he won't. He's a good horse." The spirited Prinz was also skittish about cement mixers. The first time E.E. drove a load of gravel up to dump it on the pile alongside a mixer, Prinz kept right on going. E.E. turned the team around drove them back up there. He got down and held the team while George unloaded the wagon. Eventually, Prinz became inured to this mechanical fright also. Notice the manual labor used at this time. The gravel wagon was loaded and unloaded by shovel.

Prinz indeed developed into a good work horse. George was ploughing an orchard with Prinz when he flushed a jackrabbit. Prinz ran amuck breaking loose from the plough. George had the lines wrapped around his hand and couldn't free himself. He was dragged the length of the orchard on his belly tearing up the front of his clothes. E.E. thought it was hilarious. No run-of-the-mill plough nag — Prinz. Good horse! *Good* horse.

In 1923, E.E. and Minnie Simpson went over the mountain and got married in Santa Cruz. Leitha Jones stood up with them. Minnie helped cook for A.A.'s crew of teamsters which included E.E., brother George, uncle G.W., A.A. and Barden. Minnie and Charmion became close companions. They would go down to the end of the street to Los Gatos Creek and swim. A.A. Freshour & Sons prospered. Besides doing business in building materials, they had the water wagon contract for the town for a number of years — until they voted for the wrong man. E.E. played cornet in the Los Gatos firemen's band. One job he worked on was grading a golf course using a horse drawn "Fresno Scraper." Two children were born to E.E. and Minnie. E.E. built a small house for his family on one of A.A.'s lots. They bought a model T Ford off of "Teddy" Mericle. A.A. bought an Overland Mysterie. The family took it on a touring excursion to Big Sur. E.E. served as chief mechanic. He spent much of the trip alongside the road under the hood. He said it was a mystery why it ever ran in the first place.

E.E. would arrive home from work and waiting for him at Chester Street was a little urchin who would come running to the front gate to greet him. He would say, "I'll beat you to the house Mary!" and she "Oh no you won't!" She had a funny little hopping way of running. E.E. would pretend to run along side her letting her win. Beginning in 1928, articles appeared from time to time in the Los Gatos paper reporting Mary Ellen's recurring illness. She was suffering from "mitral incompetency" — or, as the paper reported, a leaky heart valve. There was nothing the doctors could do. They sent her home from the hospital telling her parents to "just love her." Mary died in her mother's arms in June of 1929 at 76 East Julian Street in San Jose — her grandmother's home. She was named after her grandmother, Mary Ellen Simpson. Father William Keller officiated and Elvert Place directed the funeral.

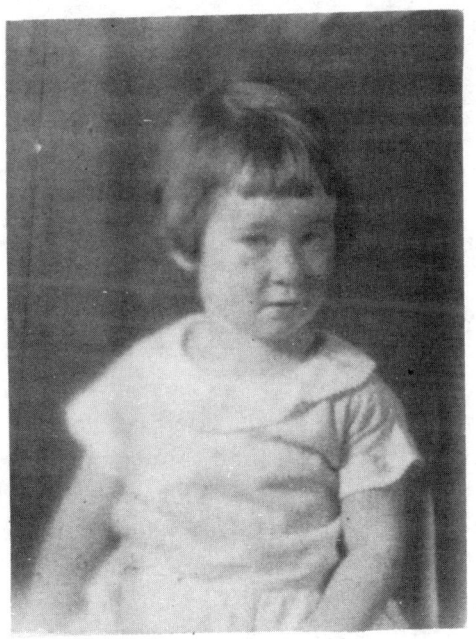

MARY ELLEN FRESHOUR   Sept. 6, 1924 – June 30, 1929.

Blond had kept his word to Min. Their baby, Charmion, was fast becoming a young lady. A.A. felt at liberty to become a suitor and won the hand of Mrs. Ella Rose. This soon led to dissension in the family and the end of *A.A. Freshour & Sons.* E.E. and Minnie bought a small place on Tully Road in Evergreen in 1929. He went to work for Foster's dairy across the road where he learned to love animal husbandry. In 1931, he moved to the San Joaquin Valley where he owned several dairy farms. He always kept a team in preference to a "Fordson." A.A. bought a small farm at Lakeport in Mendocino County and later moved back to Los Gatos then to Sunnyvale.[26] There are innumerable anecdotes about the Los Gatos Freshours and their kin and progeny. A small sample has been given.

George died shortly after he married Rosalie in 1936. He fell from a conveyor at the charcoal by-products plant of the California Packing Company in San Jose. An angle iron crossbar broke his fall. He died in O'Connor Hospital. George was known for his inveterate goodness. A.A. was devastated. Why would God take such a good boy from him and leave him with one so cussed?

At this point in our tale, we have covered two-hundred years of family history starting from 1732. In the process we have seen America's frontiers wax and wane. Having reached the Pacific shore our ancestors seem to have muddled for a while then returned inland seeking God knows what.[27] The people no longer had a *Manifest Destiny* nor any other kind of destiny. The lust for gold and the rape of the redwoods had run their course. Now they turned to California's fecund soil. Crop production around Los Gatos and throughout the Santa Clara Valley in the 1920s and 30s was phenomenal. Soon, the modern pioneers — the dustbowl Okies — made the trek west in their flivvers to work the California crops. A country tune heard on the radio went:

"Hey Okie! If you see Arkie, tell em I'm out in Californy — pickin up prunes."

THE END

NOTES

Referenced to the Bibliography

Notes on Chapter 1 — The Introduction

1. Maps of the North American Continent of that day showed the western region between the Rockies and the Pacific blank — "*Tierra Incognita.*" *e.g.* See DeVoto-Empire, pps. 56, 59-60, 247-251; Van Dorn pps. 642-3, 663; Webb, pps. 152-6.

2. Paine in *Common Sense* " 'Tis not the affair of a city, a country, a province, or a kingdom; but of a continent — of at least one eighth part of the habitable globe." and in *The American Crisis VII* "...the country is young and capable of infinite improvement, and has an almost boundless tract of new lands in store;..." See Foner pps. 17, 149.

3. After independence was declared, the US was governed by the Articles of Confederation until 1789 when the present Constitution was ratified and George Washington elected the first president. Under the Articles, the congress of the Confederation enacted the Land Ordinance of 1785 and the Northwest Ordinance of 1787. The Land Ordinance provided for surveying and selling the land of the territory and the Northwest Ordinance provided for territorial organization and development by which a section of territory would be admitted by Congress as a state. See Bailey, pps. 133-4.

4. See DeVoto - Empire, pps. 227-8, 400-403.

5. See Rupp, pps. 81-2.; Strassburger, pps. 93-5 sq. and Sturm. Primary documents are in the State Archives at Harrisburg, Pennsylvania. Also see *From the Frogmeadow*, Vol. 1, No. 1, March 1990;

6. The German Reformed Church was the state church of the Palatinate until the French armies of Louis XIV overran the area imposing the Catholic faith in the churches and universities. British policy under Queen Anne encouraged thousands of Palatines to emigrate throughout the British domain in the early 1700s. They followed the anabaptists, already in Pennsylvania, invited personally by William Penn (who was in Germany in 1677) and by his pamphlet in 1681. The Palatines arrived in huge numbers in the 1720s and 30s — preceding the Lutherans. By the late 1700s, however, the Lutherans had become the dominant of the two faiths in Pennsylvania. Both were main line reformation faiths, in contrast with the anabaptists who were separatists — essentially outlawed in their homelands by catholic and protestant alike. See: Barck & Lefler pps. 281-2.; Branch pg. 46; Klees, pps. 73-4, 137-9; Rouse, pg. 21. [continued over]

Having become Americanized, the layman found the distinction between Lutheran and Reformed obscure and they readily adapted between the churches. Note here the monumental contribution of William Penn in his "Holy Experiment." He established a "pluralistic" state. — A veritable hodge-podge of religions. There was no state religion, official or de facto. A radical concept one day to be adopted as the 1st amendment to the US constitution. Compare to Colonial Virginia where the State Church was Anglican. Governor Thomas Jefferson formulated his doctrine of separation of church and state enunciated in his letter to the Danbury Baptist Association and enacted as his *Statute of Virginia for Religious Freedom*. Koch & Peden, pps. 272-7, 291, 311-13, 332.

7. Klees pps. 142-5.; Barck & Lefler pps. 281-2.; Rupp, pg. 452.

8. So many ships crammed with Palatines docked at Philadelphia that the English Inhabitants began to fear that these people might attempt to form a separate government. To guard against this and to keep an exact tally of the number of Germans arriving, the Provincial Council, meeting at Philadelphia in Sept. of 1727, ordered all captains of ships conveying these immigrants to submit passenger lists (a windfall for genealogists!) and all foreign immigrants were ordered to take "the Declaration of Fidelity and Abjuration," (fidelity to the king and abjuration of allegiance to the Stewart pretenders and the rights of other foreign princes, prelates etc. within the realm of Great Britain or the Dominions.) See Branch pg. 49; Klees, pps. 141-2; FWP-Pennsylvania, pg. 32.

The British King to whom Hans Jerg swore allegiance was George II of the Palatinate-Hanoverian line — the German Calvinist line descended from Frederick, Elector of the Palatinate and Elizabeth, the daughter of James I. Their daughter, Sophia, married into the House of Brunswick to a nobel that became the Elector of Hanover. Their son, in the royal line of James I, was called to the British throne as King George I when Queen Anne died. This commenced the present English Royal line — the Hanoverians. They suited Parliament because they interfered little with the workings of government and prevented a rival line from threatening protestantism. The Palatine emigrants to Pennsylvania would have no problem with loyalty to a Calvinist Palatinate-Hanoverian King. The first generation would tend to be Loyalist. Succeeding generations less so. *q.v.* Hall and Albion, pps. 322-3, 426-8, chart on pg. 1009.

9. Klees' thorough presentation of the various German sects tends toward hindsight from the Pennsylvania perspective. It is excellent on their immigration to and settlement in Pennsylvania. G.H. William's work represents years of research in Europe dealing with the origins and development of the sects in Europe and is definitive in that regard.

10. The *Froschauerbible* of 1529 contained the complete cannon and became popular with the various anabaptist sects throughout Europe. It was based on Martin Luther's incomplete translations of that time with augmentation by other translators. This spurred Luther to complete his translation which was printed in 1534. In 1555, Froschauer also published an English Bible — the Thomas Bible — used in England some 50 years before the publication of the authorized King James version.

See the 1985 edition, *Encyclopedia Britannica* for a brief biography of Chrystoph Froschauer; Haller is more thorough. *q.v.* pps. 159, 162, 175-182; On a clandestine association of Basil publisher Simprecht Sorg (Froschauer) traveling with Balthasar Hubmaier to Nicolsburg, Moravia in 1526 and publishing Hubmaier's works there, see Williams, pps. 219, 816-7; For extensive data on the Froschauers of Zürich, see *From the Frogmeadow*, Vol. 1.

11. See Klees, pg. 40; In C. Henry Smith's book *Mennonite Immigration to Pennsylvania* he speaks of the well known Froschauer Bible. Also see *From the Frogmeadow*, Vol. 1, No. 7, pps. 58-60.

12. Klees pg. 220;   Everton pg. 250.

13. Rouse, pg. 23.

14. Bailey, pg. 18;   Barck & Lefler pps 58, 197-8.

15. Federal Writers Project — Pennsylvania, pg. 444.

16. For county organization see Everton pps. 314, 316. The Froschauers of Littlestown Pennsylvania were affiliated with Christ Reformed Church. The Froschauers of Fredericks County Maryland were in some cases affiliated with the Saint Jacobs (Stone) Lutheran and Reformed Church which apparently accommodated both faiths, but, there was a growing tendency for them to affiliate with an Evangelical Lutheran Church. The German Reformed Church, along with the German language, was left behind in the middle colonies when the family migrated. — And, the Froschauers became Freshours/Frushours. See Irish pg. 286 and LDS IGI microfiche on PA and MD Froschauers.

17. Bailey pg. 18;   Barck & Lefler pg. 202.

18. Branch, pps. 52-71;   Miller pg. 76.

19. Garrett, pps. 731-2.

20. The F.W.P. - Pennsylvania has a concise account of the French and Indian War. A more thorough account of the military aspect is given in Barck & Lefler pps. 463-474. For an assessment of the war as a struggle by European powers for possession of North America, see Bailey, pps. 44-59; DeVoto-Empire, pps. 220-7.

21. Barck & Lefler, pps. 468-9; Dillard. The Indians took their surviving captives to Montreal where they tortured them to death. Jean Jacques Rousseau, luxuriating in the elegant literary habitats of Europe, extolled the noble savage (whom he had never met) while, in Montreal, the Indians were forcing mothers to eat the flesh of their children. Naturalist Rousseau's compatriot, Montreal commander Louis Antoine de Bougainville wrote "What a scourge! Humanity groans at being forced to use such monsters." James Fenimore Cooper's novel, *The Last of the Mohicans*, romanticizes this conflict. See Dillard's article.

22. Tracey & Dern, pps. 380, 406

23. Historian Francis Parkman devoted a two volume work to this conflict known in Europe as the Seven Years' War. *q.v.* on the expenses: Miller, pps. 44-5, 70-4; Barck & Lefler, pps. 476-8; Bailey, pps. 89-90

24. These roads were constructed during the French and Indian War. Benjamin Franklin procured 150 wagons, horses and provisions at Lancaster for Braddock's campaign in 1755. These went on the Monocacy road to Frederick and followed the road to Ft. Cumberland from whence Gen. Braddock launched his disastrous campaign by building road north towards Ft Duquesne (now Pittsburgh.) *q.v.* Bailey pps. 56-7. Gen. Forbes, in his 1758 campaign, used the region of York as his source of supply to construct a military road from Bedford through the Alleghenies to fort Duquesne — an extension of the road from Carlisle to Bedford. Later known as the Pennsylvania Road this was the first of the national roads. Klees, pps. 162, 222; FWP-Pennsylvania, pps. 247-8, 347

25. On the Treaty of Paris of 1763 see: Barck & Lefler pps. 463-474; Miller, pps. 70-78. The map inside the covers of Miller is excellent.

26. The Pontiac War was an Indian uprising that led to the British Proclamation of 1763 which set the limit of colonial expansion at the summit of the Alleghenies. A short time later, the British ordered colonial governors to make no further grants of Crown lands — ostensibly to halt western conflict with the Indians. *q.v.* Bailey, pps. 62-3: Barck & Lefler, pps. 488-494; DeVoto-Empire, pps. 263-4; Miller, pps. 74-7.

27. Barck & Lefler, pps 58, 197-8; Rouse, pg. 68. The British astronomers Charles Mason and Jeremiah Dixon were engaged by the British government and sent in 1763 to make surveys in accordance with the governments ruling. (Astronomers were capable of accuracy not common to the surveying of the day.) The border was established in 1767 at its present location of 39°43'N. This line was to be included in the Missouri Compromise of 1820 as part of the infamous Mason and Dixon line that separated slave states from free states. It came to symbolize the separation of North from South.

NOTES

The journal kept by Mason during his 1763-68 survey of the boundary between Pennsylvania and Maryland comments on Indians. (Available as National Archives Microfilm Publication M86.) The colonial Froschauers living in this region undoubtedly had Indian neighbors.

28 Washington had more than a passing interest in real estate. He applied for warrants for himself and all the officers and soldiers of Virginia. By 1784 the greater part of his wealth lay in the wilderness. *q.v.* Garret, pg. 724. This map gives a panoramic view of Washington's holdings. He had large tracts on the James, Shenandoah and Potomac rivers in Virginia, the Monongahila in Pennsylvania and to the west along the Ohio in Virginia. Also see Branch, pps. 66-71.

29. From Koch & Peden, pps. 13-28, 722. Jefferson was consistent in the spelling "Graaf."

30. LDS IGI Microfiche for Pennsylvania Froschauer and variants. Dates range from 1746 to 1827 mostly in York Co. but a few in Lancaster and Adams. (anachronisms?) York Co. was formed from part of Lancaster Co. in 1749. Adams Co. was formed from part of York Co. in 1800. *q.v.* Everton, pps. 246, 250.

31. *q.v.* Weiser for Frederick Co. MD Freshours. On Revolutionary War Freshour veterans see Appendix A. In recent times in Green Co. TN, a gravestone was privately placed at the grave of John Freshour in the Solomon Lutheran Church Cemetery commemorating his presumed Revolutionary War service in the VA 4th Regt. He would have been a forty-five year old serving with the rank of private in the troops of another state. There is only one corresponding John Freshour compiled military record. It is the VA 4th Regt. record for the John Freshour who settled in Ross Co. OH, as born out by his Pension and Bounty Land Warrant file. [Nat. Arch. Index – Revolutionary War – Compiled Service Records, M881, Roll 973; BLWT – Pension files, W7607, BLWT 29046-160-55]

Adam Froshour appears in the German Regimental Roll of Capt. Henry Fister's Company. *q.v.* Maryland Archives - Muster Rolls, pg. 261.

32. Edited by Peter Force, Washington, 1837.

33. The metal plowshare was not used until the early 1800s. McCormack's mechanical mower reaper wasn't invented until 1834. Bailey, pg. 65, 306; Branch, pg. 47.

Wendel Freshour acquired a number of large pieces of land (140 a. to 400 a.) at Sleepy Creek in Virginia from 1773 to 1780. Simms, pps. 79, 348, 449, 451, 496.

34. On the Treaty of Paris of 1783 see: Buell; Bailey, pps. 121-4, 131; Barck & Lefler pps. 662-3, 687.

35. The Monocacy Road starts in York and follows the old Indian trail through the York Valley and thence south as indicated. An important trading route, it was followed south by many German emigrants. FWP-Pennsylvania, pg. 347; Klees pps. 156, 222; Tracey & Dern.

36. Klees pg. 220; Barck & Lefler, pg. 270.

37. Klees pg. 221; Rouse, Chapter 5.

38. Barck & Lefler, pps. 269-70.

39. Klees, pg. 220

40. The "Kentucky" rifle was the Pennsylvania rifle which had its origin in the art and ingenuity of the Swiss and Germans. The emigrating Germans brought the rifle technology with them from central Europe. The New Englanders still used smooth bore muskets and the British still used the "Brown Bess." The Hessians had rifles which was one reason the British hired them. The British were still using muskets in Jan. of 1815 at the Battle of New Orleans where Andrew Jackson's Kentucky Riflemen annihilated them. William Henry manufactured rifles for Braddock in Lancaster which became the "arsenal to the colonies." The Pennsylvania rifle was also manufactured in York. FWP-Pennsylvania, pps. 247-8, 347; Klees, pg. 212; Miller pg. 479.

41. Branch, pps. 110-123; Kincaid, Preface and pps. 41, 67-81.

42. Garrett, pps. 726-8.

43. Hunter and Hunter, pps. 792-7; Frogmeadow, Vol. 1, No. 5, Feb. 1991, pps. 37-40; On Rumsey's mill, see Strum; Garret, pps. 734-9.

44. Bailey, pps 133, 167-171; Branch, pps. 159-163.

45. Frogmeadow, Vol. 1, No. 3, June 1990, pg. 20.

46. See Appendix A.

47. "Old John" b. 1732, 1747, 1763 depending on researcher. These dates are suppositional. The identity of the parents of John Freshour Sr., immigrant to Green Co. TN, has not been established. Tradition has the Freshours and the Stevens arriving together from Pennsylvania. For his will see Appendix A-3.

48. Up until 1860, maps in text books showed the plains east of the Rockies as "The Great American Desert." *q.v.* Branch, pps. 407-8; De Voto, Wide Missouri, pps. 1-5; Unruh pg. 3.

49. The trail known variously as the Oregon Trail, The California Trail and The Mormon Trail is now known as The Oregon-California Trail. OCTA — the Oregon-California Trails Association is dedicated to preserving this important part of American history.

Notes on Chapter 2 — The Trail

1. Gibbons; Unruh, pps. 84-5, Tables 1 & 2.
2. Mattes, *The Great Platt River Road*
3. Article by Fox.
4. Generally see Pope's article; Charles Smith traveled by steamship from Cincinnatti to Westport to start his 1850 trek to California. *q.v.* Smith, C.W., pps. 9-17; The Wolverine Rangers' agent, James Pratt, purchased wagons in Chicago and had them shipped to Independence. *q.v.* Holliday, pg. 93.
5. Mattes, *The Great Platt River Road*, pg. 5.
6. F. W. P. — Oregon Trail, pps. 194-5; Paden, pps. 231-3.
7. Webb, pps. 3-9.
8. DeVoto, Decision, pg. 114; Stone, pps. 58, 60-1.
9. Stone, pg. 62.
10. Hunt, pps. 119-155.
11. Paden, pg. 416. Humbolt Sink is just south of the associated lake.
12. Article by Mary West; Graydon, pps. 6-10
13. Stewart, pps. 7-29, 36-52.
14. Graydon, pg. 14; Hunt, pps. 179-223.
15. Article by Pat Smith.
16. Graydon, pg. 9; Hunt, pps. 195, 262.
17. Graydon, pps. 9-10.
18. Paden, pg. 466.
19. Oral tradition from Mahala Jane Gann Hobbs per correspondence with Gail Benson.
20. Bryant, pg. 263.
21. Mattes — *Narratives*, Charles Hopper, pg. 41, #56, Trubody recollection, pg. 110, #281; Beard pg. 81 sq.
22. Trubody Statement; Graydon, pps. 10-13.
23. Alexander Moore's statement; Paden & Schlichtman, pps. 10-11; Bancroft - Pioneer Register, Hopper, pps. 190-1, Nicholas Gann, pg. 155. (Moore's statement appears to be the primary account from which the others are derived.)
24. Holliday, pps. 17, 53, 449-50.
25. Coy, pg. 202.
26. Graydon, foreward, pg. v.
27. Long, pps. 13-17.

Notes on Chapter 3 — Missouri Trailhead

1. Calafia is depicted on the California state seal dwarfing the large grizzly in her company. The Amazon Warrior Queen of the legendary island of California is from the *Sergas de Esplandiá* by Garci Ordóñez de Montalvo circa 1498. The early Spanish explorers applied the name of this legendary island paradise to Baja California — an apparent island. *q.v.* Chapman, pps. 55-69. The explorations and cartography of Father Eusebio Kino revealed California to be part of the North American Continent. *q.v.* Polzer, pps. 12-19; Trafzer, pps. 14-15.

The grizzly bear was very common in early California. In the summer of 1848, Charlie Hopper killed nine Grizzlies within a mile of his home near Yountville. Grizzlies were captured by the Spaniards who would lasso them with their *riatas* entangling them. They staged bear-bull fights. The *ursus horribilis* was very dangerous. The newspapers of that day carried accounts of deaths and injuries caused by encounters with them. Bear meat was commonly sold in butcher shops at Santa Cruz as late as 1885 and bears were taken as game in the Santa Cruz mountains as late as 1910. Beard, pg. 95; Koch, pps. 7-8, 188; Malmin, pg. 21; Irving, pps. 282-4; Item: Torn to Pieces by a Bear, *Daily San Joaquin Republican* (published at Stockton,) July 15, 1857, 2:3.

2. From the research of Callista Marie Martin Rau Dake by courtesy of her daughter Margaret Rau Koch. On the Rocky Mt. Fur Co. and Kit Carson's duel with Schuman see Devoto's *Wide Missouri*. Biographical sketches of the children of John and Elizabeth Freshour of Jackson Co. MO are given in Appendix B.

3. Indexed in Vineyard as Section 5, Township 47, Range 29.

4. Federal Writers Project — Tennessee, pg. 93.

5. Gillette, pps. 35-36.

6. Federal Writers Project — Tennessee, pg. 92.   **7.** *ibid.*, pg. 39.

8. Bailey, pg. 308;   Branch, pps. 246-9.   **9.** Foster, pps. 1022-3.

10. A biographical sketch of Henry Froshour is given in Appendix C.

11. Buell, The "Cherokee" River is clearly shown on his 1783 map of the United States. Also see Federal Writers Project — Tennessee, pps. 30-42.

12. Bailey, pps. 269-270; Federal Writers Project — Tennessee, pg. 42;

13. *Index to Compiled Service Records of Volunteer Soldiers Who Served During the Cherokee Disturbances and Removal in Organizations from the State of Tennessee* ... Nat. Archives Microfilm Publication M908, Roll 1.

14. Ehel, pps. 322-3, *sq.*

15. Wohleber, pg. 30; A cogent summary of the *Trail of Tears*.

16. Parkman, pg. 2.
17. Federal Writers Project — Tennessee, pps. 51-2.
18. Stewart, pps. 7-29, cf. Stone, pps. 26-31.
19. From *Narrative of Charles Hopper A California Pioneer of 1841*, by R. T. Montgomery, Bancroft Library, 1871; reproduced in Beard, pps 11-13.
20. ibid. pg. 11.
21. Parkman, pg. 3.
22. ibid. pps. 46-7; See also pg. 5 and F.W.P. — Missouri, pps. 378-9.
23. ibid.; See also Lavender, pps. 33, 36.
24. Sandburg, pps. 85, 95-7; DeVoto-Decision, pg. 203.
25. Lyman, pps. 237-242; Also see Branch, pg. 425; Bryant is excellent on John Marsh; on Rubidoux see Mattes - Road, pps. 111, 450.
26. Stone, pps. 71 sq.
27. Goodspeed, History of Cole Co., pps. 300-301.
28. ibid. Biographical Appendix, Judge W. S. Freshour, pps. 846-7.
29. US Census, 1850, Calif., San Joaquin Co., Pub. M432, Reel No. 35, Stockton District, pg. 266, dwellings 21-24.
30. Indexed by Vineyard in Sections 4 to 20, Township 47, Range 29.
31. Marion Freshour's death certificate gives his birthplace as Centerville, Johnson Co. MO;   His obituary (*The Siskiyou News*, Dec. 13, 1906, pg. 3) says Centertown, Jackson Co. MO. This data, typical of its kind, is hearsay — uncertain regarding Marion's early years and MO geography.
32. See Appendix B-3.
33. The North Carolina Regiments of the CSA had a number of Freshour soldiers. The men of east Tennessee who would not serve with the CSA were imprisoned. Many made their way at great risk through the mountains to Kentucky where Colonel Felix A. Reeve was forming the Eighth Tennessee Infantry Regiment. Sgt. George Freshour served under Capt. R. A. Ragan in Co. K recruited from Cocke County. On this and the Civil War in East Tennessee see O'Dell pps. 330-335 sq.

The Greene County Freshours didn't own field hands but did have a kitchen slave cooking for them. On this see Burgner and Huntly.

Two Cocke Co. brothers, sons of Jacob Freshour and Sarah Fronbarger were on opposite sides in the conflict. Oliver Freshour was a veteran of the Union Army and Alexander Freshour, a Confederate soldier was killed in 1863. *q.v.* Eddith Johnson's article on David Freshour, pps. 32, 34.

34. Isaiah Horn never mentions Andrew Freshour in his diary and there are never neighborhood associations in Census data or land records.

35. Ranchos were measured in leagues — 4438 acres. In 1824 the Mexican government offered to any Mexican citizen in good standing, 11 leagues. There were some small ranchos of one, two or three leagues. John Sutter and Mariano Vallejo each had a full 11 leagues. See generally Nellie Sanchez' *Spanish Arcadia,* Chapter VII. In exchange for shingling his house, Vallejo paid young Missourian George Yont two leagues — Cayumas Rancho. *q.v.* McKittrick, pps. 135-6; Sanchez, pps. 92-3. Also see Delano, pps. 125-6.

36. Frémont's position was that to require the Californians to defend their titles would result in virtual confiscation of their property — A distinct violation of the Guadelupe-Hidalgo Treaty. He held that the burden of proof should be on the squatters. McKittrick, pg. 315. See generally Josiah Royce's Chap. VI on *Land-titles and Politics.*

37. See generally McKittrick's Chapter XIX *A Travesty of Justice.*

38. Various communities claimed to have killed Murietta. *q.v.* McKittrick's quotation of Vallejo, pg. 316; Koch, pg. 114; Stone, pg. 160.

39. In looking for Freshour deeds in the alphabetized index, one would look under "Fre...." and to their surprise find Fremont, John C. in profusion. On Frémont's sudden wealth see Stone, pps. 136, 138.

40. As the Martin Murphy family before them had done, they left a slave state, Missouri for a free state, California. But they had lived with a slave holding culture in TN and MO so may have been tolerant in that regard. They were probably more interested in the incentives California offered and disliked the strife occurring in Jackson Co. Missouri. Actually, California was a *de facto* slave state — a situation that took some time to rectify. *q.v.* Nevins, pg. 79; Holiday, pg. 363n; Mattes-Road, pg. 66.

41. Monaghan, pps. 5, 16; Nevins, pg. 307 sq.

42. Sandburg, pps. 115, 123; Monaghan, pg. 7; Nevins, pps. 339-341, 393-5.

43. Sandburg, pg. 121.

44. Monaghan, pg. 61 sq.

45. Monaghan, pps. 85-106; Van Doren pg. 210.

46. Sandburg, pps. 137-8.

47. Ingenthron, pps. 40-41, 57, 95-100.

48. Monaghan, pg. 134; Ingenthron, pps. 80-91, 142-160.

49. Ingenthron, See the introduction by Kathleen Van Buskirk.

50. Monaghan, pg. 255.

51. *ibid.,* pps. 281-9; FWP-MISSOURI, pg. 53.

NOTES
433

52. The exchange of communiques between Union Commander at Pea Ridge, Brig. Gen. Samuel Curtis and Confederate Commander, Maj. Gen. Earl Van Dorn regarding reciprocal arrangements to bury the dead and tend to the wounded reflects the savage nature of the warfare. Hatred and unjustifiable killing continued after hostilities had formally ceased. *q.v.* Ingenthron, pps. 161-3, 304-7.

53. Sandburg, pps. 261-5; Monagahan, pps. 185, 204-6.

54. In 1903, the Secretary of War persuaded the Governors of most Southern States to lend the War Department the Confederate military personnel records in their possession for copying. These compiled service records and indexes are available in the National Archives. *q.v. MILITARY SERVICE RECORDS — A Select Catalog of National Archives Microfilm Publications*, pps 83-164.

Note that Confederate **pension** records are State Archive records and are **not** available in the National Archives. *ibid.* pg. 84.

55. *q.v.* Orton.

56. Lincoln had never been a national figure. He had been in the Illinois legislature for many years and had a very successful law practice in Illinois occasionally arguing cases before the US Supreme Court. In his one term as a US congressman (obtained in 1846 by collecting political indebtedness from those who preceded him) he alienated his constituency. In 1856, he lost his bid for US senate in Illinois to a Stephen A. Douglas clone — the pivotal issue being Douglas' "Nebraska" act. He first came to national attention in the 1858 senate race when he ran against Douglas and lost. His following was grass-root. He had few nationally prominent political friends (other than Douglas.) He was his own man. His election was a fluke. There were in effect two elections — one South of the Mason-Dixon line and one North which he won without a clear mandate. The North itself was fragmented as evidenced by the positions of the Lincoln Douglas debates which were widely published. In Lincoln's own words, "Only events can make a president." *q.v.* Sandburg, pps. 137-145, 154-183; Bailey, 404-412.

57. *q.v.* Safire's *He made us one nation, indivisible,* New York Times, 11 Feb. 1985, pg. A21; San Jose Mercury News, 12 Feb. 1985, pg. 7B.

Notes on Chapter 4 – Conestogas to the Wabash

1. Deduced from 1850 Census data for Henry Freshour of Gilliam twp. Jasper Co. IN and J. D. Dunn's biography. *q.v.* Battey, Jasper Co. pg. 573.

2. Paris Freshour was the father of Florence Freshour, the mother of Dorothy Inscho.

3. "Wildcat Bank" currency had become so unstable that President Jackson authorized issuance of a *Specie Circular* which required all public land purchase to be in "hard" metallic money. It became the normal legal formality to indicate in all deeds payment in coin — usually a $100 gold piece. *q.v.* Bailey pps. 227-8, 268.

4. Battey, Jasper Co. pg. 573

5. Mary Jane's stone was moved by Cliff and Nancy Freshour from a neglected and ruined cemetery to a maintained one. (Near the gravestone of Perry Mack and his second wife) They were unable to find any trace of Elizabeth. *q.v.* Havens and Walters, pps. 38-39.

6. Biographical sketches are given in Appendix D.

7. Kincaid, pps. 30-32.

8. Branch, pg. 88;   Also see Rouse, pps. 167-9.

9. Klees, pg. 226;   Rouse, pps. 230-1.

10. *q.v.* Florin.

11. Branch, pps. 322-3;   Rouse, pps. 94-8, 161-6.

12. Klees summarizes the Conestoga Wagon literature in fine prose. *q.v.* pps. 226-9

13. Federal Writers Project - Tennessee, pps. 48-49.

14. An old field stone marks Eave Freshour's grave. A gravestone for " John Freshaur, pvt 4 VA Regt., Rev War, 1863-1804," was placed in 1985. No responsible government agency or historical society has been identified.   No corresponding military, pension or BLW record has been found. Apparently this gravestone represents undocumented family tradition from unidentified sources.

15. *q.v.* Burgner & Huntly.

16. See Gillette on Tennessee pioneer lifestyle.

17. Appendix A-3.

18. Congress provided pensions for veterans of the various southeastern Indian campaigns by including them in the War of 1812 pension acts. The War of 1812 veterans from Tennessee include:

Froshour, George, [Nat. Arch. file WO 6708, BLWT 89482-120-55.] Served in the Seminole Indian War. Disability — loss of sight in one eye — wounded by an awl. m. Priscilla Williams, Sevier Co. TN. d. Mar 1871, Fayette Co. AL.

Froshour, Henry, [Nat. Arch. file WC 14295, BLWT 18823-160-50.] Served in three distinct enlistments including the Creek and Seminole Wars. m. Jane R. Finley, Shelby Co. AL. d. Aug. 1869, Washington Co. AR. See Appendix C-1.

Freshour, John, [Nat. Arch. file WC 5714, BLWT 22837-160-50.] Served in Creek Indian War. aka "Chucklehead." m. Mary Magdaline Peters, Green Co. TN. d. Nov. 1870, Green Co. TN. His pension file is a who's who of Green Co. TN. A.S. Froshour, a J.P. of Green Co. certified statements. See Appendix B-5.

Note: Those of this Tennessee generation, who could write, spelled their name "Froshour." Those who made their mark had "Freshour" and other variants bestowed upon them. The German roots were still strong. The German name Froschauer had significance. *q.v.* George F. Jones' *German-American Names,* Genealogical Publishing Co. Baltimore, 1991, pps. 29, 133; *Frogmeadow,* Vol. 1, No. 1, Jan. 1990; *ibid.* Vol. 1, No. 2, March 1990, pg. 11.

19. Edwards & Frizzel, pps. 260-1; FWP-Tennessee, pg. 297.

20. Branch, pps. 313-17; Rouse, pg. 218. Road building technology such as built the S.P.Q.R. had been dormant for 1800 years — and was now revived by Yankee enterprise. On Roman roads, see Gibbons, Edward; *The Decline and Fall of the Roman Empire,* edited by J.B. Berry, Vol. I, Pg. 39; The Heritage Press, New York, 1946. (First published in 1776.)

21. Bailey, pps. 308-9; Branch, pg. 321; Rouse, pps. 215-16.

22. Branch, pg. 283.

23. Kincaid, pps. 202-3.   **24.** *ibid.* 204-5.

25. *ibid.* 208; Branch, CH VII.

26. Bryant & Fuller, pg. 197.   **27.** *ibid.* pps. 197-8.

28. *ibid.* pps. 198-9, 205; Brice, pg. 294 sq.

29. Bryant & Fuller, pps. 19, 200-1; Brice.

30. Bryant & Fuller, pps. 20-22.

31. Smith, O. H., pps. 80-82.

32. Bryant & Fuller, pps. 206-7.   **33.** *ibid.,* pg. 23.

34. *ibid.,* pg. 204.   **35.** *ibid.*

36. Battey, Jasper Co. pg. 573   **37.** Bryant & Fuller, pps. 21-2.

38. Bailey, pps. 275-6; Van Doren pps. 158-9.

39. Branch, pps. 395-6.

40. Bailey, pg. 275.   **41.** Bryant & Fuller, pg. 197.

Notes on Chapter 5 — Indiana Prairie

1. Except where noted, the source of most of the material presented in this chapter is Battle, pps. 409-464.

2. q.v. Appendix D; US Census, Indiana, 1840, 1850, Jasper Co., Gilliam twp. and Battle, pg. 573.

3. Battle, pg. 577.   **4.** ibid., pps. 414-5.   **5.** ibid., pg. 460.

6. Holliday, pg. 93.

7. An ox is a male bovine, castrated at maturity, as opposed to a steer, which has been castrated as a calf. The growth to maturity in an unaltered state gave the ox extra thickness of the neck and extra muscle. Removal of their testicles rendered the oxen docile compared to the testosterone charged bulls. Oxen were slow but powerful. The yoked oxen were sometimes called "bull teams."

8. J.D. Dunn's biography in Battle, pg. 573; On livestock, Battle, pps. 420-1.

9. Battle, pps. 460-1.   **10.** ibid., pps. 414-5.

11. ibid., pg. 415.   **12.** ibid., pps. 416-9.

13. Bailey, pg. 306; Branch, pg. 404; Nevins, pg. 166; Van Doren, pps. 159-60.

14. US Census, 1850, Gilliam twp., Jasper Co. IN

15. Iowa Census, 1856, Jasper twp., Adams Co. IA

16. Fox, pps. 13-15; Holliday, pg. 53.

17. Bailey, pg. 308.   **18.** Fox, pg. 12-13.

19. Battle, pg. 519.   **20.** ibid., pg. 452.

21. Van Doren, pg. 207.   **22.** Sandburg, pg. 116.

Notes on Chapter 6 — Iowa Trailhead

1. Branch, pg. 468.

2. Havens and Walters, pps. 3, 12 and 24.

3. The story of Henry and Elizabeth Freshour in Iowa is resumed here. We digressed in Chapter 4 to fill in their background.

4. National Archives Civil War pension file SC 922-251.

5. See Lydia Ann in Appendix D.

6. See William in Appendix D.   **7.** See John in Appendix D.

NOTES

8. Havens and Walters, pg. 10. A reprint from the *Iowa Industrial and Immigration Bureau*, Dubuque, Iowa, 1892.

9. *q.v.* Martin & Dustin, pg. 5.

10. Ackley pps. 13, 19. (Medely was Mary Ackley's maiden name.)

11. Lewis Stout, diary. Oregon Historical Society, Mss 1059, pps. 1-9.

12. Brown, Wm. R., pps. 1-19.   **13.** Fox, pps. 12-13.

14. Mattes - Road, pps. 122-6; Martin & Dustin, pg. 6.

15. Mule teams could start earlier because buck-toothed equine dentition allowed them to feed on sparse grass. Franzwa, pg. 3.

16. Branch, pps. 475-6; also see Martin & Dustin, pg. 6.

17. Nevins, pps. 301-3. (See the "Bleeding Kansas" Map — CH-3.)

18. Nevins, pps. 304-5.   **19.** *ibid.* pg. 309.   **20.** *ibid.* pps. 481-3.

21. Branch, pg. 474.

22. Monaghan, pps. 24-6, 69-71, 90-92;   Nevins, pps. 390-2.

23. Monaghan, pg. 71. The first bridge to span the Mississippi was placed at Rock Island, IL and Davenport, IA in 1855.

24. Nevins, pg. 482.

25. Monaghan, pps. 60-8;   Nevins, pps. 381-3, 483.

26. Monaghan, pps. 105, 110-111;   Nevins, pg. 473.

27. F.W.P. - Iowa, pps. 54, 101-2, 215, 430, 486.

28. Bailey, pps. 406-7;   Monaghan, pps. 113-4;   Sandburg, pps. 157-9.

29. The Iowa-Missouri boarder had also been a disputed region. The controversy involved whether the territorial border had been set at a latitude passing through the rapids of the Des Moines River or at the rapids on the Mississippi River. The Iowa legislature set the present border in 1837. The "Honey War" over destruction of bee trees in the disputed region ensued and both state militias were called out. The U.S. Supreme Court decided for Iowa in 1851. F.W.P. − Iowa, pg. 49.

30. Nevins, pg. 166.   **31.** Monaghan, pps. 129-135.

32. Sandburg, pg. 261. The "singing" Iowa 1st Infantry fought well at Wilson's Creek. Monaghan, pps. 170-181;

33. Roster of Iowa Volunteers, IA State Archives, pps. 574, 580.

34. Ingenthron, pps. 155-60; Col. G.M. Dodge was promoted to Brig. Gen. and was Maj. Gen. at war's end. Although the Union forces won at Pea Ridge, the combat was so fierce that they suffered as much as the Confederate forces and were too depleted for pursuit.

35. See Ingenthron CH XVII on border zone march to Batesville.

36. Proctor & Scott, Vol. 31, part 1 of 3, pg. 818.

37. Nat. Arch. Civil War military record: Dow, Andrew, H4 IA Inf (UN); Proctor & Scott, Vol. 31, part 1 of 3, Gen. Osterhaus' report, pps. 598-600; Col. William's report and Leut. Col. Burton's report at Camp Ringgold, pps. 613-619. Andrew Dow is buried in grave 1204, section G of the National Cemetery at Marietta. See Appendix D-1, Lydia Ann Freshour.

38. Bailey, pg 397.

39. Iowa Census,1870; LDS IGI microfiche, Missouri.

40. Joseph T. Freshour died intestate but apparently left his affairs in order with his remaining property deeded over to his beneficiaries. He died on June 16, 1915. A deed for two lots near Soquel was recorded by L.T. Mason on June 18, 1915. The lots were deeded over to his niece Lydia Jane Freshour Bradley and her heirs and assigns. The informant on J.T. Freshours death certificate, filed June 17, 1915, was Emma Mason, address: Los Banos.

41. William A. Trubody's Narrative, By Charles L. Camp, reproduced in Beard, pps. 81-91.

42. Beard, pps. 11-13.   43. Horn, Aug. 15, 1856, pg. 31.

44. Alexander Moore Statement, Bancroft Library, Berkely, CA, reproduced in Beard, pps. 79-80.

45. US Census, 1850, CA, San Joaquin Co.

46. Reick, pg. 14;   Unruh, pps. 84-5.

47. Horn's Journal commences with his arrival in California. The first entry is Oct. 23, 1854.

48. The Bradley Bible says "Sweetwater on the way to Calif."; Obituaries in the Santa Cruz Sentinel, 22 June, 1915 and the Santa Cruz Surf, 23 June, 1915 say "native of Wyoming."; US census, 1870, CA, Santa Cruz Co., Soquel, lists place of birth for Lydia Jane as "Sweetwater on the Plains." In the same census, she appears as a domestic servant in the Adam Martin household in Pajaro twp, the place of birth given as Missouri. (She was counted twice — not an unusual occurrence.) The San Joaquin Co. 1860 census gives place of birth as Oregon [Territory.] The "Devils Gate" tradition comes from A.A. Freshour (her youngest brother), Leitha Roberts (Lydia Jane's granddaughter) and correspondence dated 9 Jan. 1975, from Maytie Wood (Lydia Jane's daughter) to Mrs. E.E. Freshour which gives place of birth as "Sweetwater, Wyoming near Devils Gate."

49. The Siskiyou News, Yreka, CA; Dec. 17, 1908, J. R. Freshour obit.; Dec. 13, 1906, Marion Freshour obit.

50. Long, pps. 13-17.

51. See the appendices for family data. The census data does not reliably report all issue from a marriage for various reasons. Children got "farmed out" quite a bit. A child born right after one census would appear on the next one (if living at home) and would be "married off" or gone off to adventure or war by the subsequent census. This is well illustrated by the Himes family. US Census, 1870, CA, Santa Cruz Co., Soquel twp., families 55 & 170; Geo. W. Himes' will, 1903, Santa Cruz Co. Probate Court, MR2.47 #1283

52. The Healdsburg Tribune, May 10, 1917, C. C. Freshour obit.

53. US Census, 1860, CA, Sonoma Co., Armalloy twp, Sebastapol.

54. q.v. Parkman.

55. Goetzmann, pps. 16-17, 101-2; Lavender pps. 26-27, 53. Bierstadt made a series of oil sketches that detailed the crafts and culture of the Sioux Indians while among them when accompanying the surveyor Lander in the Rockies near South Pass. Bierstadt was one of a number of artists who documented western exploration and emigration. Also see DeVoto, *Across the Wide Missouri* for artists of the Mountain Man era.

56. q.v. Mattes - Narratives. This work catalogs various diaries and accounts of emigrants who traveled the Platte River Road. An abstract is given and the repository of each manuscript is listed. A good research tool in a single large volume.

The OCTA COED project (Census of Overland Emigrant Documents) has created a computer data base useful to historians and genealogists.

57. There is a typed transcript. Microfilm copies are available. Mattes-Narratives, pg. 254, Mattes-Road, pps. 511, 536, Gibbons, pg. 160. A Frush enclave may be located in the vicinity of Knox Co., MO and nearby Davis Co., IA where a Lawson Frush married in 1888. This would appear to be another strain of the species Froschauer Americanus.

58. Charlie Hopper (Charles Hopper III) a. k. a. "Big Charlie" married his first cousin, Rebecca Hopper. His brother-in-law cum cousin was known as "Little Charlie." Beard, pg. 97. A number of Hoppers are included as pioneers in various histories that cover Sonoma County. It is beyond the scope of this work to untangle the Hoppers.

59. q.v. Federal Land Office Index, RG 74 B.L.M. CA, Stockton Land Office Township Tract Books 1863-1966, National Archives at San Bruno, CA. There are sixteen different parcels — most of them 160 acres, some 80 acres — recorded in T2N-R11E, T3N-R11E, under the names Andrew, Allen, George, Lewis N., Mary, Pauline, Tolman, Thomas and William Gann.

Notes on Chapter 7 — Outfitting At Omaha

1. Paden, pg. 84.

2. Martin and Dustin, pg. 7; Franzwa, pg. 3.

3. Martin and Dustin, pg. 5; Mothershead, pg. 14; Settle, pg. 40n; The J.S. Simpson family moved from Franklin Co. IN to Gentry Co. MO in 1856. Their son J.W. Simpson was born in Madison Co. IA in April of 1856. This would indicate that they followed the "Lane Trail" through Iowa into the Platte Purchase region of north west Missouri.

4. Branch, pps. 496-500; Unruh, pps. 193-6.

5. *q.v.* Bibliography. Most of these books are currently in print.

6. Capps, pg. 2; Mattes - Road, pg. 16; Branch, pg. 427; Gibbons, pg. 154. In 1849, George Gibbs apparently had with him a copy of Frémont's report of his Rocky Mountain Expedition published in 1845. *q.v.* Settle, pps. 298, 321, 324.

7. F. W. P. - Oregon Trail, pg. 32; Ackley, pg. 31.

8. Capps, pg. 2; Fox, pg. 17; Ware, pg. 5.

9. Capps, pps. 4-6; DeVoto-Decision, pg. 488 [2].

10. Capps, pg. 5; Holliday, pps. 93, 103, 118; Mattes - Road, pps. 42-3; Stewart, pps. 233-4; Unruh, pps. 329-30.

11. Capps, pg. 6; Eaton, pps. 4-5; Lavender, pps. 37-44; Stewart, pps. 106-118.

12. Mary Medley wrote her recollections many years later as Mary E. Ackley, *q.v.* bibliog.

13. Stewart, pps. 58-59, 110.

14. Dr. Anson G. Henry, letter published at Springfield in *The Illinois State Journal*, Feb. 24, 1853, 2:1-5.

15. In a letter written back to the States from Oregon, Delazon Smith gives a lengthy statistical analysis of the performance of various types of draft animals including efficiency and mortality rate. He preferred mules. Eaton, pps. 4-6.

16. Deeds recorded in Adams Co. IA. 17. Unruh, pg. 345.

18. Mothershead, pps. 15-16. 19. Newton Finley's statement.

20. Dr. Anson G. Henry, letter published at Springfield in *The Illinois State Journal*, Feb. 24, 1853, 2:1-5.

21. *ibid.* 22. *ibid.* 23. See generally Mothershead.

24. Webb, pps. 150-1; DeVoto-Missouri, pps. 418-19.

25. Potter, pg. 2.

26. Nevins, pps. 260, 431; Potter, pg. 3; John Brown's men were carring Sharps rifles at Harper's Ferry. *q.v.* Monaghan, pg. 114.

27. Potter, pg. 4.

28. DeVoto-Missouri, pg. 430 [9]; Potter, pg. 3.

29. Gillette, pg. 69. Flint locks were still in common use by the Oregon settlers in the 1850s. Martha's father Isaac Hill bought rifles of the Sharps variety at St. Louis for the train he guided to Oregon in 1852. Gillette, pps. 33-34.

30. Webb, pps. 64-5, 167-171; DeVoto-Decision, 215-6, 494 [2][3].

31. Webb, 172-178.

32. George Gibb's diary edited by Settle, *q.v.* pg. 301; Potter pps. 4-5; Stewart, pg. 229; Unruh, pps. 347-8. Two notable accounts of gun accidents on the trail are: James St. Johns diary (in Beard, pps. 32-33); Paden, pps. 206-7.

33. Unruh, pg. 144 *sq*.

34. Mattes puts 350,000 over the Platte. *q.v.* Mattes - Road, pg. 23; Unruh puts total to the west coast at a quarter million, *q.v.* pps. 84-6; Gibbons claims nearly half a million emigrants. *q.v.* pg. 154.

35. Unruh devotes a chapter to this topic. *q.v.* pps. 117-158; Mattes - Road, pps. 223-235, 515-19; Settle, pps. 40-1.

36. California State Archives, National Guard File # B 3411-5, Volunteer Cavalry Company, Santa Cruz County.

37. DeVoto-Missouri, pps. 218-220.

38. Coy, pps. 314 *sq*.; Mothershead, pg. 22.

39. Unruh, pps. 85-6.

40. Stewart, pg. 228.

Notes on Chapter 8 — Rocky Mountain Cordillera

1. Branch, pps. 409-10; Cline, 206-7; DeVoto-Decision, pg. 60; Goetzmann, pps. 45-51.

2. The Astorians got as far as present day Torrington WY in Dec. 1812. According to Stuarts diary, the party constructed a small shack and spent the rest of the winter on the bank of the north Platte River. A Wyoming Recreation Commission sign commemorates the location. The 1812 war with Britain disrupted the Astorian's enterprise in Oregon. DeVoto-Decision, pg. 53n, 485; Goetzmann, pps. 33-35; Mattes-Road, pps. 11, 284; Paden, pps. 324-5.

3. *q.v.* Irving, Introduction by Alfred Powers; DeVoto-Missouri, pg. 50; Settle, pg. 60n.

4. DeVoto-Missouri, pg. 51.

5. *ibid.* ; Capps, pg. 6; DeVoto-Decision, pg. 491 [15].

6. Cline follows Bancroft's assessment which is based on Bonneville's cover story. Bonneville is believed to have been performing reconnaissance in this disputed international territory for Andrew Jackson's War Department. Bancroft dismissed Bonneville as a womanizing profligate and a business failure and Irving as his dupe. *q.v.* Cline, pps. 168-171; DeVoto-Missouri, pps. 58-61, 110, 426-7 note 11; Goetzmann, pg. 53; Irving, Introduction by Powers.

7. The misconception of Rio Buenaventura and the nature of the Great Basin was in fact, discovered by Jedadiah Smith. Branch, pps. 408-9; Cline, pps. 157, 178-9, 206-7; DeVoto-Decision, pg. 53; DeVoto-Empire, pps. 291-5; DeVoto-Missouri, pg. 312; Goetzmann, pg. 71; Irving, pps. 148-50, 273-4, 276; Webb, pg. 154.

8. Branch, pg. 426; Stone, pg. 27; The frontispiece of Cleland's History of California is a reproduction of the western portion of the *Map of North America* published in London by James Wyld, Geographer to His Majesty, 1824. This map shows the Rio Buenaventura extended from the Salt Lake to the Pacific at a location between Santa Barbara and Monterey.

9. Goetzmann, pps. 64-72; Stone, pps. 37-38. Joe Walker and Thomas Fitzpatrick also guided Frémont.

10. Branch, pps. 301-9; DeVoto-Missouri, pps. 29-34, 96-102; Goetzmann, pps. 34-37, 40-41, 48-49;

11. DeVoto-Missouri, pps. 55-6; Ingenthron, pg. 103; Stone, pg. 59.

12. DeVoto-Missouri, pps. 55, 60.

13. Parkman, pps. 16-17.

14. Irving, pps. 47-53.

15. DeVoto-Missouri, pps. 80-85.

16. F.W.P. - Tennessee, pg. 286.

17. DeVoto-Missouri, pps. 89-90.

18. *ibid.* pg. 86.

19. Irving, pps. 53-55.

20. DeVoto-Missouri, pg. 100.

21. *ibid.* pps. 122-4.

22. Parkman, pps. 106-8. DeVoto considers this and most Beckwourth accounts apocryphal. *q.v.* Missouri, pg. 128.

23. DeVoto-Missouri, pps. 221-2, 234-6.

24. *ibid.* pps. 212-17, 237-8; Lavender, pg. 60.

25. DeVoto-Missouri, pps. 244-6.

26. F.W.P. - Oregon Trail, pps. 194-5.

27. DeVoto-Missouri, pps. 247, 251, 255.   28. *ibid.* pps. 262, 267.

29. Franzwa, pg. 4; Unruh, pps. 199-200.

30. Branch, pps. 377-382; Unruh, 75-6, 83.

31. Branch, pps. 425-7; Stewart, pps. 7-29;

32. Applegate, pps. 29-30; Van Dorn, pg. 171. This account is by Lindsay Applegate's son Jesse A. Applegate not to be confused with his uncle. These are the recollections of an Oregon pioneer who was not yet seven years old when traveling the trail.

33. Bailey, 287-292; Branch, 385-8; DeVoto-Empire, 22-26, 225-7.

34. Stone, pps. 62-76.   35. Extensively covered by Beard.

36. Branch, pps. 408-411; Cleland, pps. 57-8; Goetzmann, pg. 50.

37. Irving, pps. 355-7; Parkman, pg. 94.

38. *i.e.* The states admitted to the union. The entire country west of the Missouri River was Territory and the US was understood to be back east. The 49ers used this terminology.

39. See generally Settle. Prior to this militarization of the route to Oregon, military supervision of Indians was confined to military expeditions on the high plains. Kearny marched his dragoons in 1845 to South Pass in a display of strength. *q.v.* Parkman's description of Kearny's terrorization of the Arapahoes with his howitzer. Kearny led his dragoons to conquest of the Southwest and Southern California in 1846 via the Santa Fe and Gila Trails and returned via the Humboldt River and South Pass but left no military establishments on this return route. *q.v.* Trafzer, Yuma Frontier, CH-4; Parkman, pps. 204-5; Stewart, pps. 88-89; Unruh, pps. 160-1.

40. Mattes-Road, Intro.

41. Goetzmann, pps. 65-82. See generally Unruh, 187-8.

42. Holiday, pps. 135, 166, 188-9; Settle, pg. 323; Unruh, pps. 185, 189-193. Caravans organized along the lines of a military unit such as the Wolvarine Rangers brought their own forge with them. Holliday, pg. 119.

43. Parkman, pg. 72.

44. Mattes-Road, pps. 50-52; Unruh, pps. 111-114.

45. Eaton, pps. 156-7.

46. Franzwa, pg. 3; Lavender, pps. 49-52; Stewart, pps. 113-8.

47. The Haun family incident serves as a remarkable example. *q.v.* Paden, pps. 163-6.

48. F.W.P. - Oregon Trail, pps. 31-2; Muehl, pps. 92-3.

49. Bryant, pg. 80; Lavender, pg. 53; Parkman, pg. 57; Delano, pg. 14.

50. Eliot West, pg. 93.

51. Settle, pg. 306. Major Cross agrees in terse comments. *cf.* Bryant, pps. 78-9. See also Paden, pg. 83.

52. Stewart, pg. 159.   **53.** Muehl, pg. 93.

54. Applegate, pps. 61-2; Mattes gives many graphic accounts of trail vicissitudes. See Mattes-Road, pg. 95.

55. Applegate, pg. 67; Franzwa, pg. 3; Stewart, pg. 5.

56. The title of Parkman's *Oregon Trail* is a misnomer used to capitalize on the excitement over Oregon at the time it was published. *q.v.* Stewart, pg. 149. Parkman, fresh out of college, joined a band of Oglala Sioux and lived with them while they warred against the Pawnee and Dachota. At that time, the significance of the emigration escaped him and he went no farther west than the high plains. Nevertheless, it is an excellent resource on that region as its extensive use by DeVoto in *Year of Decision* attests. Parkman's spelling of Indian names is quaintly elaborate while DeVoto's is severly modern.

57. Applegate, pps. 67-68.

58. Camp's edition of Trubody's recollections. (Beard, pg. 86.)

59. Paden, pg. 165; Parkman, pps. 87, 223, 274.

60. Franzwa, pg. 3; Mattes-Road, pg. 89. Note that this practice was used by the American colonials in 1755 when burying General Braddock. *q.v.* F.W.P. - Pennsylvania, pps. 596-7.

61. DeVoto devotes a chapter, called *The conqueror (1837,)* to the near annihilation of the Missouri River tribes by smallpox. Over 17,000 among these tribes died leaving a stench over body-strewn village after village. The Mandan were destroyed as a tribe. The balance of power among these warring tribes was upset with the Sioux becoming dominant. DeVoto-Missouri, pps. 279-301.

NOTES

62. Mattes-Road, pps. 141, 516; Unruh, pps. 334-5.

63. Mattes-Road, Chapter XII. **64.** Settle, pg. 92.

65. Camp's edition of Trubody's recollections. (Beard, pg. 83.)

66. Nebraska Historical Marker, Scotts Bluff County Rural Teachers and Students, Nebraska State Historical Society.

67. Settle, pg. 97n; Mattes-Road, pg. 480; Paden, pg. 151.

68. Mattes-Road, pg. 518; Paden, pps. 159-60.

69. Stewart, pps. 312-13.

70. Delano, pg. 27; Stewart, pg. 229.

71. Settle, pg. 112. **72.** Delano, pg. 36.

73. F.W.P. - Oregon Trail, pps. 182-3.

74. Lewis Stout, diary. Oregon Historical Society, Mss 1059.

75. DeVoto-Missouri, pps. 366-7. **76.** Eaton, pg. 158.

77. Eaton, pps. 168-70; Stewart, pg. 59.

78. See Appendices B and D for biographies.

79. F.W.P. - Oregon Trail, pg. 31.

80. This extraordinary natural wonder is inexplicable. The Corps of Engineering geological analysis and the corresponding Indian legend are equally fantastic. F.W.P. - Oregon Trail, pg. 189; In general see Munkres.

81. Bryant, pps. 90-91; Coy, pps. 318-22.

82. Lewis Stout, diary. Oregon Historical Soc., Mss 1059, July 6th entry.

83. Appendices B and D.

84. Lewis Stout's diary, *op cit*, entries of July 4th to July 10th.

85. F.W.P. - Oregon Trail, pg. 190; Paden, pps. 215-6.

86. F.W.P. - Oregon Trail, pg. 194; DeVoto-Missouri, pg. 54; The Sweetwater flows eventually into the Gulf of Mexico. The Pacific Spring flows eventually into the Gulf of California. This flat portage lies indeed on the "Continental Divide."

87. Applegate, pps. 74-5. **88.** Paden, pg. 290.

89. Ware, pg. 25. **90.** Delano, pps. 64-66;

91. Stewart, pps. 132-6; Paden, pg. 321

Notes on Chapter 9 — Tribulation in the Basin

1. Nevada Commission on Tourism *Covered Wagon Territory* brochure.
2. Cline, pg. 170; DeVoto-Missouri, pps. 146-7.
3. Goetzmann, pps. 51-55.   4. Cline, pps. 206-7.
5. Cline, 14-15, 155-6, 159, 165. On Jedidiah Smith's return to California through the Mojave, the Indians treacherously killed 9 of his 18 men. Goetzmann says this hostility resulted from attacks of other trappers on the Mojave after Smiths first friendly encounter with them. Branch states that the attack on Smith's party was instigated by the California Mexicans who were aggravated by Smith's previous explorations in California. The Californios later jailed Smith in Monterey then released him with orders to leave California. Branch, pps. 409-10; Goetzmann, pg. 50. Cleland gives an account of the friction between Smith and the Mexican Authorities. Cleland, pps. 55-56.
6. Cline, pps. 176-7; DeVoto-Missouri, pps. 149-54.
7. Cline pg. 187; Lavender, pps. 61-2; Stewart, pps. 49-51; Stone, pps. 43-5.
8. Bryant, pps. 143, 302-3, 319-20, 450; DeVoto-Decision, pps. 61, 300, 310.
9. DeVoto-Missouri, pg. 148; Irving, pg. 275.
10. DeVoto-Missouri, pps. 432-3; Hunt, pps. 44-59.
11. Finlanda's Statement; Trubody's Reminiscences.
12. Neither were the California Indians known to be horsemen. Like the Diggers, the best use they found for the horse was to eat them. Under the aegis of the Spanish and their missionaries, the Indians were developed into productive agricultural communities. With "secularization" under Mexican rule in 1834, many of the emancipated Indians reverted to their primitive ethos and some of them maintained themselves by stealing and eating the corralled horses that were much easier to acquire than the unapproachable wild horses. Several Anglo settlers were killed by the horse thieves. The mountain men helped the Californios hunt down and kill the Indian horse thieves and themselves were privileged to take wild horses which at that time were still abundant. This, as all privileges inevitably are, was to be abused.

Bryant, pps. 433-5; Chapman, pps. 467-9; DeVoto-Decision, pg. 61.

13. The Indians traversed the Sierra on footpaths for the purpose of trading. They met at the summit of the Sierra. The Northern California Indians traded obsidian from the Shasta region with the interior Indians — for flint perhaps and the crafted specialties of various tribes.

NOTES

14. *San Joaquin Daily Republican* 1857, Aug. 11, 2:4; Oct. 18, 2:4.

15. DeVoto - Decision, pg. 337.   **16.** Parkman, pps. 168-70.

17. Stewart, pg. 275; Unruh, pps. 141-2.

18. DeVoto-Decision, pg. 338; Paden, 401-2; Stewart, pps. 178-9.

19. Stewart, pg. 163.   **20.** Trafzer, CH-4.

21. Parkman, pg. 320; DeVoto-Decision, pps. 235-242, 246.

22. Unruh, pps. 253-4, 267.

23. Hunt, pps. 154-177; Stewart, pps. 197-200 *sq.* ; Stone, pps. 108-9, 122. Note that the Mormons developed the first three roads into California, the Gila Trail, the Carson-Mormon trail and the Mormon Corridor. They didn't consider the Truckee route to be a useable wagon road.

24. Irene Paden conveys the nature of the Humbolt Road with evocative chapter titles. *"Yea, Though I Walk Through the Valley"* tells the story of the Upper Humbolt and *"Of the Shadow of Death"* relates the unimaginable severity experienced on the Lower Humbolt. Coy calls this God forsaken stretch a "veritable *Via Dolorosa*" liking it to the sufferings of Christ bearing his cross through Jerusalem to Calvary. At best, it was a tough haul.

25. Stewart's Chapter Ten on the years '50 to '59 gives many interesting statistics and notable incidents showing progressive California Trail development. *q.v.* Stewart, pps. 269-318. Unruh's "revisionist" *Plains Across* does an excellent statistical analysis and refutes traditional stereotypes with unfamiliar episodes and offbeat examples.

26. Paden, pps. 159-60; Stewert, pg. 312; Mattes-Road, Ch. X and Paden, Ch. 10 cover the ensuing punitive campaign of Gen. Harney.

27. Hunt, pps. 118-153, 236-245; See generally Helfrich & Hunt.

28. See generally Harris.   **29.** Paden, pps. 423-9.

30. *Sierra Nevada* is Spanish for *High Snowfall* or *High Snow-capped Mountain.* Cassell's Spanish Dictionary, Funk and Wagnels, New York.

31. Coy, pps. 201-2; Paden pg. 429.

32. Stone, pps. 47, 135-8.

33. *ibid.* pps. 135, 213-16, 417-23.   **34.** *ibid.* pg. 211.

35. Ackley, pg. 32; Coy, pg. 203; Hunt, pps. 167-75.

36. Ackley, pg. 33; Coy, pg. 204; Wills, pg. 76.

37. After 1828, when the Mexican government granted freedom of trade, the California ranchers became wealthy from the trade in hides and tallow with the "Boston Ships." Chapman, pps. 393, 396; Sanchez, pps. 54-5.

38. Sanchez, pps. 36-8.   **39.** Stewart, pg. 311; Unruh, pps. 332-4.

40. Stewart, pps. 314-5; Accounts vary widely. *q.v.* Mattes Narratives #s 1583, 1587, 1603 and 1609; The story from incoming emigrants is reported in the *San Joaquin Daily Republican* of Sept. 2nd, 1857. Another account, taken from the Red Bluffs *Beacon,* is given by the *Republican* of Sept. 22. The *Republican* of Oct. 16, 1857 reports that Mrs. Holloway is fast recovering and that the wound on her head has healed over also. She was reported as passing through Marysville on her way to the lower valleys. (It seems that Mrs. Holloway had become somewhat of a celebrity.)

41. F.W.P. Oregon Trail, Introduction.

42. Mattes-Road, pps. 76-81; Stewart, pps. 308-9; Delano, Ch. XXV, pps. 156-62.

43. Fox, pps. 14-15.   **44.** Delano, pps. 52-3.

45. Stewart, pg. 315-7; Unruh, pps. 151-4.

46. *San Joaquin Daily Republican* 1857, Aug. 18, 2:5.

47. *ibid.* Aug. 19, 2:3-4.   **48.** *ibid.* Oct. 8, 2:3.

49. Eaton, pps. 165, 170-1; Stewart, pps. 308-9.

Notes on Chapter 10 — Weber's Tule Marsh

1. Irving, pps. 276-7; DeVoto-Missouri, pg. 148; Stewart, pg. 42.

2. Stewart, pps. 44-6.

3. The Oregon-California trail literature gives excellent coverage of "the Trail." Owen Chochran Coy who was Professor of History, University of Southern California gives in his *The Great Trek* several chapters to the development of southern routes into California. Branch is quite global in his description of forty-niner avenues into California.

4. Adams, Calif. Highways, pg. 39. Replicas of this statue have been placed throughout the U.S. Dillon comments in his introduction to Gillette.

5. Apparently, California is sinking and Mt. Whitney is no longer the highest peak in the conterminous forty-eight.

6. Schmidt's booklet is devoted to the Big Trees road.

7. Stewart, pps. 302-3, Unruh, pg. 300.

8. See generally MacMullen; Also see Holiday, pps. 408, 411;

9. MacMullen, pps. 52-3, 56. The Delta Queen used as a tourist excursion boat on the Mississippi was built in Stockton and was originally one of the paddlewheelers plying the Sacramento. MacMullen, pps. 118-19.

10. Stewart tells the amusing story of Grove Cook, Talbot Green and his "chunck of lead." Stewart, pps. 18-29.

11. Until discovery of the New Almaden mine, the house of Rothschild, which operated the Almaden mine in Spain, had a monopoly on the world's Mercury supply, thus controlling worldwide gold and silver production. Had it not been for the New Almaden mine, all the mines of the west including those in Nevada and California would have been under foreign controll. This crucial national political issue is explained by Bulmore and Arbuckle. *q.v.* Rambo, pg. 17.

12. Bancroft's *Pioneer Register* gives brief biographies or at least accounts for all the known members of the Bartleson-Bidwell party. Some are in Rambo. The Pen Pictures series of the 1880s and 90s give many biographies.

13. *q.v.* Chapman, Ch. XXXII.

14. Dillon, pps. 207, 223-5, 230, 235.

15. Sutter rode around the property with Gulnac at the time. No effort was made to measure the land. *q.v.* Sutters deposition, *San Joaquin Republican*, Aug. 28, 1854. Vallejo's wish to see accurate surveying introduced into Alta California was not yet accomplished. The Mexican government in Alta California hardly had a system of codified law (*q.v.* alcalde Bryant) much less a regular system for dealing in land. They simply marked it off on a desino (map.) The desino shows the northern border of the grant well below the Calaveras River. Weber's survey, performed in accordance with the desino does not conform to the Mount Diablo Meridian and its related survey townships. It is an irregular botch on the San Joaquin judicial township map. It includes some fifteen square leagues including land north of the Calaveras River.

16. Tinkham-1923, pg. 49

17. McKittrick, pps. 140-3.

18. Tinkham-1923, pg. 50. Lindsey and Williams had been offered a league of land by Gulnac and built houses. After Lindsey's murder, Williams led Sutter's troops into the Sierra against the Indians. One of Sutter's men was killed. A force of Naval men were later sent to fight the Indians. Indian huts were burned and a number of Indians killed. Indian hostilities lasted from 1844 to 1847. These actions were against raiding tribes that refused to make treaties — not the peaceful San Joaquin tribes. Weber's presence marked the end of hostilities. *q.v.* Sutter's deposition, James William's deposition, Daniel Murphy's deposition, *San Joaquin Republican*, 1854, August 23, 25 and 28.

19. Tinkham-Guinn, pps. 262, sq. Apparently from Bennet B. Nell's deposition taken as evidence in the Weber Land Claim. *San Joaquin Republican,* Aug. 25, 1854, 2:4. None of the depositions taken by the California Land Commission showed Gulnac to be of weak moral character or unsound judgment. He no doubt embibed. Tinkham's "drunken sot" exaggeration is not repeated in his own 1923 edition. Gulnac considered the Land Grant to be useless since all attempts to comply with the settlement requirement had failed and time was running out. He sold Weber a piece of paper of dubious value. The conveyance grant states the price as $200 — half in silver, half in goods. q.v. Conveyance of Grant *San Joaquin Republican*, Aug. 24, 1854, 2:5. Gulnac allegedly understood that he was selling "his share" rather than the specified eleven leagues. The Land Commission attorney contended that the word "un" designating "a rancho" had been altered on the document to seemingly indicate the entire grant. This typifies the clash between the Spanish feudal concept of the relationship between land, the patrón and people and the American concept of individual ownership of small systematically subdivided parcels.

20. Tinkham-1923, pg. 49; Napoleon B. Smith deposition, *San Joaquin Republican,* Aug. 25, 1854, 2:4.

21. Bryant, pg. 364

22. According to Tinkham-Guinn. Alexander Moore says a square mile (a section, i.e. 640 acres) and two lots — perhaps between him and his father. Moore's statement; Findla's statement says "one block of town lots and such land as they would cultivate."

23. Alexander Moore's statement; Hunt, Maps 18-20 show the Stevens-Donner route. Johnson's Ranch is shown on Map 20.

24. Bancroft, *History of Calif.* pg. 556, n50. (A reference to *The California Star,* Oct. 16, 1847. q.v. Friends of Bancroft facsimile)

25. Paden and Schlichtman, pg. 10; Tinkham pps. 262 sq.; Sutter's deposition, *San Joaquin Rep.* Aug. 28, 1854; James Williams deposition, *San Joaquin Rep.* Aug. 23, 1854.

26. Alexander Moore's statement; Findlas statement says " Three or four stopped there. Some of the Indians had fever and ague, and the others were afraid to stop. two of the families who did stop changed their minds ..." Beard, pg. 65. Tinkham reports that in 1847, fifteen or twenty people residing there.

27. Alexander Moore's statement was undoubtedly Bancroft's source.

28. Tinkham-1923, pg. 50.

29. Alexander Moore's statement assumes knowledge of important California pioneers. Isaac Branham b. KY built a sawmill and distillery in MO.

He came to CA by wagontrain in 1846 with his wife and children. He and Wm. Hanks built this Lexington Sawmill which produced the lumber for construction in the San Jose, San Francisco and other Bay Area communities. Lexington was a stage coach stop before the South Pacific Coast R.R. was built. Both town and R.R. are now extinct. The town site lies under the water at Lexington Reservoir. Rambo, pps. 7, 42; Foote, *Pen Pictures*, pps. 491-4.

30. Koch, pps. 12-14, 91, 124. On the Castro sisters and the *Rancho Refugio* see Rowland's *Santa Cruz* pps. 37-8, 42.

31. Eli Moore, pre-gold-rush pioneer from Guliford Co. NC via Missouri, built a log cabin on Willow Street (now Pacific Avenue.) He is prominent in the Santa Cruz Alcalde's records. *q.v.* Bunnett, Pokriots & Reynolds. Eli Moore died in 1859 and is buried in Evergreen Cemetery. Rowland's Scrapbook, pg. 406. Item *Built For Moore Family.* Koch has Nicholas B. Gann settled at Santa Cruz in the 1840s. Koch, pg. 225.

32. Guinn — Coast Counties, Thomas Hopper biog. pps. 511-513. Also see Bunnett, Pokriots & Reynolds on Charles and Thomas Hopper at Santa Cruz.

33. Moore's statement, pg. 79 in Beard. Alexander Moore's obit. in the *Santa Cruz Surf*, Aug. 29, 1902, pg. 5:3.

34. Tinkham-1923, pg. 50.

35. Branch, Chapter XXIV, Life and Labor in the Diggins; Shank, pg. 16.

36. Paden and Schlichtman, pg. 11. A village of Indian huts was called by the Californios a rancheria.

37. Article by J. H. Carson in *An Illustrated History of San Joaquin County*, Lewis Publishing Co., Chicago, 1890. Similar accounts of the origins of Sacramento and Yuba City are given by Delano. pps. 109, 125-7.

38. Deposition of Nicholas B. Gann, Article *Evidence in the Weber Land Claim.* The *San Joaquin Republican,* Aug. 25, 1854, 2:4.

39. 1850 US Census for San Joaquin Co., CA.

40. Paden and Schlichtman, pg. 11.

41. Branch, pg. 506.

42. DeVoto-Decision, pg. 310; The Mormons had settled in Jackson Co. MO and were preparing to build their temple there. The gentiles burned their homes and drove them across the river to Cass Co. They eventually removed to Utah territory where their temple was finally constructed at Salt Lake. The animosituy smouldered for many years. Federal Writers Project — Missouri, pps. 378-9.

43. Stewart, pg. 283; Holliday pps. 276-7

44. Mitchell, pg. 50, Unruh, pps. 298-9.

45. Delano gives some "Beckwith" Crow Indian apocrypha that is even more fantastic than that given by Parkman. His biographer (*q.v.* DeVoto-MO) gives his name as Beckwourth but Beckwith is most commonly used. Delano, pps. 143-4; Devoto-Decision, pg. 61; DeVoto-Missouri, pps. 128-131; Stewart, pps. 302-3.

46. Unruh, pps. 299-300.

47. Mitchell, pg. 50.

48. Davis, Richard M., pps. 10-28; Stewart pps. 305-6.

49. Mitchell, pg. 53; Unruh, pg. 301; Hunt, pps. 236-8, Maps 24-26.

Notes on Chapter 11 — San Joaquin Trail's End

1. *San Joaquin Republican,* Stockton, 1854, July 21, 2:3.

2. *ibid.* June 22, EXTRA; July 4, 2:2.

3. *ibid.* June 28, 2:2, 2:3; July 8, 2:2; July 19 2:4; July 31, 1:1; Oct. 16, 2:2; Oct. 20, 2:2.

4. Lewis Kern arrived in Sacramento to report six incoming trains in the Carson valley "are 'down on' the Johnson's cutoff" due to tolls at the bridge and summit. *San Joaquin Rep.*, July 8, 1854, 2:2.

5. *San Joaquin Republican,* Stockton, 1854: June 12, 2:3.

6. *ibid.* August 23, 25 and 28, 2:4-5, each issue.

7. *ibid.* August 25, 2:5.

8. *San Joaquin Republican,* Stockton, 1855, April 20, 2:2-3.

9. *ibid.* May 3, 2:4.

10. San Joaquin Co. Deeds, Book A, Vol. 5, pps. 335-6. In 1864 Nicholas and Rutha sold part of section 64. She made her mark with her name given as Ruthe Malinda Gann. Book A, Vol. 14, pg. 703. In 1867 the last of the Ganns section 64 was sold, the deed being signed and notarized in Santa Cruz. Book A, Vol. 17, pps. 580-81.

11. The N.B. Gann's land of record was in Weber's rancho and wasn't particularly "up on the Calaveras" as Isaiah Horn persisted in describing it. This may have been one of Horn's idiosyncrasies — a preference for natural landmarks over obviously nearby towns. The Gann property was east of Stockton between the Waterloo road and the Linden road — as close to Stockton as to the Calaveras river.

12. Mitchell, pg. 54.
13. Adams, *The Story of Marlett*, pps. 69-70.
14. Mitchell, pps. 52, 55, 57;   Unruh, pg. 300.
15. Schmitt's booklet is devoted to the Big Trees Route.
16. Adams, pg. 70;   Mitchell, pg. 59.
17. *San Joaquin Republican*, Stockton 1857: July 3, 2:2.
18. *ibid.* July, 4, 2:2.
19. The Scandinavian Thompson knew the use of snowshoes and skis from his native land and his mail delivery exploits made him the first cross country skier of the Sierra. He was challenged to a downhill ski race and jump at Silver Mountain City. He won the race and set a jump record that he held for many years. Long, pg. 47; Schmidt, pps. 12-13.
20. *San Joaquin Republican*, Stockton, 1857: July, 19, 2:3.
21. *ibid.* July, 8, 2:2.   22. *ibid.* July, 26, 2:3.
23. See MacMullen, Chapters III, IV and VI.
24. Stone, pps. 182-5, 271-2, 349-50.
25. *San Joaquin Republican*, Stockton 1857: Sept., 24, 3:3-4; Oct., 18, 2:3.
26. *ibid.* July, 9, 2:3;   Aug., 4, 2:3;   Aug., 11, 2:4.
27. Long, pg. 23. A boundry survey subsequently proved Markley's claim to be in California. California State Historical Landmark No. 240.
28. *San Joaquin Republican*, Stockton, 1857: Sept., 24, 2:3.
29. San Joaquin Co. Deeds; Map — San Joaquin Co. Judicial Townships.
30. Located at present day Silver Creek this boom town of 2500 people was named Königsberg by the Scandinavian miners who struck silver there. The town was renamed Silver Mountain City in 1863. The town was doomed when Congress passed the Fourth Coinage Act which made gold the U.S. monitary standard and eliminated the silver dollar. Silver Mountain City became a ghost-town.

See Branch, pps. 495-6, on Sierra wagon traffic to the Comstock.

31. Long, pps. 23-25;   Schmitt, pg. 25.
32. Unruh, pgs. 56, 188 sq.; Mattes-road, pg. 335; The location of the California border was not a prevalent certitude. In a report from Kirk's road building company on the shore of Honey Lake: "The engineers express the belief that Honey Lake and Valley are in California." *San Joaquin Republican*, Stockton, 1857: Aug., 4, 2:3.
33. Stone, pps. 206-7;   Unruh, pps. 167, 173;   Long, pg. 12.

Notes on Chapter 12 — Up On The Calaveras

1. Realy, pps. 4-5, in Shank.   **2.** E.P. Joy, pg. 3.

3. Founded Feb. 1850. Courthouse was built from lumber shipped from China. California State Historical Landmark No. 264, Dept. of Pub. Works, Calif. Div. of Highways.

4. Shank, pg. 6.   **5.** Jackson, pg. 352.

6. Shank, pg. 17; Research notes on the Jenny Lind Ditch Co., including the Certificate of Corporation, compiled by the Calaveras Co. Archives.

7. Realy, pg. 3, in Shank; Shank, pg. 5.

8. Jackson, pps. 352-3;

9. E.P. Joy, pg. 6.   **10.** Sherer, pg. 279.

11. Hunt & Sanchez, pps. 459, 526-7.

12. Hunt & Sanchez pps. 421-3.

13. q.v. Newbold, John D.; *The Great California Flood of 1861-1862*, in the *San Joaquin Historian*, Vol. V, No. 4, Winter 1991; [San Joaquin Historical Society Quarterly.]

14. ibid. pps. 3-4.

15. Leon Rowland, Item: *Drouth (sic) Hit Herds*, in a 1931 issue of the *Santa Cruz Times*. [pg. 246 of Rowland's scrapbook, Special Collections of the UCSC McHenry Library.]

16. Sandburg, pps. 706-742.   **17.** Bailey, pps. 456-482.

18. U.S. census 1860, San Joaquin Co.,Castoria twp; Stockton Federal Land Office records, Nat. Arch. San Bruno, CA. Note that *Castoria* is the Spanish word for beaver. This is the region where the mountain men trapped beaver in the early 1840s — the region around the present day town of French Camp.

19. Shank, article on Chaparral School. Martin's grandchildren, Arthur, Lelia, Edith and Roland Freshour, are listed among the students and in a class picture Lelia and Roland Freshour are identified. About 1900, the school was again moved — this time two miles east — to its present location. The building presently located there is now used as a church.

20. Bailey, pps. 483-494.

21. From deeds recorded in San Joaquin County and Stockton Federal Land Office homestead records, National Archives, San Bruno.

22. Shank, pps. 10, 20.   **23.** Bailey, Chapters 24 and 25.

24. Hunt & Sanchez, pps. 534-6, 541-4.

25. Black Bart's legend engendered its share of lurid pulp — some of recent publication. Jackson's interesting account is detailed yet balanced. *q.v.* Jackson, pps. 358-61. Also see Joy, pps. 43-4, Mace, pps. 19-21.

26. Joy, pg. 45.   **27.** Mace pg. 147.

28. Petition of Fitzgerald, Sturgin and Gordon filed July 1863. Repository: San Joaquin County Surveyors office, Stockton.

29. *Old Cemeteries of San Joaquin County*, Vol. 1, pps. 38-9.

30. *The Stockton Daily Mail*, Aug. 15, 1896, pg. 11:4. Reprinted in the San Andreas paper.

31. Petition for Letters of Administration, Feb. 27, 1915, Calaveras Co. Superior Court. *The Calaveras Prospect*, Sep. 26, 1914, pg. 1:4.

32. *Stockton Daily Evening Record*, Aug. 25, 1919, — an entire column, with photo, in the section *News of the San Joaquin Valley and the Mother Lode*, pg. 1:2; Copied in *The Calaveras Prospect*, Aug. 30, 1919, pg. 1:5-6.

33. *Stockton Daily Evening Record*, Dec. 6, 1951, pg. 34:7. Photo at top of column. Arthur was inducted into the army shortly after his marriage. No issue.

34. *The Modesto Bee*, Tues., April 25, 1989, pg. B-3.

Notes on Chapter 13 — Siskiyou Gold

1. There three competing explanations of the origin and meaning of the name *Siskiyou*.

a.) Hudson Bay Company French-Canadians gave the name (meaning *bob-tailed-horse* in the Cree Indian tongue) to the place where their bourgeois, A.R. McLeod, lost animals including a bob tailed race horse when their pack train was trapped in a snow storm.

b.) The word *Siskiyou* is Indian for council grounds located in the mountains on the California-Oregon border.

c.) The Hudson Bay Company trappers used six outcroppings of rock near Willow Creek as a land mark to identify the ford on the Klamath River that they used when traveling into Central California. They called them *Six Calleuse* in French. *Siskiyou* is an English corruption of the French term.

q.v. Wales, Joseph H., *Possible origins of the Name 'Siskiyou,'* in *Siskiyou Pioneer*, Yreka, CA, Aug., 1948, pps. 42-3.

2. Rosborough, Alex J., *California's Gold Find*, in *The Siskiyou Pioneer*, Yreka, CA, 1957, Vol. 2, No. 10, pps. 64.

This issue of the *Pioneer*, subtitled *Guidebook to Siskiyou's Gold Fields*, is an excellent source of factual mining data for the mines of Siskiyou Co. as well as lore and history.

3. A fine commemorative bronze plaque is located in the schoolyard on Elm Street in French Camp. — California Registered Historical Landmark No. 668.

4. For a thorough account of Ogden and Smith and their activities related to the Siskiyou Trail development see Dillon.

5. Hunt and Sanchez, pps. 313-5

6. For a detailed history of the Siskiyou Trail see Dillon. On James Marshal see Stone, pps. 104-6.

7. OCTA has placed a trail marker in the city park in Malin, Oregon giving the history of the Applegate trail and stating: "In 1852 pioneers from the East opened a route off the Applegate Trail from the southern end of Lower Klamath Lake to the Yreka area of northern California."

8. Rosborough, Alex J., *Op. cit.*, pps. 62-6.

9. Gillette, pg. 77.

10. Thompson's Dry Diggins was named Shasta Butte City but, to avoid conflict with Shasta City, was renamed after Mount Shasta's Indian name "White Mountain" which was anglicized variously as *Ieka, Wyeka, Wyreka* and finally *Yreka* — pronounced " Why-**ree**-ka." Not to be confused with the coastal town named *Eureka* — "I have found it" in Greek.

11. Rosborough, *Op. cit.*

12. James R. Freshour never used his middle name. It was given in full as required in the Great Register of Calaveras County as James Rufus Freshour. In the last century, the name Rufus had no prejudicial ethnic implications and was considered a perfectly suitable Biblical name. It is used herein to distinguish him from other James Freshours. It is interesting that James Marion Freshour was in the Calaveras Great Register as Marion Freshour, perhaps because he was one of three James Freshours at Jenny Lind. He entirely dropped the name James as an adult. *q.v.* US Census, 1860, CA, San Joaquin Co., Douglas twp., pg 48.

13. Early records give "Frances A. McKelhany" and "Frances A. Freshour." Calaveras deeds give "Frances Annette." The records in Siskiyou Co. drop "Frances" entirely and give her name as "Annette Machelhieny" (Jas. R.'s obit.,) "Ethnet Freshour" (Marion's obit.) and "Annath [sp. ?] Michaelhaney" (Marion's death cert., Mary V. Freshour, informant.) Family tradition supports the *Michaelhaney* spelling.

14. Herzog, Frank, *River Mines,* in *The Siskiyou Pioneer*, Yreka, CA, 1957, Vol. 2, No. 10, pps. 54-56.

Presents a topographical map of the area.

15. Barton, H.J., *Value of Klamath River Mines ... 1872 - 1885,* in *The Siskiyou Pioneer,* Yreka, CA, 1957, Vol. 2, No. 10, pg. 59.

This Article tabulates the physical size of the ground worked, Number of cubic yards processed, Value taken out in $ and Average $ per yard. He comments on the methodology of the various operations. One gets the impression that this industry was labor intensive.

16. *Siskiyou News,* Jan. 23, 1886, pg. 3:4, under *Personal Mention.*

17. Marion's biog., *Siskiyou News,* May. 28, 1898, pg. 9:4.

18. *Siskiyou News,* Jan. 9, 1886, pg. 3:4.

19. *ibid.,* Jan. 23, 1886, pg. 3:4.

20. *Quartz and Placer Mining* column in the *Siskiyou News,* of May 29, 1886.

21. *Siskiyou News,* Aug. 11, 1886, pg. 3:3,4; Aug. 28, 1886, pg. 3:2,6.

22. Index to Mining Claims, Siskiyou Co. Recorder's Office, Yreka, CA.

23. The *Siskiyou News,* Feb. 12, 1898, pg. 1:3.

24. The *ibid.,* Nov. 28, 1901, pg. 1:3; *q.v.* Marion's biog. *op.cit.*

25. The *Siskiyou News,* Dec. 13, 1906, pg. 3:4.

26. *Death of Marion Freshour — One of Our Best Citizens Passes Away — Brief Sketch of His Useful Life.* A lengthy obituary in *The Siskiyou News,* Yreka, CA, Dec. 13, 1906, pg. 3:2.

27. *Siskiyou News,* Jun. 4, 1898, pg. 1:2; Jun. 25, 1898, political advertisement.

28. Nixon, Robert J., *Sheriffs of Siskiyou County,* in *The Siskiyou Pioneer,* 1959, Vol. 3, No. 2, pps. 69–71.

29. *Siskiyou News,* Nov. 12, 1898, pg. 1:3; Sept. 5, 1901, pg. 3:1.

30. *Siskiyou News,* Dec. 13, 1900, pg. 1:5. A detailed description is given. It even had a padded cell. The sheriff was frequently reported as conducting the insane to asylums in other parts of the state.

31. *Siskiyou News,* Jan. 10, 1900, Most of front page.

32. *ibid.,* Various items are from the year 1900: May 17, pg. 1:5; March 24, Apr. 4, pg. 7:1; June 13, Brevities; Jul. 20, pg. 1:4; Aug. 30, pg. 1:4; Aug. 23, pg. 1:4.

33. *ibid.,* Sept. 13, 1900, pg. 1:4.

34. *ibid.,* May 8, 1901 (on Wetzel;) June 19, 1901.

35. *ibid.,* Oct. 24, 1901.

36. *ibid.,* June 20, pg. 1, Aug. 15 and Nov. 14, Brevities pg. 5:3, 1901.

37. *ibid.,* Nov. 21, 1901, Brevities pg. 5:2.

38. *ibid.,* Jan. 16, 1902, pg. 1:5; July 24, 1902, pg. 1.

39. *ibid.*, Oct. 16, 1902, pg. 3:3.

40. *Siskiyou News*, Nov. 20, 1902, pg. 1:4. A Dec. 25th article disputed with the editor of the *Yreka Journal* on election recount. The county Superior Court denied the case of *Marion Freshour vs. Charles B. Howard*, though finding misconduct which reduced Howard's margin to 13 votes. An amendment averred misconduct in counting ballots in the Oro Fino District. The court would not allow the amendment since more than 40 days had elapsed. The higher court upheld the judgment.

Siskiyou Co. Superior Court, Civil Suits, Book 4, Pg. 216, Case 2364, In favor of defendant. Filed Jan. 27, 1903.

Reports of Cases Determined in the Supreme Court of the State of California. Bancroft-Whitney Company, San Francisco, 1904,
Vol. 142, pps. 501-5, [Sac. No. 1165. In Bank.—March 14, 1904.]
[California State Library — Law Library, Sacramento.]

41. From a supplement to the *Pioneer Press* of Etna, Fall-winter Edition, August of 1981.

42. Chester Barton wrote his critique and recollections, on August 31, 1981, in a letter to Donald Joseph Freshour, son of Joseph Jr. and grandson of Joseph Frank Freshour.

43. The coroner was the informant. The certificate stated only that he was age 50, a white male laborer, date, cause of death and that the body was removed to Yreka.

44. The *Siskiyou News*, June 22, 1907, Card of Thanks, pg. 2:2; June 27, 1907, pg. 3:6.

45. Davis, Charlotte, *Klamath River Ferry*, in *The Siskiyou Pioneer*, Yreka, CA, 1968, Vol. 4, No. 1, pps. 74-5.

46. *ibid.*

47. There is an Aug. 3rd, 1892 marriage in San Joaquin Co. between Louis Fogorcci, age 59, and Mrs. Alice Freshour, age 30. Both residents of Stockton. (Apparently the widow, Mrs. Alice Hubbard, née Freshour.) She is identified as Alice Hubbard on her death certificate.

48. *Siskiyou News*, December 17, 1908, pg. 3:5.

49. *Siskiyou News*, July 30, 1931, pg. 6:5.

50. Joseph Freshour Jr. was living in Applegate Oregon in 1918 when his son Donald Joseph was born. Joseph Jr.'s wife, Betty Head was also born at Applegate. Much of this information was provided in 1987 by Don and Ester Freshour then living on Highway 96 on the Klamath River north of Yreka in the vicinity of the defunct Gottville.

Notes on Chapter 14 — To the Rogue and Back

1. From *Wild and Scenic Rivers of the United States*, a map produced by the Cartographic Division, National Geographic Society, Washington, D.C., July 1977.

q.v. Zane Grey: Romancing the Rogue in the Nov/Dec 1992 issue of the *Table Rock Sentinel*, the bimonthly journal of the Southern Oregon Historical Society, Medford Oregon.

2. q.v. Gillette, Foreword by Richard H. Dillon.

3. Bancroft's Works, Vol. 30, (Oregon-Vol. II, 1848-1888,) Ch. X.

4. "Rf.(sic) *Camomel 64 grains; Opium 32 grains; Camphor 8 grains; Capsicum 16 grains; Pulv. Gum Arabic 4 grains — mix and make 32 pills.*" For loose bowels, a teaspoonful of Paregoric washed down with good Brandy was recommended. Dr. Anson Henry's letter, *Illinois Journal*, Springfield, Feb. 24, 1853, pg. 2:4.

5. *Illinois Journal*, Feb. 22, 1853, pg. 2:2.

6. Signed M.W.E. *Illinois Journal*, April 11, 1853, pg. 2:1.

7. Josephine County Historical Society.

8. Gillette, pps. 66-76.

9. Bancroft's Works, *op. cit.*, CH XV & XVI.

10. Genaw, *Gold Hill and its Neighbors*, pps. 36-41.

11. *Oregon Sentinel*, Jacksonville, 10 April, 1878, pg. 3:5.

12. Lacy, *Marriages*, Vol. II, pg. 3.

13. *Democrat Times*, Jacksonville, 30 Aug. 1878, pg. 3:1.

14. *Yreka Union*, 31 Aug. 1878, pg. 3:2.

15. This narrative has been gleaned from:

Criminal records, Tulare Co. Superior Court, Visalia.
Microfilm reel 1880-1881, Case 312, John Freshour, larceny, Aug., 30, 1880. (Includes indictments, subpoenas, trial transcripts, verdicts, appeal etc.)

California Supreme Court Case # 11856.
Transcript on Appeal, John Freshour, Appellant vs. Tulare Co., Respondent.
California State Archives, Roseville (Sacramento,) CA.

16. *Register of San Quentin Prison*, Printed Index — 1858-1912 and microfilm of the original register: MF 1:9(11) Roll 2, No 7471. California State Archives, Roseville (Sacramento,) CA.

17. *Tulare Weekly Times*, Visalia Calif., Sat., Aug. 31, 1878, pg 5:2.

18. *Tulare Weekly Times*, Nov. 9, 1878, pg. 5:1.

19. *Yreka Weekly Union*, Jan. 11, 1879, pg. 3:3.
Jacksonville Democratic Times, Jan. 10, 1879, pg. 3:5.

20. *Tulare Weekly Times*, July 10, 1880, pg. 5:1.

21. *Reports of Cases In the Supreme Court of the State of California*, Bancroft-Whitney Company, San Francisco, 1904, Vol. 55, pps. 375-7, No. 10502. [California State Library — Law Library, Sacramento.]

Opinion delivered 20 July, 1880 and Remittitur dated 30 July, 1880. Copies filed at Visalia, 25 Aug., 1880. *Criminal Records, Tulare Co.*, Case 312. *op. cit.*,

22. *Tulare Weekly Times*, July 31, 1880, pg. 5:1.

23. W.L. Randall was discharged from San Quentin on May 26, 1881, having served 4 years, 2 months. *Register of San Quentin Prison; op. cit.*

24. Petition and *Writ of Habeas Corpus*, both dated 30 Aug., 1880. *Criminal Records, Tulare Co., op. cit.*, Case D.

25. *Stockton Daily Evening Record*, Sat. June 22, 1907, pg. 8:2,3.

26. Recorder's office, Jackson Co., OR, Medford, Claims Book 17, pg. 140. The index gives "Jo A Freshour (Klondike)" This Quartz Claim was filed on 3 Nov., 1911. The requirement of the act of 1901 was met by digging an opening of 15 by 8 by 4 feet.

27. "Charlie" was Charles Thomas Freshour Sr. of Lodi. Family data is from the ledger of Henry James Freshour, who kept an exact record of birth and death dates for the family of James W. Freshour. He failed to mention place — only dates. A copy of this record was provided by Theresa Freshour of Sutter Creek, CA. The late Eddie James Freshour, son of Charles T. Freshour, provided a typewritten record of the James W. Freshour family as well as that of his father "Charlie." Again, no localities were given. These records gave mostly nicknames. Family lore had many of the family born in Oregon as given by informants on the death certificates. Census records were taken as more reliable in this regard.

28. James Freshour was working on the Wesley Bennett ranch in Chico twp., Butte Co. in June of 1880. He is listed as 28 and married, but Arabella and children appear not to be in the county.

29. *Ashland Tidings*, Dec. 10, 1886, Obit — Child of James Freshour of Sam's Valley. Listed in Childers and Lacy.

30. NEQ of NEQ, S29 & SEQ of SEQ, S20 T35S-R2W WWM (West Willamette Meridian.) (80 acres) Patent issued by the U.S. Land Office at Roseburg and recorded at the Jackson County Recorder's office in July of 1908.

31. SWQ of NWQ & W/2 of SWQ, S22 T35S-R2W WWM (120 acres) Issued at Roseburg and recorded at the Jackson County Recorder's office in May of 1897 by Helen Walker who had purchased the land.

32. Antioch Cemetery records held by former Sexton, Mrs. Lloyd Beers. An account of the grave markers in the small cemetery on the Morris Frick property is given in "The Forgotten Ones" by Doris Walker in the *Medford Mail Tribune* in May of 1994.
Pankey Cemetery records, Southern Oregon Historical Society.

33. *History of Sutter County*, Thompson & West, Oakland, CA, 1879. Reproduced by Howell-North Books, Berkeley, CA, 1974. pps. 92-95.

See Bancroft's *Pioneer Register* pg. 31 for Allgeier.

34. (S5 T12N-R4E MDM) Near the town of Nicolaus.

35. Sutter County marriage license and notice in *Marysville Daily Appeal*, 27 Sept., 1894, pg. 1:4.

36. No Athertons were listed in Sutter County in 1900. Only Lillie of the older children was married so it is hard to conceive of another household where she and her brood could have been. She might have been with a sister in law. James W. Freshour had four sisters.

37. E/2 of SEQ S6 T12N-R4E MDM (near his fathers quarter section)

38. *Marysville Daily Appeal*, Mar. 5, 1901, pg. 1:4 bottom. The license was filed in the Yuba County Recorders office, 4 May 1901. Witnessed by Clerk, Bowman and Willie Blue of Marysville. The bridegroom was a native of Germany and resident of Nicolaus. The bride was a native of CA and resident of Spenceville, Nevada Co. CA.

39. From James T. Leary of Sacramento, for $10, Lot 6, Block #4, town plat of Town of Nicolaus, fronting 80' on First Street by 100' depth. Notarized 29 July, Sacramento. Filed 29 August, Sutter County.

40. The 1910 census for Lodi was written very lightly, apparently in pencil, and is almost entirely illegible. The Henry J. Freshour entry was one of the few that could be read. The microfilm process used was not helpful. It is not surprising that the 1910 SOUNDEX failed to list these Freshours.

41. The only records of the cemetery are a gravestone cataloging done by the Sutter-Yuba Genealogical Society. This is an active county cemetery. There is a plat (map) of the cemetery. There is an infant grave also shown in the Freshour plot. No dates are given other than those on the gravestones.

42. Section Z, Grave 2052: Pfc. Cecil Chester Freshour, b. 9-23-1899, d. 12-18-1962, Service: 17 Aug., 1942 – 3 April 1945, Medical Detachment, Next of kin: Fred Freshour, brother, 212 E. Lodi Av., Lodi.

Notes on Chapter 15 — Sonoma to Sisquoc

1. Padre Eusebio Kino was to *Pimería Alta* (Northwestern New Spain) what Frey Junépero Serra was to *Alta California*. Kino envisioned the two regions as linked geographically, religiously, economically and politically. See generally Polzer.

2. See generally Lyman.

3. Rowland, pg. 62.

4. Chapman, pps. 463-4; McKittrick, Chapter III.

5. McKittrick, Chapter XII. Note that Mariano Vallejo was the military governor of Alta California at this time and his nephew, Juan Alvarado, was the civil governor. Their eventual rivalry caused the Mexican government to send Governor Micheltorena to succeed them both, ending "home rule". Vallejo was appointed military commander of the territory from Santa Yenez to Sonoma. The Russians attempted to negotiate for all land north of the bay to the 42nd parallel (the present Oregon border) and from the Pacific to the Sacramento River. Baron Wrangell came to California in 1834 for this purpose but failed. See Hunt and Sanchez, Ch. XII.

6. Although the Russians had discovered gold, copper and coal in Alaska, they were preoccupied with furs and neglected mining. Threatened with British invasion from Canada, they attempted to sell Alaska to the U.S. in the 1850s but the Civil War delayed the purchase, astutely negotiated by Lincoln's Secretary of State, William Seward, until 1867.

7. *Alférez* was a noncomissioned rank similar to the American rank of Warrent Officer. Vallejo was soon promoted to *tieniente* i.e. lieutenant.

8. q.v. Sanchez, In a section titled: *The Bootlegging of the Books*, pps. 226 - 232.

9. Curiously, not a saint's name. From the Spanish word *sol* meaning "sun," it was the name for the hot summer winds blowing from inland.

10. See generally Bunnett, Pokriots & Reynolds, *Records of Alcaldes*.

11. Beard, pps. 3, 96.

12. The crew that threshed at Isaiah's place was: Woods, Springer, Burgest Wall, Henry Wall, Wm. and Nick Gann, Wm. Storer and Phipps. Isaiah's grain amounted to 317 sacks of wheat and 158 sacks of barley. (Half his, half Henry Wall's — sharecropped perhaps.)

13. "Frazier" Gann was Adam Carter Gann.

14. If by "Ramona Valley" he was referring to San Ramon Creek, then he would have traveled by way of the Livermore Valley and through the Altamont Pass to Tracy. He could have gone to the north of Mt. Diablo

and followed Marsh Creek over to Byron and thence to Tracy. Either route would have been arduous in 1856. Note that this southern route from Sonoma County to Stockton was again designed to skirt the delta marshes.

15. Nicholas and Rutha Gann living some ten miles south of the Calaveras River were "up (north) on the Calaveras" relative to French Camp and Castoria Township where the Elkins and Tom and John Gann lived to the south of Stockton.

16. Payment was to the Office of the County Treasurer. This was for land described in the Certificate of Location of Leander Ransom, Locating agent of San Francisco District, as follows: Location No. 202, state School Land, Sonoma County, Township 7, Range No. 9, Sect 13, Mt Diablo Meridian being the NEQ of S13, T7N-R9W MDM containing 160 acres located for I. Horn.

17. This was for the NWQ of S21, T7N-R8W MDM.

18. C.C. Freshour also appears in the Napa census in Napa twp two months earlier (17 June) in a labor crew working for Irishman John Watson. This is apparently another case of a person being counted twice in a census — a not uncommon occurrence.

C.C. and Eunise were married at Woodland in Yolo County according to her obit. The marriage record at Woodland has C.C. Freshener married to Lavina Rice on April 4th, 1869, with the consent of her mother, Laura Rice, by W.C. Curry, Pastor ME Church.

19. Andrew's land was in S12, T26S-R12E MDM five miles north east of Paso Robles.

20. Lawson's land was in S2, T27S-R10E MDM ten miles east of Paso Robles.

21. Rowland's People File on Albert Jones. Rowlands's scrapbook item, Cholame Migration. pg. 320.

22. The document is displayed on the wall of the Museum of Mission San Diego Acalá. The document is signed:
    By the President, *Abraham Lincoln.*
    By *N.O. Stoddard*, Secretary.
    Recorded: Vol. 4; Pages 94 to 101, inclusive.
    G.N. Granger, Recorder of the General Land Office.

23. Lompoc is pronounced " Lawm-poke" by the natives. Accounts of the colonization of Lompoc appeared in the *Pajaro Times* of Watsonville in 1874.

24. See generally Best. On the Puget Sound and San Diego railroads see Best, pps. 128-148.

25. This road is still shown on modern maps of the county. The author drove on it in 1951-52 while a student at Cal Poly in S.L.O. Signs painted on boulders could still be read advertising businesses of S.L.O. There has been a succession of highways built up Cuesta Grade — all on the side of the gulch opposite from the stage road.

26. See Best, pps. 42-3, for detailed accounts.

27. Obituaries in *The Healdsburg Tribune*:
C.C. Freshour: DEATH OF A PIONEER, Thurs., May 10, 1917.
Eunice Freshour: DEATH OF MRS. FRESHOUR, Thurs., Oct. 21, 1915.
Minnie Rose Freshour: OBITUARY – FRESHOUR, Nov. 23, 1910.

28. P/O S2 T9N-R31W SBM (Santa Bernadino Meridian.)

29. P/O S28 T10N-R31W SBM.

30. Records of Santa Barbara Co. Recorder and list published in San Luis Obispo Genealogical Society, Vol 22 # 1, Spring, 1989, ISN #8756-2733. (Taken from *Ancestors West*, Vol. 4, No. 1, March 1978.)

Notes on Chapter 16 — Soquel Timber

1. Albion and Hall, pps. 291-9 on "sea dogs." Chapman, Ch. IX on Drake, pps. 261-4 on the English Buccaneers, Ch. XI on Vizcaíno.

2. See map Fig. 1.1, pg. 9; DeVoto - Empire, pps. 62-3, 284-6.

3. Father Crespi accompanied Portolá on this excursion and kept a journal that is an invaluable primary source. Father-President Serra worked at the establishment of San Diego during this time. Koch, pps. 2-3; Portolá himself kept a diary and later dictated an account to Viniegra given in Chapman. *q.v.*, pps. 225-228.

4. Chapman, pps. 220-31 on Portolá.

5. Koch, Ch. I; Rowland, pps. 5-13.

6. Chapman, pps. 246-253, 289, Ch. XXVIII.

7. Chapman, Ch. XXIII, XXIV.

8. Father Palou, in 1774, under orders from Serra traveled from San Francisco to Monterey and marked the mouth of the San Lorenzo as a prospective mission location. In 1787, the viceroy of Mexico, Juan Vicente Guemez Pacheco de Padilla Horcasitas y Aguayo, conde de Revilla Gigedo, issued an order to the head of the Franciscan order in Mexico to establish three missions in Alta California including Santa Cruz. Two thousand pesos were provided and four priests sent from San Blas. They brought the order to Fr. Lasuén. The existing Mission establishment was already overcommited but Fr. Lasuén ceremonially officiated. The mission was actually built by the military under the viceroy's order. Rowland's scrapbook, pg 246; Chapman, pg. 497.

9. Rowland, pps. 25-31, 39-43.

10. Nellie Sanchez cites the practice of the government in Mexico of dumping criminals in Alta California as the reason for the "failure" of the civic community of Branciforte. This would appear to be a misunderstanding based on the fact that the community assumed the name of its mission. Branciforte Co. was one of the original 27 counties of California created in Feb. of 1850. Within the year, its name was changed to Santa Cruz Co. Surely the name "Branciforte" did disappear from the map. Not so the industrious community. Sanchez, Pg. 8;   Koch, Ch. III.

11. Sanchez, Ch. II.   **12.** Rowland, pps. 46-8.

13. q.v. Notes on CH 12, note 15. Rowland quotes Craven P. Hester.

14. Well illustrated by Owen Coy's map in Chapman, pg. 418.

15. In 1795, lime juice was issued to all British naval vessels to stop scurvy. The Dutch had used citrus fruits to stop scurvy for several hundred years and the British learned from them. The complete absence of vitamin c in the diet for six months produces serious debility and death will soon follow. It is doubly ironic that the Spanish force under Portolá should suffer dozens of fatalities from scurvy when their Mediterranean homeland was known for citrus production and they were dying in the Mediterranean climate zone of New Spain that under the padrés would soon become famous for its citrus groves.

16. Rowland's "People File," Nicholas Gann, Jackson Bennett. Litigation was relative to Buzzell's ownership of his sawmill at Zayante.

17. Cole's Memoirs, pps. 100-4.

18. Koch, pps. 143-4;   Payne, The Howling Wilderness, pps. 3-6; Rambo, pg. 19;   Young, John V., Ghost Towns, Ch. 1.

19. Payne, pps. 10-17;   Rowland, pps. 73, 74.

20. Rowland, pps. 39-43.

21. See generally Lydon & Swift.

22. This region of the Shoquel and Aptos Ranchos on the northern shore of Monterey Bay forms a coastline arcing east to west — the Soquel Cove. Mount Diablo is due north with the Mount Diablo Meridian falling between Soquel and Aptos. Per U.S. Dept. of the Interior Geological Survey topographic maps, 7.5 Minute Series, Soquel and Laurel Quadrangles, California — Santa Cruz Co.

Quarter township (9 section) maps available from the County Surveyor's Office were compiled in 1880 and have inscribed the names of the property owners at that date. Names include G.W. Himes, J.T. Freshour, Porter, Grover, Hinh and C. McKiernan (Mountain Charlie.)

23. On the Grovers, Grover's Gulch and Glen Haven see Patten.

24. Koch, pps. 154-9; Lydon & Swift, pps. 14-17.

25. See appendix B-1 for the Himes and Baucom families. We know that these families left the San Joaquin and resided at Soquel as early as 1862-3 because of the jury duty their men folk performed at Soquel. From Rowland's "People File," Special Collections, McHenry Library, UCSC.

26. See generally Phillips biography of Cole and Cole's Memoirs.

27. Rowland's People File, Special Collections, McHenry Library, UCSC.

28. Bailey, pps. 381-4.   29. Nevins, pg. 79.   30. Kennedy, pg. 64.

31. See Stone's chapter *The Civil War Makes Its Way West.* pps. 203-7.

32. Sherer, pps. 275-7.

33. See generally Colton's *Civil War in the Western Territories.* On Johnston's refuge in Maximillian's Mexico see Proctor and Scott pps. 873, 1118, 1131-3.

34. Cole's Memoirs, pps. 154-155.

35. Information on the Santa Cruz Cavalry is from California Militia records in the State Archives and is contained in the author's *The Santa Cruz Cavalry & The Butler Guard.*

36. Proctor & Scott, Vol. 50, part 2 of 2, pps. 799, 819, 858. National Archives Records: Civil War pension record, SC 922 251. Civil War military record, Union, 8th Cal. Inf. Co. A;

37. Captain Orville Root, in Santa Cruz Cavalry monthly report to Brigade HQ, reported John Freshour, Private, Died. q.v. *The Santa Cruz Cavalry & The Butler Guard* by the author. pg. 43, items 39, 40.

38. The *Santa Cruz Local Item*, 1 Feb., 1867. Item FELL DEAD

39. U.S. Census, 1860, Napa Co. CA, Hot Springs Twp., St. Helena P.O. family 162, Alfred Musgrave, teamster age 37 from TN, wife Eliza, age 20, IL, one child Susan A., age 1, CA; Family 155, brothers Calvin, James and mother.

40. According to E.E. Freshour, his grandmother's 2nd marriage was a "hush-hush" topic so he couldn't account for Musgrave. Lietha Roberts passed on the family tradition that Musgrave "ran off with a red head." Perhaps the redhead occurred after the fact. He had taken on quite a household of step-children ranging from twin babies to teenagers — a formidable task.

41. That same year, Claus Spreckles bought Eighty-Five acres of Aptos Rancho from Rafael Castro. Both deeds were recorded Nov. 26th, 1872. The Freshour-Carravajal deed was recorded at the request of the grantees. The Castro-Spreckles deed follows the Freshour-Carravajal deed in Deeds, Vol. 15, pgs. 221-3, the Santa Cruz County Recorders office.

The Freshour-Carravajal deed was apparently concocted by J.P. Clements using information given to him by Will and Sophronia. The property description only called out bounding properties of neighbors. No legal description giving MDM referenced Section, Township and Range was given. This was common practice. The best efforts of title insurance companies have not been able to trace this deed to a prior or subsequent deed. The court house burnt down in 1894. Present records are typed copies. The Santa Cruz Land & Title Company posted this record in 1920. They judged the property to be in S15 or S16 of T10S-R1W MDM. Efforts to trace neighboring properties were likewise frustrated. Records are scant.

Notes on Chapter 17 — Steam Powered Soquel

1. Rowland, pps. 73-4.   2. Payne, pps. 17-36.

3. Generally see *Ships and Narrow Gauge Rails* by Gerald M. Best.

4. Branch, pps. 523-543;   Monaghan, pps. 343-4.

5. Bailey, pps. 519-523.   6. Stone, pps. 231-7.   7. Bailey, 519-523.

8. Lydon & Swift, pps. 22-3.   9. MacGregor, pps. 118-120.

10. MacGregor and Truesdale, pps. 324-337.

11. According to John Bradley in Santa Cruz *Sentinel* article, Feb. 11, 1965. Note that Elias Bradley of Soquel is not to be confused with Elias Bradley of Corralitos. Also, there was another John Bradley, earlier on in Santa Cruz County, who was with Waddell when he was fatally injured by a bear. q.v. *The Pajaronian*, Oct., 14, 1875.

12. A pioneer of the county, Judge Clements was married to Josefa Lodge who had inherited one-eighth of the Soquel Augmentation land grant. Judge Clements held court in a room off of the bar in Tom Mann's hotel in Soquel during the 1870s. Rowland, pps. 63-4, 69-70.

13. See generally Patten on the History of Grover' Gulch.

14. Patten, pg. 10 shows a picture of the Glen Haven class of 1888 including Lydia, Bertha and John Bradley (back row, 2nd from right.) At age 93, John Bradley contributed to Patten's book.

15. 1850 US Census, IN, Jasper Co., Iroquois twp. Family #s 6,17. W.L. Mack's obituary, *Los Gatos News*, Oct., 1, 1897, Pg 2:1.

16. Patten, pps. 5-8. Patten's description of jerkline teams

17. Koch, pps. 44-5;   Rowland, pps. 182-3.

18. Koch, pps. 71, 113, 146.

19. Koch, pps. 108-111;   MacGregor and Truesdale, pps. 248-260, 275-293.

20. The extraordinary story of the South Pacific Coast Railway is told in historical depth by two fine books: Bruce MacGregor's classic, published 1968, and MacGregor and Truesdale's *A Centennial — South Pacific Coast*, published in 1982. These books are voluminously illustrated with old photographs.

21. Koch, pps. 173-4.

22. MacGregor and Truesdale, pps. 1-5, 11, 228-9, 240.

23. McGregory and Truesdale, pg. 332; Koch, pps. 158, 174.

24. Santa Cruz Co. Surveyor's ten-chains/inch map #'s 9, 11, 13 & 15. (R1W-T10S & T11S, MDM)

25. Superior Court of Santa Cruz County, Microfilm file # 4.36.MR, Suit # 1802, Wilding, Frederick vs. F.A. Hihn, Sept. 25, 1892. The *Santa Cruz Surf*, items: 21 May 1891, pg. 3:5; 24 Sept. 1891, pg. 3:3; 25 Sept. 1892, pg. 4.

26. California State Supreme Court — Case # 14940, filed Aug. 18, 1892. [California State Archives, Roseville (Sacramento) CA]

27. *Santa Cruz Sentinel*, 23 Nov. 1878, pg. 3:3, 2:5; 22 Nov. 1884, pg. 3:2; 25 Nov. 1884, pg. 3:1.

28. Henry bought this 7.5 acre plot in 1865 and developed it into lots sold to Gough, Hannahan, Bowman, Seigman and Miller, retaining 3.3 acres for himself. None of these titles were clear. This was remedied by Congress with *An Act to quiet the title of certain lands within the corporate limits of the City of Benicia, and the Town of Santa Cruz, in the State of California*, approved July 23rd 1866. The state legislature enacted *An Act to incorporate the Town of Santa Cruz*. Approved March 31st 1866. Forms were printed and deeds recorded for all. Henry's deed also covered that part of his farm falling west of the township line and a lot he had on Front Street. Book 9, pg. 36, filed Dec. 3rd 1866. q.v. Map of Fractional T11S-R2W MDM, Embracing Santa Cruz, Surveyed by Foreman & Wright, 1866.

29. See *APPENDIX F.* q.v. McHugh's scrapbook #3, pg. 29, col 1-3; Rowland's scrapbook, pg. 264. UCSC Special collections.

30. Henry purchased this 8 acres adjacent to his brewery property from Joaquin Juarez and Paranada, his wife, in 1859. In January 1865, County Judge Blair granted this land (6.89 acres designated as lot No. 46 on the map of Branciforte made by county surveyor, A. McPherson) in pursuance of the provisions of *An act to settle the title of lands in the Village and Town of Branciforte in the County of Santa Cruz*. Approved by the Legislature April 4, 1864.

31. Santa Cruz County Surveyor map set A14-179, A15-70,

32. *Santa Cruz Sentinel*, Nov. 1, 1873, pg. 3:2.

NOTES

33. Ernst Otto's Scrapbooks, book #2, pps. 12,18; book #3, pg. 2:2. Santa Cruz Historical Museum. Rowland, pps. 213-4;

34. The Henry Bausch probate record. Santa Cruz Co. Superior Court. M.R. 2.9, case 169. The brewery was operated during this time variously by Theodore Beck, Louis Koehn and August Peter in a succession of partnerships. Annie's deed was filed on the date Henry's will was made. Santa Cruz Co. recorder, Deed Book 42, pg. 233. The deed for Henry's children was filed in Nov., 1893. Deed Book 97, pg. 166.

In a punitive breach of old-world primogeniture, Henry gave his son only one-fifth of the estate and that only after a deliberate 9 year probation. Deprived of brewery proprietorship, George resourcefully created his beer garden on the adjacent land. When the estate was finally distributed, George cut a deal with the other surviving heirs and recouped the brewery operation. What did Henry have in mind? George died of alcoholism at age 43. Perhaps his father was attempting to preclude this.

35. A.A. Freshour often recalled these gatherings according to E.E. and Minnie Freshour.

36. George Bausch probate record. Santa Cruz Co. Superior Court. M.R. 2.52, case 1440. The Santa Cruz *Riptide*, Oct. 6, 1949, pg. 17. Of Henry's other heirs, John Bausch died in 1900 and Miss Mary Bausch in 1901.

37. Koch, pps. 234-5;

38. See Appendix D-2.

39. From E.E. Freshour's reminiscences. The 1900 census gives Ralph E., Hazel B. and Edith M Barden, ages 14, 8 and 3 respectively.

40. From the tape recorded reminiscences of Leitha Roberts.

41. *Santa Cruz Surf*, 31 March 1910, pg. 5:6.

42. For a masterful discussion on this topic see *Recollections of our past* by Frank "Lud" McCrary in Big Creek Lumber 1981 Catalog. pg. 25.

43. This discussion is intended to convey the perilous nature of timber falling and the skills required. Ed Conant devotes an entire chapter to this subject in his memoirs.

44. *Santa Cruz Surf* April 9, 1897, 1:2.   **45.** *ibid.* April 10, 1897, 1:2.

46. *Sentinel* news item.   According to reminiscences of E.E. Freshour, Harvey was living on Delmas Ave. in the 1920s.

47. Dwight Wm. Grover removed to San Luis Obispo County where he founded Grover City in Aug. 1887. Family portraits, land deeds, memorabilia and the brass name plate from his Walnut St. Santa Cruz home are displayed in the Grover Beach city hall.

48. There is no official death certificate for Emily Josephine Bausch. The Bradley Bible gives her death date as Feb. 16, 1936. The record at the Santa Cruz IOOF Cemetery concurs and gives the place of death as Soquel. Her cremains were placed in the Bausch plot on May 17, 1978. Her daughter-in-law, Grace L. Bausch, had the cremains at home. Grace Bausch's conservator, Dorothy Jern of Santa Clara brought the cremains in for disposition.

Notes on Chapter 18 — Soquel to Hester Creek

1. Banks, Charles Edward, THE ENGLISH ANCESTRY AND HOMES OF THE PILGRIM FATHERS Who Came to Plymouth on the "Mayflower" in 1620 ... and the "Anne" ... in 1623.

2. The Name and Family of Conant, Manuscript Number 580, Roots Research Bureau, Ltd.

3. From the family bible record of George H. and Elizabeth Conant.

4. James Crozier Conant was named after James Crozier who appears in Stockton Directory, and Emigrants Guide to the Southern Mines, Orin F. Jackson, Printer, 1852. James Crozier is listed as blacksmith at the corner of Calif & Main. The Great Register of Voters 1866-1871, gives: James Crozier, 52, Scotland, gardener, O'Neal Twp., proved 15 years residence, 14 Feb., 1867, R & R 3560 (reregistered after 1871.)

5. MacGregor and Truesdale, pps. 1-13.

6. See Appendix G.

7. i.e. the adiministration of. This was the NWQ S22 T10S-R1W MDM. Across the road, George Washington Himes owned the SEQ S16 T10S-R1W MDM.

8. Taken from Rowland's scrapbook, pg. 11. q.v. Koch, pg. 122:1.

9. The Santa Cruz Daily Surf, 23 Aug., 1887.

10. The Santa Cruz Weekly Surf, 1 Nov., 1890, Item.

11. The Santa Cruz Daily Surf, 4 Dec., 1890, Item. The Weekly Surf, 13 Dec., 1890, Item.

12. Case No. 14941; In the SUPREME COURT of the State of California. J.T. FRESHOUR, Road Overseer of Soquel Road district, Plaintiff and Respondent, vs. F.A. HIHN, Defendant and Appellant. Four documents: 1.) Transcript on Appeal, Charles B. Younger, Attorney for Defendant and Appellant. W.T. Jeter and Julius Lee, Attorneys for Plaintiff and Respondent. Sentinel Print, Santa Cruz. Filed 18 Jan., 1892.
2.) Appellant's Points and Authorities. Sentinel Print, Santa Cruz. Filed 29 July, 1892.

3.) *Respondent's Points and Authorities.* Wm.T. Jeter and Carl E. Lindsay, District Attorney of Santa Cruz County, Attorneys for the Respondent. Printed at the "Surf" office, Santa Cruz. Filed 16 Sept., 1892.

4.) *Appellant's Reply to Respondent's Points and Authotities.* Filed 3 Oct., 1892. W.A. Woodward & Co., Printers, 12 Sutter St. S.F.
[Californa State Archives, Sacramento (Roseville) CA]

13. *Road Overseer* was the official title but it was commonly given as *Roadmaster* in newspaper accounts.

14. California Supreme Court Case No. 14941; Transcript on Appeal. *op. cit.*, pg. 27.

15. *Reports of Cases Determined in the Supreme Court of the State of California,* [No. 14941. Department Two. — August 31, 1893.] Bancroft-Whitney Company, San Francisco, 1906, Vol. 99, pps. 443-8. [California State Library — Law Library, Sacramento]

16. *West's California Digest Covering Cases From State and Federal Courts.* Volume 47A, Table of cases G – M. West Publishing Company, St. Paul, Minn. pg. Cal D-120.
[California State Library — Law Library, Sacramento]

17. This is in error. He was a member of the Wallace-Reynolds Post of the GAR and a member of the Soquel IOOF. Neither Joseph Terre nor Joseph Alfred Freshour were born in California; so, neither could qualify as a Native Son of the Golden West.

18. Koch, pg. 122; Rowland, pg. 82.

19. *Santa Cruz Weekly Surf,* Saturday, Dec. 6, 1890.

20. *The Daily Surf,* July 27, 1891.

21. See Appendix D-1, Joseph Terre, for a summary of his military record.

22. Grand Army of the Republic — The national organization of veterans of the Union Army. A picture of the Wallace Reynolds Post and their first Muster Roll appears in *Beautiful Santa Cruz* by Phil Francis published in 1896. Joseph Freshour appears in the Muster Roll but is not in the picture. The original photograph is displayed in the Veterans Bldg. in Santa Cruz. A numeral is placed on each individual in the photo and there is a corresponding list of names. There are 50 men in the photo and 132 men in the Muster Roll. According to Rowland, there was a schism in the Wallace Reynolds Post with a faction attempting to start another post at Soquel. A reconciliation occurred and the Soquel Post was never established. This, in part, may account for the small number of men in the Photo and the missing Soquel members.

23. He deeded land to Frank and Edward O'Neill (Dec., 1888,) Frank R. Dann (Dec., 1893,) and Mary C. Utter (June, 1894.) The Utter land, including 50 acres she sold to Sam and Anna Miller, went back to Joe in foreclosure and repurchase in 1896. He sold to Bernhard Bertling (Jan., 1897.) Joe purchased his retirement property from William and Hannah Oliver (Dec., 1894,) and Augusta Darling (April, 1903.)

24. Letter from Maytie Woods to E.E. Freshour, Jan., 1975. E.E. remembered his great uncle, Long Joe, as a somber old man with a tendency towards melancholia. Letha Roberts described him as a raw-boned, rugged looking individual. They were teenagers when Joe died in 1915 at age 67.

25. A photo of the "Lou" Mason home on First St. is in the Phil Walker collection.

26. The *Santa Cruz Surf*, Jan. 17, 1890, pg. 1:4. Jos. A. Miricle was a Soquel trial juror. *Santa Cruz Surf*, Column: *Soquel Yesterdays*, Feb. 13, 1890, pg. 3:4. Also see Appendix G.

27. Walter Young's memoirs, *Los Gatos Times-Observer*, 16 July, 1959. Referred to in Payne, pg. 69, as the "Franch and Miracle" mill. Note that the Frenches owned a millsite but not timberland. Miracle must have made stumpage and logging arrangements. This millsite was probably the ten acres sold to Jeret N. and Julia S. French by Edwin Fitch in Jan., 1897. Fitch apparently bought Comstock's property and parceled it out. Anderson Freshour and G.H. Conant held adjacent property. The Frenches in turn sold this parcel in May of 1905 to J.W. Simpson who had another parcel nearby, also purchased from Fitch. Santa Cruz County Deeds, Vol. 171, Pps. 145-6, grantors: J.N. & J.S. French.

28. See Rambo pg. 35, Rowland, pps. 65, 125, Koch, (on Watson,) pps. 16-17. C.P. Hester is not mentioned by Koch.

29. Namesake of Alice Edith Himes, the youngest daughter of Geo. Washington and Sarah Freshour Himes. Alice Edith Himes Gardner was age 24 when Alice Freshour was born. This tells us that A.A. and Min were well acquainted with with the Himes family.

30. E.E. Calls this the "road to Blackburn Gulch" in his reminiscences and sometimes simply refers to the entire Mountain District as "Blackburn Gulch" which can erroneously lead to the idea that they lived in the Blackburn Gulch. The stretch of road between Cahoon's and the Himes and J.T. Freshour ranches came to be known as "Cahoon's Gulch." On Cahoon see Koch, pg. 122.

31. Santa Cruz *Surf*, 25 March, 1901.

32. The 1860 CA census for Mendocino twp, Sonoma Co. gives Banner Goheen, 23 b. OH, as one of a crew of day laborers. S.M.E. Goheen came to California in 1850 when Banner was 13 years old. Unruh pg. 72.

33. Tape recorded reminiscences of E.E. Freshour. Nov. 28, 1985.

34. This was Edison A. French, M.D. of San Luis Obispo. The "Thomas" was dropped and his family only knew him as "Ed."

35. From the tape recorded reminiscences of Beatrice Simpson Dearwester. Her mother, Mary Simpson, a staunch temperance advocate, no doubt voiced negative opinions about the Donovans.

36. Mountain Lions were actually more numerous in the Santa Cruz Mountains than the more famous grizzlies. Payne, pps. 7-8.

37. From the reminiscences of E.E. Freshour. His Charlie Joon account is flagrantly apocryphal. Patten, pg. 79; Rowland's scrapbook, pg. 269.

38. From Mary Mallon Simpson's UCBB journal entries and the reminiscences of Minnie Simpson Freshour and Beatrice Simpson Dearwester.

39. Patten, pps. 12-13.

40. In another account, E.E. stated that this was the Bender house. G.W. Himes died in 1903 and the Benders may have succeeded him. *q.v.* Appendix B, Sarah E. Freshour.

41. According to E.E. Freshour's reminiscences, as far as he knew Herman Peterson was no relation to Nils Peterson.

42. Lydon & Swift, pps. 50-55.

Notes on Chapter 19 — The Bear Went Over

1. Material in this chapter is drawn from the accounts of Mr. and Mrs. E.E. Freshour and Rev. and Mrs. Edward Conant and their remembrances of stories handed down to them from James C. Conant and Anderson A. Freshour. Since E.E. Freshour was born in 1897, he would not himself remember Aggie nor her father.

2. W.L. Mack's obituary, *The Los Gatos News,* Friday, Oct. 1, 1897, pg. 2:1. *Los Gatos weekly Mail,* Sept. 30, 1897, pg. 5:3, Column:*Around Town.* Death certificates for Agnes and Wm. L. Mack are in the records of the Los Gatos Memorial Park. They would have been buried in the original Los Gatos Cemetery and their bodies among those moved to the new Memorial Park when the old cemetery was converted to commercial useage.

3. The *Los Gatos Mail,* May 8, 1902, pg. 8:3, bottom. Bruntz shows a page of the 1902 Los Gatos city directory that lists city officials.

4. *The Los Gatos Mail,* Oct. 10, 1912, pg. 4:2. *The Los Gatos News,* Oct. 18, 1912, 3:2, Column *News in Brief.*

5. *The Los Gatos Mail,* Thurs., Nov., 9th, 1911, pg. 1:3.

6. The Freshours dealt in building materials so were familiar with the building trades and described houses in structural terms.

7. James Duval Phelan, son of a forty-niner millionaire, he was elected mayor of San Francisco in 1897, U.S. Senator in 1915. His Saratoga Estate became the present Villa Montalvo Arboretum and Villa Montalvo Center for the Arts. His father, Jas. Phelan Sr., had a summer home in Santa Cruz. The son followed the trend to go over the mountain. Koch, pg. 213.

8. E.E. described in detail the embalming process, which he witnessed.

9. Koch, pg. 235. Rural Free Delivery of mail started at Santa Cruz in 1902. Until the twentieth century, the U.S. Mail system, for the U.S. population living on farms, was entirely based on delivery at the nearest Post Office. They always checked for mail when they went to town. With the new RFD system, Joe no longer had to go into the Soquel Post Office to get his mail. The towns in the Santa Cruz Mountains on the South Pacific Coast Railroad (Glenwood, Laurel, Wrights) were Post Offices for people living in the mountains.

10. His age was given as 23 when he enlisted and eleven months later, when he was discharged, his age was still given as 23 years. According to census data of 1850, 1856 and 1860, he would have been 26 to 27 years old at that time. His affidavit of April, 1913, gave his birth date as 10 Oct. 1842. By the time he died in 1915, he had his birth date 5 years more recent than the one given out by his parents to census takers.

11. Santa Cruz Co. Deeds, Grantor, Jos. T. Freshour, Book 256, pg. 457. The two contiguous lots were across the San Jose Road from the properties of Barber Darling and William Oliver.

12. Payne, pg. 16.

13. Recorded reminiscences of E.E. Freshour. Rev. J.J. Sproles was actually pastor of the Los Gatos Baptist Church. (According to sermon topics announced in the Los Gatos News during 1905.)

14. MacGregor & Truesdale, pps. 160-1.

15. The term "dark complexioned" has been used here just as the Civil War military records used it — "black" was not intended.

16. During the Cherokee removal, the Indian agents made records of each individual, recording their Indian name and its meaning and their adopted English names. These records were used in Oklahoma to later identify their descendants making claim there. Records were then established for the Oklahoma Cherokee. These records are in the National Archives. There were no Cherokee named Freshour in the removal; however, there were several Hedricks in the removal. Elizabeth Hedrick couldn't have been "removed" since she went to Indiana with her husband Henry Freshour.

See the Nat. Arch. microfilm publication M1186, *The Index and Five Rolls of Cherokee Tribe in Indian Territories,* Compiled and printed under

authority conferred by Act of Congress, Approved June 21, 1906. (INDEX: Cherokees by Blood, pps. 1-191.) The index listed 22 Ganns. No Freshours were listed. There were 7 family records for *Hedricks/Hedrick/Headricks*. These are only a few of the Cherokee microfilm records. Also see: *American Indians: A Select Catalog of National Archives Publications*, ISBN 0-911333-09-6, pps. 6,17,24,32,41,43. Some 450 rolls of Cherokee microfilm records are listed.
Also see the set of volumes: *CHEROKEE BY BLOOD — Records of Eastern Cherokee Ancestry in the U.S. Court of Claims 1906-1910*, By Jerry Wright Jordan, 1988, Heritage books, Inc, Bowie, Maryland.

17. Ingenthron, pps. 77, 128, 252; Monaghan, Chapters XVIII & XIX. Also see generally: Ehle's *Trail of Tears*.

18. In a 1941 letter to Richard Freshour of Siskiyou Co. CA, from Elizabeth Freshour of Martinsburg, WV, she adds a P.S.

"*By the way, the Freshours on our side are very dark complected people. Dark hair and eyes, but that doesn't go for us. I am the darkest and I didn't get those dark hair and eyes.*"

Courtesy of Don & Esther Freshour, Yreka, CA.

19. The dispute over this region began in 1857. Rowland, pg. 107. The boundry legislation was finally enacted in 1868. Koch, pg. 64. The Santa Cruz County Great Register of 1867 lists men from Pescadero.

20. From the Gazos Creek reminiscences of Edward Conant.

21. The lease on this farmland involved sharecroping with the owner, Wiedeman. They farmed entirely with horses. That year, 1919, they grew 1100 sacks of oats, 400 odd sacks of horse beans, 100 sacks of peas and 24 sacks of red kidney beans. Wiedeman took 750 sacks of oats and was going to take the rest. E.E. removed the remaining sacks at gun point. Wiedeman later explained that his book keeper had made an error.

22. A good map of this area as it was circa 1890-1920 is given in J.V. Young's *Ghost Towns*, pg. x.

23. Item: DEATH DUE TO ACCIDENT, *San Jose Mercury Herald*, Friday morning, Aug. 6, 1920, 1:1 top. *The Los Gatos Mail News*, Thurs., Aug., 5, 1920, pg. 3:3; Aug. 12, 1920, pg. 1:3; Death certificate.

24. From Leon Rowland's scrapbook, Special Collections, UCSC.

25. Cark Balch was Mayor of Los Gatos (1938-40.) His biog. is in the Masonic publication: *Los Gatos Lodge 292 — Centennial 1888-1988*.

26. See Appendix E for biographical sketches of the family.

27. Webb, Walter P.; *Divided We Stand: The Crisis of a Fronteerless Society*, 1985 reprint of 1944 ed., Hyperion Connection,
ISBN 0-88355-903-X.

WHEN THE GRASS SHALL COVER ME

WHEN the grass shall cover me,
Head to foot where I am lying:
When not any wind that blows,
Summer blooms nor winter snows,
Shall awake me to your sighing;
Close above me as you pass,
You will say, "How kind she was,"
You will say, "How true she was,"
When the grass grows over me.

When the grass shall cover me,
Holden close to Earth's warm bosom;
While I laugh, or weep, or sing
Nevermore for anything;
You will find in blade and blossom,
Sweet, small voices, oderous,
Tender pleaders in my cause,
That shall speak me as I was—
When the grass grows over me.

When the grass shall cover me!
Ah, belovéd, in my sorrow
Very patient, I can wait—
Knowing that or soon or late,
There will dawn a clearer morrow;
When your heart will moan, "Alas!
Now I know how true she was;
Now I know how dear she was,"
When the grass grows over me!

by INA D. COOLBRITH

WAGONS TO SOQUEL
BIBLIOGRAPHY

GENERAL BACKGROUND:

Albion, Robert G.; Hall, Walter P.,
A History of England and the British Empire, Second Edition, Ginn and Company, Boston, 1946.

Bailey, Thomas A.,
The American Pageant, Little, Brown and Company, Boston, 1956.

Barck, Oscar T.; Lefler, Hugh T.,
Colonial America, The Macmillan Company, New York, 1958.

Bartlett, R.A.; Goetzmann, Wm.H.,
Exploring the American West, 1803-1879, HANDBOOK 116, Division of Publications, National Park Service, U. S. Department of Interior, Washington, D. C., GPO, 1982 — 361-661/102

Branch, E. Douglas,
Westward — The Romance of the American Frontier, D. Appleton and Company, New York and London, 1930. Reprint, Marandell Books/Coopers Square Publishers, Inc., New York, 1969.

Buell, Abel,
1783 Map of the US, Reproduced in *The Territorial Growth of the United States*, National Geographic Cartographic Div., Washington, DC, 1987.

Chapman, Charles E.,
A History of California: The Spanish Period, The Macmillian Co., New York, 1930.

Cleland, Robert Glass,
A History of California: The American Period, The McMillin Company, New York, 1923.

Cline, Gloria Griffen,
Exploring the Great Basin, University of Oklahoma Press, Norman, 1963.

DeVoto, Bernard,
Across the Wide Missouri, Houghton Mifflin Company, Boston, 1947.

DeVoto, Bernard,
The Course of Empire, Houghton Mifflin Company, Boston, 1952.

DeVoto, Bernard,
The Year of Decision — 1846, Little, Brown and Company, Boston, 1943.

Ehle, John,
Trail of Tears Doubleday & Company; New York, 1988.

Federal Writers Project of the WPA,
IOWA - A Guide to the "Hawkeye" State, The American Guide Series, Viking Press, New York, MCMXLV. ©1938 by the State Historical Society of Iowa.

Federal Writers Project of the WPA,
MISSOURI - A Guide to the "Show Me" State, The American Guide Series, Duell, Sloan and Pearce, New York, 1941. ©1941 by the Missouri State Highway Department.

Federal Writers Project of the WPA,
PENNSYLVANIA - A Guide to the Keystone State,
The American Guide Series,
Oxford University Press, New York, 1940. ©1940 by the University of Pennsylvania.

Federal Writers Project of the WPA,
TENNESSEE - A Guide to the State, The American Guide Series, Hastings House Publishers, Inc., New York, 1959.

Foner, Philip S., edited by,
The Life and Major Writings of Thomas Paine, ©, 1945, by The Citadel Press; The Citadel Press, New York, 1961.

Irving, Washington,
The Adventures of Captain Bonneville, (originally published in 1837) Klickitat Edition, with Foreword: Bonneville and Irving by Alfred Powers; Binsford and Mort, Portland, OR. 1954

Jackson, Joseph Henry,
Anybody's Gold – The Story of California's Mining Towns, D. Appleton-Century Company, New York, 1941.

Kennedy, Elija Robinson,
The Contest for California in 1861, Houghton Mifflin Co., Boston, New York, 1912.

Klees, Fredric,
The Pennsylvania Dutch, ©, 1950, by Fredric Klees; The Macmillian Company, New York, 1961.

Koch, Adrienne; Peden, William,
The Life and Writings of Thomas Jefferson, The Modern Library, Random House, New York, 1944.

McKittrick, Myrtle M.,
Vallejo – Son of California, ©, 1943, by Myrtle M. McKittrick; Binsford and Mort, Portland, OR. 1943

Miller, John C.,
Origins of the American Revolution, ©, 1943, by John C. Miller; Little, Brown and Company, Boston, 1943.

Nevins, Allan,
Ordeal of the Union: Volume II, A House Dividing — 1852-1857, Charles Scribner's Sons, London – New York, 1947.

Royce, Josiah,
CALIFORNIA – From the Conquest of 1846 to the Second Vigilance Committee in San Francisco; Preface by Robert Glass Cleland of Huntington Library (Originally published in 1886.) Alford A. Knopf, New York, 1948.

Sanchez, Nellie Van De Grift,
Spanish Arcadia, Powell Publishing Co., Los Angeles, 1929.

Sandberg, Carl,
Abraham Lincoln — The Prairie Years and The War Years, One-Volume edition, Harcourt, Brace & World, Inc., New York, 1954.

Sherer, James A.B.,
The Thirty-First Star, G.P. Putnam's Sons; New York, 1942.

Stone, Irving,
Men to Match My Mountains, The Opening of the Far West, 1840-1900 Doubleday & Company; New York, 1956.

Van Doren, C.; McHenry, R.; editors,
Webster's Guide to American History, G. & C. Merriam Company; Springfield, MA; 1971.

Webb, Walter Prescott,
The Great Plains, Grosset & Dunlop, NY, 1972; ©1931, Walter Prescott Webb.

Williams, George Hunston,
The Radical Reformation, The Westminster Press, Philadelphia, 1962.

TRAIL LITERATURE:

Ackley, Mary E.,
Crossing the Plains and Early Days in California, Privately printed, San Francisco, CA, 1928 (Rare Books Dept., Huntington Museum, San Marino, CA.)

Applegate, Jesse A.,
A Day With the Cow Column, Ye Galleon Press, Fairfield, WA, 1990 (A reprint of the the Caxton Club edition, Chicago, 1934. First published in 1876.)

Beard, Franklin; Editor,
Charles Hopper and the Pilgrims of the Pacific, An 1841 California Pioneer, His Narrative and Other Documents.
A limited edition. Southern Mines Press, La Grange, CA, 1981

Brown, William Richard,
An Authentic Wagon Train Journal of 1853 – from Indiana to California, Privately published by Grandaughter, Barbara Wills, ©1985; Horshoe Printing, Mokolumne Hill, 1985.

BIBLIOGRAPHY

Bryant, Edwin;
Late Alcalde of St. Francisco,
What I Saw in California, Journal of a Tour By the Emigrant Route and South Pass ... In the Years 1846, 1847. (First published in 1849.) Ross & Haines, Inc., Minniapolis, 1967

Coy, Owen C.,
The Great Trek, ©1931 by the Powell Publishing Co., Los Angeles

Delano, Alonzo;
Across the Plains and Among the Diggings, Wilson-Erickson, Inc., New York, 1936

Dillon, Richard H.,
Siskiyou Trail, McGraw-Hill Book Company, New York, 1975, ©1975 by Richard Dillon.

Eaton, Herbert,
The Overland Trail to California in 1852, Capricorn Books, G. P. Putnam's Co., New York, ©1974 by Herbert Eaton.

Federal Writers Project of the WPA,
The Oregon Trail — The Missouri River to the Pacific Ocean, The American Guide Series, Hastings House Publishers, Inc., New York, 1939.

Florin, Lambert,
Western Wagon Wheels, Bonanza Books, Crown Publishing, New York, ©1970 by Superior Publishing.

Franzwa, Gregory M.,
Maps of the Oregon Trail, The Patrice Press, St. Louis, MO, 1982.

Gibbons, Boyd; Amos, James L.,
The Itch to Move West, National Geographic, Vol. 170, no. 2, Aug. 1986

Gillette, Martha Hill,
Overland to Oregon and in the Indian Wars of 1853, Limited edition with foreword by Richard H. Dillon; Lewis Osborne, Ashland, OR, 1971.

Graydon, Charles K.,
Trail of the First Wagons Over the Sierra Nevada, The Patrice Press, St. Louis, MO, 1986.

Harris, E.W.; The Nevada Emigrant Trail Marking Committee,
The Overland Emigrant Trail to California, A Guide to trail markers placed in Western Nevada and the Sierra Nevada Mountains in California. Published by Nevada Emigrant Trail Marking Committee, Inc. c/o Nevada Historical Society, Reno, NV, 1986.

Helfrich, Devere and Helen; Hunt, Thomas,
Emigrant Trails West, A Guide to trail markers placed by Trails West Inc. Along the California, Applegate, Lassen, and Nobles' Emigrant Trails in Idaho, Nevada and California. Published by Trails West, Inc.; Reno, NV, 1984.

Holliday, J. S.,
The World Rushed In, Simon and Schuster, New York, 1981.

Hunt, Thomas H.,
Ghost Trails to California, Nevada Publications, Las Vegas, NV, 1980.

Kincaid, Robert L.,
The Wilderness Road, (Originally Published, 1947 by Bobbs-Merril Company in the American Trail Series.) ©1973 by Mrs. Robert L. Kincaid, Publisher, Middlesboro, Kentucky

Lavender, David,
The Overland Migrations,
HANDBOOK 105, Division of Publications, National Park Service, U. S. Department of Interior, Washington, D. C., GPO, 1980 — 311-340/1

Mattes, Merril J.,
The Great Platt River Road, A Bison Book, University of Nebraska Press, Lincoln NE, 1987.

Mattes, Merril J.,
Platt River Road Narratives, University of Illinois Press, Champaign, IL, 1988.

Paden, Irene D.,
The Wake of the Prairie Schooner, The Macmillan Co., New York, NY, 1944; Patrice Press, St. Louis, MO, 1986.

Parkman, Francis,
The Oregon Trail, First published 1847;
Literary Guild Edition, Doubleday &
Company, Inc., Garden City, N. Y., 1946;
Viking-Penguin, 1982.

Rouse, Parke, Jr.,
*The Great Wagon Road — From
Philadelphia To the South;*
(The American Trail Series,
A.B. Guthrie, Jr., Editor.)
McGraw-Hill Book Co., New York, 1973.

Schmidt, Earl F.,
*The Big Tree Carson Valley Emigrant
Road,* Mooney Flat Ventures, Murphys,
CA, 1989.

Settle, Raymond W., Editor,
The March of the Mounted Riflemen,
Bison Book reprint,
University of Nebraska Press, Lincoln, 1989
©1940 and 1968, Arthur H. Clark Co.

Smith, C. W.; Vail, R.W.G., Editor,
*Journal of a Trip to California – Across
the Continent from Weston Missouri, to
Weber Creek, California, in the Summer
of 1850,* (Originally published in 1920.)
Ye Galleon Press, Fairfield, WA, 1974.

Stewart, George R.,
The California Trail, McGraw-Hill
Company, Inc., New York, 1962
©1962, George R. Stewart

Unruh, John D.,
The Plains Across, University of Illinois
Press, Urbana and Chicago, Illini Books
edition 1982
©1979, by the board of trustees of the
University of Illinois.

Ware, Joseph E.,
The Emigrant Guide to California,
(Originally published by J. Halsall, St.
Louis, 1849) Reprinted with introduction
and notes by John Caughey;
©1932, Princeton University Press
Da Capo Press, New York, 1972

LOCAL HISTORIES:

Bancroft, Hubert Howe,
*California Pioneer Register and Index,
1542 – 1848,* Extracted from Bancroft's
The History of California, by the
Regional Publishing Co., Baltimore, 1964.

Bancroft, Hubert Howe,
*Bancroft's Works, Volume XXX; The
History of Oregon, Vol. II. 1848-1888;*
(Originally published by The History Co.,
San Francisco, 1888) An Arno Press book;
McGraw-Hill Book Co., New York, 1974.

Battle, J. H.,
History of Jasper County, Part IV of
*Counties of Warren, Benton, Jasper &
Newton, Indiana,* F.A.Battey Co.,
Publisher, Chicago, 1883.

Best, Gerald M.,
*Ships and Narrow Gauge Rails,
The Story of the Pacific Coast Company,*
Howell-North Books, Berkeley, CA, 1964.

Brice, Walter A.,
History of Fort Wayne, D. W. Jones &
Sons Steam Book and Job Printing, Fort
Wayne, Ind., 1868

Bruntz, George G.,
*The History of Los Gatos, — Gem
of the Foothills,* Valley Publishing Co.,
Fresno, CA, 1971.

Bryant & Fuller,
Valley of the Upper Maumee, Two Vols.,
Madison, Wis., 1889
Reproduced by Unigraphics, Inc.,
Evansville, Ind., 1947

Cole, Cornelius,
*Memoirs of Cornelius Cole, Ex-senator of
the United States from California,*
Mc Laughlin Brothers, New York, 1908.

Colton, Ray C.,
The Civil War in the Western Territories,
The University of Oklahoma Press,
Norman, 1959.

Foote, Horace S.
Pen Pictures from the Garden of the World, or Santa Clara County, California, Lewis Publishing Co., Chicago, 1888.

Friends of Bancroft
[Introduction by Fred B. Rogers]
The California Star - Yerba Buena and San Francisco, Vol. 1, 1847-1848 (a reproduction in facsimilie.)
Howell-North Books, Berkeley, CA, 1965.

Genaw, Linda Morehouse,
Gold Hill and its Neighbors along the River, (Jackson Co. Oregon history) ©1988, Linda A. Genaw, Publisher, Central Point, Oregon.

Goodspeed, Publishing,
History of Cole, Moniteau, Morgan, Benton, Miller, Maries and Osage Counties Missouri., The Goodspeed Publishing Co., Boston, 1889.

Havens, Glade; Walter, Olive,
Brooks History, Brooks United Methodist Church, Brooks, IA, 1983.

Hunt, Rockwell,
Sanchez, Nellie Van De Grift;
A Short History of California, Thomas Y. Crowell Co., New York, 1937. ©1929 by Thomas Y. Crowell Co.

Ingenthron, Elmo,
Border-Land Rebellion, A History of the Civil War on the Missouri-Arkansas Border Ozark regional History Series, Book III, The Ozarks Mountaineer, Branson, MO, 1980

Koch, Margaret,
Santa Cruz County — Parade of the Past, Western Tanager Press, 1981, Santa Cruz, CA ©Valley Publishers, 1973, Fresno, CA

Lydon, Sandy; Swift, Carolyn,
Soquel Landing to Capitola-by-the-Sea, Local Studies, Vol. 22;
California History Center –
De Anza College, Cupertino, CA, 1978.

Lyman, George D.,
John Marsh, Pioneer,
©1930 Charles Scrivner's Sons,
The Chautaqin Press, NY, 1931.

Long, Ileen Price, Chairman,
Alpine Heritage, The Centennial Book Committee, The Alpine County Museum, Markleeville, CA, 1987.

Mace, O. Henry,
Between the Rivers — A History of Early Calaveras County, California, Second Edition, Conotto Publications, Jackson, CA, 1993.

MacGregor, Bruce,
South Pacific Coast, An illustrated history of the narrow gauge South Pacific Coast Railroad. Howell-North Books, Berkeley, CA, 1968.

MacGregor, Bruce A., Truesdale, Richard;
A Centennial — South Pacific Coast, Pruett Publishing Co., Boulder, CO, 1982.

MacMullen, Jerry,
Paddle Wheel Days in California, Stanford University Press, Stanford, 1960.

McCrary, Barbara, Editor,
Big Creek Lumber — A History of the Lumber Industry in the Santa Cruz Mountains, 1981 Catalog & Price Guide ©Big Creek Lumber Company, Watsonville, CA. Design and Production by Depot Hill Graphics.

Malmin, Judy Pybrum,
Corralitos, ©1982, Judy Pybrum Malmin, Publisher, Corralitos, CA

Monaghan, Jay,
Civil War on the Western Border, 1854-1865, University of Nebraska Press, A Bison Book, Lincoln and London, 1984.

Paden, Irene D.; Schlichtman, Margaret E.;
The Big Oak Flat Road, — an account of freighting from Stockton to Yosemite Valley. The Holmes Book Co., Oakland, CA., 1959

Patten, Phyllis Bertorelli,
Oh, That Reminds Me, (History of Grover's Gulch and surrounding Soquel Twp.) Big Trees Press, Felton, CA, 1970.

Payne, Stephen,
A Howling Wilderness, (A History of the Summit Road Area of the Santa Cruz Mountains 1850-1906.) Loma Prieta Publishing, Los Gatos, CA, 1978.

Phillips, Catherine Coffin
Cornelius Cole, California Pioneer and United States Senator, Printed by John Henry Nash, San Francisco, 1929.

Polzer, Charles W., S.J.,
Kino Guide II, his missions – his monuments, (Padré Kino was a notable explorer and cartographer.) Southwestern Mission Research Center, Tucson, 1982.

Rambo, Ralph,
Pioneer Blue Book of the Old Santa Clara Valley, The Rosicrution Press, San Jose, CA. ©1973 by Ralph Rambo.

Rowland, Leon,
Santa Cruz – The Early Years, Paper Vision Press, Santa Cruz, CA, 1980

Smith, O.H,
Early Indiana Trails and Sketches — Reminiscences by Hon. O. H. Smith; More, Wilstach, Keys & Co., Printers, Cincinnati, 1858

Tinkham, George H.,
History of San Joaquin County, Included in:
Guinn, J.M. - A. M.,
History of the State of California, Vol. I, Historic Record Co., Los Angeles, 1909.

Tinkham, George H.,
The History of San Joaquin County, Historic Record Co., Los Angeles, 1923.

Trafzer, Clifford E.,
Yuma – Frontier Crossing of the Far Southwest, Western Heritage Books, Inc., Wichita, 1960.

Young, John V.,
Ghost Towns of the Santa Cruz Mountains, Paper Vision Press, Santa Cruz, CA, 1979.

ARTICLES IN LOCAL HISTORIES:

Foster, Connie,
Henry Freshour, in
History of Washington Co. Arkansas, Shiloh Museum, Springdale AR, 1989.

Huntley, Harvey Jr.;
Burgner, Goldine;
XIII. Freshour, in *Lutherans in Greene County: A Bicentennial History,* Published by authors, Greenville, Greene County, Tennessee. (ca. 1970s)

Johnson, Eddith Smith,
David Freshour, in *A Look Back at the Parrotville Community,* Ruritan Club, Parrotsville, Cocke Co.,TN, May 1986.

O'Dell, Ruth Webb,
Escape from East Tennessee to the Federal Lines, in *Over the Misty Blue Hills,* Southern Historical Press, Easley, SC; Reprint, 1982.

ARTICLES IN PERIODICALS:

[The *Overland Journal* is the quarterly journal of OCTA (the Oregon-California Trails Association,) Independence, MO.]

Adams, Kenneth C., Editor,
Centennial Edition,
Sept 9 1850 — Sept 9 1950,
California Highways, Vol. 29, Nos. 9, 10. Division of Highways, Department of Public Works,
State of California, Sacramento, CA.

Camp, Charles L., editor;
William Alexander Trubody and the Overland Pioneers of 1847, California Historical Quarterly XVI, (1937): pgs. 122-143 [Reprinted in Beard.]

Capps, Michael A.,
Wheels in the West: the Overland Wagon, Overland Journal, Volume 8, Number 4, 1990, Pgs. 2-11.

Davis, Charlotte,
Klamath River Ferry, The Siskiyou Pioneer, Vol. Four, No. 1, The Siskiyou County Historical Society, Yreka, CA, 1968.

BIBLIOGRAPHY

Davis, Richard M.,
The Walker River-Sonora Crossing,
Overland Journal, Volume 6, Number 3,
1988, Pgs. 10-28.

Dillard, Annie,
"The French and Indian War in Pittsburg:
A Memoir" The American Heritage,
July-Aug. 1987, Pgs. 92-3; American
Heritage Inc., a division of Forbes Inc.,
New York.

Fox, Fred K.,
*John Mohler Studebaker's 1853 Overland
Journey from Indiana to California,*
Overland Journal, Volume 8, Number 4,
1990, Pgs. 12-19.

Garret, Wilbur E., Editor,
*George Washington's Potowmack Canal —
Waterway That Led to the Constitution,*
National Geographic, Volume 171,
Number 6, 1987, Pgs. 716-753.

Martin, Charles W. and Dustin,
Dorothy Devereux,
*The Omaha-Council Bluffs Area and the
Westward Trails,* Overland Journal,
Volume 7, Number 4, 1989, Pgs. 2-11.

Mitchell, Stewart,
Crossing the Sierra, California Highways,
Centennial Edition, Vol. 29, Nos. 9, 10.
pps 49-68. Division of Highways,
Department of Public Works,
State of California, Sacramento, CA.

Mothershead, Harmon,
*River Town Rivalry for the Overland
Trade,* Overland Journal,
Volume 7, Number 2, 1989, Pgs. 14-23.

Muehl, Ruth D.,
"The Time of My Life": Women Who
Loved The Trek, The American Heritage,
Dec. 1985, Pgs. 92-3. American Heritage
Inc., a division of Forbes Inc., New York.

Munkres, Robert L.,
Devil's Gate, Overland Journal,
Volume 7, Number 1, 1989, Pgs. 2-18.

Nixon, Robert J.,
Sheriffs of Siskiyou County, The Siskiyou
Pioneer, Vol. Three, No. 2, The Siskiyou
County Historical Society, Yreka, CA, 1959.

Pope, James Sterling,
*Still They Come: Wagon Wheels on
Paddle Wheels to the Heads of the
Oregon-California Trail,* Overland Journal,
Volume 6, Number 2, 1988, Pgs. 2-11.

Potter, James E.,
Firearms on the Overland Trails, Overland
Journal, Volume 9, Number 1, 1991, Pgs.
2-12.

Rieck, Richard L.,
*A Geography of Death on the
Oregon-California Trail,* Overland Journal,
Volume 9, Number 1, 1991, Pgs. 13-21.

Rosborough, Alex J.,
California's Gold Find, The Siskiyou
Pioneer and Guidebook to Siskiyou's Gold
Fields, Vol. 2, No. 10, The Siskiyou County
Historical Society, Yreka, CA, 1957.

Smith, Pat,
The Ultimate Family Trip, History Section,
San Jose Mercury News, Extra 2, Pg. 6, 17
June 1987.

West, Elliot,
The Youngest Pioneers, The American
Heritage, Dec. 1985, Pgs. 90-6; American
Heritage Inc., a division of Forbes Inc.,
New York.

West, Mary,
It all Started With Martin Murphy, in
Sunnyvale - A Proud History, Sunnyvale
Historical Society, San Jose Mercury News,
8 Dec. 1987. (Special Section,)

Wohleber, Curt,
THE TIME MACHINE, *1838–One
Hundred and Fifty Years Ago,* [Trail of
Tears.] The American Heritage, Sept./Oct.
1988, American Heritage Inc., a division of
Forbes Inc., New York.

GENEALOGICAL WORKS:

Bunnett, Sara A.,
SANTA CRUZ COUNTY *California Births and Deaths — 1856-1900 — From Early Newspapers*, Genealogical Society of Santa Cruz., Santa Cruz, CA, 1987

Bunnett, Sara A.,
Santa Cruz County, California Births & Deaths — from the DAILY SURF — (1901 - 1908), Genealogical Society of Santa Cruz., Santa Cruz, CA, 1989

Bunnett, S.A., Pokriots, M., Reynolds, W.D.,
Record Books of the Alcaldes of Santa Cruz, California, 1847 - 1850 (& April term, 1851.) Genealogical Society of Santa Cruz., Santa Cruz, CA, 1992

Edwards, Olga J., Frizzel, Izora W.
The "Connection" in East Tennessee, Published by the Authors.

Egle, William Henry, M. D., edited by
Names of foreigners who Took The Oath of Allegiance to the Provence and State of Pennsylvania, 1727 to 1775, ...,
Genealogical Publishing Co., Inc., 1967, Baltimore.

Everton, George B. Sr.,
The Handy Book for Genealogists, Seventh Edition, ©1981 by the Everton Publishers, Inc., Logan, Utah

Frushour, Thomas Alan, Publisher,
From the Frogmeadow,
(A quarterly newsletter.)
Nine issues — Jan., 1990 – Jan., 1993.
Temperance, MI.

Genealogical Soc. of Santa Cruz Co.,
Indexed CEMETERY RECORDS of Santa Cruz Co. California, Santa Cruz, CA, 1960
SANTA CRUZ IOOF CEM., Pg. 109;
SOQUEL PIONEER CEM., Pg. 252.

Haller, Charles R.
Across the Atlantic and Beyond — The Migration of German and Swiss Immigrants to America; Heritage Books, Inc., Bowie, Maryland, 1993.

Hunter, Katherine M. and Bernard E.
Some Notes on Berkeley Springs, West Virginia; in *Virginia Land Records*, Genealogical Publishing Co., Inc., Baltimore, 1982.

Irish, Donna R., Compiled by
Pennsylvania German Marriages, Marriages and Marriage Evidence in Pennsylvania German Churches
Genealogical Publishing Co., Inc., Baltimore, 1982.

Lacy, Ruby; Childers, Linda,
Abstracts: Ashland Tidings
Vol. II Apr 12, 1878 – Feb 12, 1885,
©Ruby Lacy, Publisher,
Ashland, Oregon, 1990.

Lacy, Ruby,
Jackson County, Oregon Records,
Vol. II Marriages, 1877 – 1888,
Compiled by Ruby Lacy, Publisher, Ashland, Oregon, 1981.

Lawson, Richard D. Sr.,
The Keesling and Smith families of Green Co. TN and Webster Co. MO,
©Richard D. Lawson Sr.,
Webster Co. MO, 1987

Maryland, Archives of,
Under the Direction of the Maryland Historical Society,
Muster rolls and other Records of Service of Maryland Troops in the American Revolution, 1775-1783. Genealogical Publishing Co., Inc. 1972, Baltimore.

Orton, Richard H., Brig. Gen,
Adjutant-General of California,
Records of California Men in the War of the Rebellion, 1861 to 1867. J. D. Young, Supt. State Printing, Sacramento, 1890.

Parker, J. Carlyle,
A Personal Name Index to Orton's "Records of California Men in the War of the Rebellion, 1861 to 1867." Gale Research Company, Book Tower, Detroit, MI 48226, ©1978 J. Carlyle Parker.

Rupp, Prof. I. Daniel,
*A Collection of Thirty Thousand Names of
...Immigrants in Pennsylvania From 1727
to 1776, With a Statement of the names of
Ships, whence they sailed, and the date of
their arrival at Philadelphia, ...*
Leipzig:Degener & Co., 1931; Genealogical
Publishing Co., Inc. 1965, Baltimore.

San Joaquin Co. Genealogical Society,
*Old Cemeteries of San Joaquin County,
Vol. 1 of 3* Stockton, CA, 1960
KIRK FAMILY CEMETERY, Pg. 38;
DRAIS FAMILY CEMETERY, Pg. 19;

Simms, Edgar B., State Auditor,
*Simms Index to Land Grants
in West Virginia.*
©1952 by the State of West Virginia

Strassburger, Ralph Beaver,
*Pennsylvania German Pioneers: A
Publication of the Original Lists of Arrivals
in the Port of Philadelphia from 1727 to
1808.* Edited by William John Hinke, 3
Vols. Pennsylvania German Society, 1934;
Reprint of Vols. 1 & 3 only, Genealogical
Publishing Co., 1966, Baltimore.

Strum, Margaret H., Edited by,
*Genealogy of the Sturm Family — A record
of the Descendants of Jacob Strum of
Sharpsburg, Maryland from 1750-1936.*
Compiled by Lloyd Elmer Strum; ©1935
Published by Margaret H. Strum, 1938,
Columbia, Ohio.

Tracey, Grace L., Dern, John P.,
Pioneers of Old Monocacy — 1721-1843.
Genealogical Publishing Co., Inc. 1987,
Baltimore.

Vineyard, Mrs. John,
Original Land Entries of Jackson Co. MO.
©The Ozark Genealogical Society; 1971,
Springfield MO

**Weiser, Frederick Sheely,
Translator, Editor,**
*Records of Marriages and Burials in the
Monocacy Church in Frederick County,
Maryland and in the Evangelical Lutheran
Congregation in the city of Frederick
Maryland — 1743-1811.,*
Special Publication No. 38,
The National Genealogical Society,
Washington, D. C., 1972

MANUSCRIPTS AND OTHER DOCUMENTS:

Bradley, Elias; Lydia Jane,
*FAMILY BIBLE: Family Record contained
in an Illustrated Polyglot Family Bible,*
Wm. Garretson & Co., San Francisco, 1869;
(Presented to Elias and Lydia Jane at their
wedding by Joseph T. Freshour with their
marriage record and the family record of
John and Sophronia Freshour.)

Findla, James,
*Statement of a few events in early days of
California as given by James Findla for
Bancroft Library, 1878,* H.H. Bancroft
Collection, Bancroft Library,
University of California, Berkeley, CA.
[Reproduced in Beard.]

Finley, Newton Gleaves,
Statement, typescript, Bancroft Library,
University of California, Berkeley, CA.

Freshour, J.T., vs. Hihn, F.A.,
*J.T. Freshour, Road Overseer of Soquel
Road District, Plaintiff and Respondent
VS. F.A. Hihn, Defendant and Appellant.*
IN THE SUPREME COURT OF THE
STATE OF CALIFORNIA, 1887,
Case # 11856, Calif. State Archives,
Roseville (Sacramento,) CA.

Henry, Anson G.,
Diary, manuscript and typed transcript,
Illinois Historical Library, Springfield, IL.

Hopper, Charles,
*Narrative of Charles Hopper, a California
pioneer of 1841.* Recorded by R.T.
Montgomery, Napa, CA, 1871, manuscript,
Bancroft Library, University of California,
Berkeley, CA. [Reproduced in Beard.]

Horn, Isaiah,
Isaiah' Horn's Journal, San Jose, Santa Clara Co., Stockton, Sonoma Co., CA; Oct. 1854 – Nov. 1871. Typed transcript by his g.g.d Ethyl Horn Smith. Lompoc Valley Historical Society.

Moore, Alexander,
A pioneer of '47, Statement of Alexander Moore of Pesdcadero. manuscript, Bancroft Library, University of California, Berkeley, CA. [Reproduced in Beard.]

Proctor, Redford, Secretary of War; Scott, Robert N., Lieut. Col., 3rd US Artillery;
The War of the Rebellion; A Compilation of the Official Records of the Union and Confederate Armies. Series I – Reports. Government Printing Office, Washington, DC, 1890.

Simpson, Mary E.,
UCBB — Uncle Carl's Baby Book; A Hester Creek family record in diary form with entries on births, christenings (with photos,) holidays, establishment of school, 1906 earthquake, etc. Mallon/Simpson records. [Author's collection]

St. Johns, James,
Diary original manuscript, microfilm, Oregon Historical Society. Portland OR. [In Beard as reprint of article edited by Geo. H. Himes.]

Santa Cruz Cavalry,
Organization Petition, Muster Rolls, Reports etc., 1863-1867. of Co. F, 1st Cav. Regt. 2nd Brig. Calif. Militia; later Co. E, 1st Cav. Regt. 2nd Brig. Calif Nat. Guard; File # B 3411-5, Calif. State Archives, Sacramento, CA

Shank, Ira C.,
History of Jenny Lind. Typescript Calaveras Co. Historical Society. San Andreas, CA.

Soquel IOOF Cemetery,
Soquel IOOF Cemetery Record Book, Soquel Pioneer & Historical Association. (This is the original ledger — mud stained from flood, but quite legible.)

Stout, Lewis,
Diary. Oregon Historical Society, Mss 1059. [Typescript. Includes *Description of the Travels From Iowa to Oregon* and *Crossing the Plains to Oregon in 1852 with Comments by Ray L. Stout,* O.H.S. Portland, Oregon.]

Tulare County vs. Freshour, John,
Tulare County, Plaintiff and Respondent VS. John Freshour, Defendant and Appellant. IN THE SUPREME COURT OF THE STATE OF CALIFORNIA, 1880, Case # 16372, Calif. State Archives, Roseville (Sacramento,) CA.

Wilding, Frederick vs. Hihn, F.A.,
Frederick Wilding, Plaintiff and Respondent VS. F.A. Hihn, Defendant and Appellant. IN THE SUPREME COURT OF THE STATE OF CALIFORNIA, 1892, Case # 14940, Calif. State Archives, Roseville (Sacramento,) CA.

Young, Walter I.,
Highland District — Santa Cruz Mountains. — 1881-1905. Memoirs written in 1957-8. Published as a weekly series in the Summer of 1959. *The Los Gatos Times – Saratoga Observer,* [Clipped and pasted into a scrapbook by Bessie Conant.]

APPENDIX A

REVOLUTIONERY WAR

VETERANS

(Documents copied verbatim)

A-1 John Freshour of Ross County, Ohio Declaration of Revolutionery War Service

Ross County
State of Ohio

On this 12th day of Oct. 1832, personally appeared before the judges of the Court of Common plea, John Freshour a resident of the county and state afore said aged 76 years on the 13th Day of May last who being duly sworn according to Law Doth on his oath make the following Declaration in order to obtain the Benefits of the provision Made by the Act of Congress passed June 7 1832 that he served two tours as a millitia man in the American Continental Service first as a volunteer of three months under Capn Scott of Militia second as a Draft for 12 months under Capn Steed a regular officer in the American Service.

From my Father's record from which I have taken this as a copy I was Born in Frederick County state of Maryland the 13th day of may in the year 1756 and when I was 14 years old my Father moved to Virginia Berkly County and in the year 1776 then I was about 20 years old there was three volunteer companies raised of which I was one of Capn Scotts company to go a three months tour to our Army which then lay in their winter quarters at Morristown in the Jersey state. Capn Thurston from Winchester was the Capn of one of these Companies and another Capn from Shepperts town I forgot his name was the Capn of another Company and Capn Scott from Martinsburgh to whos Company I belonged was the third one. About Christmas we started from Berkly county Virginia and about the middle of January we arrived at our American lines. It was then in the dead of winter. No fighting was on. Both Armies the American and the English were in their winter quarters. Nothing there to do for us. We then were billeted to houses about the country. There in the first day of March we had an Engagement with the English at a place called Miscataway in the Jersey state near Bonbrook and Middlebrook. The snow being half leg deep. The English were in an open field and we were in a Middleing large piece of woodland. We stood fire perhaps an hour and a half and we had to give way. They were more in number than us. They had cannon and we had none. One of Capn Scotts Company to which I belonged was left dead on the ground. Another of our Company who had received a dangerous wound Died soon after. Lut Cample in our Company had his arm shot off. Capn Thruston from Winchester also had his arm shot off. We then stand yet till the last Day of March then was Discharged and went home.

In the year 1778 in the month of March my Capn of Militia was called upon to Draft three men of his Company and have them ready to be sent on a Certain Day to Martinsburgh which was our County town, and from there to be sent on to our Continental Army to serve a tour of 12 Months as a Draft (in) the Continental Service, — this caused a great Dread on the most of the Company. Then I and some more of the Company Made a proposal to the Capn and the Company that we would throw in 2 Dollars a piece and if every one of the Company would do so we would stand no Draft but let 3 of the Company take that money and serve the tour of 12 Months as a Draft in the Militia Service, — and in a little time they were all agreed to do so. Then I and two more of the Company took the money, Bought our selves some good cloathe and went to Martinsburgh where all the Drafts had to meet on a Certain Day in the Month. From there we started the last week in March or the first in April for the army which then lay at the Valley Forge on School Kill (sic) 12 mile on this side of Philadelphia. we arrived at our Army about the Middle of April. the English army then lay in Philadelphia and vacated Philadelphia the 18 of June that same year 1778 and made for New York. I had been laying 3 or 4 weeks under the Doctor sick. Washington immediately with his whole army followed the English army. All the sick in the Army were carried in wagons in the country about to farmers barns. Orderly men and Doctors were appointed to move and care for the sick. Washington with his army overtook the English Army at Monmouth in the Jersey and there had a battle. I could hear the cannons from where I lay sick in the hospital which was about 23 miles. Then the English Army went on to New York and our army crossed the North river and went on the White Plains in York Government as it was called then perhaps 25 or 30 miles above the City of New York, about the middle of July. All them that were in the hospitals which had got able to travel of which I was one were collected out of the different hospitals together and taken to our Army which was then at the White Plains and many of us being very weak, It took us between two and three weeks to get there.

There we lay about 2 months then General Malenburgh with his Brigade to which I belonged at that time was sent up the North river and stationed on General Puttnam's farm right on the bank of the North river on the other side. There we staid till about the first of Dec. There I stood sentry at General Puttnam's apple mill and cider press. There I and a great many others with some of our officers crossed the North river to do a tour of 2 days work at the fort called West Point which lies pointedly on the bank of North river on this side about 2 mile above General Puttnams farm which is on the other side. Albany lies about 90 mile higher up river. There the tidewater goes and comes every 24 hours. About the first of Dec. we left that place went down on the other side of the river how far I do not know then crossed the river and came about 2 weeks travel south through the Jersey state to where there was a great piece of woodland. There we struck our winter quarters and about Christmas we lived in our cabins which we had to build and about the last of March or first of April all them that were Drafted belonging to the Virginia troops were Discharged and sent home.

General Mulenburgh *Brigade Genl*
Col Neval......................*of Regt*
Capn Stark *belonging to his Company*

Court Finding (written very illegibly)

He continued after the war to reside in the Northern part of Berkley County Virginia near Bath now Morgan County Virginia and was there about 20 Years. That he removed to Hocking in the state of Ohio where he resided for f__? years and removed from there to Paint Creek in the County of Ross where he still resides.

He received a discharge from Col Neval, a discharge from Capt Steed and likewise a discharge from Capt Scott all of which discharges since ?_____? destroyed ? by time and accident ? That he has no documentary evidence to prove the facts stated in this declaration and that he knows of no person who's testimony he can provide, he hereby relinquishes every claim what ever to a pension or annuity except that ?_____? as as the pension roll of the agency of ...?

(continued page missing)

A-2   Application — John Freshour's Widow

Ross County
State of Ohio

On this 22nd day of November AD 1857, personally appeared before the Supreme Court of Ohio, held in and for the County of Ross and in open court, Margaret Freshawer, a resident of Ross County aforesaid, aged seventy nine years on the 3rd day of April AD 1857, and being first duly sworn according to law, doth on her oath, make the following declaration in order to obtain the benefit of the provisions made by the Act of Congress passed on the 7th day of July 1838, granting pensions to widows of persons who served during the Revolutionery War, and of the Joint Resolution of Congress of the 3rd day of March AD 1851, in relation thereto.

That she is the widow of John Freshawer, deceased, who was a soldier of the Revolution, and who entered the service of the United States in Berkley County, in the State of Virginia, and served as a private in the Virginia Militia she believes in the company commanded by Captain Steid or Stipp; That she does not know the year in which her said husband entered said service nor the Regiment to which he belonged; but she recollects of his telling her that he served at one time one year and at another time three months; that her said husband, John Freshawer drew a pension in his lifetime, amounting to fourty three dollars and thirty three cents per annum, which he continued to draw up to the time of his death; that she believes his pension certificate was dated about the month of October in the year 1833, and that said certificate entitled him to draw a pension from and after the 4th day of March 1831; that he then resided in Ross County in the State of Ohio, and continued to reside there until his death; that he died in said County of Ross on the 13th day of October 1841; that she is not able to provide any evidence of her said husband's service, but referrs to the proofs on file in the pension office in Washington City, upon which her said husband's pension certificate was granted and issued, as proof of the fact; that she was married to the said John Freshawer on the 27th day of September 1791, in Shenendoah County in the State of Virginia, and that her name before marriage as aforesaid was Margaret Funkhauser; She further declares that she is still the widow of the said John Freshawer.

Margaret (*her mark*) Freshawer

In testimony whereof I Angus L. Fullerton Clerk of said Supreme Court have herewith set my hand and affixed seal of said Court this 22nd day of November AD 1857
Angus L Fullerton, Clerk

A-3 John Freshour of Green County, Tennessee Last Will & Testament

In the Name of God. Amen

I John Froshaur Sener of the County of green and State of tennefsee farmer being vary Sick and weake in body but in Parfect mind and menany thanks be given unto god Caling into Mind the mortality of my Body and Knowing that all men is ones to Die Do make and ordain this my Last will and testament that is to Say prinsabally and first of all My wife Eave frushour Shall have the plantation I Now Live on in prosefsian afs long afs She Remains My widow and to have all the profits of the same Dureing her widow hood and She is to keep two of the horses and three Cows and all my Sheep and all my hogs and all my hausehold furneture:: Secondly My three Daughters Namely Mary Susanah & Marget is to have Eaight Pounds apese out of My Eastate afs the other garls has had a bed and a Cow:: thirdly and after My My wife's Death or at the End of hur widowhood the plantation and all that I have willed to her Shall be Solde at publick Sale by my Executors and the Money Divided in Eqsuel Sheres amongs all my Children onely that the part that falls to My Daughter Elizabeth the Executors Shall Not give it to Peter Rader but they Shall Buey a Pese of Land and Let the Said Rader Settel onit afs long afs he Lives and then My Executors Shall Makeover the Same to thire Children:: fortehly My plantation that My two Sons Lives on Namely gorge and John is to be divided in to two partes between them and it is to be Divided afs folles begining at the Mouth of the Spring branch thence up Said branch till against the upper End of Johns barn thence a Strate Corse to the Line Next to Hutchasions onely the Saw Mill and the Land that Lies on the North Side of the Crick Excepted and if tha take the aforsaid Land gorge frushour Shall pay one hundred and Eaighty Dollers to My Executors to be paid in three payments the first payment is Eaight Munts after My Death and the Next in Six munts after that and the third payment is in six munts after that and the payments Shall be in Equel Divisions and John frushaur Shall pay to My executors the Sum of three hundred dollers to be paid in three payments one hundred Dollers in Each payment to be paid at the Same times that gorge is to pay his payments then My Executors Shall Make them Deeds to the Said Land afs thay are Now Setled:: fifthly the first Money that Comes in My Depts Shall be:: paid:: Sixtly the Next that is Colected to the amount My Son Jacob frushour Shall have Sixty Pounda because he has had No Land:: Saunthly and all the Money that is Comind to My estate after the afore Said payments is Made Shall be Divided afs fast afs it Can be Colected in Eqsel Sheers amongst all my Children Namely Eave Stephens Jacob frushour

Ealizabeth Rader gorge frushour John frushour Catrin winters Magdolena faust Mary frushour Susanah frushour Margit frushour and when the other part of My Eastate that is Resaevaed in the first Sextion and the Sawmill and the Land on the North side of the Crick that is Excepted in the fourth Sextion Shall be Sold agreeabel to the conditions of the third Sextion it Shall be Divided in like manner in Eqsuel Sheers amounst all My Children afs before mentioned afs loan afs My Executors Can Collect it agreeabel to thare Sale and I do ordaine my wife Eave frushour John frushour and Joseph winter my Lawfull Executors and I Do hereby uterly Disalow Revoke and Disannull all and avary other testament wills lagecces Beqseeaths and Executors in any ways before Named willed and beqsueathes Ratifing and Conferring this and No other to be my Last will and testament in witnefs whareof I have hereunto Set my hand and Seal this Second Day of March one thousand Eaight hundred and one

Signed Sealed published pronounsed
and Declared by the aforesaid John frushour
afs his Last will and testament in the
preasents of ufs who in his preasents and
and in the preasents of Eachother have
here unto Subscribed our Names

                         his
            John $\mathcal{F}$ frushour Sen $\{S\mathcal{EAL}\}$
                       mark

test:
John Lescollet
Zogren Greg?

Copied verbatim in the interest of historical accuracy.

A-3 *(continued)*

John Freshour of Green County, Tennessee Codicil — Last Will & Testament

A Codicil to this Will

Beit known unto all men by these Preasents that I John Frushour Sener of the County of green and State of tennefsee farmer have made and Declared My Last will and testament in writing bareing Date the Second Day of march one thousend Eaight hundred and one I the Said John frushour Sener by these Preasents Codiciel Do Ratify and Confirm my Said Last will and testament and do further give My two Sons Namely Gorge frushour and John frushour a Longer time to pay the Money for thare Land they Shall pay it in three payments afs it is Mentioned in My will onely thare first payments Shall be in three years after My Death the Second payment in Six munts after the first payment the third payment in Six munts after the Second payment this Codiciel Shall be a judged apart of my Last will and testament and all things tharein Mentioned Shall be afs fully and ampely proformed afs if it haid been writen Down in my Said Last will and testament afs witnefs My hand and seal this third Day of March one thousand Eaight hundred and one

                    his
John $\mathcal{F}$ frushour Sener   {$\mathcal{SEAL}$}
                    mark

test:
Giles Parman
Creton Lassatlan?

Copied verbatim in the interest of historical accuracy.

APPENDIX B
BIOGRAPHICAL SKETCHES
MISSOURI

B-1   Jackson Co.

These are the children born to **John** and **Elizabeth Smith Freshour** in Greene Co. Tennessee and reared in Jackson Co. Missouri:

Thomas Freshour (b. 1821 TN) married Harriet Alice Offutt (b. 1825 VA) in Lafayette Co. MO in July 1846. (Her parents lived in Lafayette Co.) Their first three children, born in Missouri, were: Sarah E. b. 1847, Martha E. b. 1850 and James W. b. 1853. Martha E. apparently died as an infant. Their other children, born in CA, were: Thomas I. b. 1860. Harriet Alice b. 1863, Mary b. 1866 and Margaret b. 1869. The Thomas Freshours were living in Elkhorn twp. of San Joaquin Co. CA in 1860. Harriet's brother James Offutt was living with them. Thomas bought 160 acres in Oct. 1866 and 80 acres in 1868. (S21 and S16 T4N-R7E) He registered to vote in Elliot twp. in 1867. In 1870 their locale had been redesignated Liberty twp. Their eldest daughter had married and Offutt was also gone. The Thomas Freshours sold in Jan. 1873 and moved to Calaveras Co. where he was registered to vote as a farmer residing near Milton in 1875. His son James William Freshour registered as a farmer residing at Jenny Lind. Two other Freshours had preceded them to the Jenny Lind area. Thomas' brother Martin and James R. Freshour with his son Marion were previously registered. In 1874, James Offutt homesteaded 160 acres purchased from Martin Freshour. In 1880, Jas. Wm. Freshour was working on a farm in Chico twp., Butte Co. His wife, Sarah Arabella Atherton was born at Verona — in south Sutter Co. Her father was Englishman Wm. Atherton of Jenny Lind. The Thomas Freshours next appear in Jackson Co. OR. Thomas and his son James W. were granted homesteads in twp 35 in Sam's Valley near Medford OR in 1890 and 1893 respectively. Thomas Freshour died in March of 1896 in Butte Co. CA at the age of 76. A single grave in the Chico Cemetery was purchased By Jas. W. for his father. In 1897 widow, "Harriette" Alice Freshour of Butte Co., deeds over the Sam's Valley land to a purchaser in Butte Co. Harriet was at Scottsburg in Douglas Co. OR in 1900 with gnd. son Charles in her household. Clark and Harriet Alice Freshour McAfee were established on a nearby farm. J.W.'s daughter, Lillie A. Freshour married Geo.W. Parker of Nicolaus, Sutter Co., in 1894. J.W. with Addie and Henry Freshour are in the Parker household at Nicolaus in 1900. Addie Freshour married rancher, David H. Cramer, of Nicolaus in 1906. Charles Freshour owned property in Nicolaus and purchased the Freshour plot at the Nicolaus

Cemetery when Harriet Freshour was buried there in 1908. In 1920 James W. and Bell Freshour were living at Lodi. Charles and their other sons were then living there. James W. Freshour was buried in the Nicolaus Cemetery in Dec. of 1922. His grandson, James W. Freshour, son of Frank Walter Freshour, resides at Modesto. Many descendants of James W. Freshour are found at Lodi. Henry James Freshour was in the produce business with his son Terry Richard for many years at Stockton.

Rutha Malinda Freshour (b. 1824 TN) married Nicholas Broyles Gann in April of 1846 at Jackson Co. MO. There was a profusion of Ganns in Green Co. TN, Jackson Co. MO and finally in CA — always neighbors to the Freshours. Broyles was probably his mothers maiden name. (A Nicholas Broyles paid tax in 1814 in Washington Co. TN which is adjacent to Green Co. A Broyles wagon train family settled in Butte Co. CA. They originated in Washington Co. TN.) Nicholas Gann homesteaded land in twp 47 of Jackson Co. MO in Dec. 1836 at the age of 29. He married Rutha at age 39. She was 22. Her name is given variously as Ruth, Ruthy and Rutha. The German name *Ruthe* was a common name among the Freshours and, following the German pronunciation (Ruth-*eh*,) came to be spelled Rutha in English. They had a child Mahala Jane who claimed to have been born in 1841 in Pike Co. MO perhaps to a previous marriage. Their other children were William Henry b. 1847 near Stockton CA, Mary Elizabeth b. 1851, Martha Rosanna b. 1854, John H. b. 1856, all in San Joaquin Co. CA, Adam b. 1859 and Nicholas B. b. 1863 Santa Cruz CA.

Mahala Jane recalled that her family came to California in 1847 in the Hopper wagon train when she was a 6 year old. Santa Cruz historian Margaret Koch says that Nicholas B. Gann lived between the San Lorenzo River and the Graham Hill Road where he settled in the 1840s. — Until the '49 gold rush. Nicholas and Rutha are in the 1850 and 1852 San Joaquin Co. census. Rutha's name is given as Malvina and Gann misspelled as "Gant" in the 1850 census. Mahala Jane is shown as age 8 and William as 3 the census being in Oct. The Ganns bought land in Weber's Rancho in 1853. In 1854, Nicholas gave a deposition to the Land Commission regarding C.M. Webers land claim. Nicholas and Rutha sold some land back to Weber in 1855. The rest they sold in 1864 and 1867 after moving back to Santa Cruz. Rutha's name on the deeds was given as "Ruthe Malinda Gann" and she made "her mark." They gave power of attorney to Tom Gann in 1858 in San Joaquin Co. Mahala Jane married Samuel K. Hobbs at her fathers house in O'Neal twp. in Sept., 1857. In 1860 and 1870, the Ganns are in the Santa Cruz Co. census. By 1880 Nicholas and Rutha had moved a few miles south to Soquel — to spend their senior years near Rutha's sisters and cousins. Nicholas B. Gann died in 1887 and Rutha M. Freshour Gann died in 1890. They are buried in the Soquel IOOF Pioneers Cemetery.

APPENDIX B

Lawson Henderson Freshour (b. 1827 TN) went west as did all his sisters and brothers. According to Isaiah Horn's journal, Lawson Freshour was in San Jose, apparently living there, in Dec. 1854. After Isaiah's father died in 1856, Isaiah's brother Greenberry moved with his mother to Sonoma Co. Isaiah moved his family from San Jose up to the Russian River to be near his mother. Lawson Freshour and William Gann traveled with them. They camped along the way, in Sept. 1856, and crossed the bay on the Carquinez Ferry. They paid $8.50 ferriage for a wagon with two horses, 3 cows, a mare and a horse. Lawson, William and Isaiah's brother Greenberry Horn helped him locate land at Dry Creek near Geyserville and settle on it. The implication was that Lawson and William also settled there at that time. This was the last mention of Lawson Freshour in the Isaiah Horn diary. There are 1862 and 1863 land grants to Isaiah Horn (in T7N-R9W) and to Greenberry M. Horn (in T7N-R8W) in Sonoma Co. — None for Lawson. Lawson Freshour is farming at Corrilitos in Santa Cruz Co. in 1867 — near his sister Emaline Baucom and his mother. He was in San Luis Obispo Co. and paid taxes in 1874 on 160 acres (S2 T27S-R10E MDM) west of Hot Springs (Paso Robles) where Andrew Freshour was also living. [see Appendix B-4.] Lawson moved to Santa Barbara Co. and in 1877 his Hot Springs property went to the state for taxes. Lawson owned 80 acres 10 miles east of Sisquoc (S2 T9N-R31W SBM) which he let go to the state for taxes in 1879. He sold 160 acres nearby on the north fork of La Brea Creek (S28 T10N-R31W) to the Goodchild brothers in 1885. Lawson was listed at Sisquoc in the Great Register of Santa Barbara Co. in 1890. Lawson died in the Santa Barbara Co. Hospital at the age of 72 in Sept. of 1897. He was single.

Malvina Freshour (b. 1829 TN) married William Fagan sometime prior to the 1850 MO census. Wm. Fagan was deeded land (S6-T47-R29) in Jackson Co. MO in Nov. of 1849. In the 1850 census, they are next door neighbors to the John and Elizabeth Freshour family in Jackson Co. MO. Since she fits the 1840 census for a female 10-15 years old we have supposed her to be a member of that family. The Wm. Fagans probably came to CA in 1854 with the Freshours. Isaiah Horn, in an August 1856 diary entry, mentions Lawson Freshour going to visit William Fagan.

Sarah E. Freshour (b. 1831 TN) married George Washington Himes (b. 1821 IN) in April of 1849 in Van Buren twp. of Jackson Co. MO where they appear (as Hanes) in the 1850 census. Their children were: Margaret Elizabeth b. 1844 (from prev. marriage) Mahala Jane b. 1850, Emaline b. 1854 MO, James Rufus b. 1855 MO, Ruth Missouri b. 1857 MO, Sarah Ann b. 1859 CA, George William b. 1861 CA, Edward b. 1863 CA, Clarissa Frances b. 1865 CA, Laura Ellen b. 1867 CA, Julia Omnie b. 1869 CA and Alice Edith b. 1871. They moved to CA sometime between 1857 and 1859.

In Jan. 1861 the G.W. Himes lived in San Joaquin Co. where daughter Elizabeth age 16 m. James Madison Dover. The J.M. Dovers moved to Santa Cruz Co. settling at Soquel. The Dovers later moved to Bakersfield. The Himes owned 160 acres near Soquel (SEQ S15 T10S-R1W MDM) and were reported in the *Weekly Surf* (Dec. 6, 1890) as having lived on that ranch for 25 years. Their neighbor across the road was Joseph Terre Freshour. In the 1870 census, they are in the next house from Sophronia and her nine children. (Sophronia owned 160 acres.) In 1870 their daughter Ruth was in the household of Wm. and Mahalia J. Ryder who are shown in 1880 as Wm. and M.J. Rider (sic.) Sophronia Freshour is shown as housekeeper for his brother Chas. Rider next door. Sarah E. Himes died in Jan. of 1886 and George W. Himes died in Aug of 1903. They are buried in the Soquel IOOF Pioneer Cemetery. The will of G.W. Himes gives the married names and place of residence for the children of George Washington and Sarah E. Freshour Himes.

Martin Freshour (b. 1833 TN) married Mary Ann Gentry in March of 1853 in Jackson Co. MO. A land record (S5-T47-R29) is there for Martin in Oct. 1854. They had eight children. Thomas b. 1854 MO d. prior to 1860. They were in CA when their second child Sarah Ann was born according to the 1860 census but her gravestone says that she was born in May of 1856 in Jackson Co. MO. Their other children, all born in San Joaquin Co. CA, are: Martha Jane b. Oct. 1858, Mary Elizabeth b. 1860, William Andrew b. 1864, Clara Evaline b. 1867 and Emma Rey b. 1871.

Martin and Mary Ann were living in O'Neal twp. of San Joaquin Co. in 1860. John and Sophronia Freshour are their neighbors. Joseph Freshour, age 21 b. IN, is in the household of Martin and Mary Ann as a farm hand. This undoubtedly is Joseph Terre, brother of neighboring John. Martin is registered as a voter in Douglas twp. in Aug. 1866. Martin and Mary Ann are neighbors, in 1870, to Annette Freshour and children; James R. absent, probably in the mines. Martin transferred his voter registration from San Joaquin to Calaveras Co. in Oct. 1872 giving his residence as Jenny Lind. Martin and Mary Ann homesteaded the land once belonging to Jas. R. at Stone Corral near Jenny Lind. This Freshour property straddles the county line. Martin's two eldest daughters died as children, Sarah Ann dying in 1863 at the age of 7 and Martha Jane in 1868 at the age of 10. Martin and his daughters are buried in the Kirk Family Cemetery nearby in San Joaquin County. The area is bounded by Highway 26 and the Calaveras River.

Other Freshours living at Jenny Lind were James R. and his son Marion and Martin's brother Thomas. By 1875, all, except Martin, had moved away. Three of Martin's children were married at nearby Stone Corral or Jenny Lind. Mary Ann died at Stockton in Aug. of 1896. Martin m. Mrs. Cecelia Boardman in Nov. 1899 in San Joaquin Co. Martin died a widower in 1914 in the Co. hospital in San Andreas and is interred in the Kirk Family Cemetery. At that time daughters Clara Neal and Minnie Christy were living at Jenny Lind, Emma Wolf was living at French Camp, near Stockton, and William A. Freshour was living at Ripon, between Stockton and Modesto, thus establishing the Ripon Freshours.

Emaline Freshour (b. 1836 MO) married Joshua Baucom in Sept. of 1853 in Jackson Co. MO. She was lacking one month of being 17 and he was 21 years of age. Joshua Baucom is listed in the 1860 and 1870 census as Joseph Baucom b. 1832 in TN. Their children were Sarah E. b. 1854 MO, John J. b. 1857 MO, Mahala Jane b. 1859 San Joaquin Co. CA, Emily E. b. 1862 CA, Ruth Frances b. 1864 CA, James William b. 1867 CA and the five youngest born in Santa Cruz Co. CA: Joseph Marion b. 1869, Mary b. 1872, Thomas b. 1874, Charles F. b. 1876 and Edward b. 187x. In the 1860 Census Joseph and Emaline were in Elkhorn twp. of San Joaquin Co. and a close neighbor was Thomas Baucom with wife and 5 children following the TN, MO, CA pattern. — Probably an older brother. Emaline's brother, Tom Freshour, is in the same twp. Listed in the household with Joseph and Emaline is Emaline's mother Elizabeth Freshour, age 65. She is still with them in the 1870 in Soquel twp. her age given as 84 — an apparent error. Joseph Baucom served jury duty in Soquel in 1863. The Baucoms lived in the community of Corralitos in Soquel twp between Soquel and Watsonville. The Great Register of 1867 shows: Joseph Baucom, 35, TN, Pajaro; Reese Baucom, 37, TN, Soquel.

Joseph Baucom was a Pvt. in the Santa Cruz Cavalry throughout that organizations existence — from 1863 to 1867. Pvt. Reese Baucom was a member until October of 1866 when the unit was reorganized. John Baucom was listed as a new member at that time but never continued.

In 1875, the judicial townships were reorganized and Corralitos became part of Pajaro twp. "Josiah" and Emaline Baucom were in Pajaro twp in 1880 with six children and their son, John Baucom age 25, was working on a nearby ranch. Elizabeth Freshour, died in 1876 and is buried in the Baucom family plot in the Watsonville Pioneer (IOOF) Cemetery. John J., James W., Thomas and Charles F. Baucom married and settled around Corralitos. Joseph Baucom died at Corralitos in Sept. 1907. His son Joseph Marion died in 1908. Emaline married again — to C.M. Whiteman. Emaline Freshour Baucom Whiteman died in 1914 at Corralitos. She and Josiah are buried in the IOOF Pioneer Cemetery at Watsonville.

These are Tennessee people reared in Missouri. They generally moved to California as young married adults in the 1847 – 1857 decade. This completes the biographical sketches of the children of John and Elizabeth Freshour of Jackson County Missouri.

B-2   Cole Co.

Judge William S. Freshour (b. 1815 NC) moved with his parents to TN as an infant and lived there on his parents farm until 1835 when at the age of 20 he went to MO. Moved to Callaway Co. MO, m. Elizabeth Wells 1837. They had one son b. 1843 d. 1859. Judge and Mrs. Freshour reared 4 orphan children.

William S. Freshour engaged in merchandising in Boone Co. and then moved to Cole Co. and built a store. The village of Centre Town (now Centertown) was platted at that site. In 1851, Judge Freshour borrowed $2500 from *James Freshour*, his brother "who had gone to the State of California in 1849 and who returned in 1851 with a fortune that he had made in that State. Afterward he returned to that State, and now [*1889*] is living there."

The Judge operated the store until 1860 "when he lost $10,000 in slaves and other property, but be it said to his credit that Judge Freshour had his will drawn up before the *Emancipation Proclamation*, giving his slaves their freedom and $300 in money at his death."

He served as justice of the peace for a number of terms. He was elected judge of the county court in 1879, served two years, but declined a second term. He was captain of militia commanding mustering companies at several annual musters. In 1889, the Judge owned nineteen stores and dwellings in Centre Town and 800 acres of land about the village.

John Freshour (presumably the brother to the Judge) b. 1819 TN, m. 1849 to Parmelia C. Allen. They had five children in 1860 all born in MO. William Henry b. 1841, Elizabeth b. 1844, Emily b. 1846, John b. 1848 and Missouri b. 1851.

No other data is given on *James Freshour*. Data given here on Wm. S. and John Freshour are incomplete. They are not CA immigrants.

B-3   Cole Co. / Jackson Co.

There is another *Wagon Train* Freshour that apparently has Cole County connections. Although married in Jackson County, Missouri, he doesn't fit the John and Elizabeth Freshour family.

James Rufus Freshour. (b. April 1826 Hancock Co. TN) At 2 years of age moved with his parents to Missouri. m. Jackson Co. MO, Mar. 1852, Frances Annette McKelhany (b. 1836 IL.) They had two children in MO; James Marion Freshour b. 1853 MO and John William Freshour b. 1855 MO. Three other children were born in CA; Joseph Frank Freshour b. 1857 in present day Alpine Co. CA, Noah b. 1861 d. 1861 Calaveras Co. CA and Alice Freshour b. 1862 Calaveras Co. CA.

There is a James "Freasure," 21, TN, in the 1850 CA census for San Joaquin Co. A group of four adjacent families (in Dwellings 21 - 24) are those of Sampson Hitchcock, Nicholas Gant (sic), Sam'l Campbell and John D. Gann respectively. James Freasure is in the Campbell household. The census index gives his name as "Freisare." Hitchcock, Gann, Wm. Fagan, John and son Martin Freshour and Charlie Hopper were neighbors in MO, all owning land in Range 29, twp 47 in Jackson Co. James R. Freshour's obituary states that he came to California in 1847 — returning to Missouri to return again to California in 1857. This data tends to fit the brother James Freshour of Judge W.S. Freshour of Cole Co. MO.

James R. Freshour's son Marion's place of birth is given variously as Centertown in either Jackson or Johnson Co. MO. Centertown in Cole Co. MO was the home of the Judge William S. Freshour family. — Another association of James R. Freshour with Judge William S. Freshour.

James R. and Francis A. Freshour are in Douglas twp. of San Joaquin Co. in the 1860 census. That year they purchased a parcel in Elliott twp. that straddled the San Joaquin/Calaveras county line. (We encountered two such parcels. The other one Martin Freshour sold to Offutt.) The Calaveras Great Register (of voters) of 1866 shows James R. Freshour's occupation as miner although he owned ranch land. Later, Martin Freshour homesteaded the former San Joaquin/Calaveras land of James R. Freshour. In 1872, James R. and his wife Annette arrived at Yreka in the Siskiyou Co. gold country in northern CA. Three years later they moved up to the Klamath river near Gottville. James R. Freshour died at Gottville in Dec. of 1908 at 82 years of age. He was preceded in death by his wife Annette and two sons John and Marion. Joe died in 1931. Most of the family are buried in Evergreen cemetery at Yreka. Their descendants have continuously lived in Siskiyou county to the present day.

B-4 Johnson Co.

Another Wagon Train Freshour family was located in Johnson Co., MO., adjacent to Jackson County to its southwest.

Andrew Freshour b. 1810 TN, m. Jane Marcum (b. 1810 VA) Johnson Co. MO Mar. 1837. Andrew Freshour appears on the 1848 Cass Co. tax list. Andrew and Jane were in Madison twp of Johnson Co. in 1850 with five children. Eliza Jane b. 1838, William F. b. 1840, Christopher Columbus b. 1843, Mary M. b. 1845 and Nancy E. b. 1848. In 1860, Andrew was in Amalloy twp of Sonoma Co. CA with his four children, Wife Jane apparently deceased. Eliza Jane Freshour m. Benjamin W. Scott in Santa Rosa, Sonoma Co. in Nov. of 1858. Andrew was farming in Liberty twp of San Joaquin Co. in 1868. C.C. Freshour m. Eunice Lavina Rice with her mother's consent in Woodland, Yolo Co. in April, 1869. In 1870 Andrew Freshour lived at Estrella in Salinas twp of San Luis Obispo Co. with Hot Springs as P.O. C.C. and Eunice and newborn son are with him and Mrs. Rice and son are next door. Daughter Mary M. Wright with husband and children are nearby. In 1880 seventy-two year old Andrew lived at Arroyo Grande in S.L.O. Co. with the Wrights and seven children in the household. "C.C." Freshour was a notable resident of the Geyserville and Healdsburg area in northern Sonoma Co. Four sons and three daughters survived him there.

Andrew Freshour tended to associate with N.C. Hoppers.

B-5 POSTBELLUM MISSOURI FRESHOURS

After the War of the Rebellion (1861-1865,) other Freshours came from Green Co. TN and settled in MO to stay.

Jacob James Freshour b. 1841 Green Co. TN and wife Sarah Catherine Renner m. Green Co. TN 1860 and their children and his mother moved from Green Co. TN in 1871 to Webster Co. MO along with the Bowers and Renners. Jacob J. was the son of Jacob A. Freshour b. 1814 TN and Regina Bowers and grandson of John "Chuckle Head" Freshour and Magdalena Peters.

Regina Bowers Freshour died in Morgan, Laclede Co. MO. Mary Magdolena Freshour, Regina Elizabeth Freshour, Susan Emmaline Freshour, Iranious Sylvanious Freshour and Laura Etter Freshour all married in Seymour, Webster Co. MO. Iranious S. "Uncle Bud" Freshour was an only son and he had only a daughter so this Freshour line died out.

The St. James, Green Co. TN — Phelps Co. MO Raders descended from Peter Rader and **Elizabeth Freshour** who also made the move in 1871. The town of Rader in NE Webster Co. took its name from them.

Partial data are presented since these are not CA immigrants.

B-6   POSTBELLUM MISSOURI FRESHOURS

(*continued*)

A Freshour family left Cocke Co., TN in 1885 to live in MO for about eight years then moved to Yamhill Co., OR.

George Freshour (b. Feb., 1844, TN) and wife, Isabel (b. June, 1853, N.C.) m. TN, 1878 (per 1900 census,) moved to Missouri circa 1885. Their children were: John H., b. Aug., 1884, TN; Marian L., b. Apr., 1886, MO; Nellie J., b. Feb., 1888, MO; Minnie L., b. Mar., 1890, MO; Cora G., b. Sept., 1892, MO; and Hariette, b. July 1893, OR. The family moved to Yamhill Co., Oregon in the fall of 1892 or spring of 1893. Isabel claimed seven children, all of them living in 1900. Next door was Wm. & Mary Booth married only 6 months. Mary, possibly dau. of George and Isabel, was b. June, 1882.

LDS-IGI lists: George Freshour, m. Ezabelle (*sic*) Arms, Cocke Co., TN, 2 Oct., 1883.

These MO to OR immigrants are not really of the wagon train era. They apprear to have many Oregon descendants. Search discontinued.

APPENDIX C
BIOGRAPHICAL SKETCHES
ARKANSAS

C-1   Washington Co.

In 1832, this family traveled by flatboat from the Hiwassee River in Eastern Tennessee to Ft. Smith Arkansas on the Arkansas River at the border of present day Oklahoma — A remarkable feat.

Henry Froshour (b. 1789 PA) married Jane Finley (b. 1797 NC) in 1821 in Shelby Co. AL. Their first four children, Dempsey, Ruth Ann, Dorcas Isabella and Mary, were born in GA. The Froshours moved to TN 1829-31 where Nancy was b. They moved to Washington Co. AR in 1832 where Martha H. and Barbara were b. All six daughters married — five of them in Washington Co. — and reared families. One was a Civil War widow and remarried. Son Dempsey was deaf and dumb and lived with his parents his entire life.

This was the *Henry Freshour* of War of 1812 fame. He volunteered three times establishing three military records. He volunteered at Knoxville in Nov. 1812 for three months and later volunteered at Blount Co. TN in Sept. 1813 for three months. He was discharged at Blount Co. TN. He also volunteered in Oct. 1814 for a term of six months being discharged in the spring of 1815 in Blount Co. TN. Although indexed in military records as Freshour, he spelled his name Froshour. His record shows that his occupation was blacksmith and mechanic, his height 5 feet 10 inches, hair - black, eyes - black and complexion - dark. (Nat. Arch. BLW 18823-160-50, WC14295) Tradition says he was "black dutch."

Henry did gunsmithing in AR during the Civil War. Washington Co. is just south of the Pea Ridge Battlefield and in the border warfare area. Apparently Henry survived the war by maintaining neutrality and repairing guns for both the Union and Confederate troops. He held property across the OK border where he could legally race horses — a life long interest.

Henry Froshour d. 1869 Washington Co. AR, Jane Finley Froshour d. 1881. They are buried with son Dempsey in Lewis Cemetery, Washington Co. AR. (From Connie Foster, *q.v.* Bibliography.)

Although not Wagon Train Freshours we include them because they depict a mode of travel from East TN to the frontier.

APPENDIX D

BIOGRAPHICAL SKETCHES

IOWA

D-1   Jasper Co., IN – Adams Co., IA

These are the children of **Henry** and **Elizabeth Freshour** reared in Indiana and positioned at the Iowa trailhead in 1857: (We include an account of Elizabeth's son J.D. for the historical insight it provides.)

"**J.D. Dunn,** farmer and stock raiser, was born in Green Co. TN Aug. 15, 1820 and is the only child of James and Elizabeth (Hedrick) Dunn, natives of TN ... the former died of yellow fever in 1821, and his widow afterword married Henry Freshaur .... Our subject came to this State [IA] with his mother when twelve years old; his education was neglected, having to work at farm work, which he followed until manhood; after which he worked at teaming from Fort Wayne to Toledo and Logansport. In 1840, he came to this [Jasper] county, and the next fall managed a breaking team with five oxen, which he followed for thirteen summers. He also bought and sold claims, and his first purchase of land for himself was forty acres ... and finally bought his present place of 153 acres, ... Nov. 26, 1839 he married Miss Rachel Campbell, of Stark Co. OH, dau. of James Campbell, a pioneer of this twp. Mr. and Mrs. Dunn in the early days, made their own clothing from their own fabrics, and otherwise experienced the hardships of the pioneer. ..."

John Freshour (b. 1825 Green Co. TN) and his twin George were 14 years old when they moved from Ft. Wayne to Jasper Co. IN. John Married Catherine Golesberry at Jasper Co. IN after the 1850 census. Catherine died in Jasper Co. in July of 1852. In 1853 John married Sophronia South (b. 1832 OH) in Jasper Co. (Sophia means *wise* in Greek. Sophronia means *wise-minded* i.e. sensible. Both names were common in the last century.) John and Sophronia had nine children: William Henry b. Jan. 1854 Jasper Co. IN, Joseph Alfred b. Sep. 1855 Adams Co. IA, Lydia Jane b. Jul. 1857 "Sweetwater on way to Cali'a," Rhoda Ann b. Feb. 1859 San Joaquin Co. CA, George Wesley b. Nov. 1860 O'Niel twp. San Joaquin Co. CA, Emily Josephine b. Nov. 1862 Santa Cruz Co. CA, Mary Francis b. Nov. 1864 Santa Cruz Co. CA and twins Rutha Malinda and Anderson Arthur b. Mar. 1867 Soquel twp. Santa Cruz Co. CA.

John and Sophronia owned a city lot in the newly platted town of Brookville, now Brooks, in Jasper twp. of Adams Co IA. They sold it in

August of 1856. They bought 46 acres in adjacent section 18 in Dec. 1855 which they sold in Mar 1856. No deeds were recorded for them in San Joaquin Co. CA. John enlisted in Co. F, Santa Cruz Cavalry, 1st. Cav. Reg't. 2nd. Brigade, C. M. (California Militia) in Dec. 1863 and was serving in that unit at the time of his death. John Freshour died in Jan. 1867 at 41 years of age. He died near Porter's Tannery in Soquel. Tradition says he was mounting his horse at Porter's Tannery and was stricken with a heart attack. His obit. says he had gone for a doctor for his wife and on his return his horse fell with him, near Porter's Tannery, through a bridge which collapsed. He got the horse out and proceeded home. He later went out to the stable to inspect his horse for injury and suddenly died of heart failure. Comparison of tradition to documented record is instructive. He died two months before the twins were born. Brother Joseph Terre purchased a plot of eight graves in the Soquel IOOF cemetery at this time. Besides the twins, Sophronia was left with 7 other children ages 3 through 13. Sophronia remarried in July of 1868 to Alfred Musgrave and bore a daughter Martha Ellen Musgrave b. May 1869 Santa Clara Co.

In 1870 Sophronia and her children are next door to George W. and Sarah E. (Freshour) Himes. Alfred Musgrave is listed in a different household. Sophronia and her son William H. sold 160 acres in Soquel twp of Santa Cruz Co. in Nov. 1872. Sophronia owned a home in Soquel which she deeded over to F. A. Hihn in 1879. She had her own cabin on John Bradley's property and finally moved in with Elias and Lydia Jane at Capitola Heights where she lived out her years. Sophronia died in 1915 at the age of 83 and is buried in the Soquel IOOF Pioneer cemetery next to John.

George Freshour (b. 1825 Green Co. TN) married Elizabeth Ann Davis (b. 1831 IN) in Jasper Co. IN in 1849 (after 1850 per US census of that year.) In Sept. 1853 George and Elizabeth deeded to James Mitchel for $75, 40 acres in S3 T30N-R5W in the presents(sic) of Paris C. Freshour. Their first child Henrietta was born in 1852 in Jasper Co. IN. George and Elizabeth had eight more children born in Jasper twp. of Adams Co. IA: Francis M. b. 1856, William Perry b. 1857, Lydia Ann b. 1860, James b. 1863, ..., Elmer b. 1871. George and Elizabeth lived out their years in Adams Co. IA. George died in 1873 at age 48 leaving Elizabeth with five children to provide for. Elizabeth died in 1920 at close to 90 years old at Brooks IA leaving three surviving children; Mrs. Henrietta Dentler, Mrs. Lydia Riford of Rawlings WY and Elmer Freshour. She was also survived by eight grandchildren. Elizabeth was buried at the Brooks cemetery. William Perry Freshour d. Des Moines 1919, m. Alice Minnie Lemon and they had sons Fred and Ralph b. 1892 Des Moines. Ralph was the father of James Freshour of San Jose CA b. 1930 Chicago.

APPENDIX D

Mary Jane Freshour (b. 1827 Greene Co. TN) married Perry Mack (b. 1826 PA) in July 1847 in Jasper Co. IN. They moved to IA at the same time George and John moved there. Perry and Mary Jane had seven children the first four being born in Jasper Co. IN and the last three in Adams Co. IA. Their children were: Mary b. 1848, John A. b. 1849, George W. b. 1850, Alice C. b. 1853, Liamanes b. 1856, Sarah E. b. 1858 and Elmer Ellsworth Mack b. 1862. Note that the first two boys were named John and George in the Hans Jörg tradition. In the 1870 census, Perry's brother William L. Mack and his wife Sarah Jane and their daughter Agnes C. are living with Perry and Mary Jane in IA. The W.L. Macks are in Soquel CA in 1880. Agnes is then married to Joseph Alfred Freshour, the son of John and Sophronia. Perry and Mary Jane's sons John A. and Elmer Mack migrated to CA as did their uncle W.L. Mack. John A. Mack with wife and three children appear in Soquel twp. in 1880. Elmer became a close friend of his first cousin Anderson A. Freshour. Elmer Mack m. Clarissa F. Himes dau. of G.W. and Sarah E. (Freshour) Himes in 1884 in Santa Cruz Co. CA. (See Appendix B-1.)

Mary Jane (Freshour) Mack died ca. 1869 and Perry remarried in July of 1875 to Eliza Wheeler. Perry was a member of the GAR having served in Co. D, 29th IA Infantry. Perry died July 1892 in Brooks IA and was buried next to Eliza.

William Freshour (b. 1829 Green Co. TN) went to IA with the rest of the IN Freshours and appears, at 26 years of age, in the 1856 IA census in the household of Perry and Mary Jane Mack along with Lydia Ann. There is no other record of him. He may have taken the trail to CA. William Freshours were not uncommon in CA but they always develop a different identity upon scrutiny. One that might fit is Pvt. William Freshour of Co. I, 2 Reg't California Cavalry. He enlisted as a US Volunteer on Nov. 24 1864 at Camp Bidwell near Chico in Butte Co. CA. This unit was famous for Indian fighting in Nevada. The Regimental Muster and Descriptive Roll dated Feb. 26, 1865 at Camp Bidwell gives place of birth: Howard Co. Tenn., Age: 30 yrs., Occupation: laborer, Eyes: hazel, hair: dark, Complexion: dark, height: 5 ft. 10 1/4 in., Mustered out at Sacramento CA June 24, 1866 with Company. Only muster roll records are available for this man; There is no pension record. He appears too young to be our subject but he may not have actually known his own age. This was common. Joseph Terre Freshour wasn't too sure of his. (cf Wm. son of Andrew, Appendix B-4.) The reference to Howard Co. TN is a mystery. The penmanship is good. This could be Howard Co. MO. The physical description is a prototypical Tennessee Freshour. *This is an unfinished search.*

Joseph Terre Freshour (b. 1838 Ft. Wayne, IN) never married but led a very interesting and productive life. He left Iowa with John and "Safrony" as a 19 year old and must have found the trip quite an adventure. He would have been his full height for several years as is often the case with Freshours — he was 6 foot 2 inches tall. In later life the family distinguished him from his nephew Joseph Alfred Freshour by calling him "Long Joe." He appeared in the 1860 CA census in O'Neal twp San Joaquin Co. in the household of Martin Freshour. He was listed as a farmer (ranch hand perhaps.) John and Sophronia lived in the same twp. He moved to the Santa Cruz area on the coast when they did. He was one of 61 men that organized the Santa Cruz Cavalry in June of 1863. He became 3rd Sergeant in Nov. 1863 when the unit was accepted as Co. F, 1st Cav. Reg't. of the California Militia. He was serving with this unit at its last muster of Jan. 1868. He was absent from the Santa Cruz Cavalry while he served with the US Army. In Nov. 1864 he enlisted at Watsonville, Santa Cruz Co. for the 8th Reg't, California Volunteers, US Army. He mustered into Co. A, 8th Reg't., California Infantry at Ft. Point, San Francisco. He appeared in the Regimental Description Book as Age - 23 years; height - 6 feet 2 inches, Complexion - Dark; Eyes - Dark, hair - Dark. Where born - Ft. Wayne Ind, Occupation - Farmer. Note that the age which he gave was inconsistent with data on his early years — which he didn't have access to as we do. This was to cause him difficulty later. He was appointed Sergeant in Dec. 1864. He served at Ft. Vancouver Washington Territory on the Columbia River with some D.S. at Cape Disappointment. He mustered out of U.S. Army service in Nov. 1865 at Ft. Point and rejoined the Santa Cruz Cavalry serving with his brother, John, and many other Soquel men.

In the 1870 Soquel twp. Santa Cruz Co. census J.T. Freshour is living alone two houses away from Sophronia's large household perhaps looking after them since his brother John had died a few years before. His occupation is given as shingle maker. In the 1880 census, he is boarding and working in the W.A. Young sawmill near Soquel. He became Roadmaster of Soquel twp. supervising the construction of new roads in the area. He was involved in lawsuits regarding public use of roads originally built as private logging roads. He received a Civil War pension in his later years. He spent his last years in a place outside of Soquel above the cemetery on the Soquel-San Jose road. He had a wagon and hauled wood. He slipped on his steps at home and broke his thigh. The doctor put him in Seabright Sanitarium where he died on June 16, 1915. He died intestate but left his affairs in order. His remaining real estate was deeded to Lydia Jane Bradley. "Emma" (Emaline Freshour) Mason and L.T. Mason acted as next of kin and fulfilled his final wishes. Joseph T. Freshour was a member of the Soquel IOOF and the Wallace-Reynolds Post of the GAR in Santa Cruz. He is buried in the Soquel IOOF Pioneer cemetery next to John and Sophronia.

APPENDIX D

Alfred Henry Freshour (b. 1841 Jasper Co. IN) was 13 years old in 1854 when he arrived in Adams Co. He was 20 years old in 1861 — the ideal age for soldering in the War of the Rebellion. He enlisted at Quincy IA on the 28 Oct. 1861 in the 4th Reg't of IA Infantry to serve 3 years. He was 5 feet 8 inches high, Dark complexion, hazel eyes, auburn hair and a farmer by occupation when he mustered in as a pvt. in company H. In June of 1862 he was given a certificate of disability for discharge at Batesville AR because of an enlarged heart. The certificate gave the above data. He is listed in the Roster of Iowa Volunteers, Co. "H" as follows:

Freshour, Alfred. Age 20. Residence Quincy, nativity Indiana. Enlisted Oct. 28, 1861. Wounded in hip slightly March 7, Pea Ridge, Ark. Discharged July 21, 1862, St. Louis, Mo.

In Feb. 1865, **Alfred H. Freshour** married Rebecca Ann Evans b. 1850 IN. They had three children; Charles E. b. 1866, Joseph Marion b. 1867 and Jessie Lemuel b. 1869. These were the only children they were able to have since Alfred Henry Freshour died in Nov. 1872 at the age of 31 years. He is buried in Adams Co. IA. He was a member of the GAR. Charles E. is the grandfather of Cliff Freshour of Prescott, Adams Co. IA.

Lydia Ann Freshour (b. 1844 Jasper Co. IN) was 10 years old in 1854 when she arrived in Adams Co. She was 17 years old in 1861 when the Civil War started. She married Andrew I. Dow in April of 1863 in Adams Co., IA. Dow served with Alfred Freshour in Co. H, 4th Iowa Reg't. He was severly wounded in combat and died in the hospital at Marietta Georgia in Sept., 1864. In May of 1866, in Adams Co., Lydia married Samuel A. Young who served with Perry Mack in Co. D, 29th Iowa Reg't. He was discharged in Aug. 1865. They lived in Adams Co. IA until 1873 when they moved to Beloit KS. In 1883, they moved to Ft. Collins, CO where they spent the remainder of their lives except for a brief sojourn at Tie Siding, Wyoming. Their children were: Mary Belle b. 1867, Wm. Henry b. 1869, Fannie b. 1871, Rosa b. 1873, Nellie C. b. 1875, Grace b. 1877. Samuel Young died in July of 1921 and Lydia died in June of 1923 at Ft. Collins. They were preceeded in death by their youngest daughter Gracie who died at age nineteen. Lydia was pensioned as Andrew Dow's widow and received Samuel Young's pension after he died. Mary Bell was married to Frederick Christman. The Christmans lived out their years at Ft. Collins and the family was prominent in the area. Nellie C. Young married Frank Shelt at Ft. Collins in Jan. of 1908.

This completes the biographical sketches of the children of Henry and Elizabeth Freshour of Jasper County Indiana. The *History of Jasper Co.* says that Henry and Elizabeth Freshour went to IA and died there. There is no record of them in IA.

D-2   Jackson Co., MO – Adams Co., IA

Henry Freshour b. TN and **Amanda Henney** b. N.C. were married in Jackson Co., MO in 1856. These are the children who were living with them at Brooks IA in 1870.

Lucinda Freshour (b. 1857 MO)   m. George Hatch 1877 in IA.

Emiline Freshour (b. 1858 IA) married Lewis Tracy Mason in 1886 at Soquel, Santa Cruz Co., CA; both residents of Soquel, he aged 29, she was 28. L.T. Mason was the son of Sylvester J. Mason and brother of Charles S. Mason — land owners and neighbors to Joseph Terre Freshour. L.T. was a close friend and associate of J.T. Freshour. The L.T. Masons left Santa Cruz Co. after the earthquake of 1906. They purchased land (SWQ S25 T10S-R10E MDM) near Los Banos in Merced Co. in Dec., 1906. L.T. bought a 2nd S25 parcel in partnership with Benjamin Halsey at that time. The Masons kept a home at 551 University Avenue in Palo Alto while L.T. Mason Jr. attended Stanford University beginning in the fall of 1911. They are in the City Directory of 1913. Amanda Freshour lived with them and died at Palo Alto, CA in March of 1913 and was interred at Los Banos. She had been in CA since 1882. The *Palo Alto Times* gave her obituary and the card of thanks signed by Mr.& Mrs. L.T. Mason gave her name as Amanda L. Freshour. In 1914, L.T. and Emma sold their Los Banos property and bought another nearby parcel (S36 T10S-R10E MDM) in 1916 from Miller & Lux. Emma Mason of Los Banos was the informant on Joseph T. Freshour's death certificate in 1915. (Which accurately gave Elizabeth Headrick as J.T.'s mother.) L.T. Mason recorded deeds for J.T. Freshour upon J.T.'s death. Emiline Freshour Mason died in 1922 and Lewis T. Mason died in 1923 at Los Banos and both are interred with Amanda Freshour in the Mason plot in the Los Banos Cemetery. L.T. Mason Jr. died in 1932 and is buried with his parents.

Thomas Andrew Freshour (b. Sept. 1860 MO) Thomas was living in Soquel Twp., Santa Cruz Co. in 1900. He was single and his mother, Amanda, age 75 was in his household. Thomas died Apr. 1909 at Los Banos, Merced Co. CA. He had been in CA since 1882 and was at Los Banos nine months prior to his death at age 48. His occupation was lumberman. L.T. Mason purchased the Mason family plot in the Los Banos Cemetery for his brother-in-law's burial.

APPENDIX E

BIOGRAPHICAL SKETCHES

CALIFORNIA

E-1   Santa Cruz Co.

These are the children of pioneers **John** and **Sophronia Freshour** born to them in Indiana, Iowa, Wyoming and California and reared in O'Neal Township of San Joaquin County and Soquel Township of Santa Cruz County.

William Henry (b. Jan. 1854, Jasper Co., IN) "Will" was three and a half years old when he arrived in California in 1857 and was age 8 when his parents moved from San Joaquin Co. to Soquel. He was 13 years old when his father, John, died in Jan. 1867 making Will the man of the house. In the 1870 census Sophronia Musgrave is the head of the household with 16 year old William H. Freshour listed next, Musgrave having left. In Nov. 1872, William H. and Sophronia Freshour deeded over 160 acres in twp. 10 of Soquel Township to Jose Maria Carravajal and Mariano Soto for one hundred dollars in US gold coin. Will married Irena Beswick (b. 1861 MO) in Apr. 1876 in Soquel at the residence of the brides parents. Will and Irena had only one child — Harvey Freshour. They appear not to have been in Santa Cruz Co. during the 1880 census but Will is listed as a teamster at Soquel in the 1884-5 County Directory. They were living in Santa Cruz in early 1897. His Sisters Ruby Freshour and Emma Bausch and brother George Freshour were living there at that time.

Will and his family moved to Glenwood in late March of 1897 to live at Bowen's Mill where he was employed with Nicholas Gann to cut timber. On the afternoon of April 8th, a heavy gust of wind toppled the redwood he was ready to fall and he fell trying to jump out of the way and was crushed and instantly killed. A coroners jury found it to be an accident. The funeral was at George Freshour's house in Santa Cruz. He was interred in the cemetery plot of his brother-in-law, George Bausch, in the Santa Cruz IOOF Cemetery. Irena continued to live in Santa Cruz. Will died at 43 years of age and his son was apparently in his late teens. It was reported in Oct. of 1898 that Harvey Freshour returned to San Jose after visiting his Mother and friends in Santa Cruz. A Harvey Freshour was living in the San Jose area in the 1960s.

Joseph Alfred (b. Sept. 1855, Jasper Twp, Adams Co., IA) Joe arrived in CA in time for his 2nd birthday and was age 6 going-on 7 when his parents traveled from Stockton to Soquel. He was attending school at Soquel at age 14 in 1870. In March of 1876, Joseph A. Freshour, age 20, married Agnes C. Mack, age 14, at the residence of the brides parents near Soquel. In 1880, Joe and "Aggie" are next door to Aggie's parents, the William L. Macks, and Sophronia's household. They then had children C.M. (Caliste) b. Aptos, May 1877 and J. Edwin (Eddie) b. Aug. 1979. Effie was born after 1880. Joe was listed twice in this census, also being listed in Jared Comstock's sawmill crew as a teamster. His uncle, "Long Joe," was listed in W.A. Young's sawmill. Joe went to work for the San Jose Water works in 1890 and moved to Los Gatos. The W.L. Macks also moved to Los Gatos. Agnes died in February of 1892 and was the first to be buried in the Freshour-Mack burial plot at Los Gatos. Her father W.L. Mack died in September of 1897. His profession was given as wheelwright.

In 1900, Joe and his two adult children, Edwin and Effie, are living with the widowed Sarah Mack. Caliste was married to Fred Barryman and the couple had an infant son in April of 1900. His father, Englishman Arthur Barryman, was also living at Los Gatos with his Mexican wife Canula. Caliste and Fred had four children, Fred Jr., Charlie and two daughters. Fred Barryman ran a plumbing shop in Los Gatos which Fred Jr. later took over. The Barryman plot is adjacent to the Freshour-Mack plot in the Los Gatos Cemetery. Elmer Mack was living with his wife and three children at Los Gatos in 1900. John A. Mack was W.L. Mack's brother. His son, William P. Mack, moved his photography business from Capitola to Los Gatos.

The 1920 census shows Joe living at Alma with his wife, Scotswoman Bella. Joe Freshour was employed by the San Jose Water Co. tending their Lexington reservoir and patrolling by horse and buggy the trestled redwood flume that ran down to a lower reservoir near Los Gatos. An automobile coming down out of the Santa Cruz Mountains swerved to miss an oncoming auto, on July 11, 1920, and struck the rear of his buggy throwing him against the dash. He complained of pains which worsened ending in his death on the 4th of August. A coroner's jury declared his death from a ruptured liver to be the result of an accident. At 63 years of age he was survived by his wife, Bell Cassels Freshour, son Eddie and daughter Caliste Barryman both of Los Gatos and Effie Mason of San Mateo.

Eddie worked for the San Jose Water Co. before moving to Colusa County. John Edwin Freshour, a dairy farmer at Williams, died in 1941 and was interred at Los Gatos. He was survived by wife, Maria B. Freshour, and two step sons, his sisters, Mrs. Fred Barryman of Los Gatos and Mrs. George Mason of Burlingame. His obituary was printed in the Santa Cruz Sentinel. The Joseph Alfred Freshour family was remembered at Soquel.

Lydia Jane (b. July 1857, on Sweetwater R., Nebraska Terr. — now WY) "Jenny," as her youngest brother A.A. called her, arrived in San Joaquin Co. CA as an infant and was about age 5 when her parents moved to Soquel. She was age ten when her father died and at age 13 was in Sophronia's household in July of 1870 in Soquel. She attended school that year. Counted twice in 1870, she is also shown in the household of Baden farmer Adam Martin of Pajaro twp. In April of 1874, Lydia Jane Freshour, age 17, married Elias Bradley, age 46, (b. Geagua Co. OH,) at the residence of the bride's mother at Soquel. Bradley was a teamster in the Great Registers of 1867 and 1882. Joseph T. Freshour was witness and presented the couple with a Bible inscribed with a record of the wedding and the Indiana Freshour family record. Elias called Lydia Jane "Liddie." Their six children, born at Soquel, were John Wesley b. Feb. 1875, Lydia Ann b. Mar. 1877, Bertha May b. Apr. 1881, Luzern (Ernie,) b. Oct. 1884, Harvey Rupert b. Jan. 1888, and Maytie Pearl b. Nov. 1890. The Bradleys reared their family in Glen Haven (Grover's Gulch) and ca. 1908 moved to nearby Capitola Heights where they and Sophronia lived out their years. Elias died in Dec. of 1912 and was interred in the Freshour plot at the Soquel IOOF Cemetery.

Teen age John Bradley worked as "swamper" on an eight-horse team lumber wagon for Frealon Grover. He later worked for the Cowell ranch. He remained single helping to support the Bradley family. Lydia Ann married Nelson Jones (b. N.B. Canada) in March of 1895. Their children were Leitha Laurel b. Dec. 1895, Wilbur Nelson b. Jan. 1900, Glenn Robert b. Mar. 1904 and Erma Estell b. Dec. 1907. The Jones built a house on Porter St. in Soquel and were living there when the 1906 earthquake occurred. The Bradley Bible was handed down to their daughter Leitha who was married to Porter Roberts. (no issue.) Harvey Bradley married Marian Lathrop in 1922. They had a son Arnold. Harvey died at Woodland in 1951. Maytie Pearl continued to live with her parents at Capitola Heights and cared for her grandmother, Sophronia, and her mother, Lydia Jane, when they were both dying. The Los Gatos Freshours took the train over the Santa Cruz Mountains to pay their respects. Sophronia at age 83 suffered general infirmity and a broken hip. Gangrene set in. Lydia Jane was age 57 when she died of carcinoma of the stomach in June of 1915 — five days after her uncle, Joseph T. Freshour, had died at Seabright Sanatorium. One month later Sophronia died. All three were interred in the Freshour Cemetery plot at Soquel where John Freshour had preceded them by 48 years.

Maytie married Oliver Woods at Santa Cruz in Jan. 1916. Their three children were Clifford Bradley b. Lompoc, Jan. 1917, Ruthie Pearl b. Los Alamos, Sept. 1918 and Alta May b. Lompoc, May 1921. Maytie and her three children lived among the Freshours at Los Gatos for a while but finally settled at Watsonville.

Rhoda Ann (b. Feb. 1859, at Stockton, San Joaquin Co., CA) was named after Sophronia's sister, Rhoda South. She was three years old when her parents moved from the San Joaquin Valley to Soquel. Rhoda was eight years old when her father died. In 1870 at age 11, she is in Sophronias household and has attended school that year. "Annie" Freshour, age 16, married Charles Maran/Marcen, age 24, both of Soquel, in March of 1875. Annie Morrison, age 19 of Soquel, married Richard Marion Beswick age 23 of Gilroy, in Sept. of 1878. The Beswick family is shown in Gilroy in 1870 with Richard (b. 1855, MO) the eldest of four children at age 15. Richard was listed in the Santa Cruz Co. Great Register of 1882 as a teamster, age 27, from Soquel. In Will Freshour's obituary, his sister, Mrs. Richard Beswick, was reported at Gilroy in 1897. The Beswicks eventually moved over to the vicinity of Lathrop in San Joaquin Co. Annie maintained contact with her sister Lydia and the Soquel Bradleys. This is evident from a group photo including Soquel, Los Gatos and Lathrop Freshours and from entries in the Bradley Bible. The Beswicks of Lathrop had children Walter, Percy, Clara and Ethyl (m. Hain.) Richard died in Nov. of 1911 at age 56. Percy died from being kicked in the groin by a mule the day before Christmas in 1916. Walter died in an attempt to climb through a barbed wire fence with a shotgun in Nov. of 1918. Rhoda Ann Beswick died at age 85 at Lathrop in June of 1944. She outlived Richard by 33 years. She is buried in East Union Cemetery. Pearl Hain was the informant.

George Wesley (b. Nov. 1860, O'Neal Twp, San Joaquin Co., CA) "G.W." was age 9 in Sophronia's household and attending school at Soquel in 1870. A farm laborer at age 19 he was the man of the household, Will and Joe being married and on their own in 1880. The 1882 Great Register lists G.W. (age 22) as a Soquel woodsman as did the 1884-5 County Register. He was in San Joaquin Co. and married Martha Jane "Mattie" Buchannan (b. Mar. 1858, CA,) on Dec. 31, 1890. Mattie had 6 sons by her marriage to M.A Speaker. To these were added three of G.W.'s children, Clyde, Birdie Violet b. Jan. 1892 and Gladys. G.W.'s home was at 18 Trescony St. in Santa Cruz in 1897. G.W. and Mattie moved to Santa Rosa where Gladys was born in Feb. 1901. Mattie died Easter Sunday in March of 1910 at Santa Rosa. Interment was at the Santa Rosa Rural Cemetery. G.W. joined the Freshours of Los Gatos where he drove team for A.A. Freshour. Birdie married William Stout of San Jose in 1911 at Santa Cruz. Gladys later married Al Billicks. The Billicks settled at Galt south of Sacramento where they reared Georgeann, Annabelle, Johnny, Martha and Billy. Clyde and Birdie were without issue. Teamster George Wesley Freshour lived his last years at Galt and died in Feb. 1947 in the Sacramento Co. Hospital from accidental burns from an oil heater. He was interred in Cherokee Memorial Park at Lodi.

APPENDIX E   515

Emeline Josephine (b. Nov. 1862, Santa Cruz Co., CA) "Emily" was attending school in Soquel in 1870 and, at age 17 in 1880, was keeping house in Sophronia's household while Sophronia was listed as a border and housekeeper at the Chas. H. Ryder household. Emeline Freshour, age 19, resident of the Town of Branciforte, married George H. Bausch, age 22, of Santa Cruz in April of 1883 at Soquel. George was the son of Henry Bausch listed in Santa Cruz in 1870 as beer manufacturer from Hesse Darmstadt and employing brewers from Prussia and Wertenberg. The 1882 Great Register shows father and son together in business as brewers. Both were named George Henry Bausch but the elder Bausch went by the name "Henry" and the younger by the name "George." With the death of Henry Bausch in Nov. 1884 his son took over the business. Henry Bausch was buried in Holy Cross Cemetery. The Bausch Brewery and Bausch Gardens were at the corner of present day Soquel Ave. and Ocean St. The brewery was well known to Santa Cruz residents who sent youngsters with pails to fetch fresh yeast for baking their bread. The Freshour clan frequented "Emma" and George's establishment. The Bausches 4 children were Mabel, Eva D. b.1886, Ruby b.1891 and a son, Eddie. Eva and Ruby died, both at age seventeen. The Bausches eventually sold the brewery. George Bausch, age 43, died at Santa Cruz in Dec. 1904 and is interred in the Bausch plot in the IOOF Cemetery. Eddie Bausch ran a bar in San Jose. Emma Bausch moved to San Jose and later to San Francisco. Emily J. Bausch, age 73, died at Soquel in February of 1936 and her cremains were interred in the Bausch plot in May of 1978 when daughter-in-law, Grace L. Bausch, was placed under the conservatorship of Dorothy Jern of Santa Clara, CA.

Mary Francis (b. Nov. 1864, Santa Cruz Co., CA) "Mae" Freshour grew up and attended school at Soquel and, at age 15 in 1880, was keeping house with her sister in Sophronia's household. We have no information on her early adult years. In the 1890s she was a member of the Santa Cruz Salvation Army and was romantically involved with another Salvation Army soldier — Charles F. Carrington. Their marriage at the Advent parsonage was announced in the *Santa Cruz Surf* of 28 Jan. 1895. They wore their uniforms. She was age 30. Mae (Mary Francis) Carrington died Dec. 30 1895. The funeral was conducted at her residence on Branciforte Ave. in east Santa Cruz and she was interred in the Soquel IOOF Cemetery. She died the day following the birth of her daughter Mae H. Carrington. Mae Carrington was reared by Sophronia while she was able then "Myrts" (Martha Ellen) Musgrave Barden and her husband Charles Barden became foster parents to Mae. (*q.v.* Musgrave below.) Mae Carrington married Frederick N. Scott. The Scotts had a daughter, Bula Mae. About a year later, Nov. 1917, Mae Carrington Scott died at Willits, CA.

Rutha Malinda (b. Mar. 1867, Soquel Twp., Santa Cruz Co., CA) Twin to A.A. Freshour, because of her coloring she was known as "Ruby." The Germanic "Rutha" had not been used by the Indiana Freshours. She was perhaps named after Rutha M. Gann of the MO branch. (q.v. App. B-1) Ruby was attending school at Soquel with A.A. at age 13 in 1880. She remained single and lived at Santa Cruz in 1897. In a portrait she appears to be wearing a uniform; so, may have been in the Salvation Army with her sister Mae. She underwent surgery in Nov. 1902, from which she never recovered, dying from asthenia (weakness) — no doubt from loss of blood. (Classification of blood types was discovered in 1901 and successful transfusions later became practical.) Ruby died at age 35 and was interred in the Santa Cruz IOOF Cemetery near the Bausch plot and later her remains were moved to the Bausch plot near her sister, Emma Bausch, and her niece, Ruby Bausch.

Anderson Arthur (b. Mar. 1867, Soquel Twp., Santa Cruz Co., CA) was named after Sophronia's brother, Anderson South. Twin to Ruby and a typical "blockheaded Dutchman," he was known to the Freshour family as "Blond." To business associates, he was "A.A." Born two months after their fathers death, the twins, at age 3 are in Sophronia's household in 1870 and they are age 13 and attended school at Soquel in the 1880 census. A.A. grew to manhood working in the logging operations around Soquel.

Anderson A. Freshour, age 25, married Minerva J. Conant, age 15 years and 5 months, both of Soquel, married in March of 1890 at Soquel. Written consent of the brides mother, Elizabeth Conant, was on file. Nelson Jones and Miss Lydia Bradley, both residents of Soquel witnessed the ceremony performed by C.H. Darling, Pastor M E Church. Nelson and Lydia were married a short while later. Minerva Jane's brother, Jim Conant, drove bull team for Grover at Soquel and later drove his own team of horses over the Santa Cruz Mountains hauling lumber from Soquel to Los Gatos.

The children of "Min" and "Blond" Freshour were: James "Jimmy," b. March 1894, Soquel, d. Sept. 1894, buried in Soquel IOOF Cemetery; Alice Edith b. Mar. 1895, Everett Edison b. July 1897, Mabel Elizabeth b. Jan. 1901, George William b. May 1902, Hazel Fern b. May 1905, all born on Hester Creek, and Charmion Celetis b. Mar. 1912, Los Gatos.

Around 1895, Blond and Min moved up on the Soquel-San Jose Road in the Hester Creek district below the summit of the Santa Cruz Mountains. They lived on the "Reed place" and on the "Donovan place." A deed filed by neighbor J.W. Simpson, cites an adjacent property owned by Anderson Freshour and another owned by G.H. Conant. Simpson bought his property from 49er Jarret French, the father of George French. Millwright George French and C.B. "Curt" Miracle, operated a sawmill in the vicinity. A.A. and his brother-in-law, Jim Conant, worked at the Miracle-French mill. George

French was married to Min's sister, Mabel Conant (aunt Mame.) A.A. played his concertina at dances at the Frenches. George H. and Elizabeth Conant lived nearby. Elizabeth died in Oct. of 1901 from pneumonia and was buried in the Soquel IOOF Cemetery. The French-Conant-Freshour community lived there until after the 1906 earthquake. The San Andreas Fault at the summit is less than three miles away.

    A.A. and George French moved their families back down to Soquel where A.A. worked for the Loma Prieta Mill on Hinkley Creek and French went to work for Herman Peterson at Soquel. A.A. helped remove the Loma Prieta Mill to Mill Creek at Swanton. He filed saws for that mill until 1909. Miracle started a lumber company at Campbell with French's help. A.A. worked there then went to their lumber yard at Los Gatos ca. 1910. He cut off the end of an index finger while operating a shingle making machine.

    Shortly after her last child, Charmion, was born at Los Gatos, Minerva Jane, at age 35, died while undergoing goiter surgery at the Santa Clara Co. Hospital in Oct. 1912. She was buried in the Soquel IOOF Cemetery. Blond had promised Min that he would not make the children live under a stepmother. He would take his family over the Santa Cruz Mountains to visit the Bradleys and Jones and his mother, Sophronia.

    George and Mabel French, with George H. Conant, moved to Mountain View. French was head sawyer for the Campbell Redwood Lumber Co. at Gazos Creek in 1917. A.A. was a woodsman at Gazos Creek until the mill failed in 1919 then took up farming at nearby Bean Hollow on the coast. The Freshours moved to a ranch at White House in 1920 then moved to Scott's Creek near Swanton where A.A., George and E.E. worked with a two-man saw felling redwoods which they split into grape stakes. They then moved to Bonny Doon and then back to Los Gatos. A.A. worked for Casaletto then went into the teaming business hauling construction materials. This became *A.A. Freshour & Sons.*

    A.A. married Mrs. Eleanor Rose ca. 1929. She called him "Andy." The A.A. Freshours lived at Lakeport on Clearlake for a while. Andy retired and was living in Sunnyvale when Eleanor died ca. 1936. He moved to Oakland to be with his daughters, Hazel — Mrs. Andrew Mellin and Alice — Mrs. Aljo Barry. Charmion was Mrs. Walter Vienop of Napa and Mrs. Mabel Kilborn was at Foresthill. E.E. married Minnie Simpson and became a farmer in the San Joaquin Valley. A.A.'s son, George, was employed by the California Packing Co. He fell from a conveyor at their charcoal by-products plant at San Jose and died in O'Connor Hospital from the injuries in July of 1936 at age 36. He had been recently married to Rosalie and left no issue. He was interred at Oak Hill Cemetery. A.A. Freshour, age 85, married Jenny Barnett, age 84, at Oakland in June of 1952. They both died in April of 1960. A.A. was interred at Oak Hill Cemetery at San Jose.

A.A. and Ruby Freshour were born two months after their father John died in January of 1867. John's widow, Sophronia South Freshour, married Alfred Musgrave at Soquel in July of 1868.

Martha Ellen Musgrave (b. May 1869, Santa Clara Co., CA) Martha was born during Sophronia's brief marriage to Alfred Musgrave who allegedly "ran off" with a red head. (surname Redhead?) Not being able to afford a divorce, Sophronia continued to use the name Musgrave and reared Martha Ellen as one of her family. Charles B. Barden, age 29, b. TN, married "Ella Mossgrove," age 20, both of Santa Cruz, in July of 1890. Barden worked at the Bausch Brewery and lived across from the brewery on Ocean Street. In 1900, Charles Barden lived with Ella M. and Earl, age 7, at Los Gatos. Sophronia Freshour, age 53, is in their household with May [Carrington] Barden, age 4. Daughters Zay and Thelma were born to the Bardens at Los Gatos. The Bardens became foster parents to Mae Carrington when Sophronia moved to Capitola Heights to live with the Bradleys. Martha was known to the Los Gatos Freshours as "Myrts." Martha Ellen Barden died at Los Gatos in Nov. of 1911. In the early 1920s, Charles Barden worked driving team for the *A.A. Freshour & Sons* of Los Gatos.

John and Sophronia took in John's teenage brother, Joseph Terry Freshour, when they moved from Indiana to Iowa in 1854 and the two brothers remained close thereafter. See Appendix D-1. Joseph Terry remained single, his family being his nieces and nephews. He lived out his years at Soquel, always near Sophronia and her family. The Indiana Freshour line vanished from Santa Cruz County when Joseph T. Freshour died in 1915 except for the Bradley-Jones line. The other descendants moved to the Bay Area or the interior of the state.

The biographical sketches given above draw from the Bradley Bible and from the octogenarian reminiscences of Everett E. Freshour and Leitha Jones Roberts (granddaughter of Lydia Jane Freshour Bradley) and are supported by research in the public records.

APPENDIX F

Part Of
THE FRACTIONAL TOWNSHIP MAP
of SANTA CRUZ

P/O **T11S-R2W MDM**   [Surveyed by Foreman & Wright, 1866]

The Lands of Henry Bausch.

The following two pages show the San Lorenzo River and the East Santa Cruz (Branciforte) land lying between it and the R1W western boundary. The western tip of Henry Bausch's farm is bounded by Cooper St. and the "Branciforta River." This property extends well into R1W as shown in the author's revision that follows. Henry Bausch also owned land bounded by Water St. and what was then Burnett St. This was parceled out to several owners by 1866 with a portion retained by Bausch. By 1884, he had sold that. Note the alley named Bausch St. The bridges of that day weren't very hard lived. Some were rickety and even the better ones succumbed to flood water. Burnett St. was replaced by Ocean St. which jogged to give it a perpendicular approach to Branciforte Creek. The new Ocean St. divided the former land of Philip Legett.

The Bausch Tract was laid out, including May Street, in 1867. By 1893, only three lots were sold and May St. was not constructed until 1906 when the tract was reestablished. A portion of the tract was taken to form part of the Branciforte School lot. Ocean St. intersects Soquel Road at a right angle but does not run north to south. In fact, the survey township boundary angles across Ocean Street to pass through the Bausch brewery site. This map reflects the Henry Bausch estate as settled in 1893. Note Henry's home shown as Annie Bausch's lot. [*Data on Bausch Tract taken from Old City 98 maps A14-179 and A15-50.*]

Comparison to modern maps reveals that the San Lorenzo River at this locale has been apparently straightened — perhaps by dredging. Cooper St. lost its former importance as the streets on the Santa Cruz side of the river went through a series of revisions. Burnett St. and its bridge disappeared. River St. is relatively modern. East of Ocean Street, Cooper street became Soquel Road. Some of this probably occurred when the covered bridge pilings were driven creating a reliable San Lorenzo River bridge. Arcan St. then became Bridge St. (Note Arcan's lot.) Santa Cruz streets were among the topics covered in Leon Rowland's column.

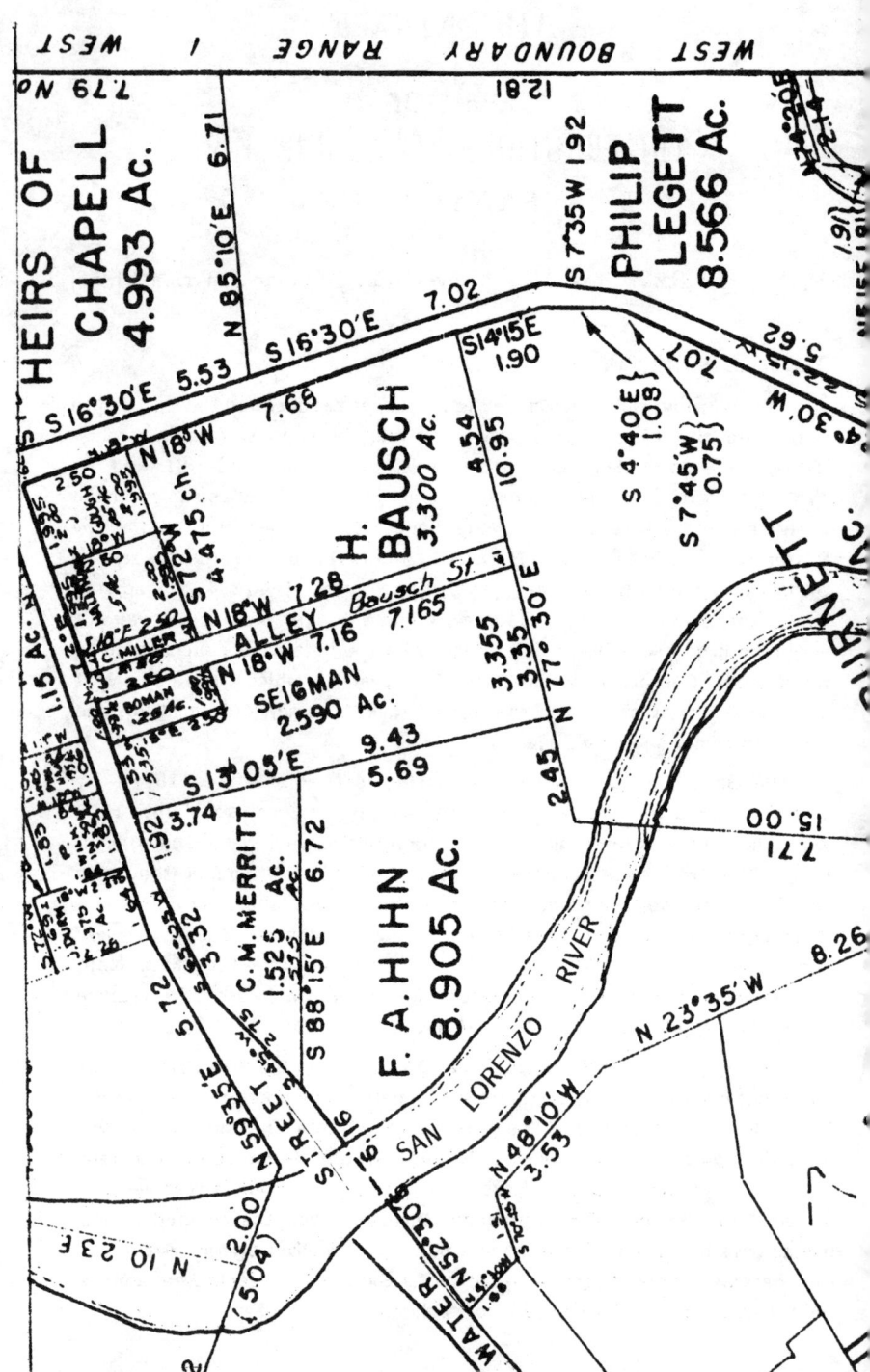

APPENDIX F

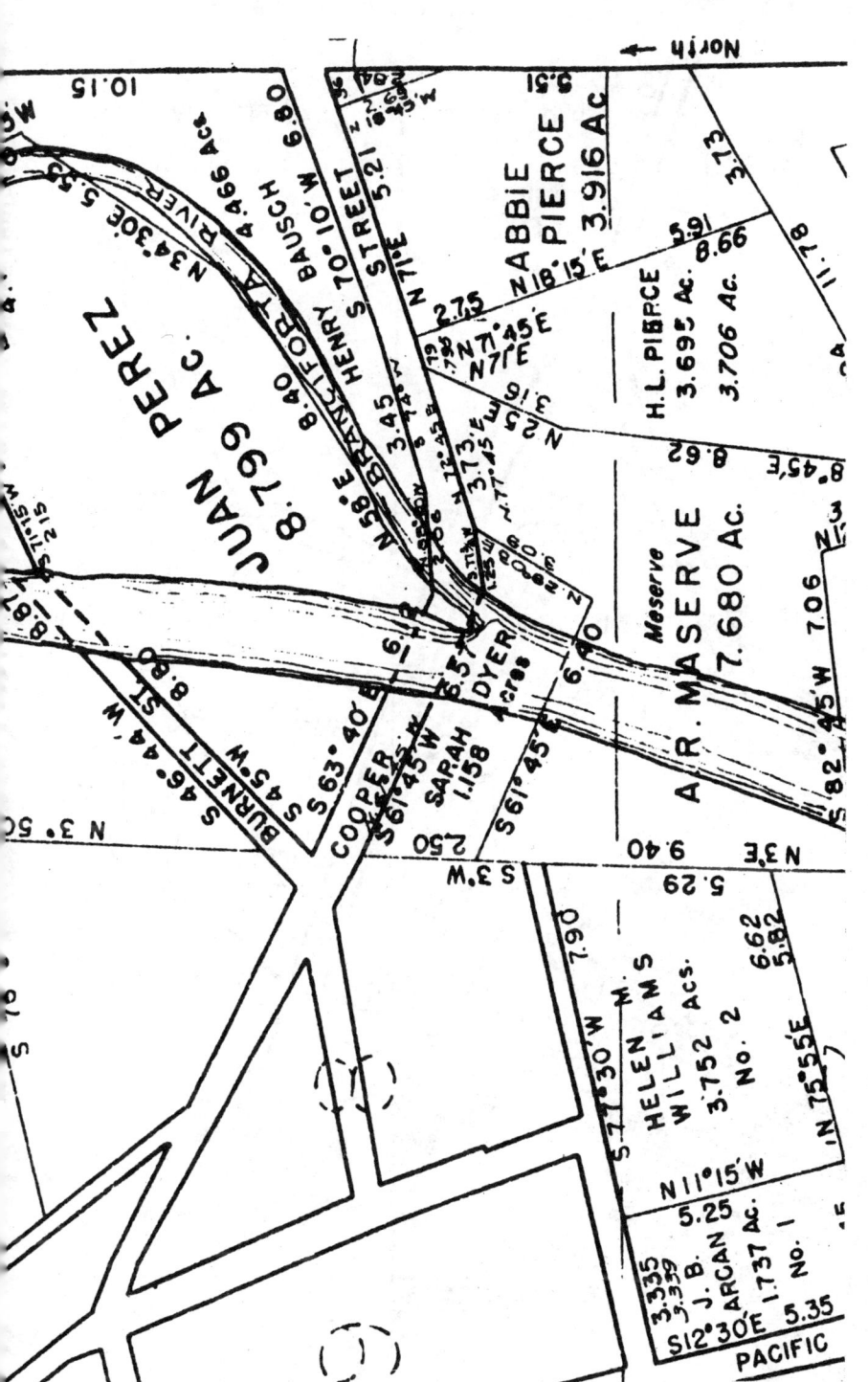

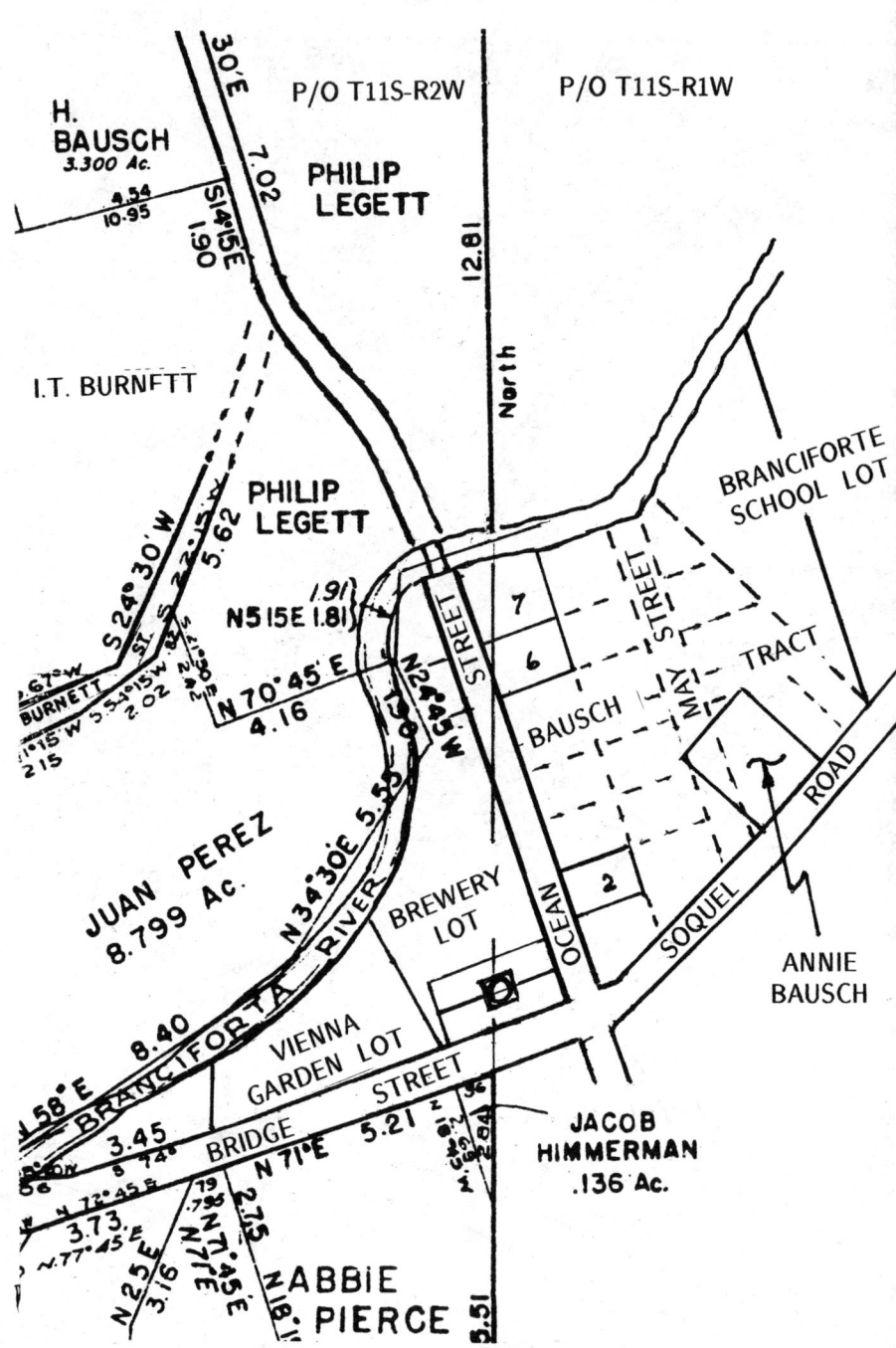

APPENDIX G

GROUP PHOTO — ODD FELLOWS LODGE No 137
SOQUEL

Santa Cruz Co., CA [From the Phil Walker Collection.]

Lodge Officers .... **Soquel Lodge of 1892**

APG — H.V. Angell
NG — Charles Spreckelsen
VG — Ed West
Rec. Sec. — Charles S. Mason
M. Guard — Frank Daubenbis
Out Guard — W.P. Chase
RSNG — L.T. Mason
LSNG — W.S. [or O.W.] Shafer

Fin. Sect. — George French
Treas. — Schuler Peck
Warden — Simon Ewing
Conductor — C.B. Miracle
RSVG — Charles Givens
LSVG — George Strickland
RSS — J.D. Esty
LSS — L.M. Barnes

Lodge Members [As numbered on the photograph.] **Soquel Lodge of 1892**

1. Alfred Bowman
2. Anderson Freshour
3. ...
4. ...
5. ...
6. I. Fleisig
7. Marshall Doane
8. O.M. Ellis
9. George Hart
10. Ernest Eschleroth
11. ...
12. Dick Mason
13. C.B. Miracle
14. Henry Daubenbis Sr.
15. Addie Wyman
16. ED Noble
17. S.J. Mason
18. William Ryder
19. Frank Tarleton
20. John Lyman
21. George Parker
22. O.W. Shafer
23. Henry Daubenbis Jr.
24. C.T. Kirkpatrick
25. J.T. Freshour
26. C.S. Adams
27. ...
28. ...
29. [David M.]? Rice (from Aptos)
30. Judge Nicols
31. ...
32. B.F. Parrish
33. Robert Hussey
34. Fred Wyman
35. Luther Elsmore
36. J.D. Esty
37. L.M. Barnes
38. Ed Green
39. William Hall
40. ...

[continued]

41. Uriah Thompson Sr.
42. Nathan Hart
43. Thomas Curran
44. ...
45. Harrison Murdock
46. C.W. Jensen
47. C.S. Mason
48. Lena Hall
49. Mrs. Ellis
50. Ione Wyman
51. Lizzie Chase
52. Sarah Fleisig
53. Ethel Bowman
54. ...
55. ...
56. Julia Daubenbis
57. Mrs. Wm. Brown
58. Mrs. Marshall Doane
59. ...
60. ...
61. ...
62. ...
63. Simon B. Ewing
64. Annie Martin
65. ...

66. Emma Mason (Mrs. Chas.)
67. Sarah Britton Smith
68. Mrs. George Ord
69. Schuler Peck
70. Emma Mason (Mrs. Lewis T.)
71. Ed West
72. Rose Pauls
73. Mrs. Lou Parrish
74. H.V. Angell
75. Eva Strickland
76. Chas. Spreckelsen
77. L.T. Mason
77A. Della West
78. Mrs. Ellis
79. Mrs. Green
80. ...
81. Mrs. W.J. Nash
82. Mrs. Ewing
83. Mrs. Givens
84. Ephriam Chase
85. Jack Smith